Reading Heidegger

Studies in Continental Thought
John Sallis, general editor

Reading Heidegger

COMMEMORATIONS

Edited by John Sallis

Indiana
University
Press

BLOOMINGTON AND INDIANAPOLIS

The paper used in this publication meets the minimum requirements of American
National Standard for Information Sciences—Permanence of Paper for Printed
Library Materials, ANSI Z39.48-1984.
∞ ™
Manufactured in the United States of America

Library of Congress Cataloging-in-Publication Data
Reading Heidegger : commemorations / edited by John Sallis.
p. cm. — (Studies in Continental thought)
Includes bibliographical references and index.
ISBN 0-253-35053-0 (alk. paper). — ISBN 0-253-20712-6 (pbk. : alk.
paper)
1. Heidegger, Martin, 1889–1976. I. Sallis, John, 1938–
II. Series.
B3279.H49R36 1992
193—dc20 91-27080

1 2 3 4 5 97 96 95 94 93

CONTENTS

Acknowledgments

The papers collected here were presented at the international conference held at Loyola University of Chicago on September 21–24, 1989, in observance of the hundredth anniversary of the birth of Martin Heidegger. I would like to express my gratitude to Loyola University for the generous support provided from the Loyola-Mellon Fund and the Loyola Endowment for the Humanities. I am also grateful to the National Endowment for the Humanities for the major funding provided for the conference. Thanks also to all those who took part in the conference and to those who assisted with it. My thanks especially to Dennis Keenan and Nancy Fedrow for their unstinting work in coordinating the various phases of the conference. Thanks also to Kristine Sandy and Kathryn Sallis.

John Sallis

References to Heidegger's Text

REFERENCE IS BY VOLUME NUMBER (WHERE APPROPRIATE)
AND PAGE NUMBER (UNLESS OTHERWISE INDICATED).

GERMAN TEXTS

EM   *Einführung in die Metaphysik.* 2nd ed. Tübingen: Max Niemeyer Verlag, 1958.

GA   *Gesamtausgabe.* Frankfurt a.M.: Vittorio Klostermann, 1975ff.

GA 2   *Sein und Zeit* (1927)
GA 4   *Erläuterungen zu Hölderlins Dichtung* (1936–1968)
GA 5   *Holzwege* (1935–1946)
GA 9   *Wegmarken* (1919–1961)
GA 13   *Aus der Erfahrung des Denkens* (1910–1976)
GA 15   *Seminare* (1951–1973)
GA 20   *Prolegomena zur Geschichte des Zeitbegriffs* (SS 1925)
GA 21   *Logik. Die Frage nach der Wahrheit* (WS 1925/26)
GA 24   *Die Grundprobleme der Phänomenologie* (SS 1927)
GA 26   *Metaphysische Anfangsgründe der Logik im Ausgang von Leibniz* (SS 1928)
GA 29/30   *Die Grundbegriffe der Metaphysik.*
     Welt—Endlichkeit—Einsamkeit (WS 1929/30)
GA 34   *Vom Wesen der Wahrheit. Zu Platons Höhlengleichnis und Theätet* (WS 1931/32)
GA 39   *Hölderlins Hymnen "Germanien" und "Der Rhein"* (WS 1934/35)
GA 40   *Einführung in die Metaphysik* (SS 1935)
GA 51   *Grundbegriffe* (SS 1941)
GA 52   *Hölderlins Hymne "Andenken"* (WS 1941/42)
GA 53   *Hölderlins Hymne "Der Ister"* (SS 1942)
GA 54   *Parmenides* (WS 1942/43)
GA 55   *Heraklit* (SS 1943 and SS 1944)
GA 63   *Ontologie. Hermeneutik der Faktizität* (SS 1923)
GA 65   *Beiträge zur Philosophie. (Vom Ereignis)* (1936–1938)

H   *Heraklit.* Seminar WS 1966/69 (with Eugen Fink). Frankfurt a.M.: Vittorio Klostermann, 1970.

HK   "Die Herkunft der Kunst und die Bestimmung des Denkens" (published in *Distanz und Nähe, Reflexionen und Analysen zur Kunst der Gegenwart*, ed. Petra Jaeger und Rudolf Lüthe, Königshausen & Neumann, 1983, 11–22.)

HW   *Holzwege.* 3rd ed. Frankfurt a.M.: Vittorio Klostermann, 1957.

ID   *Identität und Differenz.* 3rd ed. Pfullingen: Günther Neske, 1957.

KM   *Kant und das Problem der Metaphysik.* 4th ed. Frankfurt a.M.:

	Vittorio Klostermann, 1973.
N 1, *N* 2	*Nietzsche.* 2 vols. Pfullingen: Günther Neske, 1961.
OA	*De l'origine de l'oeuvre d'art:* Première version inédite. Authentica, 1987. German text with French translation by Emmanuel Martineau. (Lecture presented in Freiburg i. Br. on 13 November 1935.)
S	*Vier Seminare.* Frankfurt a.M.: Vittorio Klostermann, 1977.
SA	*Schellings Abhandlung über das Wesen der Menschlichen Freiheit (1809).* Tübingen: Max Niemeyer Verlag, 1971.
SD	*Zur Sache des Denkens.* Tübingen: Max Niemeyer, 1969.
SG	*Der Satz vom Grund.* Pfullingen: Günther Neske, 1957.
SP	"Nur noch ein Gott kann uns retten," *Spiegel*-Gesprach mit Martin Heidegger am 23. September 1966, in *Der Spiegel,* Nr. 23/1976.
SU	*Die Selbstbehauptung der deutschen Universität.* Frankfurt a.M.: Vittorio Klostermann, 1983.
SZ	*Sein und Zeit.* 9th ed. Tübingen: Max Niemeyer, 1960.
UKa	"Vom Ursprung des Kunstwerks. Erste Ausarbeitung." *Heidegger Studies* 5 (1989).
US	*Unterwegs zur Sprache.* Pfullingen: Günther Neske, 1959.
VA	*Vorträge und Aufsätze.* 2nd ed. Pfullingen: Günther Neske, 1959.
W	*Wegmarken.* Frankfurt a.M.: Vittorio Klostermann, 1967.
WD	*Was Heisst Denken?* Tübingen: Max Niemeyer, 1954.
WP	*Was ist das—die Philosophie?* Pfullingen: Günther Neske, 1956.
ZS	*Zollikoner Seminare,* ed. Medard Boss. Frankfurt a.M.: Vittorio Klostermann, 1987.

ENGLISH TRANSLATIONS

BP	*The Basic Problems of Phenomenology,* trans. Albert Hofstadter. Bloomington: Indiana University Press, 1982.
BT	*Being and Time,* trans. John Macquarrie and Edward Robinson. New York: Harper and Row, 1962.
BW	*Basic Writings,* ed. David Farrell Krell. New York: Harper and Row, 1977.
EGT	*Early Greek Thinking,* trans. David Farrell Krell and Frank A. Capuzzi. New York: Harper and Row, 1975.
IM	*An Introduction to Metaphysics,* trans. Ralph Manheim. New Haven: Yale University Press, 1959.
NE 1–4	*Nietzsche.* 4 vols., reprinted in 2 paperback vols., ed. and trans., David Farrell Krell. San Francisco: Harper Collins, 1991.
PLT	*Poetry, Language, Thought,* trans. Albert Hofstadter. New York: Harper and Row, 1971.
QT	*The Question Concerning Technology and Other Essays,* trans. William Lovitt. New York: Harper and Row, 1977.
R	"Preface" (by Heidegger) to: William J. Richardson, *Heidegger:*

Through Phenomenology to Thought. The Hague: Martinus Nijhoff, 1963.

SAU "The Self-Assertion of the German University," trans. Karsten Harries. *The Review of Metaphysics* 38 (1985).

TB *On Time and Being,* trans. Joan Stambaugh. New York: Harper and Row, 1972.

Reading Heidegger

JOHN SALLIS

Introduction

These texts are commemorative. They commemorate the hundreth anniversary of Heidegger's birth. All were in fact written for a conference celebrating this event. The conference took place in Chicago on September 21–24, 1989.

In 1955 Heidegger himself took part in a commemoration in Messkirch celebrating the anniversary of the birth of the composer Conradin Kreutzer. Heidegger's address on this occasion was later published as *Gelassenheit*. At this *Gedenkfeier* Heidegger observed that to celebrate one who has been called to create works requires, above all, duly honoring the works. In the case of a composer this is done through the performance of his works; it is done—in Heidegger's words—by bringing the works of his art to sound.

The case of a thinker is different, the character of the appropriate commemoration less apparent in advance, less easily determinable beforehand, its determination perhaps inevitably broaching already the commemoration itself. A thinker does not create works: he leaves neither poems nor music to be brought to sound in celebratory performance; nor does he produce anything to be exhibited, that is, set up in such a way that its *Gestalt* can shine forth most radiantly as the work of truth. Such ways in which truth can occur, its taking place in a work, Heidegger distinguishes from the ways in which truth comes into play in thinking, namely, in the questioning and saying of the thinker, in that saying in which the thinker would be bound to the questionable.[1] It is a matter of a saying that, cast as questioning, brings to sound that which is already silently bespoken in the withdrawal, the essential questionableness, of the *Sache* itself. It is a matter of a saying in which that essential questionableness would come to be cast into the word. It is a matter of the inscription of Being, of writing the truth, though in a sense that precedes and, in the end, displaces the common opposition between speech and writing.

To celebrate a thinker requires, then, duly honoring his texts. This can be done only by reading those texts in such a way as to let them resound in the questionableness that is their element, only by reading them in such a way as to reengage them with the *Sache* that they would let sound and to reinscribe them in the element of essential questionableness.

Hence celebration as engaged reading, as readings that would engage Heidegger's texts today, celebrating them by lending them a contemporary voice, celebration as ventriloquy. It is a matter of an engagement of Heidegger's texts now, *after Heidegger,* an engagement that cannot but draw into question the very sense of this *after,* posing over it a question mark that will cast its shadow across this and every other sustained effort to think after Heidegger. First of all, simply because Heidegger is also, in Nietzsche's phrase, an author born posthumously. At least as author of the series of remarkable lecture texts *(Vorlesungen)* that have appeared since the *Gesamtausgabe* was launched in the mid-1970s. These texts compel a rereading and a rethinking even of those among the previously published texts that once seemed most settled, most secured by decades of interpretation. Without such texts as *The Basic Problems of Phenomenology* and *The Metaphysical Foundations of Logic,* who could even have begun to suspect what turnings and overturnings, advances and retreats, drawings and withdrawings from the history of metaphysics, occur in Heidegger's move to the limit of *Being and Time?* That limit, in all its insecurity and its power of recoil, comes still more forcefully into play in Heidegger's massive treatise *Beiträge zur Philosophie,* held back since the late 1930s and only recently published in the *Gesamtausgabe.*

It is especially to the texts appearing for the first time in the *Gesamtausgabe* that the conference in Chicago and the present collection are addressed. Among these texts there is one that bears especially on the effort to read Heidegger engagingly. It is a text consisting only of two short paragraphs and entitled *Was Heisst Lesen?* Listen to Heidegger's answer to the question about reading posed in this title:

> That which is sustaining and directive in reading is gatheredness [*Sammlung*]. To what is it [i.e., reading] gathered? To what is written, to what is said in writing. Authentic reading is a gatheredness to that which, unbeknown to us, has already claimed our essence, regardless of whether we comply with it or withhold from it. (*GA* 13: 111)

Two points are to be underlined. First, reading essentially involves coming to be *gathered* to what is *said* in writing, in the text. Second, reading, thus understood, is *responsive*—that is, the gatheredness of reading is not something that one simply initiates; rather it is a response to a certain claim, a demand, already made upon the would-be reader. This is why the question—in all the polysemy reflected upon it by another title, *Was Heisst Denken?*—is not simply translatable. It asks: What is reading? What does it mean to read?—but also: What calls for reading? What calls forth reading? Venturing to read this text, one might then say: reading is *responsive gatheredness.* Thus it is akin to hearing, which in another text Heidegger calls "gathered hearkening" *(das gesammelte Horchen)* (VA 214). It is also akin to memory, which in *Was Heisst Denken?* Heidegger describes as a matter of coming ardently to be gathered to that which essentially speaks to all thoughtful meditation (*WD* 92). Hence a reading that both listens attentively and remembers responsively. Reading as commemoration.

There is perhaps no saying what such reading requires, especially when—as so often with Heidegger's—the texts are openly, even structurally provocative of such reading. One thinks especially of all the texts that somehow efface themselves: for instance, by crossing out the word *Being* while still letting it remain legible; or by retracting something like the propositional character of a text, something that a common reading would declare inseparable. One thing is certain: as one comes to read these texts, gathering oneself responsively to them, they come to appear more and more uncommon, even stranger. Indeed, one might well say that Heidegger is, as Nietzsche once said of himself, "a teacher of slow reading." His texts require—I cite from Nietzsche's Preface to *Morgenröte*—that "gold-smith's art and connoisseurship of the *word* which has nothing but delicate, cautious work to do and achieves nothing if it does not achieve it *lento*. . . . This art . . . teaches to read *well*, that is to say, to read slowly, deeply, looking cautiously before and aft, with reservations, with doors left open, with delicate eyes and fingers. . . ."[2]

Nonetheless, it is not only a matter of slow reading but also—though perhaps it comes to the same thing—of engagement, of a reading that would be engaged with the way of thinking bespoken by Heidegger's texts, reengaging those texts with the *Sache* that they would let sound, letting them resound, even if in a tongue that cannot but sometimes sound somewhat strange. Reading may take the form of questioning, for instance, a questioning that would reenact or translate the questioning enacted in those texts; or a questioning that would use the very resources of those texts in the effort to locate within them certain blind spots, residues of dogmatic assertion. And yet, one cannot overlook a series of discussions that have begun to gauge the immense complexity of such a stance of questioning, a series of discussions that go back to a conference on Heidegger that David Krell organized in Essex in 1986,[3] discussions that were extended and elaborated in Jacques Derrida's *De l'esprit: Heidegger et la question* and given a still further turn in a now well-known footnote in *De l'esprit* addressed to Françoise Dastur.[4] I refer to the discussions pertaining to the question of the question, to the privilege of the question in Heidegger and to all that can be said against such privilege, to what Charles Scott has said most succinctly in writing of Heidegger that "he is in a question that is not his."[5] I refer also to Heidegger's explicit denial of that privilege in a passage in *Unterwegs zur Sprache*, which reads: "The proper bearing of thinking is not questioning but rather listening to the promise of that which is to come into question" (GA 12: 165). Not questioning but, first, listening, hearing—akin to reading, responsive gatheredness, commemoration.

Heidegger calls it also originary thinking (*das anfängliche Denken*). In a passage, one of his most astonishing, that comes toward the end of the afterword to *Was Ist Metaphysik?*, he describes such thinking as a thinking that squanders, lavishes, expends itself (*verschwendet . . . sich*) upon Being for the truth of Being. Because it answers to the need to preserve the truth of Being, because it gives itself up for the sake of the truth of Being, such thinking—says Heidegger—occurs "in the freedom of sacrifice." He continues: "Sacrifice, removed from all compulsion because arising from the abyss of freedom, is the lavishing (*Verschwendung*) of the essence of man in the preservation of the truth of Being for beings" (GA 9: 309f.). In sacrifice, he says, there takes place a concealed thanks (*der verborgene Dank*), and thinking becomes thanking.

A thinking become thanking. In a word, commemoration. Hence these commemorative texts, which celebrate the opening brought by Heidegger's thought, offering thanks for that way that, as Jacques Derrida said nearly twenty years ago, constitutes an original, irreversible advance.[6]

NOTES

1. See "Der Ursprung des Kunstwerkes," *GA* 5: 49. See also the simpler formulation given in the earlier version that Heidegger presented in Freiburg in 1935 [*De l'origine de l'oeuvre d'art* (Première Version Inédite [1935]), ed. Emmanuel Martineau (Authentica, 1987), 44].

2. Friedrich Nietzsche, *Morgenröthe,* in vol. 6 of *Werke: Kritische Gesamtausgabe,* ed. G. Colli and M. Montinari (Berlin: Walter de Gruyter, 1971), 9.

3. The papers presented at the conference are published in *Research in Phenomenology* 17 (1987). See especially Jacques Derrida, "On Reading Heidegger," 171–85.

4. Jacques Derrida, *De l'esprit: Heidegger et la question* (Paris: Galilée, 1987), 147–54.

5. Charles E. Scott, *The Language of Difference* (Atlantic Highlands, N.J.: Humanities Press, 1987), 87.

6. Jacques Derrida, *Positions* (Paris: Les Éditions de Minuit, 1972), 73.

I

IN THE WAKE OF
BEING AND TIME

RODOLPHE GASCHÉ

1. Floundering in Determination

Thought as well as proper life in language are "especially prone to succumb to the danger of commonness," Heidegger writes in *What Is Called Thinking?* If this is so, it is because language, and thought too, has a tendency to drift away into the obvious or self-evident—into ordinary thinking and the common meanings of words. Common terms easily take the place of proper terms—of the words inhabited by language and thinking (*gewohnte Worte* as opposed to *gewöhnliche Worte*). More precisely, as if driven by frenzy, common terms usurp "the place of language properly inhabited and of its habitual words." Yet, says Heidegger, such "floundering in commonness (*Taumel im Gewöhnlichen*) . . . is not accidental, nor are we free to deprecate it. This floundering in commonness is part of the high and dangerous game and gamble in which, by the essence of language, we are the stakes" (*BW* 365). Consequently, thought cannot simply push aside current meanings of words in favor of the proper ones. It must face this floundering in its very inevitability, and in such a manner that it can show that these words and thoughts are not unrelated to the words of language inhabited by thinking. As we will see, Heidegger conceives of the relation in question as one in which customary signification is rooted in the originary meaning of a word or thought (and, conversely, as one in which that decisive meaning falls away). Yet does this attempt to come to grips with the inevitable language-slide successfully reverse its course? Or is the manner in which floundering in commonness comports with genuine thought perhaps more insidious and more complex than the possibility of retracing the original significations of common words or thoughts would make it seem? What if precisely the possibility of getting ahead of the game, of resisting the floundering in commonness, would perpetuate that very same floundering? Or, if thought's chance of coming into its own by leading the common terms back to their proper and inhabited meanings would depend not only on a reproduction, but perhaps a multiplication of commonness? It is true that such multiplication of common terms and thoughts in the very process of their overcoming could be a (partly or totally) calculated game. Yet the proliferation of commonness may also escape all strategy, and no longer be accountable in terms of what has been called, hitherto, *common*, ordinary. Indeed, such a proliferation of ordinary meanings results, as suggested, from the very attempt to assess the same logic which rules the binary opposition of the common and the proper. Hence, the question arises as to what relation "properly" exists between the manifold ordinary terms to which one must resort in order to retrace the ordinary back to the original and the very process of derivation itself. In addition, one may wish to ask, is such multiplication necessary, accidental, or neither? Perhaps one should also regard the nature of this latter as floundering precisely because it may no longer represent a simple opposite to genuine thought, if, indeed, successful thought does not go without it?

These are among the questions on which I would like to elaborate in this paper which I conceive of as an inquiry of sorts into the mood of *Being and Time*. However, a warning is called for at this point. I will not only engage the questions alluded to from a specific angle by concentrating on one term only, on its inescapable floundering in common meaning and on Heidegger's "inability" to secure a proper meaning for it, but will also limit myself, for reasons of space, to the first half of *Being and Time*. Since the term I shall discuss is that of determination (*Bestimmung*), I will thus have to forego the exploration of this term's temporal, destinal, and historical implications.

When used in philosophical discourse—by Kant for instance—the expression *Bestimmung*, as Heidegger notes in *The Basic Problems of Phenomenology*, is "not arbitrary (*beliebig*) but is terminologically defined: determinatio." The immediate source for this term in Kant is Baumgarten, yet its history reaches back through Wolff and Leibniz to Scholasticism and antiquity, Heidegger adds (*BP* 35). In the conceptual history of "determination" with which Heidegger is concerned, the term is a formal-apophantic category. A determination is a predicate of what, in the grammar and general logic pertaining to assertions, is called a subject (*BP* 126). It enlarges the concept of a thing—that is, its what-content (and not a thing in its empirical manifoldness). Through determination a thing (or rather its concept) becomes demarcated from another thing. *Omnis determinatio est negatio*, Spinoza wrote and thus set the framework within which the formal-apophantic category of determination had to be understood. Since the eighteenth century, *Bestimmung*, which translates the Latin *determinatio*, has had, in the technical language of philosophers writing in German, the meaning of a conclusive fixing or settling of the content of concepts by demarcating them with the help of marks, characteristics, or predicates from other concepts. Thus wherever the notion of *Bestimmung* appears in a philosophical text, it is not, as Heidegger aptly remarks, an arbitrary concept or word, and that is true as well in the text of *Being and Time*. Yet although Heidegger's elaborations focus in that work on the formal-apophantic nature of *Bestimmung*, he has already broadened the scope of this notion beyond its meaning in the tradition to which I have alluded, so as to include within its horizon predication not only of the what-content of the *concept* of things but also of *things* in their actuality, existence, or extantness. The notion in question is thus treated as a category of epistemological realism in addition to its serving to assert the nature of essences or possible things. Undoubtedly, this extension of the scope of the notion in question responds to specific historical reasons, in particular to Heidegger's debate with Neo-Kantianism. Yet, considering the perspective of fundamental ontology that informs Heidegger's discussion of

Bestimmung in *Being and Time*, the broadening of that notion may have still another, and perhaps more essential, purpose.

A first definition of *Bestimmung* is given in *Being and Time* in chapter 13 when Heidegger proceeds to describe knowing of the world (*Welterkennen*) as a mode in which Being-in is exemplified. Knowing, he writes, is a "way of determining the nature of the present-at-hand by observing it." Heidegger tells us here that the act of making determinate is primarily an interpretive perception (*Vernehmen*) constituted by addressing oneself to something as something and discussing it *as such*. Therefore, determination presupposes "a *deficiency* in our having-to-do with the world concernfully." Indeed, determination is based on a "fixed staring at something that is purely present-at-hand," on an attitude towards the world, in other words, that becomes possible only if all ordinary ways of relating to the world have been blended out. Something like *Bestimmung* can become envisioned only if the world is encountered in such a way that entities present-at-hand reveal themselves "purely in the *way they look*" (*BT* 88). At first, determination as an interpretive perception is nonpropositional. However, what is perceived and "made determinate can be expressed in propositions, and can be retained and preserved as what has thus been asserted" (*BT* 89).

It is while discussing assertion as a derivative mode of interpretation in both chapter 33 of *Being and Time* and in the Marburg Lectures on *Logik. Die Frage nach der Wahrheit* (Winter 1925–26), that Heidegger refines this definition of *Bestimmung*, its characteristics and presuppositions, but especially the ontological realm in which it obtains. In the analysis of assertion, determination becomes defined as a mode of "pointing out," (*Aufzeigung*, or *Aufweisung*) in which something present-at-hand is predicated of something that itself is present-at-hand. As assertion, determination is a mode of discovering (*Entdecken*), of ἀπόφανσις. Yet, what it discovers, what it makes thematic as Heidegger calls it in *Logik*, is the present-at-hand as present-at-hand. Thus predicative, or determining, assertion is a constricted mode of discovering. Heidegger writes in *Being and Time:*

> It is not by giving something a definite character that we first discover that which shows itself—the hammer—as such; but when we give it such a character, our seeing gets *restricted* to it in the first instance, so that by this explicit *restriction* of our view, that which is already manifest may be made *explicitly* manifest in its definite (*in seiner Bestimmtheit*) character. In giving something a definite character, we must, in the first instance, take a step back when confronted with that which is already manifest—the hammer that is too heavy. In "setting down the subject," we dim entities down to focus in "that hammer there," so that by thus dimming them down we may let that which is manifest be seen *in* its own definite character as a character that can be determined. (*BT* 197)

But by focusing in on a thing as something present-at-hand, which paves the way for any access to properties or the like, one does not only dim down or blend out the thing's nature as something ready-to-hand but also veils or covers up readiness-to-hand (*BT* 200). In his lectures on *Logik* (1925–26) Heidegger adds that in determining-letting-something-be-seen as merely present-at-hand, the proper character of Being of this something (in this case its readiness-to-hand) withdraws. Giving the example of a piece of chalk, he remarks that "if the determination: this piece of chalk is white, is made in conformity with the meaning that determination and assertion have in asserting, then this way of letting this thing be seen is possible only on the basis of a *re-concealing (Wiederverbergens)* of the piece of chalk as a with-what of one's dealings" (*GA* 21: 158). By reconcealing the way we have been relating to the piece of chalk in our unthematized everyday dealings with it, and by thus purely *concentrating* on its presence-at-hand, it becomes possible to let this piece be seen from characteristics drawn from the object itself that are themselves present-at-hand. Heidegger writes: "In determining assertion the as-what from which the determination takes place, namely white, is drawn from the given about-what itself" (*GA* 21: 156). This mode of predication, in which the characteristics that let something be seen assertively are drawn from the thing itself, is what Heidegger calls *Bestimmung*. Determination as assertion is constituted by "communication," or speaking forth. Of "communication" in which one makes assertions, Heidegger notes that it "is a special case of that communication which is grasped in principle existentially" (*BT* 205).

The very fact that, in determining assertion, the "what" that is said of something is "drawn *from that* which is present-at-hand," reveals that the as-structure that characterizes assertion as a derivative mode of interpretation "has undergone a modification." Since determining assertion becomes possible only when the ready-to-hand is veiled as ready-to-hand, so that properties or the like can come into view, the "as" "in its function of appropriating what is understood . . . no longer reaches out into a totality of involvements" (*BT* 200). Compared to the "as" of an interpretation which understands circumspectively—the primordial existential-hermeneutical "as"—the "as" in determining assertion has been leveled to "just letting one see what is present-at-hand, and letting one see it in a definite way. This leveling of the primordial "as" of circumspective interpretation to the "as" with which presence-at-hand is given a definite character is the speciality of assertion." This derivative "as" that constitutes the structure of determining assertion, is called the apophantical "as" (*BT* 201).

Determination, therefore, is not a primary discovering. In *Logik,* Heidegger emphasizes that "assertive determination never determines a primary and originary relation to what is." Because it is derivative on the originary as-structure of circumspective understanding and is the result of a leveling modification, it can never "be made the guiding thread for the question regarding Being." "Determination," he concludes, "is itself as well as its whole structure a derivative phenomenon" (*GA* 21: 159–60).

If determination is thus a restrictive mode of discovering that presupposes modified structures of understanding and a reduction of the world to the present-at-hand, then what is the status of the word *Bestimmen* in the discourse of *Being and Time?* Indeed, Heidegger not only demonstrates the derivative character of determination as a concept and a mode of interpretation but also continues to make use of the terms *bestimmen* and *Bestimmung* (as well as numerous words of the same root) in a variety of ways. I shall try to address the question regarding the status of the notion of *Bestimmung* in *Being and Time* by suggesting that it is not merely a question of stylistics and not simply a theoretical question, but that it concerns the *Stimmung* (the mood and/or the coherence) of Heidegger's discourse. Heidegger, while discussing the leveling of primary understanding in determining assertion in his Marburg Lectures on *Logik,* makes a distinction that may give us a lead on how to approach the question of the word *Bestimmen* in the work of 1927:

> When I say: This piece of chalk is white, then this assertion about something with which I am dealing, is not an assertion that as such would primarily relate (as far as its content is concerned) to my dealings. If I said, while writing: The chalk is too hard . . . then I would make an assertion *within* my performance (*Verrichtung*), within writing. . . . This assertion: "The chalk is too sandy," is not only a determination of the chalk, but at the same time an interpretation of my behavior and of not being able to behave—of not being able to write "correctly." In this assertion I do not wish to determine this thing, that I hold in my hand, as something that has the properties of hardness or sandiness, but I wish to say: it *hinders* me in writing; thus the assertion is interpretatively related to the writing activity, i.e., to the primary dealings of writing itself, i.e., it is assertion as interpretation of Being-in—as Being-alongside. (*GA* 21: 157)

Undoubtedly, when Heidegger, in *Being and Time,* engages the problem of *Bestimmung* as one that has served as the guiding thread for the question of Being from Greek antiquity to Husserl as well as for the sciences, his conclusion that *Bestimmung* is a derivative phenomenon primarily relates to the subject matter under discussion. But this assertion is made as well in the process of developing, arguing and writing *Being and Time,* and thus is also, especially in consideration of what this work is all about—the question of Being—a statement regarding his argumentative and writing performance. That *Bestimmung* is a derivative phenomenon, then comes to mean that assertive determination is an obstacle when trying to come to grips with the question of Being while Heidegger was writing *Being and Time.* Indeed, if the determining mode of assertion is not appropriate for dealing with the question of Being, this mode, as well as the word *Bestimmung* itself, inhibits (*hemmen* is Heidegger's word) the very performance of elucidating the question of Being. Yet, as we shall see, *Bestimmung* as a term, if not as a concept, appears throughout *Being and Time,* and thus the question arises as to the status and function of this term in the production of Heidegger's work. Why must Heidegger continue to use the philosophical language of *Bestimmung;* how do the uses of that term relate to what he himself has established about its notion; and how does Heidegger's own explicit or implicit account of his continued use of the term do justice to its manifold appearances or occurrences in *Being and Time?* These are among the questions that I would like to touch upon.

Heidegger, in *Being and Time* (but elsewhere as well), makes frequent and seemingly innocent use of the terms *bestimmen, bestimmt,* or *Bestimmung* in their common meaning of "to define," "to characterize," "to qualify." Certainly, on repeated occasions he makes an arbitrary (*beliebig*) use of it. He employs it as well in the sense of "certain," "specific," or "determined," for instance, when he writes: "These Others, moreover, are not *definite* (*bestimmte*) Others" (*BT* 164). And, at times, *bestimmt* has the meaning of "intended" or "destined for," as when we read "that along with the equipment to be found when one is at work, those Others for whom the 'work' is destined (*bestimmt*) are 'encountered too'" (*BT* 153). In all these cases, the term is used in a casual, ordinary way.

A definitely more technical use of *Bestimmung* occurs in Heidegger's text when the task of phenomenological description or interpretation becomes characterized as one of determining the structures of its objects (in paragraph 14, for example). In this latter case, *Bestimmung* means "in die Berstimmtheit bringen," to give definiteness to, or "to raise to a conceptual level the phenomenal content of what has been disclosed" (*BT* 117, 179). Although *Dasein*, the object of the phenomenological analysis of *Being and Time*, is thoroughly different from objects present-at-hand, Heidegger continues to characterize his whole investigation as an *existentiale Bestimmung*, as an attempt to exhibit the *Grundbestimmungen des Daseins*. Yet even more questionable is a third type of reference to the concept of determination.

The meaning of Being, its structures, are said to "lie beyond every entity and every possible character (*seiende Bestimmtheit*) which an entity may possess" (*BT* 62). Hence the meaning of Being "demands that it be conceived in a way of its own, essentially contrasting with the concepts in which entities acquire their determinate signification (*Bestimmtheit*)" (*BT* 26). But Heidegger does not only characterize phenomenology as the *Bestimmungsart* of Being; Being itself is to be made determinate, according to the essential determinative structures for the character of its Being (*seinsbestimmende*) (*BT* 38). At stake in such an analysis is Being's originary *Sinnbestimmtheit* (its "temporal determinateness") which has to be made thematic in an overcoming of "the very indefiniteness (*Unbestimmtheit*)" in which vague and average understanding holds Being, by means of a return to "those primordial experiences in which we received our first ways of determining the nature of Being (*Bestimmungen des Seins*)" (*BT* 40, 25, 44).[1]

One may perhaps wish to object here that this use of the notion and word *Bestimmung*, with reference to what the analytic of Dasein is to achieve and to Being itself, is not to be taken literally, that the term is used between quotation marks, so to speak. Yet, although in *Logik* Heidegger had clearly stated that Being is not an object for any possible *Bestimmung*, (*GA* 21: 160) he does not make the slightest effort in *Being and Time* to counter any misunderstandings that could result from his talk about *Seinsbestimmung* and *Seinsbestimmungen*, as opposed to his hyphenation of the word (*Be-stimmung*) in *Was ist das—die Philosophie?*, for instance. Supposing that, in the context of the question of Being, the notion of determination should have another, more originary signification than its current and metaphysical use, it never becomes distinguished from its metaphysical double. Why this neglect in a work that prides itself on reaching beyond the established philosophical and scientific distinctions even at the price of neologisms? In determination, one recalls, something (present-at-hand) is characterized in terms of properties drawn from this something itself. It is a mode of assertion that lets something be seen from itself. Is Heidegger's neglect to attend to the specific meaning that determination ought to have when used with reference to Being, perhaps rooted in an unresolved problem regarding the phenomenological characterization of what shows *itself by itself*—Being, first and foremost—on the one hand; and on the other, the letting-be-seen of what is present-at-hand by means of determinations drawn exclusively *from that* which is given in such a manner? Has Heidegger, indeed, fully clarified, in *Being and Time,* the relation between the wealth of the demarcating traits that come into view when that which shows itself to a phenomenological glance is allowed to show itself by itself, and "the abundance of things which can be discovered by simply characterizing them (*ein neuer Reichtum des im reinen Bestimmen Entdeckbaren*)" in the theoretical glance by which the world becomes dimmed down to the uniformity of what is present-at-hand (*BT* 177)? In any case, the very fact that Heidegger has relegated the concept of determination to the derivative domain of the present-at-hand and to a mode of letting-be-seen in terms of characteristic properties drawn from the thing itself requires that the "improper" references to this concept in *Being and Time* be some-how accounted for.

In *What Is Called Thinking?*, Heidegger remarks that the common meaning of words that have usurped their proper meanings is "not totally unconnected and unrelated to the proper one. On the contrary, the presently customary significa-tion is rooted in the other, original, decisive one" (*BW* 366). Yet the technical meaning of *Bestimmung* that Heidegger has limited in a categorical way to the sphere of the present-at-hand, is at best *Bestimmung's* proper metaphysical sense. It is, as we have seen, a mode of relating derivative of a more fundamental mode, and thus there is nothing originary to it. *Bestimmung* as a philosophical *terminus technicum* is just as common as its customary signification. But is there then a proper signification of *Bestimmung,* a signification in which that word would *prop-erly* be thought and inhabited? It must be noted here that the derivation and limita-tion of *Bestimmung* in *Being and Time* does not yield a proper meaning of that word. No fundamental meaning of *Bestimmung* is produced in this work to account for the juxtaposition of its different usages by showing them to be derivative of its proper meaning.[2] As a result, there is a certain disparity between the various occurrences of the word in question in *Being and Time,* a disparity that would be considerably complicated if one were to include in this investigation the addi-tional, and major, signification of *Bestimmung* as vocation or destination. If, how-ever, all these manifold usages of *Bestimmung* (and its variants) are not unconnec-ted and unrelated, it is certainly not because of some more originary meaning of the term. Another law than that which commands the relation of the improper to the proper must regulate their distribution. Let me recall that assertive determi-nation is a derivative mode of interpretation that presupposes and replaces the more primordial mode of interpretation in circumspective understanding. Under-standing, together with state-of-mind (*Befindlichkeit*) are the two constitutive ways in which Dasein *is* its "there," and are equiprimordial with discourse (*Rede*). State-of-mind is one of the basic ways in which Dasein's Being is disclosed to it as its "there." Such disclosure takes place in what is called "our mood, our Being-attuned (*Stimmung, Gestimmtsein*)" (*BT* 172). Heidegger writes: "In having a mood, Dasein is always disclosed moodwise as that entity to which it has been delivered over in its Being; and in this way it has been delivered over to Being which, in existing, it has to be" (*BT* 173).[3] Such disclosure, Heidegger adds, is not knowledge in the sense of being known *as such*. The "that-it-is" disclosed to Dasein in its Being-attuned does not express "ontologico-categorially the factuality belonging to presence-at-hand." Whereas the latter "becomes accessible only if we ascertain it by looking at it," the "that-it-is" disclosed in Dasein's state-of-mind by contrast has to be conceived "as an existential attribute (*existenziale Bestimmtheit*) of the entity which has Being-in-the-world as its way of Being." In Being-attuned, Dasein "is brought before itself," not as beholding itself, but as "finding itself in the mood that it has" (*BT* 174). In this prereflexive and precognitive mode of finding itself, Dasein experiences its *thrownness*, that is, the facticity of always already being its own "there" (not as such, not abstractly, but) in a specific way, as belonging to a determined world, and as being alongside determined intraworldly things. This "that-it-is" in which Dasein finds itself in the mood that is has (*als gestimmtes Sichbefinden*), and "which, as such stares it in the face with the inexorability of an enigma," (*BT* 175) represents, by its very facticity, the matrix for existential-hermeneutical understanding (according to the as-structure), as well as for its derivative, apophantical interpretation. In Being-attuned, Heidegger continues, Dasein has, in every case, already disclosed "*Being-in-the-world as a whole, and makes it possible first of all to direct oneself towards something*" (*BT* 176). But if Being-attuned permits directing oneself towards something in the first place, it is because Dasein encounters the world in such a way that what it encounters can "matter" *to* it (*von innerweltlich Begegnendem angegangen werden kann*). Only because in Being-attuned the world is experienced as one that can "affect" us, can understanding be primarily circumspective, and under given circumstances, "just sensing something, or staring at it" (*BT* 176).

In other words, *Stimmung* is the condition not only of possibility of circumspective interpretation but also of its modification and leveling in determining assertion as well. Without the primordial disclosedness of *Stimmung* or *Gestimmtheit*, and its matrical structures, no such thing as *Bestimmung* would be possible. *Stimmung*, in a sense prior to all psychology of moods, that is, in the sense of a fundamental *existentiale*, is thus the original, decisive thought and word upon which *Bestimmung* (the thing and the word) are based. With *Stimmung* we thus seem to have found a proper and fundamental mode of 'awareness' to which the technical philosophical term as well as the customary term of *Bestimmung* can be connected according to a scheme of deduction; still, it is not a proper meaning of *Bestimmung*. Even where *Bestimmung* is properly understood (as in *Being and Time*, but especially in *The Question of Truth*), it never becomes a proper word, a word inhabited by thought (a *gewohntes Wort* as opposed to a *gewöhnliches Wort*). Thus, although with *Stimmung* we have in principle a proper deduction of the possibility of *Bestimmung*, the problem I alluded to remains.

There is no proper use of *Bestimmung* that would justify Heidegger's speaking of *Seinsbestimmung,* or of *Bestimmungen des Seins.* The disparity remains.

Let me add at this point that with the derivation of *Bestimmung* from *Stimmung,* Heidegger has also accounted for the possibility of "*stimmen*" in the sense of *Übereinstimmung,* and thus for the question of truth as ὁμοίωσις or *adaequatio.* Propositional truth is rooted in the accordance between a determining assertion and what it is about. But since determining assertion is based on a definite modification of the primordial hermeneutical as-structure of interpretation, "truth, understood as agreement, originates from disclosedeness" (*BT* 266). In the explicit exhibition of the derivative character of the phenomenon of *Übereinstimmung* (section 44, section b), Heidegger secures his derivation by demonstrating that this phenomenon is, in the same way as *Bestimmung,* limited to the realm of the present-at-hand. *Übereinstimmung* is not only a relation between two terms that are both present-at-hand but also the relationship of agreement in *Übereinstimmung* is itself present-at-hand (*BT* 267).

Yet if truth as agreement is a function of determining assertion which is itself rooted, as far as its possibility is concerned, in the *Gestimmtheit* of state-of-mind (as well as in understanding), *Gestimmtheit* or *Stimmung* must be conceived as a primordial way of *Beziehen, Bezug,* relationship. Indeed, the three essential determinations of *Stimmung*: (1) Dasein's thrownness or facticity; (2) the disclosure of its Being-in-the-world as a whole; and (3) the fact that something can "matter" to it (its *Angänglichkeit*)—constitute existentially Dasein's openness to the world. In *Stimmung,* in the attunement of a state-of-mind, Dasein which experiences *itself* always already factically (knowingly or not), is shown to be capable of being "affected" by the world and of directing itself towards things in a world that in every case has already been disclosed to it. Dasein's Being-attuned in a state-of-mind, is the existential a priori of all possible linkage, connecting, or relationship.

For lack of time and space I must forego here the temptation to show that Heidegger's understanding of *Stimmung* in *Being and Time* is a recasting of Kant's notion of transcendental apperception from a fundamental ontological perspective. Such a demonstration would have to base itself on the discussion of transcendental aesthetics in his Marburg Lectures on *Logik.* "All determination and all thinking is a connecting of a given manifold," Heidegger remarks here (*GA* 21: 308). And "Determination is synthesis, synthesis is gathering together (*Zusammennehmen*) in a unity" (*GA* 21: 294). Heidegger makes these statements with respect to formal intuiting, and asks, consequently, what it is that ultimately makes a connecting of the manifold possible. Such connecting by intuition and understanding is possible only if there exists something like unity in general. For Kant, Heidegger writes, this unity is the transcendental unity of apperception—that is, "the originary a priori of all connecting, that is, of all determining, and hence the a priori of the possibility of determining the manifold as such" (*GA* 21: 322).

Stimmung is, existentially speaking, the most primordial unity that *Being and Time* resorts to, an originary mode of relating from which *Bestimmung* as a restricted mode of discovering, and truth as *Übereinstimmung,* follow. As such, it is at once the enabling condition of logical determination and truth as agreement, of all characterization, definition, description, etc.—i.e., the arbitrary common meaning of *Bestimmung* as well as of all *stimmen* (about which Heidegger only speaks disparagingly as indicative of a merely formal mode of relating and correctness). This concept of *Stimmung* will be replaced by Heidegger later on with the less subjective notion of *Grundstimmung*,[4] and, in particular, with the notion of *Stimme*, in the sense of the *(lautlose) Stimme des Seins*. What is true of Stimmung, namely, that it must be understood beyond all psychology of moods, is also true of *Stimme*, although the original basic meaning of the verb *bestimmen* in Middle High German was "to name by voice, to fix by voice."[5] The *Stimme* toward which Heidegger retraces the possibility of determination and truth as accordance is not primarily voice. *Stimme*, as Heidegger uses it, must be understood verbally, actively, as minimal cohering, minimal agreeing. As he will say later, *Stimme* puts into *Stimmung*, which itself disposes thought to correspond appropriately to what speaks to it. Thus, what becomes *gestimmt*, attuned to Being, whether in *Stimmung* or in thinking, can always also become articulated linguistically.

With this I circle back to the question of Heidegger's use of the term "determination" in *Being and Time*. The expansion of the term to include epistemological predication of things now appears to have provided Heidegger with a sufficiently generalized background to be able to derive all forms of determination (philosophical, epistemological, and commonsensical) from one primordial unity—the unity of attunement. It is a derivation that takes the form of a grounding through exhibition of the modifications that the originary unity undergoes in the various types of determination.

If it is a general principle, as Heidegger claims in section 29, that from an ontological point of view one must "leave the primary discovery of the world to 'bare mood,'" then even the "purest *theoria* has not left all moods behind." But as he notes in *Was ist das—die Philosophie?*, not only theory—that is, not only the conceptual grasp of a world dimmed down to the uniformity of the present-at-hand—but also philosophy is attuned. And so is Heidegger's *Being and Time*. This work, to take up the language from the Cerisy conference of 1955, is attuned to the "voice," the *Stimme* of Being. Its task, as Heidegger notes from the outset, is to lift Being out of its forgottenness and to reawaken an understanding of the meaning of the question of Being. Undoubtedly, *Being and Time* corresponds to the "voice" through a very definite mood, but also, and primarily, through a very definite sort of cohering, of having a unity in a specific way. One way in which *Being and Time* achieves this unity is by exhibiting *Stimmung* as that which sets the term(s) for determination. But does this a priori synthesis account for all determinations as well as for the manifold ways in which *Stimme* is said, and in particular in Heidegger's text? Has Heidegger, indeed, explained with this model of originary cohering his continued use of both the term and concept of *Bestimmung* with respect to the question of Being? Undoubtedly, from *Stimmung* all other (determined) forms of determinations have been successfully derived. But is such essential derivation capable of accounting for the problem that I have tried to point out? The improper or, more precisely, *common* use of a word such as "deter-

mination" in formulations like *Seinsbestimmungen* or *Bestimmungen des Seins* remains an inhibition (*Hemmung*) to thinking—to thinking nothing less than the
ways in which Being attunes. Apart from the technical meaning of *Bestimmung*,
no proper meaning of the word can come to the rescue of the philosopher. Yet
Heidegger uses it, as he does so many other variations of the word. Inescapably,
he *must* do so and thus flounder in commonness. However, the thinker would
have to account for such floundering by exhibiting the language-slide between the
proper and the improper. But what if no habitual meaning of determination is
to be found? The model of essential derivation to which *Stimmung* yields in *Being
and Time* and which makes it such a powerful synthetic tool seems to be either
too finely or too loosely knit a synthesis to account for the paradoxically inevitable
improper use that Heidegger must make of the term in question. What becomes
visible here is that such improper reference to *Bestimmung* in the context of the
question of Being can only be accounted for if the manifold forms of determination
are no longer gathered together according to the traits of letting-something-be-seen
from itself, as itself, or from the negative modalities thereof. In other words, another model must be found than that by which determination properly points out
essences (or of things *as such*)! The limits of the originary synthesis of *Stimmung*
would come even more poignantly into view were one to emphasize the numerous
terms Heidegger summons in *Being and Time* that have the root part: *stimm-*.
From both a subject-related and a performative perspective all these words and
notions contribute to the thought of *Stimmung* and ultimately to that of Being.
It is not a question, as one may easily infer, of faulting Heidegger's achievement
in *Being and Time,* and especially not of there being linguistic limits to properly
expressing something that has already been properly thought. Rather it is to argue
that the rigorous development of something like an originary synthesis that would
account for all forms of determinations cannot but flounder, not only because
of its inevitable recourse to improper usage of the terms to be derived but also
because of the variety of ways in which these terms must be used do not fall
under the binary oppositions that organize the various stages in the deduction.
Still, the very idea of an originary synthesis calls upon us to think together this
inescapable floundering and what in such floundering is positively achieved.

Yet Heidegger's evocation of a floundering in commonness as part of the high
and dangerous game of thinking and speaking does not master the diversity and
disparity of all the ways in which *Stimme* is being said. The binary opposition
of the proper and improper, of the habitual and the common meaning of words,
and perhaps of philosophical thought and common sense, cannot serve to bring
order to the manifold in question. If thought flounders when we try to come to
grips with determination, it is because the very necessity of formulating an
originary synthesis such as *Stimmung,* for instance, cannot avoid producing a proliferation of precisely what has to be derived—a plurality of not only improper
but also sharply different notions of determination (and by root related words)—
different because of tone, style, tense, and, in particular, levels of argumentation.
A certain lack of coherence thus comports with the coherence that *Stimmung*

makes. This incoherence, which the philosophical schemes of derivation and binary opposition fail to master, must nonetheless be accounted for.

Stimmung as the ultimate a priori of all connecting, would indeed have to be the starting point for such an elucidation of the way(s) in which *Stimmung* itself comports with a certain incoherence. It is an incoherence that, unlike the improper, does not stand in a symmetric relation to its opposite and that thus escapes binary determination. Hence the kind of accounting that I call for cannot consist of tying originary *Stimmung* up with such things as *Stimmungslosigkeit, Verstimmung,* etc., which Heidegger, in chapter 29, has effectively accounted for. Nor can it be a question of linking *Stimmung* to some equiprimordial disunity, discord, disharmony, etc., *if* these values continue to receive their meaning from within the horizon of unity, harmony, accord, etc. Rather it is a question of tying *Stimmung,* as originary synthesis and its successful derivation of *Bestimmung* and *Übereinstimmung,* to the floundering of thinking—not only to the improper, common use of *stimm*-related terms but also to all the major irreducibly different occurrences of *stimm*-related terms that result from the phrase regimens (to use a Lyotardian term) and the metaleptical shifts in argumentation that are required in demonstrating the originarity of *Stimmung* in the first place. Such floundering does not take place in improperness or impropriety. It is a floundering congenital with the dangerous game of thought Heidegger talked about. If this game consists in establishing *Stimmung* as the originary synthesis for all possible *Bestimmung,* then to tie this game up with the manifold and heterogeneous occurrences of *stimm*-related words in *Being and Time* would mean to think the becoming of *Stimmung,* the coming into its own of originary *Stimme* from a beyond not only of its synthetic achievement, its character of state-of-mind but also of its possible verbalization. Beyond the minimal cohering of *Stimmung* and *Stimme*—in their *Er-stimmung* or *An-stimmung,* perhaps—a mesh of relations would thus emerge that would no longer be simply attuned, synthetic, or originary. Rather than seeking some sort of accordance, some even deeper *stimmen* between *Stimmung* and the manifold "voices" in Heidegger's text, the accounting in question would instead have to take the form of a mesh—of what Heidegger, on several occasions, has referred to as a *Geflecht.*

N O T E S

1. *An Introduction to Metaphysics* refers even to Being as "determinate, wholly indeterminate Being (*Sein als das bestimmte völlig Unbestimmte*)" (*IM* 78).

2. Certain developments in "On the Essence of Truth" (*BW* 113–41), and also the hyphenation of *Be-stimmung* in *Was ist das—die Philosophie?* suggest that there is perhaps a proper meaning of that word, upon which the technical (and current) meaning of the term is dependent.

3. In a handwritten comment in the margins of his own copy of *Being and Time,* Heidegger notes with respect to the quoted passage: "dass es zu seyn hat: Bestimmung!" (*GA* 2: 56). I translate: "that it has to be: destination!" Being attuned to, disclosedness, and

destination are thus intimately interlinked. It is a fine example of how the temporal meaning of determination becomes tied into Heidegger's attempt to foreground the question of determination in that of state-of-mind, in moods.

4. See in this context Michel Haar, *Le chant de la terre* (Paris: L'Herne, 1985), 88ff.

5. See, for instance, G. Drosdowski et al., eds., *Der Grosse Duden* (Mannheim: Dudenverlag, 1963).

MICHEL HAAR

2. The Enigma of Everydayness

Translated by Michael B. Naas and Pascale-Anne Brault

The sun is new everyday

Heraclitus

That which is *ontically* so familiar in the
way Dasein has been factically interpreted
that we never pay any heed to it, hides
enigma after enigma existential-ontologically.

Heidegger, *Sein und Zeit*

What is everydayness? Is it simply what the history books call "everyday life": a set of practices that govern private and public life at a specific time and for a specific people? Is it not first of all a constitutive structure, original and unavoidable, of all Being-in-the-world? In everydayness, Heidegger says, Being-with-others prevails over the Being-one's-self which we could be. We are other than our own possible selfness. In everyday encounters and affairs, we act, think, and are like the "they" is: I am spontaneously like anyone else would be in my place. Everydayness refers to an indefinite substitutability of roles, situations, gestures, and words, which, far from remaining external to me, constitute my first "my"-self. From day to day we are not only like the "they" is, but, in our most intimate being, we are the "they"-self. The anonymous structures of the world push me aside, eclipse and replace me as "subject." To be in the mode of everydayness is thus not simply to conform, to be *like* everybody else, to be guided by the most commonly accepted behavior. It is, rather, to be *first of all other than oneself*, not to have subjectivity for oneself. "*Proximally,* it is not 'I', in the sense of my own Self, that 'am', but rather the Others, whose way is that of the 'they'" (*SZ* 129). *Proximally [zunächst]*, even when I say "I," what I express and do belongs to a "we-they think, a we-they act, a we-they live in such and such a way." This is one of the meanings of *Verfallenheit*, fallenness, the other being

Dasein's self-identification with a *thing of the world,* either a being simply given there present-at-hand (*Vorhandenes*) or a tool or instrument ready-to-hand (*Zuhandenes*).

What is enigmatic about the phenomenon of everydayness if not the fact that it is *inaugural and secret* (that it goes unnoticed or is considered "normal")? Does the enigma of the everyday thus stem simply from its self-dissimulation? But would this not then be the enigma proper to all truth understood as a process of unconcealment whose heart is concealed? Perhaps we can get closer to the enigma by asking: But why *must* it be this way? No doubt because this dimension of the everyday is primordial and necessary. But why then *must Dasein* fall *from the start* into the grips of the others and become subjected to the hidden tyranny of thingness and the "they?" Why is it that it is not only the existence that just "hangs on from day to day," that abandons itself to chance and is thereby lessened, weakened, and tired but also *all existence* subject to the rhythm of daily life and "ephemeral" in the literal sense is given over to this destitution or abasement in which it "contents" itself, as Heidegger says, to a Being-with-others that is common, levelled, and indifferent to its own alienation? Because under the famous rubric "Being-with-others" the analytic is not a "critique" of repeated gestures, sedimented habits, or the constant rehashing of the same words and ideas. It has to do, rather, with a *first destitution* which is *prior* to Being-one's-self. Everyday Being-in-the-world forces us from the start to make *our own* the paths already laid out and trodden, the behaviors already prescribed, the ideas already accepted. So once again, why is this, since it seems that everyone wants honestly, lucidly, and with all his energy to "find himself" (as the "they" says!)? Why, since everyone flatters himself with having his own opinion about what is said in the papers and considers himself to have a certain degree of personal "leeway" within the "social" constraints which no one challenges? For does not everyone believe himself capable of escaping the "average and ordinary" [*durch-schnittlich*]) being which, he thinks, is proposed to him without being imposed upon him?

But how in fact would one escape it, Heidegger asks. Through entertainment, work, solitude, travel, romance? Would this not still be to follow the "models" of behavior dictated by the "they," ways of behaving that have been "prescribed by Being-with-one-another" (*SZ* 370)?

Why is Being-together spontaneously and fundamentally diverted from authentic self-accomplishment? Why is it initially difficult, if not impossible, for us in everydayness to bring to each other mutual enrichment such that through an exchange with others we might discover our own particularity?

Is not the Heideggerian depreciation of collective existence, "public" in the sense of simply Being-with, the continuation of a theme obscurely derived from the Platonic distrust of *doxa,* that is, of the opinion of the majority or the masses? Is not the fact that everydayness is seen as a denial of the self, an ontological "apostasy,"[1] a retaking up of the traditional theme of the *Many* as the fall, dispersion and bad fragmentation of the *One* or the *Good?*

The first section of *Sein und Zeit* shows that the "they" is an unavoidable ontological structure of Dasein. Even if it can, "in an existentiell manner, 'surmount' everydayness," (*SZ* 370),—that is, overcome it here and there personally or concretely through some stroke of genius, some creative gesture or burst of inspiration, or, who knows, through some sort of aberrant behavior—the everyday fundamentally dominates and determines it. The "they" always constitutes the first and essential being of Dasein in relation to which any deviation is marginal and from which any exceptional act, bound to be recuperated sooner or later, detaches itself only for a brief moment.

Dasein does not escape the everyday, even and especially if it refuses to be guided by it. "Everydayness is determinative for Dasein even when it has not chosen the 'they' for its 'hero'" (*SZ* 371). Thus the attempt to escape the authority of the "they," through, for example, entertainment, would still be a recognition of its domination over the Dasein which I am (or can be). The same thing goes for abandoning oneself to the "they," for being sick of it or wanting to master it. "In everydayness Dasein can undergo dull 'suffering', sink away in the dullness of it, or evade it by seeking new ways in which its dispersion in its affairs may be further dispersed. In the moment of vision, indeed, and often just 'for that moment', existence can even gain the mastery over the 'everyday'[2]; but it can never extinguish it [*auslöschen*]" (*SZ* 371).

Just as I can leave one *Stimmung* only by means of a counter-*Stimmung*, so I can leave the everyday only by means of a counter-everyday. If we are burning in the heart of everydayness from a monotonous though inextinguishable fire which constantly overtakes us, is it not because this is the obscure flame of temporality that touches us *zunächst und zumeist*, proximally and for the most part, to use the expression constantly repeated in *Sein und Zeit*?

But why? Why can we dominate the everyday only for an *instant*? Is this instant already the "moment of vision" [*Augenblick*] of authentic temporality wherein future, present, and past are found melded together in an ekstasis? But why then does this instant not "hold" like the moment of resoluteness? Why is it itself ephemeral? Why, especially, this first fall, prior to all mineness? Why the enigmatic "fallenness" of an ownness not yet known or attained? Why is Dasein, if it *can* win itself, or can "never win itself; or can do so only 'in appearance'" (*SZ* 42), always *already* dispersed into various worldly "concerns?" As much as Heidegger emphasizes in section 9 of *Sein und Zeit* that the two modes of *authentic* and *inauthentic* Being do not express a difference of more to less, of a greater to a lesser or more inferior Being, the description of the "they" in sections 26 and 27 is largely pejorative since inauthentic, everyday-Being is called "deficient," and the "they" is said to obscure, smother, and level all true possibility for Being by reducing any discovery to the already-known.

The enigma of everydayness is thus multiple. The *original* lowering of Dasein cannot be deduced but can only be phenomenologically noted and described. Enigmatic as well is the attachment, the irresistible inclination, the "temptation," as Heidegger says, which Dasein has for its own loss in the "they." Is this because the "they" doesn't die? Is it because the "they" is able to provide a reassuring explanation for all phenomena? But if Dasein is *Jemeinigkeit, in each case mine*, how can and must it fall from the beginning into non-mineness and, thus, forget its own essence? No doubt it is once again possible to respond that this fall comes from the fact that mineness produces anxiety. But what could be meant by an a priori fleeing in the face of an anxiety which 'one' (or the "they") has never known?! A strange Dasein it is that exists always already in a time that is not its own, even though it can never really become an authentic self, able to have itself in its entirety, except through an experience of the anxiety-ridden annihilation of all that is around it, through the trauma caused by the disintegration of the everyday world (pleonasm!) in its entirety! And enigmatic yet again is the primacy of facticity over transcendence; facticity first in the sense of a raw fact of Being, then in the sense of being surrounded or imprisoned by the Being of natural beings, and finally in the sense of being caught up in the paths, destinations, identities, and realities already established.

If Dasein is not a being of the world, if its Being is light, openness, *Lichtung,* how can it be fallen to the level of substances and things, deprived of its "natural" light, since its essence is to ek-sist far from itself, in view of itself, outside of itself? This self-reifying in-sistence of the ek-sistent is indeed enigmatic. Enigmatic also is the possible and initially nonvoluntary conversion through anxiety of an existence primordially fallen. Enigmatic too is the fact that our daily immediacy must make such a long detour, passing by a sphere so distant that it in fact envelops the entire world itself. Enigmatic finally (but is this the last enigma?) is the endless and inevitable oscillation between the ownness possibly won or rewon and the profound Neuter in which all existence is bathed. Because even if Dasein is authentic, that is, resolved to project upon the finite horizon of its own mortality the possibilities of the world that it has appropriated and has the courage to retake up and repeat again and again, it can never escape nor release itself once and for all from the everyday!

But is everydayness *really original?* Is there not concerning this crucial point an underlying doubt that gives to the entire work its impetus to push further on? The first section of *Sein und Zeit* clearly gives ontological primacy to the We-They. In the we-they the analysis discovers the source of all *significance [Bedeutsamkeit]*, that is, of the set of the systems of relations which constitute the world. Functioning like a transcendental subject, the "'Realest' subject of everydayness" (*SZ* 128), but concrete, factical, endowed with the highest concretion, (it is even designated as *"ens realissimum"* (*SZ* 128), "the 'they' itself prescribes that way of interpreting the world and Being-in-the-world which lies closest" and it "itself articulates the referential context of significance" (*SZ* 129). So it is not surprising to read on the following page that the "they" is found at the origin of the meaning of the Being of *all* worldly beings—first, because the being simply *present-at-hand* (*Vorhandenes*) is the result of a reduction (of a reduced vision of the being available or ready-to-hand (*Zuhandenes*); and, second, because in the common interpretation of everydayness Dasein is itself interpreted as a being simply present-at-hand. The refusal to understand the authentic one's-self as simply present-at-hand cannot make the "they" as supremely real subject disappear. That is why *"Authentic Being-one's-self* does not rest upon an exceptional condition of the subject, a condition that has been detached from the 'they'; it is rather an *existentiell modification of the 'they'—of the 'they' as an essential existentiale"* (*SZ* 130). Notice that Heidegger says: "an existentiell modification." And yet in the second section, after having gained both the existent*ial* possibility for Dasein to be an authentic totality through Being-toward-death and the existentiell possibility to be an authentic whole through anticipated resoluteness, it appears that these truly original possibilities had been *covered over* by the interpretations of the "they." From the moment when a "being-possible-as-a-whole" comes to light, *the analysis shifts*. The "they," public time, and the world now get their meaning from this new ground which is clearly not a supporting ground (a substance or a subject) but Dasein as possibility. My own possibility is *higher* than the solidified reality of the "they." This latter is "an *existentiell modification* of the authentic Self" (*SZ* 317, emphasis mine). The contradiction in the words is only in appearance insofar as the "they" was only in appearance the realest subject.

It would thus be possible to show that the reversal that governs the entire architectonic of *Sein und Zeit* rests upon a presupposition which is non-phenomenological, since it is not originally derived from a mere description of the phenomena of the *world* but from a preconceived notion of Dasein. This presupposition is none other than that of an authentic Self. The "they" is derivative from ownness. It is the appearance whose essence is ownness, the unshakable and nonhypothetical ground, the unique source of the world. From the first sketches of *Sein und Zeit* onward, Heidegger's principle of analysis is that manifest and polymorphous phenomenality hides and *covers over* the Originary-One. Being and truth are to be rewon from the coverings-over which are part of the movement and structure of manifestation. Thus Heidegger writes as early as 1923: "To everydayness belongs a certain averageness [*durch-schnittlichkeit*], the 'they,' in which the ownness [*Eigenheit*] and the possible authenticity [*Eigentlichkeit*] are kept covered over [*sich verdeckt halt*]" (*GA* 63: 85). Heideggerian phenomenology consists in discovering this true primordial ownness which the tradition, fallenness and forgetting, but also the unfolding of the world itself, keep covered over. The deconstruction of everydayness will thus have to reveal its *specific* mode of covering over. So what is this powerful mechanism, this great force of forgetting which works to dissimulate ownness? It is not, paradoxically, indifference to oneself but indifference to the other.[3] And this, in the very coming together of acting-with or caring-with.

A double covering over of the Other in work and in "ethics" constitutes the foundation of the everyday. Indeed, Dasein forgets its own possible care (*Sorge*), the concern to be itself and to unify its own time, by throwing itself into *Besorgen*, busied activity always looking to produce something or other, and *Fürsorge*, solicitude always looking to procure something for the other. These two activities are always for and with others, but in truth they are indifferent to the Other. There is no everydayness without the alterity of the Other being implied, invoked, or used, and yet at the same time, repressed, neglected, and finally denied. Everydayness is founded upon a "deficient" mode of Being-with-one-another (*Miteinandersein*).

The reality of everydayness is the world itself understood as a system of practical ends, as the network of functional and operational relations, that is, the world as a system of calls, to everyone in general and no one in particular, to work with a view toward something. In the *Prolegomena*, everydayness is more precisely defined as "the busied activity in the world with-one-another" (*GA* 20: 336). If the primordial discovery of the world is linked to affectivity (anxiety, fear, joy), everydayness is characterized by the affective neutrality that has always already admitted that the only thing that counts is the task to be accomplished. The being of the everyday world is in accord with the work to be done; it is joined in the common interest and it works to reactivate and reiterate the relations of functional interaction. Dasein ceases to be everyday when it is idle! Its everyday name is that of its occupation. Well before the analyses of Jünger (*The Worker,* 1932), Heidegger affirms that the *common* name of man is the worker. "In its everyday preoccupations Dasein is proximally and for the most part, always and each time, that at which it works [*das was es betreibt*]. One is what *one* does. [*Man* selbst ist was *man* macht]. The everyday interpretation of Dasein derives from that which each time constitutes its occupation as the horizon of this interpretation and its denomination. *One* is a shoemaker, tailor, professor, or banker" (*GA* 20: 336). What characterizes everyday Dasein is the fact that it has no *proper* name: its name changes according to the work it does. Work and everydayness are identical; those who work and share their everydayness are interchangeable.

In its daily work Dasein is intrinsically anonymous; it has no identity or interiority of its own. It is essentially replaceable by others insofar as they can perform the same tasks as it. Thus everydayness does not at all include the private sphere; familial relations, for example, remain indetermined as far as their possible authenticity is concerned. Everyday existence is always *outside, extrovert, public.*[4] The everyday is not the home. Must we then say, like Blanchot, that "if it is anywhere, it is in the streets"?[5] Is it not rather everywhere that one works? Everydayness would thus be in offices and workshops but not in museums and churches! It would be more *dense* in the city than in the country, a function of the *density* of work and of the instrumental and operational networks. In any case, everydayness signifies "publicness," that is to say, an interpretation that is common, exterior, irresponsible and necessarily superficial: "insensitive to every difference of level and of genuineness" (*SZ* 127), "publicness" establishes a false transparency which "obscures everything." It passes off all the phenomena of the world as having been, for a long time already, "well known and accessible to everyone," precisely because their equipmental meaning and practical uses are evident. Thus excluded from the definition of everydayness are, first of all, non-work-related attitudes and familiar gestures which are continually rebegun, for example, sleeping, getting up, washing, dressing, eating, reading, etc. (To which mode of Dasein do they belong if not to a *neutral* mode with respect to authenticity or inauthenticity? Must we say that eating out in a restaurant belongs to everydayness because one needs professionals, but that preparing a meal alone for oneself does not belong to it?) Excluded as well is all that belongs to a nonequipmental relation with nature, as, for example, taking a walk in a garden. (Would swimming in a pool be closer to everydayness than swimming in the ocean? And what about hunting and fishing as nonlucrative "sporting" activities which do not aim at procuring food? Would fishing be a sort of parody of everyday life which is supposed to be utilitarian, teleological, and serious?) The everyday must belong to an "intersubjective" human world, as Husserl would say. If it is understandable that the earth as the substructure of the world that escapes the world (except for the artist or the poet, as Heidegger will later say) be excluded from the everyday, it is odd that the alternation of day and night does not belong as such to everydayness, no more than the sun, the light, the seasons, the rain, or the wind do.

Houses and shelters against the rain, boats and airplanes, belong to everydayness, but not the rain, the heat and the cold, the sea, and the air themselves. The sun is an exception in that it marks the beginning and the end of the work day and lends itself to counting the hours, either directly on a sundial or indirectly on a watch. In *Sein und Zeit* the sun is considered phenomenologically as a nonfabricated "tool," a sort of instrument of work given by nature.[6] Everydayness is extranatural. Its daily sense is determined solely by the day of the world and not by the light of the day. In everydayness the sun is not new everyday; it shines upon nothing new because everything that is of *public utility* ceases to be new the moment it functions.

Everydayness, if it is outside of nature, is not, however, "social." It is founded upon a Being-with-others which existentially determines Dasein, even if no Other is in fact present-at-hand. "Even Dasein's Being-alone is Being-with in the world. The Other can be *missing* only in and for a Being-with" (*SZ* 120). "So far as Dasein *is* at all, it has Being-with-one-another as its kind of Being" (*SZ* 125). This Being-with originally takes, because of the primacy of praxis and equipmentality, the mode of Being of *common "concerns."* "Concern" (*Besorgen*) means ontically to be concerned with such and such an affair, to tend to such and such a need, to be involved in an activity aimed at procuring such and such a thing in the world. Ontologically, as an existential, it is to project one's "care" into the world. But procuring something *for another Dasein* is the result not only of concern (being preoccupied by the "material" availability of things, by the techniques for working with what is at hand), but of "solicitude" (*Fürsorge*). "Concern is a character-of-Being which Being-with cannot have as its own . . . " (*SZ* 121). *The Other calls for solicitude.* To be concerned (even if only for oneself) by food and clothing comes from solicitude and concerns Being-with—even more so when it is a question of feeding, clothing, caring for or helping others. But as the analysis notes, " . . . Dasein maintains itself proximally and for the most part in the deficient modes of solicitude" (*SZ* 121). What is this deficiency? It is nothing other than the "indifference" that characterizes ordinary solicitude. Ordinary solicitude is indifferent not to the objects to be provided but to the *place* of the Others in the concern that concerns them directly. It is indifferent not to that which the Other needs but to the "care" which the Other should take upon himself in this activity of procuring something. While concentrating on things, inauthentic solicitude seeks in fact to substitute itself for the Other in order to dominate him. "This kind of solicitude takes over for the Other that with which he is to concern himself" (*SZ* 122). Heidegger opposes to this "substitutive-dominating solicitude" an "anticipatory-liberating solicitude," that does not claim to take away from the Other his "care"; rather it helps him clearly understand it so that he can go freely toward it.

The various modes of Being of the "they" described in section 27, i.e., the inauthentic care to differentiate oneself from others, complacency regarding averageness, levelling, "publicness" that renders everything accessible and on the same level, all these various modes come from the *in-difference* with which Dasein endeavors to be *nobody*, to tear itself away from its own situations and decisions. "The 'they' has always kept Dasein from taking hold of these possibilities of Being. The 'they' even hides the manner in which it has tacitly relieved Dasein of the burden of explicitly *choosing* these possibilities" (*SZ* 268).

Does not the Heideggerian analysis amount to saying that the fall into everydayness is useful, pragmatically necessary, but "immoral"? The Good is elsewhere, in the Unique that I alone can discover; it is to be found not "in me," in my interiority, but in the world through the constant projection of my own temporality. Heidegger carries out a critique of the 'I' as substance, but he considers, perhaps in obedience to an exigency that comes from the oldest metaphysical source, that the complete unification of Dasein is the absolute *telos*. Dasein must be "protected *[schützen]* against its tendencies toward fragmentation [*Zersplitterung*]" (*SZ* 351). The bad plurality of affairs, concerns, or *pragmata* is opposed to the good singularity of my care in the face of my own possibility for death. Resoluteness turns its back on this fluttering about, on this constant pursuit of novelty, on indifference, in order to attach itself to the repetition of possibilities taken up as my own, in order to find the "constancy of Self," the "stability of existence," "the Self's resoluteness *against* the inconstancy of dispersion" (emphasis mine) (*SZ* 390).

The whole question is lodged in this refusal: Can I find my own being *against* everydayness? Why is it necessary to exclude "everyday things" from the authentic experience of Being? Is not authenticity modelled after the *myth of the hero*, the cult of the exceptional state, as the *instant* when existing Dasein sees itself ecstatically in its totality? Does not Heidegger expressly say that in the authentic retaking up of past possibilities "Dasein may choose its hero" (*SZ* 385)? Is it not rather that it chooses itself as its only hero?

Is it not necessary, in order to be done with Platonism, with the eternal schism, to learn anew to *love* the everyday? How could we, even from Heidegger's point of view, project only what we have chosen? What would we then do with facticity and chance? Is not the *amor fati* which teaches to "will that which I was forced to do," wiser than the radical and total depreciation of the everyday, wiser than the struggle with and suspicion of *ordinary Being*?

If authenticity were an heroic fiction, would not its counterpart, "everydayness," be just as fictive?

Listen to what seems to be Nietzsche's anticipated, albeit excessive, protest against this fiction, a protest just as intense and violent as the fiction itself and as the entire tradition:

The fantastic and delirious pathos with which we have valorized the most exceptional acts has as its counterpart the absurd indifference and contempt in which we enshroud obscure and everyday actions. We are the dupes of rarity and we have thus depreciated even our daily bread.[7]

NOTES

1. The word is taken from Robert Brisart. "La métaphysique de Heidegger," in *Heidegger et l'idée de la phénoménologie* (Dordrecht: Kluwer, 1988), 219.

2. Cf. *SZ* 56: "Being-in-the-world has always dispersed itself or even split itself up into definite ways of Being-in."

3. Indifference also because of a lack of distinction. Cf. *SZ* 118: "The Others are those from whom, for the most part, one does *not* distinguish oneself—those among whom one is too."

4. "No one in everydayness is himself. . . . The averageness of everyday Being-there implies no reflection on the 'I' ("Le concept de temps," in *Heidegger* [Paris: L'Herne, 1983], 30–31).

5. Maurice Blanchot, *L'entretien infini* (Paris: Gallimard, 1959), 362.

6. Michel Haar, *Le chant de la terre* (Paris: L'Herne, 1987), 56–58, and *SZ* §80.

7. Friedrich Nietzsche, *Aurore, Posthumous Fragments* (Paris: Gallimard, 1970), 353–54; also in *Sämtliche Werke, Kritische Studienausgabe,* Band 9, 3, (89) (Berlin: Walter de Gruyter, 1980), 70.

JOHN SALLIS

3. Deformatives

Essentially Other Than Truth

What if truth were monstrous? What if it were even monstrosity itself, the very condition, the very form, of everything monstrous, everything deformed? But, first of all, itself essentially deformed, monstrous in its very essence? What if there were within the very essence of truth something essentially other than truth, a divergence from nature within nature, true monstrosity?

How could one then declare the truth—if it were monstrous? How could one even begin—as I have—to ask about a monstrous essence of truth? Would not the language of such declarations and questions have to become monstrous in addressing—and in order to address—such truth? Would not the deformation of truth, the operation of its deformatives, engender a deforming of language? Would it not require a commencement of deformative discourse?

There is perhaps no discourse more inextricably entangled in what it would address than discourse on the essence of truth. There is perhaps no questioning less capable of detachment from what it would interrogate. For to ask the philosophical question "τί ἐστι . . .?", the question "What is it?", is to ask about the essence; and thus in the question "What is the essence of truth?" one merely repeats what is asked about, merely doubles the question. To say almost nothing of the way in which questioning is always already engaged with truth prior to any question: in coming to question one is already oriented to truth, that engagement from a distance constituting the very condition of the question. Heidegger has much to say about such engagement—for example, the following, which I excerpt from that part of *Beiträge zur Philosophie* entitled "The Essence of Truth": "The essence of truth grounds the necessity of the *why* and therewith of questioning" (*GA* 65: 353). There will always already have been a response to the essence of truth—a believing (*Glauben*) the *Beiträge* calls it—whenever questioning commences. Questioning will never have been simply outside the truth, other than the essence of truth, essentially other than truth.

Can there be, then, a question of an other? Under what conditions can the question of an essentially other than truth be raised? According to the *Beiträge* this question, the question of the relation of truth to an other, is inhibited, even prohibited (*verwehrt*), as long as ἀλήθεια is conceived in an originary way, *anfänglich begriffen als Grundcharakter der* φύσις, says Heidegger. One can ask about such a relation, he continues, only after the originary essence of ἀλήθεια has been given up and truth has become correctness (*GA* 65: 329–30). Thus the question of an other, of that which would be essentially other than truth, would not be an originary question. It would arise only in decline, in a falling away, in a certain return from engagement with the originary essence of truth.

It is a strange question, this question of the other of truth. For what could be more obvious than that truth has an other, an opposite, namely, untruth or error? Yet, what is the sense of other that is taken for granted when error is declared the other of truth? Can the sense of other be so rigorously stabilized that error can be declared simply *the* other of truth? Can the sense of otherness be restricted to opposition? Can the sense of opposition be itself rigorously controlled, its polysemy utterly reduced?

It will prove especially difficult to control the pairing of essence and other. One may say of course that error is essentially other than truth in that it falls simply outside truth itself, outside what truth itself is, outside the essence of truth. Indeed, in his most sustained discourse on the essence of truth Heidegger reaffirms this externality affirmed by both common sense and metaphysics. And yet, his reaffirmation is limited, not to say ironic, first of all because there is no simple outside: as the mere negation, the symmetrical opposite of truth, error is not essentially other but is dependent on the determination of truth. It is not essentially other than truth but only the other side of the determination of truth, the mere opposite.

Thus it is that when Nietzsche comes to think that final possibility with which the possibilities of metaphysics would finally be exhausted, he thinks truth as "*the kind of error* without which a certain kind of living being could not live."[1] This inversion, Nietzsche's reversal of Platonism, the end of metaphysics, proclaims that truth is error, that truth is untruth. In the *Beiträge* Heidegger repeats this proclamation, even though he encloses it within a double warning, marking it as captious and as too easily misunderstood. Nonetheless, it bears repeating, he grants, in order "to indicate the strangeness" of what is to be undertaken in this connection, the strangeness of what Heidegger calls a new projection of essence (*Wesensentwurf*) (*GA* 65: 351). The project is to reopen the essence of truth, redistributing the opposites. It is a matter of bringing a second moment into play along with the Nietzschean moment of inversion, of releasing a moment of displacement by which the very *Ordnungsschema* governing the opposition between truth and error would be transformed (cf. *GA* 43: 260). Now truth and untruth would be thought together differently; and through this deforming of the essence of truth thinking would come to *twist free* of the metaphysical opposition.

Such thinking of the essence of truth is carried out most rigorously in the text "On the Essence of Truth." What I propose is a rereading of this text—or rather, here, an indication of the schema of such a rereading—one that would focus on the moment in which the text twists free, one that would trace the displacement in which the mere opposite would become a proper untruth and would come to deform truth itself.

One should not underestimate the strangeness of this text, first presented as a public lecture in 1930 and repeatedly revised before finally being published in

1943.[2] If one compares the published text of 1943 with the still unpublished lecture of 1930, the impression of strangeness is enhanced. The double text, enclosing a period of thirteen years, becomes even stranger if one unfolds within it another discourse on truth belonging within this period, the one contained in the *Beiträge* (1936–38) under the title "The Essence of Truth" (*GA* 65: 327–70). In the latter, for example, one finds a curious sequence of indications assembled under the title: *Worum es sich bei der Wahrheitsfrage handelt* (one might translate loosely, since it cannot strictly be translated: What the question of truth is all about) (*GA* 65: 338). The first indication in the sequence reads: "not a matter of a mere modification of the concept." The second reads, surprisingly, strangely: "not a matter of a more originary insight into the essence." The third continues: "but rather a matter of *den Einsprung in die Wesung der Wahrheit*"—a matter, one may say in lieu of the impossible translation, of stepping into the essential unfolding of truth. The indications become still stranger, the fourth reading: "and consequently a matter of a transformation of the Being of man in the sense of a *derangement* [*Ver-rückung*] of his position among beings." What is the question of truth all about? Human derangement, madness!

The strangeness of the text "On the Essence of Truth"—I refer to the published text of 1943—is less apparent, at least at the beginning. The objections by which common sense opposes any question of the essence of truth are sounded; and it is declared that common sense has its own necessity, that it can never be refuted by philosophy. Yet, almost from the outset a displacement of the common commences, giving way finally to the uncommon declaration of the proposition "The essence of truth is the truth of essence." What is perhaps strangest is the pairing of this declaration with a certain retraction. Heidegger says of the proposition: "It is no proposition [*Satz*] at all in the sense of a statement [*Aussage*]" (*GA* 9: 201). But if the proposition "The essence of truth is the truth of essence" is also not a proposition, then what is to be said of it, through it? A most uncommon saying: "the saying of a turning within the history of Being."

In its formal structure the text "On the Essence of Truth" displays a certain symmetry. It is divided into nine sections. The first four develop the question of the essence of truth. This development is gathered up in the fifth, the central section, which is entitled "The Essence of Truth." Then come, finally, four sections that appear to extend or round out what has been established, addressing the question of the relation of philosophy to the essence of truth and especially the question of untruth.

In the movement of the text, however, there is a certain eccentricity that finally transforms—or rather, deforms—this formal structure. Thus, most notably, the question of untruth is not simply reserved for the final sections of the text but is in play from the beginning, in play at least in Heidegger's ironic declarations of the legitimacy of deferring, if not excluding, its consideration. This operation of the question of untruth throughout the text cannot but produce, in turn, a certain doubling of the center, hence finally a decentering of the entire discourse, even a monstrous decentering.

A certain uncommon movement is broached from the outset of the text. Heidegger begins: Vom *Wesen* der Wahrheit ist die Rede. The discourse concerns the *essence* of truth. Heidegger italicizes *Wesen* (*essence*) and so in this opening calls attention to it. In a sense the entire opening section of the text is addressed solely to this word *essence* and to what is said in it. Heidegger observes that in asking about the *essence* of truth, one is not concerned with any specific kind of truth but rather disregards, abstracts from, the differences between, for example, scientific truth and artistic truth, attending rather to the one thing that distinguishes every truth as truth. That one thing that all truths have in common would constitute the *essence* of truth. Thus, essence means: the common—in Greek: κοινόν.

In this connection Heidegger also refers to common sense (*der gemeine Menschenverstand*). He not only refers to it but also speaks (almost) with its voice, and one realizes from the outset that various voices—a polyphony—are to be heard in this text. Heidegger voices—as a question—the objections that common sense makes to the question of essence: "Is not the question of essence the most inessential and superfluous that could be asked?" (*GA* 9: 177). It is as if common sense—opposing the question of the common—were in opposition to itself. Yet the opposition that Heidegger stresses is that between common sense and philosophy, an opposition that is in a sense irresolvable: "Philosophy can never refute common sense" (*GA* 9: 178). Near the end of "On the Essence of Truth" Heidegger will again speak of common sense, and it will be necessary to consider what bearing the questioning ventured in Heidegger's text has on common sense and whether this questioning bears on it in any other than a purely extrinsic, negative way.

What first broaches an uncommon movement is a marginal comment written by Heidegger in his own copy of the third edition (1954) of "On the Essence of Truth" and now, along with other marginal comments, included with the text in the *Gesamtausgabe*. These marginal comments are not simple additions to the text, and their function cannot be limited to mere clarification. Not only do they introduce in the margin of the text later developments in Heidegger's thought that presuppose the way laid out in the text; but also within the text itself many of the marginal comments produce a disordering, announcing at the outset of a development in the text a result that is to be reached only by way of that development. For instance, at the beginning of section I Heidegger sets out to consider what one ordinarily understands by the "worn and almost dulled word 'truth'" (*GA* 9: 178–79). Yet, before he can even begin to declare what this most ordinary understanding is, the text is interrupted by a marginal comment keyed to the word *truth:* the comment refers *truth* to *clearing* and, hence, leaps over the entire development just commencing that will be required in order to translate the discourse on truth into a discourse on clearing. The marginal comment carries out the translation instantaneously; its discourse, disordering the text, is heterogeneous with the discourse of the text—or rather it renders the text a scene of double writing.

A similar disordering, a drastic foreshortening, is produced by the marginal comment keyed to the word *essence* in the opening sentence of "On the Essence of Truth." The comment reads: "Essence: 1. quidditas—the what—κοινόν; 2. making-possible [*Ermöglichung*]—condition of possibility; 3. ground of the making-possible" (*GA* 9: 177). Thus, prior to the determination of essence as the common, as κοινόν, the comment indicates that this initial determination is not the only one that will come into play, that there are at least the two other senses of essence mentioned in the comment. Thus, the text is to put into question not only the essence of truth but also the very sense of essence. It could not be otherwise, granted that Heideggerian reading of Plato that links the determination of truth as ὁμοίωσις to the determination of Being as εἶδος, hence to the determination of *essentia,* essence. Thus is the text "On the Essence of Truth" oriented from the beginning to that nonproposition to which it will finally lead: the essence of truth is the truth of essence.

One finds, then, in the text "On the Essence of Truth" a *double series* of redeterminations, beginning with the ordinary concept of truth and the common sense of essence and then proceeding to the more originary determinations mentioned in the marginal comment.

Heidegger begins by circumscribing the ordinary, i.e., the common, concept of truth. What one ordinarily understands by *truth* is that which makes a true thing true, more specifically, that by virtue of which a thing or a proposition is true. As such, truth has, then, the character of accordance or correspondence (*Übereinstimmung*). In the case of a thing it is a matter of accordance with a certain preunderstanding; for example, true gold, genuine gold, is gold that accords with what one understands in advance by *gold.* In the case of a proposition, it is a matter of accordance with that about which the proposition is asserted, of correspondence with the thing spoken of. Heidegger traces this concept of truth back to its origin in the medieval definition: *veritas est adaequatio rei et intellectus.* Here there is a double accordance rooted in the medieval conception of the relation between God, nature, and man. A thing is true only if it accords with the divine idea, with the archetypal idea in the divine intellect; in this case truth consists in the accordance of the thing with the divine intellect (*adaequatio rei ad intellectum*). But in the case of the human intellect, that is, of human knowledge as expressed in propositions, the structure is more complex: on the one hand, a human idea is true by according with the divine idea, just as anything creaturely is true by according with the divine archetype; on the other hand, a human idea is true by according with the thing known, and it is in this connection that truth consists in *adaequatio intellectus ad rem.* The connection is this: a human idea can correspond to the known thing only on the basis of a double correspondence (of the human idea *and* of the thing) to the divine idea. As Heidegger writes: "If all beings are 'created', the possibility of the truth of human knowledge is grounded in the following: that thing [*Sache*] and proposition measure up to the idea in the same way and therefore are fitted to each other on the basis of the unity of the divine plan of creation" (*GA* 9: 180–81). A marginal comment puts it still more succinctly: "Because of correspondence with the creator, therefore [correspondence] *among themselves* (as created . . .)" (*GA* 9: 181). By thus tracing the common concept of truth back to its medieval origin, Heidegger carries out a kind of desedimenting of it, referring it to this, its "most recent," origin in such a way as to broach its *Destruktion*. In order to disrupt the obviousness that common sense takes it to have, he shows that this concept of truth is rooted in medieval ontology, in a certain interpretation of Being, and that, consequently, the concept of truth as accordance (correspondence) is anything but obvious when, as in modern thought, it comes to be detached from that interpretation of Being. By linking the allegedly ordinary concept of truth to its medieval origin, by demonstrating its historicity, Heidegger indicates that outside medieval ontology it is not at all obvious what is meant by accordance of an idea with a thing, of a statement with that about which it is said. By desedimenting this concept of truth, he releases its questionableness: "What is it about statements that still remains worthy of question [*Fragwürdiges*]—granted that we know what is meant by accordance of a statement with the thing? Do we know that?" (*GA* 9: 182).

The irony is more veiled in what Heidegger says at this first stage about untruth. But only slightly so: Heidegger links what is said about untruth to the very obviousness that the entire discussion has aimed at subverting. It is considered obvious that truth has an opposite, namely, untruth, which would, then, consist in nonaccordance. Heidegger concludes that untruth, so conceived, "falls outside the essence of truth." He continues: "Therefore, when it is a matter of comprehending the pure essence of truth, untruth, as such an opposite of truth, can be put aside" (*GA* 9: 182). As mere opposite, untruth belongs outside; its consideration can be left aside or at least deferred until the essence of truth has been secured.

What drives Heidegger's text on to its second stage is the question: What is meant by *accordance* (*Übereinstimmung*) in the definition of truth as accordance of a statement with the thing about which it is made? How can there be an accordance between a statement and a thing, considering how utterly different they are? Heidegger's answer reaches back to Husserl's *Logical Investigations:* such accord is possible only because the statement is not just another, though utterly different thing, but rather is a moment belonging to a comportment to the thing about which the statement is made. Heidegger's formulation is most concise in the 1930 lecture text: "It is only because the statement is also a comporting [*Verhalten*] that it can in its way accord with something." What kind of comporting occurs in the assertion of a true statement? A comportment, says Heidegger, that presents the thing as it is. Or rather, since he writes the word with a hyphen, *vor-stellen*, distinguishing it from *vorstellen* in the modern epistemological or psychological sense, let it be said that such comportment sets the thing there before us as it is. But what is thus required? What must be involved in a comportment that—in the appropriate sense—presents the thing as it is? Heidegger answers—I cite the 1943 published text:

> This can occur only if beings present themselves along with the presentative statement so that the latter subordinates itself to the directive that it speak of beings *such-as* they are. In following such a directive the statement conforms to beings. Speech that directs itself accordingly is correct (true). (*GA* 9: 184)

What is required, then, is "a binding directedness [*eine bindende Richte*]" to things, a subordination of speech to them in such a way that one speaks of things in just *such* a way *as* they are.

At this juncture let me double the text, bringing into play alongside the published text of 1943 the original lecture text of 1930. For in the earlier double of the text one finds a different formulation of the same matter. Heidegger refers to two characteristics of such comportment as occurs in the assertion of a true statement: on the one hand, revealing or making manifest (*Offenbaren*) and, on the other hand, letting-be-binding (*Verbindlich-sein-lassen*). Thus, such comportment reveals things, shows them as they are, *and yet* is bound precisely by those things. Heidegger raises the question of the relation between these two characteristics, the question as to which is prior. In a sense it is less a question than a paradox that one might formulate as follows: one's comportment would have to be bound by the things, governed by them, in order to reveal them *as* they are; and yet, that comportment could be bound by them only if one had already revealed them so as to take one's bearings from them as they are. This paradoxical formulation indicates the necessity of Heidegger's conclusion: "The two characteristics of comportment, revealing and letting-be-binding, . . . are not two at all but rather one and the same." They must, then, be thought together, thought as one and the same.

In the 1943 text Heidegger gathers up the requirements that must be met in order that comportment be such that true statements can arise in it; he gathers them in the phrase "openness of comportment (*Offenständigkeit des Verhaltens*)." He concludes: "But if the correctness (truth) of statements becomes possible only through this openness of comportment, then what first makes correctness possible must with more originary right be taken as the essence of truth" (*GA* 9: 185). Such is, then, the second pair of determinations in that double series: more originary than the common essence is essence as *making-possible;* and more originary than truth as accordance (correctness) is the essence of truth as openness of comportment.

Heidegger's move to the third stage seems quite classical: it is a regress from the openness of comportment to the *ground* of that openness. In the 1943 text the move is carried out very quickly, requiring only a few sentences. Let me attempt to reinscribe those sentences—still more economically—by extending the doubling of the text, again bringing into play the description of open comportment provided by the 1930 text. The first of the two characteristics, revealing beings, involves presenting them, setting them there before—and so over against—us; that is, it involves setting them within what the 1943 text calls "an open field of opposedness [*ein offenes Entgegen*]," "an open region [*das Offene*]" (*GA* 9: 184). The other characteristic of such comportment, letting beings be binding, involves maintaining a binding or pregiven directedness toward those beings so as to present them *as they are*. Thus, the openness of comportment requires a certain *engagement* in the open region and a certain *openness* to what is opened up there, namely, to the beings to which speech would submit. Such engaged openness is to be called *freedom*. Thus, the ground of the making-possible of truth as accordance is freedom. Heidegger concludes that the essence of truth is freedom.

Such is, then, the third pair of determinations in the double series: essence as *ground* and the essence of truth as *freedom*.

The essence of truth is freedom: Heidegger observes that this proposition cannot but seem strange. Strange—not merely because it offends common sense by appearing to submit truth to human caprice, but because, far beyond the reach of common sense, it broaches in the word *freedom* an opposition that borders on the unthinkable, an engaged openness, an engagement that "withdraws in the face of beings in order that they might reveal themselves" (*GA* 9: 188–89). Will these ever have been thought as one and the same? Can freedom be thought as such?

It would appear that freedom comes to be thought in the move toward the center of the text "On the Essence of Truth." The very title of the fourth section, "The Essence of Freedom," appears to indicate the course of the further regress that such thinking would follow: from freedom to the essence of freedom. Indeed Heidegger asks explicitly: "How is this essence of freedom to be thought?" (*GA* 9: 187–88). Yet, at the beginning of this section, he also hints that this regress will be a *double move:*

> Consideration of the essential connection between truth and freedom leads us to pursue the question of the essence of man in a regard which assures us an experience of a concealed essential ground of man (of Dasein), and in such a manner that the experience transposes us in advance into the originarily essential domain of truth. (*GA* 9: 187).

Thus, it is to be: (1) a move to the (concealed) essential ground of man, this ground presumably constituting the essence of freedom; and thereby (2) a transposition to a domain of truth that Heidegger ventures to call "originarily essential."

Heidegger begins by identifying freedom as *letting-be:* freedom lets beings be the beings they are and so has the character of letting-beings-be (*das Seinlassen von Seiendem*). Letting-be is not of course a matter of neglect or indifference. In one marginal comment, he explains that it is "not negative"; rather, in the formulation given in another marginal comment, it is "to allow what is present its presence, to bring nothing else . . . in between" (*GA* 9: 188). It is, however, no mere dealing with beings, no tending, managing, or even preserving, but requires that one "engage oneself with the open region and its openness [*das Offene und dessen Offenheit*] into which every being comes to stand" (*GA* 9: 188). Heidegger adds that in the beginning of Western thought this open region was conceived as τὰ ἀληθέα (he translates: *das Unverborgene*, the unconcealed) and its openness as ἀλήθεια (*Unverborgenheit*, unconcealment). One cannot but note also the connection with the phenomena of world and disclosedness (*Erschlossenheit*) developed in *Being and Time*.

By introducing letting-be, Heidegger reorients somewhat those two opposed moments that were found to drive the concept of freedom almost to the point of contradiction. In place of an engagement in revealing, in presenting beings, that would be coupled with a withdrawal, a holding back, so as to be bound by beings, engagement is now thought preeminently as engagement *in the open region,* whereas it is a matter of withdrawal *in the face of the beings* that come to presence in that open region. It is still a matter of thinking these together, even if also in their difference:

> To engage oneself with the disclosedness [*Entborgenheit*] of beings is not to lose oneself in them; rather, such engagement withdraws in the face of beings in order that they might reveal themselves with respect to what and how they are and in order that presentative correspondence might take its standard from them. (*GA* 9: 188–89)

Such engagement, which sustains letting-be, has the character of exposure (*Aussetzung*) to beings as such in the open; it is a matter of being set out into the open region in which beings come to presence. It is a matter of being *ek-sistent,* of standing outside oneself, out into the open in which beings come to presence.[3] Heidegger insists that, when conceived as ex-posure, as ek-sistence, freedom can no longer be regarded as a property of man but rather must be considered that which first lets man be *as* man: "Man does not 'possess' freedom as a property. At best, the converse holds: freedom, ek-sistent, disclosing Da-sein possesses man . . . " (*GA* 9: 190).

Hence one movement of the double move: to the concealed essential ground of man, namely, freedom as ek-sistence—that is, the essence of freedom determined as ek-sistence.

But in this determination of the essence of freedom how is the sense of essence determined—if I may continue for the moment to mark with the word *sense* a question belonging to a region in which this word cannot but become ever more questionable. Most remarkably and in utter contrast to the previous three stages, Heidegger now says nothing whatsoever about the sense of essence, not even in his marginal comments. Yet, something can be said—even if with all the withholding that the matter here exacts, even if such reticent saying also borders on the unthinkable, reproducing the opposition that would be said in the word *freedom,* reproducing it as freedom of speech. Something can be said if one sets side by side two almost identical propositions bearing on the determination of freedom. The first reads: "the essence of freedom manifests itself as exposure to the disclosedness of beings." The other: "Freedom is . . . engagement in the disclosure of beings" (*GA* 9: 189). Both freedom and the essence of freedom are the same—namely, exposure to or engagement in the disclosedness or unconcealment of beings. Thus, the essence of freedom is freedom—that is, freedom itself, freedom proper. In the word *essence* one is now to hear: the "itself," the proper.

And yet, what is most remarkable is that this would-be delimitation of freedom itself, of freedom proper, has precisely the effect of disrupting the "itself," the "proper." For to be ek-sistent, to be engaged in, exposed to the unconcealment of beings, is to be referred beyond oneself, referred *essentially,* one might venture—not without also withholding it—to say. It is to be outside oneself, ecstatic, in a manner that cannot leave the "oneself," the proper, the essence, intact.

Thus it is that Heidegger writes: freedom "receives its own essence from the more originary essence of uniquely essential truth" (*GA* 9: 187). Let it be said: freedom is submitted to unconcealment, to ἀλήθεια. This submission constitutes the second moment of the double move: a transposition to the originarily essential domain of truth. Hence, the double move as a whole consists in the regress to the essence of man (freedom, ek-sistence) *and then,* precisely because it is ek-sistent, ecstatic, in the referral of this essence beyond itself, what one would like to call its *essential* reference beyond itself (were the reference not deformative both of essence and of its doubling). One could say that there is a deeper sense in which freedom is not a property of man (were the deformation of essence, now broached, not also a deformation of sense, of the sense of sense, to say nothing of the implied order of depth): freedom, as ek-sistence, is the very *dispropriation* of the essence of man.

Thus it is, too, that at the center of "On the Essence of Truth," in that section in which the entire movement would be gathered under the title "The Essence of Truth," so little is said. What one finds there is a discourse that bespeaks unmistakably the submission to ἀλήθεια, a discourse on attunement (*Stimmung*), the very way of being submitted to the open, to ἀλήθεια. It is *almost* as if at its center the text "On the Essence of Truth" had come essentially to its end. Almost as if it would require still only perhaps some final rounding out.

Almost—but not quite.

For at the center there is also another discourse, a discourse on untruth, one that resumes a subdiscourse that has haunted the text all along its way toward the center. Even after the regress to freedom as the essence of truth, the question of untruth is addressed in nearly the same form as at the outset: untruth is declared both the opposite of truth and the non-essence of truth and, with an irony that anticipates what is to come, it is said to be excludable "from the sphere of the question concerning the pure essence of truth" (*GA* 9: 187). Then, following the disruption of freedom proper that is announced under the title "The Essence of Truth," Heidegger introduces an untruth that would consist, not in mere nonaccordance, but in covering up or distorting (in a certain opposition to letting-be). Then, most decisively, he withdraws untruth from the domain of the merely human. Untruth, too, must be referred beyond all proper freedom, beyond man himself: "The non-essence of truth cannot first arise subsequently from mere human incapacity and negligence. Rather, untruth must derive from the essence of truth" (*GA* 9: 191). To think the essence of truth will thus require thinking also the non-essence (un-truth). Thus begins—at the very threshold of the center—the decentering that drives the text onward: not only the decentering already under way, the decentering of man, the decentering by which he is displaced, dispossessed, in the direction of originarily essential truth; but also now—still more disruptively—a decentering of truth itself, a displacement by which it ceases to be simply (properly) set over against its opposite (untruth). It is a decentering of opposition as such that now drives the text onward.

Onward to the would-be center—which, contrary to what its title and the apparent symmetry of the entire text would suggest, culminates not in a declaration of the essence of truth, of truth proper, but rather in a discourse on untruth. This discourse proclaims a still more intimate adherence of untruth to truth: "Letting-be is intrinsically at the same time a concealing [*Das Seinlassen ist in sich zugleich ein Verbergen*]. In the ek-sistent freedom of Dasein . . . there is concealment [*Verborgenheit*]" (*GA* 9: 193). Thus is broached a monstrous decentering of the essence of truth, an opening of it to an other that would no longer be merely a symmetrical opposite but that would be intrinsic to it, that would belong to it. Thus, at its center the text broaches a monstrous decentering, which cannot but deform the text itself. From this point on it will become ever more monstrous—beginning with the passage from the would-be center to the remaining sections of the text, a monstrous transition that is not a passage or transition at all but a leap. A marginal comment marks it as such—as "the leap into the turning (that essentially unfolds in *Ereignis*) [*der Sprung in die (im Ereignis wesende) Kehre*]" (*GA* 9: 193).

Hence the monstrous phrase that follows this leap—the phrase with which Heidegger refers to concealment as: the un-truth that is *most proper* to the essence of truth. Now untruth belongs most properly to the essence of truth, belongs to what would have been the proper of truth, had that very proper not been disrupted by the submission of freedom to ἀλήθεια. It is time to read the discourse onto which the phrase opens:

> Here non-essence does not yet have the sense of inferiority to essence in the sense of the general [*das Allgemeine*—what is common to all] (κοινόν, γένος), its *possibilitas* (making-possible) and the ground of its possibility. Non-essence is here what in such a sense would be a pre-essential essence. But "non-essence" means at first and for the most part the deformation [*die Verunstaltung*] of that already inferior essence. Indeed, in each of these significations the non-essence remains always in its own way essential to the essence and never becomes unessential in the sense of something indifferent. (*GA* 9: 194)

Truth becomes monstrous: a deformation of what is natural (i.e., of the essential); a divergence from nature, something unnatural, within nature (non-essence within essence). Here the sense of essence is disrupted so decisively that it erases its very designation as a disruption of *sense,* namely, by disrupting the very operation of the concept of sense as well as the sense of concept. Concealment as non-essence is a deformative so decisive as to require that one begin to write differently, that a deformative writing commence.[4] One would say that now the structure of essence is such that the non-essence belongs to it rather than falling outside it, that essence is such as to include non-essence within it. But one would have also to pair with such saying an unsaying that would grant the deformative effect upon such words as *such, within,* and *itself.* Little wonder that, when Heidegger comes finally to propose the answer to the question of the essence of truth, he must pair that proposal with a denial that it is a proposition.

Let me extend the discourse in that direction by mentioning—all too briefly—three moments in the discourse on untruth that has now commenced.

The first is the extension that the deformative move undergoes through the introduction of *errancy*. Thus would Heidegger name—alongside the concealment already introduced into the essence of truth as its proper non-essence (*eigentliche Un-wahrheit*), what he now calls *the mystery* (*das Geheimnis*)—another form—or rather, deform—of untruth belonging to the essence of truth, belonging to it as its essential counter-essence (*das wesentliche Gegenwesen*). Hence, there is a doubling of untruth, into non-essence and counter-essence. But, in turn, errancy is determined as a double movement. On the one hand, it is a concealing of concealment, that is, a covering up of the mystery that holds sway throughout Dasein's engagement in the open. On the other hand, it is a turning toward readily available beings, away from the (concealed) mystery: "Man clings to what is readily available and controllable even where ultimate matters are concerned" (*GA* 9: 195). Thus is man left "to his own resources," in a kind of abandonment or destitution (*Seinsverlassenheit*).

Hence, there is not only a doubling of untruth but even a redoubling inasmuch as errancy is thus determined as a double movement. Such proliferation of deformatives cannot but deform ever more the essence of truth, inasmuch as essence in all its senses hitherto—thus, one would like to say: essence in its essence—has been determined primarily in relation to unity, not duplicity. But now, as truth becomes essentially duplicitous, it becomes also ever more monstrous.

The second extension gives an indication of the force of the disruption. Heidegger writes:

> But to speak of non-essence and untruth in this manner goes very much against the grain of ordinary opinion and looks like a dragging up of forcibly contrived *paradoxa*. Because it is difficult to eliminate this impression, such a way of speaking, paradoxical only for ordinary *doxa* (opinion), is to be renounced. (*GA* 9: 194)

Such a way of speaking, this double talk about an essential non-essence, *speaks against* ordinary opinion, literally contra-dicts common sense. For common sense insists on the mutual exclusion of opposites, that one cannot have, in the same connection, both truth and untruth, certainly not as constituting the very essence of truth. This mutual exclusion is precisely what is enforced by the so-called law of non-contradiction. Little wonder that Heidegger proposes a certain indirection or renunciation: he is speaking against the law of non-contradiction. Could there be a discourse more monstrous than one that dares contradict the law of non-contradiction?

The third extension indeed attests to something still more monstrous. Now it becomes a matter not only, as the 1930 text expresses it, of letting the non-essence into the essence, but of putting into question the priority of the essence proper over the non-essence. The 1930 text denies such a priority, granting instead that concealment is "as old as the very letting-be of beings." The 1943 text goes still further and reverses the priority:

The concealment of beings as a whole, untruth proper, is older than every openedness of this or that being. It is also older than letting-be itself which in unconcealing already holds concealed and comports itself toward concealing. (*GA* 9: 193–94)

Thus it is said—and will soon have also to be unsaid—that within the essence of truth non-essence is older than what was previously called essence, untruth older than truth—the word *older* here replacing all the words with which a thinking short of such deformity would still attempt to say such orderings. The *Beiträge* says the same differently: "The essence of truth is un-truth"—a saying that, even if risky, serves nonetheless, as the *Beiträge* continues, "to bring nearer the strangeness of the strange essence of truth" (*GA* 65: 356).

In the final section of "On the Essence of Truth" Heidegger proposes an answer to the question of the essence of truth.[5] The proposal takes the form of a translation. The proposition—it will also be declared not a proposition—to be translated is introduced as follows: "The question of the essence of truth finds its answer in the proposition: *the essence of truth is the truth of essence*" (*GA* 9: 201). In preparation for translating this proposition, Heidegger establishes four points: (1) The subject of the proposition, though written at the end, is: *the truth of essence*. In the translation the proposition will be rewritten accordingly, inverted. (2) In *the truth of essence,* essence is to be understood verbally: as *wesen*. Here there is already a problem of translation, of translating *wesen* into English, or rather, an impossibility, in face of which one can only resort to some such locution as: to unfold essentially. (3) In *the truth of essence, truth* says: sheltering that clears (*lichtendes Bergen*). In turn, *sheltering that clears* simply says the essence of truth as it has finally been determined in Heidegger's text: unconcealment (clearing) as including double concealment (mystery and errancy), which might be written as ἀ-λήθεια. Such sheltering-that-clears Heidegger identifies as the *Grundzug* of the Being of beings: its basic character, to be sure, but, more literally, the basic draught, drawing, movement, by which beings can come forth in their Being, come to presence. Putting (2) and (3) together, one may translate *truth of essence* as saying: *sheltering-that-clears* (i.e., the drawing of ἀ-λήθεια) essentially unfolds. . . . (4) In *the essence of truth,* as this occurs in the proposition to be translated, essence means whatness and truth is understood as a characteristic of knowledge, i.e., as accordance.

These preparations let one see that the proposition *the essence of truth is the truth of essence* encompasses the full course through which "On the Essence of Truth" has moved. Heidegger's translation makes this explicit: "Sheltering-that-clears is—i.e., lets essentially unfold [*lässt wesen*]—accordance between knowledge and beings" (*GA* 9: 201). But then, having translated the proposition, Heidegger abruptly denies that it is a proposition: "It is no proposition [*Satz*] at all in the sense of a statement [*Aussage*]" (*GA* 9: 201). Presumably, one is to understand: it is not a proposition, a statement, because it is a saying of that which first makes possible all propositions in the sense of statements with their claims to be in accordance with things.

At the outset and indeed throughout "On the Essence of Truth" Heidegger refers to the opposition between philosophy and common sense (*der gemeine Verstand, der gesunde Menschenverstand*). By voicing—as an ironically endorsed question—the opinion of common sense that the question of essence is "the most inessential and superfluous that could be asked" (*GA* 9: 177), he alludes to a very traditional interpretation of this opposition: that philosophy is *eine verkehrte Welt,* standing common sense on its head. The opposition is one that philosophy cannot simply dissolve; common sense has, to be sure, its own weapons, most notably, the appeal to obviousness. Philosophy cannot refute it, says Heidegger, for it is blind to the essence of philosophy (in the language of the 1930 text), or (according to the published text) "deaf to the language of philosophy" and "blind to what philosophy sets before its [own] essential vision" (*GA* 9: 178). Furthermore, common sense constantly threatens to ensnare philosophy:

> Moreover, we ourselves remain within the sensibleness of common sense to the extent that we suppose ourselves to be secure in those multiform "truths" of practical experience and action, of research, and belief. We ourselves intensify that resistance which the "obvious" has to every demand made by what is questionable. (*GA* 9: 178)

Or in the more direct language of the 1930 version:

> The common understanding, who is that? We ourselves, even and precisely philosophy, we ourselves who now conjecture about the question of the essence of truth as about just any other question, which we tend to pose just like the question of the weather or any such thing.

One could say, then, that common sense is not just an opposite set decisively and securely outside philosophy; rather, the opposition between philosophy and common sense is such that it also opens up *within philosophy itself.* Thus would the non-essence of philosophy (common sense) belong to its essence, the deformation of essence thus coming to determine philosophy itself, or rather, in strictest terms, to deprive it of itself, submit it to dispropriation.

A traditional name for this non-essence that invades the essence of philosophy is *sophistry.* Heidegger alludes to the relevant configuration:

> However, in the same period in which the beginning of philosophy takes place, the *marked* domination of common sense (sophistry) also begins. Sophistry appeals to the unquestionable character of the beings that are opened up and interprets all thoughtful questioning as an attack on, an unfortunate irritation of, common sense. (*GA* 9: 199)

Heidegger leaves it unsaid whether he takes the opposition between philosophy and common sense (sophistry—though certainly it is not *simply* common sense) to represent a decline from another thinking that would be free of such opposition or whether such opposition is to be regarded as necessarily belonging to any thinking, however displaced it may be from the beginning of philosophy.

There is something about the 1930 version of Heidegger's text that I have left unsaid until now: the title "The Essence of Truth" is given only as the *second* of two titles and even as such is placed in parentheses, as a subtitle subordinated to the first of the titles, the main title: "Philosophizing and Believing" (*"Philosophieren und Glauben"*). Furthermore, Heidegger announces in the opening paragraph that

> the task of the lecture is stated by the main title. The main title says what is to be dealt with, philosophizing and believing, thus not philosophy and theology. The subtitle states how we are to set about the task . . ., [viz.,] by questioning concerning the essence of truth.

Heidegger asks: "But is believing not then already excluded?" He answers: "Certainly, and yet we deal also with believing in passing over it in silence." Indeed, there is only silence: after the opening paragraph, believing is not mentioned again. And in the 1943 version of the text there is only the most passing of references to believing.

In order to elucidate this strange situation, one must turn to *Beiträge zur Philosophie,* specifically to the section entitled "Belief and Truth" (*GA* 65: 368–70—§237). Let me deal—very schematically—with a series of points: (1) Heidegger refers, first of all, to the task of the section: to conceive the essence of believing on the basis of the essence of truth. The affinity with the stated task of the 1930 lecture is evident. (2) Focusing on believing and noting its opposition to knowing (*Wissen*), he offers the following characterization: believing is a *Für-wahr-halten* of something that withdraws from knowledge; to believe is to hold as true (to hold to be true) something that withdraws from insight. Heidegger mentions the example of believing a report whose truth cannot be directly confirmed. (3) But then he asks: What is authentic knowing (*das eigentliche Wissen*)? His answer: it is that knowing "which knows the essence of truth and thus only determines itself in the turn from out of this essence." It is *das Sichhalten im Wesen der Wahrheit*; or, in the terms of "On the Essence of Truth," ek-sistence. (4) Heidegger calls this knowing "essential knowing [*das wesentliche Wissen*]" and gives it priority over all believing: it is more originary than every believing, for the latter is always related to something true (*ein Wahres*) and hence presupposes knowing the essence of truth. He adds that such knowing is no mere representing of something encountered (*vorstellen*—written now without the hyphen). (5) And yet, he continues: "If one takes 'knowing' in the prevailing sense of representing [*vorstellen*] and possession of representations, then essential knowing is indeed not a 'knowing' but a 'believing.'" One could say: essential knowing is a believing because it is linked, not just to *something* that withdraws, that is concealed, from insight, but to the very concealment in the draught of which things can come to be concealed, to withdraw from insight, the concealment that Heidegger has identified as the (double) non-essence belonging "properly" to the essence of truth. (6) Heidegger concludes: "This originary believing is not at all a matter of accepting that which offers immediate support and makes courage superfluous. This believing is rather a persisting in the uttermost decision [*Ausharren in der äussersten Entscheidung*]."

No doubt, then, the main title of the 1930 lecture was not simply a rhetorical means for linking the lecture to the particular audience to whom it was delivered (to the Faculty of Protestant Theology in Marburg). And yet, one cannot but wonder that the theme expressed in that title remains so undeveloped and, in the version published in 1943, disappears entirely. Was it perhaps a believing that proved so monstrous that it had to come to be called otherwise? For example, by a word that already, inconspicuously appears in the 1930 text: *Gelassenheit*.

Then Heidegger would have said *from* the strange essence of truth, beginning from the truth of essence, that dispropriation for which even ek-sistence and ecstasis (to say nothing of believing) seem still too centered: no longer letting-be, but being-let, or rather having (always already) been let (into the open in which beings can come to presence). Yet the strangeness that sounds in *Gelassenheit* when it is heard with the ears of technological man resounds, in the end, from the strange essence of truth, from "the strangeness of the strange essence of truth."

In the wake of this strangeness—a wake that has perhaps only just begun, a wake in which we are to mourn nothing less than the passing of truth itself—what is to become of the essentially other than truth? No longer is it the mere opposite that could be kept securely outside the essence of truth. Nor is it an other that truth could appropriate in such a way that the otherness would be retained within a new unity attesting the priority of truth. Nothing is kept more explicitly at a distance from Heidegger's text(s) on the essence of truth than dialectic. The untruth that is essentially other than truth remains essentially other even within the essence of truth; in the words used in the *Beiträge,* it remains as something oppositional (*als Widerständiges*) within the essence of truth (*GA* 65: 356). It is even—as Heidegger would say in that perhaps most monstrous saying—something within the essence of truth that is older than truth itself.

Thus, what is essentially other than truth belongs to the essence of truth, even though within that essence its otherness is preserved, not just dialectically but as oppositional, even as older than truth. Presumably this is why—to return to that passage in the *Beiträge* to which I referred earlier—the question of the relation of truth to another is prohibited as long as ἀλήθεια is thought in an originary way.

This prohibition is what allows Heidegger to broach a discourse on the possibility of experiencing errancy itself (*die Irre selbst*) in such a way as to escape being drawn into (along by) it (*GA* 9: 197). To experience it thus would be to overcome its essential otherness. Yet how could one experience errancy itself? Is there errancy *itself,* errancy proper? What of the prohibition that would have the effect of holding it within reach of such an experience?

Is it perhaps just this prohibition that we shall have to ponder in that still immeasurable wake that marks the passing of truth itself? Not to question, perhaps not even to think, but to ponder, to weigh, to test the weight of the prohibition against saying an other so essentially other that it would not belong to the essence of truth, an other that would be outside the essence of truth without becoming again a mere opposite unable to withstand the logic of appropriation. An other that would engender, not πόλεμος, but outrage. An other so essentially other than truth that it would be absolved from truth, as absolutely as madness can be. Let us, then, ponder whether what the question of truth is all about is in the end akin to madness.

NOTES

1. Friedrich Nietzsche, *Der Wille zur Macht*, ed. Peter Gast and Elizabeth Förster-Nietzsche (Stuttgart: Alfred Kröner, 1959), §493.

2. In a note in *Wegmarken* Heidegger explains that the work first published in 1943 "contains the repeatedly revised text of a public lecture, which was thought out in 1930 and presented several times under the same title (in the fall and winter of 1930 in Bremen, Marburg a.d.L., Freiburg i.Br. and in the summer of 1932 in Dresden)" (*GA* 9: 483). According to the *Nachschrift* that I have examined of the Marburg version, the lecture was presented there to the Faculty of Protestant Theology. Also, despite Heidegger's remark in the note in *Wegmarken*, "The Essence of Truth" was only the subtitle in this version of the lecture. I shall return below to this question of titles.

3. This analysis parallels that found in "On the Essence of Ground" (1929), though the language of the latter remains closer to *Being and Time*. In the 1929 text the concept of freedom is introduced following the development of the concept of world: "The passage beyond beings to the world [*Der Überstieg zur Welt*] is freedom itself. . . . Freedom alone can let a world hold sway for Dasein . . ." (*GA* 9: 163–64). This passage beyond beings to the world Heidegger also calls transcendence.

4. Also a double writing, a rewriting or rereading of Heidegger's text that would release into it what certain rhetorical strategies (primarily irony) hold in reserve up to the center. For though untruth comes into play as proper to the essence of truth only at the center of the text, it cannot but have been in play (even if as repressed) in all the determinations retraced from the beginning of the text.

5. *Wegmarken* includes a remark indicating not only that the text of "On the Essence of Truth" goes back to the 1930 lecture but also that the first paragraph of the Note that concludes this text was added in the second edition (1949); a shorter version of this remark is also found in the later separate editions of the text, for example, in the fourth edition (1961). In the first edition (1943) the section entitled "Anmerkung" is not numbered (so the text has only eight numbered sections), and it is treated as a note, set in smaller print after a blank half-page marking the end of the text itself. A comparison of the version of the Note found in the first edition with the version in all later editions shows that in fact the first *two* paragraphs of the later version replace a single paragraph that in the first edition refers the text to the 1930 lecture and connects it to the task of reflecting on the truth of essence. Thus the link between the essence of truth and the truth of essence, which comes to be forged in the extended first paragraph added to the concluding note in the second edition, is already traced as task in the first edition. What is marked by the second, very brief paragraph added in the second edition is the disruption that that task as initially traced underwent: "Already in the original project the lecture 'On the Essence of Truth' was to have been completed by a second lecture 'On the Truth of Essence'. The latter failed for reasons that are now indicated in the 'Letter on Humanism'" (*GA* 9: 201). (The reference is presumably to the much-discussed passage regarding the turn: "The adequate execution and completion of this other thinking that abandons subjectivity is surely made more difficult by the fact that in the publication of *Being and Time* the third division of the first part, 'Time and Being', was held back. . . . Here everything is turned around. The division in question was held back because thinking failed in the adequate saying of this turning [*Kehre*] and did not succeed with the help of the language

of metaphysics. The lecture 'On the Essence of Truth', thought out and delivered in 1930 but not printed until 1943, provides a certain insight into the thinking of the turning from 'Being and Time' to 'Time and Being'" (*GA* 9: 327–28). Even though the task of a reflection under the title "On the Truth of Essence" that would have completed "On the Essence of Truth" (in a manner presumably analogous to that in which "Time and Being" would have completed "Being and Time") "failed," the first paragraph added to the second edition shows unmistakably that it was a matter, not of disrupting the link and abandoning reflection on the truth of essence, but of recognizing that the reversibility of that link had never been simply deferrable and that thinking the truth of essence could never have been held in reserve as a task, that it cannot but have commenced already in "On the Essence of Truth," even at the cost of proving to have deformed a certain project that that text would have been supposed to carry out.

II

HEIDEGGER AND PSYCHIATRY

WILLIAM J. RICHARDSON

4. Heidegger among the Doctors

When all is said and done, this is the story of a friendship—a friendship first between two men but also between the disciplines they represented. Both the men and their separate disciplines are familiar to us: on the one hand, Martin Heidegger (philosopher); on the other, Medard Boss (Swiss psychiatrist), founder and high priest of the so-called daseinsanalytic method of psychotherapy. To be sure, these two have been discussed jointly before, but what makes their relationship worth reconsideration here is the recent (1987), still untranslated, and relatively unknown publication of the seminars given by Heidegger at Boss's invitation to the psychiatrists of Zurich over a ten-year period (1959–1969).

Although both men originally intended that these seminars be published only after their deaths, Boss eventually changed his mind so that he could preside over editing them. At any rate, there they are—protocols from the seminars, corrected and emended by Heidegger, followed by Boss's personal record of numerous conversations between the two men over the years, and finally some selected letters from Heidegger to Boss for good measure—all in all a rather full record of a friendship. Because of the general unfamiliarity with the book, I propose first to offer a brief summary of its content, then to thematize one issue in particular, namely, the daseinsanalytic critique of the Freudian unconscious, and finally to conclude with an exploratory reflection on this critique.

The earliest record we have of the relationship between Boss and Heidegger is a letter dating from 1947. Heidegger had been suspended from his teaching responsibilities by the ongoing denazification process, and the only published work we have from that period is the "Letter on Humanism" written in response to Jean Beaufret's questions from Paris two years earlier. When Boss requested permission to visit him that summer, we may presume that Heidegger welcomed the stimulus that would come from another inquiring mind from another country and from another discipline. At any rate, the two men—fourteen years apart in age—hit it off famously, so much so that the very reserved Heidegger could bring himself to write: "If it were possible to find the opportunity to support my capacity for work (*Arbeitskraft*) with a *little* box of chocolates, I would be very grateful" (ZS 299). Life for Heidegger must have been austere in 1947.

What brought Boss to Heidegger? A general dissatisfaction with the training he had been given in face of the clinical cases he had to deal with, and the discovery in Heidegger's analysis of the human phenomenon (Dasein) in *Being and Time* of certain concepts that proved very helpful. His professional formation had hardly been deficient. He was trained in psychiatry by the two Bleulers at Burghölsli. He had begun his analysis with thirty-odd sessions with an ailing Freud in 1925, finished it with Karen Horney in Berlin, was taught by Reich, supervised by Sachs, Fenichel, Jones, among others, and for ten years participated in a biweekly seminar with Carl Jung. One would have to assume that he was acquainted with the best analytic thinking of the day, but dissatisfied he certainly was. For a time, he thought that the Eastern thought of India might help and even tried to learn Hindi in order to study it. But then he discovered *Being and Time,* and his commitment to it became total.

Twelve years would pass before Boss got around to proposing the seminars. Meanwhile, he and Heidegger became fast friends. They would vacation together with their wives—visiting Italy, Sicily, the Aegean Islands, and Greece—or sometimes they would simply take a work-vacation together a week at a time in Boss's getaway home at Lenzerheide in the Alps near Davos. Boss learned much from their conversations, of course, and finally decided that his experience of Heidegger the thinker should be shared with others. Heidegger agreed to lead some seminars, and several times each semester for the next ten years he would spend a week or so in Zurich offering two three-hour sessions each time to fifty to seventy psychiatrists, most of them relatively innocent of philosophy of any kind, let alone his own.

What does Heidegger do in these seminars? In a word, he offers psychiatrists a crash course in some of the fundamental concepts of *Being and Time* that had first fired Boss's enthusiasm. And who is more capable than he to do it? Those concepts by now are current coin and easily recalled. Heidegger is interested in the meaning of Being (*Sein*) as different from beings (*Seiende*) that it lets be; and he proceeds by a phenomenological examination of a particular being among the rest, namely, human being that he calls Dasein that must somehow know the answer to the question since it is able to ask it. Under examination, Dasein reveals itself as a phenomenon whose nature it is to-be-in-the-world. Heidegger examines first what is meant by world and then what is meant to be "in" such a world. As for the world itself, it is to be understood not as the sum total of everything that is but as a horizon within which beings are encountered, a matrix of relations interior to which beings have their meaning for humans. Eventually this matrix of meanings would be conceived of as the matrix of comprehensibility, of whatever is articulable by speech.

For Dasein to be "in" such a world implies several different existential, i.e., structural, components: one structural component that discloses/projects the world as total meaningfulness (*Verstehen:* "understanding"), one that discloses beings within the world through affective disposition (*Befindlichkeit:* "state of mind"), and finally one that permits Dasein to articulate in speech what it affectively understands. This last component Heidegger calls *Rede*, but since this is his translation of the Greek λόγος, I think it better simply to anglicize the Greek, hence, as "logos"—understanding thereby the structural component through which it is able to let something be seen in words. As a structural component, then, logos shares Dasein's nature as Being-with-others, and this is the foundation of its capacity to interact with other Daseins through the mediation of speech (*Mitteilung:* "communication"). It goes without saying, of course, that the structural component of logos shares in the radically temporal character of Dasein, whereby in advancing resolve Dasein lets the future come through its past, letting beings (including itself) become manifest in the present. The implications of all this are as far-reaching as the phenomenology, which justifies it, is complex.

What does Heidegger do, then, with the psychiatrists? He tries to follow the advice he gives Boss as he prepares to be a Visiting Professor at Harvard: "You must succeed in bringing about a change of viewpoint in your auditors, in awakening [in them] the sense in which questions must be asked" (*ZS* 324). He recommends a meditation on space and spatiality as a good way to start, and that is exactly how he begins the seminars. The analysis of space (and eventually time) add nothing but a certain freshness to the treatment of the issues in *Being and Time*. What is interesting is the rigor of his pedagogical method. Sessions proceed with homely examples of cups and tables. Are they here? Or there? Or where? Are they now? Or then? Or when? What is where? What is when? It is often very Socratic, and tough-minded—but also clear and very philosophical. Boss offers us a specimen:

HEIDEGGER: How does Dr. R. relate to the table before him?
LISTENER A: He is sitting behind it and looking at it.
HEIDEGGER: At one with this, the "nature" of Dr. R.'s Dasein also reveals itself—but as what?
[Five minutes of silence. . . .]
HEIDEGGER: I remain silent because it is senseless to want to lecture you about Dr. R.'s existing. Everything depends on your learning to *see* the matter for yourselves, that you are patiently attentive to the matter, so that it may reveal itself to you in the totality of its own proper meaningfulness.
LISTENER C: Dr. R. is separated from the table by an interval of space.
HEIDEGGER: What, then, is space?
LISTENER D: The distance between Dr. R. and the table.
HEIDEGGER: What is distance?
LISTENER E: A definition of space.
HEIDEGGER: What, then, is space as such?
[Ten long minutes of silence. . . .][1]

One can hear the participants grumbling. At one point Heidegger grumbles a little himself to Boss: "Either the analysis becomes too 'abstract' for the participants, or—when it becomes 'concrete' for them, I, for my part, talk about things about which, professionally speaking, I understand nothing" (*ZS* 343). There is, however, one illuminating formula in the very first session that slowly will be orchestrated: "To exist as *Da-sein* means to hold open a domain through its power to receive/perceive (*Vernehmen-können*) the meaningfulness of those [things] that are given to it and address [Dasein] in virtue of [Dasein's] own luminosity" (*ZS* 4).

The seminars as a whole, then, resonate profoundly with *Being and Time,* but certain new themes, or at least new explicitations, emerge that are worth more attention than we can give them here. The first of these is the distinction, important for psychotherapy, between *Vergegenwärtigung* ("rendering something present") and *Erinnern* ("recalling" it). The first deals with what *Being and Time* refers to as Dasein's *Sein bei* other beings, i.e., of being able to be "near" them, not by being physically "alongside" of them but because of its privileged access to their Being that lets them *be* near (*ZS* 90). This will enable him to explain certain parapraxes (like forgetting one's umbrella) without resorting to the notion of some unconscious wish.

More important is Heidegger's examination of psychosomatic phenomena, which leads him to an analysis of the human body, notably missing from *Being and Time*. Heidegger distinguishes clearly between body as *Körper* and body as *Leib*. The limit of the former is one's skin, the limit of the latter is the horizon of the World for Dasein as Being-in-the-world (*ZS* 112–13). Thus he tells Boss:

> We cannot "see" because we have eyes, rather we can only have eyes because according to our fundamental nature we come to presence as beings that see. Likewise, we could not be bodily (*leiblich*) in the way we are unless our Being-in-the-World always already consisted fundamentally of a perceptive/receptive relatedness to something that addresses us out of the Open of our World, [that Open] as which we exist (*ZS* 293–94).

This permits Heidegger to give a new reading to such a phenomenon as "stress" (e.g., *ZS* 185). When Boss reminds him of Sartre's criticism that *Being and Time* contained only six lines about the body, he replies that this had been for him the hardest of all problems to solve and that he knew of no way to say any more about it at the time (*ZS* 292). In any case, the analysis here is important and cries out for careful comparison with the work of Merleau-Ponty.

A third theme worth our attention is Heidegger's critique of Ludwig Binswanger. One will recall how the "psychiatric daseinsanalytic" of Binswanger penetrated the American scene in the sixties through the sympathetic presentation by Rollo May under the guise of "existential psychoanalysis." Binswanger, and then May, claimed that Heidegger's conception of Dasein as Being-in-the-world was its foundation. Binswanger liked this much of Heidegger's project but felt that Heidegger's conception of Dasein was too solipsistic, that the notion of "care" as its fundamental thrust was too sociological, and that both must be supplemented by the experience of love. Heidegger dismisses all this by saying that Binswanger missed the point that the experience of Being-in-the-world was fundamentally openness to Being as such, that this openness was essentially shared with other Daseins, that "care" was not some form of social welfare service but designated the existential-ontological structure of Dasein in its unity as such, and that whatever is to be said about the nature of love, it must be grounded in this structure (*ZS*

236–42). He remarks that Binswanger had subsequently acknowledged that he had "misunderstood" Heidegger's thought but insisted that it had been a "productive" misunderstanding (*ZS* 151). So be it!

Let that suffice to characterize the sweep of the book as a whole. More particularly, what is to be said about the unconscious as Freud has taught us to understand it? For Heidegger, Freud is a classic example of the modern (broad sense) scientific mind, a mind that is totally oblivious to the Being-dimension of the objects it deals with, i.e., the mysterious process within them that lets them come to presence and reveal themselves to us as what they are. It is interested in their object-character, their objectifiability, their capacity to be conceptualized in representations, measured, calculated, controlled.

He finds the historical paradigm for this mentality jointly and in complementary fashion in the physics of Galileo and the philosophy of Descartes. Galileo, he claims, was interested in neither the apple nor the tree but only in measuring the fall. For his project of the physical world, after he rejected the metaphysical physics of Aristotle, was one of the absolute homogeneity of space and time that permitted him to measure, calculate, and predict movement with mathematical instruments that were increasingly available. The philosophical complement of this, of course, was the insight of Descartes. Insisting on a humanly verifiable and unshakable foundation of certitude, he found it in the self-validating self-consciousness of the *cogito*. This for Descartes, then, was the foundation-ὑποκείμενον-*subjectum,* completely closed in upon itself. Everything else became accessible only by being represented to the self-conscious subject and by it, i.e., as an object.

Both axes of the paradigm converged, of course, in Kant. On the one hand, Kant was able to formulate the conception of nature by which Galileo and others had operated but which they could not articulate, i.e., as the "conformity to law of all experiences in space and time."[2] On the other hand, Kant could investigate the conditions that must prevail in the enclosed self-consciousness of Descartes that would enable it to discern the laws that governed its experience of nature that was presumably "outside" its own enclosure. If he distinguished consciousness as "empirical" and consciousness as "pure," this was only part of the analysis. The essential element was that the objects of experience were what they were (their Being as Kant conceived it) only in relation to the conscious subject that represented them. This was a form of idealism, Heidegger points out, and he insists that Husserl was part of the same tradition, his contribution to it being, after the inspiration of Brentano, the notion of intentionality (see *ZS* 189–91). Once Husserl's experience of consciousness is stretched out to the transcendental level to become Transcendental Subjectivity, it becomes what Binswanger understood by Being-in-the-world. That is why Heidegger separates himself from it so radically.

To Heideggerians, this is pretty dull stuff—it is such old hat! Already implicit in *Being and Time,* this conception of history begins to be articulated in the inaugural lecture of 1929, "What is Metaphysics?", and has been repeated times beyond number in the later period after World War II. But Heidegger thrusts it again on these poor doctors as a way of saying what he thinks of Freud and the unconscious. The fact is that it was Boss who introduced Heidegger to Freud's metapsychological work and, according to Boss, Heidegger "couldn't believe that such an intelligent man could write such stupid things, such fantastical things, about men and women."[3] For Heidegger, Freud's metapsychology is merely the application of a Neo-Kantian conception of science to human being (ZS 260). What Freud is looking for is an explanation of human phenomena through an unbroken chain of causality (ZS 7). When he cannot do this on the level of consciousness, he postulates an unconscious—at best a pure hypothesis (ZS 214). Result: the "fatal distinction between conscious and unconscious" (ZS 319) is born and, alas, seems here to stay.

To stay? Well, if the Freudian unconscious is only the underside of a Cartesian conception of consciousness as an encapsulated ego-subject, what happens if this Cartesian model is scrapped? Does not the unconscious go too? Of course it does— and that is exactly Heidegger's position. For Dasein is not fundamentally an ego-subject. Dasein is the clearing in which all beings (including itself) may appear and reveal themselves as what they are. That is why for Dasein to exist "means to hold open a domain through its power to receive/perceive (Vernehmen-können) the meaningfulness of those [things] that are given to [Dasein] and address [Dasein] in virtue of [Dasein's] own luminosity" (ZS 4). Heidegger often describes this dwelling in the clearing as a "sojourn," or Aufenthalt. He describes it this way:

Dasein is always to be seen as Being-in-the-World, as the caring about things (Besorgen) and caring for (Sorgen) [other Daseins], as the being-with the human beings it encounters, never as a self-contained subject. Moreover, it is always to be seen as standing within the clearing, as sojourn with the things that it encounters, i.e., as disclosure for those beings that come to the encounter. Sojourn is always at the same time a comportment with (Verhalten zu). . . .

One cannot ask about some 'porter' (Träger) [who carries] this comportment, rather the comportment carries itself. This is the wonderful part of it. 'Who' I am now can be said only through this sojourn, and always at the same time in the sojourn lies what I sojourn with and with whom and how I comport myself with [them]. (ZS 204–205)

In another register, this comportment is a function of the existential structures already delineated in Being and Time, still remarkably functional in Heidegger's thought in the sixties:

[Befindlichkeit (translated either as "state of mind" or as the "ontological disposition")] is the de-termining attunement of its here-and-now relation to the World, to its With-Being with other humans (Mitdasein der Mitmenschen) and to itself. Befindlichkeit founds any actual feeling, whether of well-being or its opposite (Wohl-und Misbefinden), but is in turn itself founded in the exposure of humans to the totality of beings. This already says that to this exposure (Geworfenheit: thrownness) belongs the understanding of beings as beings; but likewise there is no understanding that is not [itself] already thrown. . . .

Thrownness and *understanding* belong reciprocally together in a correlation whose unity is determined through *language (Sprache)*. Language here is to be thought of as saying *(Sagen)*, in which beings as beings, i.e., from the viewpoint of their Being, show themselves. Only on the ground of the correlation of thrownness and understanding through language as saying is mankind able to be addressed by beings. *(ZS* 182–83)

Language, then, not simply in the sense of *communication (Mitteilung)* (*ZS* 183) or even of verbal articulation *(Verlautbarung)* (*ZS* 232) but in the sense of saying *(Sagen)* is essentially a showing forth *(zeigen)*, or rather a letting-show-forth *(sich zeigen lassen)* or be seen *(sehen lassen)* of the beings one encounters within the World as beings (*ZS* 117, 126). And the reverse is also true: "Every phenomenon shows itself [to the phenomenologist] only in the domain of language" (*ZS* 83). In a word, "language is the original openness of whatever is that is preserved in different ways by mankind. Insofar as humans [are together with other Daseins] and remain essentially related to other humans, language is, as such, dialogue *(Gespräch)*" (*ZS* 183). It is understandable why Heidegger recalls his famous formula from the *Letter on Humanism:* "Language is the house of Being" (*ZS* 226).

All of this put together adds up to the conception of Dasein as a self. For Heidegger, the word stands for Dasein as Being-in-the-world insofar as it remains the same throughout the entire historical process. But this does not make it a substance, still less a subject. Its permanence consists in the fact that "the self can always come back to itself and find itself in its sojourn still the same" (*ZS* 220). Hence, it is essentially a temporal process. "The selfhood of Dasein is only in the manner of tim-ing" (*ZS* 220)—but a tim-ing process that takes place always in a determined situation, surrounded by the beings revealed to it within the clearing that is its world. Essentially temporal, Dasein is likewise essentially historical *(geschichtlich)*: "[I call] historical the style and manner with which I comport myself with regard to what comes to me, to what is present and to what has been. Every power-to-be-/do *(Seinkönnen)* something is a determined confrontation with what has been with a view to something coming towards me, and to which I am resolved" (*ZS* 203).

What does the word "I" add to the experience of historicizing Dasein as a self? This is not of itself a testimony to consciousness but simply the naming of the self as it is experienced by itself at any given moment. "For the Greeks, 'I' is the name for a human being *(Mensch)* that adjusts to the limits [of a given situation] and, thus at home with himself *(bei sich selbst)*, is *Himself*" (*ZS* 235). To become "conscious" in such a condition will mean trying to determine "how this original being-intimate-with *(Sein bei)* [other beings] . . . hangs together with other determinations of Dasein" (*ZS* 143). What then does "consciousness" mean for Heidegger? "Standing within the clearing [of Being] does not mean that human being stands in the light like a post, but the human Da-sein *takes up a sojourn* in the clearing and 'concerns' itself with things" (*ZS* 188).

All of this is well and good, but how does it play as psychotherapy? Just to get the flavor of it, I propose two vignettes: (1) a specimen of pathology; (2) an example of dream-interpretation.

First, a case of repression. Heidegger himself suggests a way to understand repression. For Freud, Heidegger claims, this meant simply the hiding (*Versteckung*) of a representation, whereas for Heidegger it implies an "ecstatic-intentional" relationship to the world. Thus, it is characterized by a refusal to accept what is pressing upon One.

> Repressing is a looking away from, . . . a fleeing from, . . . hence no mechanically represented shoving away, so to speak of psychic conditions [or] letting disappear of psychic material. In repression, what approaches a human being is so little avoided that much rather the repressed material confronts the repressing agent for the first time in an especially stiff-necked way. (*ZS* 357)

As an example, Boss offers the following case from his clinical experience:

> A nineteen-year old girl passed by a flower nursery on her way to work every day. A young, handsome gardener who worked there seemed obviously interested in her; each time she passed he would look at her for a long time. The girl became excited whenever she was near him, and would feel herself peculiarly attracted to him. This attraction bewildered her. One day she stumbled and fell on the street directly in front of the entrance to the nursery. From then on both her legs were paralyzed.[4]

In an interview Boss summarizes his analysis of the case:

> This was a neurotic way of relating to the world because she wasn't free in her whole existence, and especially in her relationship to men. She was brought up to believe that all men were dangerous and evil so she couldn't get close to a man, let alone have any feeling for a man, any loving feeling. She therefore always felt compelled to flee from men. In this instance, she saw a man who for some time had attracted her. When she suddenly saw this man nearby and coming even closer to her she just collapsed. And this hysterical paralysis, this paralysis of the legs was nothing other than a block, a blocking of her possibilities for moving toward him. She was completely shocked by this man who could arouse a little bit of love in her. Her shock was not merely a symptom but a way of being in and of itself, a being frightened by, and being prohibited from, relating to a man because until then she had only seen men as terrifying creatures, as wild animal-like beings which would swallow her up. She was so panic stricken and shocked that her whole existence was blocked from carrying out her possibilities for a loving relationship with this man.[5]

We get perhaps a clearer sense of the method if we consider the daseinsanalytic approach to dreams. The approach is strictly phenomenological. It is assumed that the capacity to dream is a structural component of Being-in-the-world, and the analyst is interested in the manifest dream rather than its latent content. The reason is that in speaking about latent content we are not speaking about dreaming but only about a selected number of waking thoughts associated with the events of dreaming, while the manifest content manifests the dreamer while dreaming, i.e., strictly as a phenomenon.[6]

By way of illustration, let us look at Boss's interpretation of a dream of Heidegger's. The dream (repeated at long or short intervals since his student days): "He was in the situation of his matriculation examination at the *Gymnasium* in Constance. All the professors who had examined him at that time were once more physically present before him and harassed him with relentless questions." Boss comments:

> It is specific of our dreaming state that the meaningfulness that appears to us addresses us mostly from sensorily perceptible present beings, which, moreover, do not belong to our own existing. For example, in Heidegger's dreaming, he is addressed primarily by his matriculation examiners. In the following, more clear-sighted waking state, we may be addressed by the same 'fulfilled meanings' but from more characteristic, much more central facts, or better, 'givens', of our existing. So Heidegger's waking perception, too, expanded and focused to an ever clearer awareness of the meaningfulness of being examined, but in an incomparably more comprehensive way than previously in the *Gymnasium*. He came to see how he had long been examined out of the center of his being, which consisted primarily of a fundamental ability to think (*des Denkenkönnens*). It brought him enough suffering that in his waking state he was exposed to the never slackening demand emanating from this center of his being that he endure and pass the maturity examination of his philosophizing. However, his dreaming vision was so highly constricted that of all possible examinations of maturity only that of his high school matriculation examination could occur to him. The repetition disappeared only after he had deepened and broadened the traditional interpretation by antiquity of *Sein* as *Anwesen* to the discernment of *Ereignis* which shows *Sein* and *Menschenwesen* as belonging together in an indivisible identity, as *vereignet* ("ordered") *zugeeignet* ("assigned"), *übereignet* ("appropriated") to one another. His own proper and fundamental self-realization was evidently reached with his waking discernment of that state of affairs which revealed itself to him in *das Ereignis*. . . . If this lightning-like revelation of the *Ereignis* had not corresponded to the true completion of his selfhood, how could it be at all comprehensible that Heidegger forthwith not only never again dreamt of having to stand the scrutiny of his *Gymnasium* examiners but, now waking, found his way out of the earlier constant pressure to think, and into a wise, serene composure in the depths of his heart.[7]

This is all very edifying and it will do for now. We will come back to it later.

What are we to conclude, then, about the existence of the unconscious? If it is true that the unconscious of psychoanalysis is no more than an unbroken chain of psychic causality that by hypothesis accounts for the gaps in conscious experience, it is no wonder that Heidegger will have no part of it. But is that the only way to understand the nature of Freud's discovery?

I suggest that the answer is "no." For we have now another reading of Freud that neither Heidegger nor Boss took account of, that of Jacques Lacan. For Lacan, what Freud discovered in the unconscious was not an unbroken chain of psychic causality but the hidden power of speech, and that it is structured not really like a thermodynamic machine but like a language. If Freud's thinking had been clearly presented to Heidegger in these Lacanian terms, would he still have been so hostile to it?

I put the matter that way, because during the fifties a strong effort was made in France to arrange a dialogue between these two lions that did not quite work.

Note Heidegger's comment to Boss after the receipt of Lacan's *Écrits:* "For my part, I am not yet ready to read the obviously baroque text. I am told, however, that it is causing the same kind of stir in Paris as (in its time) Sartre's *Being and Nothingness*" (ZS 348). Later (1967), after receiving a letter from Lacan, he comments: "I think the psychiatrist needs a psychiatrist" (*ZS* 350). When a student of Heidegger was once introduced to Lacan precisely as such, Lacan's only response was: "Heidegger is not interested in psychoanalysis."

However that may be, Lacan, the psychoanalyst, was certainly interested in Heidegger, at least in the early part of his teaching career. In the famous "Discourse at Rome" of 1953, "The Function and Field of Language and Speech in Psychoanalysis"[8] (considered by most the *Magna Charta* of his future work), the allusion to Heidegger is explicit. For example, when discussing memory, Lacan observes: "in Heideggerian language one could say that both types of recollection constitute the subject as *gewesend*—that is to say as being the one who thus has been"[9] and he gladly makes his own Heidegger's famous formula about "being-unto-death."[10] Eventually, he would back away from this mode of expression but he acknowledged to the end that Heidegger's work, in particular his conception of language, was "propaedeutic" to his own.[11] In fact, in 1956 he translated personally into French Heidegger's landmark essay on the *Logos* of Heraclitus,[12] where Being, under the guise of Heraclitus's *Logos,* is interpreted as language itself in its origins, the aboriginal language. As I understand Heidegger's development, this is where it becomes clear that the language problematic of the later period is simply the natural complement to the conception of logos as an existential component of Dasein in *Being and Time,* i.e., after the so-called "turning (*Kehre*)" in his thought. It is this essay that permits Lacan to claim an ally in Heidegger when he says that human beings do not speak language but language speaks them.

Does this mean that they are saying the same thing? Obviously not! We have a sense of what it means for Heidegger. What does it mean for Lacan? The shift to a focus on language and its structure began for Lacan in the early fifties with the discovery of the work of Lévi-Strauss. It was from Lévi-Strauss that he took the word "symbolic" to describe the order of language: its structure and its laws. This he quickly distinguished for purposes of psychoanalytic theorizing from what he called the "imaginary" component of the psychoanalytic subject (that dimension that deals with images—any form of sensible representation) and from what he called the "real" (that dimension of experience that is impossible to represent at all, whether in language or in images). This distinction, he claimed, was warranted by Freud himself and has become one of Lacan's major contributions.

When Lacan claims that language speaks the human subject, it is obviously the symbolic order to which he is referring as Other than the subject. There is no need to recall here that Lacan's conception of this Other of language derives from Saussure; that this Other is organized by the laws of language discovered by Saussure and his followers; that the principles of the unconscious governing dream formation discovered by Freud (e.g., displacement and condensation) follow the same pattern as the laws of metonymy and metaphor in linguistics as developed by Saussure and his followers; or that Lacan uses such facts to justify his claim that the unconscious is structured like a language. There is no need, either, to insist here that these laws—or rather *the* Law—are not abstractions but are inscribed in human culture itself and determine the subject through signifying chains forged by one's ancestral past, family history, social milieu and, as time goes on, the record of one's own personal odyssey as its frustrated desire searches for a lost object through the mediation of language. More specifically, the signifying chains of the symbolic order that determine Heidegger's dream as reported include all the signifiers of his origins and destiny—mother, father, teachers, milieu, friends—all those possibilities of Dasein's Being-in-the-world that he himself described in *Being and Time* as coming from one's heritage, one's milieu, or one's individual choices (see *SZ* 12)—all those details of Heidegger's genealogy and cultural background that people like Victor Farias and (more reliably) Hugo Ott have been calling to our attention. And it is the same symbolic order that supplies to Boss the pattern by which to interpret the dream.

Now it is the symbolic order, thus individuated, that Lacan claims is the structure of the unconscious that Freud discovered. This is the language that speaks the subject, rather than the reverse. For the subject of psychoanalysis, Lacan claims, is the linguistic subject. Linguists like Benveniste distinguish two modes of subject: the spoken subject, i.e., the subject of the spoken word as spoken that remains as part of the spoken discourse; and the speaking subject that recedes in the very act of speaking. It is the latter that for Lacan is the subject of our parapraxes, lapses, dreams, etc.,—i.e., the unconscious as subject that sabotages beyond our control what we consciously intend to say and do.

All this was clear to Lacan by 1953, so if two years later he took time out of a busy teaching and clinical schedule to personally translate Heidegger's *Logos* essay, one has to surmise that he felt that this essay supported his case. In a way it certainly does. For Lacan, the id of Freud (the *Es* of *Wo Es war soll Ich werden*) translates as *ça: ça pense, ça parle*. For Heidegger: *die Sprache spricht. C'est ça!* For both, language speaks the human thing. For Heidegger, Being-as-*Logos*, in Dasein as its clearing, speaks through beings, inviting Dasein to let them be seen as what they are by bringing them into words. For Lacan, the process is less poetic. For the symbolic order is a chain of signifiers that refer less to individual signifieds (as is the case in Saussure) than they refer to one another and as such produce the subject of language. In the words of Benveniste: "It is . . . literally true that the foundation of subjectivity is in the exercise of language."[13] The linguistic subject as such, then, is an *effect* of the signifying chain. Thus a sign "represents something for someone," but "a signifier represents a subject for another signifier."[14] Hence, "the effect of language is the cause introduced into the subject. By this effect [the subject] is not cause of itself. For its cause is the signifier without which there would not be any subject in the real. But this subject is what the signifier represents, and it could not represent anything except for another signifier."[15] To be sure, there is a causality here, but in the order of language, not in the order of thermodynamically styled psychic energy.

What are we to infer from all this? Clearly remaining in the Cartesian tradition to the extent that he calls a human being a subject at all, Lacan in no way conceives of this subject as an encapsulated ego of consciousness. As a subject of the unconscious, it dwells in intersubjective space, in the domain of social discourse (*le lien social*), the locus of the Other. Hence, such a subject of language must not be thought of as inside the speaker more than outside him—that is why one of the repeated metaphors for the subject is the Moebius strip, where inside and outside are one. This is a long way from Heidegger's conception of Dasein as guardian of language, the "house of Being," but it is a long way, too, from his conception of the Freudian unconscious as an unbroken chain of psychic causality.

It is obvious that these two conceptions cannot be conflated, but can they be taken to complement each other? I think so—at least I shall try to think so—though I wish to insist that there is no way to reduce one to the other without destroying both. In the first place, given the vast difference between the problematics that concern them, Heidegger's question about the difference between Being and beings is an existential/ontological problem, i.e., on the level of Being (according to the terminology of *Being and Time*), while Lacan's question about the structure of the unconscious in psychoanalysis is clearly an existentiell/ontic one (i.e., on the level of beings)—no more ontic than Boss's daseinsanalytic psychotherapy that Heidegger enthusiastically endorses (*ZS* 161)—but ontic nonetheless. As a result, all of Lacan's claims for the exhaustive comprehensiveness and ultimacy of the symbolic order (e.g., "there is no Other of the Other,"[16] i.e., no metalanguage, no metasymbolic) are equally ontic claims. They are statements made about the ultimate structure of the Many (Heraclitus's πάντα), or, in our day, about the order of technology, not about the One (Heraclitus's Ἕν)—still less about the difference between them, which is Heidegger's only concern.

Lacan's question is different from Heidegger's, then, but there is much that they can offer each other. In Lacan, the ontic emphasis risks becoming no more than that, and Lacanian psychoanalysis needs to be reminded of its "unavoidable, inaccesible" grounding in Being as much as any of the natural sciences. Again, Heidegger's conception of truth as ἀλήθεια that reveals itself and hides itself at once—not only hides but confounds itself in "errance"—is in my view absolutely indispensable to psychoanalysis. And since Lacanian analysis claims to make no philosophical pretensions of its own, a philosophical view that can share its fundamental engagement with the functioning of language and yet find a way to take account of the freedom (*some* kind of freedom), historicity, and the illusion, at least, of unity in human beings could be salutary indeed.

But Lacan has something to offer to daseinsanalysis, too. In the first place, it suggests a method for exploring the language dimension of psychotherapy that daseinsanalysis apparently lacks and at the same time offers the chance to tune in on a wealth of clinical experience (Freud's plus Lacan's) otherwise inaccessible to it. If only by offering a challenge to daseinsanalysis by forcing it to take seriously such terminology as "symbolic," imaginary," and "real," a Lacanian perspective could provide a much-needed service.

A case in point: Heidegger's dream! Boss seems quite pleased with his interpretation of it, but a Lacanian, I think, would be less so. For the examiners obviously represent the Other—one would want to know more about this Other. How was it experienced otherwise? In 1921, as Heidegger describes it, he was trying "to follow a way which was leading [he] knew not where. Only the immediate prospect was known to [him], for this was continually opening up, even if the field of vision often shifted and grew dark" (*US* 91). This, too, was an experience of an Other. And at another time Boss describes an incident on their first trip together to Assisi:

> Each morning during our 10 o'clock walks, Heidegger would fall silent and be inaccessible to my desperate attempts to cheer him. I feared I had offended and wounded him in some undiscoverable way. In the meantime, I had become aware of Heidegger's extreme sensitivity to the finest nuances of the atmosphere of people. After several repetitions of this apparently ill-humored behavior, I broke the silence to ask directly what I had done to incur his displeasure. Heidegger was highly astounded. "Absolutely nothing!" he replied. "Always at this time of day '*das Denken*' comes over me. Then, if I do not want to do myself painful violence, I have to surrender myself to it.[17]

This, too, was an experience of the Other. What about this Other? Is this the Other that in Boss's view came to articulation as *Sein, Anwesen,* and *Ereignis*? Then what about the Other that came to expression in 1933 when, as the first Rector of the University of Freiburg after the Nazis came to power, Heidegger sold out, at least for a time, to the rhetoric of Nazi ideology? What about that Other then—who, or what, was that? All of this, too belongs to his *gewesend* self, the self that he has been. "'Who' I am now can be said only through this sojourn, and in the sojourn lies at the same time what I sojourn with, and with whom and how I comport myself with them" (*ZS* 205). "Every-power-to-be/do something is a determined confrontation with what has been with a view to something coming towards me, and to which I am resolved" (*ZS* 203).

I realize that this is an ugly question. But we cannot responsibly talk about "Heidegger among the Doctors" today without acknowledging the fact that both as a man and as a thinker he is very much in the dock. He not only sold out to Nazism for a while in the thirties but never subsequently repudiated anything he said or did during that time. What is there to say about the experience of that Other then? The question is, of course, very complex. It is first of all an historical question (what really happened?); a philosophical question (the nature of the Other?); a politicophilosophical question (what is the relation between philosophy and politics); an ethical question (what ought he to have done?); and a psychodynamic question (how did it happen?). Most of these aspects have already been widely discussed. His relationship to the daseinsanalyst Boss, however, invites us to examine the psychoanalytic aspect of the issue: is there any way to understand Heidegger's Nazi behavior psychodynamically—not to condemn him, nor to exonerate him, but simply to understand the truth of what happened?

If we turn to Boss and the daseinsanalysts, what have they to say? If there is no unconscious—no way to talk about anything but unthematized possibilities—

then must not Heidegger accept full responsibility for what he did or did not do? Or, at any rate, does not Boss's own assessment of him need a little touching up?

> In the tireless, never-flagging patience and forbearance with which Heidegger endured and fulfilled this undertaking, even unto the limits of his physical possibilities, is to be found the unshakeable evidence of the greatness of his own humanity. With [Heidegger's] conduct toward our Zollikon circle, he demonstrated unequivocally that he not only knew how to write and speak of that highest form of humanness in the relation to others, namely, of that selfless *vorspringende* caring which frees the other to his own selfhood, but that he also knew how to live it in an exemplary way.[18]

For a psychoanalytic view, at least a Lacanian view, the matter may be different. If one can accept the distinction between symbolic, imaginary, and real and explore it here at least for heuristic purposes, then it might be plausible to surmise that in the onrush of the real in that turbulent spring of 1933 Heidegger got stuck in the imaginary and was swept up by events before the symbolic gave him distance from them. I would hypothesize that Heidegger simply became intrigued with what seemed on the level of fantasy to be the embodiment of his own thought in a tangible, historical movement. The narcissistic lure included the reflection of himself as thinker, as doer, as *Führer* in a revolutionary movement that promised to return to the source of Greek thought reincarnated in the genius of his own people. The result: frozen fascination—perhaps even self-hypnosis—for a time. Captured by the imaginary, he would have remained its prisoner until the symbolic has its way with him and he was able, at least according to his statement of 1945, to see Nazi ideology for what it was—a radical form of the Nietzschean nihilism that must be overcome.[19]

Does this hypothesis make sense? Certainly it will not quell the controversy about the intrinsic nature of Heidegger's thought and its possible relation to his politics, but I find it suggestive for two reasons. In the first place, it transposes the discussion into a fresh context, the context of the psychic structure and personal history of this man who did what he did. It would be fascinating to study his "psychohistory," but beyond some anecdotal data concerning his devotion to his mother and relationship with his wife, we simply do not know enough from a clinical point of view even to speculate responsibly about what really happened to him along his way. But if such data ever were to become available, then the Lacanian categories of symbolic, imaginary, and real would be, I submit, the instruments with which to begin.

A second reason why I find this hypothesis attractive is, in a sense, a confirmation of the first. John Sallis, elsewhere in this volume,[20] leads us to infer that the *Stimme* of Being that reaches us immersed in everydayness is the voice of ἀλήθεια that reveals itself as the monstrosity of truth. But when I hear Heidegger talk about λήθη as "older" than the essence of truth, I hear what Lacan means by the real. And when he speaks about the *a-* of ἀλήθεια, I hear the revelation of the world that is structured—better, perhaps, determined—by the imaginary and the symbolic. Madness in these terms would not be the experience of some

Other of the essence of truth but simply the foreclosure of the symbolic that leaves us helpless before the real. One way to ponder the monstrosity of truth, then, might be to ponder it in the oblique—not by finding words to express it, but by meditating its event in Heidegger himself *as* a struggle with the negativity of truth, and by considering the long way that followed the debacle of 1933, including its inscrutable silence, as an effort to wrestle the monstrosity of ἀλήθεια into some symbolic form.

NOTES

1. Medard Boss, "Martin Heidegger's Zollikon Seminars," trans. Brian Kenny, *Review of Existential Psychiatry and Psychology* 16 (1978–79): 10–11.

2. Immanuel Kant, *Critique of Pure Reason*, trans. Norman Kemp Smith (New York: St. Martin's Press, 1965), B 165.

3. Erik Craig, "An Encounter with Medard Boss," *The Humanistic Psychologist*. Special Issue: ed. Erik Craig, *Psychotherapy for Freedom, The Daseinsanalytic Way in Psychology and Psychoanalysis* 16 (1988): 34.

4. Medard Boss, *Daseinanalysis and Psychoanalysis*, trans. Ludwig B. Lefebre (New York: Basic Books), 117.

5. Cited by Craig, "An Encounter with Medard Boss," 47.

6. Ibid., 203–16.

7. Boss, "Martin Heidegger's Zollikon Seminars," 13–20.

8. Jacques Lacan, *Écrits. A Selection*, trans. Alan Sheridan (New York: Norton, 1977), 30–113.

9. Ibid., 47.

10. Ibid., 103.

11. Jacques Lacan, *The Four Fundamental Concepts of Psychoanalysis*, trans. Alan Sheridan (New York: Norton, 1978), 18.

12. Martin Heidegger, "Logos (Heraclit, Fragment 50)," trans. Jacques Lacan, *La Psychanalyse* 1 (1956): 59–79.

13. Emil Benveniste, *Problèmes de la linguistique générale* (Paris: Gallimard, 1972), 262ff.

14. Jacques Lacan, *Écrits* (Paris: Seuil, 1966), 840.

15. Ibid., 835.

16. Lacan, *Écrits. A Selection*, 311.

17. Boss, "Martin Heidegger's Zollikon Seminars," 8.

18. Ibid., 10.

19. Philippe Lacoue-Labarthe, *La fiction du politique* (Strasbourg: Association des publications près les universités, 1987), 39–40.

20. See John Sallis, "Deformatives: Essentially Other Than Truth," in the present volume.

III

QUESTIONING
ETHICS

CHARLES E. SCOTT

5. Nonbelonging/Authenticity

The word *nonbelonging* as I wish to use it does not suggest a determinant relation to belonging. We *can* think of the word in such a way that it refers to a state that is necessarily related to but different from another state called belonging. But we shall take *nonbelonging* to cancel this connection and lose its meaning as it appears to fulfill its meaning. *Nonbelonging* refuses a conjunction with belonging in the process of seeming to signify such a connection. If *nonbelonging* were a state to which we belonged, it would be comprehensible. We could define the space that separates it from belonging, and we could place and familiarize ourselves with the distance that separates belonging and nonbelonging. The strangeness of nonbelonging could be located. But *nonbelonging* in the 'sense' that I am taking it would be lost in the familiarizing process. As we lose the 'sense' of nonbelonging and its familiarity, and as we lose our thought of it, perhaps a different thought will emerge, one, no doubt, that we will also lose.

Both *dwelling* and *abyss* are words that arise as Heidegger speaks of dasein's proper appropriation of its mortal temporality. The words unsettle each other: one does not dwell in an abyss, and the continuities of dwelling appear to replace the formless chaos named by *abyss*. Dwelling and abyss do not belong to each other, and their nonbelonging pervades authenticity. Does their nonbelonging unsettle a familiarity of dasein with its own propriety as Heidegger describes it in *Being and Time*? If *Eigentlichkeit* means that dasein comes to dwell in familiarity with its mortal temporality—if dasein's open release in and to its temporality defines the proper space of its existence—abyss and anxiety would be properly located in that space and *nonbelonging* would be an inappropriate word to use when speaking of dasein's proper existence. If, on the other hand, dasein's temporality means that abyss prevails in an erasure of the space of propriety, how are we to think properly of authenticity? And of dasein's dwelling? How might dasein belong to itself? How is *Being and Time* to be read if dasein's propriety possesses no proper space and if *Eigentlichkeit* overturns itself in its own movement and possesses neither *eigen* nor *keit*?

First, is there a case to be made for nonbelonging in Heidegger's account of authenticity? The second part of *Being and Time* shows that dasein is the unifying basis for its own self-disclosure and authenticity. The strong implication is that as dasein comes properly to appropriate its mortal temporality, it may be taken to belong to its being. In section 53, the last section of part 2, chapter 1, he sketches out what he will have to establish, namely, that dasein's existential structure makes possible an individual's proper (*eigentliche*) being to death. Because this possibility is dasein's own—is constitutive of dasein—it is said to be *eigentlich* or proper, true, and essential. The name of this condition for the possibility of an individual's proper, mortal way of being is the disclosiveness of situated understanding. *Disclosiveness* is to be read in Heidegger's sense of showing forth, opening up, or clearing; and *understanding* is to be read in his sense of dasein's alert, projecting ability to be: dasein's constitutive ability to be is a forecasting process of disclosure that manifests temporality as it projects forward, and in that sense understands, in its historical, social situtation.

Heidegger interprets dasein's ability to be in the language of possibility, however, and this language makes problematic the sense in which dasein can be said to belong to its being. In this context it is not a possibility for a future realization of something determinant, nor is it a possibility that takes place at a distance from dasein and can be known objectively by contemplation. Dasein's proper and true ability to be is mortal possibility and is characterized as the possibility of the impossibility of existence: being to death. Dasein's world-openness, its clearing for the self-showing of beings, is an ability to be that is sheer, mortal possibility. Possibility (*Möglichkeit*), Heidegger says, is disclosed (*unverhült*) as the impossibility (*Unmöglichkeit*) of existence. Being to death, then, is the "meaning" of dasein's ability to be. "Death, as possibility, gives dasein nothing to be 'actualized', nothing which dasein, as actual, could itself be." *Meaning* thus does not suggest any kind of supersensible world or a world made familiar in dwelling. To belong to being to death is to belong to nothing at all as one dwells in the familiarity of one's world.

Vorlaufen, or running ahead, is, with *proper, possibility, understanding,* and *being to death,* the fifth organizing term of this section. It addresses the movement of being to death and possibility. "Being to death as running ahead in possibility first of all *makes possible* this possibility and makes it as such free." Dasein's ability to be discloses itself in the running ahead of being to death. It is a movement in which the most extreme possibility of human being, its death, is brought forth and uncovered in its possibility. What is most dasein's own, its ability to be, is not *something* to be realized. Dasein's propriety regarding its being for Heidegger is not a matter of the self's actualizing itself. There is no self there when dasein's ability to be is addressed. Its movement is one of running ahead to its impossibility in its mere ability to be. It is not a movement of self-constitution or of the unfolding of an essence that has a nature to unfold or of a truth that is to finds its adequacy in an identity that is constituted on the basis of truth's form or content. The movement of dasein's proper and true possibility is mortal temporality in its difference from the possible identities that we might become, the possible lives that we might lead, and the selfhood that we might achieve.

The movement of mortal temporality is dasein's most essential (*eigenste*) possibility for interpreting its proper existence (*eigentliche Existenz*). Existential understanding, in contrast to interpretation, is found in the projective aspect of dasein's temporal movement. Human being, in its care, continuously projects and designs (*entwirft*) in the midst of its relations. Heidegger has shown in section 31 that its projective character opens up (*erschliesst*) in and to the world as well as reveals the being of dasein as possibility of not being. Projection is being possible. In the section at hand he indicates in a preliminary sketch (*Entwurf*) that the temporality of understanding and its projective character (*Entwurf*) are revealed in its mortal running ahead. Heidegger's intention is to show how dasein "auf eigenstes Seinkönnen sich entwerfen kann"—how dasein can project itself on and by its most proper ability to be. Running ahead shows itself as the possibility for understanding the most proper, uttermost ability to be. If he can show this possibility *and* let it be shown in his account of it, he will have an interpretation that is designed after the temporal and mortal design of dasein's understanding and one that invokes the thought of an abysmal temporality that comes into its own as it passes away. He will then be in a position to show how dasein might live in a way that, like the interpretation of *Being and Time*, opens to its being. Dasein's temporal and mortal movement, its *Vorlauf,* would then be the basis for the way we design our lives, a basis that evacuates itself in its mortality, and a basis that exceeds the possibilities for dwelling and belonging.

This basis has no definitive or determinate nature. Dasein's most proper course of conduct takes place as it lets its disclosure disclose itself in whatever activity one undertakes. Heidegger says that his own work must uncover the structure of running ahead in death as dasein's truest possibility. If his writing succeeds and is proper to dasein, it will be responsive to its own "vorlaufenden Erschliessen," to its own understanding *in* running ahead disclosively. That does not mean that the correctness of Heidegger's analysis will be guaranteed if he is true to the being of dasein. It means that an anxious desire for correctness will be experienced in the mortal possibility of dasein's being, which in its occurrence is not subject to correctness or incorrectness; and although Heidegger does not entirely face his own anxiety regarding unity, the impact of his account means that the book's project regarding unity is also in question by virtue of dasein's mortality of design. On the basis of dasein's movement, as Heidegger finds it, even the language of being, running ahead, and design do not escape the unfixing quality of dasein's disclosure. Its truth—the self-disclosure of mortal temporality—comes most clearly to bear as it puts itself in question in consequence of its own claims. Dasein's disclosive running ahead in mortal temporality and the ek-stasis that it constitutes undercut any predisposition to complete certainty, most particularly that predisposition that inclines one to canonize Heidegger's writings or to think on *their* basis rather than on the basis of their possibility for no possibility at all. Heidegger's interpretation of dasein is not the result of "staring at meaning" and coming up with the best reading of the meaning of life. It is designed, rather, to express dasein's ability to be in its disclosive being to death. It clears the way for dasein's world-openness as the temporal course of being to death. The account of dasein's authenticity takes its departure from the finite, temporal movement that is the condition of possibility of both meaning and no meaning, that is, from the questionableness of meaning in being to death. Heidegger's own account, in its discipline, suggests that an abysmal aspect suffuses his project of a definitive descriptive account of dasein. *Being and Time* is a book that cannot belong to the circumscription of its own words and thought. It is indefinitely beyond itself in its mortal temporality.

When dasein's *eigenste Möglichkeit* (most proper possibility) is named death (*SZ*, p. 263), the meaning of *most proper* or *ownmost* or *most essential* is thus interrupted. Dasein's *eigenste* ability to be, its truest can-be, is not something that properly can be said to be its own in the sense of a property at its disposal. Nor is its truest capacity to be self-relational found in the sense that a subject relates to itself. The continuity of self-relation is ruptured by a course of coming to be that does not reflect or represent the self. It rather discloses human being as non-self-like possibility without identity or subjectivity. Dasein is clear (*offenbar*) not only in its difference from its everyday self-understanding but in its difference from selfhood. There is a wrenching (*entrissen*) quality in dasein's deathly openness. It lives out its existential understanding as it is torn from the meanings and values by which it makes its way in its society and as it is torn from its inherited interpretation of itself as self-founding. In this wrenching aspect dasein lives its disclosure of its being in the midst of its activities and connections. It stands out of—ek-sists—everything that it lives for. Dasein's deathly openness ek-sists its selfhood as well as its ethos.

Dasein in its most proper possibility is not finally defined by its linkage to people or things. This is not to say that it is not linked to people and things. It is found *only* in social, historical matrices, in its metaphysical history and technological age, and in language that bears the forgetfulness of being. It occurs only in multiple human connections. But dasein is in excess of its definitive way of being. The human world's ability to be, its clearing for all beings, interrupts both dasein's history and the matrix of connections, not in the active sense of doing something to the history and matrix, but in the sense of pervading and making possible the matrix without being identical to the matrix or having an existence independent of the matrix. Playing on *Vorlaufen,* we can say that being-in-the-world's ability to be courses through the connections of our individual lives as difference from connections and yields their fragility, their mortality, their disconnection in the midst of their connections. When Heidegger says that dasein's possibility runs forward as dasein's future, is dasein's ability to be, and is being to death, he means that dasein goes forward in this interruption: to go in its most proper being means that in moving into its future dasein never leaves its being to death, its possibility for no possibility. Its futural movement is being to death. "Es geht um sein eigenstes Sein"—it goes about its most proper being. One can see why interpreters have often mistaken this claim to mean that dasein is individually alone in its mortality and that Heidegger is a modern stoic who holds that humans must accept the fate of death with singular courage. But we also see that dasein, as an intrinsically social, historical, and worldly being, is a being marked by difference in its being from the totality of its relations and values. *In* its relations and values dasein is the opening, the *erschliessen,* of its ownmost incapacity to own its being by affirming who it in fact is. It comes into its own by the disownment of the priority of its selfhood in the way it is a self.

How is this interruptive nonrelatedness to be lived? What is proper to it? The paradox in this part of Heidegger's analysis is found in his claim that by disowning the sufficiency of one's connections and identity vis à vis dasein, one owns not only one's history and world but also one's being. Just as Nietzsche's self-overcoming in his account of the ascetic ideal echoes the theme of self-sacrifice, Heidegger's interpretation echoes the same thing. The individual individuates itself by discovering the singularity of its being to death and by living its connections with a sensibility informed by that singularity. One loves in the fragility of loving, not in the assumption of its founded meaning. One affirms values with the understanding that one and one's values are able not to be in the possibility of their affirmation. Nothing replaces the individual's life in its living. But rather than thinking in a connection between self-giving and universal principles, Heidegger thinks in the interruption of the meaning of our lives by the mortal *possibility* of living and finds in owning the being's interruption of our lives that we may disown the theoretical and existential sufficiency of our selves for defining our being or our ability to be. Individuation means living responsively in the world with the *eigenstes Möglichkeit* of being to death, which interrupts one's historical and community identity and puts in question the meaning of life. This is saying something quite different from the statement that the individual must die his or her death alone. In owning one's being one owns no one, and that 'no one' is both the truth of one's being and nonbelonging. No one, no history, no community, no subjectivity authorizes the individual's life. The question is how we are to think of being without authority and meaning for life, without self-relational meaning. When Heidegger says that an individual is forced by the forward run (*Vorlaufen*) of existence to take over its most proper and true being in possibility, he is saying that the individual's world and life are decentered and ruptured by the individual's resolve. In this open resolve the thought of selfhood, subjectivity, and self-constitution are set aside. In open resolve one opens out in the world in the "understanding design" of dasein's mortal openness. We are finding that in belonging to its being dasein belongs nowhere in addition to belonging to its everyday world and cultural tradition.

Dasein's situation is thus not one in which it constitutes itself and gives itself familiarity primarily by means of realizing a given potential for selfhood. In intrinsically (*eigentlich*) lacks reality and is able to come into specific kinds of living only by virtue of the historically formed world-relations in which it finds itself. The 'wholeness' of its being is found in the stream of possibility—not a determinant possibility for a specific way of being that dasein may realize in more or less appropriate ways. Possibility is never surpassed, even momentarily, by some form of dwelling. Rather, given its history, the very activity of self-constitution proliferates dasein and moves it away from its wholeness and unity, a wholeness that is found in its attunement "to the nothing of the possible impossibility of its existence." Dasein's true (*eigenste*) situation is found in an attunement that has neither subject nor object. It is the mood of sheer, mortal possibility: anxiety. The thought of whole and unity is pushed by Heidegger to a breaking point as he shows that human being finds its unity in nothing present or realizable. In speaking of this opening to dasein's whole ability to be, Heidegger uses a middle voice phrase: "die Angst ängstet sich *um* das Seinkönnen des so bestimmten Seienden und erschliesst so die äussereste Möglichkeit": "Anxiety (is) anxious in the midst of the ability to be of the being that is so disposed and opens up the uttermost possibility." Anxiety discloses dasein's ability to be in a wholeness without substance and in the figuration of possible impossibility. Dasein is most true, that is, it is its own disclosure, in possibility that opens to all values and meanings and stands out from everything that makes an individual's life worth living. The thought of grounding thus falls away in the anxiety that grounds the thought. In anxiety nonbelonging displaces any space that might locate it.

The title of section 53 is *Existenzialer Entwurf eines eigentlichen Seins zum Tode (Existential Projection of a Proper Being to Death)*. We have emphasized that *Entwurf*—projected design—is closely associated with *Vorlauf*—the running ahead of dasein's possibility as being to death. This section appropriates dasein's proper *Vorlauf* in its *Entwurf* by developing an interpretation based on dasein's existential understanding of its mortal temporality, and in that process prepares to break the traditional thoughts of unity, wholeness, and ground. These thoughts are projected in the forward run of dasein's anxious possibility and can no longer suggest a transcendental grounding for value and meaning. Human being is uncovered in the process whereby the traditional and everyday senses of self and transcendence are ruptured by anxiety, which is the modal aspect of dasein's ungrounded mortality.

In this rupture both dasein and *Being and Time* stand out of the context of belonging. *Stand out* itself is in question. Dasein has no unambiguous stand in its anxiety, and *Being and Time* has no unambiguous place to stand beyond its historical determination. In reference to dasein's determination we can say that it stands out of its familiar world and its self. But there is no determined transcendental field in which to take another stand, no additional and firmer world in which to ek-sist and come to a more proper home. The recoil in the metaphysical history in which *Being and Time* is conceived is radical in the sense that while the book is completed in anticipation of a fuller and more complete account of its own enabling history, and while the authorship of the book is admittedly within the metaphysical lineage that it puts in question, its limits fade out in the possibility that gives it its space of disclosive communication. It does not recoil into a higher truth or into the possibility of greater accuracy and truthfulness. It recoils into no perspective or world view, into no place that can provide a higher standpoint for clarification of belonging. Belonging as it does to an accountable history, *Being and Time* also moves with a timing that gives it no teleological meaning to provide a greater meaning to its history. It finds an ending to its history in the language that gives expression to the *Vorlauf* of its lineage. Neither dasein nor *Being and Time* can belong to the being that discloses them, that is, they cannot belong to their own disclosure, and this nonbelonging appears as mere vacancy as mortality interrupts the determinant connections of their lives.

We can make a case for modifying this radicality. We can point out that dasein's being is metaphysical even as it breaks the hold of metaphysical thinking. We can rightly say that in *Being and Time* dasein's being belongs to the question of being and that that question arises in a quite specific lineage. In this sense nonbelonging might be said to belong to the history of metaphysics, that anxiety and the possibility of no possibility are phenomena *within* this history. Anxiety and the possibility of no possibility occur in a quite determinate way: they belong to a tradition that constitutes dasein. We might further point out that in authenticity dasein comes to dwell in a determinant manner by an open vulnerability to its mortal temporality, that nonbelonging is given a home in its appropriated disclosure.

And yet in the process of uncovering this determination, *Being and Time* finds itself uncovered, opened out beyond its history into no history, no determination, no familiarity. This opening out, when made familiar by thematization, impels thought in strange, but presumably fulfillable directions. But these directions take their direction from the nondirection of dasein's opening out, and belonging as Dasein does to this transformation, it finds that *in* its belonging it belongs nowhere. Its history is locatable only by reference to its own locations, and its locatability is grounded in nonlocatable indeterminacy. Dasein's belonging belongs to nonbelonging, which provides nothing.

Nonbelonging puts Heidegger's thought at an edge that is dangerous in the perspective of the values and meanings that tells us what is right and wrong at the most fundamental level of our culture. When our essential determinations are undetermined—when our belonging is ungrounded—and when the basis of our creative and ethical passions is experienced as abysmal and unbased, we, in experiencing the importance of universality that is our heritage, are given to believe that the value of life itself is in question. The exhilaration of living at the edge, the passions associated with risk, the freedom of being uprooted: these enlivening spurs to perception and a sense of being that frighten us and awaken our sensibilities to the narcotic of normalcy at its best also forecast the possibility of disruption and catastrophic loss of order. It is not a friendly struggle when we find that at the edge of belonging we can expire with an intensity of living that makes anemic the satisfactions that ordinarily stir in us the deep emotions associated with dedicated affiliation. To live with our ethos and hence with our identities at the limit of recognition threatens exhaustion as well as exhilaration. It is one thing to read the *Duino elegies* or *On The Essence of Truth* in the full assurance of belonging deeply to a way of life that makes clear who we are to be; it is quite another to feel the ungrounding of what grounds us and to be on the line of belonging in the abyss of nonbelonging. How are we to be properly ourselves when we find nonpropriety in the circumference of our being?

The issue is joined in Heidegger's account of *Eigentlichkeit* and *Uneigentlichkeit* in which the propriety of ethics is put in question at the same time that ethics appears to be inevitable. The term *eigentliche* refers to specific ways in which an individual relates to its being. What is the proper way for dasein to live with regard to its being? How is it to constitute itself in its being, which interrupts the very meaning of self-constitution with its possibility of no self at all, a possibility that is dasein's and is most properly so? Our issue is, how does dasein's nonbelonging put ethics in question as Heidegger establishes dasein's proper way to be vis à vis its being?

The tension that we have to work with in *Being and Time,* when we consider dasein's propriety regarding itself, its authenticity, is found in Heidegger's emphasis on dasein's ontological structure as the unifying origin, in the sense of condition for the possibility, of all relative, ontic ways of existing, and in his showing that this ontological structure and its account are in question by virtue of dasein's own disclosure. Dasein's ontological structure provides the basis for raising the question of being, for interpreting its historicity, and for showing how it might exist appropriately with regard to its being. But the basis is more like abyss than like anything that can be properly called normative. Given our inherited senses of ultimate meaning for reality and the intrinsic value of human existence, this discovery appears at first nihilistic. If we have no solid reference to support the values of individual lives, then anything can be justified. Anything has, of course, been justified in our history, including the most severe repressions, torture, extreme cruelty, wars, and the morbid enslaving and destructive segregation of vast groups of people. The proliferation of norms whereby we justify certain values and contend against other values mirrors our fear of what the world would be like if we lacked an adequate basis for justifying our values and realizing the best possibilities of ourselves. The tension in Heidegger's thought between the seach for a normative basis for thought and the discovery of a 'basis' that puts that search in question arises directly out of the fear to which our tradition responds by supporting its ideals and highest hopes with a combination of axioms, authorizing disclosure, and careful judgment.

The tension in Heidegger's thought puts in question the combination of axioms, authorizing disclosure, and judgment, as well as the belief that with a proper normative basis for our values we can hope to overcome the destructive proliferation of violently opposing ways of life. The question we are approaching is whether people can find options to grounded normativity as the basis on which they come to be who they 'should' be. Do options to the traditionally ethical ones arise for our language and thought when the tension between ontological grounding and being that cannot be a ground, but is like an *ab-grund,* defines the space for thought? Does Heidegger's account of the basis for authenticity twist free of its ethical desire for grounding presence?[1]

Heidegger's analysis shows that our 'natural' identities are formed within complex histories and communities that structure our identities as though the inherited values were absolute. It further shows that their conceptual structure is based on the assumptions that being is continuing presence and is simple, that time is linear and quantifiable, that death is the endpoint of life, and that human being has a kind of nature that is available to objective discovery. Our everyday "fallen" lives are thus the basis of traditional metaphysical thought and the means of evaluation accompanying it in the name of ethics.

The normal is "uneigentlich"—improper, not true, not essential—and "verloren," lost. When we hold in mind that the possibility of ethical thought and action is found in traditional 'normalcy' and its history, we see the cutting edge of Heidegger's thought concerning dasein's resolve: as we turn to the possibility of *Eigentlichkeit,* authenticity, we are turning away from ethics as we know it even as we turn to dasein's determining itself in relation to its mortal disclosiveness. Nonbelonging interrupts both our heritage of ethics and the possibility of making authenticity into a new ethics. This turning away from ethics is no less than a twisting free of a body of selfhood that is given in its investment in not knowing its being or its propriety vis à vis its disclosure to which it cannot belong. It is a turning that occurs *in* dasein's authenticity. Heidegger's position is far stronger than one that provides only a formal basis for determining what our normative values should be. This metaphysical strategy of formal-positive determination is changed by his thought, which is under the impact of mortal temporality's ekstasis vis à vis belonging and dwelling. The question is whether we are able even in our authenticity to recognize the range of our suffering and pleasure or the meaning of the institutions and disciplines by which and in which we become who we are in the expectation of belonging to a way of dwelling that is appropriate to our being.

The "voice" of dasein's possibility "calls" in the midst of our involvements. Heidegger uses the experience of conscience, not its contents, as his phenomenal field. In his account, we undergo a calling away from our identities and selves to the possibility of our being. This call is corrupted by religions and moralities to seem as though it were calling to a specific way of life or ethos and as though it were initiated by specific violations that arouse guilt in a given individual. But the call itself discloses not the power of an ethos but the difference of human being, in its being, from its traditional ways of life. One undergoes, in the disclosiveness of dasein, a continuous "call" to its propriety, its *eigenste Selbstseinkönnen,* its most appropriate ability to be itself. Dasein's call to itself is like a voice that comes to dasein in the midst of its traditional life, like an appeal or summons to undergo the difference, in its being, from its self. "It gives dasein to understand" that its being is found in the disclosiveness of its ability to be in its possibility of no possibility at all, not in its values or in the objects of its religious and philosophical projections. The voice of conscience, as the disclosure of dasein's being in the midst of its everyday values and standards, functions to make those values and standards uncertain and to "call" dasein to its difference from who it is in its efforts to be someone recognizable in its culture.

The wrenching away from dasein's self and the interruption (Heidegger says breaking into) of our identities by the call of conscience are constitutive movements of dasein that put it in touch with itself. Dasein's self, Heidegger says in section 57, is clearly not in the call of conscience which presents neither a person nor a definitive and definite way of life. Nothing familiar is encountered. In our experience of ourselves we ordinarily say that we are lost when we find no landmarks or customs to which we can relate with familiarity. But on Heidegger's account we begin to find ourselves when we are dislocated and displaced by the disclosure of our being that has no 'stand', no name or heritage in our environment. The wrenching movement and displacement are aspects of the disclosure of being in our everyday world and is hence both our inauthentic and authentic existence.

In this "call" we begin to hear the "understanding" that constitutes the *Vorlauf* of our finitude. There is no observer, no judge, no clear definitions or standards. But instead of being lost we are homing in on our being. This wrenching movement means in the context of *Being and Time* that we are being freed from the "lostness" of our familiar world of cultural inheritance and from the surveillance of our identities that make us who we are. To be *eigentlich*—proper to our being—and attuned to our being in our everyday lives, we have to overcome the monopolizing power of valences and exigencies that define who we are.

Heidegger's account of the call of conscience provides for his interpretation the possibility of this overcoming, this twisting free. It further establishes the difference that constitutes our lives and shows that in this difference we, as culturally determined identities, have access to the being whose erasure is part of who we are traditionally to be. To trust our meanings and values by giving them axiomatic status, to stake our lives on them, and to know ourselves in their mediation is to forget our being and the possibility of living appropriately as the being that we are. Only by the severity of the wrenching, twisting movement out of the surveillance and authority of our normalcy and identity can dasein come into its own. But its own is not something defined by belonging. Dasein, in its history, has been on an edge that it has sought to erase; and, coming to its own, dasein finds both the edge and its attempted erasure in the range of identities that it can be. The call of dasein's being, on Heidegger's account, is a call from its history in which the *danger* of its best establishments reveals a mortality that *Being and Time* finds difficult to speak in the radicality and terror that its history has bestowed upon it. And in being proper to its being, dasein finds itself without the ballast that it has come to expect in the technological tradition that makes possible the language of authenticity.

If the being of dasein were determinant and if it provided immediately a nature to be realized by individual action, ethics would not be put in question. We could in principle find out what our nature is and how to meet its standards. But since dasein, in being called to itself, is called to a being whose meaning is mortal temporality and thus has no intrinsic, determinant meaning at all, the structure of ethics as such is in question. To be in question does not mean that we may hope for a time when ethics will be abolished and we will live a higher life, unstressed by the difference between our being and our cultural lives. The "lostness" of everyday life is not to be lost, on Heidegger's account. It does mean that as we follow unquestioningly the patterns of our best ideals and values in a state of mind that knows, at least in principle, what is genuinely and universally good and bad, we are lost to our being and to our mortal indeterminacy. We cannot expect that such a life will unconsciously and inevitably override its mortal temporality by, for example, organizing our environments in systems of value that create totalities of meaning that are invested in ignoring both their own being and the meaning of their being for totalizing meanings. Whereas in the traditional thought of subjectivity one expects some type of self-realization consequent to conformity to the reality of the subject—whatever the subject might be—in the instance of *Being and Time* authenticity means the disclosure of human-being-in-question without the possibility of resolving the question or the problems that follow it. Is it possible that our systems of self-realization and self-sacrifice for higher values make inevitable a maiming of human life that is recognizable only when our best ways of being are profoundly disturbed by the nonpresence of our being? Do our axiomatic values at their best constitute a blindness to who we are and what we do? Does the disclosure of our being and its appropriation, along with the pain and disruption that constitute it and follow it, make possible a profound and thoroughgoing uncertainty that itself reveals the limits of ethics?[2]

The question of ethics in the context of *Being and Time* is a way of being that is concerned in the world and with other people. It happens in language and practice and comes to itself as an individual who is already constituted by relations. The difference of being and everyday existence takes place only in world relations. Hence the emphasis on continuously twisting free of cultural domination *in* cultural life, never outside of it. The terminus is not a life that is withdrawn from culture and history, nor is it found in projected experiences that are ahistorical and purged of corruption. The aim involves an individual's being-with-others in a specific environment and history and attuned in its relations to the *Vorlauf* of its being without presence. The "perversion" that inevitably occurs in our standards for living is found in their insensitivity to their mortal temporality.

Heidegger articulates his interpretation in the traditional language of being-as-presence. Existential understanding is "given." Being "presents itself." Dasein "comes to itself." His interpretation is no less involved in the wrenching, twisting recoils than in dasein's authentic movements. In association with this articulation, Heidegger shows that as being presents itself, no subject or substance or nature is disclosed. The possibility for no possibility is disclosed. Mortal disclosure takes place. As dasein comes to itself, no specific course of action is indicated. The given existential understanding has neither a subject nor an object. Dasein's being does not name anything present; rather it names mortal, temporal disclosure that forecasts itself as temporal possibility rather than as a standing nature. The language of presence in this text is thus in a process of twisting free from its own inevitability in the tradition in which it occurs and in which Heidegger thinks. This movement articulates dasein's movement recoiling toward the possibility of authenticity in which nonbelonging is no less invoked than dasein's propriety regarding itself.

The issue of dasein's coming to itself is thus one of dasein's allowing its difference in its being vis à vis the status of its life. In this difference Heidegger finds the opening of nonbelonging and the questionableness of the manner in which we establish systems of value. If an individual can allow and affirm its mortal temporality, in contrast to the invested obfuscation of mortal temporality, and can also allow the *question* of the meaning of being in its historical identity, if it can want the 'address' of its being in spite of wanting a sense of continuous and meaningful presence, it can, perhaps, come to appropriate the difference of its own being as it decides its daily issues. This alertness is like a person's affirming or loving another person with a full sense of mortality in the relationship.[2] Or it is like experiencing the validity of a system of values without a sense of certainty or universality. Nothing specific is there to will in dasein's owning its being—hence the anxiety to which Heidegger gives attention. Allowing its being, dasein allows the "calling forth" of its continuous need to take care, given its primordial lack of stasis. This allowing, given the constitution of its identity, is like dasein's unburdening itself of traditional resistances and opening itself to the inevitability of being without foundations. Resoluteness thus cannot be conceived in terms of self-constitution. Rather, self-constitution requires a basis for validation, and authentic experience itself falls into question as dasein comes into its own through its disclosure of its incapacity to belong to its being.

The middle voice gives articulation to dasein's ability to be, its understanding, and its wanting to have conscience, each of which constitutes a manner or *Weise* of disclosiveness (*Erschlossenheit*) that also is not a subject or object with regard to an action. We are in a position to see that in open resolve (*Entschlossenheit*) and authenticity (*Eigentlichkeit*) disclosure discloses and time times, that Heidegger's emphasis is not on self-constituting action or intentional action but on the (self-)disclosure of dasein's disclosiveness in which nothing belongs to no one. Dasein's disclosiveness is its being. It is being to death, the possibility of no possibility, the *Vorlauf* of no continuing presence. Dasein's being is *its* difference from the finite continuity of its identity and its being in the world. In its most proper being, no 'I' controls and no one belongs to being.

'I' is always situated in a locality of specific determinants. It does not enjoy the benefits of an ontologically founded ideal that can guide it to right decisions. Decisions are made in the power of the values and possibilities for action that are allowed by the situation. This is not a version of historical relativism, however, since the ontological indeterminacy of the specific situation is made inevitable by dasein's being, not by the control of history. The proliferation of values and meanings that characterize our history has its meaning in dasein's being, in its ability to be, as we have seen. The 'I' that resolves properly opens to its being in its situation, twists free from the control of predominant standards of judgment by attending resolutely to its being, and makes its judgments and commitments in the loosening of the bonds of the everyday by virtue of concerned and open regard for its being. As dasein lets itself be called forth in its most proper being, the 'I' is modified by the non-I of its being. It becomes strange to itself in its clarity of purpose and certainty, and it acts forthrightly in understanding the collapse of clarity in its being. No less situated, no less concerned or committed, the individual's attunements and expectations, its perceptiveness, satisfactions, and priorities are conditioned by, as it were, an open door to mortal time that lets in an element different from the presence and totality of value. It acts, but now in the questionableness of the possibility of its actions and in the transgressions of being that mark its living. To be this way is to be resolved, and to be resolved is to attest to the nonbelonging of being in the value-laden situation that one lives in and through.

The tension in this paper—between Heidegger's language and the language that I have used to speak of nonbelonging—mirrors a tension in *Being and Time:* the book's language is facing more than it can articulate; it belongs to a tradition that begins to be overturned within it; it speaks with anxious obsession in the presence of the mortal temporality that conditions it and that it dreads. This tension, as much as the book's discipline and claims, reveals the nonbelonging that invests *Being and Time*'s tradition as an edge of risk, an edge that puts in question all the effort required to reach the edge. And it forecasts a manner of speaking and thinking that might be alert to kinds of suffering to which we are blind when we belong at a secure distance from something that properly explodes our familiar world into nonbelonging.

NOTES

1. I take the term *twist free* from David Krell's translation of *Herausdrehung* and from John Sallis's use of the term in "Twisting Free: Being to an Extent Sensible," *Research in Phenomenology* 17 (1987): 1–21.

2. In pathological grief, for example, a person is often traumatized by the interruption of death, and the grief is less over the loss than over the mortality that infuses the other and one's relation with the other.

ROBERT   BERNASCONI

6. Justice and the Twilight Zone of Morality

In *Being and Time* Heidegger excused himself from the task of providing a history of the concept of truth on the grounds that it could only be written on the basis of a history of ontology (*SZ* 214). If after 1930 he repeatedly ventured what at least on the surface look like sketches of the history of the concept of truth, it was not because he had in the meanwhile completed a history of ontology. It would be more accurate to say that Heidegger came to recognize that the history of truth could not be separated from that of ontology. For a decade at least, he sought to present the history of ontology in terms of a history of truth. The result was not the history of truth as a concept but the history of truth in its Being. It was thus a history of the essence of truth in that unique Heideggerian sense of the phrase such that in due course and with appropriate caution it would have to be thought of as a history of the truth of essence. One of the reasons for that need for caution is the difficulty of understanding how a term such as "history" might be understood in conjunction with the phrase "truth of essence." Would such a history of truth be *Historie* or *Geschichte?* And if *Geschichte*, would it be *Geschichte* in the sense of *Geschick?*[1] In other words, is this history of essence a story that strives to present above all a coherent picture of a continuous history? Or is it to be thought of as governed by the discontinuities of the sending of Being? Furthermore, at what point must truth be thought in terms of ἀλήθεια? Many years later Heidegger would acknowledge that "ἀλήθεια thought *as* ἀλήθεια has nothing to do with 'truth'; rather, it means unconcealment." He continued, "What I then said in *Being and Time* about ἀλήθεια already goes in this direction. Ἀλήθεια as unconcealment had already occupied me, but in the meantime, 'truth' came in between" (*H* 260). It is possible that what Heidegger understood as having intervened was precisely his attempt to write the history of the essence of truth, notwithstanding the fact that there were a number of instances in the 1930s and 1940s, particularly in the lecture courses, in which Heidegger warned his students that when he said truth in the context of the history of the transformation of its essence, they should hear it in terms of ἀλήθεια.

I am not proposing to pursue these questions directly. The history of the essence of truth, if I may be allowed to call it that provisionally, is not really my topic here, although it will prove easier to expel it formally than it will be to keep it from returning uninvited. It will suffice to begin by rehearsing the outline of that history as it is to be found in "Plato's Doctrine of Truth,"[2] an essay that spans the period 1930 to 1943. Heidegger identifies four stages in Plato's allegory of the cave from the *Republic*. One's journey begins with being chained in the cave. Then one is released from one's chains so that one can look around, before being forced into the sunlight, and finally one is returned to the cave. Each stage is correlated with its own kind of truth, or rather, its own kind of unconcealment. For Heidegger's reading assumes that for Plato, as for his predecessors, the self-evident and fundamental experience of ἀλήθεια is that of unconcealment. Heidegger's argument is not that ἀλήθεια as unconcealment disappears in Plato. Even though it comes under the yoke or mastery of the idea (*W* 135–36), it maintains a position (*Rang*) (*W* 130). That is to say, after Plato, "the essence of truth does not unfold from its own essential fullness as the essence of unconcealment, but is displaced (*sich verlagern*) to the essence of the *idea*." None of this is explicit in Plato. The passage between them is left unsaid by Plato. Although ἀλήθεια is said, ὀρθότης or correctness is meant. Truth is both unconcealment and correctness, the correctness of perceiving and asserting based on ὁμοίωσις, the agreement of knowledge with the thing itself. The recognition of this ambiguity is a crucial moment of Heidegger's reading, although it is readily overlooked in the effort to distill Heidegger's approach to the level of a doctrine.

For most of "Plato's Doctrine of Truth," Heidegger confined himself to a reading of a few pages of the *Republic*, but at the end of the essay Heidegger briefly continues the story beyond Plato. The same ambiguity identified in Plato is also to be found in Aristotle where ἀλήθεια is set in opposition to ψεῦδος in such a way that truth as the correctness of an assertion is opposed to its falsity. To characterize the main epochs of subsequent metaphysics, Heidegger provides only three quotations and a minimal commentary. In Aquinas, ὁμοίωσις becomes *adaequatio*. Aquinas's location of truth in the understanding, following Aristotle, is subsequently sharpened by Descartes. Finally, Nietzsche, of whom the most is said, defines truth as incorrectness of thinking. Truth is a kind of error insofar as thinking necessarily falsifies the real by stabilizing or fixing becoming through representation. Nietzsche's conception of truth does not overturn ἀλήθεια; rather it is said to be the most extreme consequence of the transformation of truth from the unconcealment of beings to the correctness of sight. It is therefore only a change in the determination of the Being of beings as idea (*W* 139). In that way Heidegger could be said to be pointing to what is sometimes referred to as the unity of metaphysics.

The history of the transformation of the essence of truth was not the only story that Heidegger was telling at the time. There were the stories Heidegger told to the German people about their role in the future of their country. I shall briefly return to this later, but only after I have introduced another story that Heidegger was telling, one that intersects with the story about ἀλήθεια and also perhaps the story of the *Volk*. It is the story of δίκη. The story has to be collated from a number of Heidegger's essays and lectures from this period. It has never been told as a story, not even by Heidegger it seems, and the first task will be to reconstruct its outline from Heidegger's scattered remarks. I will give the most attention to the roles of Anaximander and Nietzsche in this story, even though it has been the appearance of a discussion of some of the intervening stages in a recent volume of the *Gesamtausgabe* that gives the clue to its importance.

Δίκη was among the first words of philosophy. Or, more precisely, the only sentence that survives from what is often called the oldest philosophical text known to us includes this word. Heidegger's interpretation of Anaximander is best known from his essay "The Anaximander Fragment."[3] Although in a 1941 lecture course Heidegger also takes up the Anaximander fragment, the references to δίκη are curtailed.[4] I shall therefore focus on the 1946 essay, albeit only to give a very partial account of it.

The fragment is preserved by Simplicius who cites it from Theophrastus. In Burnet's *Early Greek Philosophy*, one of the commentaries Heidegger consulted, the fragment as found in Simplicius via Theophrastus is translated as follows: "And into that from which things take their rise they pass away once more, 'as is meet; for they make reparation and satisfaction to one another for their injustice according to the ordering of time', as he says in these somewhat poetical terms."[5] Theophrastus' phrase, "in these somewhat poetical terms," encourages scholars, including Burnet, to judge the phrase in single quotation marks to be Anaximander's actual words and not just a paraphrase.[6] Heidegger decides that the direct quotation is briefer still.

Heidegger restricts the fragment to the phrase: ". . . κατὰ τὸ χρεών. Διδόναι γὰρ αὐτὰ δίκην καὶ τίσιν ἀλλήλοις τῆς ἀδικίας."[7] Heidegger, after careful consideration, renders it, ". . . entlang dem Brauch; gehören nämlich lassen sie Fug somit auch Ruch eines dem anderen (im Verwinden) des Un-Fugs" (*HW* 342). In the English translation of Heidegger's essay this is translated in turn as ". . . along the lines of usage; for they let order and thereby also reck belong to one another (in the surmounting) of disorder" (*EGT* 57). Heidegger's translation of δίκη as *Fug* can be rendered in English as "order" or possibly "juncture," although both words suggest themselves more from desperation than conviction. Other commentators use the more conventional translation of "justice" or, like Burnet, "reparation." Heidegger's translation is governed by a specific interpretation. What is at stake in this interpretation of Anaximander's saying?

Heidegger from the outset contests the standard interpretation of the fragment according to which nature is being described in terms that derive from the human sphere. He dismisses the accusation that Anaximander's "moral and judicial notions get mixed in with his view of nature." The criticism is anachronistic. Ethical or judicial issues were not at that time interpreted in terms of disciplines (*HW* 304; see also *GA* 51: 99). If there are no boundaries to be drawn between, for example, ethics and physics as disciplines, "then there is no possibility of trespass or of the unjustified transfer of notions from one area to another" (*HW* 305). But does that mean that law and the ethical are not at issue here at all? Heidegger carefully guards against such a claim. "Denial of such boundaries between disciplines does not mean to imply that in early times law and ethicality were unknown" (*HW* 305). This can be clarified with reference to the contemporaneous essay, *Letter on Humanism*. Heidegger there tries to disengage his thinking from the disciplines of ontology and ethics in order to think the truth of Being. This thinking, which Heidegger remarks could be called "original ethics," and which he says had already been attempted in a preliminary way in *Being and Time* under the title of "fundamental ontology," moves in the realm from which law and ethicality derive or from which they are assigned. As Heidegger wrote of νόμος, it is "not only law but more originally the assignment contained in the dispensation of Being" (*W* 191). Similarly, in the Anaximander essay Heidegger attempts to hear in the key words a more "original" meaning than their subsequent moral or juridical meaning would allow.

Heidegger speculates that the words criticized by Theophrastus as poetic were δίκη, τίσις, ἀδικία and διδόναι δίκην (*HW* 304). What underlies Theophrastus's judgment is not just his understanding that these words have primarily a moral or juridical meaning but also the assumption that by beings (τὰ ὄντα) Anaximander means natural things in the narrow sense (φύσει ὄντα) (*HW* 305). Together the two assumptions result in a reading of the sentence as some kind of metaphor. Heidegger's diagnosis is that this reading is a consequence of the divorce of thinking from poetizing that took place with metaphysics (*HW* 303 and 343). Heidegger offers an interpretation of the fragment in which these same words speak through the language of subsequent Greek thought, specifically through φύσις and λόγος, ἔρις and μοῖρα, ἀλήθεια, and ἕν. "In the language of these fundamental words, thought from the experience of presencing, these words from the Anaximander fragment resound: δίκη, τίσις, ἀδικία" (*H* 325; *EGT* 39). The words deemed by Theophrastus to be inappropriate for philosophical thinking at its highest level are found to permeate the very words from which philosophy originally drew its inspiration. The fundamental words of Parmenides and Heraclitus, and thus of Western thinking generally, are from the outset words which, according to an old tradition, are derivative and thus extraneous to fundamental thinking. Heidegger in his reading of the fragment wants to upset that tradition and in such a way as to counteract the tendency to diminish the contribution of the early Greek thinkers.

On Heidegger's interpretation, the Anaximander fragment is concerned with Being (*GA* 51: 123). Τὰ ἐόντα, in the sense of "the present, whether present or absent" (*das gegenwärtig und ungegenwärtig Answesende*), is designated by him as the unspoken, the unsaid in what is said in the Anaximander fragment. This establishes a continuity between the fragment and the thinking that follows it in the West. Heidegger writes of τὰ ἐόντα that "This word names that which from now on, whether or not it is uttered, lays a claim on all Western thinking" (*HW* 324). For Heidegger, the Greeks thought Being in terms of presencing, and the words δίκη and ἀδικία are to be construed with reference to it. Δίκη is associated with the idea of presencing as a lingering or tarrying. Such a conception is distinct from a notion of presence as permanence or persistence, but the two are not in simple opposition to each other. The fragment appears to be concerned with the relation between the two modes of presencing. Lingering in the former sense is recognized as an arising which subsequently passes away, and thus it recalls in certain respects Heidegger's attempt to articulate φύσις in its Greek sense. But persisting is also a kind of lingering, and Heidegger describes ἀδικία as an insurrection (*Aufstand*) on behalf of sheer endurance (*HW* 328). Heidegger thus reads the fragment as foreshadowing the idea of Being as permanence which appears to govern Western metaphysics, while at the same time he claims that this idea is thought by Anaximander as bound to an idea of presencing as arising and passing away, an idea that Western metaphysics neglected.

Heidegger does not arrive immediately at the translation of δίκη as order (*Fug*) and ἀδικία as disorder (*Unfug*). His initial translation employs the terms juncture or jointure (*die Fuge*) and being out of order (*aus der Fuge sein*) (*HW* 327). The translation changes when Heidegger moves from understanding the fragment as saying that ἀδικία is the essence of what is present (*HW* 328)[8] to understanding it as saying that the presenting of what is present is a surmounting or coming to terms with ἀδικία (*HW* 335).[9] Heidegger uses the word *Verwindung* rather than the more forceful *Überwindung* in order to convey that ἀδικία is not put to one side once and for all, but is the nonessence (*Unwesen*) that belongs to the essence of presencing (*GA* 51: 119). Just as Heidegger understands Anaximander's fragment as concerned with Being, so Heidegger's essay should be understood as an attempt to engage in thinking the truth of Being. That is why Heidegger's reading of Anaximander's fragment does not culminate in δίκη. Nor for that matter does it focus on τὸ ἄπειρον, which is most often the central focus of Anaximander's commentators. The word that Heidegger identifies as "dictated to thinking in the experience of Being's oblivion" is τὸ χρεών. Heidegger translates it as *der Brauch*, which in the absence of a noun formed from the verb "to brook" is usually translated "usage" (*HW* 340). This is the word that is assigned to the thinker of the truth of Being. But it would be wrong to think of the different words, δίκη, ἄπειρον, and χρεών, as alternatives from which one must be selected. With the word τὸ χρεών Anaximander, according to Heidegger, thinks the dispensing of justice and injustice, or rather, because these terms might return us to distinctions and realms which have been displaced, juncture and disjuncture. "Usage distributes juncture and reck in such a manner that it reserves for itself what is meted out, gathers it to itself, and secures it as what is present in presencing" (*HW* 339). For Heidegger, to think δίκη in its relation to τὸ χρεών is not only to bring it into relation with the beginnings of philosophy, such that it allows us to proceed to a reading of Parmenides and Heraclitus (*HW* 341), but it is also to understand it in terms of what still remains to be thought in the assignment of the truth of Being.

Heidegger appears to make little attempt to follow the thought of δίκη into Parmenides or Heraclitus. So far as I am aware, it is only in the summer semester of 1935 in *An Introduction to Metaphysics* that Heidegger joins the company of the many scholars who juxtapose these three early thinkers of δίκη. In this context he introduces his translation of δίκη as *Fug* or juncture. In the previous semester Heraclitus' fragment 80 had been understood to be saying that right is strife so that δίκη was translated as *Recht* (*GA* 39: 126). A few months later fragment 80 was understood to say, "It is necessary to keep in view both setting apart as essentially bringing together and juncture as diverging" (*EM* 127). What stands between the two translations is Heidegger's reading of Sophocles' *Antigone*, and in particular the famous chorus on human being. Heidegger, at the outset of his reading of Sophocles, rejects the translation of δίκη as "justice" or "norm" on the grounds that it gives the word a juridical and moral meaning at the cost of its basic metaphysical content, which he understands as the originary collectedness of φύσις (*EM* 123). Furthermore, Heidegger understands Sophocles' word τὸ δεινόν in terms of the relation between τέχνη as the violence of human know-how and δίκη as the overpowering juncture. The human being is in a violent struggle with δίκη as the overpowering. There are victories and defeats as the human being is tossed between juncture and disjuncture but no final victory (*EM* 123). It is not hard to recognize an echo of Anaximander in this account, even if it is one that Heidegger himself does not acknowledge explicitly.

What Heidegger does acknowledge is a much less obvious proximity between Anaximander and Parmenides. The reciprocal relation between τεχνη and δίκη that Heidegger found in the chorus from *Antigone* is understood by him to be the same as the belonging together of thinking and being in Parmenides (*EM* 126). Heidegger finds support for this in Parmenides' reference to Δίκη as holding the keys to the gates of the paths of night and day. He interprets this as referring to the path of being that discloses, the path of appearance that distorts, and the path of nothingness that closes off. Beings open themselves only insofar as the juncture of Being is preserved and protected. "Being as δίκη is the key to beings in their conjunction (*Gefüge*)." Heidegger will never again make so pronounced a statement about δίκη as this one from *An Introduction to Metaphysics*, but from this point on the word begins to take on an importance within his retrieval of Western metaphysics.

This importance is already reflected in the following year, in the lecture course, *The Will to Power as Art*, in which Heidegger marks a transformation in the essence of δίκη which parallels the more famous transformation in the essence of ἀλήθεια. Once again the transformation takes place in Plato's *Republic*, albeit on this occasion the political dimension of the *Republic* is recognized in a way that perhaps reflected some of Heidegger's own political aspirations and disappointments. According to Heidegger, Plato's *Republic* is an attempt to show "that the sustaining ground and determining essence of all political Being consists in nothing less than the 'theoretical', that is, in essential knowledge of δίκη and δικαιοσύνη" (*N* 1: 193). Knowledge of δίκη is philosophy itself, with the consequence that philosophers should rule the state (*N* 1 194). This does not mean that philosophers should conduct the affairs of state. It does mean, however, "that the basic modes of behavior that sustain and define the community must be grounded in essential knowledge, assuming of course that the community, as an order of being, grounds itself on its own basis, and that it does not wish to adopt standards from any other order." The passage deserves more attention than it has been given in the current debates concerning the intersection of Heidegger's philosophy with Nazism. It should not be forgotten that when Heidegger made this observation he had already experienced what he understood as a series of rebuffs to his offer to help guide the development of National Socialism. However, if Heidegger understood his own public support for Nazism and his attempt to shape its direction as itself modeled on the role of the philosopher in Plato's *Republic*, and there is clear evidence that he did, then his account of the history of the transformations of ἀλήθεια and of δίκη should have led him to be suspicious of this appeal to Plato. The use of such a model could be more readily accommodated within the thinking of *Being and Time*, or indeed almost any philosophy prior to it (except perhaps Nietzsche's), than it could within his later thinking, in which the sense of history is more radical and the suspicion of old models more acute.

Heidegger introduces δίκη into his discussion of the *Republic* by denying, as he had already done in his discussion of Anaximander and Parmenides, that it is a moral or legal concept. Once again it is conceived as "the conjoined juncture of the order of Being" (*N* 1: 227). Heidegger writes, "Δίκη is a metaphysical concept, not originally one of morality. It names Being with reference to the essentially appropriate articulation of all beings" (*N* 1: 194). Heidegger stresses the importance of retaining the metaphysical sense of δίκη for a reading of Plato. But when Heidegger says that δίκη is a metaphysical concept, the context shows that this cannot be taken to mean that it belongs to Western metaphysics. Nor can the phrase be understood as meaning that it is an "ontological" concept as opposed to a moral or juridical one. It is metaphysical in the sense of the word elucidated at the end of "What Is Metaphysics?". Or, rather, it corresponds to what in the *Letter on Humanism* comes to be called either "original ethics" or "fundamental ontology." So when Heidegger indicates, albeit only in passing, that in the course of Plato's *Republic* there is a transformation from the metaphysical sense of δίκη to its moral sense, this could perhaps also be understood as a passage from "original ethics" to morality, although he does not say so explicitly. Heidegger writes, "To be sure, δίκη slips into the twilight zone of morality precisely on account of the Platonic philosophy" (*N* 1: 194). If such a passage could be confirmed, and the attempt to do so goes beyond what I am attempting here, it would be a decisive moment in the history of Western metaphysics.[10] Quite how decisive becomes clear from the subsequent history of metaphysics.

This history, as it relates to the question of justice, is outlined in the 1942–43 lecture course on Parmenides. Initially, Heidegger shows little or no interest in Parmenides' account of δίκη here. Heidegger bypasses the opening lines of the poem where δίκη is introduced. Nor does Heidegger pause over his translation of δίκη as *Fug* in line 28 of the poem,[11] although in the context of a discussion of Plato's *Republic*, Heidegger does return to the translation of δίκη in Parmenides as *Fug* to suggest that the Greeks might have heard in it echoes of δείκνυμι as showing and δικεῖν as projecting. On this occasion it is not so much δίκη as *iustitia* that attracts Heidegger's attention. Elsewhere, Heidegger thematizes justice almost always to renounce it as a topic because it was not an adequate translation for δίκη. Here *iustitia* is introduced in its own right and, as we shall see, δίκη is put to one side. Even so, Heidegger's discussion of justice might readily be overlooked. This is because the chief focus of that part of the course in which it appears is the history of the transformation of the essence of ἀλήθεια. Indeed it is Heidegger's fullest statement of that history for the period after Plato.

Much of the discussion is dominated by the question of translation, first of all from Greek into Latin, a process which almost always in Heidegger marks a loss without compensatory gain.

The Romanization not just of ἀλήθεια but of ψεῦδος is understood as a "transformation of the essence of truth and of Being" and as a genuine event in history (*GA* 54: 62). The polemical aspect of Heidegger's discussion is most pronounced when the Latin word passes into German. So, for example, Heidegger dismisses *falsch* as *ein undeutsches Wort* (*GA* 54: 57). *Falsum* is inadequate as a translation of ψεῦδος, because it does not capture the connotation of disguise, the sense of something appearing to be other than it is (*GA* 54: 64), Heidegger uses the word "pseudonym" to illustrate his point (*GA* 54: 44, 52–53). Although a pseudonym does in certain respects conceal the real name of the person, Heidegger, using Kierkegaard as his example, suggests that it should at the same time reveal what the author of the specific text is in truth. The Latin *falsum* is, like *veritas*, divorced from the issue of concealment and unconcealment which underlies the Greek experience of "truth." *Falsum* is associated with deception and Heidegger notes the German word *Trick* is also to be regarded as "un-German." This time the word has been borrowed from English, a fact Heidegger at the height of the Second World War regards as somehow peculiarly appropriate (*GA* 54: 60). Heidegger even debates whether *Wahrheit* is "un-German." He hesitates to agree with the Grimm brothers that it is, but he does so finally, not on etymological grounds, but because its meaning has been determined by the Christo-Roman term *verum* (*GA* 54: 69). Nevertheless, Heidegger is on this occasion not content merely to mark the loss that takes place in the translation.

In the Parmenides lecture course, Heidegger goes further than elsewhere in determining the positive content of *verum*. *Verum* is the upright (*das Aufrechte*) that is directed from above (*GA* 54: 71). It is related to *rectum* from *regere* to rule and hence carries a judicial meaning that is brought to the surface in the word *rectitudo*. Relating *verum* to *iustum* in the sense of law or right, and observing that Roman law (*ius*) also belongs to the essential realm of the command, Heidegger finds that both true and false are determined by the *imperium*, the command, and thus move in the essential realm of justice (*GA* 54: 59, 66). Heidegger comments, in what is his only direct reference to δίκη in this part of the discussion, "For that reason *iustitia* had a completely different essential ground from δίκη, which presences (*west*) in terms of ἀλήθεια" (*GA* 54: 59). At first sight the reference to δίκη appears to be merely negative. There is a gulf between δίκη and *iustitia*, a gulf that might seem to exclude a history of the essential transformations of δίκη of the kind I am trying to expose. And yet the clarificatory phrase added by Heidegger, that δίκη presences in terms of ἀλήθεια, reverses that judgment because it directs attention back to the transformations of ἀλήθεια in its essence. Δίκη gives way to *iustitia* as ἀλήθεια gives way to *verum*. Just as the latter change does not mean that the essencing of truth in the history of Western metaphysics is governed simply by ἰδέα without reference to ἀλήθεια as unconcealment, so the essencing of δίκη in the history of metaphysics is not wholly supplanted by δικαιοσύνη in its moral or juridical sense. Nevertheless, the articulation of this continuity threatens to transform *Seinsgeschichte* into *Historie*. The essential difficulty is underlined by another passage from the lecture course, in which Heidegger writes, "Roman *veritas* has become the 'justice' of the will to power. The circle of the essential history of the metaphysical conception of truth has closed. However, ἀλήθεια remains outside of the circle" (*GA* 54: 78).

In "Metaphysics as History of Being," a text written in 1941 and first published in 1961, Heidegger hints at a connection between the transformation of the essence of truth and theology (*N* 2: 421–23). This suggestion is further developed in the Parmenides lecture course. The political *imperium* gives way to the religious *imperium* of the Roman Curia (*GA* 54: 67). Its commands take the form of ecclesiastical dogma that divides people into believers and heretics and gives rise to the Spanish Inquisition. Heidegger associates the determination of the true as what is certain with Luther, who poses the question of whether and how someone can be certain and assured of eternal salvation. It is a question of whether and how one can be a "true" Christian, a question already posed in the Middle Ages by Aquinas, as Heidegger shows. The question of *iustitia* becomes a question of *iustificatio* or *Rechtfertigung* (*GA* 54: 75). Heidegger's familiar association of the beginning of modern metaphysics with Descartes's *certitudo* is here extended to include discourses of rightness and justification. Descartes is identified as a thinker concerned with the right use of reason (*usus rectus rationis*) as the faculty of making judgments (*GA* 54: 76). That use of reason which is not right is false in the sense of error. In Kant the question of the right use of reason is characterized by Heidegger as a "will to secure certainty" (*Wille zur Sicherung der Sicherheit*).

Heidegger completes the discussion in the Parmenides lectures of 1943–44 with a reference to Nietzsche. Western metaphysics is said to have achieved its pinnacle in Nietzsche's grounding of the essence of truth in certainty (*Sicherheit*) and justice (*Gerechtigkeit*) (*GA* 54: 77, 85). This brief reference, like that in "Plato's Doctrine of Truth," draws on the lecture course from the summer of 1939 entitled "Nietzsche: The Will to Power as Knowledge." The 1939 lecture course is in some ways the most important of Heidegger's discussions of justice, but it only reveals its significance for the question of the history of (the essence of) justice in the context of the other texts already discussed. Heidegger remarks that it can be shown that Heraclitus's thought of δίκη sparked off Nietzsche in his reflections and constantly ignited his thinking. Two points are important. First, Heidegger, evoking the distinction between *Historie* and *Geschichte*, insists that he is not interested in questions of influence. Such historiological (*historisch*) observations are secondary. What is at issue is "the historical determination that the last metaphysician of the West obeys."[12] Second, Heidegger remarks on the absence in Nietzsche of any attempt to articulate the relation of justice to the essence of truth (*N* 1: 632). Heidegger is quite explicit that his own aim here is to think the essence of truth to the extreme and to show it to be the point at which the thought of justice becomes inevitable (*N* 1: 633). Heidegger's claim is that its necessity can be shown by an "historical reflection" (*geschichtliche Besinnung*).

The schema that governs Heidegger's reading of Nietzsche in this lecture course is set out in the context of his account of the concept of chaos. Heidegger observes that Nietzsche does not adopt the primordial Greek sense of chaos as the measureless, the groundless yawning-open. He follows the modern sense of chaos as the jumbled or tangled (*N* 1: 562–63). In addition, however, there is a further sense of chaos "originating from the basic position of Nietzsche's thinking." According to that third sense, chaos names "a peculiar preliminary projection of the world as a whole and for the governance of that world" (*N* 1: 566). There is therefore a "double meaning" to chaos in Nietzsche.[13] Chaos is "the inexhaustible, urgent, and unmastered abundance of self-creation and self-destruction," either thought originally as that in which law and its negation, unlaw, are first formed and dissolved, or thought superficially as it is encountered in the impression of confusion (*N* 1: 569). This is the basis on which Heidegger shows that Nietzsche's thought of chaos is both metaphysical, insofar as it falls short of Hesiodic chaos, and yet is not entirely confined to metaphysics by virtue of an ambiguity that escapes the oppositions and inversions in which Nietzsche is otherwise held (*N* 1: 617–18). Heidegger explains this in terms of the ambiguity of Nietzsche's concept of truth. The true, as a fixing or securing of what is in the course of becoming, is a denial of chaos, the truly actual. Hence Heidegger's gloss on Nietzsche's statement that "Truth is the kind of error without which a certain kind of living being could not live."[14] Heidegger explains, "With respect to chaos, 'the true' of such a truth is not appropriate to that chaos; hence, it is untrue, thus error" (*N* 1: 619).

It is not only because Heidegger's treatment of chaos best shows the schema with which Heidegger was operating at that time that I am making it the basis for my attempt to recover what he has to say about Nietzsche on justice. Nietzsche's thoughts on chaos and on justice are, according to Heidegger, essentially related. The association is made through the concept of truth. In 1942 in "Plato's Doctrine of Truth" Heidegger quotes the same passage from *The Will to Power* that I have just quoted. He identifies it as the beginning of the unconditional fulfillment of the history of metaphysics (*W* 139, 142). But "Plato's Doctrine of Truth" fails to specify what the 1939 lecture course makes clear, that the culmination of Nietzsche's attempt to think the essence of truth must be found in what Nietzsche calls "justice": "Nietzsche thinks the essence of truth at the outermost point as something he calls 'justice'" (*N* 1: 632. See also *N* 2: 20). Heidegger insists on this, in spite of the fact that Nietzsche's most decisive thoughts on justice belong to the period of *Thus Spoke Zarathustra* and are relatively few in number. Furthermore, as Heidegger acknowledges, Nietzsche was, in his final years, completely silent about what he called justice (*N* 1: 632).

Nietzsche failed to make explicit the connection between the thought of justice and that of the essence of truth (*N* 1: 632). Heidegger set himself the task of doing, or at least beginning to do, what Nietzsche was unable to do. The task is to penetrate the historical roots of the metaphysical question of truth so that it becomes clear why the thought of "justice" becomes inevitable after the abolition of the distinction between a true and an apparent world (*N* 1: 633–34). Heidegger takes two routes to this outermost point of the essence of truth. The first route is in terms of Nietzsche's understanding of truth as a holding-to-be-true. According to Heidegger, and the importance of the point is more readily apparent in the context of the Parmenides lecture course, such holding-to-be-true is usually thought of in terms of command (*Befehl*). The law of contradiction is such a command, the positing of a measure in the form of an imperative (*N* 1: 607–09). Heidegger poses the question of whether one can dispense with a standard (*Mass-gabe*) without succumbing to arbitrariness (*N* 1: 635).

For himself, Heidegger refuses the question because it seems to be formulated in such a way as to retain a standard against which the dispensing of standards is to be judged (*N* 1: 648). He attributes to Nietzsche another answer: "holding-to-be-true takes its law and rule from justice" (*N* 1: 643). The answer is metaphysical in that "justice" is here being taken metaphysically as the fundamental character of a thinking that is constructive (*Bauen*) or commanding, exclusive, and nihilative (*N* 1: 639–41).

The other route Heidegger takes returns to the issue of the fixing or securing of chaos. Heidegger identifies the securing of permanence (*Bestand*) as assimilating and giving human direction to chaos. This assimilation not only recalls the struggle between τέχνη and δίκη; it corresponds to the Greek ὁμοίωσις. At the culmination of metaphysics, the essence of truth as ὁμοίωσις does not collapse but attains an exclusiveness it lacked when it operated within the orbit of the distinction between the true and the apparent world (*N* 1: 635–36). Nietzsche gives the essence of truth "the *metaphysical* name" justice (*N* 1: 637), although he may not have understood the historical reasons that led him to do so. According to Heidegger, after the publication of *Thus Spoke Zarathustra* Nietzsche thinks the essence of truth "always and everywhere . . . in terms of its ground of possibility, in terms of justice" (*N* 1: 637–38). Heidegger says "always and everywhere," even though he had earlier acknowledged that the word "justice" is rare in Nietzsche. If Heidegger's account is somewhat strained at this point, it is because, as with the other discussion, everything here is subordinated to establishing that Nietzsche's text remains governed by metaphysics.

What does Nietzsche understand by "justice"? Heidegger again issues the warning that the term cannot be given a juristic or moral meaning (*N* 1: 636). To approach Nietzschean *Gerechtigkeit* one must put aside Christian, humanistic, enlightenment, bourgeois, and socialist morality (*N* 2: 197, 325). Ordinances of this kind are familiar in Heidegger and can never completely succeed. The difficulty of translating *Gerechtigkeit*—because all the likely candidates justice, righteousness, justification, and so on, have what Heidegger at another time might have called different ontic commitments—is not entirely negative. The history of justice shows that the languages of the *imperium* and the curia are also under scrutiny in this discussion. Meanwhile, Heidegger defines justice for Nietzsche as the unitary connection (*Zusammenhang*) of what is right, in the sense of the precise, the fitting, what gives direction (*N* 1: 637). Justice determines right and wrong from the standpoint of its own power and does not use an independent measure to help decide what is right and what is wrong (*N* 2: 198). It is the ground of the possibility of every kind of harmony of human beings with chaos, be it through art or knowledge (*N* 1: 638, 647–48). "Justice is the preconstructive allotment (*Zuteilung*) of conditions, that firmly secure a preservation, that is, an attaining and maintaining" (*N* 2: 327). Such an allotment "precedes all thinking and acting."

In employing these phrases Heidegger seems to point forward to the *Letter on Humanism* with its attempt to move into a realm prior to thinking and acting, as well as its attempt to pass beyond the distinction between ontology and ethics by reference to the prior realm of so-called "fundamental ontology" or "original ethics." But the suspicion persists that the ontological sense remains privileged, and not just here in respect of Nietzschean *Gerechtigkeit*, but also in those places where Heidegger attempts to purify δίκη of its moral meaning.[15] Insofar as *Gerechtigkeit* is understood as occupying a place in the history of truth—or even in a history of the essence of truth—then it is being determined not just metaphysically (in terms of the history of Western metaphysics) but also ontologically in the narrow sense. Only insofar as Nietzschean *Gerechtigkeit* is heard as recalling δίκη does it attain the ambiguity that would enable it to exceed the limitations of such a history.[16]

In the lecture, "The Will to Power as Knowledge," Heidegger does not appear to find an ambiguity in Nietzsche's word "justice." He thus appears to close off the possibility of finding a Nietzsche who is not simply metaphysical, a possibility that had opened up with the ambiguity of Nietzsche's understanding of chaos. That he closes off this possibility is in conformity with the general tendency of Heidegger's reading of Nietzsche at this time, reflected in the lecture course by the statement that the "will to power in its *most profound* essence is nothing other than giving Becoming the permanence (*Beständigung*) of presence" (*N* 1: 656).

And yet in other texts from the same period, even those in which the focus remains directed to the permanence of presence, this is understood to give rise to other possibilities, which he sometimes refers to as "the transition to another beginning" (*N* 2: 29). So, for example, in *The Eternal Recurrence of the Same and the Will to Power*, Heidegger appears to go further. The two lectures that go under this title were intended as a conclusion to all three courses on Nietzsche, although they were never delivered. The thrust of these remarks is the claim that Nietzsche "overcomes metaphysics" only in the limited sense of transforming it into its final possible configuration (*N* 2: 16). In this context, in clear anticipation of the account given ten years later in "The Question concerning Technology," Heidegger provides an analysis of the age of consummate meaninglessness, where meaninglessness is understood as the "lack of the truth (clearing) of Being" (*N* 2: 20). Truth as "justice" is understood as the supreme will to power, the anthropomorphism of the unconditioned rule of human beings over the earth (*N* 2: 20).[17] This, the extreme position of Western metaphysics, marks the dominance of τέχνη. In terms of *An Introduction to Metaphysics*, it is the apparent, *but impossible*, victory of τέχνη over δίκη. Justice arises as the word of the last metaphysician precisely at the time when the loss of δίκη is most extreme. Nietzsche's word *Gerechtigkeit* is at once the extreme oblivion of δίκη and yet for that very reason, according to a familiar Heideggerian law, it provides the possibility for recalling δίκη.

However, such remarks are isolated and only sketchily outlined. For the most part the question of truth intervenes and occupies the main focus. Indeed, it is in respect of Nietzsche's determination of the essence of truth that Heidegger ultimately denies that justice can "be raised to the rank of the main heading in Nietzsche's metaphysics" (N 2: 331).[18] The reason is that "in Nietzsche's thought it remains veiled as to whether and how 'justice' is the essential trait of truth." Nietzsche says enough to enable Heidegger to attribute the thought to him but not enough for the inevitability of that thought to emerge from a reading of Nietzsche. Nietzsche *should have* thought truth as justice. He needs to have done so. It is the thought that has its ground in "the historical determination that the last metaphysician of the West obeys" (N 1: 632). Nietzsche cannot attain this thought but he poeticizes (*gedichtet*) the ideal of the thinking of the last metaphysician in the figure of Zarathustra. Here there is another hint of the relation between "justice" and poetic thinking, albeit understood very differently from the way Theophrastus construed it.

Why is it inevitable that justice should have been the last word of metaphysics? It is not possible to address this question with the resources of metaphysics alone, that is to say, with the resources of truth. The last word of metaphysics should have been justice because the first word of that thinking from which metaphysics divorced itself is and is not justice. More specifically, it is δίκη. Only engagement with the thinkers before metaphysics—Anaximander, Parmenides, Heraclitus— lets metaphysics appear in its unity and completeness. Conversely, it is metaphysics that lets δίκη, ἀλήθεια, and λόγος be tied together in a story. Heidegger can exhibit the inevitability of Nietzsche's obligation to think justice only by including in his narrative what he at the same time acknowledges does not belong to the story. Heidegger seems to admit as much. "Are we not forced into historical classification, which comes from without and looks only backward, or even into the historiological miscalculation (*Verrechnung*) of history, which is always captious and usually carping?" (N 2: 329). The story draws the premetaphysical into metaphysics, establishing a false continuity. Heidegger tries to resist this consequence by rejecting the translation of δίκη as justice. He must equally deny the translation from δίκη to *iustitia*. And that is perhaps why he left the history of the essence of justice scattered throughout his work, waiting to be discovered by the scavengers who came together a full century after Heidegger's birth and a full century after Nietzsche inevitably should have thought, and perhaps almost thought, truth as justice.[19]

NOTES

1. See, for example, N 2: 235. For further discussion of the distinction between *Geschichte* and *Historie* and the difficulty of maintaining it, see Robert Bernasconi, "Descartes in the History of Being: Another Bad Novel?" *Research in Phenomenology* 17 (1987): 75–102.

2. W 109–44. Because this essay is so familiar and because it is not the real subject of this paper, my reading shall be brief and will not reflect all the nuances of Heidegger's text. See Robert Bernasconi, *The Question of Language in Heidegger's History of Being*

(Atlantic Highlands, N.J.: Humanities Press, 1985), 15–27; John Sallis, "At the Threshold of Metaphysics," in *Delimitations* (Bloomington: Indiana University Press, 1986), 170–85; and the essay by Adriaan Peperzak in the present volume.

3. "Der Spruch des Anaximander," *HW* 296–343. In a note Heidegger explains that the essay is drawn from a longer treatise composed in 1946.

4. *GA* 51: 98–99, 118–20. However, the discussion, particularly of the textual problems, are not sufficiently extensive to satisfy the reference to such discussions in "The Anaximander Fragment" (*HW* 314). This suggests further more extensive discussions in other yet to be published lecture courses.

5. John Burnet, *Early Greek Philosophy*, 3rd ed. (London: A. and C. Black, 1920), 52. Heidegger read Burnet in German translation.

6. Other commentators who begin the quotation from κατὰ τό χρεών include Heidel, "On Anaximander," *Classical Philology* 7 (1912): 233; and J. B. McDiarmid, "Theophrastus on the Presocratic Causes," in *Studies in Presocratic Philosophy*, ed. D. J. Furley and R. E. Allen (London: Routledge & Kegan Paul, 1970), 1: 190–93. Attribution of the whole passage to Anaximander is defended by Paul Seligman, *The 'Apeiron' of Anaximander* (London: Athlone Press, 1962), 66–83.

7. Heidegger explicitly notes his agreement with Franz Dirlmeier's delimitation of the text, while at the same time distancing himself from the reasons he gives (*HW* 344): "Der Satz des Anaximandros von Milet," *Rheinisches Museum für Philologie* 87 (1938): 376–82. The phrase expelled by Heidegger is defended by, for example, G. S. Kirk: "Some Problems in Anaximander," in *Studies in Presocratic Philosophy*, 1: 345–46, and Charles H. Kahn, *Anaximander and the Origins of Greek Cosmology* (New York: Columbia University Press, 1960), 170–71.

8. Even if recent commentators have tended to dismiss the interpretation which has Anaximander saying that existence is an injustice, the interpretation has maintained a certain resilience, as Gregory Vlastos has shown, "Equality and Justice in Early Greek Cosmologies," in *Studies in Presocratic Philosophy*, 1: 76–80.

9. See further Marlène Zarader, *Heidegger et les paroles de l'origine* (Paris: Vrin, 1986), 91–95.

10. The argument that there is an abrupt transition when at *Republic* 331c Socrates describes Cephalus's speech about δίκη as a speech about δικαιοσύνη is argued by Eric Havelock in *The Greek Concept of Justice* (Cambridge, Mass.: Harvard University Press, 1978), 308–23. For the context, see also Havelock, "Dikaiosune: An Essay in Greek Intellectual History," *Phoenix* 22 (1969), 49–70.

11. *GA* 54: 13. For discussions of this lecture course, albeit with a very different focus from the present one, see A. Lowit, "Le 'principe' de la lecture Heideggerienne de Parmenide," *Revue de Philosophie Ancienne* 4:2 (1986): 163–210; M. S. Frings, "Parmenides: Heidegger's 1942–43 Lecture Held at Freiburg University," *The Journal of the British Society for Phenomenology* 19:1 (1988): 15–33; and Véronique Fóti, "Aletheia and Oblivion's Field: The Parmenides Lectures," unpublished lecture, delivered to the Society for Phenomenology and Existential Philosophy, Pittsburgh, October 1989.

12. *N* 2: 632. Reiner Schürmann in a brief but helpful discussion of justice in Heidegger reads this passage as a denial of "any kinship" between Nietzschean "justice" and Heraclitean δίκη. He appears to believe that this is a necessary consequence of the fact that "the concept of justice translates 'truth as ὁμοίωσις' for the age of closure (*N* 1 632f)," *Heidegger on Being and Acting: From Principles to Anarchy* (Bloomington: Indiana University Press, 1987), 364 n. 62. However, as I try to show, this would eradicate the ambiguity of the history of Being in respect of Western metaphysics. As with the thought of chaos, Nietzsche's word "justice" is metaphysical and yet not entirely confined to metaphysics but heard from beyond it. This parallels the way the Anaximander fragment is said to lay a claim of subsequent thinking while at the same time being reducible to it.

13. Heidegger had already in 1937 observed "a dual significance" (*eine zweifache Bedeut-*

ung) in Nietzsche's concept of chaos, but it does not appear to be conceived in the same way as the double meaning (*Doppelbedeutung*) identified two years later (*N* 1: 569). Only in the first of the two cases does Heidegger explicitly observe that Nietzsche "fails to liberate himself from the traditional sense of chaos as something that lacks order and lawfulness" (*N* 1: 349–50).

14. Friedrich Nietzsche, *Sämtliche Werke. Kritische Studienausgabe*, Band 2 (Berlin: Walter de Gruyter, 1980), 506, 34 [253].

15. Levinas, who clearly differentiates what he calls "ethics" from Heidegger's retrieval of the Greek ἦθος, suggested in a recent essay that in spite of himself Heidegger could not succeed in eradicating the ethical from Anaximander. "It [love] puts into question the ego's natural position as subject, its perseverence—the perseverence of its good conscience—in its being. It puts into question its *conatus essendi*, the stubbornness of its being [*étant*]. Here is an indiscreet—or 'unjust'—presence, which is perhaps already an issue in "The Anaximander Fragment," such as Heidegger interprets it in *Holzwege*. It puts into question the 'positivity' of the *esse* in its *presence*, signifying, bluntly, encroachment and usurpation! Did not Heidegger—despite all he intends to teach about the priority of the 'thought of being'—here run up against the original significance of ethics?" ("Diachronie et representation," *Revue de l'Université d'Ottawa*, 55:4 [1985]: 92; trans. R. Cohen, "Diachrony and Representation," in *Time and the Other* [Pittsburgh: Duquesne University Press, 1987], 108–109).

16. The echo of δίκη in *Gerechtigkeit* thus belongs among those moments in Heidegger in which the ethical exceeds the "twilight zone of morality." I have explored other cases in, for example, "Deconstruction and the Possibility of Ethics," in *Deconstruction and Philosophy*, ed. J. Sallis (Chicago: University of Chicago Press, 1987); "The Fate of the Distinction between Praxis and Poiesis," *Heidegger Studies* 2 (1986): 111–39; and "The Double Concept of Philosophy and the Place of Ethics in *Being and Time*," *Research in Phenomenology* 18 (1988): 41–57.

17. On the relation of Nietzsche's *Gerechtigkeit* and technology, see further Schürmann, *Heidegger on Being and Acting*, 192–93.

18. David Krell has shown that the importance Heidegger gives to *Gerechtigkeit* in Nietzsche is not quite as idiosyncratic as it might at first appear. He does this by showing that previous writers on Nietzsche had already come to focus on the term. See the analysis to *Nietzsche. The Will to Power as Knowledge and as Metaphysics* (New York: Harper & Row, 1979), 272–74. Nevertheless, Heidegger gives Nietzsche's thought of justice an entirely different role from either Ernst Bertram or Alfred Baeumler. The task that Heidegger assigns to *Gerechtigkeit* is one that he and he alone could have identified, relying as it does on his unique conception of *Geschichte*. Nothing that can be found in Bertram and Baeumler prepares one for the role Heidegger gives to Nietzsche's *Gerechtigkeit*. They had cited the relevant Nietzsche texts but their discussion is at another level. It is almost certainly they, for example, whom Heidegger has in mind when he dismisses the observation about Nietzsche's debt to Heraclitus as *historisch*. See Bertram, *Nietzsche. Versuch einer Mythologie* (Berlin: Georg Bondi, 1929), 114–16, and Baeumler, *Nietzsche der Philosoph und Politiker* (Leipzig: Phillip Reclam, 1931), 65–70.

19. The reading of Heidegger's 1939 lecture course, "The Will to Power as Knowledge and as Metaphysics," was developed for a graduate seminar held at the University of Essex in the spring of 1988. The essay is dedicated to the members of that seminar, my last at Essex.

DAVID FARRELL KRELL

7. Where Deathless Horses Weep

> . . . We often have occasion to observe
> how repugnant it is for a horse to trample
> a living body underfoot; an animal never
> encounters without disquiet a dead member
> of its own species: there are even some
> that extend to their dead a kind of
> interment . . .
>
> > Jean-Jacques Rousseau, *Discours sur*
> > *l'origine et les fondements de*
> > *l'inégalité parmi les hommes*

Several years ago Charles Scott sent me the draft of a paper on Heidegger and ethics.* In it he cited a passage from Homer's *Iliad* on horses and ethics. It was clear that in questions of ethics horses had the edge over Heidegger. For the passage Scott cited is one of the most stunning in all of Homer. It appears twice (not surprisingly inasmuch as a third of all Homeric verses are repeated verses), first in the sixth song, as Paris gallops through the city on his way to the plain of battle, and then in the fifteenth song, as his brother Hektor spurs the Trojans to their most successful counterattack. The passage, we would say, elaborates an extended metaphor, and it runs as follows:

> As when in its stall a steed that's had its fill of fodder
> Breaks free from its halter and sprints spiritedly
> > across the field
> Toward its accustomed bathing place
> > in the swift-flowing river:
> It is all power. Head held high, mane
> Fluttering to its shoulders, sleek
> > with the fiery spark of youth;

*Now published as "Heidegger and the Question of Ethics," in *Research in Phenomenology* 18 (1988), 23–40, the nascent form of a book-length project entitled *The* Question *of Ethics: Nietzsche, Foucault, Heidegger* (Bloomington and Indianapolis: Indiana University Press, 1990). I would like to dedicate the present chapter to Charles Scott. My thanks also to Michael Naas for his Homeric horsemanship, so much more skillful than my own.

Its limbs carry it lightly
to the herd's familiar grazing ground.

The words that drew Scott's attention to the passage are εἰωθώς (cf. εἰωθότος, ἔθω) designating the spot where the horse "customarily" bathed, and ἤθεα (cf. τὸ ἦθος), referring to the herd's "familiar" pasture (νομός), its habitat, its "haunts." These words suggest that horses not only *live* but also *dwell*, and that they dwell in nearness to what Heidegger, after Heraclitus, calls the δαίμων. Whether horses have "character," or "ethics," or even worse, "morality," would no doubt be secondary questions for Heidegger; that is to say, not really *questions* at all. What the horses have is *freedom*, now that the halter has been torn; freedom and the pride of power in their sleek flanks.

Yet I abandon this passage and its wild steeds now to the man—or centaur— who uncovered it for us. I shall be concerned here with a different passage, and with different horses. They are daimonic horses, albeit under yoke; not prancing free, but standing motionless. They are horses who mourn.

I .

Patroklos is dead. A not so very forthright god stripped him of his armor and left him dazed and naked before the lances of not so very brave men. Apollo, concealed in a cloud of fog, struck him in the back, knocked off his helmet, undid his armor, lopped off his lance, shattered his shield, and let the Trojans clean up the mess.

Human beings are like olive trees. Not the ancient trunks but the tender shoots thrusting from them. These mere slips are transplanted to a lonely place, a vale bubbling with water. Homer depicts the destiny of such an olive shoot as follows:

Stately tall it grows, rustling softly in the cool
    of every wafting wind,
Bristling with shining blossoms;
Until a wild whirlwind looms, of an instant,
Uproots the shaft and stretches it out on the earth.
Il. 17, 53–58

Three words in these last two lines begin with the existential prefix ἐξ=: ἐξετάνυσσε, from τάνυμαι, "to stretch out"; ἐξέστρεψε, from στρέφω, "to twist and tear out"; and ἐξαπίνης (=ἐξαίφνης), "sudden, instantaneous, looming on or out of the instant." The instant is the ecstatic rapture or remotion in and from which Plato seeks ineffable insight (see *Parmenides* 156d and Letter 7, 341d), the rapture that yields all the existential words of Aristotle's treatise on time (*Physics* 4, 10–14). It is the instant of *Entrückung* or rapture by which Heidegger hopes to name the animatedness of a temporal yet untimely existence.

Patroklos succumbs of an instant. The finality of death veils him (κάλυψε), his psyche streams from his limbs down to the House of Hades, cut off from manly strength and youthful nobility, lamenting its lot.

An instant earlier, on the field of combat, Patroklos wielded Achilles' weapons, wore his armor, and drove his horses. Or, rather, it was Achilles' driver, Automedon, who handled the horses for Patroklos.

And what horses they are! Under one yoke, the dappled and the dun, both as fleet as the wind. Indeed, they were sired by Zephyros the Westwind upon the Harpy Podárgē as she grazed in a green meadow on the banks of Okeanós, on the outermost rim of earth. Attached to the chariot as a trace-horse is yet a third steed, Pédasos by name. Of Pédasos the poem says, in one of its most puzzling lines, "Even though he was mortal [θνητός], he could keep up the pace of immortal horses" (*Il.* 16, 154: ἵπποι ἀθανάτοι). Pédasos soon demonstrates his mortal heritage: Sarpedon casts his lance at Patroklos but misses, striking Pédasos instead; the horse whinnies, collapses in the dust, and breathes forth his θυμός (*Il.* 16, 467–69). Thus it is not the mortal steed but one of the immortal horses, one of the Harpy's lineage, the dun, who later warns Achilles of his impending demise. Scolded a second time by the driver, Automedon, for reasons we shall soon hear about, the dun lowers his head and speaks with the human voice granted him by the shimmering goddess Hera:

> We will rescue you, for the moment, brave Achilles.
> Yet nigh is the day of your demise. We are
>   not to blame.
> But the great god and the mighty fates [θεός τε
>   μέγας καὶ μοῖρα κραταιή]. . . .
> For we race with the panting Westwind,
> Whom they say is swiftest. Yet to you it is allotted
> To be laid low by a man and by a god.

Erinýes now silences the steed's resounding, foreboding voice. Achilles is piqued that a horse should play his seer. "I know my part," he snarls, and drives the horses off to battle.

One can understand Automedon's scolding and Achilles' anger. For earlier on, in the thick of the battle for Patroklos' corpse, the immortal horses suddenly lost heart and stood stock-still.

> Yet the horses of Achilles, standing apart
>   from the battle,
> Weep the moment they learn that their master
> Lies in the dust, laid low by the hand
>   of murderous Hektor.

No matter how hard Automedon flails them with the whip, curses or coaxes them, they do not move. I come now to the passage that stands as the crypt of my own remarks:

> But just as funeral stele stand fixed above the tomb,
> As monuments to the dead man or woman,
> They stand motionless and motionless hold
>   the splendid car.

Their heads are lowered to the ground, tears of mourning
Run hot from their lids, so painfully do they
Miss their master. Their luxuriant manes spill
Over the ring of the yoke and are soiled in the dust.
  It was a painful sight for Zeus, Son of Chronos,
To see these weeping steeds. Sadly he shook his head
  and said to his heart:
  "Ah, you wretches! Why did we ever give you
    to King Peleus,
A mortal, you who are ageless and deathless?
Was it so that you could share in the sufferings
  of these unhappy humans?
For, truly, there is nothing more wretchedly lamentable
  than human being,
Amid all the beings that breathe and creep
  on the earth."

Il. 17. 426–47

The profoundly moved yet unmoving horses—like the marbles of a pediment frieze in the Acropolis Museum at Athens—are immortal steeds. Death does not touch them; no spear can dislodge their life. Yet even immortal horses are susceptible where mortality is concerned: immortal Zeus regrets his brother's having given immortal horses to the mortal Peleus, the immortal horses who now weep for Patroklos. The words *mortal* and *immortal* open and close line 444 of song seventeen. They cause that line to seesaw from mortal humanity to deathless divinity, with horses as the fulcrum. These horses are the vicarious sufferers of human death, sharers in the human disaster (*Il.* 17, 445: δυστήνοισι . . . ἀνδρασιν), which the song now from the mouth of Zeus goes on to name with unequalled, calamitous clarity: οὐ μὲν γάρ—it must be a Parmenidean pronouncement, we suppose, anachronistically, a pronouncement of and by being: οὐ μὲν γὰρ τί πού ἐστιν ὀιζυρώτερον ἀνδρός, the pronouncement employing the onomatopoeic word for lamentation, wailing, keening (*Il.* 3, 408: ὀϊζύω); "for nothing anywhere is more wretchedly lamentable than man"; here the line breaks, only to have the next line complete the thought with its first word, πάντων, "of all"; and after the strangely inverted prepositional phrase, ὅσσα τε γαῖαν ἔπι, "of all things the earth upon," comes the cruel close and the collapse of the elevated diction: πνείει τε καὶ ἕρπει, "all that breathes and creeps." The German translation of the entire phrase has: "Denn kein anderes Wesen wirklich ist mehr zu bejammern / Als der Mensch von allem, was atmet und kriecht auf der Erde." If toward the end of his life Gustav Mahler had seen and heard these lines, we would have had yet another glorious song-symphony *von der Erde.*

Mortals mourned by immortal horses. Do we—with our canned horsemeat and our saccharine religions—have any hope of hearing or reading these lines? So much of *The Iliad* is explicitly devoted to the initiation of mortals into their mortality, initiations from the horse's mouth or from a fellow human's. In case Aeneas has failed to notice the teeth and skulls cracked by bronze spear-tips, the eyeballs rolling in the dust like forlorn marbles, brains oozing up the implanted shaft of spear, Meriones informs him, "You too are born mortal, θνητὸς δε νυ καὶ σὺ τέτυξαι" (*Il.* 16, 622). And poor Hippotheos, whatever his relation to horses and gods, serves as perhaps the first exemplar of what Heidegger was to call the *unbezügliche* or "nonrelational" character of death: "For soon enough there rushed upon him the misfortune from which no one could rescue him, however much he may have desired it" (*Il.* 17, 291–92). Or Hektor's farewell to Andromache: "No mortal, whether noble or common, ever outruns μοῖρα, from the moment they come to be" (*Il.* 6, 448–49). Or, finally, Odysseus' cheerful goodbye to his Phaeacian hostess, Queen Arete: "Fare ye well—until the days of dotage and death, which are the human lot" (*Odyssey*, 13, 59–60).

Yet the most humane of these mortal initiations comes once again from Achilles's deathless steeds, not only from their mouths but also from their hearts and eyes. Motionless with mourning (ἑσταότες πενθείετον), they stand there with troubled heart, *bekümmert im Herzen*, ἕστατον ἀχνυμένω κῆρ (*Il.* 23, 283–84). That is precisely the phrase used to describe Achilles's grief over Agamemnon's seizure of Brisēïs (*Il.* 19, 57); or the mourning of the men who lay Patroklos's corpse on the pyre (*Il.* 23, 165); or the terror of the goatherd Melanthios when the sowherd Eumaeus strings him up to the rafters (*Od.* 22, 118). More than "troubled," then, in each case; let us say, "profoundly anxious." *Bekümmerung* is a kind of being stunned, *gebannt*, or dazed, *benommen*, by the most frightful of κῆρες. Yet if we so much as mention *Bannung* and *Benommenheit*, we are thrust back (or well forward) onto the fundamental concepts of metaphysics as Heidegger conceives of them in his 1929–30 lecture course.

2.

Life, just-plain-life, Heidegger seems to suggest in *Being and Time*, is Dasein deprived of care, *Sorge*. He should not have implied that, and he knew it. His enmity toward "philosophy of life" and his own initial move toward a "philosophy of existence" in an effort to escape from the blind alley of the former must be understood as anxiety in the face of its problem: how to prevent two millennia of heady philosophy from condemning human beings to a life above the eyebrow line. In the face of this problem, intensified by the Neo-Kantian and positivist obsessions with epistemology and rigorous science, Heidegger too stands there with troubled heart. Whatever the achievements of the fundamental ontology in *Sein und Zeit* may be, they do not ease this trouble. For if care is the existential-ontological structure of Dasein, then Dasein minus *Sorge* equals, not just-plain-life, but zero. When in 1929–30 Heidegger once again takes up the question of life by examining the comparative world-relations or access-to-beings of stone, animal, and Dasein, he is, I suspect, oppressed by the sense of his earlier failure to confront *Lebensphilosophie*. The quandary will continue to afflict him throughout his lectures on Nietzsche. For no recourse to the categories of body and soul, matter and form, sense and spirit can come to the aid of existential analysis. If Dasein is some body who is alive, its life will be a matter of care, time, and death. Yet what of a life that is unlike Dasein, *undaseinsmäßiges Leben?* The life of a horse, for instance? If deprived of care, will horses also be deprived of death?

Of course horses are deathless! Only Dasein dies. Horses merely perish. Well, then, are Achilles' horses deathless because they are immortals or simply because they are animals? Are they gods or dogs? With such questions we are perhaps at the very nerve of Western ontotheology. When Heidegger tries to sever Dasein from the animal, or to dig an abyss of essence between them, he causes the whole of his project to collapse back into the congealed categories and the oblivious decisions of ontotheology. Yet when he opens up—if only for a brief moment— the "ring of de-inhibitions" that links the animal to its limited, impoverished world, opens it up to the possibilities of *time* and *death*, a formidable contingency arises to confront his analysis. It is the chance that may well end all existential analysis and induce a different kind of meditation, a meditation on the trail of the daimonic, following two sets of traces, to wit, those of overpowering power, *das Übermächtige*, and the holy, *das Heilige*. These two sets of traces converge in the capacity to mark time and to die, and also in the capacity to share a peculiar kind of pain, the capacity to mourn. You will think now, because I mention mourning, that I am speaking of someone other than Heidegger. I am speaking of Heidegger. Pain, mourning, and being able to die: *Schmerz, Trauer und das Sterben-KÖNNEN.* And that means the capacity to be a horse.

In a moment I shall read those passages in the 1929–30 lecture course in which the forged ring of animal life, which is the ring of the yoke and halter of ontotheology, cracks and opens. Heidegger himself recognizes the necessity of the fissure in the ring, the tearing of the halter, and the escape of the captive animal. Yet because I will soon lose myself among the trees, the *Buchstaben* of Heidegger's text; because I will be unable to see the forest, the swift-flowing river, the pasture; let me state quite baldly, in thesis form, what I think all this touches on.

1. Even before the mid-1930s Heidegger recognizes the import of Hölderlin's intimation that only as figures of *mourning* can gods become present in a destitute time. However, mourning marks the *mortals*, who sooner attain to the abyss.

2. Mourning, pain, and joy will by the 1950s become something other than *Grundstimmungen:* they will become the variable μέλος of language, the singing that sustains the saying of language.

3. The capacity to mark time and to die will by then be something other than existential structures: they will announce the very bestirring (*Regung*) of propriation (*Ereignis*), the arousal that grants time and being throughout the epochal history of being.

4. If and when the capacity to mourn abandons thinking, if and when any sort of hope in the rescuing power of history, philosophy, fatherland, emancipatory discourse, or the unending conversation survives, meditation on the δαιμόνιον will succumb to demonic political power. Not only in 1933 but also in 1989.

5. Effective against such virulent hopefulness may well be a capacity of mourning that is thoroughly contaminated by a kind of mirth, marred by a peculiar mania,

a certain kinky humor. My guess is that such mourning will reflect less sobriety and equanimity than equinimity, horse-sense along with a certain kind of horseplay.

Enough, however, of grand gestures: Monty Python galloping through *The Holy Grail* on coconuts. Let me slow down and examine the ring of de-inhibitions, *den Enthemmungsring*, the ring of the animal's access to beings, as it cracks and opens to time and death.

3 ·

The three sections of Heidegger's 1929–30 lecture course that will concern me here are section 61, which tries to bring to a conclusion the analysis of the organism; section 62, which reiterates the openness to the world that characterizes animal behavior, even as benumbed behavior; and especially section 63, which raises an objection to the thesis concerning the animal's impoverished world. The objection, I believe, is not met. It is circumvented in a way that both challenges the analysis and drags it back into the realm of ontotheology—the tradition that extends, let us say, from Paul to Schelling. The objection, unmet as it is, indicates that the course's entire undertaking is a colossal failure, a *daimonic* failure (see *GA* 29/30: 264).

Section 61c concedes that the effort to delineate the essence of the animal organism is "incomplete." The description of benumbed behavior (*Benommenheit*) fails to render in a positive way the peculiar animation or animatedness (*Bewegtheit*) of life. A whole series of questions remains to be taken up; for example, the Hegelian question of the individual organism's relationship with its species and its specific history. (It is remarkable that both here and in the *Beiträge zur Philosophie* Heidegger remains almost entirely within the confines of *Hegel*'s meditation on the mating process and species identity, without ever citing Hegel's extraordinary analyses.) Yet there is one question on which the entire analysis of organism and world-relation hangs, one "moment," Heidegger says, "which belongs to the innermost essence of life, and which we designate as *death*." He continues: "The touchstone [*Prüfstein*] for determining the suitability and originality of every inquiry into the essence of life and vice-versa [the life of essence, or of the creature] is whether the inquiry has sufficiently grasped the problem of death; and whether it is able to bring that problem in the correct way into the question concerning the essence of life" (*GA* 29/30: 387).

Two remarks. First, recall the parallel passage in Heidegger's *Nietzsche* lectures (*N* 1: 460; *NE* 2: 195) in which the problem of *the nothing* is declared the *Probierstein* that determines whether we gain entry into the realm of philosophy or remain barred from it. What might seem to be a merely regional issue, a matter of "theoretical biology," is in fact the existential-ontological project, the project of philosophy *tout court*. Second, recall that Heidegger's attempt two years earlier to identify the unified horizon of ecstatic temporality failed to confront what Heidegger called, in a classic understatement, the "difficult problem of death" (*GA* 24: 387). Once again it is death that should reveal the innermost animatedness and vitality of life's essence, its élan, its *Schwung* and *Schwingung*, precisely as it should have revealed the existential truth of *time*. Yet rather than confront the challenge, Heidegger here falls back on the distinction between *Sterben* and *Verenden*, "dying" as opposed to "perishing." Benumbed behavior "prescribes *altogether determined possibilities* [ganz bestimmte Möglichkeiten] of *death*, of *coming-to-death*" (*GA* 29/30: 388). Although Heidegger employs the plural here, *Verenden* remains the sole possibility of animal life. He immediately relates this problem (as he does in *Sein und Zeit*) to the theoretical-biological thesis of immanent death. Like Freud, Heidegger is much exercised by the death that is in life, *in sich selbst*; unlike Freud, Heidegger is careful not to go too far, *zu weit*, with the thesis of immanent death. (Clearly, a long story waits to be told here, a story recounted perhaps on a stack of postcards, the story of *Heidegger* and what Derrida has called "the menace of the psyche," but I cannot tell it now.)

If section 62 insists on the openness (*Offensein*) of benumbed behavior and the access-to-beings that an organism indubitably exhibits, it is also forced to fall back onto a position that *Sein und Zeit* itself showed to be inadequate. The animal does not experience being *as* being, does not have access to beings *as such* (*GA* 29/30: 390–91). Here and throughout the final hours of the lecture course Heidegger appeals to the animal's lack of ἀπόφανσις, its lack of λόγος, as the secret of its benumbed behavior in an impoverished world. Not the hermeneutic-as but the apophantic-as comes to dominate—and undo—fundamental ontology; furthermore, as Heidegger himself here suspects, the labors to establish a *Grundstimmung* for metaphysics will all have been in vain. Human beings are no longer those who are benumbed by anxiety in the face of their uncanny existence (see the references to *Sein und Zeit* in my "Daimon Life," *Research in Phenomenology*, 17 [1987], p. 51, n. 14); nor are they the beings who are bedazzled by the overpowering power of the δαιμόνιον (see *GA* 26: 13); rather, human beings are once again those who have the word and who take the floor to declare that animals inhabit an impoverished world, that their being is absorbed in a circle of drives and a ring of de-inhibitions within which they dispatch their prey and propagate their species, bedazzled, un-bothered, and be-wildered. Perhaps also be-witched. Which is what bothers Heidegger.

Section 63 is entitled (*nota bene*, not by Heidegger) "Self-objection against the thesis of the animal's not-having a world as a deprivation and of its being poor, and the nullification [*Entkräftung*] of this objection." Brave words, words of a solicitor. Yet something else is happening to Heidegger's text and to his entire effort. There will be no "nullification" of the objection, but only an infinite postponement of the difficult problem of death. A postponement, but also a change of venue for Heidegger's meditation, in the direction of Schelling.

What is wrong with the thesis of world-poverty? Clearly, it is blatantly anthropocentric: the animal's behavior appears to be benumbed only against the backdrop of a more vigorous and vital stance toward beings as such; its world reflects a deprivation only against the backdrop of a richer, more abundant openness to being. However, as Heidegger will insist throughout his *Nietzsche* lectures, especially in the third, the charge of anthropomorphism-anthropocentrism is essentially duplicitous, for it always presupposes that a thinking could—if only it were rigorous enough—erase the human backdrop, expunge the horizon of existence. Heidegger's self-imposed task is to think the "positive side" of this duplicitous state of affairs (*GA* 29/30: 394). It is not that the thesis concerning the animal's world-poverty goes too far and has to be "wound down" or even "renounced"; it is that a certain possibility has to be "left open" (*GA* 29/30: 395). Heidegger hints at that possibility in two passages, the first early on in the "self-objection", the second at its culmination. The first passage:

> If deprivation [*das Entbehren*], in certain of its transformations, is a suffering [*ein Leiden*]; and if a being deprived of world, and poverty, belong to the animal's being; then a suffering and a sorrow [*ein Leiden und ein Leid*] would have to permeate the entire animal kingdom and the realm of life in general. Biology knows absolutely nothing about this. To fabulate on such things is perhaps the poets' privilege [*Von dergleichen zu fabeln, ist vielleicht ein Vorrecht der Dichter*]. (*GA* 29/30: 393)

Which fabulists is Heidegger thinking of? He does not say. Yet who can read this passage and not be reminded of the fabulous Schelling and his *Schleier der Schwermut*, the veil of melancholy draped over all life, the veil spun in vain in order to occlude the bifurcated essence of God.

If *I* seem to be spinning veils—and tales—here, if *I* appear to be a mere Schleier-macher, let this second passage unsettle you as much as it unnerves me:

> The fact that biology knows nothing of this is no counterproof against metaphysics. That perhaps only poets occasionally speak of it is an argument that metaphysics dare not unleash. In the end, one does not really need Christian faith in order to understand something of those words that Paul (in Romans 8:19) writes concerning the ἀποκαραδοκία τῆς κτίσεως, the creatures' and all creation's longing gaze [*von dem sehnsüchtigen Ausspähen der Geschöpfe und der Schöpfung*]; for the ways of creation, as the Book of Ezra (4: 7,12) also says, have in this eon become narrow, mournful, and arduous [*schmal, traurig und mühselig*]. (*GA* 29/30: 396)

The word *sehnsüchtig*, "longing," cannot but lead us (as it presumably led Heidegger) to Schelling. Something else, an Other, *ein Anderes*, will also soon lead us there. Note for the moment the fabulous use of Paul, whose faith one need not share in order to grasp the suffering and the longing that pervade life, Paul being here corroborated by the apocryphal, fabulous Book of Ezra: Old and New Testaments, as well as authentic and apocryphal scriptures, conjoined to testify to—or to fabulate upon—the ways of life and all creation. Which are *traurig;* "Sad, sorrowful," we would normally say. Today I render it more literally as "full of mourning." Continuing the passage:

> Nor do we need any sort of pessimism in order to be able to develop the *world-poverty of the animal as an intrinsic problem of animality itself.* For with the animal's openness to that which de-inhibits [*Offensein . . . für das Enthemmende*], the animal in its benumbed behavior is essentially exposed to an Other [*wesenhaft hinausgestellt in ein Anderes*], something that can never be revealed to it as either a being or a nonbeing, yet which, de-inhibiting, and with all the transformations of de-inhibition that it encom-

passes, introduces an *essential shattering* into the essence of the animal [*eine* wesenhafte Erschütterung *in das Wesen des Tieres*].

Two remarks. *Hinausgestellt in ein Anderes*. Is that not at least reminiscent of *Hinausgehaltenheit in das Nichts*? What is this essential shattering of animal life? We will not understand the openness and the world-relation of benumbed behavior, will not understand the organism, "as long as we fail to bring into play the fundamental phenomenon of the life-process, and thereby of death [und damit des Todes]." After several years have passed, Heidegger will identify this fundamental phenomenon of life as a "bestirring" (*Regung, Erregbarkeit*), and he will continue to associate these words with "shattering" (*Erschütterung*). To feel the force of this essential shattering, one would have to trace the use of the words *Scheitern* and *Erschütterung* in *Sein und Zeit* as the touchstones of existential analysis as such, but also in the 1935 *Einführung in die Metaphysik*, where Dasein is defined as shattering in the face of the overpowering, the uncanny, the daimonic. And, of course, also in the 1933 rectoral address, where "the most intense stirring" meets with "the most extensive shattering." A massive undertaking, and a dispiriting one, a shattering one. Allow me to take a shorter route, another route, a route into the Other.

4.

Where deathless horses weep. Horses? Which horses?

Perhaps the blinded horses of Peter Shaffer's *Equus*, though with tears, not gore, in their eyes. Perhaps Jewel's horse, in *As I Lay Dying*—Jewel and Jewel's horse, Faulkner's "two figures carved for a tableau savage in the sun":

> When Jewel can almost touch him, the horse stands on his hind legs and slashes down at Jewel. Then Jewel is enclosed by a glittering maze of hooves as by an illusion of wings; among them, beneath the upreared chest, he moves with the flashing limberness of the snake.
>
> (chap. 3, "Darl")

Perhaps Jewel's horse, for who can forget the horse that kicks and bites like an immortal mortal?

Not, however, Raskolnikov's nag, not the piteous horse, the dray horse that Nietzsche conjures in a letter dated May 13, 1888, to Reinhart von Seydlitz:

> Yesterday I dreamed up an image of *moralité larmoyante* [a weepy moralism], as Diderot puts it. Winter landscape. An ancient drayman, with an expression of the most brutal cynicism, harsher still than the winter that surrounds him, relieves himself upon his own horse. The horse—the poor, berated creature—looks about, grateful, *very* grateful—.
>
> (*Briefe*, 8, 314)

No, not the gratefully submissive whipping-horse of a lacrimonious morality, but a horse that weeps, a horse perhaps that mourns a man who collapses in the streets of Torino.

Perhaps also the spirited sorrel ridden by a woman only the most pinched and embittered souls would deny was outrageously beautiful, a woman who even riding bareback could reach from her mount the first cherries of summer and who said that when she bit into the first cherry the first drops of blood began to flow and she was not really surprised because the time was as ripe as the cherry but startled nonetheless by the drops as always never really expecting them and who in this instant—stretched out in it so suddenly—thought or rather felt four things in her life to be perfectly consonant: the cherry, the blood, the friend she loved starkly, and the horse; which four things in their unity she invited him to contemplate, knowing full well that he would be as baffled and bewitched in that fourfold as she was.

Horses? Which horses?

Why should any horse, whether animal or god, care about Patroklos? What immortal mortal animal or mortal immortal god could share in his plight, which is twofold: first, that he is older than Achilles yet loves him as a younger man would, the most trying situation for a Greek male, as Alcibiades (and Socrates?) knew well; second, that a god has knocked him silly from behind, and men from front, back, and side, wherever like vultures they can get in on the kill. Yet it is not out of shame over their Olympian kin that these horses weep, nor in rage at the blackguards who strike that defenseless body. Not shame and rage, but persistent, unsuccessful mourning of a being they can neither introject nor incorporate. Mourning as longing.

At the culminating moment of his 1936 lectures on Schelling, Heidegger considers Schelling's daring thesis that the essence of ground in God is longing, *die Sehnsucht*. He can no doubt sense the resistance in his hearers, their twitching flanks, their spooked eyes; he employs every rhetorical trick he knows in order to overcome their skittishness:

> The essence of ground in God is longing? We can scarcely restrain the objection that this statement projects a human condition onto God—. Ah, yes! *But*: it could also be otherwise. For who has ever verified the supposition that longing is something merely human? And who has ever refuted thoroughly and with sufficient reason the possibility that what we call *longing*, which is where we are, in the end is something other than we ourselves? Does not longing conceal something that denies us *any* grounds for limiting it to humankind, something that would sooner give us cause to grasp it as that in which we human beings are unfettered *out beyond ourselves* [über uns weg *entschränkt*]? Is it not precisely longing that proves the human being to be Other, other than a mere human being? (*SA* 150)

To the resurgent cries of *Schleier-macher! Schleier-macher!* Heidegger could retort—although he never would, but then why not?—that the "beyond" of "out beyond ourselves," the *weg* of *über uns weg*, is precisely the *animal*'s de-inhibited openness to beings (*GA* 29/30: 364). Likewise, the *Regung* or "bestirring" of longing in the ground of God's essence has everything to do with the untrammeled, unfettered essence of just-plain-life: *Regung* is destined to be a word in Heidegger's theoretical biology (see especially *GA* 54: 237–38), in his Schellingian meditation on ontotheology (see *SA* 151, 159, 161), and in the language of φύσις and *Ereignis* (see *US* 257–58, 264). Not just anyone's God, but Schelling's and Hölderlin's God, on the verge of discovering its flanks, its sexes and sexualities, its fatal commitment to mortality, its ineluctable subjection to the granting, the bestirring of time and being. And a mortality whose "fundamental mood" would be *Schmerz* rather than suffering and sorrow, an impossible mourning that is always and everywhere a *Sehnsucht*, a langor and a longing. Less a "fundamental mood" than a melody, *eine Weise*; perhaps what Whitman called a threnody.

Pain, mourning, and the ability to die. If death invades animal life too and shatters it, what blindness and what wisdom was it that long ago sang ageless, deathless horses? That confused mortals with immortal steeds? That granted the immortal horse a mortal voice, borrowed from immortal Hera, and where did *she* get it from?

Never mind the voice. Mind equine tears, the water shed, the impossible, impassable watershed.

What world-relation do these mournful horses have? Freud says that in mourning the *human* world suddenly becomes impoverished. What would Heidegger say? What world-relation do these weeping horses have? Answer: they sustain *every possible* relation.

First, that of stone:

> But just as funeral stele stand fixed above the tomb,
> As monuments to the dead man or woman,
> They stand motionless and motionless hold
> > the splendid car. . . .

Second, that of the god:

> It was a painful sight for Zeus, Son of Chronos,
> To see these weeping steeds. . . .
> > "Ah, you wretches!"

Third, and finally, inevitably, that of humankind:

> "Was it so that you could share in the sufferings
> > of these unhappy humans?
> For, truly, there is nothing more wretchedly lamentable
> > than human being,
> Amid all the beings that breathe and creep
> > on the earth."

IV

THRESHOLDS

JIRO WATANABE

8. Categorial Intuition and the Understanding of Being in Husserl and Heidegger

My aim in this paper is twofold. First, I want to elucidate one of the most important aspects of the complex relation between Husserl and Heidegger and thereby bring to light certain similarities and differences between these two philosophers. This elucidation will constitute the major portion of my paper. But, second, I will also offer some critical comments on the analytic philosophy of language. Thus, my discussion is not only a philosophical-historical study but also is oriented toward a systematic philosophical reflection, even though the latter can be only briefly mentioned at the end of the paper.

I.

It is well known that in 1907, while still a student in the Gymnasium, Heidegger as "awakened" to the "question of Being" by the writings of Brentano (*R* x, *US* 92, *SD* 81). It is known too that during the winter semester 1909–10, while a theology student in Freiburg, Heidegger checked out from the university library Husserl's *Logical Investigations,* expecting this work to provide him with a "decisive challenge in the questions provoked by Brentano." The young Heidegger "read this book over and over again in the following years," as he later recalled (*SD* 81ff.). After he turned in 1911 to the study of philosophy, he once again felt moved to "work closely through Husserl's text" on the occasion of Rickert's seminar on Lask (*SD* 83). "Even after the publication of Husserl's *Ideas 1,*" continues Heidegger's account, he felt himself "bound" by the "unwavering fascination of the *Logical Investigations*" (*SD* 85). Consequently, we may suppose that the young Heidegger first learned the phenomenological way of thinking through his study of the *Logical Investigations.*

But what was it about the *Logical Investigations* that so fascinated Heidegger? After Husserl succeeded Rickert at Freiburg in 1916, Heidegger's main concerns crystallized as his "familiarity with phenomenology grew, no longer merely through literature but by actual practice" (*R* xii). This change came about through "dialogues with Husserl" that "provided the immediate experience of the phenomenological method" (*R* x). Finally, Heidegger could leave behind "merely reading about" phenomenology and could grasp the "fulfillment of the way of thought" that was phenomenology (*SD* 85). Heidegger's interest in the "*Logical Investigations* was renewed, above all in the sixth investigation of the first edition," when in 1919 he found himself "teaching and learning in a close relation with Husserl" (*SD* 86). The sixth investigation centers on categorial intuition, about which Heidegger says: "The difference between sensuous and categorial intuition discussed here revealed its importance for determining the 'multiple meanings of entities'" (*SD* 86). Accordingly, there should be no doubt that Heidegger's long-lived interest in the *Logical Investigations* at last resolved itself into a focus on the thematic of categorial intuition. One can say, without exaggeration, that categorial intuition constitutes one of the most important fundamental questions shared by Husserl and Heidegger.

2 .

Now just what is categorial intution? What role did it play in the formation of Heidegger's thinking about Being? In the 1925 lecture course *Prolegomena to the History of the Concept of Time* (*GA* 20), Heidegger dealt with Husserl's phenomenology in detail, and in particular with categorial intuition. He lists three main fundamental discoveries of phenomenology: "intentionality, categorial intuition, and the original sense of the a priori" (*GA* 20: 34). More precisely, as Heidegger himself remarked, "the correct grasp of the categorial" is closely connected with the "discovery of intentionality," so that both are almost "one and the same" (*GA* 20: 80); conversely, "the discovery of categorial intuition" no doubt makes it possible to "seize more sharply the a priori" (*GA* 20: 98). Thus, the problem of categorial intuition undoubtedly constitutes the center of the three discoveries.

There are certainly many aspects to categorial intuition, but I will deal with it here only insofar as it is deeply interwoven with the problem of Being. This approach will enable me to elucidate the fundamental questions of Heidegger and Husserl in such a way that the similarities and differences of the two thinkers can become apparent.

In this regard I would like to submit three theses. First, categorial intuition contains the germ of the problem of ontological difference. Second, if a Being or state of affairs grasped in categorial intuition is not, for Husserl, to be regarded as subjective, even less would this be the case for Heidegger, for whom a grasping in categorial intuition could only be considered as a self-showing of beings themselves (*Sichzeigen des Seienden selbst*). Third, whereas Husserl's understanding of categorial intuition remains oriented toward assertion (*Aussage*), such an orientation is for Heidegger unsatisfactory; thus, Heidegger wanted to expose a ground even deeper than assertion and to think through more radically the problem of truth thereby brought to light. Along this path he eventually reached the standpoint in *Being and Time,* namely, that fundamental thinking of truth and the attempt to unfold the understanding interpretation (*die verstehende Auslegung*) of Dasein as a deeper fundament than assertion.

3 ·

What is the relation of categorial intuition to the problem of the ontological difference?

According to Heidegger, intuition means: "the simple grasping of the bodily-given, as it shows itself" (*GA* 20: 64); in the "shows itself" of this definition one can already hear a slight Heideggerian nuance, but I leave this point to one side today, for, since Kant, intuition has been defined as "that through which knowledge is in immediate relation with objects."[1] However, for Husserl there is not only "sensuous" but also "super-sensuous (i.e., raised above sensuousness, or categorial)" intuition;[2] moreover, categorial intuition must lie, as Heidegger points out, in each "most ordinary" experience (*GA* 20: 64), even in the simplest perception, insofar as it becomes as "expressed assertion" (*GA* 20: 65, 75).

For example, when we say along with Husserl that "This paper is white," then we can surely see this "white paper" with our eyes and touch it with our hands, but we cannot confirm by sensuous intuition *that* this paper *is* white, *that* it *is* so, the so-called "state of affairs." That which we "mean" (*bedeuten*) and "signify" (*signitiv meinen*) by the "little word 'is'," i.e., something "corresponding" to the word "Being," cannot be found by us in sensuous perception. That is to say that "Being is absolutely imperceptible." Nevertheless, there is no doubt that we certainly "seize" and "grasp" every state of affairs. In fact, Being is not sensuously perceptible, but "self-given" "in the fulfillment which at times invests the judgment, the becoming-aware of the intended state of affairs." Being is hence "self-given" to a certain extent in the "perception of the state of affairs," i.e., in a "state-of-affairs-giving-act," in short, in "categorial intuition." This intuition, in which Being and its state of affairs are given, is a type of categorial intuition.[3]

Heidegger similarly writes that when a person makes an assertion such as "This chair is yellow," the perceptual assertion is not fully "demonstrable via perception" (*GA* 20:77). He continues, "I can see the chair, but I can never in all eternity see the 'is' in the same way that I see the chair" (*GA* 20: 77); further, "color is something sensuous, real," Heidegger writes; "one can see colors, but not *being*-colored." Finally, Heidegger concludes "Being, on the contrary, is nothing of this sort; thus it is nonsensuous, not real" (*GA* 20: 78).

Kant had already declared that "Being is no real predicate,"[4] a statement that holds not only for "existential Being," but also for "predicative and attributive Being,"[5] and thus for "Being in the sense of the copula" (*GA* 20:78). Husserl had already stressed this by declaring: "I can see colors, but not *being*-colored. I can feel smoothness, but not *being*-smooth. I can hear a tone, but not its *being* as it sounds." Further, "Being is nothing *in* the object, but also nothing attaching *to* an object." Being is "in the real sense overall" no "inner" or "outer" "feature."[6]

This thought of Husserl's is doubtlessly linked closely with Heidegger's problematic of the ontological difference. Heidegger himself writes in *The Basic Problems of Phenomenology:* "We can always easily imagine and represent to ourselves a being from any domain." But "can one represent to oneself something like Being? Does one not deceive oneself in such an attempt? In fact, we are at first baffled and find ourselves clutching at thin air. A being—that's something, a table, a chair, a tree, the sky, a body, some words, an action. A being, yes, indeed—but Being? It looks like nothing." Heidegger continues: "We must confess that under the heading of Being we can at first think to ourselves nothing. On the other hand, it is just as certain that we are constantly thinking Being. We think Being just as often as, daily, on innumerable occasions, whether aloud or silently, we say 'This *is* such and such', 'That other *is not* so', 'That *was*', 'It *will* be'. In each use of a verb we have already thought, and have always in some way understood, Being" (*GA* 24: 18).

Along these lines, Heidegger says in *Being and Time:* "In all knowledge or assertion, in every relation to beings, in every relation with one's own self, use is made of 'Being', and the expression is thereby 'without further ado' understandable. Everyone understands: 'The sky *is* blue'; 'I *am* happy', and so forth. But this average understandability merely demonstrates that this is ununderstandable"; for "'Being' cannot have the character of a being" (*SZ* 4). Surely, "there are many things which we designate as 'being', and we do so in various senses" (*SZ* 6), but Being is "that which determines beings as beings, that on the basis of which beings are already understood, however we may discuss them in detail. The Being of beings 'is' not itself a being" (*SZ* 6). Later in *Being and Time* Heidegger writes: "Beings are, quite independently of the experience by which they are disclosed, the acquaintance in which they are discovered, and the grasping in which their nature is ascertained. But Being 'is' only in the understanding of those beings to whose Being something like an understanding of Being belongs" (*SZ* 183). Thus, Being can be apprehended and grasped only in our understanding of Being; consequently, the question of Being can be taken up only by turning back to Dasein, which understands Being, by clarifying the understanding of Being as a fundamental structure of Dasein. This requires an "existential analytic of Dasein" (*SZ* 13). It is already clear that hereby Heidegger has begun to lay the foundation of his thinking of Being.

4 .

I now proceed to my second thesis. In the *Logical Investigations* Husserl had already emphasized that the concept of Being, although apprehended in our "judgment," is nevertheless not obtained "through reflections" on certain judgments.[7] Heidegger stresses this character of categorial intuition and points out that Being, although non-real and non-sensuous, cannot be identified "straightaway" with "the spiritual in the subject," that is, with the "immanent, the conscious, the subjective"; he insists that this precisely is "the original sense of the discovery of categorial intuition" (*GA* 20: 78ff.). The discovery of intentionality had already shown that one is directed toward a being, so that what is self-given in categorial intuition is evidently "nothing psychic," but "an original objectivity" (*GA* 20: 80). Correspondingly, Heidegger strongly criticizes the Neo-Kantian misunderstanding stemming from passages in Husserl[8] in which the "categorial" is introduced as "form" in opposition to the "matter" of the "sensuous" (*GA* 20: 96). It would be a fatal mistake if one thought that the "spontaneity of understanding" as the categorial became a "formative principle of perceived matter" (*GA* 20: 96). On the contrary, according to Heidegger, the categorial forms are "nothing made out of conscious acts," "nothing constructed by the subject," but they present an object "more originally in its 'in-itselfness'"; they "constitute" a new objectivity; the constituion means "letting an entity be seen in its objectivity" (*GA* 20: 96ff.). Thus the thing itself (*die Sache selbst*) can be seen in categorial intuition in its essence (*Sachlichkeit*); one could say that precisely in this way Heidegger prepares a new way for genuine phenomenological-ontological investigations. What was carried out by the Husserlian phenomenology of "acts of consciousness" is now held by Heidegger to be the "self-showing" of a present entity, its "revealing" and "unconcealedness" (*SD* 87). Herewith, the problem of ἀλήθεια, which had already been thought for ages by "Aristotle" and "Greek thinking," comes into the purview of phenomenology.

In fact, Heidegger himself acknowledges that in his appropriation of the phenomenological method "a renewed study of the Aristotelian treatises (especially Book 9 of the *Metaphysics* and Book 6 of the *Nicomachean Ethics*) resulted in the insight into ἀληθεύειν" (*R* x); and in *Being and Time* Heidegger also suggests that truth as unconcealedness was already alive for the Greeks, especially in the above mentioned books of Aristotle (*SZ* 225). Therefore, Heidegger's appropriation of phenomenology was closely connected with the discovery of the Greek concept of truth as ἀλήθεια. It was thus that he came to formulate his own fundamental thoughts on Being and truth.

5.

I will now address my third thesis, that concerning the problem of truth. Since this problem is very complicated, I will present only some special features whereby this problem became important for Heidegger in his critical confrontation with Husserl's thought. Indeed, it was via the problem of truth that Heidegger departed from Husserl's phenomenology. I want to support this thesis by referring briefly to two of Heidegger's lecture courses prior to *Being and Time*.

First of all, in the *Prolegomena to the History of the Concept of Time* Heidegger writes that if, in categorial intuition, an empty intention turns out to be founded in a thing (*Sache*), then both the emptily intended and the originally intuited "come to coincide with each other" (*GA* 20: 66); this "identifying fulfillment" or "evidence" contains the problem of "truth and Being" (*GA* 20: 69ff.). Here one should observe that for Heidegger it is valid, first of all, to separate "two concepts of truth and consequently two concepts of Being" (*GA* 20: 73). For example, when we say: "This chair is yellow," we can stress at first the Being in the "*being*-yellow" and mean that the chair "is *really* and *truly* yellow" (*GA* 20: 71, 73). "Truth signifies here so much as *Being, being*-real"; "True means here hence so much as *making*-the-knowledge-*true*" (*GA* 20:71). Truth is thus the Being itself that makes knowledge true. Here Being is "subsistence of identity," that is, the "subsistence and stasis of a state of affairs in the truth-relation" (*GA* 20:

72). According to Heidegger, this concept of truth originated with the Greeks (*GA* 20: 71, 73).

Second, when we stress the being-*yellow*, that is, "the belonging of a predicate to a subject," then "copula-Being" comes into view; in this case Being is apprehended only as a "structural moment" or a "relation factor" in a state of affairs (*GA* 20: 72). On this occasion truth is considered to be only a "phenomenon" that would have to be studied in conformity with an "assertion" (*GA* 20: 73). And, in fact, truth has been traditionally regarded as "belonging to an act of asserting," that is, "to a predicative, relational act" (*GA* 20: 73). But the "truth of a relational act is only a definite sort of being-true" (GA 20: 78); originally for the Greeks the "simplest perception" was called true (*GA* 20: 73), for in this case one can touch (θιγεῖν) an entity in its truth. Thus does Heidegger undercut traditional thinking regarding truth and Being in his attempt to resituate this problem on a ground more fundamental than assertion.

The same tendency can be recognized in a clearer and more detailed manner in the 1925–26 lecture course *Logic;* here again Heidegger reads Husserl's *Logical Investigations* with regard to the question of truth. He focuses on the result of Husserl's critique of psychologism, namely, that the "judged sense of a judgment" is "no real occurrence," but "an ideal Being, validity (*Geltung*)" (*GA* 21: 46). But even in this case truth is considered to be the "truth of a proposition," that is, the "validity of an assertion" (*GA* 21: 22, 25); furthermore, validity is equated with the "reality of true propositions" (*GA* 21: 77). Yet precisely here, Heidegger contends, the "essence of truth" is not thought at all (*GA* 21: 73).

Generally speaking, Heidegger claims in this lecture that "contemporary" logic—indeed the entire tradition of logic—is a "logic of validity" (*GA* 21: 62, 78, 79, 124). He maintains that traditional logic is based primarily upon an "expressed proposition," namely, upon an assertion (*GA* 21: 134). Here there is only a semblance of inquiry into the essence of truth (*GA* 21: 78, 82). To counter this semblance and to broach a genuine thinking of the essence of truth, Heidegger undertakes to develop a "philosophical logic" (*GA* 21: 55ff., 124).

Such a logic would be oriented, not toward assertion, but toward the "intuitive knowing of a being" itself (*GA* 21: 99ff.); it would focus especially on the analysis of "demonstration" in which the emptily intended and the intuited "coincide with each other" (*GA* 21: 107), that is, on the problem of "evidence" (*GA* 21: 108); this logic would endeavor to clarify the origin of "truth qua identity" (*GA* 21: 109), since "validity" would now be reduced to "truth in the sense of identity" (*GA* 21: 111). Thus would Heidegger carry out his "return to Aristotle" (*GA* 21: 109).

In this return it becomes manifest that in Aristotle the "proposition is not the locus of truth," but that on the contrary, "truth is the locus of propositions" (*GA* 21: 135). Therefore, in Aristotle—as opposed to the tradition—a proposition qua assertion is considered from the standpoint of "uncovering and covering over," that is, as "letting an entity be seen" (*GA* 21: 133, 163), that is, as "uncovering an entity" (*GA* 21: 169). Looking for textual evidence to support these points,

Heidegger masterfully refers to the ninth book of the *Metaphysics* in which Aristotle says we can "touch [θιγεῖν]" the "simple essence" of a being as "itself" and "in itself" (*GA* 21: 180, 182, 190). We gain genuine proximity to it, "let it be seen," and "perceive" it (*GA* 21: 181). In this manner, the Being of an entity comes to be "uncovered" (*GA* 21: 181). However, the possibility of "covering over" or "disguising" appears only in the case of complex entities (*GA* 21: 185).

The same position is suggested in *Being and Time*. There Heidegger said that in Aristotle both the "αἴσθησις" as well as the "pure νοεῖν" are the "primordial kind of uncovering" (*SZ* 226) and thus are "true" in this sense (*SZ* 33); in particular, the pure νοεῖν can never be "false," but "can at worst remain a non-perceiving, ἀγνοεῖν" (*SZ* 33). Only when we "hark back to something else in our pointing out," that is, only within a "synthesis-structure," does there appear a "possibility of covering over" (*SZ* 34).

In this discussion we should recognize that "assertion is not the primary 'locus' of truth," but that on the contrary, "assertion is grounded in Dasein's uncovering, or rather in its disclosedness" (*SZ* 226). Assertion is grounded primarily in the "way of Being in which Dasein can either uncover or cover up" (*SZ* 226). Consequently, assertion is only a "derivative mode of interpretation" (*SZ* 153ff.); this interpretation is in turn only a "development of understanding" (*SZ* 148ff.). Therefore, every assertion must be grounded in Dasein's understanding interpretation, in which the "fore-structure" of understanding and the "as-structure" of interpretation (*SZ* 151) are intimately connected as a unified phenomenon in which the true "circular structure" of understanding works productively (*SZ* 153). So we must reject a levelled-off "apophantical 'as'" and turn back to a living "existential-hermeneutical 'as'" (*SZ* 158). All our knowing must be grounded in this understanding interpretation of Dasein that alone can confirm something as really true. This concludes Heidegger's criticism of the logic of validity in Husserl's sense.

6.

The above-sketched thought of Heidegger's—namely, that in order to grasp a state of affairs and, along with it, the Being of a being, one must return to a living understanding of Being, that is, to Dasein's understanding interpretation—supplies us with a means to criticize the levelled-off concept of Being that is widespread today in analytic philosophy of language. Here a few brief comments must suffice.

Since Russell's theory of descriptions, or indeed since Frege, it has been generally maintained that there are three meanings of Being: "the 'is' of existence," "the 'is' of predication," and "the 'is' of identity."[9] Russell's theory of descriptions takes up Being in the sense of existence (that is, in what Heidegger would call presence-at-hand [*Vorhandenheit*], and states that "everything that has been said about existence is sheer and simple mistake," that "all traditional metaphysics is filled with mistakes due to bad grammar."[10] According to this allegedly revolutionary opinion, the "fundamental meaning of existence" is given to us only when "any propositional function" is "possible" or "sometimes true." In short, "existence is essentially a property of a propositional function."[11] In Carnap's words, "existence can be predicated only in conjunction with a predicate, not in conjunction with a name."[12] This theory is central to the analytic philosophy of language.

But the theory is only apparently plausible. Its importance consists in its attempt to apply Ockham's razor to the destruction of metaphysical entities in defense of a common-sense realism. But if examined more precisely, it proves to be a completely perverted theory of Being, which, far from solving the problem of Being, does not even pose it correctly.

This theory insists that, in order to confirm whether something exists or not, one must first construct its "propositional function"; when there is something that fills this function, making it possible or true, then one can say that "there is at least one value of X for which that propositional function is true."[13] In this manner, Russell alleges, one can really get at the concept of Being.

However, one can criticize this theory from three points of view and demonstrate thereby that it fails to pose correctly the problem of Being.

First, one must point out that the concept of Being is already contained in the propositional function itself. The propositional function can be expressed thus: "something that *is* so and so," or "X, such that X *is*. . . . "[14] Clearly, here we begin to catch sight of the concept of Being, not, to be sure, in the sense of existence, but in the sense of the copula, that is, the 'is' of predication. Without this Being in the sense of the copula, Being in the sense of predication cannot work. However, as Heidegger has shown, the Being of the copula is only a "structural moment" in an assertion (*GA* 20: 72); the "is" of predication or the phenomenon signified by the copula really depends on Dasein's understanding of Being (*SZ* 160). In fact, if we had no understanding of Being in conjunction with, for example, the concept of *being*-free, we could not judge at all whether there really *is* something in this world that *is* free. The understanding of Being and of *being*-free must therefore precede any judging whether there really *is* something that *is* free. Without such understanding of Being, one could never judge whether there *is* indeed in this world anything that corresponds to a propositional function. Everything depends on the difficult question of Being; without deliberately posing the question of Being, no logic, however refined and sophisticated, can produce anything, for then it simply relies on assertion and on mere mechanical and rational manipulation.

Second, this theory maintains that one gets the concept of existence only when a "propositional function" turns out to be "possible or true."[15] But on what basis can one recognize such possibility or truth? Is it enough that one goes back, as Kant said in his critique of the ontological argument, only to the "conjunction with one of my perceptions," or, more generally, to "the context of the whole of experience,"[16] or to "sense-data"?[17] By no means. For the fact of being-free can never be sensuously confirmed: in order, then, to reach a decisive conclusion concerning being-free, one must refer back, as Heidegger says, to Dasein's understanding of Being regarding this state of affairs and so, generally speaking, to the "experience of consciousness" in the broad sense that Husserlian and Hegelian phenomenology give to this expression. Without considering this understanding of Being, without such phenomenological-ontological consideration of human being and of the world as such, one cannot indicate the ultimate horizon in which something in this world could be considered possible or true.

Third, one can point out that the Russellian theory contains a hidden circularity. Russell holds that one gets "the fundamental meaning of existence" only when one knows that "there is at least one value of X for which that propositional function is true."[18] This entails that the meaning of existence (that is, of Being) presupposes the meaning of "there is" (that is, of Being). It is clear that here we find the *definiendum* already in the *definiens;* this is doubtless a circularity.

And yet, in a sense this case only confirms what Heidegger says: that the circularity of understanding belongs essentially to the structure of Dasein as is quite inevitable (*SZ* 153). If, for example, we ask: "What *is* 'Being'?, we keep within an understanding of the 'is'" (*SZ* 5). The inevitability of such prior understanding of Being is indicative of the complexity that the development of the question of Being will involve, even though at the same time it is precisely the assurance of "a positive possibility of the most primordial kind of knowledge" (*SZ* 153). For the development of such knowledge mere logic will never suffice. The task is rather to clarify the meaning of Being by recourse to that being. Dasein, that always already has an understanding of Being.

NOTES

1. Immanuel Kant, *Kritik der reinen Vernunft*, (Hamburg: Felix Meiner, 1956), A 19/B 33.
2. Edmund Husserl, *Logische Untersuchungen* (Tübingen: Max Niemeyer, 1922), 2: 143.
3. Ibid., 131–44.
4. Kant, A 598/B 626.
5. Husserl, 2: 137.
6. Ibid.
7. Ibid., 140.
8. Ibid., 136.
9. Bertrand Russell, "The Philosophy of Logical Atomism," in *Logic and Knowledge*, ed. R. C. Marsh, (London: George Allen & Unwin) 245; G. Frege, *Funktion, Begriff, Bedeutung*, ed. G. Patzig, (Göttingen: Vanderhoeck), 36n., 68, 73.
10. Russell, "Philosophy of Logical Atomism," 186, 269.
11. Ibid., 232.
12. R. Carnap, "The Elimination of Metaphysics through Logical Analysis of Language," in *Logical Positivism*, ed., A. J. Ayer. (New York: Free Press, 1959), 74.
13. Russell, 232.
14. Ibid.
15. Ibid.
16. Kant, A 601/B 629, A 600ff./B 628ff.
17. W.O.V. Quine, "Russell's Ontological Development," in *Essays on Bertrand Russell*, ed. E. D. Klemke (Urbana: University of Illinois Press), 12ff.
18. Russell, 232.

FRIEDRICH-WILHELM VON HERRMANN

---

9. *Being and Time* and *The Basic Problems of Phenomenology*

Translated by Parvis Emad and Kenneth Maly

When the manuscript of *Being and Time* was originally delivered to the printer, on April 1, 1926, it included a text for division 3 of part 1, entitled "Time and Being." As Heidegger was reading proof for the book, he realized that this last and most important section of the book was not worked out as well as it needed to be. Thus, in early January, 1927, he withdrew that portion of the text. It is for this reason that *Being and Time* appeared (in April 1927) *as* the first half—without division 3 of part 1. At that time Heidegger had hoped that within a year he would be able to elaborate and clarify the thought process of division 3—that would then have been published as part 2 of *Being and Time*.

This is the background for Heidegger's designating his lecture course for the summer semester of 1927 a "new elaboration of division 3 of part 1 of *Being and Time*." Thus *The Basic Problems of Phenomenology* is explicitly intended as the crucial continuation of *Being and Time*.

Given these facts, we are confronted with the question: To what extent is the lecture course text of 1927 (with which the publication of the *Gesamtausgabe* began, in November 1975) a new, second elaboration of division 3 of part 1 of *Being and Time?* In order to answer this question, we first need to know what the thematic of that division of part 1 was meant to be. We do not have the first elaboration that Heidegger discarded. However, the published first half of *Being and Time* has within it enough indications and directives for the path that thinking was to take in division 3. These indications and directives allow us to answer the question raised above, namely: What is the actual relationship of *The Basic Problems of Phenomenology* to *Being and Time* and to the systematic outline for *Being and Time* that is given in section 8?

I find these indications as follows:

1. in the above-mentioned section 8,
2. in the brief foreword to the treatise,

3. in the introduction, whose task is the exposition of the question of being and whose fifth section offers a glimpse into the direction that the first half with its three divisions takes,
4. in the title to the first half, and
5. finally, in section 83 (the last section of division 2), that leads into the third division.

By clarifying the question of the inherent relation of *The Basic Problems of Phenomenology* and *Being and Time,* I intend to get a firm insight into the inner systematic as well as the way of the fundamental-ontological elaboration of the question of being. It is only by a full and reliable knowledge of the systematic structure of the fundamental-ontological elaboration of the question of being that we are capable of sufficiently understanding the transition to the elaboration of the same question in terms of the history of being as it occurs in *Beiträge zur Philosophie.*

PRELIMINARY INDICATIONS OF THE THIRD DIVISION, "TIME AND BEING," IN THE FIRST HALF OF *BEING AND TIME*

FOREWORD TO *BEING AND TIME* AND ITS REFERENCE TO THE THEME "TIME AND BEING"

In the foreword to *Being and Time* the basic question of the treatise is immediately named and emphasized—by means of italics—as *the question concerning the meaning of being.* The phrase "meaning of being" initially says: being as being, being as such, or being itself in the sense that properly belongs to it. The phrase "meaning of being" says something different from the question concerning a being as a being or a being in its being. If the question of the meaning of being is to be raised anew, then the word *anew* tells us that, although the question takes up the traditional inquiries of Parmenides, Plato, and Aristotle, it does so by abandoning from the outset the traditional mode of inquiry as an inquiry into beings in their being, *in favor of* the more originary question of being as such.

The foreword also tells us that the intention of the following treatise is "to work out concretely the question of the meaning of *being.*" This statement of intention points ahead to the entirety of the treatise with its two parts, of which only the first part was published to begin with. Therefore, the foreword tells us that the provisional goal of the treatise would be "the interpretation of *time* as the possible horizon of any understanding of being whatsoever." The words *being* and *time* are also put in italics here, in order to tell the reader how to understand the title "Being and Time": time as that horizon within which being as such is understood. If we inquire into the meaning of being as such, then time proves to be the meaning of which we are inquiring; and time is that in terms of which, in any comportment toward beings, we understand from the outset the being of those beings. It is noteworthy that at this juncture in the foreword, where the fundamental words *being* and *time* are mentioned for the first time, the fundamental words *understanding of being* are also introduced to set the direction. The question is about the meaning of being as such. And time is to be shown to be this meaning: time as the horizon within which being—as what is always understood in any understanding of being—gets determined temporally. Thus the foreword indicates most concisely and formally that, in the process of its elaboration, the fundamental question of "being and time" will turn into the question of "time and being." That is, the fundamental question of "being and time" turns into the question of how, in the understanding of being, being gets determined temporally within the horizon of time.

THE TITLE OF THE FIRST HALF OF *Being and Time* AND ITS PRELIMINARY INDICATION OF THE THEME "TIME AND BEING"

The title of the first half of *Being and Time* reads: "The Interpretation of Dasein on the Basis of Temporality and the Explication of Time as the Transcendental Horizon of the Question of Being." By considering the "Outline of the Treatise" as given in section 8, we see how the theme that is mentioned in this title spreads over various sections of the first part. This title repeats what was made clear in a preliminary and formal way in section 5 of the introduction, namely, that elaboration of the question of the meaning of being—i.e., the question of being—branches off into two tasks, dividing the treatise into two parts. After naming for the first time the title of the first part, Heidegger announces its structuring into three divisions. We immediately see that the first half of the title—before the conjunction "and"—gathers together that theme which is dealt with in the first two divisions. The "Interpretation of Dasein on the Basis of Temporality" takes place in two stages. In conjunction with the guiding question of the meaning of being, the first stage—the "Preliminary Fundamental Analysis of Dasein"—uncovers Dasein as constituted in its ownmost mode of being as that which understands being—Dasein in its existential-ontological structures that constitute *Existenz* as that which understands being. Proceeding phenomenologically, this uncovering is a "fundamental analysis" because it lays open the fundamental (i.e., essential) structures of the being of *Existenz*, which understands being. However, this uncovering is "preparatory" because it prepares for the most original interpretation of the being of Dasein that follows in division 2 entitled "Dasein and Temporality." It is here that the meaning of the being of Dasein, which remained concealed in division 1, is shown to consist in Dasein's temporalizing temporality.

However, the demonstration of the existential temporality of Dasein—the meaning of its being—is not the same as responding to the guiding question concerning the meaning of being as such, which includes the meaning of being of all beings that are not Dasein. The response to this fundamental question of *Being and Time*—a response that is served by the existential ontological analytic of Dasein in division 1—is the task set for division 3. The second half of the title of the first part—which follows the conjunction "and"—points to the task: "The Explication of Time as the Transcendental Horizon of the Question of Being." The word *horizon* was already mentioned in the foreword—time as a horizon—but it is now more closely identified as a transcendental horizon. The adjective "transcendental" is derived from the noun "transcendence": transcending, surpassing, or stepping beyond. Transcendence in this sense is the central determination of *Existenz* in its enactment as that which understands being. As existing, Dasein has already surpassed or stepped beyond the being that it itself is as well as that being that is other than itself but toward which it (Dasein) comports itself essentially in its self-being. Dasein has always already stepped beyond *to* the disclosure of being as such, to being in totality, in order to return from this existentially and transcendentally disclosed disclosure back to beings as beings. Dasein understands being in its (Dasein's) *Existenz* and in the existentials that constitute *Existenz,* insofar as being in totality is disclosed, open, and lit up in these existentials and in their enactment. Being as such—being in totality—is the being of *Existenz* as well as the manifold modes of beings other than Dasein, which are disclosed and lit up along with *Existenz* and its enactment. But something like a horizon belongs to Dasein's transcendence; and this requires that this horizon be characterized as a transcendental horizon. The horizon of Dasein's *Existenz,* within which Dasein transcends beings and understands being, is that disclosed horizon (*Gesichtskreis*) within which Dasein understands the disclosure and lighting up of being. But if time is this lit-up horizon for an understanding of being according to Dasein, then Dasein understands the being that is disclosed within the horizon of time. i.e., temporally.

Time needs to be explicated as the transcendental horizon—specifically, from out of the aforementioned temporality of Dasein. If, in its *Existenz* as that which understands being Dasein transcends beings, then transcendence is grounded in turn in the temporality of Dasein. To put it differently, Dasein transcends beings in the enactment of temporalizing its temporality. And if in its enactment of transcendence Dasein opens out onto the disclosed horizon of time, then time is the horizon of existential temporality. As horizon, time belongs essentially to existential temporality, so that—after division 2 uncovers existential temporality— division 3 can uncover time as the horizon, or horizonal temporality, from out of the existential or transcendental temporality. The existential or transcendental temporality and horizonal time are inseparable. In this togetherness, they make up the essence of time or original time—whose derivative is that time that is familiar to us and is guided by the now and which Heidegger calls ordinary time.

The Preliminary Indication of the Third Division, "Time and Being," in Section 5 of the Introduction

Because section 5 of the introduction provides an introduction to the first part of the treatise *as well as* an initial, formal view of the main steps in thinking in all *three* divisions, therefore—and correspondingly—its title not only names the theme of the first two divisions that contain the analytic of Dasein in the narrow sense but also names the theme of the third division, "Time and Being." The phrase, "ontological analysis of Dasein," in the title of section 5 corresponds to the phrase "interpretation of Dasein on the basis of temporality" in the title of the first part. Likewise, the phrase "laying open of the horizon for an interpretation of the meaning of being in general" in the title of section 5 corresponds to the phrase "explication of time as the transcendental horizon of the question of being" in the title of the first part.

Paragraphs 9 to 14 of section 5 present an initial, if only formal, view of the theme of the third division "Time and Being." This presentation offers us the important clue that in "Time and Being" the question of the meaning of being—one which guides the analytic of Dasein—will be provided in two clearly separate steps.

The phenomenological uncovering of the meaning of the being of Dasein as temporality that temporalizes itself is the "ground for obtaining" (*SZ* 17) the response to the guiding question concerning the meaning of being in general—and not only the response to the question of the meaning of the being of Dasein. Based on temporality as the meaning of the being of Dasein, this question inquires into the meaning of the being of all beings other than Dasein, toward which Dasein comports itself on the basis of its existential-transcendental temporality. Dasein comports itself toward these beings only from out of a previously understood being that is disclosed and lit up in Dasein's understanding. But if the being of beings other than Dasein is disclosed and lit up in the enactment of a temporality that temporalizes itself, then the horizonal disclosure of the being of beings other than Dasein is temporally disclosed and lit up *along with* the existential disclosedness of *Existenz*. While existential disclosedness of *Existenz* is temporally disclosed as temporality, the disclosure of the being of beings other than Dasein that is understood within that temporality is temporally disclosed as the horizon of time. Because in understanding its being as temporality Dasein is shifted into the horizonally disclosed time, Heidegger speaks of the existential or transcendental temporality as an ecstatic temporality. Starting from the ecstatic temporality that is uncovered in division 2, division 3 must now "bring to light" (*SZ* 17) the horizon of time that belongs to temporality. Thus the first of the two steps of thinking the theme "Time and Being" consists in "an original explication of time as the horizon of the understanding of being in terms of temporality as the being of Dasein which understands being" (*SZ* 17). To put it differently, this first and decisive step in the analytic of division 3 fills out the ecstatic temporality which is disclosed in division 2, showing it *as* the time horizon which belongs essentially to temporality. To sum up, the content of the first step of "Time and Being" is this uncovering of time that temporalizes itself horizonally in the ecstatic temporality as the horizon for understanding the being of beings other than Dasein.

The second step, whose formal characterization is given in paragraph 11 (of section 5), brings to full fruition the result of the first step. On the "basis of the question of the meaning of being" (*SZ* 17), i.e., on the basis of the explication of time carried out in the first step as horizon of ecstatic temporality, the second step must show "that and in what way the central problematic of all ontology is rooted in the phenomenon of time correctly viewed and explicated" (*SZ* 17). But what does this mean, seeing that the central problematic of all ontology is rooted in the phenomenon of horizonal time, uncovered from out of ecstatic temporality? The twelfth paragraph responds to this question. Being "is grasped in terms of time" (*SZ* 17).

After division 2 grasps Dasein's ownmost mode of being from out of the original time as ecstatic termporality, the task is to grasp the being of beings other than Dasein in terms of ecstatic horizonal time. But the being of beings other than Dasein is not uniform; rather it shows a manifold of differentiated ways (modes) of being (which Heidegger also calls "modi"). If being is to be grasped in terms of time, then it must be shown that and how "the various modes and derivatives of being, in their modifications and derivations," are made intelligible in light of horizonal time temporalized in ecstatic temporality. Heidegger distinguishes modes or ways of being from derivatives of being. These latter are those structures of being that prove to be variations of the primary modes of being. Thus the task that the second step faces in the context of the theme of "Time and Being" consists in making visible "being itself," i.e., the manifold modes and derivatives of the being of beings other than Dasein in their *temporal* character. But it is important to note the emphasis, namely, that "being itself"—i.e., being as such—has a "temporal" character of its own. Because this character is determined from out of original time as the unity of ecstatic temporality and horizonal time, the term *temporal* in reference to being as such cannot mean "to be in time." To be in time indicates a manner in which *a* being is in time. For its part, to be in time—the intratemporality of beings—comes out of (is derived from) original time out of which being as such receives its temporal meaning. Considering the "original determination of the meaning of being"—i.e., of the being of beings other than Dasein, "its character and modes" which stem from ecstatic-horizonal time—Heidegger speaks of a "*temporal* determination" (*SZ* 19). While he uses the Latin word-construction *temporale* to characterize terminologically the horizonal phenomenon of time, he uses the German word *zeitlich* to think the determination of the meaning of *Existenz* and its modes as they evolve out of the ecstatic phenomenon of time (i.e., from temporality). Thus Heidegger distinguishes terminologically and technically between the "temporal (*Zeitliche*) interpretation" of Dasein (*SZ* 378) in its being and the temporal (*temporale*) interpretation of the being of beings other than Dasein. The second step in the context of the third division "Time and Being" is summed up in the phrase "working out *the temporality of being* (*Temporalität des Seins*)" (*SZ* 19).

SECTION 83 OF THE SECOND DIVISION AS TRANSITION TO THE THIRD DIVISION, "TIME AND BEING"

The title of this section, like that of section 5 and the whole first part, indicates both the theme of the first two divisions *and* the theme of the third division of the first part. The phrase "existential-temporal analytic of Dasein" refers to the first and second divisions. What follows the conjunction "and"—"the fundamental ontological question of the meaning of being in general"—points to the theme of the third division. Right in the first paragraph Heidegger emphasizes that "the exhibition of the constitution of the being of Dasein" in the first two divisions did not occur for its own sake, but remains the "way" whose "goal" is "to work out the question of being in general" (*SZ* 436).

The last paragraphs of section 83 direct the way to the task that emerges out of what is achieved at the end of the second division and relates to the upcoming third division—precisely, *as* the task that is decisive for the whole project of *Being and Time*. First, the treatise affirms what it has achieved in relation to the fundamental question of the meaning of being by way of the analytic of Dasein. The treatise demonstrated phenomenologically that "being [. . . is] disclosed in the understanding of being" (*SZ* 437). By bringing into thinking's field of view the basic phenomenon of disclosedness, i.e., clearing as the disclosure belonging to being—its truth (unconcealment)—this treatise not only renders visible being in terms of beings (as the tradition does), but renders visible being as such. In Dasein's understanding of being, being is disclosed and opened up. "Understanding" in the phrase "understanding of being" belongs to Dasein itself as a fundamental mode of existing Dasein. The analytic of Dasein shows that this "understanding" has the structure of a thrown projection. Being in general, being in totality, is opened up in the enactment of thrown projection. From out of the multiplicity of modes of being—which includes the unity of the concept of being as such—the analytic of Dasein first of all allows the thematization of the mode of being of *Existenz*, of *Mitdasein*, and along with these the mode of being of beings other than Dasein—as handiness (*Zuhandenheit*) and extantness (*Vorhandenheit*). In doing this, the analytic of Dasein only touches upon the mode of being of life and of ideal beings. Disclosure of being which is opened up existentially and transcendentally "makes it possible that, as existing being in the world, Dasein comports itself *to beings*." In reference to Dasein's comportment to beings, disclosure of being as such is "prior" to these beings and "nonconceptualizeable" and at the same time is not explicit and is nonthematic. However, the being toward which Dasein comports itself from out of the existential disclosedness of being in totality—a disclosure that remains concealed to Dasein—comes up against Dasein as an innerworldly being, something handy (*zuhanden*), extant (*vorhanden*), or living (*lebendig*), as well as a being that *as Existenz* is and is not itself, but is the other.

The understanding of being as understood and disclosed is enacted in the mode of thrown projection, like all understanding befitting Dasein. Both the disclosing understanding of Dasein's being in the world *and* the disclosing understanding of the being of beings other than Dasein are possible in a way that befits Dasein as thrown projection only from out of the "original constitution of the being" of Dasein, from out of its ecstatic temporality (*SZ* 437). Hence, the first crucial step in the third division, "Time and Being," requires a phenomenological exhibition of "an original mode of temporalizing of ecstatic temporality itself." But this mode of temporalizing must show itself as a mode of temporalizing that makes possible "the ecstatic projection of being as such" (*SZ* 437), i.e., it temporalizes the horizon of time (horizonal time) and temporally projects the being of beings other than Dasein—that is, discloses this being. Thus it must be shown how "a way of original *time*" leads from ecstatic temporality "to the meaning of *being*"— but that means how original time proves phenomenologically to be that horizon that endows all characteristics and modes of being and their derivatives with their temporal meaning.

THE BASIC PROBLEMS OF PHENOMENOLOGY AS THE SECOND ELABORATION OF THE THIRD DIVISION, "TIME AND BEING"

The fact that the text *The Basic Problems of Phenomenology* deals with the investigation of the theme of time and being is shown explicitly in the discussion of the title in section 4 of the introduction. As Heidegger puts it: "The entire stock of basic problems of phenomenology in their systematic order and their foundation" amounts to a "discussion of the basic question of the meaning of being in general and of the problems arising from that question" (*BP* 16). Thus he names both of the main steps of the elaboration of the theme of time and being—steps that we have differentiated by going through pertinent texts of *Being and Time*. The first step consists of a discussion of the fundamental question of the meaning of being in the narrow sense, i.e., a phenomenological explication of horizonal time on the basis of ecstatic temporality. The problems that emerge from the fundamental question indicate clearly what *Being and Time* mentions only implicitly, as the temporal interpretation of the characteristics, modes, and derivatives of the being of beings other than Dasein. These brief preliminary allusions to the third division did not explicitly state that, in order for the treatise to interpret temporally the characteristics, modes, and derivatives of being from out of the horizon of original time, the structure, characteristics, and modes of being must first be established in systematic outline. Establishing such an outline is what essentially occurs in the second step of dealing with the theme of time and being and what leads to the insight that there are four basic problems that emerge from the fundamental question concerning the meaning of being in general.

At this point we may already claim that the discussion of the fundamental question and the four basic problems that emerge from that question make up the central core of "Time and Being"—and not only in its second but also in its first elaboration. In the design of the lecture course, which is divided into three parts, this central core is set aside for part 2 and carries the title: "The Fundamental-Ontological Question of the Meaning of Being in General. The Basic Structures and Basic Ways of Being" (*BP* 23, 225). We may surmise that Heidegger dealt with the fundamental question in the first discarded elaboration of "Time and Being," by way of explicating horizonal time out of ecstatic temporality and by addressing the temporal treatment of the four basic problems directly and immediately after the systematic analysis of the second division. By contrast, the second elaboration manifests a significant deviation. Here, right at the beginning of section 1 of the introduction, we learn that we cannot get to the basic problems of phenomenology directly, "but rather by way of a detour of a *discussion of certain individual problems*" (*BP* 2). These problems have to do with "some characteristic theses about being that have been advocated in the course of the history of Western philosophy since antiquity," whose "specifically inherent content . . . is to be critically discussed, so that we may make the transition from it to the above-mentioned basic problems of the science of being" (*BP* 15). Basic problems of the phenomenological science of being are to be "sifted out" from the historically transmitted theses on being and determined in their "systematic interconnection" (*BP* 1). This constitutes the content of the first part of the lecture course entitled "Critical Phenomenological Discussion of Some Traditional Theses about Being" (*BP* 25, 27). The advantage of this approach to the four basic problems and to the basic question—which Heidegger characterizes as a detour—is that it lets us see how the basic question of being as such and its meaning, as well as the four basic problems that emerge from this question, grow out of a radicalization (deepening)—i.e., from a repetition (*Wieder-holung*)—of traditional metaphysics and ontology.

But the "Outline of the Course" given in section 6 of the introduction specifies still a third part, with the title "The Scientific Method of Ontology and the Idea of Phenomenology" (*BP* 23). Its task is to develop the structure, characteristics, and modes of being as such in terms of the theme of phenomenology and to develop the idea, i.e., the concept of phenomenology by considering how phenomenology deals with its theme (*BP* 1, 3). As with the first and second parts, that are divided into four chapters, part three also was to have four chapters. After accomplishing the analytic of Dasein and responding to the basic question that guides this analytic, and after dealing with the four basic problems that emerge from that question, Heidegger now proceeds to reflect upon "the ontical foundation of ontology and the analytic of Dasein as fundamental ontology," on "the a priori character of being and the possibility and structure of a priori knowledge," on "the basic components of phenomenological method: reduction, construction, deconstruction," and on "phenomenological ontology and the concept of philosophy" (*BP* 24). We are certainly not wrong in assuming that the content of this third part in its concluding reflection on the idea of phenomenology also belonged to the broad theme of "Time and Being" in its first elaboration. For as is possible in no other way, the section in the introduction of *Being and Time* devoted to method can initially discuss and offer only the "preliminary concept of phenomenology" (*BP* 34). As a preliminary concept, it is a provisional one, which points ahead to a complete concept of phenomenology to be given later. This complete concept of phenomenology to be given later. This complete concept of phenomenology is what is designated as the idea of phenomenology.

RESPONDING TO THE FUNDAMENTAL QUESTION OF THE MEANING OF
BEING IN GENERAL

The four historical theses about being (being is not a real predicate; *essentia* and *existentia* belong to the constitution of the being of a being; the basic ways of being are the being of spirit and the being of nature; and the being of the copula) are various theses about a being in its being. Thus they are metaphysical theses. However, concealed in each of these theses is a fundamental-ontological basic problem, i.e., a basic problem of being. The basic problems that are thus concealed can be unveiled and worked out only if we first pose "the *fundamental question* of the whole science of being" and respond to "*the question of the meaning of being in general*" (*BP* 16). A critical interpretation of each of these four traditional theses leads us in each case to an initial, formal indication of the fundamental-ontological basic problem. Reflection on the way taken in the second part of the lecture course—in discussing the basic question and the basic problems emerging from this question—proves to be the same as we know it from *Being and Time*.

Being as such, and along with it the meaning in question, are given in our understanding of being, in understanding the being of a being that we ourselves are and that is called *Dasein* because of its understanding of being. The being which is opened up in understanding makes it possible for Dasein to comport itself toward the being that it itself is and also is not. Understanding of being has the "mode of being of human Dasein" and is the way in which Dasein is structured in its being (*BP* 16). Only when we unveil and determine the constitution and structure of the being of Dasein as that being which *understands being* is there a prospect "of comprehending in its structure the understanding of being that belongs to Dasein" (*BP* 16). Only a most original clarification of the structure of Dasein can lead us to ask the two questions regarding the understanding of being in their interconnectedness and to respond to them. The first question is: What is it that makes this understanding of being possible at all? And the second question is: Whence—that is, from which previously given horizon—does Dasein understand being? Accordingly, the fundamental-ontological analytic that unveils (uncovers) the understanding of being inquires not only into that understanding that is peculiar to Dasein but also into the being that is understood in understanding, i.e., into the understandability of being.

This brief reflection on the way that is to be followed leads to the following insight: the question of the meaning of being in general, i.e., the analytic of Dasein's understanding of being, presupposes "an analytic of Dasein ordered to that end." This analytic must first work out the basic constitution of Dasein (as does care in the first division of *Being and Time*) and then lay open the meaning of the being of Dasein (as temporality in the second division of *Being and Time*). This reminder of the two partial tasks of the analytic of Dasein is followed by a crucial reflection on the path that leads from the analytic of Dasein to answering the fundamental question of the meaning of being in general under the title "Time and Being."

The meaning of the being of Dasein is ecstatic temporality. Understanding of being belongs essentially to Dasein's being and its constitution of being. This understanding of being that belongs to Dasein's being comes from the meaning of the being of Dasein, from temporality. Understanding of being as a thrown projection takes place as an original way of ecstatic temporality's temporalizing. However, the understanding that is (thus) temporalized is not without the being that is understood in this understanding. Thus it is not only understanding that is temporally determined but also the being that is understood in this understanding, the being of beings other than Dasein, toward which Dasein comports itself in such and such a way. "Hence there arises the prospect of a possible confirmation of the thesis that time is the horizon from which something like being as such becomes intelligible" (*BP* 16, 17). As horizon, time belongs to ecstatic temporality, to the extent that this time-horizon is disclosed or lit up in the temporalization

of ecstatic temporality. Here too the fundamental-ontological interpretation of
being as such is characterized in terms of time, i.e., as a temporal interpretation.

With this Heidegger indicates the direction that the lecture course will take
in its crucial second part. This part both works out the fundamental question
by demonstrating the horizonal time that belongs to ecstatic temporality, and discusses the four basic problems as problems of temporality (*Temporalität*). Taking
a quick look at the division of the second part as projected in section 6, we find
that the four chapters correspond to the four basic problems. But we do not find
a specific chapter devoted to the fundamental question that should have been dealt
with prior to the four basic problems. The first chapter is entitled "The Problem
of Ontological Difference" (*BP* 24, 27). But when we look more closely, we find
that sections 19 to 21 work out and respond not only to the question of the ontological difference but also—as announced—to the fundamental-ontological question
concerning the meaning of being in general. It is only in the last section of this
chapter, section 22, that the basic problem of ontological difference is discussed
as a basic problem of the temporality of being.

Thus we can say that the first elaboration of "Time and Being" follows *directly*
from the analytical results of the second division of *Being and Time*. Because
ecstatic temporality in its possible ways of temporalizing was uncovered in division
2, division 3 can go directly to a presentation of the task which was formulated
at the end of section 83: uncovering that original way of temporalizing of ecstatic
temporality that projects being in general in terms of horizonal time. But the
second elaboration of "Time and Being" does not choose the direct path. The
peculiarity of the manner in which Heidegger proceeds in the second elaboration
consists in the fact that, beginning in the first part and continuing into the second
part, major segments of the analytic of Dasein are unfolded, namely, those segments that are absolutely necessary for responding to the fundamental question
of the meaning of being. In other words, the presentation of the theme "time
and being" takes place at the same time as the essential segments of the analytic
of Dasein from the first two divisions of *Being and Time* are reworked. This manner
of proceeding has the advantage that it does not presuppose the knowledge of
the first half of *Being and Time*. Heidegger could not take it for granted that
participants in the lecture course had appropriated the first half of *Being and
Time* since this work had just been published.

In order for Heidegger to respond to the fundamental-ontological question of
the meaning of being in general in the first chapter of the second part the notion
of ecstatic temporality first had to be uncovered and then introduced into the
lecture course. To this end, Heidegger chose a remarkable approach—remarkable
insofar as it is not the approach used in the second division of *Being and Time*
but precisely reverses that approach. In "Dasein and Temporality" Heidegger proceeds from care to temporality as original time in order to show how the ordinary
now-time—the only time to which we are usually accustomed—emerges from
original time. At the beginning of the second part of *The Basic Problems of Phenomenology*, Heidegger goes the opposite way, proceeding from the decisive conceptual determination of the ordinary time in Aristotle and returning step by step

to the original domain of ecstatic temporality. (This occurs in sections 19 and 20.) Near the end of section 20 Heidegger proceeds with a phenomenological explication of time as the horizon of understanding being from out of ecstatic temporality. He introduces the horizon of original time by turning his gaze toward "ecstases of temporality (future, past, and present) which are not simply shifts to . . . , not, as it were, shifts to the nothing but rather—as shifts to . . . because of the ecstatic character of each of them—they each have a *horizon* which is prescribed by the mode of the shift . . . the mode of future, past, and present, and which *belongs to the ecstasis itself*" (*BP* 302). Heidegger characterizes as "horizon" or "horizonal schema of ecstasis" the whereunto of the shift or the whither of the ecstasis (*BP* 302). The ecstatic unity of the ecstases of temporality correspond to "the unity of its horizonal schemata" (*BP* 302). For this reason Heidegger no longer speaks only of an ecstatic temporality, but also of an ecstatic-horizonal temporality. Dasein's transcending makes possible its understanding of being. But if Dasein's transcending "is founded on the ecstatic-horizonal constitution of temporality" (*BP* 302), then this temporality is the condition of the possibility of *understanding* of being as well as the condition of the possibility of being itself as a being which is understood, i.e., disclosed and lit up. This insight concludes section 20, "Temporality (*Zeitlichkeit*) and Temporality (*Temporalität*)."

Thus in the following section, 21, entitled "Temporality (*Temporalität*) and Being," Heidegger can show in an initial but fundamental way that ecstatic-horizonal unity of temporality temporally projects the being of beings that are other than Dasein. Right at the outset Heidegger emphasizes that temporality (*Temporalität*) is "the most original temporalizing of temporality (*Zeitlichkeit*) as such"—the most original within a richly articulated base of origin. Section 83 of *Being and Time* also speaks of this "original manner of temporalizing of temporality." As a fundamental response to the basic question, section 21 of *Basic Problems* offers "*a temporal [temporale] interpretation of the being of those extant entities most near to us, i.e., the being of handiness*" and shows, "in an exemplary way with regard to transcendence, how the understanding of being is temporally [*temporal*] possible" (*BP* 303, translation altered). The being whose being is projected as handiness within the horizon of original time comes up against Dasein in its concernful dealing with it. This dealing has its own temporality, which is a rendering present that retains and awaits. But it is not this temporality, but rather the more original temporality of understanding of being, that projects—and that means discloses—the handiness of the being with which Dasein is concerned. Like each way of temporalizing of temporality, the original way of temporalizing of temporality—which makes possible understanding of being—is the unity of the three ecstases of future, past, and present. The ecstasis of rendering present is decisive for the temporal projection of handiness. The direction of the shift of this emphasis aims at the *horizon of Präsenz* which is peculiar to this ecstasis. Here Heidegger makes the following crucial statements:

That which lies beyond the ecstasis as such, on the basis of its shifting character and as determined by that character—or, more precisely, that which in general deter-

mines the *whither of the "beyond itself"* as such—is *Präsenz as horizon.* Präsenz
is not identical with the present; but, as *the basic determination of the horizonal
schema of this ecstasis,* it joins in constituting the complete time-structure of the
present. The same thing applies to the other two ectases, future and past . . . ."
(*BP* 306)

In conjunction with the ecstases of future and past, the ecstasis of present projects
handiness as such onto the horizon of Präsenz. By being praesentially projected, the
being of the being that we encounter as innerworldly is understood temporally. Thus
Heidegger can state the principle: "*Accordingly we understand being from the original
horizonal schema of the ecstases of temporality.*" (*BP* 307)

The First Basic Problem: The Ontological Difference of Being and Beings

Heidegger tells us that the four basic problems of phenomenology, or of phenomenological fundamental ontology, originate from the fundamental question.
How does the first basic problem, the problem of ontological difference, originate
from the fundamental question? To what extent is this basic problem the first
of the four basic problems? Fundamental ontology is the philosophical science
of being as such, and *not simply* the philosophical science of beings as beings.
But being as such is nevertheless being of beings. However, itself not a being,
being is in its core different from beings. That is why we speak of being itself.
As differentiated from beings, being nevertheless determines beings *as* beings.
Without being, beings would not be manifest and intelligible as beings. Therefore,
we must find out how to grasp the difference between being and beings and,
furthermore, how to account for the possibility of this difference. Conceptual clarification of the difference between being and beings also requires that we determine
how being is different from beings but nevertheless belongs to beings, in that
it makes beings manifest. Only after we enact the difference between being and
beings clearly and transparently can we obtain the theme of fundamental ontology,
i.e., being as such and its meaning. Once this is obtained, we find that we have
also clarified to what extent the ontological difference between being and beings
is the first basic problem. Only after we have thoroughly and basically clarified
the difference between being and beings can we discuss the other three basic
problems, all of which concern being as such. The significant section 4 of the
introduction, "The Four Theses about Being and the Basic Problems of Phenomenology," offers a formal indication of the fundamental question and of the four
basic problems that originate from this question. It also shows that clarification
of the ontological difference depends upon a prior and explicit clarification of
the meaning of being is general, i.e., how ecstatic-horizonal temporality makes
possible the differentation of and from beings (*BP* 18). The task announced in
section 4 is met again in section 22. In its enactment of *Existenz* Dasein understands being, comports itself toward beings according to this understanding, and
thus experiences beings as beings. The difference between being and beings breaks
through, in the enactment of Dasein's *Existenz,* as a difference which is implicitly

known. As an implied understanding of being as the being of beings toward which Dasein comports itself existentially, the difference of being and beings "has the mode of being of Dasein" (*BP* 319). Therefore, the mode of being of *Existenz* can also be characterized thus: "to be in the enactment of this difference" (*BP* 319, translation altered). But because *Existenz* is enacted as self-temporalizing of ecstatic-horizonal temporality, the difference between being and beings is temporalized in the temporalization of temporality. Differentiation of being and beings is enacted in and along with the temporalization of ecstatic-horizonal temporality, in which disclosure of being as the being of *Existenz and* the being of handiness is opened up ecstatically-temporally (*zeitlich*) and horizonally-temporally (*temporal*). This takes place in such a way that beings become discoverable as handy through disclosure of praesentially projected handiness. The difference between being and beings turns out to be the difference between disclosure of a temporally determined handiness and discoveredness of a handy being as what is present.

It is important to note that the difference between being and beings can "be known expressly and explicitly and, as known, be interrogated and, as interrogated, investigated and, as investigated, conceptually comprehended" (*BP* 319) only because it is enacted on the gound of temporality and is always already temporalized with it. Only to the extent that the difference between being and beings is always already preontologically there, "*latent in Dasein's Existenz*"—i.e., is uncovered in Dasein—can this difference be made explicit and thematic. Because being "becomes a possible theme for comprehension (*logos*)" in this philosophical thematization, the explicitly enacted difference between being and beings is called "ontological difference" (*BP* 319).

THE SECOND BASIC PROBLEM: BASIC ARTICULATION IN BEING

The first basic problem—the ontological difference of being and beings just discussed—is worked out in terms of Kant's thesis that being is not a real predicate. The second basic problem is worked out in terms of a critique of the thesis of medieval ontology—whose roots go back to Aristotle—that constitution of the being of every being includes both a whatness (*essentia*) and a being-extent (*existentia*).

But to the regret of all who are interested in a complete elaboration of fundamental ontology and in the theme of "Time and Being," we find that the second elaboration of "Time and Being" is also incomplete—especially since the treatment of the second, third, and fourth basic problems is missing. One reason for this was external: the semester ended.

Nevertheless, we can derive the main thrusts of Heidegger's elaboration of the last three of the four basic problems, on the one hand, by considering section 4 and, on the other hand, by dealing with relevant chapters of the first part. (In each chapter of the first part the third section initially works out the fundamental-ontological basic problem by way of a phenomenological critique of the inadequacies of the traditional thesis.) Following this approach, we can gain insight into the other three basic problems, thus gaining an understanding of the inner systematic character of the four basic problems of phenomenological fundamental-ontology as they originate in the fundamental question.

It is above all medieval ontology—with its doctrine of *distinctio realis, modalis,* or *rationis*—which states the thesis that to every being belongs a whatness (*essentia*) and a way of being (*existentia*). Medieval ontology understands whatness and being-extant (being real) as ontological characteristics of beings. At the same time, this thesis comes up with a universal ontological claim, namely, that it pertains *to each and every being,* including humans. Medieval ontology states this thesis dogmatically. This ontology *does* indeed consider the *distinctio* in detail but it fails to inquire into its possible origin. It is this question of the origin that leads to the second fundamental-ontological basic problem. Its elaboration shows that whatness and way-of-being pertain in a wide sense to being itself and that being as such (and not only being of beings) "is essentially articulated" by both of those ontological determinations (*BP* 18). However, if being as such as being of beings other than Dasein is disclosed temporally, then the meaning of being already disclosed as temporal horizon must answer the question "why every being must and can have a what, a τί and a possible way of being" (*BP* 18). The problem of basic articulation of being is "the question of the necessary *belonging-together of whatness and way-of-being* and of *the belonging of the two of them, in their unity, together with the idea of being in general*" (*BP* 18).

However, the traditional universal ontological thesis of dividing the being of beings into whatness and extantness must be restricted and modified. However, restriction and modification do not aim at the division of being as such, but rather at the dogmatic claim that all beings have only one mode or kind of being, namely the *existentia,* and that beings differ from one another only through their whatness and not through their kind of being (cf. *BP* 119 ff.). The first being not to remain within this universally formulated thesis of the tradition is that being whose mode of being is not *existentia,* but rather *Existenz,* that being which understands being. It is this mode of being that is most proper to Dasein which does not allow the ontological constitution of Dasein to have something like reality or whatness (*quidditas, essentia*). The mode of being of *Existenz* points, not to the whatness, but to the whoness of Dasein. Who Dasein is in each case is determined in accordance with how it comports itself in its being toward this being. The being of Dasein is never articulated in terms of *essentia* and *existentia* but in terms of the distinction of *Existenz* and whoness.

Likewise, the traditional thesis of the *distinctio* of being in *essentia* and *existentia* is invalid for all beings that are other than Dasein. The necessary restriction and modification of this thesis extends even to beings other than Dasein because these beings too are not generally and uniformly extant in the whatness respective to each. *Existentia* is also not the only mode of being of beings other than Dasein but only one way of being among many. And because this mode of being prescribes the corresponding whatness of beings, only the mode of being of extantness (*existentia*) can *traditionally* prescribe thinghood. By contrast, the mode of being of handiness prescribes as its corresponding whatness that which Heidegger calls *Bewandtnis.* A third mode of being of beings other than Dasein is life, which prescribes the independent whatness of a living being—a whatness that can be grasped neither as thinghood nor as *Bewandtnis*. Finally, as the fourth mode of being of a being other than Dasein, Heidegger mentions *Bestand* and *Beständigkeit*, i.e., "constants" and "constancy," which are the mode of being of geometrical and arithmetic relations. This mode of being also prescribes an independent whatness of these beings. The traditional problem of *distinctio*, which fundamental ontology transforms into the problem of the basic articulation of being, proves to be a very complicated problem. For as far as the basic articulation of being as such is concerned, we are dealing with the division into *Existenz* and *Mitdasein*, on the one hand handiness, extantness, life, and constants—while on the other hand we are dealing with whoness, *Bewandtnis*, thinghood, and the whatness of living beings as well as of constancy.

However, we can understand the second basic problem only after we grasp it in connection with the first basic problem. The problem of the basic articulation of being "is only a more specialized question concerning the ontological difference in general" (*BP* 120). In its difference from beings, being is not simple, but articulated—and not in a singular manner but in manifold ways. The articulation, varying as it does in accordance with each mode of being, participates in the difference between beings and being and thus in the ontological difference. Everything that pertains to the articulation of being must be thought in terms of the ontological difference of being and beings.

The Third Basic Problem: Modifications of Being and the Unity of Its Multiplicity

The third basic problem is worked out in a critical discussion of the central thesis of modern ontology that begins with Descartes. According to this thesis, the basic modes of being are *res cogitans* (the being of spirit) and *res extansa* (the being of nature). When we outlined the second basic problem, we had to anticipate a portion of the third basic problem, namely, the multiplicty of the modes of being. Exposition of this basic problem proceeds from the observation that, in addition to its whatness (which is now only a part of the thematic), every being has a way-to-be. The third basic problem is concerned with a systematic fundamental-ontological thematization of modes of being. Tradition states that the "way-to-be" has the same character for all beings. However, the fundamental-ontological critique of this thesis demonstrates a multiplicity of differentiated modes of being. In particular, this critique reveals the mode of being which is incomparably peculiar to human beings, as the mode of being of *Existenz*, that being which understands being.

At first sight it looks as if the modern ontology of Descartes and Kant had already put forth—for the first time—this difference between the mode of being of spirit and person, on the one hand, and the mode of being of nature and reality on the other. But, if we look more closely, we see that that difference is, strictly speaking, not a difference between modes of being but a difference in the whatness of beings. Modern ontology, too, knows only one mode of being, namely extantness; and it is on this basis that this ontology differentiates *res cogitans* from *res extensa,* person from thing. But if there are several modes of being, then we must ask which are the basic ways of being. Moreover, we must ask "how the multiplicity of ways-of-being is possible and how it is at all understandable from out of the meaning of being" (*BP* 18). And finally the question emerges as to "how we can speak at all of a unitary concept of being, despite the multiplicty of ways-of-being" (*BP* 18).

As we saw in connection with the second basic problem, Heidegger differentiates five—or six—basic ways of being in all: *Existenz, Mitdasein,* handiness, extantness, life, and constants. As a mode of being, *Mitdasein* does not mean others who exist as Dasein does but the mode of being of the other. As a mode of being, *Mitdasein* is not only a variation of my own mode of being (of *Existenz*) but also a specific and irreducible mode of being on the basis of which I encounter the other as a stranger.

The traditional distinction of being in *res cogitans* (person) and *res extensa* (reality) is made under the "guidance of an overarching concept of being" according to which being means extantness (*BP* 176). The radical difference between Dasein's constitution of being and the constitution of beings other than Dasein is manifest only in the fundamental ontological difference between modes of being of *Existenz* and extantness in the wider sense. But the mode of being of Dasein and the mode of being of beings other than Dasein prove to be "so disparate that it seems at first as though the two ways of being are incomparable and cannot be determined by way of a unified concept of being in general" (*BP* 176). It is a question of "the unity of the concept of being in reference to a possible multiplicity of ways-of-being" (*BP* 176). Because discussion of the third basic problem does not exist, the question concerning the unity of the concept of being is left without an answer. Nevertheless, the entire discourse of the fundamental-ontological inquiry and its thinking process allow us to respond to this question. The unity of the concept of being is given in the unity of the meaning of being in general, i.e., in the unity of the ecstatic-temporal (*zeitlich*) and horizonal-temporal (*temporal*) disclosure or clearing of being in general.

THE FOURTH BASIC PROBLEM: THE TRUTH-CHARACTER OF BEING

The fourth basic problem emerges in a critical discussion of the thesis on the being of the copula which, since Aristotle, belongs to logic and its history. In the proposition S is P, "is" connects S to P. Any apophantic *logos* thus conceived is either true or false. This means that being true or not being true is connected to the being of the copula. Logic recognizes the connection between being and truth only in this form that is established in various ways. But this form can serve as a point of departure for getting at the fundamental-ontological problem that resides in the truth-character of being as such. The showing which occurs in the predicative proposition is a predicative disclosing of beings, which as such is founded in a prepredicative, primary disclosing of these beings. Truthfulness of the proposition is a predicative truth that is founded in the prepredicative truth of beings, i.e., in their prepredicative manifestness.

Prepredicative discovery of beings is, in turn, rooted in the understanding of the being of those beings to be discovered. It is disclosure of beings which belongs to the *Existenz* of Dasein that makes possible the primary discovery of beings and the discoveredness or truth of these beings. But it is disclosedness itself which is the most original phenomenon of truth. Discoveredness as truth (unconcealedness) of beings, which in turn grounds the predicative truth of a proposition, is what is founded in disclosedness as the truth (unconcealedness) of being.

Manifestness as unconcealedness belongs to being as its own truth. Thus it must be said: "Being is given only if there is disclosure, that is to say, if there is truth" (*BP* 18). But there is only truth as manifestness of being "if a being exists which opens up, i.e., which discloses . . . " (*BP* 18). This opening up belongs "to the mode of being of this being" (*BP* 18); it belongs to the thrown projection and to the ecstatic horizonal temporality of Dasein. There is being "only when truth exists, i.e., when Dasein exists" (*BP* 222). For only with Dasein is disclosure opened up ecstatically and horizonally—a disclosure in which alone there is being. There is not being without disclosure, without its manifestness as its truth. But then this means: "being and truth [are] essentially related to each other" (*BP* 223). However, because disclosure is opened up ecstatically-temporally (*zeitlich*) and horizonally-temporally (*temporal*), the truth of being itself is constituted according to time (*zeithaft*).

Having brought out and clarified the systematic and fundamental structuring of the question of being in its fundamental-ontological mode, we can now turn our gaze to the same being question as it gets worked out within the context of the history of being—as presented in *Beiträge zur Philosophie (Vom Ereignis)* (*GA* 65). In this context let me simply formulate a series of questions, without going into them here: What becomes of the fundamental question of the meaning of being when it gets elaborated within the history of being? In what way does the question of the unity of *Zeitlichkeit* and *Temporalität* get transformed? In what way does the ontological difference between beings and being get transformed? What changes occur in the basic articulation of being itself and in the problem of the multiplicity of being's ways and their unity? And, finally, what happens to the truth-character of being?

DAVID WOOD

10. Reiterating the Temporal

Toward a Rethinking of
Heidegger on Time

Is it possible to share Heidegger's sense of the scope and importance of the time question and yet be unhappy with the course of his development of that question, especially after the twenties? Time is of central importance to philosophy: first, because very many philosophical questions can be reformulated as questions about time; second, because the various forms of philosophical questioning can be distinguished by their general orientation toward time; and, finally, because both what we call *life* (or *existence*) and what we think of as *world-time* can be dramatically illuminated by the ongoing project of analyzing temporal structures.

Yet, although it is Heidegger who has most powerfully formulated such a critical place for time (both for understanding the philosophical tradition and in our continuing to *think*), I share with Derrida the sense that there is a lingering commitment to something like the privilege of presence in his thought, particularly exhibited in the continuing quest for the primordial. I seek to re-engage with the task of articulating the temporal, a task that Heidegger frames in terms of the transcendental horizon for the question of Being, while at the same time dismantling these very terms and the trajectory they supply to Heidegger's thought.[1]

This paper has something of the shape of a spider's web after the struggle with the fly—there are some ragged holes and many signs of recent disturbance. When Hegel writes, "A mended sock is better than a torn one. Not so with self-consciousness."[2] I would like to think that the same can be claimed for writing.

Heidegger's effective subtitle for *Being and Time* was: "The Interpretation of Dasein in Terms of Temporality, and the Explication of Time as the Transcendental Horizon for the Question of Being" (*SZ* ix). I am not alone in having been captivated by these words and their promise. And yet the book that opened with the big question ends with questions that one would think it ought to have answered: "How is the [ecstatic] temporalizing of temporality to be interpreted? Is there a way which leads from primordial *time* to the meaning of *Being*? Does *time* itself manifest itself as the horizon of *Being*?" Three and a half years later, in *Kant and the Problem of Metaphysics*, and particularly in section 4, the project of fundamental ontology is restated, repeated, perhaps for the last time. After that the problem of time and temporality *as such* recedes.[3] When time reappears, in the lecture

"Time and Being" (1962), it is virtually unrecognizable.

I cannot attempt here a reconstruction of Heidegger's own path, but I would like nonetheless to venture a few remarks on what we could call a temporal repetition of Heidegger's project. The complexity of the issues involved is formidable, and I cannot claim to have even begun to address them all, let alone to have any adequate articulation of them. But I hope at least to indicate a certain direction of thought.

I begin from three senses of unease. First, that Heidegger's thinking about time and temporality in the twenties opened up paths not taken, and that we might come to find these paths compelling. Second, that there are some very general philosophical dangers attached to the path Heidegger did take in pursuing the question of Being. Third, and more specifically, at the point at which, arguably, a key temporal concept does emerge—with the *Geschick des Seins*, the destiny of Being—there is a serious danger of the ratio of darkness to light becoming overpowering. My attitude toward Heidegger is, at least superficially, not unlike Heidegger's to Husserl, when he continued to read his *Logical Investigations* long after Husserl had moved on.

I will try to present these sources of unease as at least plausible grounds for a return to Heidegger's thought of the twenties. The scope of this paper is not limited to a redirecting of our reading of Heidegger. But the breathtaking scope and depth of his own attempts both to rethink the major philosophers of time—particularly Aristotle, Augustine, Kant, and Hegel—as well as the rest of the tradition, make him *indépassable*.

Finally, and most difficult, I want to suggest ways in which it might be possible to think of Being, the a priori, transcendence, the ontological difference, primordiality—all the values which drive Heidegger forward after 1929, and drive him away from time and the temporal—in a very different way.

This last part is the most speculative and the least complete. It represents a preparedness to take what one might call the heroic (perhaps suicidal) course of trying to accommodate and translate all of Heidegger's "ontological" concerns rather than simply treating them as symptoms of some sort of folly. It would involve saying of these what Heidegger says of the traits of the common conception of time, that ". . . they are not simply arbitrary fabrications and inventions. The essence of time must itself make these kinds of conceptions possible and even plausible" (*GA* 26: 198).

THE PROJECT OF *BEING AND TIME*

I began by referring to the very brief period in which the project of *Being and Time* flowered and faded. In fact we could push this back to the summer of 1924, and Heidegger's lecture "The Concept of Time," or to his lecture course on *The History of the Concept of Time (GA* 20) in the summer of 1925, which has been called his "proto-*SZ*."[4] The published version of this course prepares us for the care Heidegger takes to prepare the way for the project and also for his subsequent repeated failure to complete the outline of his course. Here he manages only a final fifteen pages dealing with "The Exposition of Time Itself," after three hundred closely corresponding to the first half of *Being and Time* as we know it. He discusses particularly the relation between death, authenticity and Dasein's being a whole.

This relation sets the theme for much of the second division of *Being and Time*,[5] which is heavily structured by the search for a way of understanding Dasein as a whole, by the distinctions between authentic and inauthentic temporality, between *Geschehen* (Historizing) and *Geschichtlichkeit* (Historicality), and by the need to both describe and account for the ordinary concept of time and to contrast to it an ecstatic-horizonal one. But there is a wider frame to these discussions which Heidegger describes as follows: "Our aim is . . . to work out the question of the meaning of *Being* and to do so concretely. Our *provisional* (vorlaufiges) aim [emphasis mine] is the interpretation of *time* as the possible horizon for any understanding whatsoever of Being." The place of time in the text is from the very beginning, subservient to the question of the meaning of Being. If time were not seen as the key to the meaning of Being, it would not be entertained. The term that bears the weight here is *vorlaufiges,* which means *provisional,* but also *temporary, for the present* and (even more amusingly in English), *for the time being.* What does this tell us? Let us leave aside the fact that he understands his own text as a treatise with a purpose and a path, in which, we might suppose, the discussion of time is to be subordinated to the question of Being according to a quite traditional temporal schema. The important thing is that Heidegger is introducing the relation between Being and Time in terms of priority, difference, and deferment. And his treatment of time in his subsequent three lecture courses consistently bears out this subordination.

The most obvious thing to learn from this is how misplaced it would be to complain when Heidegger turns away from time and the temporal in pursuit of the question of the meaning of Being. For not only at the beginning of *Being and Time* but in many other places, he repeatedly insists on the ontological interest he has in time, and how this cannot be in the ordinary sense of *being extended in time,* which would not distinguish us from rocks. If that is so, the restricted nature of Heidegger's interest in time is hardly one we could challenge. But there is one possibility that this intimate link of priority, deferment, and difference between Being and Time occludes. It is the possibility that Being might be nothing other than Time. As a guiding proposition this would caution against the turning away from time in pursuit of the question of Being. It might enforce a kind of discipline on what one thought it possible to say about Being. For the implication would be that everything that one previously thought one could build *on* ecstatic temporality, one would have to think through it. One would have to develop ways of thinking in which mapping, overlayings, interweavings, readings, harmonic co-ordination, would substitute for foundational ones. Being would be nothing but a way of timing.

The distinction between *Zeitlichkeit* and *Temporalität,* for example, which is fundamental to the working of *Being and Time,* is presented in terms of an "as" relation. Heidegger writes that "*Temporalität* means *Zeitlichkeit* insofar as *Zeitlich-*

keit itself is made into a theme as a condition of the possibility of the understanding of being and of ontology as such" (*GA* 24: 324). These two terms do not, as Heidegger puts it, quite coincide. And in 1936, in a rare return to such language, this slippage turns into a gulf, and he links *Temporalität* and *Ereignis*.[6] My point is: what would it be to think in temporal terms this very *as*-relation between *Zeitlichkeit* and *Temporaltät*? What would it be like to fold back time onto itself, to thicken and stratify it rather than depart the scene? But let us return to *Being and Time*. Part I, the only published part ends, as we have said, with the question as to whether "time itself manifest[s] itself as the horizon of Being" that the book set itself to answer. In 1927 in *The Basic Problems of Phenomenology*, we find a phenomenological working through of medieval ontology in relation to Kant, and (in chapter 4) he addresses the fundamental ontological presuppositions of logic. In part 2, we move from "traditional discussions" back to fundamental ontology, but more particularly, Heidegger immediately broaches the problem of the ontological difference through Time, *Zeitlichkeit* and *Temporalität*. At the end of this part 2, Heidegger's tone is very different from that of *Being and Time*. This time, having taken the route through Kant's conception of the transcendental, he can claim to have shown that " . . . time is the primary horizon of transcendental science, of ontology, or in short, it is the transcendental horizon. It is for this reason [he goes on] that the title of the first part of the investigation of *Being and Time* reads 'The Interpretation of Dasein in Terms of Temporality, and the Explication of Time as the Transcendental Horizon for the Question of Being.'" The very last section seems to sum things up most satisfactorily. He describes phenomenology as "Temporal or transcendental science" (contrasted with positive science), and he begins to link the transcendental temporality required to think the "a priori" to the Platonic conception of anamnesis.

Aritstotle makes an appearance in *The Metaphysical Foundations of Logic*, but this time the central figure is Leibniz, and again it is the problem of Transcendence that ushers in the discussions of time. Now famously, Heidegger affirms the essential neutrality—prior to any concrete, including sexual factuality—of Dasein in *Being and Time*, and he describes Dasein as essentially dispersed. More importantly, and though some have wished to underplay this, Heidegger thinks through again the idea of fundamental ontology, and argues for "a special problematic which has for its theme beings as a whole . . . [and which would deal with] the metaphysics of existence . . . [and even] the question of an ethics" (*GA* 26: 199). This he calls metontology. He describes it as arising within "the essence of ontology itself and is the result of its overturning [*Umschlag*], its *metabole*" (*GA* 26: 199). Now, it is not wholly clear what this refers to, and Heidegger does not to my knowledge explicitly come back to it, though the transformation of the fundamental question in *Introduction to Metaphysics* would seem to reflect this ontic dimension. But one way of reading it would be as a sign of what is to come, namely, the breakdown of the very project of fundamental ontology, which runs parallel to the move away from time and the transcendental.[7] There are, I believe, other seeds of the move away from time in the last sections of this book. But I ought to make explicit what I mean by *moving away from time and temporal,* because it reflects my whole orientation toward Heidegger. In the difference between *Zeitlichkeit and Temporalität* there is the beginning of a fascinating lexical movement which one might almost call Hegelian. *Temporalität* is *Zeitlichkeit* insofar as . . . (as we have suggested above). The Hegelian version would be that *Temporalität* is the *truth of Zeitlichkeit.* When I talk of moving away from time and the temporal, I mean moving away from the continued reference back to *Zeitlichkeit,* and the increasing preparedness to discuss *Temporalität* on its own, and finally to abandon it in favor of overtly atemporal language. But what would it be to be faithful to the complexities of the *existentiell* and *Zeitlichkeit?*

Let us look at one of the seeds of this development, bearing in mind that Heidegger thinks he has now *shown* that time is the transcendental horizon for the question of Being, that he has answered the last question in *Being and Time.* In section 12 ("Transcendence and temporality") Heidegger confronts what he sees as a danger, namely, that we may come to see the three temporal ecstases—making-present, coming-towards, and having-been—as having a unity which after all has some kind of presentness itself, so that one could finally say that this ecstatic unity is what time *is.* He has previously countered this by saying that *time temporalizes (itself),* which avoids in its linguistic expression suggesting a reduction of time to identity.[8] Here, and he is specifically trying to differentiate his position from Bergson and his *élan vital,* he suggests that "the unity of the ecstases is itself ecstatic." Again, trying to capture this, he writes: "Temporalization is the free oscillation of the whole of primordial temporality; time reaches and contracts itself." Heidegger also tries to transcendentalize, one might say, the idea of *horizon* (as when it is said that time is the horizon for the question of Being). Each *ecstasis* is both a being-carried-away, an overcoming of barriers, and produces a kind of closure, or horizon. Heidegger suggests we think of there being a primordial horizonal unity corresponding to the unity of the *ecstases.* He calls this horizonal unity *ecstematic.* I must now quote the paragraph that follows in full:

> This ecstematic unity of the horizon of temporality is nothing other than the temporal condition for the possibility of *world* and the world's essential belonging to transcendence. For transcendence has its possibility in the unity of ecstatic momentum. This oscillation [*Schwingung*] of the self-temporalizing ecstases is, as such, the upswing [*Überschwung*] regarded as [swinging] toward all possible beings that can factically enter there into a world. The ecstematic temporalizes itself, oscillating as a worlding [*Welten*]. *World entry* happens only insofar as something like ecstatic oscillation temporalizes itself as a particular temporality. (*GA* 26: 270)

The response we have to this kind of discourse determines the way we think about Heidegger's whole trajectory. And I confess I find myself at something of a loss for words. Perhaps I could resort to the minimal coherence of a *string* of comments. I think this passage is seminal in connecting the work of the twenties to the later concerns, particularly the return to the question of Time in "Time and Being." In the word oscillation there are strong adumbrations of the later discussion of the *Zuspiel,* the interplay between the three dimensions of time, which he calls "the true extending, playing in the very heart of time" (*TB* 15). This would give us a stronger sense of the continuity of Heidegger's project. So too would the parallels between this upswing and the *es gibt* and *Geschick*. Heidegger's discussion of the way an ecstatic horizon opens up a certain space could be said to presage the remarks about freedom, and about destiny and fate.

What this suggests is at least that, even if we read these texts of the late twenties as working within a problematic that is about to be shattered, that they already prepare the way for this shattering. And this preparation is accomplished by certain very specific moves that Heidegger makes, one hesitates to say *almost without thinking*, but certainly repeatedly, and without accompanying justification. What I am talking about is the announcement of the requirement of *unity* of a differentiated set that he has already analyzed transcendentally. This unity cannot, however, be ontic, nor can it be transcendental in any sense that would carry the burden of a deeper sense of presence. So it has to be understood in a way that would not have these drawbacks. Heidegger hits on *free oscillation* as a way of describing this new deeper nonobjective unity. This then allows the parallel construction of a corresponding horizonal (ecstematic) unity. And the celebratory paragraph we quoted is the result.

Now I must confess to lingering Kantian worries about this language; it is not clear to me that opposing a *way of thinking* to philosophical method can allow one to dispense with certain constitutive rules of intelligibility. In fact there are rules that *drive* as well as constitute this discourse. But in formulating them it will become apparent that my analytic intentions are predatory.

We *could* say that Heidegger assumes not just the value but the fact of *unity* here, and that by doing so, he evinces a prejudice in favor of the simple and the stable. We could claim that this prejudice is metaphysical and argue that this in itself is a reason to treat much of his later work with suspicion. But equally we could say that this is not simple prejudice—it is a way of justifying the march of a certain reflexive, syntactic intensification, in which simples get divided, divided things get opened out, the opened out divided things get drawn together into a unity, that unity then divides (oscillates) and moves (swings). And if we graft onto this the *Geschick des Seins,* we would find a rhythmic approaching and withdrawal of what oscillates and swings.

Heidegger has a defense against the charge of metaphor,[9] which essentially claims that the ontic meaning (of *house*, say) which we might think was proper, is actually only fully grasped through a kind of meditative thinking. In this case, the fact that the regions and movements addressed by this discourse cannot be found within what we call space and time, within the world, is a confirmation, not a refutation, of their sense, for it is the possibility of space, time, and world that is the issue. However, this only opens, if you like, a *logical* space; it does not tell us how to understand what is being said. We can undoubtedly link Heidegger's discourse to the limit discourse of other philosophers (think of Husserl on time as an Absolute Flux) and, if one thinks of oscillation, swinging, and vibration, there are undoubtedly echoes of Christian mysticism. But this only compounds the problem.

I have elsewhere charged that tapestry we call the philosophical tradition with a lack of interest in the complexity of time. My general project could be described as a persistence in the attempt to translate the transcendental into the temporal by dropping assumptions about linearity, unidimensionality, and so on. Nietzsche's account of the eternal recurrence is in this respect exemplary. The consequences for Heidegger's own quasi-transcendental discourse about temporality is highly contentious, but basically it would mean treating each of his moves as pointing to and indeed exemplifying the possibility of levels of intensification (and dispersion) of ontic time. Just to give one absolutely concrete example: the relation between the unity of the three ecstases and the three ecstases would be no different in kind from the relationship between a chord and the three notes from which it was composed, or perhaps, better, a tune and its notes. Again, the relation between *Zeitlichkeit* and *Temporalität* would be no different in kind from the relation between a sound and its being repeated as a note. This is what was meant above by *folding back*. Heidegger's whole discourse is, however unwillingly, a conceptual construction that points away from the temporal toward its conditions of possibility. My question is whether a complex account of existential time might not be able to accommodate all that Heidegger wants to say. Surely Heidegger begins with *the everyday (or philosophically commonplace) view of everyday time*, to which he then opposes alternatives. But what if everyday time were actually multi-stranded (not just entangled[10] in some negative sense); what if the units and styles of its measurement were not only not unifiable, but never thought to exhaust our everyday understanding. What if there were a fundamental problem of escaping from our models of time which needs to be resolved before we describe authentic time and primordial time?

I will not attempt to summarize the last major volume in this series of reworkings of *Being and Time*, but suffice it to say that Heidegger's 1929 *Kant and the Problem of Metaphysics* continues to pursue the intimate connection between time and fundamental ontology through a reading of Kant. His assessment of the importance of the transcendental imagination in the first critique and its fate in the second edition is such as to suggest that Kant's defense of reason here meets an abyss, from which he turns away—the essential finitude of man. Heidegger tries to show the inherently temporal character of Kant's laying of the foundation of metaphysics (i.e., transcendence). Heidegger treats the transcendental imagination as a ground for the unity of sensibility and understanding which is "also the root of both stems." This "root" grows out of primordial time. And this primordial time can be seen to unify the three modes of pure synthesis—pure apprehension, pure reproduction, and pure recognition—as the temporalizing of time. "Ontological knowledge," he writes, "is made up of 'transcendental determinations of time' because transcendence is temporalized in primordial time" (*KM* 191). Heidegger later offers us a succinct review of *Being and Time*, focused on the problem of philosophy as forgetting. But this treatment of Kant does not so much advance the course of fundamental ontology, to which he is still here committed, as demonstrate his ability to translate Kant into his own terms, hence the remark of Cassirer[11] that he reads Kant as a usurper. The three pages of questions with which he ends the book (and which ask about the way forward from Kant to Hegel that would reinstate "Logic as the system of Pure Reason"), raise in sharpened form the limitations posed by Dasein's finitude and restate the primacy of the question of Being as that of our friendship toward "the essential, the simple, and the stable" (*KM* 239). The *Basic Problems* ended with a long quotation from Kant defending philosophy against the philosophy of feeling; the *Metaphysical Foundations of Logic* takes us back from Leibniz to Plato with a quotation from the *Republic* linking transcendence and Being; and the *Kant* book ends with a quotation from Aristotle—to the effect that what we have always sought and has always eluded us is Being. Heidegger, in other words, demonstrates an extraordinary persistence in maintaining the focus on the question of Being, and on the question of time as a necessary path to pondering that question. In articulating these doubts about the later course of his thinking, I asked whether or not the very intimacy Heidegger insists on between Time and Being was not a subtle exclusion of the possibility that they might be one and the same (by which I do *not* mean that they belong together). In this light, and in the light of the course of his later development, consider this final quotation from *Kant and the Problem of Metaphysics:* "If the problematic of metaphysics is designated as that of Being and Time [*Sein und Zeit*] the explication which has been given concerning the idea of a fundamental ontology makes it clear that it is the conjunction "and" in the above title which expresses the central problem" (*KM* 235). My claim is that this problem had already been resolved by the subordination of Time to Being at the very beginning of *Being and Time*. What then could the question of time mean? He concludes: "Neither Being nor time need be deprived of the meanings which they have until now, but a more primordial explication of these terms must establish their justification and limits" (*KM* 235). This sits most uneasily with the claim made in a number of places in these books that the words time and temporal no longer have their ordinary meanings. Heidegger's central move, which appears in the Kant book (*KM* 233–34) and elsewhere is to argue that the *a priority* of Being is a temporal determination requiring a different sense of time to be thought. What we have to ask is whether the engine of primordiality which generates these other times is not itself questionable. This, surely, is the point of Derrida's claim[12] that no alternative conception of time will escape from being metaphysical. To dig deeper, to find an even earlier time, may indeed attract these difficulties. My question would be whether we are still operating not with models of everyday time, but everyday models of time, which need radical revision.[13]

It is this possibility that I would like to have opened up by an all too brief review of the way in which Heidegger continued to pursue the project laid out in *Being and Time*. Using words that will perhaps give a hostage to fortune, Heidegger after this period finds other horses to ride in pursuit of the question of Being, and allows the gap between time and its ontological appropriation to grow to the point at which the latter separates off and takes on a life of its own. I, on the other hand, at least imagine another way forward, in which we do not so much supplement the ordinary concept of time with authentic and primordial additions as we explore further the structural complexities of the temporal in the hope that the question of Being might be, if not solved, at least dissolved in the process. Furthermore, I am not convinced by the necessity or the propriety of the release of the Being question from the horizon of Time, and I would like in the second section to explain why.

TURNING AWAY FROM TIME

I am, of course, not the first to want to rethink the path that leads from *Being and Time*. More than anyone else, Heidegger himself did that. Indeed, the very path he took was the product of such continuing reflection. In his *Letter on Humanism* he answers the question of whether *Being and Time* was a blind alley with a powerful and indignant affirmation of its problematic: the truth of Being. But the only references to time in this response are in the importance of persistence, patience, and warning against illusory measures of progress. In "The End of Philosophy and the Task of Thinking," he says he has been trying "again and again since 1930 to shape the question of *Being and Time* in a more primordial fashion . . . to subject the point of departure in *Being and Time* to an immanent criticism" (*SD* 61).[14] He floats the idea of substituting the title *Opening and Presence* for *Being and Time,* but such a translation would not free us from questioning. We would still have to ask: "But where does the opening come from and how is it given?" The book, he seems to be saying, is or has a destiny. His fidelity to its *Sache,* the matter of thinking, is unchanged. But, again, there is no reference here to time or temporality, while there is a great deal of talk of the open, the free open, lighting, *Präsenz,* and so on. It is as if the reference to the *transcendental horizon* in the original formulation of the project of *Being and Time* has not simply been dropped, but in its death has spawned a productive *space* of questioning that has entirely displaced time and temporality. If this is so, it is because time as it is dealt with in *Being and Time* has become inessential—a possible solution to a problem that remains, unsolved. Time, the harlot of philosophers through the ages, has been ditched when found wanting.

Of course, this is not quite true. Time has been displaced only in the sense that its place has shifted. It remains, wedded as ever to ontological duties, and it appears in the form of destiny. But as Heidegger will explain in "Time and Being," *time* now means something very different. I shall argue that this new determination of time in terms of the thinking that comes to a head in "Time and Being" represents a loss as much as a gain.

To do this, I will first nibble away at some of the basic assumptions that drive Heidegger's thought and argue that the weakness of these pillars importantly affects the viability of the later Heidegger's choice of language, and hence the move away from *Zeitlichkeit.* I shall be attempting, against the tide, to take up a certain distance from Heidegger. The general form of this distance is to say that the central thrust of Heidegger's later thought is corrupt, and that this corruption is not eliminable by any repair work. This corruption is an *unthought* in his texts which yet sustains them.

There are two aspects or dimensions to what I am calling corruption here.

In each case, we are concerned with a feature of *thinking* which importantly compromises its purity. This essential corruption forces us, I believe, to reassess what is undertaken in its name, and what it excludes. For it is hard to accept that it can exclude at one level what already corrupts it at another. The two directions of corruption I have chosen to discuss are: (1) ontic discourse, and (2) the "machinery" of Heidegger's thought. I will argue that the ontic roots of Heidegger's language from *Sorge* to *es gibt* fatally injure attempts at a thinking that would, in his words, think "Being without reference to beings." And I will argue that it is possible to begin to give an account of the hidden law of Heidegger's thought, of which he says he is not in command (*GA* 13: 9–13). (Those who object to this law being called machinery would be endorsing what I want to say about ontic discourse.) The combined consequence of such essential corruptions is in effect to pose a series of questions: Does not the attempt to ask the question of Being rest on the possibility of a privileged language, or at least a language privileged in its relation to language? Is the claimed continuity of the matter of thinking any *more than* that of lexical daisy-chains that join ownness to appropriation, to property, to belonging, to hearing, to giving, to the gift, and so on? And what possible ground can there be for privileging *this particular chain*. These questions are not gratuitous. If it is the lure of this discourse—together, it must be said, with the luminotopological discourse of opening, clearing, and lighting—that permits the displacement of time and the temporal, then a certain abrasion of that lure might draw us back to the point at which time would have a different future.

I will begin with some doubts about Heidegger's ontic discourse. By ontic discourse I mean particularly the chain of terms associated with property and dwelling: giving, sending, granting, bestowing, preserving, withholding, belonging, withdrawing, nearing, abiding, opening, spacing, etc. In my view it is a fundamental intellectual obligation to retain a certain exteriority in reading Heidegger, even if one cannot simply go around him, and even if the very idea of exteriority to such a thinker is essentially problematic. And if, one by one, or in small clusters, we can learn to follow and perhaps operate with each of these terms, there comes a time when we begin to notice the common space they occupy—which we could call the space of a primitive economy—an economy prior to mediated exchange, prior to money, prior to representation, and so on.[15] Heidegger not only never *pauses* over this language, but he also never questions or thinks it as a whole, understandably perhaps. But I do not see how we can avoid thinking it.

Allow me, if I may, to pose a methodological question. What is it to reflect like this on Heidegger's language? What kind of event is it to come to hear another refrain amid the notes? This question, I would claim, is absolutely central to understanding what is and what is not happening in Heidegger's *On the Way to Language*, and in a curiously redoubled way. Heidegger announces, at the beginning of "The Nature of Language," his aim "to bring us face to face with the possibility of undergoing an experience with language," an experience in which our usual unthinking use of language is disturbed. Does the dawning sense that a certain discourse is wedded to a particular unspoken economy count as such an experience? I will return to this question a little later in my discussion of Heidegger's machinery.

The primitiveness of this discourse is not thematic for Heidegger for the simple reason that it is through what we could almost call its gift of certain possibilities of syntactic transformation that he can pursue his speculative dehiscence of the *is*. The word Being (*Sein*) itself offers certain possibilities—more in German than in English—while the verbal form of the *is* suggests a much greater wealth of expansion, especially through the rich articulation of tenses. And the two divisions of *Being and Time* could be said to be structured first by an articulation of Being, and second, by an expansion of the *is* through the complexities of tense. Our capacity to position ourselves through the use of complex tense is an extraordinarily fruitful field for philosophical inquiry. The diverse possibilities languages provide for this would suggest different kinds of temporal openness. Heidegger is clearly also concerned with *mood,* both in *Being and Time* and later in his discussions of activity and passivity. We may suppose that the possibility of dehiscence of the *is* in directions other than tense is part of what drives the turn after the twenties.

The interpretation of the other *is*—of identity—as belonging-together points in the same direction.

Heidegger is working his way through the manifold meanings of Being by pursuing tense and mood in the *is* of existence and predication, and by a kind of relational deconstruction of the *is* of identity. The moment of translation (especially of Parmenides, Heraclitus, and Anaximander) is the point of maximum vulnerability to such a dehiscence. It is not clear to me that Heidegger always made the distinctions I am making here, but the project of the dual dehiscent articulation of the *is* is clear.

The tension between the articulation of these two *is*'s both affects the internal organization of *Being and Time*—especially the subjection of *Zeitlichkeit* to considerations of identity through authenticity and the struggle between *Zeitlichkeit* and *Temporalität*, between *Gegenwärtigkeit* and *Anwesenheit,* and between the Heidegger of the twenties and the later Heidegger.

The dehiscence of the *is* of identity into questions of belonging, possession, gift, and so on is a double gesture. Introducing the relationality of belonging into identity involves difference, irreducible division. This difference is contained, first by its articulation within the static lexicon of primitive (premercantile) economy in which the relationship between the self and what Kierkegaard called the constituting Power is articulated in terms of primitive economic relations, and second, by its subjection to a time ultimately determined by considerations of identity. This primitive relational lexicon derives its positive power from the thought that it could reverse the condensation effects locked into identity, or presence. But the caged creature is only released into a pen, in which the bars are stronger and the locks more secure.

What is put into play in this lexicon of giving, belonging, bestowing, etc., are various contained forms of identity-constituting and identity-generating relationships. But their containment is assured from the outset. It is assured by the economy that frames this lexicon, which essentially excludes representation, signs, structure . . . and we might add, writing, excludes the outside, and in particular excludes, in an important respect, time. When Heidegger returns to time (in "Time and Being") it is to bind it to space, to displace it, to emasculate its possibilities.

The containment of this economy is assured—in the sense that the law of enchainment that would add terms to the series states that no new term shall introduce dispersion, or representation; no new term shall introduce alien currency into the economy.

Heidegger, on the occasion of his refusal of the Berlin chair in March 1934, in what is undoubtedly a political statement too, wrote of his work, "being intimately rooted in the life of the peasants" (*GA* 13: 10). It is here, too, that he talks of the fundamental way in which he is not in command of the hidden law of his own work and of peasant existence wanting to be left to its own law.[16]

Enormous questions open up here. We would have to work through Heidegger's relation to Dilthey's *Weltanschauung-philosophie,* and the whole refusal of psychologism, anthropologism, and so on. But the question has to be asked: What is the hidden law of his work, and what is the law of the peasants' existence, and what connection can we make between the law of this *dwelling* and the lexicon of primitive economy that Heidegger deploys in his thought. Even accepting Heidegger's valuation of "simple rough existence,"[17] his own concern with *dwelling* might suggest radically different forms of primitivism generating radically different base lexicons. Nomadic herdsmen and fisherman might come up with the tent and the boat of Being respectively, and joking apart, the associative chains attached to such modes of dwelling could be quite different. Heidegger has, I claim, attempted the dehiscence of Being (as identity) through belonging, having, reaching, sending, etc.—through primitive modes of human interaction refigured as modes of mediated self-relation, and developed with a certain autonomy. As primitive forms, we might suppose they would be at least universal and hence philosophically illuminating. But they are not presented as a lexicon at all, let alone as a primitive stratum. They are deployed as ways of articulating Being without representation, without, one could say, writing. The hidden law here is that Being shall not be contaminated, corrupted through articulation. Articulation shall not pass through the ontic in any essential way. This lexicon cannot be linked to a particular economy of existence. But what then do we do with Heidegger's reference to an inner relationship, the intimate rootedness of his work in peasant life? Can we seriously leave things there?

Heidegger explicitly refuses to be bound by the ontic roots of his terminology. The example of care (*Sorge*) in *Being and Time* springs to mind most readily. But the motif of purification, of decontamination, is not only itself infected with the very same difficulty of shedding the ontic but it also relies on the possibility of subjecting the play of language to psychic pacts (agreements between writers and readers to understand a word in a certain way). This seems wholly implausible in itself but even more so on Heidegger's view of language.

These difficulties are, I claim, serious impediments to our continuing to naively deploy the discourse in which the later Heidegger has schooled us. That we continue to do so may best be understood within the wider discourse of investment.[18]

The second dimension of essential corruption I have described is the *machinery* of Heidegger's thinking. I use this word, of course, provocatively, to suggest that we might begin to think the unthinkable: that what Heidegger calls thinking might be structured in ways it does not (and in some ways cannot) itself think, ways indeed that it explicitly excludes.

In *Memoires for Paul de Man*[19] Derrida offers us a very subtle discussion of the massive upsurge in artifical memory and indeed of the technology of memory in the course of a comparison between Heidegger's claim that science does not think and de Man's own account of the relation between thinking and techno-memory. There is one particular sentence I would like to pick up on. Derrida has commented on Heidegger's strategy of separation and subordination of *science* to thinking, and goes on: "The Heideggerean argument which operates everywhere to justify this division and hierarchy, when it is reduced to its essential schema, has the following form and can be transposed everywhere: 'The essence of technology is nothing technological.'" What interests me in this is the idea of a "schema that operates everywhere"[20] in Heidegger's thought. It might even help us get clear about the "hidden law" that commands his work. But more interestingly it would surely take us to an outside inside Heidegger's work. Heidegger cannot understand himself as operating a machine. He cannot allow that thinking could be reduced to an algorithm, or a cluster of them. But what about us? What if we were to say "The essence of thinking is nothing thoughtful." I do not mean that Heidegger has not thought about thinking: the play between thinking and thanking (see *WD*) is clearly some sort of expansive articulation of thinking, and the various ways in which he distinguishes it from reasoning, calculation, etc., show the same concern for its differentiation. And, of course, it is Heidegger who declares that the most thought-provoking thing is that we are still not thinking (*WD* 3). But does it have no secret law of its own? Could there not be machinery operating, something without intrinsic value that generates sequences of sentences in ways judged productive? When Heidegger writes that "all metaphysics leaves something essential unthought: its own ground and foundation," can *we* not answer that this very pursuit of ground and foundation is the unthought in thinking? Consider the crucial moves in "Time and Being" in which the *es gibt* emerges.

> We do not say: Being is, time is, but rather: there is Being and there is time (*es gibt Sein* and *es gibt Zeit*). For the moment we have only changed the idiom with this expression. Instead of saying *it is*, we say *there is, It gives*.
>
> In order to get beyond the idiom and back to the matter, we must show how this *there is* can be experienced and seen. (*SD* 5)

We could look also at the parallel moves in "The Principle of Identity": After quoting and quickly translating the crucial Parmenidean fragment—"Das Selbe namlich ist Vernehmen (Denken) sowohl als auch Sein." ("For the same perceiving [thinking] as well as being.")—he tells us that Parmenides does not help us hear what τò αὐτό says. And yet "We must acknowledge the fact that in the earliest period of thinking, long before thinking had arrived at a principle of identity, identity itself speaks out in a pronouncement which rules (*Verfugt*) as follows: thinking and Being belong together in the Same and by virtue of this Same. "Unintentionally [Unversehens] we have here already interpreted τò αủτó, *the Same.* We interpret Sameness to mean a belonging together" (*ID* 18). This he goes on to say has now been fixed, but quite what it means is unclear. We have to take a closer look and "let the matter speak for itself."

If we judge these sequences of sentences in terms of the links from one to the next, we can only suppose that part of the Heideggerean text is missing. Then we realize that what legitimates these sequences are Heidegger's references to *saying* and to the *matter* of thought.

But a less tendentious way of understanding what is going on would be to say that a certain machinery is in operation and that it is this machinery that guides the sequencing of sentences. I have tried to capture what is happening here in the phrase: aleatory opportunism feeding a meditative program governed by powerful recursive principles.

One such group of principles would include:
• Seek the third that dissolves static representational dualisms.
• Pursue such discourse as allows the articulation of subject/object relationships in ways that undermine any simple distinction.
• Transform questions of identity into transactional ones.

Such principles can be characterized by the drive to the primordial. I have already discussed this in the first section, with reference to the claim that "Temporalization is the free oscillation of the whole of primordial temporality . . . " In "Time and Being" (*TB* 15–17) after Heidegger has reached three dimensions, he asks for the *source* of their unity, which proves to be the "interplay [*Zuspiel*] of each toward each." Not content with that, he asks about the *giving* in the "es gibt sein" and discovers "an extending opening up," and then asks *what gives* to which the answer is *Ereignis*, appropriation. Heidegger's genius lies in the modulation of these moves, but the underlying schemata involved are not too difficult to discern.

If as it has been said,[21] Heidegger's work is in the last analysis (which never comes) the most rigorous defense of presence, that is only the name for the clustering (perhaps belonging-together!) of a diversity of operations, procedures, devices, which are not only in principle capable of repetition, but whose often predictable repetition constitutes Heidegger's opus. It could be said, then, that Heidegger's texts are textual productions generated by the recursive application of a small number of procedures.[22] If these play at least a part in what is called thinking, they are not themselves thought through. This is our task, and Heidegger's necessary fate. We might perhaps here return to the question I raised above, about Heidegger's discussion of undergoing an experience with language. Heidegger's strategy here is familiar. He opens up a radical opposition to a taken-for-granted attitude, and then gives a *particular specification of the alternative*. It is then only too easy to lose sight of the space opened up. In this case (see *US* 157ff.), Heidegger is engaged in inducing in us an inversion of our usual sense of being subjects in control of language, by suggesting that we will arrive at the essence of language by "undergoing an experience with language." By listening we will hear language speaking, we will experience the "granting that abides in Saying." Words will be seen not just to name preexisting items in the world, but to give them being, to arise with them. But what of the listening that listens to *grant, abide, obey, summon* and so on, and hears reactionary politics, or hears theology, or hears the worldview of the peasant farmer? Such a listening is no less a radical break from the ordinary use of language, it is no less an experience which one can undergo with language. Derrida once said that he did not see eye-to-eye with Heidegger on language; it was perhaps just such a change of ear that he was alluding to.

These two corruptions, forms of constitutive exteriority of Heidegger's texts, are intended to give us pause in considering the fate of time in the later Heidegger, and to give some reason for a reprise of the abandoned program.

TIME AS DESTINY

Heidegger makes great play of the destiny of Being, the *Geschick des Seins*. I begin with what I could only call a strong allergy to the language of both fate and destiny; perhaps my ear is more Nietzschean than Heideggerean (perhaps more like a nose!). Beginning as I do with a much lower tolerance of what sounds, despite Heidegger's denials, like secondhand Hegelian machinery, and with a much more positive welcome to chance and the messiness of Being, I want to look at a small selection of his remarks on destiny as a symptom of the dangers of his allowing his thinking about time to be totally subordinated to ontology.

I want all too briefly to distinguish three approaches to destiny: existential, ontological, and textual. The first two I attribute to Heidegger, and the last I associate at least with the name Derrida. In each of the first two approaches I want to argue for importantly contestable assumptions, which when brought out and taken seriously would transform them into more modest and plausible areas of investigation.

The existential approach to destiny, which already appears in a strong form in Nietzsche, can be found in section 74 of *Being and Time* (on Historicality), and of course Heidegger is riding heavily on etymological echoings here. I will quote only a short passage:

> Destiny is not something that puts itself together out of individual fates, any more than Being-with-one-another can be conceived as the occurring together of several Subjects. Our fates have already been guided in advance, in our Being with one another in the same world and in our resoluteness for definite possibilities. Only in communicating and in struggling does the power of destiny become free. (*SZ* 384)

What Heidegger is trying to achieve in this section is a synthesis of the idea that the repetition of tradition opens up our destiny, that Dasein's ecstatic temporality is the ground for historizing, that destiny cannot be just a summation of individual fate, and that a community can realize its destiny through communication and struggle.

The distinctive function played by destiny in this passage is to provide a way of transcending the mere arithmetic addition of individual fates, and to introduce the presumption of a *terminus ad quem* into a community's historical reflection. The strategy of Heidegger's thought here, as elsewhere, is to provide what looks like a solution to what seems to be a pressing problem, and represent it as *the* solution.

My central claim is this: the word *destiny* functions in such a way as to imply that there is a truth, or a space of truth, to be won by such struggle. Even if every word prescribes a law, this one is essentially legitimating in its function, and when Heidegger talks about the power of destiny becoming "free through communication and struggle," he is eliding the importance of coming to some collective vision of the future, with success in discovering one's true destiny. This elision eases, though it does not prescribe, the slide into totalitarian thought because the need to arrive at and enact the truth can easily be made to override questions as to how one arrives at it. Hence the leadership principle. Remember Parmenides' goddess: "Come, I will tell you—and you must accept my word when you have heard it. . . ."[23]

Heidegger, it is only fair to say, would repudiate any such direct reading. He writes, for instance, "Always the destining of revealing holds complete sway over man. But that destining is never a fate that compels. For man becomes truly free only insofar as he belongs to the realm of destining, and so becomes one who listens and hears, and not one who is simply constrained to obey" (*QT* 25). This draws on his account of freedom to be found in "On the Essence of Truth." And Heidegger is quite right to insist that we cannot think of truth or freedom except within what for the sake of speed we can call an opening. But nothing requires that disparate openings historically coincide or that this or that opening is compelling.

Unless we are to have philosopher-kings it is important, I claim, to keep separate

1. the continuing need for revolutionary thought,
2. the need for radical change at certain times in history,
3. the impossibility of giving a wholly rational grounding for any particular projection of the future,
4. the supposition that there are privileged revelations of destiny.

Perhaps we need a god to save us from believing that there is no conflict among poets. But we also need to ask whether poetic eschatology should be privileged over that of economists or ecologists. And then we must ask: who privileges, where, and when?

It could be said that what I mean by patience is the avoidance of risk. There are times, surely, when we have to risk all to win all. Consider Nietzsche on Wagner's Bayreuth, "the event which lies like strange sunlight upon recent and immediately coming years, designed for . . . a future age," and which "must transform every notion of education and culture in the spirit of everyone who experiences it . . . a curtain has been raised on a future in which there are no longer any great and good things except those which all hearts share in common."[24] Nietzsche bet on Wagner, and lost. This is what he wrote later: "This essay is full of world-historical accents. This is the strongest 'objectivity' possible. The absolute certainly about what I am was projected on some accidental reality— the truth about *me* spoke from some gruesome depths."[25] And Heidegger even wrote, ". . . we must produce the illusion, as it were, that the given task at hand is the one and only necessary task" (*GA* 26: 201). What is beyond dispute is that no model of action is adequate that does not address questions of risk, crisis, investment, commitment, decision, failure, death . . . but also the most radical opening of one's relation to the future, one for which Reason always comes too late.[26] Time may always be revolutionary, but there are *also* revolutionary times, in which action can legislate, and not just follow rules. But genuine absence of rational grounds for projecting the future must not spawn metaphysical simulacra in the form of destiny. Destiny is *at best* the name of a projectable space of possibility within which my (or our) actions would make sense.

This takes me on to consider Heidegger's use of the *Geschick des Seins,* the destiny of Being, Being as destiny. Everything I have already said about the privileging of a primitive economics applies here too.

Reference to the *Geschick des Seins* is meant to translate the *es gibt (Sein)* into historical terms, as the fluctuating of Being as gift, giving and withdrawal, to complete the process of withdrawal from the stage of existential analytic represented in *Being and Time,* and it is meant to occlude the importance of "history" not only as a sequence of events, but even as understood in the accounts of historicity in *Being and Time.*

Heidegger's central and continuing task is to think "Being without [reference to any foundational relation to] beings." The surpassed, "metaphysical" account did, however, have one advantage—of offering a distinctive and constitutive *relation* against which Being could be clarified. The *Geschick des Seins* relocates this relationality in a movement of giving or sending, and holding back of withdrawing. This is not what we ordinarily think of as history, thought it may look like it. Heidegger writes: "Being does not have a history in the way a city or a people have a history. What is history-like in the history of Being is obviously determined by the way in which Being takes place and by this alone . . . this means the way in which *es gibt Sein*" (*TB* 8). Sending is defined as "a giving which gives only its gift, but in the giving holds itself back and withdraws." "What is historical in the history of Being is determined by what is sent forth in destiny and not by an indeterminately thought-up occurrence" (*TB* 8–9). The theme of the accidental is pursued more explicitly when he writes: "The sequence of epochs in the destiny of Being is not accidental, nor can it be calculated as necessary . . . What is appropriate shows itself in the destiny. What is appropriate shows itself in the belonging together of the epochs. The epochs overlap each other in their sequence so that the original sensing of Being as presence is more and more obscured in different ways" (*TB* 9). Heidegger is clearly right when he says that these remarks are to be referred back to *Being and Time,* section 6, the discussion of the history of ontology, and not to the later discussion of historicality.

The reason is surely this: Heidegger has taken his own expression—"the destruction of the history of ontology"—and thought it through more deeply. The result of that pondering is the attempt first to eradicate any sense of linear chronology or teleology in "history," and second, to think through the double genitive of the "of" in the history *of* ontology, through the implications of the *es gibt (Sein)*.

It is hard to take Heidegger seriously when he writes of Being withholding itself and turning away. Of course, he means to shock. But it is surely too much of a *reaction* to a predominantly subjectcentered tradition, and as a *reaction*, flawed. The discourse of destiny importantly attests to both the structural invisibility of the conditions of what appears, and the transformation in history of the deepest forms of those conditions. But the story of scene-changing in a transcendental theatre is not convincing. In particular, Heidegger's supposition that *epochs* would be prior to and would condition the shape and fate of representation is undermined by the very narrative.

In his essay "Envoi," Derrida asks whether the repetition of envois (epochs, sendings . . .) including that of representation itself might not be subject to an unthought law of representation, namely, the constant repetition of the envoi, the great Greek epoch. This question would affect "not only the whole ordering of epochs or periods in the resumed unity of a history of metaphysics or of the West [but also] the very credit we would wish as philosophers, to accord to a centered and centralized organization of all the fields or all the sections of representation grouped around a sustaining sense of a fundamental interpretation."[27] This is not just a problem about Heidegger's formulation of the epochality of Being. It is a problem about *what it is* he is trying to formulate. And yet it is arguably the question of formulation, and then commitment and reception of thought, that actually provides a locus for the very saga Heidegger is relating. Does not the discourse of the *Geschick des Seins* capture rather well the risks of reading, writing, and translation?

This very treatment of Heidegger makes it perfectly clear how important to him is this question of the reception of his thinking, and it is not at all difficult to treat giving, withholding, concealing, and so on, as a language for articulating the drama and the stakes of writing, reading, being read, translating, interpreting, etc.

This issue clearly did concern Heidegger. There are numerous remarks offered in guidance to the reader or listener—to ignore the propositional form—to follow the movement of showing (at the beginning of "Time and Being") and that "the Saying of Appropriation in the form of a lecture remains . . . an obstacle" (*TB* 24). And his readings and translations of Parmenides again make appeals to special principles (e.g., listening to the saying) to violently recoup the losses embodied in centuries of tradition. I would suggest as a project for some other day that a careful study be made of the point-by-point structural parallel between what Heidegger says about the destiny of Being and what he says about writing as transmission. The issue is already problematized elsewhere, particularly in Kierkegaard and Nietzsche. And it is of course discussed in Derrida's essay "Mes Chances."

In "Mes Chances," Derrida transforms his promised topic—psychoanalysis and literature—into proper names, through whose destiny as signs the problematic of chance and necessity can be thought through more generally in a "*logos* or *tropos* of envoi." The link between Heidegger's *Geworfenheit* (thrownness) and its *Zerstreuung* (dispersion) (in the *Metaphysical Foundations of Logic*) allows him to introduce, at least as a model, the essential iterability of a mark, by which it is continually divided and multiplied, which, as he puts it, "imprints the capacity for diversion within its very movement." If we suppose that this structure of the trace or mark is not only, if you like, fundamental, but also pervades every "constituted identity," then the effect would be to introduce intrinsic deviation or dispersion within any such determination as destiny. Writing about Freud, Derrida says "In the destination [*Bestimmung*] there is thus a principle of indetermination, chance, luck or of destinerrance. There is no assured destination precisely because of the marks and the proper name."[28] By the introduction of chance, and in particular, the alignment of the question of destiny with the structure of the trace, Derrida has exploited the connection Heidegger insists on between thinking and Being and language in ways Heidegger would not have anticipated. If Derrida has a hand in shaping Heidegger's destiny it will not have been entirely by chance because the centrality of language for Heidegger always made it a hostage to fortune.

At the risk of being labeled one of the last men, from whom nothing great or good ever comes, and who, as Nietzsche put it, sacrifice the future to themselves, I would like to suggest the possibility of converting this whole discourse of destiny and chance into a more cautious domain of reflection.

In saying this, I am trying to respond to what Phillipe Lacoue-Labarthe[29] described as the suspicion with which one must always now read Heidegger. I am proposing a cool, modest, gently analytical (with a small *a*) approach to these questions because we cannot as philosophers divorce the style and shape of our pronouncements from the wider possibilities of their rhetorical transformation. The wider public discourse of destiny is not separable from wars of mass destruction. I do not mean the *word* destiny, but its confident use. There is an important difference between mentioning it, discussing it, analyzing it, making it the site of questioning and so on, and its approved use even in the course of what claims and promises to be a program of radical interrogation.

Let me give an example, which will raise far more problems than it resolves, but one which we must, I believe, confront. In *Ecce Homo* ("Why I Am a Destiny" [*Schicksal*]) Nietzsche did not write "there will be a wailing and gnashing of teeth"—a problem, as he might have put it, for dentists. He wrote "there will be wars the like of which have never yet been seen on earth." What does this mean? What do we tell our students it means? Or ourselves? He writes of geological upheavals, of the advent of "great politics," and talks of the war of truth against the lies of millenia. I will not here discuss the performative rhetoric of apocalyptic discourse. I will confess that what I and what I suspect many other teachers of Nietzsche have explained is that the war he is describing is one carried out in books, conferences, debates, arguments, and so on. It is the struggle against lies, against stupidity, against smallness, against morality—the struggle to overcome *man*. And we clearly separate this from the struggles that have littered our century with trenches, camps and burnt-out cities, struggles that still gnaw at our consciences and plague our screens. We make this distinction, we draw these lines. But what if the fate of the lines we draw, as philosophers, in our thinking and writing and speaking, is to be immediately overrun by the scene of their reception? What would such a fate mean for responsibility?

In the first paragraph of "Why I Am a Destiny" (*Ecce Homo*), Nietzsche wrote "I am no man, I am dynamite." (He was repeating a description made of him by a reviewer of *Beyond Good and Evil*, which perhaps holds a lesson for reviewers.) Pursuing this question of responsibility just a step further: just before Nietzsche was writing, when dynamite had only just been invented and introduced into the United States, legislation was enacted which, for the first time introduced the principle of Absolute Liability for the consequences of its use. Strong high fences, warning notices, and taking all reasonable care were no defense against a claim for injury (or death) from dynamite. Intentions and precautions were no defense.

If the word destiny is typically linked to a rhetoric of arousal, then *destiny* in this sense has a destiny. Quite apart from our doubts about its metaphysical legacy, the speed with which it can be deployed in the cause of political and military mobilization surely ought to give us pause. Our precautions, our warnings, footnotes and so on, are no safeguard if destination is, precisely, not able to guarantee the preservation of identity, but is intrinsically divided, delayed, diverted.

What then would this discussion about destiny tell us about time? If we read Heidegger literally, not very much. The real continuity of this later work with *Being and Time* is that the question of time is only a means to another end—that of awakening and preserving a certain experience of the truth of Being.

I promised at the outset that I would suggest ways in which we might come to think of Being, the a priori, transcendence, the ontological difference, and so on, in a new way. I will now pursue these matters a little further.

The obvious way in which to rethink Being, the ontological difference, etc., is to follow the path already beaten by Derrida, who offers us powerful strategies for undermining both the character of the primitive and the primordial as well as the textual drive that takes us in these directions. Derrida's classical gestures here centered around a kind of parodic substitution of an impossible origin within a transcendental framework. This is the legacy of *differance*, trace, supplement and so on. In "*Ousia* and *Gramme*" Derrida explicitly repudiates the idea of another, primordial time that could underwrite ordinary time. In doing so, he brings ruin to much of the language of the later Heidegger. But of course part of what is questioned is the very idea of the transcendental (or quasi-transcendental) framework. I want to suggest a way of expanding the erosion of the transcendental other than this substitutive displacement. This would attempt to reopen the field of *intratemporal constitution* by pursuing forms of interreferential and articulatory complexity. In a graded series of levels, this would involve attempts to articulate the temporal forms of transition, dehiscence, difference, repetition, interweaving, entanglement, superimposition. As well as the Derridean displacement of the origin (in favor of repetition, and *differance*), I am suggesting we pursue the possibilities of multiplicity of temporal series, of the complexity of their constitution, of the capacity for crossdetermination of one series by another, etc. Such an account will take considerable analytical work, and I cannot take it further here. What drives this thinking is what I would call my *principle of all principles*—that it is always to soon to abandon the resources of the temporal. And the continued use of terms like horizon, spacing, transcendence, even ecstasis, requires of us at the very least a textual circling back, to break open and rearticulate their temporality.[30]

Let me give two examples of persistence with or fidelity to the temporal. First, Heidegger often asks us not to read his work as a series of propositions but rather to "follow the movement of showing." It would not be difficult to present this request as absolutely critical for our entire understanding of Heidegger, what a military commander would think of as a bridge that *had to kept open*. But what is it to "follow a movement of showing?" What is it to come across this request again and again? Or at both the beginning and at the end of a paper? Consider:

1. *Showing* is already a repetition that renews or recovers by a return that repeats a more original sense of allowing to be seen. (See Heidegger's account of phenomenology in section 7 of *Being and Time*.)

2. A *movement of showing* is a textual movement both in the sense of the continual vertical upsurging movement[31] (what Heidegger would call presencing) that sustains the text at each instant, and in the sense of a movement of succession (and the transcendence of succession) through the course of the text.

3. *Following* such a double movement will subject it to the most complex processes of ongoing and reflexive temporal synthesis and releasement, which no result will quite capture, and yet which cannot be quite distinguished from the series of the results of such readings, and so on.

4. *Responding* so resonantly to this double movement of the text will itself both bring to bear the most complex coordination of hidden and overt agendas, pasts and futures, and itself be taken up into that tangle of ear and eye and nose by which we will subsequently live and act and . . . read. I am trying to suggest we can translate "following the movement of showing" into a language that gives voice to an open coordination of rhythms within rhythms and repetition of repetition, a cotemporal *fracticity*.[32]

I would now like to offer a second example of the kind of repetition of the temporal I am suggesting—that of the ontological difference. This again is a central notion for Heidegger. My line of thought is this: it may be vital to be able to shift from ontic discourse, discourse about beings and their relation to each other, to discourse about Being, about *Ereignis*, about the *es gibt*, about withholding, etc., but that does not preclude what could be called back-door entanglements between the ontic and the ontological. One way of explaining this would be to insist on exacting the pound of flesh from the debt owed by the ontological to ontic language, to insist that there is no proper way of paying off this debt, that giving, withdrawing, responding, turning away, *bind* the ontological to the ontic in ways Heidegger appears to resist. I consider it may be vital because I would treat this very attempt at an articulation of temporal fracticity as a radical shift from everyday models of time, a shift famously adumbrated by Augustine. But this discontinuity is not the announcement of another realm at all. The transcendental, if you like, is nowhere else but *in* the empirical. (see Merleau-Ponty's *Invisible*).[33] The best model for this unity of absolute distinctness *at a time* and wider continuity, is offered, I believe, by the Moebius strip (a flat ribbon, twisted once and joined in a circle) at any point of which there are two quite distinct sides, which are yet, when traced through, seen to be only a single surface. This neither proves nor explains anything, but it illustrates how one might begin to think *transcendence within temporality.*

One radical criticism of the position outlined here would be to suggest the need for another reading of Heidegger's itinerary after the twenties showing that he is engaged in this very project.[34] On this reading,[35] time does not disappear, but continually erupts—as overcoming the spirit of revenge (in Nietzsche), as reserve and efficiency (in "The Question Concerning Technology"), as thanking and commemoration (in *What is Called Thinking?*), as restitution (in "The Anaximander Fragment"), as founding and presencing (in *On the Way to Language*), and so on. Perhaps it is a sign of some lingering nostalgia on my part to want a more systematic and programmatic treatment of temporality than this, one which would reconstruct the geological formation that gives rise to this archipelago of instances. Temporality will become the infinitely complex site of the *re-* from which the spectre of primordiality will have been finally banished, never to return.

NOTES

1. I have pursued these themes more fully in *The Deconstruction of Time* (Atlantic Highlands, N.J.: Humanities, 1989).

2. G.W.F. Hegel, *Werke* (Frankfurt a.M.: Suhrkamp, 1970), 2: 558.

3. It does not disappear entirely. William McNeill has pointed out to me, for example, a late reference to authentic and inauthentic temporality in Heidegger's 1934–35 lecture course on Hölderlin's "Germania" and "Rhine" poems.

4. See Thomas Sheehan's invaluable study—"Heidegger's Early Years: Fragments for a Philosophical Biography"—in *Heidegger: The Man and the Thinker* (Chicago: Precedent, 1981). See also Theodore Kisiel's "On the Way to *Being and Time*," *Research in Phenomenology* 15 (1985).

5. See *The Deconstruction of Time*, part 3.

6. In *Beiträge zur Philosophie* (*GA* 65). I have William McNeill to thank for this reference.

7. Heidegger, however, insists on the necessary tie between metontology and fundamental ontology (*GA* 26: 199).

8. See Jean-François Courtine's "Phenomenology and/or Tautology," included in this volume.

9. See, for example, "Brief über den 'Humanismus,'" in *GA* 9.

10. Recalling Heidegger's account of his "attempt to interpret Augustinian (i.e., Helleno-

Christian) anthropology in the light of . . . the ontology of Aristotle," it is perhaps not surprising that Heidegger (see esp. *SZ* 178) has the same worries about *entanglement* as Augustine (see, for example, "Thou wilt increase, Lord, Thy gifts more and more in me, that my soul may follow me to Thee, disentangled from the birdline of concupiscence; that it rebel not against itself, and even in dreams not . . . through images of sense, commit those debasing corruptions, even to pollution of the flesh . . ." (*The Confessions of St. Augustine*, trans. Edward Pusey [New York: Collier, 1961], 10: 173). Heidegger's attempts to purify *Verfallen* (esp. *SZ* §38) of its *negative* connotations have to be judged in the light of his retention of so much of Augustine's topology. And if theology were *essentially* a certain topology? Perhaps we have not got rid of God if we still . . .

11. See his review in *Kant-Studien* 36, no. 1/2 (1931): 17.

12. "*Ouisa* and *Gramme*," in Jacques Derrida, *Marges de la philosophie* (Paris: Éditions de Minuit, 1972), passim.

13. For a fuller account of this project see *The Deconstruction of Time*. The question of *complexity* is obviously central here. Coming after Heidegger's praise of the simple and the stable, it is obviously a crucial question. The issue is whether greater complexity can make for the kinds of difference that make a difference. And that question, too, requires thought. If what is required is a difference of *level*, we have to ask whether the differentiation of levels is as sharp as one supposes, and whether that sharpness is not itself the product of detemporalization. This suggestion has of course extraordinary consequences, for it would affect the ontological difference itself, on which Heidegger pins so much. The claim would be this: that differences of *level* are only ever local, and that there is no guarantee that they can be sustained over time, or in the dispersive recontextualization that is the lot of language. For a model that proves nothing, but shows everything, consider the Moebius strip, which has at any point two clearly distinct sides, but until it is cut these sides are in fact one continuous side. I owe this example, of course, to Lacan.

14. See Parmenides: "It is all the same to me from what point I begin, for I shall return again to this same point," in Kathleen Freeman, *Ancilla to the Pre-Socratic Philosophers* (Oxford: Blackwell, 1966), 42.

15. A very different diagnosis could be drawn from Levinas, for whom the locus of all that I have called a primitive economy, would be the face-to-face relation, in which I am always already called (on) by the Other. But would it really *save* the Heideggerian text to relocate it on Levinasian terrain?

16. Consider Derrida's "the writer writes *in* a language and *in* a logic whose proper system, laws, and life his discourses cannot dominate absolutely . . ." (*Of Grammatology*, trans. Gayatri Spivak [Baltimore: Johns Hopkins University Press, 1974], 158). This claim, which itself *repeats* (rewrites) something of the turning inside out of the sock of language that Heidegger attempts in "The Nature of Language" (in *US*), can be allowed to turn back onto Heidegger's own discourse.

17. We must never forget that unlike his peasants, Heidegger keeps leaving the mountains and *returning*. The *valuation* of simple rough existence is never itself simple. Heidegger is entangled in sentimentality, despite his disclaimers.

18. The question of investment in Heidegger (both our investment in his work and the way certain kinds of economic prejudices work their way through his work) must await another occasion. As far as the latter is concerned, I think we need to think about (1) the dangers he sees in the *Bestand*, the standing-reserve that characterizes the *Gestell*, enframing (2) the rejection of any neutral currency (such as meaning) in language. Could Heidegger's work be a refusal of money? Marc Shell's *Money, Language and Thought* (Berkeley: University of California Press, 1982) deserves wider philosophical attention.

19. Jacques Derrida, *Memoires for Paul de Man*, trans. Cecile Lindsay, et al. (New York: Columbia, 1986), 108–90.

20. Cf. Derrida's reference to "the germinal structure of the whole of Husserl's thought" (*Speech and Phenomena*, trans. D. Allison [Evanston: Northwestern University Press, 1973],

3).

21. By Jacques Derrida in *Positions*. I perhaps ought to say that I have the same preference for the early Derrida as I have for the early Heidegger, and as Heidegger had for the early Husserl . . . A study is needed of "The Early and the Late: the Finitude of Thought," dealing also with the early and the late Hegel, Schelling, and Marx, arguing for some general truths of thanatography: opening and closing?

22. The specification of these rules is here very gestural and incomplete. My confidence in recommending the elaboration of these rules to others is based, not just on what could be called rogue "experience with language," in which one becomes aware of the machinery of Heidegger's staging, and the sense of the organizing economy of his language, but also on the premise that there *must* be such rules (by which I mean, minimally, insistent patterns of repetition), if the language is to make sense. In consequence, what I am saying cannot be a criticism of Heidegger as such. What it does take issue with is his own understanding of what he is doing, of what thinking *could* be.

23. Freeman, 42.

24. Nietzsche, *Richard Wagner in Bayreuth,* in *Untimely Meditations,* trans. R. J. Hollingdale (Cambridge: Cambridge University Press, 1983), 249.

25. Nietzsche, *Ecce Homo,* trans. Walter Kaufmann (New York: Random House, 1967), 275.

26. Crucial texts here would be "The Origin of the Work of Art," and the title essay in Derrida's *Psyché: Inventions de l'autre* (Paris: Galilée, 1987).

27. Derrida, *Psyché,* 136–37.

28. "My Chances; Mes Chances," in *Taking Chances: Derrida, Psychoanalysis and Literature,* eds. Joseph Smith and William Kerrigan (Baltimore: Johns Hopkins, 1984), 16.

29. Phillipe Lacoue-Labarthe, *La fiction du politique* (Paris: Christian Bourgeois, 1987).

30. This movement of circling back is of course itself *temporal,* and it raises the question of whether we should not be able to rethink the movement back to the ontic outlined in Heidegger's discussion of metontology (in the appendix to *GA* 26, section 10) in essentially temporal terms.

31. A way of thinking through such a vertical *movement* that relied less on the idea of presencing could perhaps be found through the doctrine of a double axis of language, of which the paradigmatic, or substitutive, would generate the *verticality* here described.

32. "Fracticity" is a new word. It suggests the fractal quality of facticity—that deeper inquiry does not reveal simplicity but ever more complexity.

33. See Merleau-Ponty's *Le visible et l'invisible* (Paris: Gallimard, 1964).

34. Allergy to the language of fate and destiny, and doubts about the language with which the *Geschick des Seins* is elaborated should not be misunderstood as a general hostility to the risks Heidegger increasingly takes in his own use of language. If, as I claim, existential temporality is essentially plural, polyphonic, then the language of *Stimmung*, attunement, tone, awaits us. And if time is the persistent brinking of otherness (perhaps, specifically, the Other) then the language of opening, lighting and clearing would become increasingly seductive. Thinking knows no mantric words, nor does it proscribe. What justifies and sustains it is its persistence in returning to the source of its sustenance: time.

35. Tina Chanter points the way in her important paper "Metaphysical Presence: Heidegger on Time and Eternity," presented to the Society for Phenomenology and Existential Philosophy, October 1989, at Duquesne University, Pittsburgh.

V

PHILOPOLEMOLOGY

JACQUES DERRIDA

11. Heidegger's Ear

Philopolemology
(*Geschlecht* IV)

Translated by John P. Leavey, Jr.

. . . als Hören der Stimme des Freundes,
den jedes Dasein bei sich trägt

Heidegger, *Sein und Zeit*

. . . as in hearing the voice of the friend
whom every Dasein carries with it

Translated by Macquarrie
and Robinson

. . . écoute qui s'ouvre à la voix de l'ami
que tout Dasein porte auprès de lui

Translated by Vezin

. . . comme l'écoute de la voix de l'ami
que chaque Dasein porte auprès de lui

Translated by Martineau

. . . l'ouïr de la voix amie, que tout être-là
porte en lui-même

Translated by Boehm and de Waehlens

I .

The friend is silent. This friend. Keeps silent. Here, at least, *this* friend says nothing. One could nearly conclude from this, from then on, that this friend utters nothing determinable: Heidegger evokes nothing said by or no saying, however friendly, of the friend. The voice of this friend does not necessarily speak. This friend could be aphasic. One could even be physically deaf without ceasing to carry [*porter*] its voice *bei sich*, with oneself, through its voice. With oneself does not mean right next to oneself. With oneself does not mean the nearest, the closest, nor in oneself. In its strict grammaticality, the phrase says that Dasein carries with it the friend itself, and not only its voice: "als Hören der Stimme des Freundes, *den* jedes Dasein bei sich trägt" (*SZ*, § 34, p. 163). Through its voice that I hear, I hear the friend itself, beyond its voice but in that voice. I hear and carry the friend with me in hearing its voice. Of course, *bien entendu*, Dasein "carries" the friend itself, but not the friend in its totality, in flesh and blood. Dasein carries it, one might say, in the figure of its voice, its metonymic figure (a part for the whole). What about this rhetoric that seems to complicate the grammar without, however, contradicting it? For it is indeed the friend and not its voice that I hear. What about this exemplary part that seems to be valid for the whole? Why does the voice play this role? And why does hearing assure this presence of the friend permanently carried by Dasein "bei sich"? The question of this privileged metonymy will no longer leave us.

Where then is this voice? Where does it come from? It seems to be neither in us, nor outside us, but within the friend. Neither in our ear, nor outside our ear. But what does "bei sich tragen" mean to say? Where is an ear? What is the inside and the outside of an ear? What is it, for an ear, to (be) open? What is it to prick up one's ear [*tendre l'oreille*]? To hear [*entendre*] or not to hear? To be deaf, not to be able or to be unwilling to hear, perhaps in the sense in which Heidegger will speak later (1933–34), about Hölderlin's *Der Rhein*, about mortals that turn, as is said in French and English, a "deaf ear" (*das Überhören*)? Unlike gods and poets, "Mortals hear like those that cannot hear (*als nicht-hören-können*); their understanding [*entente*] is the *deaf ear* (*das* Überhören) and the will-not-to-hear (*Überhörenwollen*)" (*GA* 39: § 14, p. 200; I cite this decisive passage immediately for fear of not having the time to devote all the necessary attention to it here later, as well as to what is said of *Überhören* and of misunderstanding, mishearing, *sich Verhören*, in the lecture *Logos* [1951], or to what is said of the ear in *Der Satz vom Grund* [1955–56]).

Where then is the ear that we lend, as is said in French and English, in particular the ear we lend to the voice of the friend? What is the ear, in the literal [*propre*] sense, if there is such a sense? What, properly speaking, is the ear, the ear as such and in its singularity? It is true that, however elliptical Heidegger's little phrase, it seems already to assure us that we do not even take the initiative in lending or pricking up the ear to the voice of the friend. Through this voice, Dasein carries the friend with it, whether it wishes to or not, whether it knows it or not, and whatever its resolution. In any case, what matters here is not what the friend's voice says, not its said, not even the saying of its said. Hardly its voice. Rather what matters is the hearing (*das Hören*) of its voice. *Das Hören* is the principal theme of this chapter. And this hearing could not open Dasein to "its ownmost potentiality-for-being (*sein eigenstes Seinkönnen*)," if hearing were not first the hearing of this voice, the exemplary metonymy of the friend that each Dasein bears close by itself (*bei sich trägt*). The enigma is situated perhaps not far, very close by, if not within these few words, "bei sich" and "tragen." Let us not forget that the expression *bei sich* will have struck, in the German tongue, the statement [*énoncé*] of one of the most obscure things, nothing less than absolute knowledge at the end of Hegel's greater logic, the pure concept as it conceives itself, "the simple being to which the idea determines itself . . . and [that] is the concept that, in its determination, remains close by self (*das einfache Sein, zu dem sich die Idee bestimmt . . . und ist der in seiner Bestimmung bei sich selbst bleibende Begriff*)."[1]

This friend does not speak, but is also invisible. The friend does not appear [*paraît, apparaît*] any more than it comes to speak or to a decision [*il ne prononce ou ne se prononce*]. The friend has no face, no figure [*figure*]. No sex. No name. The friend is not a man, nor a woman; it is not I, nor a "self," not a subject, nor a person. It is another Dasein that each Dasein *carries*, through the voice it hears, with itself (*bei sich trägt*), neither within itself, in the ear, in the "inner ear," inside a subjective interiority, nor far away, too far from the ear, for one can also hear from afar, in an exterior space or in some transcendence, but in its vicinity [*parages*], at a distance that is neither absolute—absolutely infinite— nor null in the absolute proximity of an ownness [*propriété*], nor then determinable according to some objective unit of measurement in the world. This carrying-distance [*portée*] of the voice, this *être-à-portée de voix*, as one would say in French, this being within earshot of the voice, appears of another order.

That perhaps is what one can be authorized to say, in order to begin, about the friend such as it is apparently named, only once named, in a brief parenthetical clause of *Sein und Zeit*. This allusion seems unique, remains so brief and so enigmatic that almost no one has lent it any attention or even judged it necessary to stop at it, except, to my knowledge, Christopher Fynsk, Jean- François Courtine, and Jean-Luc Nancy to whose brief and recent incursions[2] I pay tribute as I am getting ready today to engage myself in a direction that was not theirs.

The friend, then, seems named once in *Sein und Zeit*, but keeps silent even if its voice is *evoked*. The friend does not appear, has the visibility of no determined figure or face, has no subjective, personal, sexual status; one cannot even decide if the friend is living or dead. When I say that the friend is named, that is still too much, for it has no proper name; the friend calls perhaps, but is not then called, and nothing permits one to suppose that the friend is singular even if the common noun that designates it, "the voice of the friend," is grammatically singular. "The voice of the friend" seems rather to confer on it a kind of oneness that does not exclude plurality. A friend is always the friend. This friend is always the friend. As will be seen, a certain singularity remains required; this friend is not the concept *friend*, nor the friend in general. The friend thus commonly named is not called; the author of *Sein und Zeit* does not address the friend, does not say to it, as Hölderlin or Aristotle in famous apostrophes, "O, friend," "O, friends." One then can hardly say that the friend is named by Heidegger in *Sein und Zeit*. I prefer to say that the friend is only evoked. Why only *evoked*? For three reasons:

(1) First of all, because of the furtive and enigmatic brevity of the passage. The passage of the word "friend," rather than of the friend, in a parenthetical clause, is as suspended as it could be in a poetic evocation, without well-marked premises or consequences.

(2) Evoked, next, because the friend itself is not the one named in such an abstract and indeterminate way, not the friend in itself and *in toto*; by metonymy, so to speak, by figure, is evoked just a part of the *figure* of the friend, in the general sense of the word "figure" and in the sense in French of *figure* as "face," *visage*: evoked not in itself, *en soi*, such as it is, this figure, this face, the figure of the friend such as the friend is in itself, but the voice of the friend *by* me, *by the Dasein* I am, by a certain ear of the Dasein each of us is. And still the question remains open of knowing whether the ear can here be named by figure or in the literal [*propre*] sense, indeed beyond this rhetorical alternative. The problem of the literal or figurative sense of the ear (but also of the eye) of thought will be thematized in *Der Satz vom Grund* (chap. 6; I have spoken of that elsewhere and perhaps I will have time to come back to it today from another point of view). The friend's voice, the friend in its voice is not in itself [*en soi*], but in me, but not even *in me* as Dasein, for Dasein is not a "self," not an "I," and Heidegger specifies that this friend whose voice I hear, this friend is carried by every Dasein "bei sich," with itself, close by itself. The voice of the friend is neither within itself, nor designated as itself, nor within me, nor in a Dasein that could include it as a part or a moment of its own proper constitution, in its very own ear, even if the friend's being-carried seems in effect constitutive of Dasein, for Heidegger does say of *every* Dasein. The enigma of the "bei sich" excludes at once exclusion and inclusion, transcendence and belonging, the exteriority of an absolute stranger and the intimacy of the completely near, distance and proximity. The friend whose voice I hear is not here present, not even present now on the telephone, even if it is *there*, however, taking part in the being-*there* of Dasein, and so in the *Da* of *Sein*. It is then difficult to assign a site to this voice of the friend by every Dasein. And we will not know what the ear of Dasein is inasmuch as we will not know what hearing (*hören*) this voice of the friend or hearing in general signifies. The difficulty is doubled or imprinted again in the word "trägt." Although the voice is not within it, Dasein carries the friend in carrying its voice. Dasein carries with it the friend, its voice or the hearing of this voice of the other friend as if these three constituents, hearing, voice, the other-friend, formed in the silent displacement of the same chain, as it were, a unique carrying of this carrying-distance of the voice [*une seule portée de cette portée de voix*].

But what does "carry" (*tragen, porter*, bear) mean in this case? Carry not in the sense of carry within oneself, but carry by oneself (*bei sich*), carry without carrying, carry the other? Carry some other thing than oneself in the difference and yet in a certain proximity between what carries and what is carried? What can an ear help us to hear and understand on this subject? Far from being able to comprehend starting from some other thing, from more familiar schemas, what is this carrying-distance of the voice of the friend by every Dasein, perhaps it is starting from this hearing of the voice of the friend by oneself [*auprès de soi*] for Dasein that one will be better able to hear and understand what not only friend, but also Dasein, "voice," "carrying-distance," "being-by," and "ear," etc., mean. To begin to read the carrying-distance of this "Tragen" with the seriousness it calls for, it would be necessary to neglect nothing of the thinking attention that Heidegger accords to the German semantics of *Tragen* and to all the potential resources that he exploits on this or with which he plays, as he will do in particular much later, on a motif that is not just any motif, since it is a matter of nothing less than difference, of one of the names he gives to difference (*Unter-schied*), to wit, *Austrag*.

Without having the time to engage myself in this here, I only recall that this singular writing of *Tragen* is deployed in particular in *Die Sprache*, precisely, the text in *Unterwegs zur Sprache* that dates from 1950, and so from 23 years after *Sein und Zeit*. Its title, *Die Sprache*, thus reproduces a part of the title of the chapter of *Sein und Zeit* in which we read this evocation of the voice of the friend that every *Dasein bei sich trägt*, namely, "Dasein und Rede. Die Sprache." In *Die Sprache*, without in fact [*même*] neglecting the idiom of "carrying to term," as is said of a child "carried to term" by its mother, in French "*porté à terme*" and in German "*ein ausgetragenes Kind*," Heidegger describes what I shall call the singular spacing of the call (*Ruf*). Like the voice of the friend, carried with Dasein by Dasein, the call is neither in the ear nor far from the ear, is neither near nor far away. And to describe this topics or this atopics, Heidegger calls to the light of day [*fait venir au jour*] all the enigmas in gestation in the semantics of *Tragen*. Let me select, for lack of time, a few lines in accordance with what is called in them by the friend's voice thus carried. I cite the lines in German, but I shall not translate them; rather I shall hold myself between translation and paraphrase. In *Die Sprache*, Heidegger listens in to a Trakl poem, as he will do again elsewhere, at the place where Trakl also speaks of the brother and of the stranger in a text I spoke about some years ago. The sentences I am going to read follow the famous passage that says "Die Sprache *spricht*. Dies heißt zugleich und zuvor: Die *Sprache* spricht. Die Sprache? Und nicht der Mensch? . . . Der Ruf ruft zwar her. So bringt er das Anwesen des vordem Ungerufenen in eine Nähe. . . . Das Herrufen ruft in eine Nähe. Aber der Ruf entreißt gleichwohl das Gerufene nicht der Ferne, in der es durch das Hinrufen gehalten bleibt. Das Rufen ruft in sich und darum stets hin und her; her: ins Anwesen; hin: ins Abwesen" (*US* 20–21): Speech *speaks*. That also and first of all means: *speech* speaks. Speech? And not man? . . . The call calls indeed to come here. It thus brings to proximity the presence of what beforehand was not called. . . . The call to come calls to a proximity. But, for all that, the call does not uproot what it calls from the distance in which what is called remains held by the call that carries itself toward it. The call calls in itself and thus always goes and comes; here, toward presence, there, toward absence.

Everything said here of the call and its spacing, of its relation to distance and to proximity, to presence and absence, to "neither-inside-nor-outside," seems to me to suit what was already said of the *Rufcharakter des Gewissens* or of *Das Gewissen als Ruf der Sorge* (§§ 56–57) in *Sein und Zeit* ("The character of conscience as a call," "Conscience as the call of care"), as well as what was said of the voice of the friend that every Dasein carries with it (*bei sich trägt*)— in a site that is neither included nor excluded, neither interior nor exterior, neither near nor far, what already differs from a certain concept of the Aristotelian φιλία that is always tied to the values of presence, proximity, familiarity. Just as well in *Sein und Zeit* as in *Die Sprache*, the analysis of *Ruf* must no doubt be brought into contact with this little phrase on the voice of the friend, on the carrying-distance [*portée*] of this voice. I shall say, abusing a little the French idiom, that the *rapport* between these two *portées* of the voice is to my mind more than an analogy or a coincidence. I will come back to this.

And farther on, still in *Die Sprache*, following again the motif of the *Geviert* that gathers (*versammelt*: this will once more be my guiding thread) *das Dingen der Dinge* ("the thinging of things"), Heidegger advances in the space that relates or refers *Tragen* to *Austragen* as carrying (to term) [*portée*], gestation, bringing into the world that brings to term or to birth, and to *Austrag* as difference or διαφορά. Διαφορά signifies at once difference (*Unterschied*), but also the *differend*, disagreement, the dis- by which one *is carried* to one side, by which one is separated in *being carried along* in the discord. In διαφορά, as in rapport, relation, reference, difference, there is the reference to *ference*, to carrying [*portée*], to the Greek φέρω or the Latin *fero*, to διαφέρω (I differ, I defer, I separate, and I carry, I bear, to the end). I cite again: "Die Dinge tragen, indem sie dingen, Welt aus": "Things, as they unfold their thing-being, bring into the world, carry the world (to the world)." "Unsere alte Sprache nennt das Austragen: bern, bären, daher die Wörter 'gebären' und 'Gebärde'. Dingend sind die Dinge Dinge. Dingend gebärden sie Welt" (*US* 22): "Our old tongue names this 'carrying to term' (*Austragen*) bern, bären, from which come the words 'Gebären' [give birth, carry to term, deliver, bear children: all gestation] and 'Gebärde' [gesture, deeds, behavior, how one carries oneself, comportment]. In unfolding their thing-being are things things. In unfolding their thing-being, they [here I risk a neologism] 'gest' ['*gestent*'] world [they carry it during gestation, carry it to term, give it a comportment, a countenance, a figure, a face, a gesture]."

Now the other name of what carries the world to the world and to term in the *Austrag* is the gathered unity or intimacy of the dif-ference (*Unter-Schied* that Heidegger writes here in two words) or of the διαφορά. I am again going to read and, if not translate, at least paraphrase a passage in which this constellation of difference gathered into unity, of *tragen, Austrag* and *Nachträglichkeit*, of *walten, gönnen*, and of *Ereignis* should introduce us "nachträglich" (25 years behind) to the thought of friendship that is announced in the little phrase of *Sein und Zeit* I am just now trying to approach. At the same time, in this passage, the selection or the cutting out I must do for lack of time will follow the course of concepts and words that will be, I think, indispensable for us to approach the configuration of φιλεῖν, πόλεμος, λόγος, on the path of thinking of Heidegger. The names of these concepts then are *tragen, Austrag, nachträglich, walten, gönnen, Ereignis*. They all resist translation, which is why the violence of my gesture will consist not only in cutting out but in paraphrasing rather than translating.

Heidegger has just said that the world accords to things the favor of their essence or their unfolding. The word that is important here to me is *gönnen*; we'll see why shortly and how it translates for Heidegger the very movement of φιλεῖν in φύσις, as he follows its traces in Heraclitus: "Diese [Welt] gönnt den Dingen ihr Wesen. Die Dinge gebärden Welt. Welt gönnt die Dinge" (*US* 24). The world offers, gives, let us rather say accords, to things their being, their essence, the unfolding of what they are. I prefer the word "accord" to the word chosen by the French translators ("offer") [or the English translator ("grant")] to translate *gönnen*. For we find in this word, besides the sense of generous gift, that of accord, of ἁρμονία, of harmony as accord quasi musical and perceptible to a certain ear. This harmony will be of importance to us shortly in our reading of Heidegger's Heraclitus. Then this world accords to things their being. Things carry the world (to term or in gestation: *die Dinge gebärden Welt*). The world is the accord of things, world equals accord of things (*Welt gönnt die Dinge*), the world accords things in the double sense of giving things, giving to things their essence but also their accord.

Farther on one sees appear the *walten* that, as we'll shortly see, will have long commanded all the thought of the Heraclitean πόλεμος as Heidegger interprets it. Intimacy, interiority (*Innigkeit*) that gathers the world and things is not a confusion (*Verschmelzung*). This intimacy prevails, imposes itself or its force, indeed its violence; it rules or dominates (*waltet*); it *l'emporte*, I would say in French, or in English, it *carries the day*, only where the inside (*das Innige*), world, and thing are purely separated, disjoined (*rein sich scheidet*), and remain disjoined, separated, dissociated (*geschieden bleibt*). In the middle of the two, in the between that separates world and thing, in their "inter," in this *Unter* of the *Unter-Schied*, in the *dis-* of the *dif-ference*, the separation carries the day (*in ihrem inter, in diesem Unter- waltet der Schied*). Then, after insisting on the fact that dif-ference (*Unter-Schied*) must no longer be heard here as the name of a general concept holding for all possible differences, but as *this* difference, the one and unique (*als dieser Eine. Er ist einzig.*), Heidegger names this difference "der durchtragende Austrag," what carries to term, in the sense of birth and gestation, what always carries and includes [*comporte*] the other itself in and up to separation but in the intimacy of the difference. The intimacy of the dif-ference (*Die Innigkeit des Unter-Schiedes*) is what unites or unifies the διαφορά (*das Einigende der Διαφορά*). If one takes into account that in the words διαφορά or *difference*, then in Greek as well as in Latin, the division or separation is in *rapport*, like *rapport* and the word "rapport" itself, like relation, with the *portée* or the *port* of *porter* (φέρειν, *fero*), one finds more than justification and necessity for what resembles the play of Heidegger with the semantics of *tragen*, when he writes for example: "Die Innigkeit des Unter-Schiedes ist das Einigende der Διαφορά, des durchtragenden Austrags. Der Unter-Schied trägt Welt in ihr Welten, trägt die Dinge in ihr Dingen aus. Also sie austragend, trägt er sie einander zu": The intimacy of the dif-ference is the uniting of the διαφορά of what *carries to term* in having *carried* through and through. Dif-ference carries to term the world in its becoming-world, carries to term things in their becoming-thing. Carrying them thus to term, it relates them one to the other. *Der Unter-Schied*, the dif-ference does not mediatize after the fact [*après coup*] (*vermittelt nicht nachträglich*) in connecting world and things with the help of an added-on mediation (*durch eine herzugebrachte Mitte*). Dif-ference first discovers (*ermittelt*), makes world and things accede, as mediation (*als Mitte*), to their being (*Wesen*), that is, to their mutual rapport (*in ihr Zueinander*), whose unity it carries to term (*dessen Einheit er austrägt*) (*US* 25).

The German semantics of *Tragen, Austrag, Nachträglich*—which we are following here as the problematics of *Unter-Schied* or difference and which I am trying to translate into the Latin semantics of *port*, of *rapport*, of *relation*, of the *portée*, of *porter à terme* (carrying to term), of *comportment*, etc., with a view to problematizing and better interrogating the phrase of *Sein und Zeit* that we will not lose from view (*das Hören der Stimme des Freundes, den jedes Dasein bei sich trägt*)—Heidegger tends to want to protect this semantics, justly, against a certain Latinization. It is necessary to insist on this, because the whole historial perspectivizing of φιλεῖν, of πόλεμος, and of λόγος—whose reconstitution I would like to try to sketch—essentially implies, as we will see, a sort of Greco-German alliance and a foreclosure [*forclusion*], indeed the diagnosis of a decay of φιλεῖν into *amicitia*. Where we are, in *Die Sprache*, Heidegger underscores that *Unter-Schied* is no more a distinction between objects (*Gegenstände*) of our representation (*Vorstellen*) than it is a relation between world and thing. If "relation" has the same etymology as the *ferre* of difference or reference, like the whole family of "port," "*porter*," "rapport," etc., one sees that it is a matter of dissociating the thought of *tragen* and of *Austrag* from every *relational distinction*, indeed from every objective "dimension," for Heidegger next takes analogous precautions concerning the Latin word *dimension*. I paraphrase again a passage before coming back to the voice of the friend with Dasein concerning which we already know we must avoid speaking of proximity or distance, of relation or distinction, of inside and outside, of objectivity and subjectivity. In the last passage I am getting ready to paraphrase again, *Ereignis* and *Gönnen* appear, which gather what at once will be more and more inseparable in Heidegger's thought (a thought of the *Ereignis* that would be less a mode of being [*eine Art des Seins*] than being would be a mode of *Ereignis* [*eine Art des Ereignisses*][3] and a thought of that gift accorded or according that, as we'll see, Heidegger has never ceased to place in the heart of φιλεῖν). Here then is this passage. It marks that all that "Unter-Schied" is not, all that from which "der Unter-Schied" must be carefully distinguished is said in Latin: "Der Unter-Schied ist weder Distinktion noch Relation": "The *Unter-Schied* is neither distinction nor relation" (*US* 25).

"Das Wort 'Unter-Schied' meint demnach nicht mehr eine Distinktion, die erst durch unser Vorstellen zwischen Gegenständen aufgestellt wird." The word *Unter-Schied* then no longer signifies a distinction established between objects by our representation only. "Der Unter-Schied ist gleichwenig nur eine Relation, die zwischen Welt und Ding vorliegt, so daß ein Vorstellen, das darauf trifft, sie feststellen kann." The dif-ference is just as little a simple relation present between world and thing and such as the representation can establish it after encountering it. "Der Unter-Schied wird nicht nachträglich von Welt und Ding als deren Beziehung abgehoben." Dif-ference is not abstracted after the fact (*nachträglich*) from the world and the thing as their rapport. "Der Unter-Schied für Welt und Ding *ereignet* Dinge in das Gebärden von Welt, *ereignet* Welt in das Gönnen von Dingen" (*US* 25). The untranslatability culminates in this sentence: Dif-ference for world and thing *ereignet* . . . things in the gesture of gestation of the world, it *ereignet* the world in the gift accorded of things.

This detour through an overloaded context permits beginning to read *Tragen* and *gönnen*. This "carrying" and this "according" (in the double sense of the gesture of according a gift or a favor, *gönnen*, and of the harmonic accord) will have marked the Heideggerian thought of φιλεῖν. I hope that this detour will not seem too long nor anachronic when, returning nearly a quarter century earlier, we must try to hear what this brief and elliptical allusion to the voice of the friend that each *Dasein bei sich trägt* says.

(3) There was a *third reason* why I said this friend was only "evoked." This extracted or abstracted part of the friend that Dasein carries with it, neither near nor far, neither in nor outside of it, neither in the ear, however "inner," nor outside the ear, is not just any part of the friend. It is what can permit *evocation* in general, to wit, the voice. What is evoked in this furtive or fleeting but doubtless decisive evocation is a vocation, indeed a call within self [*en moi*], *Ruf* or rather *Stimme* that will then be able to compose with all sorts of possibilities (*einstimmen, Einstimmigkeit, Stimmung, Bestimmung, Übereinstimmung, Verstimmen, Verstimmtheit, Verstimmung*). Besides, a little earlier (*SZ*, § 29), analyzing *Die existenziale Konstitution des Da* and *Das Da-sein als Befindlichkeit*, Heidegger devotes long and keen analyses to *Gestimmtheit* and to the fact that in *Gestimmtheit* it is always already according to the dimension of a *Stimmung* that Dasein is disclosed (*erschlossen*) as the being [*étant*] that is in its being delivered over (*überantwortet*, handed over, abandoned) as the being that has, in existing, to be (*SZ* 134–35). Since it is going to be a question of the friend and of friendship, and since I do not know yet what name to accord what some will be tempted to call a feeling, sentiment, affect, passion, or πάθη, it is necessary to begin by recalling the connection between *Befindlichkeit* (a word for which no good translation exists: "state of mind," "disposition," "*disposibilité*," "affection"), the tonality of *Stimmung*, the being-delivered-over of *Überantwortung* and the being-thrown of *Geworfenheit*. As Heidegger recalls (*SZ*, § 29, p. 137), *Befindlichkeit* is not a state of the soul, a psychic quality that would then be projected onto things or persons. Since the little phrase on the voice of the friend belongs to a long analysis of *Mitsein* in the modalities of *Mitteilung, Mitverstehen*, and *Mitbefindlichkeit*, nothing that concerns the friend would come under then a psychology, no more

than a social science or human science in general, indeed an anthropology. It is Dasein and not ψυχή, man, self, nor subject, conscious or unconscious, that carries the friend in its voice or rather in hearing this voice.

Since the convention or the contract (in any case, the suggestion of John Sallis) wants me to privilege here a certain rapport of Heideggerian thought to the Greek tradition, I shall underscore three traits concerning Aristotle.

First, Heidegger refuses to determine *Befindlichkeit* as the place of affects or feelings, at least in the psychological sense of the term. And he then refers positively (*SZ*, § 29, p. 138) to the fact that Aristotle has not studied the πάθη in a psychology but in a rhetoric, a rhetoric itself understood as a hermeneutic, "the first systematic hermeneutic of the everydayness of *Miteinandersein*." It is in the same chapter that Heidegger mentions just as positively the tradition of Scheler, which goes back to Augustine and Pascal: one has access to the truth or to knowledge on the basis of love or charity and not the reverse (*SZ* 139).

And yet, *second*, everything that in this evocation of the friend depends on an analytic of *Sprache* and λόγος comes immediately after and thus supposes a critique or rather a "destruction" of the Aristotelian interpretation of λόγος. In the conclusions of the immediately preceding chapter (*SZ*, § 33, p. 159), Heidegger regrets that Aristotle's first phenomenological impulse in the analysis of λόγος was interrupted or broken to become a simple theory of judgment, of connection or separation of representations and concepts. Among other things, this means that everything in the future that will articulate, in an essential way, in Heidegger's thought λέγειν or λόγος and φιλεῖν will claim to come back to a pre-Aristotelian, in truth, a pre-Platonic, hearing of λόγος. Not only does the evocation of the voice of the friend follow a critique of the Aristotelian limit in the interpretation of λόγος, but it will also be followed by an analogous reservation (*SZ* 165) about the definition of man as *animal rationale*, ζῷον λόγον ἔχον, a definition that, Heidegger says, is not false but covers over or dissimulates the phenomenal ground from which this definition of Dasein is uprooted. This double reservation regarding Aristotle does not prevent Heidegger from defining the voice of the friend in such a way that only the opening of a Dasein is up to it. Dasein being the essence of man then is not contradictory to the Aristotelian proposal according to which there is friendship par excellence (πρώτη φιλία or τέλεια φιλία) only between men: not between gods and men, not between animal and man, not between gods, not between animals. On this point, Heidegger would remain Aristotelian: Dasein alone has a friend, Dasein alone can carry it *bei sich*, man alone as Dasein pricks up, opens, or lends an ear to the voice of the friend, since this voice is what permits Dasein to open itself to its own potentiality-for-being. The animal has no friend, man has no friendship properly so called for the animal. The animal that is "world poor," that has neither language nor experience of death, etc., the animal that has no hand, the animal that has no friend, has no ear either, the ear capable of hearing and of carrying the friend that is also the ear that opens Dasein to its own potentiality-for-being and that, as we will hear in a moment, is the ear of being, the ear for being.

The difference between animal and Dasein passes there again through the possibility of the "as such" (*als*) and of understanding or comprehending (*entendre, Verstehen*). Elsewhere I have tried to problematize Heidegger's analyses in this place. I shall underscore and generalize here only this remark: whether a matter of the hand, of feet, eye, sex, or ear, the Heideggerian phenomenology of Dasein's body, in what is more original and more necessary in that phenomenology, supposes precisely the phenomenological as such or the phenomenological "as such." The structural difference between Dasein and non-Dasein, for example the animal, is the difference between a being open to the as such and a being that is not, and therefore is "weltarm," world poor. In one stroke [*Du coup*], the voice of the friend, and consequently friendship in general, gives itself to be heard and understood [*entendre*] only in the phenomenological space of the "as such." No friendship outside a world in which "Verstehen" and phenomenology are possible. And the animal, if something like that existed that had some unity, will have no ear. No ear capable of hearing.

Nevertheless, *third*, the very moment he confirms this Aristotelian philosopheme, Heidegger clearly intends to return to a pre-Aristotelian, indeed pre-Platonic, hearing of λόγος, that is to say, to an experience of φιλεῖν more originary than that of the Platonico-Aristotelian φιλία. What does this claim signify? Up to what point is it sustained? It is surprising, yet all the more significant, that Heidegger often speaks of φιλεῖν but practically never names φιλία; and when, for example in the seminar of 1943–44 on Heraclitus, he does so, translating φιλία by *Gunst*, Plato and Aristotle, the great philosophers of φιλία, will not even be evoked.

Neither friendship nor φιλία are expressly named, it seems to me, in *Sein und Zeit*, in particular in the little phrase around which we are circling. Heidegger does not speak of friendship, of the concept or the general essence of friendship, but of the friend, of someone, of a Dasein in the singular whose voice alone (a partial object, perhaps a psychoanalyst would say) opens in a way the hearing of Dasein.

Why and how does it "open" Dasein? No doubt because a voice of the other, the other itself, is carried by every Dasein thus "bei sich," not in it, nor outside it, but "*bei sich*." The order of the existential analytic here is the following: no discourse (*Rede*) without (hearing) understanding [*entendre*], in the sense first of comprehension (*Verstehen, Verständlichkeit*), no understanding agreement [*entente*] or *Verstehen* without hearing (*Hören*). Hearing is constitutive of discourse, but does not consist in an acoustic phenomenon of the physiopsychological order; hearing has no need of the "inner" or "outer" ear in the organic sense of the term. Hearing is the "primary and authentic opening of Dasein for its ownmost potentiality-for-being (*Das Hören konstituiert sogar die primäre und eigentliche Öffenheit des Daseins für sein eigenes Seinkönnen*)" (*SZ* 163). What the ear is, the essence and the destination of Dasein's ear, will be understood starting from this *Hören*, and not the inverse. And Heidegger names the hearing of the voice of the friend in the same phrase, in order to make explicit [*expliciter*] this opening of Dasein to its ownmost, its most authentic potentiality-for-being. If hearing the friend's voice constitutes Dasein's opening to its ownmost potentiality-for-being, that means there is no Dasein without it, no properness, indeed no self-proximity of Dasein without this "bei sich Tragen" of the different other, of the other-different as friend but of the other. Dasein has an ear and can hear then only insofar as Dasein carries "bei sich" the friend, the voice of the friend. No ear without friend. No friend without ear.

Dasein's opening to its *ownmost* potentiality-for-being, as hearing the *voice of the other as friend*, is absolutely originary. This opening does not come under a psychology, a sociology, an anthropology, an ethics, or a politics, etc. The voice of the other friend, of the other as friend, the ear that I prick up to it, is the condition of my own-proper-being. But this voice nevertheless defines the figure of an originary sharing [*partage*] and an originary belonging, of a *Mitteilen* or of everything that is, as Heidegger says in this passage, "shared" (*geteilt* [*SZ* 164]) with the other in the *Mitsein* of discourse, of address and response. Shared [*commune*] belonging, in difference, is immediately inscribed, like a kind of originary socius, in what passes, through the ear, from *Hören, hearing,* to *Hörigkeit* as obedient listening—the other-friend, the other as friend being there already, its voice at least already having sounded, as if it dictated a kind of law the moment Dasein comes to its own potentiality-for-being—and to *Gehörigkeit,* to belonging. There would not be any properness, any proper potentiality-for-being of Dasein without this voice of the other-friend yet so difficult to situate in the topology of its "comportment," so to speak, in what it carries with it, in it outside it, in its "bei sich tragen," that is, "in" or "with" a certain ear for which the distinction between inside and outside is so *unheimlich.* Dasein hears (*hört*) because it can comprehend or hear, *entendre,* in the sense of understand (*verstehen*). As understanding being-in-the-world (*In-der-Welt-sein*) with the other (*mit den Anderen*), Dasein listens to (*"hörig"*; a word that Heidegger leaves between quotation marks to underscore the play from hearing/listening as "hören" to listening to as obedience, indeed submission or subjection). And in this obedient listening (*Hörigkeit*), there is indeed Dasein's belonging: Dasein is from then on "zugehörig," belongs already to what could be called the belonging or sharing of the community ("Als verstehendes In-der-Welt-sein mit den Anderen ist es dem Mitdasein und ihm selbst 'hörig' und in dieser Hörigkeit zugehörig" [*SZ* 163]: As understanding being-in-the-world with the other, it [Dasein] is attentively or obediently listening to *Mitdasein* and itself. And in this obedient listening it belongs, or it is partner, it participates or shares).

But what I am anxious to insist on, before provisionally leaving this inexhaustible paragraph, is that this singular friend that every Dasein carries and hears "bei sich," no more represents friendship in general than it is necessarily friendly. The voice is not friendly, first because it is the voice of the friend, of someone, of an other Dasein responding to the question "who?" What defines the "voice of the friend," then, is not a quality, the friendly characteristic, but a belonging. But because this voice is not necessarily friendly, one ought not conclude for all that that the voice of this friend is neuter or neutral. Why? The voice of the friend is not reduced to the phoneme or to the acoustic phenomenon, does not merge with the noise perceived by an animal ear or auditory organ. This voice is an essentially understandable voice, the possibility of speech or discourse. It is essentially marked, like everything found at the opening of Dasein, by a certain *Stimmung* and by *Befindlichkeit*. It has then a tonality or a modality that one would call, in a language not very Heideggerian, affective. But here this voice says nothing determined. Heidegger lends it no remark. Nor as voice is it, regarding essentials, a kind of witness, that eye of conscience that accompanies, keeps watch over, and oversees, if at least the perceptive, visual, and cognitive, indeed theoretical connotation of attestation or testament is valued. But if it is not an eye of conscience, it is not either the inner voice of conscience, for this voice is not interior. One would not be able to pose on this subject questions of a critical or deconstructive type that recourse to the monologue or to the purely inner voice of the *ego* in Husserl's *Logical Investigations* could call for. Here there is no phenomenon of ideal self-presence in the inner voice. It is really a matter of the voice of the other.

One of the most difficult questions in deciphering this paragraph is a question that can just as well be qualified as logical, rhetorical, philological, indeed poetic. It concerns the status of this allusion to the voice of the friend in the demonstrative chain of the paragraph and finally step by step in the chain of the chapter and the book. A philological or poetic question: if the voice of the friend is only one example among others of the "bei sich tragen" of the other by every Dasein, is there behind this example a kind of more or less poetic τόπος, a quasi-citation? Even if, as is unfortunately my case for the moment, I cannot recognize the literal detail of a very determined citation, one can always think of a τόπος rather current, not only in everyday language but in numerous literatures that will have, under one form or another, named a "voice of the friend." Even if there is no hidden citation, in the strict sense of the word "citation," Heidegger doubtless makes at least a kind of virtual reference to current expressions, "the voice of the friend," the "bei sich tragen," recurrent expressions, allusions to a τόπος, but justly to underscore the enigmatic and necessary character of the τόπος, of the place to which this τόπος refers, to wit, a voice that is situated neither inside nor out of Dasein, neither near nor far, a voice that participates as it were in the opening of the Da-, of Da-sein, and that takes the exemplary form of a voice, in the very absence of the voice's carrier. This response to the question that I called, for want of anything better, philological or poetic leaves it unsolved and even relaunches the question of the exemplarity of this example. Why would the voice of the friend be a better example of this situation, of this topology of Da-sein? One definitely understands the necessity to take up the example of a voice of the other in a chapter entitled *Da-sein und Rede. Die Sprache*. But why a "voice of the friend"? Why not the enemy? The lover? The father, the mother, the brother, or the sister, the son or the daughter or so many other figures still, all also "speaking"? Everything happens as if the friend were not one figure among others, and therefore could play an exemplary role for being the figureless [*le sans-figure*], or as is said in French *le figurant* or similarly in English, the figure-head, that individual being no one can be anyone, the exemplary, then at once singular and general, configuration of every possible other, of every possible figure, or rather of every possible voice of the other. Every voice of the other is in some way the voice of the friend, figured by the voice of the friend for Dasein. For Dasein alone can and must have a friend that speaks. Dasein alone has an ear for the friend that speaks.

Here is imposed on me a logicorhetorical dimension of the same question, the question of exemplarity. After the evocation of the friend, when Heidegger speaks of "Aufeinander-hören," of listening-to-one-another *in general*, has the friend been only one example among others (and then why this example rather than another or than the contrary example)? Or else does Heidegger also speak of the other as the voice of the friend, such that the exemplarity functions here in another sense, not in the sense of the example among other possible examples, but of the exemplarity that gives to be read and carries in itself *all* the figures of *Mitdasein* as *Aufeinander-hören*? All the figures of *Mitsein* would be figures of the friend, even if they were secondarily unfriendly or indifferent. The internal structure of chainings in this short paragraph does not seem to me to permit by itself alone deciding between the two hypotheses. Rather, if I orient myself toward the second, that is because a larger context, the one I am now going to try to recognize, seems to indicate that for Heidegger φιλεῖν, on the nonpsychological, nonanthropological, nonethicopolitical plane of the existential analytic and above all of the question of being or φύσις, welcomes within itself, in its very accord, many other modes than that of friendliness, but as well opposition, tension, confrontation, rejection, indeed, we will come to this, if not war, at least *Kampf* or πόλεμος. And it seems reasonable to think that Heidegger still speaks of the other as the voice of the friend when, immediately after the evocation of that voice, he concludes his paragraph in this way: "Listening to one another, which constitutes *Mitsein*, has for possible forms: following (*Folgen*), accompanying (*Mitgehen*), the negative modes of not-hearing (*des Nicht-Hörens*), of opposition (*des Widersetzens*), of defying (*des Trotzens*), of turning away (*der Abkehr*)" (*SZ* 163). In the hypothesis I am going to follow, these negative modes could still determine the hearing of the voice of the friend. To be opposed to the friend, to turn away from it, to defy it, to not hear it, that is still to hear and keep it, to carry with self, *bei sich tragen*, the voice of the friend.

Consequently, if one still goes no further than *Sein und Zeit*, than so to speak the premises of the course I would like to sketch, one can say that there is neither opposition nor contradiction between what is said of the voice of the friend as exemplar of *Mitsein* as *Aufeinander-hören* and what is said near the end of the book about struggle (*combat, Kampf*) as the essential form of *Miteinandersein*, of community (*Gemeinschaft*), and of the people (*Volk*). That is because the voice of the friend does not exclude opposition, because it does not oppose itself to the opposition that there is no essential opposition between φιλεῖν and *Kampf* or, as will be said later, πόλεμος.

Before leaving *Sein und Zeit*, I would like to situate around the word *Kampf* not only a motif that does not at all contradict the evocation of the friend's voice as the opening of Dasein as *Mitsein*, but on the contrary, prolonging it, announces very precisely the thematization so insistent of struggle (*Streit*, πόλεμος, and above all *Kampf*) in the *Rectorate Discourse* (1933) and in the *Introduction to Metaphysics* (1935). Section 74 of *Sein und Zeit* (*Die Grundverfassung der Geschichtlichkeit*), which, once more, makes explicit Dasein's own proper potentiality-for-being, would call for a long and meticulous reading. I retain from it one single trait. Compared to sharing or communication (*Mitteilung*) and on the same level, to the same degree, struggle (*Kampf*) is how the power (*Macht*) of destiny (*Geschickes*) is set free. This destiny (*Geschick*) is here the *Geschehen* of Dasein as *Mitgeschehen*, the historiality of or as being-with. The *Geschehen*, the historial event, so to speak, that of which historiality is made, to wit, *Geschichtlichkeit* whose fundamental constitution Heidegger analyzes here, is common or shared historiality under the form of community (*Gemeinschaft*) and the people (*Volk*). The common destiny of the community or the people sets free its power (*Macht*) in the sharing, the communication (*Mitteilung*), to be sure, but also both quite as much and quite as originarily, in the struggle (*Kampf*). This power that is thus set free in the common or shared struggle is also superpower (*Übermacht*), namely, the movement of a finite freedom that assumes, in the impact [*tranchant*] of a choice (*Wahl*), the nonpower (*die Ohnmacht*) of the turning away or of the being-turned-away (*Überlassenheit*). The motif of choice (*Wahl*) is at once indissociable from that of resolution, of authenticity of resolution or decision (*Eigentlichkeit der Entschlossenheit* [*SZ* 383]), but also of heritage (*Erbe*). Dasein, as it throws itself by anticipation toward death, inherits and chooses. The inherited possibility is at the same time chosen (*aber gleichwohl gewählten Möglichkeit überliefert* [*SZ* 384]).

All these possibilities—choice, tradition both inherited and chosen, authentic resolution also determined, in the same chapter (*SZ* 383), as the "projecting of oneself toward one's own being-guilty [or being-liable, being-accountable]—a project that keeps silent and is ready for anxiety (*das verschwiegene, angstbereite Sichentwerfen auf das eigene Schuldigsein*)" (*SZ* 385)—all that is at once historial, because shared in the being-together or with-one-another, in *Miteinandersein*, but also shared in the struggle and as struggle (*Kampf*). And so, just like "the voice of the friend," *Kampf* belongs to the very structure of Dasein. It belongs to its historial structure and thus, this must also be explicitly stated, to the subjectivity of the historial subject. For let us not forget what question announces section 74 on "The fundamental constitution of historiality (*Die Grundverfassung der Geschichtlichkeit*)":

> *to what extent and on the basis of what ontological conditions does historiality belong,*
> *as an essential constitution, to the subjectivity of the "historial" subject?* (inwiefern
> und auf Grund welcher ontologischen Bedingungen gehört zur Subjektivität des
> "geschichtlichen" Subjekts die Geschichtlichkeit als Wesensverfassung?) (*SZ* 382; Hei-
> degger's emphasis)

This section resonates historically in both the most acute and serious way with what is announced or found in gestation in Germany and Europe from 1927 to 1933. This resonance is not necessarily a consonance or a correspondence and remains to be interpreted. But in any case the discourse that is organized around *Volk* and *Kampf*, in *Sein und Zeit*, but also and above all in the *Rectorate Discourse* (1933) and in the *Introduction to Metaphysics* (1935), is not at all contradictory to the evocation of the friend's voice some 220 pages earlier, although, to my knowledge once again, those are the only two occurrences of the word *Freund*[4] and the word *Kampf* in *Sein und Zeit*. No contradiction, no opposition, I was saying, and first because opposition itself, but also resistance, disobedience, insubordination (*Widersetzen*) are described as essential possibilities of "listening-to-one-another" (*Aufeinander-hören*), of faithful or docile hearing (*Hörigkeit*), and of belonging (*Zugehörigkeit*), in which remains exemplary the hearing of the voice of the friend that each *Dasein bei sich trägt*.

If the voice of the friend, and then the reference to the friend, is as essential to Dasein's own-proper-being qua *Mitsein* as are the community, the people, and struggle (*Kampf*), it is no doubt logical to conclude from this that there is no friend that is not itself Dasein responding in return to the same description and the same conditions: no friend outside of the possibility of speaking, hearing [*entendre*], entering the *Miteinander* of *Auseinandersetzung*, no friend outside of belonging to a community and to a people (*Volk*). It is not entirely excluded, nor is it certain that belonging to the *same* community or to the *same* people, the experience of the *same* tongue, or the participation in the *same* struggle is the requisite condition for a voice of the friend to be carried *bei sich* by Dasein. That is not certain, no doubt it is excluded by the analysis of hearing (*Hören*) and of the pricked-up ear (*Horchen*) that immediately follows the evocation of the friend's voice. To prick up the ear is not to hear auditory sensations and noises, sonorous complexes, acoustic phenomena that could give rise to a psychology. No, we prick up our ear toward what is beyond the ear, the open ear, *over there*, in the world, *beside* [*auprès de*] what is for example usable in the world (again the expression *bei*, this time underscored: beim *innerweltlich Zuhandenen*) or *beside* what is heard [*entendu*]. We do not hear hearing but the heard and then what is understood: Dasein is essentially what hears in understanding, that is, in being beside what is heard in the sense of understood (*beim Verstandenen*) (*SZ* 164). It is by this, by the opening, the ear's opening, the opening of Dasein to its own proper potentiality-for-being and the opening of the ear as Dasein's ear, it is by this, through the ear, that Dasein carries the voice of the friend *bei sich*, but that it also carries itself beside [*auprès des*] things in the world and first beside what is heard and understood (beim *innerweltlich Zuhandenen* or *beim Verstandenen*). All the enigma of this topics of Dasein's ear and of the *Da* of *Sein* passes through this semantics of the *bei*, of this *beside*, this *auprès de* whose vicinity is neither the very close nor the infinitely distant.

Heidegger gives some rather interesting examples of what is heard and understood when we prick up our ear and when, from then on, beyond the acoustic phenomenon and noise, we are *by, beside* (*bei*), what is outside us. These examples are of two orders: on the one hand, things that are in the world as "innerweltlich Zuhandenen," and on the other hand, the discourse of the other. The first series associates modern technomilitary themes (the creaking wagon [*den knarrenden*

Wagen], the motorcycle, the marching column [*die Kolonne auf dem Marsch*] [*SZ* 163–64], then again the motorcycle and still the wagon) and nontechnological but no less significant themes (the north wind, the crackling fire, the woodpecker tapping the tree). Concerning the discourse of the other, we are in advance with the other (that is to say, outside ourselves) beside the being (*bei dem Seienden*) (*SZ* 164) on which the discourse bears [*porte*], even if we do not understand what the other says, even if the other speaks a foreign tongue, even if we hear unintelligible (*unverständliche*) words: this unintelligibility, for example, that of a foreign tongue, does not prevent us from understanding that we are dealing with an intelligible language that bears on the beings *beside* which Dasein can stand. This remark permits one to think that the voice of the friend whose originary and constitutive character we have analyzed must doubtless speak a language [*langue*] and belong to a *Volk*, but through this voice the tongue of a foreign people can be spoken. The friend can be a stranger, but like all Dasein it belongs to a community and a people, is engaged in a history, a *Geschehen* that is a *Mitgeschehen*, and in a struggle. Like every voice, and thus like every ear, those of the friend.

2 .

Starting from there, I shall try to show why and how φιλεῖν (I do not say φιλία) and πόλεμος (most often translated by *Kampf*) will never be either excluded or opposed in Heidegger's path of thinking. This path of thinking *traverses* (I leave to this word all its equivocation) a historicopolitical space and time that must not be forgotten or placed between parentheses but about which we must avoid haste and stereotypes. Instead of proceeding in a continuous and chronological manner, I thought it more propitious to a certain demonstration to start again from a text relatively late and distant from *Sein und Zeit*, then to come back progressively or regressively toward the texts closer to *Sein und Zeit*, those of 1933 and 1935, the *Rectorate Discourse* and *Introduction to Metaphysics* and certain texts on Hölderlin.

I start again then from the later texts. One of the first affinities between the thematics of *Sein und Zeit* in the configuration that we have just recalled (*Stimmung, Gestimmtheit, Befindlichkeit, Sprache, Rede, Hören, Hörigkeit, Zugehörigkeit, Ruf* and *Stimme des Freundes*) and the thematics of *Was ist das—die Philosophie?* (1955–56), passes, I would say, through the ear. On one hand, its thematics is the determination of φιλοσοφία as hearing the voice and the call of being, correspondence, accord, but also on the other hand, the reinterpretation of "destruction" as hearing. The response to the question "Was ist das—die Philosophie?" consists in a correspondence, an *Entsprechen*, with that toward which philosophy is underway (*unterwegs*). To respond or correspond to philosophy, to reach this *Entsprechen*, we must lend an ear (*hören*), Heidegger says, to what philosophy has already said to us in speaking to us, in addressing itself to us in a sort of summons [*assignation*] (*was die Philosophie uns schon zugesprochen hat*) (*WP* 21). On this condition will there be response, correspondence, responsibility, dialogue, tradition (*Entsprechung, Gespräch, Überlieferung*). Heidegger describes all that passes through a first *hearing* of the address, of the addressed summons, also as a process of appropriation *(Aneignung)* and of transformation. I underscore this to mark strongly the role of the ear in such appropriation. The word *Aneignung* is used at least twice in this context, and something more remarkable still, not only to designate the welcome of the tradition but also its "destruction." Decon-struction, or rather 'Destruktion,' is also an experience of the appropriation of the tradition, and this deconstructive appropriation signifies first, it calls itself, it calls, *heißt:* "open our ear *(unser Ohr öffnen).*" I cite this important paragraph *(WP* 22):

> Solche Aneignung der Geschichte ist mit dem Titel "Destruktion" gemeint. 'The word *"Destruktion"* aims at such an appropriation of history.' Der Sinn dies Wortes ist in *Sein und Zeit* (§ 6) klar umschrieben. 'The sense of this word is clearly delimited in *Sein und Zeit* (§ 6).' Destruktion bedeutet nicht Zerstören, sondern Abbauen, *Abtragen* [I underscore this last verb, of course] und Auf-die-Seite-stellen—nämlich die nur historischen Aussagen über die Geschichte der Philosophie. 'Destruction does not signify demolition that puts in ruins, but de-construction *(Abbauen)*, clearing away [or carrying away *(déport)*, I shall not say deportation, but displacing in order to remove is in question], to put aside historicizing statements on the history *(Geschichte)* of philosophy.' Destruktion heißt: unser Ohr öffnen, freimachen für das, was sich uns in der Überlieferung als Sein des Seienden zuspricht. 'Destruction means: to open our ear, to render it free for what, handed over to us in the tradition, is addressed to us or addresses to us its injunction as being of beings.'

To open the ear in order to appropriate the tradition of philosophy, to corre-spond to the call of the being of beings, to open the ear in order to appropriate also while "destructing," that is an experience that can give us to *entendre* (to hear and to understand) what the same text says in 1955 of symphony and harmony, of φιλεῖν as συμφωνία and as ἁρμονία. *Was ist das—die Philosophie?* does not name φιλία, and that is no doubt not by chance. Heidegger is pushed by a "destruc-tive" necessity to try to hear and understand [*entendre*] φιλεῖν before the Platonic and Aristotelian φιλία. He translates φιλεῖν, of which he speaks a great deal, by *das Lieben*, loving, before any distinction between the loving of love and the loving of friendship, what in French, in a seminar I am devoting to these questions, I call *aimance*. What is rather funny [*drôle*] is that the modern Greek translation of Heidegger's text retranslates in its turn *Lieben*, not by φιλεῖν, but by ἀγάπη, ἀγάπαν, which gives some peculiar sentences. When Heidegger writes: "Φιλεῖν, lieben bedeutet hier im Sinne Heraklits: ὁμολογεῖν, so sprechen, wie der λόγος spricht, d. h. dem λόγος entsprechen" *(WP* 13): "φιλεῖν, loving, signifies here, in the Heraclitean sense, ὁμολογεῖν, speaking as λόγος speaks, that is, to corre-spond to λόγος," the modern Greek says: "φιλειν, ἀγαπῶ, σημαίνει ἐδῶ . . . τὸ ἡρακλείτειο νόημα: ὁμολογεῖν, νὰ ὁμιλοῦμε ἔστι ὅπως ὁμιλεῖ ὁ Λόγος, δηλαδὴ νὰ ὁμολογοῦμε πρὸς τὸν Λόγον."

When Heidegger links together the question "What is philosophy?" and that of φιλεῖν, it is a matter of getting back to that moment, which was not only a moment in time but a dimension of the experience of being and of λόγος where the experience of φιλεῖν and even of the φιλόσοφος has not yet given rise to φιλοσοφία. Here one form of the same question that Heidegger does not formulate in this way but for which if you wish I would take responsibility could be: how does one hear and understand (*entendre*) (and this hearing understanding is not only the understanding of the sense of a word, but also an experience without limit) a φιλεῖν that not only is not yet φιλία but about which philosophy, still too young or come too late for that, has no authority to question, since it is born itself of something like an event unexpectedly coming over φιλεῖν and over the understanding agreement [*entente*] of φιλεῖν? What about φιλεῖν before φιλία and φιλοσοφία? "*What about φιλεῖν?*" and not "What is φιλεῖν?" or "What is the essence of φιλεῖν?" for the question form τί ἐστιν "what is?" does not hold the ultimate competence. It itself is rendered possible *de jure* by a movement of φιλεῖν. We are going to see how, according to Heidegger, it would already be in the sphere of influence [*mouvance*] of φιλεῖν.

We are caught in the ring of a circle insofar as, when questioning about philosophy, we have already taken a look over philosophy (*wir schon einen Einblick in die Philosophie genommen haben*) (*WP* 11). The ring of this circle has already engaged us in the Greek tongue that is not one tongue among others. Why is it not one tongue among others? The response to the question, as obscure and authoritarian as it seems, in any case for me, is indispensable to the intelligence of what Heidegger will say about φιλεῖν in the word φιλόσοφος, such as Heraclitus, Heidegger says, will probably have struck, stamped it (*geprägt*, ἐκτυπωθεκε, says the modern Greek translation). The Greek tongue alone, Heidegger says, is λόγος. From then on, in that tongue, what is said (*das Gesagte*) merges in a remarkable way with what the said names (*nennt*). The said of saying and the named would immediately merge, so that the language would be immediately transparent, transgressed toward the thing itself, without the sometimes opaque or indirect mediation of the verbal signification (*Wortbedeutung*). Heidegger writes what I have just given you without conviction but as the premise of what is going to follow:

> When we hear a Greek word with a Greek ear (*Wenn wir ein griechisches Wort griechisch hören*), then we are docilely following its λέγειν, its immediate exposition (*seinem unmittelbaren Darlegen*). What it exposes is there before us (*Was es darlegt, ist das Vorliegende*). Through the word heard with a Greek ear (*durch das griechisch gehörte Wort*), we are immediately *by* the thing present there before us (*unmittelbar bei der vorliegenden Sache selbst* [I underscore the "by," the "*bei*"]), and not first *by* a simple verbal signification (*nicht zunächst bei einer bloßen Wortbedeutung*).

Supposing that such is demonstrated, *concesso non dato*, I fail to see how, from then on, that could not be said of every tongue from the moment one hears with the ear, so to speak, of that tongue. But let us leave this. The question that matters more to me is the following: what can λέγειν, when we lend to it a Greek and friendly ear, give us to hear and understand [*entendre*] in this history or in this fable of φιλεῖν? Heidegger then hears the word φιλοσοφία. This word would be originarily an adjective, formed on the model of φιλάργυρος, "the one who loves money," the friend of money (*silberliebend*); φιλότιμος, friend of honor (*ehrliebend*). It is important that this be an adjective, in the first place because, when Heraclitus strikes this word, φιλοσοφία does not exist: "for Heraclitus, there is not yet any φιλοσοφία (*für Heraklit gibt es noch nicht φιλοσοφία*)." The ἀνὴρ φιλόσοφος is not what one would call today a philosopher, "a 'philosophical' man (*ein 'philosophischer' Mensch*)" (*WP* 12). The ἀνὴρ φιλόσοφος is the one that loves σοφόν, "ὅς φιλει τὸ σοφόν." Now what does φιλεῖν mean? The response essentially implies the λόγος, whence the necessity of the detour of a short while ago. No φιλεῖν without λόγος or without λέγειν. Then, I shall add, no φιλεῖν without hearing. "Φιλεῖν," Heidegger says, "lieben bedeutet hier im Sinne Heraklits: ὁμολογεῖν, so sprechen, wie der λόγος spricht, d. h. dem λόγος entsprechen": "φιλεῖν, loving, signifies here, in the sense of Heraclitus, ὁμολογεῖν, to speak here as λόγος speaks, that is, to correspond to Λόγος". Φιλεῖν, then, is to accord oneself to the λέγειν of λόγος, to hear and respond to it. This given accord is indeed a responding, a corresponding, an *Entsprechen*, an understanding [*entente*] through correspondence in the order of *Sprechen* or *Sprache*, of λόγος, according to the same (ὁμολογεῖν). One could already carp, although I won't, about what opens the possibility of φιλεῖν in the experience of correspondence but also of corresponsibility, in a nonsubjective sense and perhaps nonhuman, nonpsychoanthropological, nonmoral and nonpolitical sense. Responding, co-responding would be φιλεῖν, as co-responding with or to λέγειν and not first with some individual or collective *subject*. At least there would be correspondence with someone or a few only insofar as a correspondence in language, tongue, λέγειν and *Sprache*, will already be engaged, opened, or rather opening. It would be necessary to think correspondence according to λέγειν in order to have access to the correspondence called personal, friendly, or loving in general. (From there one would be easily led, I note in passing, to that Aristotelian proposition that is situated nevertheless in a place apparently derived with respect to this one here—according to which the ἐνέργεια of φιλία, the presence in act of friendship, requires that one speak to the other in its very presence. Friendship exhausts itself in ἀπροσηγορία, immediate non-hailing [*noninterpellation*], nonapostrophe, nonaddress, when one does not speak directly enough to the friend.) The correspondence Heidegger speaks about in order to define homology, ὁμολογεῖν, *Entsprechen*, as correspondence with λέγειν, is the accord of voices, harmony, unison, *Einklang*, with σοφόν: ἁρμονία. Moreover, *Einklang* is found retranslated in modern Greek by συμφωνία. It is not only the understanding [*entente*] of the word φιλεῖν that must then pass through the ear and preferably the Greek ear, it is φιλεῖν itself. "Dieses Entsprechen steht im Einklang mit dem σοφόν. Einklang ist ἁρμονία": "This correspondence is in accord with σοφόν. Accord is ἁρμονία." "Dies, daß sich beide ursprünglich einander fügen, weil sie zueinander verfügt sind, diese ἁρμονία ist das Auszeichnende des heraklitisch gedachten φιλεῖν, des Liebens": "This, that one being joins together[5] with the other in the reciprocity, that the two originarily join together because they are enjoined one to the other, this ἁρμονία characterizes φιλεῖν as Heraclitus thinks it, loving (*des Liebens*)" (*WP* 13).

In this harmonization, a being (*Wesen*) is joined together or up (*sich fügt*) with another. This syn-harmony perceptible to a quasi-musical ear (the modern Greek translates *sich fügen* by συναρμόζεται, συναρμόζονται) supposes the reciprocity of the there-and-back, the going and coming of exchange (*wechselweise*). A serious problem when one tries to draw the consequences of this mutuality in the moral and political field of friendship. What would be the political carrying-distance [*portée*] of a thought or an experience of φιλεῖν that would no longer respect this law of reciprocity and would appeal to dissemblance, heterogeneity, dissymmetry, disproportion, incommensurability, nonexchange, the excess of every measure and thus of all symmetry? All these words are not synonyms, of course. A democracy to come should give to be thought an equality that is not incompatible with a certain dissymmetry, with heterogeneity, or absolute singularity, an equality even requiring them and engaging them from a place that remains invisible but that orients me here, from afar, no doubt beyond the Heideggerian aim [*propos*].

In reciprocity (*wechselweise*), a being joins up and together with another, and the two, *beide*, one and the other in the two, *both* (French has neither *beide* nor *both*) *sich einander fügen* originarily (*ursprünglich*) (*WP* 13). This *originary* harmony then is not constructed, derives from nothing, is a consequence of nothing. But above all, Heidegger reckons with the play so difficult to translate between *sich fügen* and *verfügen*, which means to order, arrest, decide, affect, enjoin, assign. The two, both join together originarily because an injunction is made and received, a mission assigned. This happens not only to the two, to the both of the two, nor only to both as one *and* the other or as one *or* the other, but to the both-two, *one another*. That is enjoined to them with the violence without violence of a law that assigns one to the other, promises them, recommends them, adjusts one to the other, as one another. *Fügen* implies a *Verfügen*, an adjustment that is not simply natural, in the sense derived from the word "nature," but natural in the sense in which φύσις is opposed neither to λόγος nor to νόμος. The justice of a law or of a commandment assigns the adjustment of two beings in the harmony of φιλεῖν. This justice has already spoken in the correspondence or the promise of φιλεῖν, lovence [*aimance*] before every distinction between love [*amour*] and friendship [*amitié*], before every Aristotelian distinction, I shall add, between the three types of φιλία. That is what it would be necessary to hear and understand [*entendre*], with a Greek ear, of *Einklang*, ἁρμονία or συμφωνία, of the choir of the two, the both, one-another with what gives or calls music, assigns one another to the hymn, assigns the hymn to one another in tempo [*en mesure*], according to the accuracy [*justesse*] of the note and tone.

Heidegger, who speaks more often of the hymn than of music, then makes a second knot in order to tie, tighten, weave his interpretation of φιλεῖν at work in Heraclitus's ἀνὴρ φιλόσοφος before all φιλοσοφία and before all Platonic or Aristotelian φιλία.

Since, in the sense of *Lieben*, of ἁρμονία, and of *Verfügen*, the ἀνὴρ φιλόσοφος loves σοφόν, it remains to determine what σοφόν means in Heraclitus. Now if I said that Heidegger tightens up in the same sense the woven knot of his interpretation, that is because he also finds again in σοφόν this bond, this unity of the One, the gathering that joins up that he had already thematized in φιλεῖν and in ἁρμονία. And from this One of the σοφόν, he has no trouble in finding again the One that gathers of λέγειν, of λόγος, that he had already put to work or rather recognized at work in the ὁμολογεῖν of φιλεῖν, as he had also discovered, some years before, in Dif-ference (*Unter-Schied*, διαφορά, or *durchtragende Austrag*, in *Die Sprache*, US 25). With a discreet but efficacious, sweet and violent agility, in a single paragraph, Heidegger takes up again with being, re-ties the knot with being, weaves all these motifs with that of being. At the end of a very brief path, lovence [*aimance*], *Lieben*, φιλεῖν, λόγος or λέγειν, ὁμολογεῖν, ἁρμονία—and being, that will be *the same, the gathering of the same: Versammlung, Sein*, Λόγος. The concatenation seems impeccable and indivisible. Once again it is a question of the ear. Let us listen.

"The ἀνὴρ φιλόσοφος loves (*liebt*) σοφόν. What this word says for Heraclitus is what is difficult to translate. But we can elucidate it according to the interpretation of Heraclitus himself [*nach Heraklits eigener Auslegung erläutern*, a word translated in modern Greek by ἑρμηνεία]." Heidegger then is going to take the *example* of what Heraclitus calls *one* σοφόν in order to say what *the* σοφόν was for Heraclitus. The hermeneutics of Heraclitus concerning σοφόν becomes then what *one* σοφόν, *this* σοφόν of Heraclitus, says, what Heraclitus says *in the form* of *one* σοφόν. Heidegger continues: "*Demnach sagt* τὸ σοφόν *dieses*": "In conformity to which σοφόν says this": "῝Εν Πάντα, 'One (is) all' ('*Eines [ist] Alles*')." "'All' means here: Πάντα τὰ ὄντα, the ensemble, the all of beings. ῝Εν, the One (*das Eins*) means: the one, the unique, what unites all (*das Eine, Einzige, alles Einigende* [the same words as for qualifying dif-ference, *Unter-Schied*, διαφορά, and *Austrag* in *Die Sprache*]). But united is every being in being (*Einig aber ist alles Seiende im Sein*). Σοφόν says: every being is in being. In order to say it more sharply (*Schärfer gesagt*): being *is* beings [*Das Sein* ist *das Seiende*: Heidegger underscores or italicizes the "*ist*" and comments on his gesture]. Here 'is' (*ist*) speaks transitively (*spricht 'ist' transitiv*) and signifies as well 'gathered' ('*versammelt*'). Being gathers beings in that it is beings (*Das Sein versammelt das Seiende darin, daß es Seiendes ist*). Being is gathering— Λόγος (*Das Sein ist die Versammlung—*Λόγος)" (*WP* 13).

What is then said in a finer, sharper way and must be heard clearly, with a finer ear than the common ear, is thus at once this *transitivity* of being, of the "ist," and the fact that this transitivity is exercised under the form of *gathering*. Heidegger accuses then the deafness of our modern and common ear before the extraordinary thing that he nevertheless just understood, heard (*hören*), and gave to be understood. Heidegger's ear then divides itself. More precisely, it is divided in two. There is a deaf ear like that of everyone today (Heidegger speaks in that case of what sounds "for our ear," ["für unser Ohr"]), and this ear perceives as "trivial" what has just been heard or said. The other ear over-hears the unheard through the deafness. And we find again the whole semantics of *Hören-Gehören*, of hearing-belonging, that we had questioned in *Sein und Zeit* around the voice of the friend. The fact is, *Versammlung*, gathering, is also a question, in being itself, of *Hören*, of Λόγος, and of *Gehören*. I cite: "Every being is in being

(*Alles Seiende ist im Sein*). To hear that (*Solches zu hören*) is what sounds (*klingt*) trivial, if not insolent to our ear (*für unser Ohr*). For no one has the need to care about beings belonging to being (*daß das Seiende in das Sein gehört*). Everybody knows it well: a being is something that is" (*WP* 13–14).

When he says "our ear," Heidegger understands by implication, of course [*bien entendu*], "your ear," in any case the ear of those (I can also be one of them, he seems to say, at least through one of my ears) that hear neither being, nor the ontological difference, nor the λόγος as gathering, nor then the φιλεῖν of σοφόν. And not to hear—here, for this "we" of "our ear"—is also to be blind, is no longer to see the splendor of what amazed the Greeks. For what is most amazing (*das Erstaunlichste*), for the Greeks, what has provoked the θαυμάζειν of which speak Plato in the *Theaetetus* (155d) and Aristotle in *Metaphysics* (A2, 982b12ff.) (*WP* 24–25) is precisely that the being remains *gathered* in being and *shines* in being's splendor. But we could always not hear this correspondence, this *Entsprechen* between being and beings starting from the address (*Zuspruch*) of being. Being can be heard or not heard (*gehört oder überhört*). Once it is heard, it can be said or be still. To be in the correspondence (*Entsprechen*) is to hear (*hören*) the voice or the call of the being of beings (*die Stimme des Zuspruchs*); it is to pay attention (*achten*) to that voice as soon as one is first disposed or accorded to it (*bestimmt, abstimmt*) (*WP* 23).

To better hear and understand [*entendre*] this passage on *Hören* and *Überhören*, on hearing and turning a deaf ear, no doubt it would be necessary, but we do not have time for it here, to follow closely at least some of the pages devoted to Hölderlin's *Der Rhein* in the seminars of 1933–34 (*GA* 39, § 14, pp. 194ff.). Very rich, these pages distinguish among the ordinary modes of hearing. The Gods hear in compassion (*erbarmende*), mortals are in the not-understanding, not-hearing, the *Überhören* as *Nichthörenkönnen* or *Überhörenwollen*, the "not-hearing" as "not-being-able-to-hear" or "unwilling-to-hear." Heidegger analyzes then what being accessible through the ear means, as he will do in similarly important passages from *Logos* and *Der Satz vom Grund* (chap. 6). And he comes to distinguish in sum *three* experiences of understanding [*entente*]. If the Gods hear in compassion (*erbarmend* is a word from Hölderlin) according to *Erhören*, which also means to answer; if there is also the *Überhören* of the mortals that cannot or do not want to hear; there is also, third, the hearing of the poet that is neither the *Erhören* of the gods nor the *Überhören* of mortals. This ear of the poet stands firm beside the origin that the poet has a passion for. The poet is steadfast in hearing what originarily and properly happens (*was da eigentlich geschieht*) and what in general "is" (*überhaupt "ist"*) (*GA* 39: 201). This ear of the poet, which is distinguished from that of the gods as well as from that of the common of the mortals, greatly resembles the ear Heidegger sketches or evokes in *Was ist das—die Philosophie?* It hears the "ist" before or at the origin of philosophy.

Is this analogy justified? I am tempted to think so. We could say then that the ear pricked up toward the originary φιλεῖν is for Heidegger an interior ear, an ear *of the inside*; not in the sense in which anatomy objectively describes and localizes what it calls the "inner ear," but in another sense. This ear would be an ear of the inside because it just has no need of external, sensory, or metaphorical sonority. Of the ear of the inside, Heidegger speaks literally at least in two highly significant contexts, in particular from a political point of view.

(1) The first is precisely the seminar of 1934–35 on Hölderlin's *The Rhine* that I just alluded to and whose "Preliminary Remark" speaks of "that history that is opened on the struggle (*Kampf*) in which the coming or the flight of the god will be decided." Now in this important sequence that unfortunately I cannot reconstitute, Heidegger speaks of "the ear of the inside" in order to define the poet's hearing that, unlike the common hearing of the mortals and the gods, stands firmly by the origin: the origin *insofar as it is and such as it is*. This ear of the inside stands and remains firm because it hears what *stands* and *consists* beyond contingency. This ear is poetic (*dichtende*) because it hears *in advance* just what it causes to burst forth. It *gives* itself to hear what it hears [*Elle* donne *elle-même à entendre ce qu'elle entend*]. It is *dichtende* because it speaks, says, poetizes itself. It is interior in that it produces in some way of itself what it hears: it hears it in advance, is in advance of what it hears and gives to be heard, as if the ear were speaking or were speaking itself, hearing itself speak in advance, fore-telling itself, outside of all conscious or speculative reflectivity, outside of all absolute identity, indeed all proximity, with itself:

> Das standhaltende Hören ist das Dabeibleiben mit dem inneren Ohr. Wobei? Beim Ursprung, bei seinem Entspringen als solchem, d.h. bei dem, was er und wie er eigentlich *ist*. Das standhaltende Hören hört nicht dieses und jenes als Einzelnes, sondern hört, was im zu Hörenden eigentlich Bestand hat und den Bestand ausmacht. Solches hört es über das Zufällige hinweg im voraus heraus. Das standhaltende Hören ist als dieses Im-voraus-heraushören das *dichtende* Hören. (*GA* 39: 202)

I give up translating this passage, save, approximately, its last phrase: "The hearing that stands firm [the *stehen* of *Stand* resonates with the previous *Bestand*], insofar as this hearing carries outside what it hears in advance, is hearing that is poetic/poetizing, that poetizes."

(2) The second context in which Heidegger speaks of the inside ear is much later, but it is politically as significant. He begins with "Meine Damen und Herrn," at the beginning of the *Vorlesung* of June 20, 1952. The text corresponds to the transition from the fourth to the fifth hours of *Was heißt Denken?*:

> Ladies and Gentlemen!
> Today at Freiburg the exposition "Prisoners of War Speak" has been inaugurated.
> I ask you please to go to it, in order to hear this mute voice (*diese lautlose Stimme zu hören*) and to let it no longer go outside your interior ear (*und nicht mehr aus dem inneren Ohr zu verlieren*).
> Thinking is faithful thinking (*Denken ist Andenken*). But faithful thinking is something other than a fleeting actualization of the past (*Vergegenwärtigung von Vergangenem*).
> Faithful thinking considers what reaches us (*Andenken bedenkt, was uns angeht*).

We are not yet in the space suitable for reflecting on freedom, nor even for speaking of it, so long as we *also* close our eyes on this annihilation of freedom (*Vernichtung der Freiheit*). (*WD* 159)

It is necessary then to see, but also to hear, from the inside ear, ours, what this annihilation signifies of our freedom that, still in 1952, in its mute speaking (*lautlose Stimme*), the memory of our prisoners of war can say to us.

From 1934 to 1952, at least, whatever particulars these dates answer, the inside ear was then an explicit theme. Evidently this is not the sensory or sensitive ear [*sensitive ou sensible*]. No more than the hand is this an organ with which graspable or perceptible things are received or perceived. Here we are dealing with the same schema that permitted distinguishing Dasein's hand, always engaged with speaking and λόγος, from the ape's prehensile organs. And that is why the ear is called interior. But that the ear does not belong to the order of sensory exteriority does not mean that it is, for all that, the innermost ear of the intellect or of reason, a function of the intelligible of which the sensory ear would be only a metaphor here. This interior ear is neither sensory, nor intellectual, nor the metaphysical metaphor that will have assured in the tradition the transfer from one to the other. In this respect, the major and most explicit texts doubtless remain, it seems to me, a passage of *Logos*, that lecture from 1951 on fragment 50 of Heraclitus, and a passage from chapter 6 of *Der Satz vom Grund* (1955–56). Around Heraclitus's fragment that will soundly support the remark of *Was ist das—die Philosophie?* (οὐκ ἐμοῦ ἀλλὰ τοῦ Λόγου ἀκούσαντας ὁμολογεῖν σοφόν ἐστιν Ἑν Πάντα), Heidegger advances in 1951 one of the densest, most active and gathered interpretations of *Logos*. For lack of time, I shall keep only some gestures that turn around the ear. First of all, the affirmation according to which the "speaking of the tongue (*das Sprechen der Sprache*)" that has its essence in λέγειν as *legen* ("to lay," *étendre*) is determined neither on the basis of the φωνή, nor on the basis of the σημαίνειν (*VA* 204; *EGT* 64), in other words, comes under neither an acoustics, a phonetics, or a phonology, nor a theory of signification. Let us not forget that Heraclitus's fragment spoke of hearing or acoustics and said: "οὐκ ἐμοῦ ἀλλὰ τοῦ Λόγου ἀκούσαντας," what Heidegger hears and translates in this way: "'When you have not only lent me your ear (*Wenn ihr nicht mich [den Redenden] bloß angehört habt*), but when you hold yourself in a belonging capable of hearing (*sondern wenn ihr euch im hochsamen Gehören aufhaltet, dann ist eigentliches Hören*), that is authentic hearing'" (*VA* 209; see *EGT* 67). Nowhere are hearing and belonging, *Hören* and *Zugehören*, more tightly associated than in this reading of Heraclitus. And whether it is a matter of *Versammlung* or of *Sein*, this always passes through the λόγος and concenters itself around λόγος. At bottom logocentrism is perhaps not so much the gesture that consists in placing the λόγος at the center as the interpretation of λόγος as *Versammlung*, that is, the gathering that precisely concenters what it configures.

Next, and consequently, the ear is not for Heidegger an organ of the auditory sense *with* which we hear. Hearing (*das Hören*), in the authentic sense, is a gathering, a self-recollection (*Sichsammeln*) toward the word [*parole*] that is addressed to us (*Anspruch, Zuspruch*). The gathering of hearing is done starting from the address and not from the organ of hearing. We hear when we forget the ears and auditory sensation in order to carry ourselves, through them, toward what is said and of which we are part (*gehören*). In other words, Heidegger unceasingly recalls to us that *Hören* (*entendre*, hearing understanding) must be thought starting from listening or lending an ear (*Horchen*), and not the inverse. Everything is played out in the difference between *hören* and *horchen*. In order to hear (*hören*) what *hören* means, it is necessary to listen, to hearken (*horchen*), and not only hear. "Das Hören ist erstlich das gesammelte Horchen. Im Horchsamen west das Gehör. Wir hören, wenn wir ganz Ohr sind": "Hearing is first a gathered hearkening. The heard has its being in hearkening. We hear when we are all ears." This gathering in "all ears" [literally in the "all ear"] is why we do not hear *with one* or *two* auditory organs. As he will repeat in *Der Satz vom Grund*, Heidegger underscores that we do not hear because we have ears, but we have ears because we hear. And when we speak of thinking as hearing or hearkening, this is not a metaphor (*Übertragung*) transferring a "properly so-called" or allegedly authentic hearing [*audition*] onto the spiritual plane (*auf das Geistige*). Finally, we find again here the thread of the meditation on *Überhören*. Not hearing or misunderstanding, mishearing (*überhören* or *sich verhören*), is an essential possibility of hearing: "So gehört zum eigentlichen Hören gerade dieses, daß der Mensch sich verhören kann, indem er das Wesenhafte überhört" (*VA* 206; see *EGT* 65): "Thus it belongs properly to hearing precisely that man can hear wrongly (mishear) insofar as he mishears the essential."

Der Satz vom Grund includes in this regard another essential gesture. Not only because every interpretation of the *Nihil est sine ratione* is displaced around a changing of tone (*Ton, Tonart*) of the "nothing" toward "is" and of "without" toward "reason," a changing of intonation the hearing of which makes us perceive a harmony (*Zusammenklang*) between *Sein* and *Grund*, but because Heidegger rejects there the sensible/intelligible opposition as well as the rhetoric it commands, in particular the concept of metaphor. This concept exists only "within the boundaries of metaphysics" (*SG* 89). For a long time and on several occasions having tried to situate and analyze this passage, I will make do here, in the present context, with underscoring two points on its subject, namely, that *on the one hand* this movement is again that of a going back from Plato to Heraclitus, and that *on the other hand* it is as valid for the eyes as for the ears, or rather for the eye and for the ear, for as I have shown on the subject of hands, the passage from the plural or the dual to the singular is essential here.

(1) To go back toward Heraclitus: after recalling that thinking must grasp through the gaze what we have properly heard in intonation, thinking grasping with the gaze just what is heard, Heidegger writes: "Thinking is a grasping through hearing that grasps through gazing," in conformity with "ancient doctrines," for example: "What, in the being, constitutes what it possesses of its own properness, Plato names ἰδέα, the aspect of the being and what is seen by us. Earlier, the

properness of the being Heraclitus had called λόγος, the speaking of the being, to which we respond in hearing. These two terms show us that thinking is hearing and seeing (*daß das Denken ein Hören und ein Sehen ist*)" (*SG* 86).

(2) If "with," hearing *with* the ear, seeing *with* the eye, no more signifies the instrumentality of the agent than in the expression *Mit-sein*, that is as valid for hearing *with* the ear as for seeing *with* the eye. The examples are musical. In the first place, the Bach fugue we would never hear if we heard "with" our ears sound waves come to strike the tympanum. In the second place, Beethoven's deafness that did not prevent him from hearing more things and things greater than before. "*We* hear, not the ear. . . . Our organ of hearing is a condition in certain regards necessary, but never its sufficient condition, never the presenter and giver of what properly must be perceived" (*SG* 87–88). In the meantime, Heidegger had given himself over, in passing, he said, to an etymological digression. Perhaps some will find this digression no longer exempt from political import [*portée*]. The digression concerns in effect the vocable *dumm*, then also *Dummheit*, a word whose misfortune one knows has been assured by Heidegger's belated confiding about his indulgence for Nazism in its Hitlerian episode (*eine große Dummheit*, he said). In the same passage of *Der Satz vom Grund*, directly after the allusion to Beethoven, Heidegger notes: "Let's say in passing that *taub* ('deaf'), *tumb* [from which comes today *dumm, Dummheit*] are equivalents of *stumpf* ('blunted'), which explains why we find again the same *tumb* in Greek under the form τυφλός, 'powerless to see,' thus 'blind'" (*SG* 87).

Therefore, in 1955, in *Was ist das—die Philosophie?* when he says "we," "our ear," Heidegger designates several ears and several hearings: we who find trivial the statement "Alles Seiende ist im Sein," we are mortals that cannot and do not want to hear and rather remain in the deafness of *Überhören*. We are not gods, nor at this point philosophers yet. But we should then be rather on the side of the poets, who stand firm close by the origin of what "is" (*ist*) and hear it, transitively, as poets.

At the point where we are, before even all φιλοσοφία and all φιλία, no longer can φιλεῖν, εἶναι, and λέγειν be disjoined. Lovence (*aimance*) would be this transitivity of being in which, closest to symphony, one gathers and collects oneself, one-another say lovence (*aimance*) to themselves. They declare they are in love according to the ὁμολογεῖν. They do so all the more originarily, intensely, with the just and sweet force of a destiny, since we are there before the distinction between love and friendship, before the friendships (the three friendships of Aristotle), before every subject, all anthropology, all psychology of the passions, and perhaps even, we are coming to this, before *Eros*, erotic desire or at least a certain inquisitive and jealous tension, a certain *Streben* of *Eros*.

What in effect happens between on the one hand the experience of φιλεῖν, at the Heraclitean moment of λόγος as *Versammlung*, and on the other hand the origin of φιλοσοφία?

What happens then, as one could say in a language that is not literally Heidegger's, but that seems to me not to betray it, is the drama of a scission, a separation and a discord. The gathering, the harmony, the homology, and the φιλεῖν of λόγος were threatened in their unity, the wonder was lost. And a few alone, small in number, tried to save σοφόν from [*contre*] the Sophists, from men of the market-place of culture and of common sense. What common sense, that marketplace of culture, forgets or does not hear (*überhort*) is precisely φιλεῖν, λόγος, *Sein*, *Versammlung*, the wonder before being's splendor in which beings appear. That is what the Greeks had "to save and protect (*retten und schützen*)" before the aggression (*Zugriff*) of the marketplace, of sophistry, of sophistry's intelligence and rhetorical cleverness. Instead of astonishing, the sophists had an intelligible explanation all ready: for everything and everyone. They brought [*apportaient*] that explanation onto the market (*auf den Markt*), both the place of public opinion and the auction room of opinions, the places of auctioneering, of the cry and prattle. In this rapid and incisive way of describing the complicity between the sophist understanding (*Verstand*) and the free market of opinions, one sees dawn a reservation with regard to a certain democratization that would resemble a vulga-rization, which associates the sophist understanding and commerce, the majority and political liberalism, indeed parliamentarism, one could almost say the "media." Despite other important differences I would like to come back to, there would be in those differences an affinity between Heidegger and Schmitt. When Heidegger speaks of the saviors of "φιλεῖν" that have taken responsibility for λόγος and being, for the essential *Versammlung*, he says "a few," the small number of those that, as men or free subjects could make a choice about this, have taken on themselves such a responsibility, the responsibility of responsibility, the respon-sibility of corresponding in *Entsprechen* with being, λόγος, and φιλεῖν. Small in number, they have taken on themselves the salvation of the most astonishing (*die Rettung des Erstaunlichsten*). Heidegger does not even say—and one should not say—that they have *taken on themselves* such a responsibility, as men or free subjects could. This responsibility has come upon them. It happens to those very rare Greeks to make their path toward σοφόν: "The protection (*die Rettung*) of the most astonishing (*des Erstaunlichsten*)—beings in being—happened (*geschah*) thanks to a few that took the path toward what is more astonishing there—namely σοφόν." These few strove (*strebten*) toward σοφόν. Heidegger underscores the word *strebten*. This tension proper to the few (*durch ihre eigenes Streben*) will have awakened, then maintained in them this nostalgia (*Sehnsucht*) for the lost σοφόν (*WP* 14).

This nostalgia is the origin of philosophy. It is a reaction to the loss of the originary φιλεῖν, of the ὁμολογεῖν, of the correspondence with λόγος. One could even say that every *philosophical*, for example Aristotelian, determination of the πρώτη φιλία or of the τέλεια φιλία inhabits the space of mourning, but also of reactive nostalgia, sometimes triumphant as mourning can be, the space of semideafness that still hears [*entend*] without hearing any longer the ὁμολογειν of the originary φιλεῖν. Because it grows hollow in this nostalgia and this inner division, in this loss of the originary *Versammlung* of λόγος, the φιλεῖν of φιλοσοφία is no longer the φιλεῖν whose memory is nevertheless kept. Philosophy would stand in the tensing of this nostalgic tension that would make of itself a search, a quest, an investigation, a *Suchen*. This *Suchen* is an ὄρεξις, the tension of a desire. In everyday language, ὄρεξις is even a desire for food. From ἀμονία or συμφωνία, one has passed to the desire strained toward satisfaction, accomplishment, completude, the reconstitution of a totality, restoration, The ὄρεξις is strained. Ὀρέγεσθαι is to strain [*tendre*], to strive toward [*se tendre vers*], to await [*attendre*], to be strained [*être tendu*], *streben*. It is the movement of return toward the lost place, the suffering of νόστος, a "nostalgia of/for being," to cite in another sense the title of the book of a French philosopher, Ferdinand Alquié, whom the students of my generation were still reading and who would not be considered a militant Heideggerian. Heidegger does not give here any example of the interpretation of ὄρεξις by philosophers like Plato or Aristotle. Such examples can be multiplied. Let us think of what Phaedon says about the ὄρεξις of the soul, when the ψυχή, breaking with the senses, first with hearing and sight, then with pain and pleasure, ready to send the body packing (χαίρειν τὸ σῶμα), as well as commerce and exchange, etc., becomes strained in the desire of being, the desire of what is (ὀρέγεται τοῦ ὄντος) (65c). This ὄρεξις defines for Plato the one that is "truly a philosopher" (ἀληθῶς φιλόσοφος).

Φιλοσοφία seeks then *after*. Φιλοσοφία comes *after*, is later than the symphony, mourns the harmony of the originary *Einklang*. This delay *eroticizes* the philosophical search, goads on the properly philosophical question, and determines φιλεῖν in tension with *Eros*. And with this unexpected arrival of a philosophical *Eros* plunged into mourning, we are not far from the question of *Geschlecht*, one could even say, you are going to see why, of the *Geschlecht* of the question. Heidegger describes the moment, the now of philosophy searching for, seeking *after* being in this way: "Σοφόν—the being in being (*das Seiende im Sein*)— is now properly sought (*wird jetzt eigens gesucht*). Because φιλεῖν is no longer an originary symphony with σοφόν (*nicht mehr ein ursprünglicher Einklang mit dem σοφόν ist*), but the particular tension of a searching *after* σοφόν (*sondern ein besonderes Streben* nach *dem* σοφόν), the φιλεῖν τὸ σοφόν becomes 'φιλοσοφία.' Φιλοσοφία whose tension (*Streben*) is determined [destined, *bestimmt*] by Eros" (*WP* 14).

With this erotization of the questioning *Streben*, in the inquisitive tension toward σοφόν, toward the ῞Εν Πάντα, the being that is gathered in being, the question upsurges: "What is the being insofar as it is?" With this question is philosophy born, which did not exist so long as φιλεῖν was in harmony with σοφόν and in homology with λόγος. Heraclitus and Parmenides were not philosophers, not because they were *not yet* philosophers, philosophers in the future, but because they were "the greatest thinkers (*die größeren Denker*)" (in modern Greek μεγαλύτεροι στοχαστές, which signified rather in ancient Greek the seers, those that see and conjecture clearly). Why are they the greatest thinkers? Not because they had been capable of some exploit, of a heroic *Leistung* (*WP* 15), but because, in a completely other dimension, they are found in the accord of φιλεῖν, in symphonic harmony, in the *Einklang* or homology with λόγος and the ῞Εν Πάντα. They were the thinkers of φιλεῖν as λόγος, that is, as the gathering of being. The erotic step [*pas*] toward philosophy was accomplished later, by others, Socrates and Plato in the first place. This first step toward philosophy was prepared, but because it just missed being paralyzed by sophistry.

The noun φιλία does not appear in this passage written around 1955 in the tracks [*trace*] of Heraclitus. The insistence bears [*porte*] on the infinitive or the verbal substantive, on φιλεῖν as λέγειν. But if this fact is significant, if it marks perhaps that φιλία is already too philosophical, too Platonico-Aristotelian, that fact can also be interpreted as the effacement or the retreat [*retrait*] from a previous use. The noun φιλία was in effect present, and even frequent, right in the title of certain chapters of the seminar devoted to Heraclitus in 1943–44, a seminar that remains, it seems to me, the massive and then still invisible base of these remarks of 1955, invisible at least in France where this lecture was given at Cerisy-la-Salle. Section 6 of *Die Wahrheit des Seins* (*Heraklit, GA* 55: 127ff.) bears twice, in *a* and *b*, the noun φιλία in its subtitles, with the words *Gunst* and *Gönnen* as equivalents (we encountered them a short while ago in *Die Sprache* [in *Unterwegs zur Sprache*]), favor and the accord of the favor, the gift accorded, the offering or the grace accorded: "Die φιλία ist das Gönnen der Gunst, die etwas schenkt . . ." (*GA* 55: 129): "φιλία," Heidegger says thus in 1943–44, "is to accord a favor that offers something." We will read what follows in a moment. But before coming to that text of 1943–44 that uses the noun φιλία, whereas Heraclitus, it seems to me, never uses anything but the verb φιλεῖν, I would like to propose two remarks on the appearing of *Eros* that we just saw pass very quickly in *Was ist das—die Philosophie?*

First remark. The gravity of this elliptical allusion to *Eros* can be evaluated in countless ways. Its implicit context is so rich. But in supposing a sort of pre-erotic moment of φιλεῖν does not Heidegger point to a sort of *Lieben* or lovence [*aimance*] that would still stand not only short of φιλία and of the different types of friendship distinguished by Aristotle (according to virtue, political interest, or pleasure), but short of the distinguishing mark [*insigne*] and the enigmatic distinction between love and friendship, this last resembling perhaps in its canonic model, as I have tried to show elsewhere, the homo- or monosexual de-erotization [*désérotisation*] or sublimation of fraternity, that is, of the virile duo. Where then, in this respect, is the voice of the friend placed, the friend that each *Dasein bei sich trägt?* Is this voice pre-erotic or not? What can that mean? What about its *Geschlecht* and its rapport to fraternity?

The *second remark* is induced by the first, and I shall also leave it in the preliminary stages [*en chantier*]. It concerns the place, the status, and the moment of *Sein und Zeit*. This book, opened with a reference to Plato's *Sophist*, is dedicated to the question of being's sense (*die Frage nach dem Sinn von Sein*) that is to be posed again while renewing it (*erneut zu stellen*), for we do not always know what the word "being" "properly" (*eigentlich*) means (*SZ*, foreword, p. 1). Does such a book, dominated as it is by this question and by all the modalities of the questioning search, through *Gefragte, Befragte, Erfragte*, does such a book belong, as one would be tempted to think, to philosophy such as it will have been situated in 1955 by *Was ist das—die Philosophie?*, to φιλοσοφία in its post-Heraclitean moment, in the tension of *Suchen* or *Streben* that is erotic, plunged into mourning, questioning, yet nostalgic, *after* the loss of originary ὁμολογεῖν and originary φιλεῖν? Or else does *Sein und Zeit* already try to pass this limit in order to go back, as certain signs also let it be thought, short of that limit? I do not believe one can respond with a simple "yes or no" to the question posed in this form. Moreover, there it is a matter of the question of the question, as I have tried to show in *Of Spirit*.[6] If the status and the moment of *Sein und Zeit* overflow this hypothetical frontier from both sides, and such would be the force of this inexhaustible event, then one can draw from it at least one consequence, the only one that interests me here for the moment, to wit, that the brief evocation of the friend's voice in *Sein und Zeit*'s section 34 shakes or oscillates between two times. The evocation is the between-time of these two times that are not in time: before and after the philosophical *Eros* of the question, at the birth of this *Eros* that the evocation will also have *carried*. If *Sein und Zeit* were the book of the friend, it would also be the most and the least erotic book given us to read in this century.

After these two remarks, I return to the use of the noun φιλία in the seminar on Heraclitus of 1943–44. Sections 5 and 6, which form its most immediate context, would merit by themselves alone much more than a long lecture. I will limit myself then to some indications.

(1) Heidegger has just (*GA* 55: § 5, pp. 110ff.) translated or interpreted Heraclitus's fragment "φύσις κρύπτεσθαι φιλεῖ" in the German statement: "'Das Aufgehen dem Sichverbergen schenkt's die Gunst.'" *Gunst* is the word that will next (*GA* 55: § 6, p. 127) be exchanged with the word φιλία. In other words, the accorded gift is here the self-concealing of φύσις, that is, of what rises, opens out, emerges, blossoms (*aufgeht*), or inversely the "rising" of what is concealed. Φύσις is an essential relation between apparently contradictory traits (*Aufgehen/Untergehen, Aufgehen/Sichverbergen*: rise/set, show/conceal). And φιλεῖν, φιλία, *die Gunst* is what accords, as a gift, one to the other. The audacity of this interpretative translation of "φύσις κρύπτεσθαι φιλεῖ" by "Das Aufgehen dem Sichverbergen schenkt's die Gunst" is dictated by the ear, by a penetrating listening (*Hinhören*) that while advancing from the inside toward the inside accords itself to the most initial (*anfänglich*) (*GA* 55: § 5, p. 125).

(2) Heidegger values here the noun φιλία because he wants to say something about friendship (*Freundschaft*) and not only about φιλεῖν. He wants to speak about friendship in its rapport with philosophy and education. Concerning "φύσις . . . φιλεῖ," he recalls that he has translated φιλία τοῦ σοφοῦ, in a preliminary way, by "friendship for what is to be thought (*Freundschaft für das Zu-denkende*)." But if the translation of σοφόν by "what is to be thought" remains provisional, what is the φιλεῖν of φιλία, or the φιλία of φιλεῖν? How are these words to be translated? "We now translate φιλεῖν in Heraclitus's sentence" (φύσις κρύπτεσθαι φιλεῖ), Heidegger says (*GA* 55: 128), doing then what he says and saying what he decides to do in hearing what is dictated to him by his ear that

is intimately penetrating according to the originary *Hinhören*: "Jetzt übersetzen wir das φιλεῖν im Spruch des Heraklit mit 'die Gunst schenken'": to accord favor or grace. But in their originary sense, this favor, this grace, this gesture that consists in according (*Gunst, Gönnen, Gewähren*)—we must not hear and understand (*verstehen*) them in their secondary and accessory sense, however related, of favoring (*Begünstigen*) or protecting (*Begönnern*). How then are we to hear and understand this accorded grace? To respond to this question, Heidegger writes a phrase that I cite and try to translate because it strangely resonates, across a certain interval, with the little phrase of *Sein und Zeit* and with its immediate context. One finds in the phrase the other, the being of the other, the belonging (*gehören*), and the enigmatic purport [*portée*] of "carry" (*tragen, porter*): "Das ursprüngliche Gönnen ist das Gewähren dessen, was dem anderen gebührt, weil es zu seinem Wesen gehört, insofern es sein Wesen trägt" (*GA* 55: 128): "Offering in an originary way is to accord to the other what comes back to it [what is due it] because that belongs to its being [or essence] insofar as that carries [supports, bears, carries with it, includes, *trägt*] its essence."

The grace of this friendship leaves the other, lets it be, gives it what it has and what it already is. Nothing more and nothing less: this grace gives it what it has or what it already is, to be sure, but what it has and what it is only in the offering and according to the listening of this friendship. That is why, no doubt, this resonance "bei sich" of the friend's voice is essential to Dasein's own potentiality-for-being about which *Sein und Zeit* spoke to us. This grace: essential and light, since it lets be the other that it permits to be; grave but almost useless and inaudible, like an aphonic voice for an interior ear; discreet and inconspicuous but decisive, constitutive. Essential then also to its freedom, for what this grace of φιλία accords to the other is nothing less than the birth [*eclosion*] of freedom proper (*eigene Freiheit*) to the being thus accorded. There is certainly a reciprocity in the being thus accorded (*das wechselweise gegönnte Wesen*) (*GA* 55: 128), in the being thus freed for itself by such a friendship. But this reciprocity does not signify that one can be substituted for the other and that this substitution is a testimony of friendship, for example in the case of necessity, of distress, or of danger. In Dasein's being-one-for-the-other, manifestations or proofs of friendship are not required. It is even necessary that in acting each renounce exercising an influence, Heidegger specifies. One would be mistaken if one thought that such an offering of being is a matter of course, as if Dasein then were nothing other than a *Vorhandensein*. No, this ontological offering, this *Gewährung des Wesens* to the other requires knowledge and patience. One must be able to wait for the other to *find itself* in the unfolding of its being. One must accept that for its part the other does not attach any great importance to this self-discovery (*aus dieser Wesensfindung kein Aufhebens macht*) (*GA* 55: 129).

This insistence resembles the commentary, fifteen years later, of the little phrase from *Sein und Zeit*, where it is a matter of the "füreinander Dasein," of the structural character of the bond of friendship, of its rapport with the being of Dasein and its freedom, of the .espectful, silent, almost voiceless discretion of this consonance effaced up to renunciation. The root of this renunciation is described in an admirable formula whose analogue will be found later in Lacan. Φιλία, Heidegger says in short, gives the being that φιλία is not. Φιλία gives to the other, recall what he said just before, what already belongs to the other, but φιλία for all that is no less required by Dasein as such. "Die φιλία ist das Gönnen der Gunst, die etwas schenkt, was ihr im Grunde nicht gehört und die doch Gewähr geben muß, damit des anderen Wesen im eigenen verbleiben kann" *(GA* 55: 129): "Φιλία is to accord a grace that makes the offering of something that at bottom does not belong to it and whose guarantee it must nonetheless give [for which it carries the responsibility] so that the being of the other can remain in what is proper to it." Φιλία is in short the other's proper, the gift to the other of what is to the other its very own proper or properness. And what then is due it. But this due escapes no doubt the dimension of the contracted debt. In *Der Spruch des Anaximanders* (1946), Heidegger also says that justice (δίκη), which he also translates by *Fuge* (joint, accord, coupling) is given, and he wonders how what is unfolded in ἀδικία, injustice or disjoining, can give justice, δίκη, in other words, can give what it does not have, and the question becomes: "Kann es geben, was es nicht hat?" "Can it give what it doesn't have?" *(HW* 329: *EGT* 43). It is necessary to pose the question and to respond if, why, and how such a gift, the gift itself, is possible or necessary: the gift of what one does not have as the only gift possible.

That for Heidegger is "the essential and concealed ground of all education." But by that very thing, insofar as this friendship is also philosophy, friendship for what is to be thought, φιλία is what gives to every historial people *(geschichtliche Volk)* a regard for the essential *(GA* 55: 129). This allusion to the historial *Volk* and to education is the trait that one would be tempted to call the most political in this 1943 text.

(3) But in order to avoid any misunderstanding, any mishearing, and any precipitation over this word "political," one must immediately specify that Heidegger is doubly careful concerning all human, subjective, anthropological, and psychological interpretation of Heraclitean φιλεῖν that upholds this whole discourse. Φιλία must not first be heard and understood [*entendue*] as human, subjective, or objective comportment. That would be an anachronism. Heidegger goes so far as to say that the anthropological or psychological point of view would be foreign even to Aristotle. What in modern times is called anthropology or psychology doubtless depends in his eyes, as one knows, on a metaphysics of subjectivity, on the interpretation of man as subject. He can thus declare that psychology did not exist for the Greeks, that Aristotle's Περὶ Ψυχῆς has nothing to do with psychology, that the fulfillment of metaphysics transforms that work [*celle-ci*] into psychology, that psychology and anthropology are the last word of metaphysics, that psychology and technics go together like the right and the left. And even that Christianity (and then, we can conclude from this, every Christian concept of friendship, of the "neighbor" or the "brother") constitutes the first stage in the formation of the passions for the subject of psychology *(GA* 55: 130). Whatever once more may be the case of this epochal distribution and of all the problems it poses,

there appears to be little doubt that Heidegger always claims to speak here of φιλία, as he spoke of the friend's voice fifteen years earlier, in a space that is no longer, or not yet, that of the *ego* or the *alter ego*, of the ethicopolitical person or subject, of the ἄνθρωπος of anthropology or of the ψυχή of psychology, to say nothing of the God of ontotheology.

(4) As regards the gods, but also *Eros*, I must neglect, for lack of time, what Heidegger says in the same passage about sentence 15 of Parmenides that names the *Eros* of the gods. *Eros* here is, when one thinks according to the essence, Heidegger says, "der dichtende Name für das denkende Wort 'die Gunst'" (*GA* 55: 132): "the poetic [poetizing] name for the thinking word that is said [or called] 'grace.'" For this fourth and last point of reference, I shall not speak of *Eros* but of Ἔρις, which will introduce me onto the other slope [*versant*] of this reading. The other slope that is in truth only the same, fold according to fold,[7] or fold according to false fold (or crease [*faux pli*]). If the grace, the favor, or the gift of friendship, *die Gunst*, is accorded to φύσις and through φύσις in its double movement of self-opening and -closing, of blossoming forth [*eclosion*] and dissimulation, of *Aufgehen* and *Untergehen*, of *Aufgehen* and *Sichverbergen* or *Sichverschließen*, then the conflict and the discord are neither strangers nor opposed to the grace of friendship. No more than *Kampf*, at the end of *Sein und Zeit*, was opposed to what it nonetheless is opposed to, namely, the voice of the friend. Here the grace accorded, *die Gunst*, is also the fundamental trait of Ἔρις, of discord (*der Grundzug der* Ἔρις, *des Streits*). On condition, of course [*bien entendu*], that one think Ἔρις, discord, in an originary way and not under the form of current and commonplace representations like what is placed opposite the adversaries in prejudice, detriment, quarrel, or disagreement (*Ungunst, Mißgunst, Hader, Zwist*) (*GA* 55: 133). In thinking the truth of being (and this part, *Hauptteil*, of the seminar on Heraclitus is entitled *Die Wahrheit des Seins*), one could say that Ἔρις is also the truth of φιλία, unless it also be the inverse, perhaps in the sense in which Blake inscribes in a hardly legible way in the manuscript of the *Marriage of Heaven and Hell*: "Opposition is true Friendship."

3.

What would be the marriage of heaven and hell in Heidegger's world? In 1955, on the foundation of a reading of Heraclitus continued at least for a dozen years, *Was ist das—die Philosophie?* unfolds then or folds back up on itself the essential affinity, indeed the equivalence, between φιλεῖν and λόγος, φιλεῖν and φύσις. The folding back up of λόγος is also the consonance of being as gathering (*Versammlung*), ἁρμονία, *Einklang*, etc.

Now exactly twenty years before, in the Freiburg summer seminar that will give rise to the publication of the *Introduction to Metaphysics*, this time again, this time already, Heidegger is tuned in to Heraclitus—to that fragment 53 on the πόλεμος that will have been the subject in the summer of '33 of a correspondence with Carl Schmitt. And he seems to say the contrary, something that resonates at first hearing as the contrary of what he will say twenty years later. This time he says not that φιλία and λόγος, φιλεῖν, ὁμολογειν, and λέγειν are the same, he says "Πόλεμος und λόγος sind dasselbe" (*EM* 47): "Πόλεμος and λόγος are the same." If φιλία and λόγος are the same in 1955, if πόλεμος and λόγος are the same in 1935, are not φιλία and πόλεμος always the same?

A philosopher or a historian pressed to appear in the press would press to send a press communiqué to all the press agencies in order to put forward his or her last discovery. And one would immediately read in *The Nation, Newsweek, The Village Voice*, the *Frankfurter Allgemeine Zeitung, Le Monde*, or *Liberation* some definitive sentences: whereas after the war, in 1955, Heidegger says of the λόγος that it is friendship itself, in 1935, right in the Nazi period, the author of the *Rectorate Discourse*, two years after his resignation, declares war again. He says without embarrassing himself about the same λόγος that it is not friendship but πόλεμος. Referring to the same λόγος, he declares war before the war and at the apogee of Nazism. Then after the war and the end of Nazism, there he goes declaring peace, multiplying the declarations of love and friendship, singing unity, the ῝Εν Πάντα of being that gathers in concord, harmony, and homological correspondence. The same press communiqué would find in this the confirmation, in 1935, of that thought of struggle, of combat (*Kampf*) that oriented the *Rectorate Discourse* two years before.

That is not false. And I am not saying that this press dispatch would be misled or misleading. But it is advisable to decelerate things a bit, if at least one still wants to read and to think what one claims to judge. Before regarding more closely the passage from the *Einführung . . .* I just cited, it is advisable in effect to recall what was said of *Kampf* in the *Rectorate Discourse*. Not that the word *Kampf*, any more than the word *Führer*, lets itself be totally determined in itself, in its sense and in its sense effects, by a context then dominated by a *Führer*, author of a certain *Mein Kampf*, in an ideological ground from which it receives and in its turn supplies the irrigation. But the use of the same words cannot not be contaminated by this irrigation, above all the moment Heidegger took part in the restructuring of the university in accordance with the "Führerprinzip." Heidegger has not been able not to play with a difference of sense and sense level in order to maintain the most serious equivocation, the only equivocation, alas, he believed possible or necessary at that moment. Thought of the *Kampf*, discreetly put in place in *Sein und Zeit*, as we have seen, is introduced in force toward the end of the *Rectorate Discourse* at a striking moment. Why "striking" [*marquant*]? The word *prägen* (to mark, strike, leave an imprint), so frequent in Heidegger, will also be useful in 1955 concerning the word φιλόσοφος forged, stamped (*geprägt*) by Heraclitus. Here, always in the name of gathering, Heidegger defines what must gather the German university, and gather it originarily into *one striking* force, with *one* trait. This striking force, at once unified and unifying, is struggle (*Kampf*).

Heidegger has just defined the three services, the three obligations (*Bindungen*) that, through the people, bind to the destiny of the State in a spiritual mission (*durch das Volk an das Geschick des Staates im geistigen Auftrag*). These three services (the service of labor, military service, and the service of knowledge) are of equal rank and equally originary (*gleichursprünglich*) for being-German, the German essence (*dem deutschen Wesen*) (*SU* 16). (I would pose here, between parentheses, to whoever would be shocked in all good conscience by what Heidegger says of the originary and indissociable coordination of these three services or prescriptions, the following question: How and *according to what criteria* would we be able *in all rigor* to dissociate them in *our* existence as citizens, and even as teachers, in the modern democracies of the industrial age, before or after the two world wars? Where, even in an industrial democracy, passes the rigorous frontier between knowledge, armies, and productive labor in general? This parenthesis is not intended to minimize the evident and serious engagement of Heidegger with Nazism. One must never do that. What the *Rectorate Discourse* says, *in this context*, about the three services, is compromising enough by itself. But if one does not forget that in our so-called democratic context no discourse—even were it with another tone—succeeds in *rigorously dissociating* the scientific, the military, and labor [skilled or industrial] or can praise one without the other, then one measures things otherwise, one at least avoids the good conscience or ridicule.) It was then necessary to wonder what coordinated, thus gathering, these three duties among themselves and at the same time what originarily related them to the essence of being-German. That this gathering is a "striking force" (*prägende Kraft*) [*SAU* 478 reads "formative force"—trans.] and that this force is of the order of the *Kampf* (*SU* 18)—all that does not only recall the end of *Sein und Zeit*. As soon as *Kampf* is presented here as the force of gathering, this statement from the *Rectorate Discourse* announces what will be said two years later in the *Einführung* . . . just before the phrase "Πόλεμος und λόγος sind dasselbe": "Die Auseinandersetzung trennt weder, noch zerstört sie gar die Einheit. Sie bildet diese, ist Sammlung (λόγος). Πόλεμος und λόγος sind dasselbe" (*EM* 47): "The debate with the other [*Auseinandersetzung*, "fighting, combating, or struggling with one another" will be the translation established by Heidegger for Πόλεμος] does not dissociate the unity, no more than it destroys it. On the contrary that debate forms the unity, is the gathering (*Sammlung*) (λόγος). Πόλεμος and λόγος are the same."

Der Kampf then is what gathers the three duties. As these duties are originarily equal for being-German, one can logically and without abuse say that struggle gathers being-German in the unity of its triple mission. That is consistent, once more, with an explicit proposition of *Sein und Zeit* (§ 74) on the community of destiny of *Mitdasein* as *Volk*: it is a community of struggle. Here the community of struggle, for example, the *Kampfgemeinschaft* between masters and students, gathers everything in keeping the opposition open. This structure always interests Heidegger: dissension maintains, gathers, accords. "Only struggle holds the opposition open," he says: "Der Kampf allein hält den Gegensatz offen" (*SU* 19), and the "holding" (*halten*) is no less decisive than the opposition. We are not far from Carl Schmitt for whom a group gathers and identifies itself, thus reaching the State, that is, the political [*au politique*] as such, only insofar as it keeps itself in opposition, an opposition so radical, touching its very being, that it must have its own being as its stake, in other words, a total war in which the people can risk absolute disappearance. The people must thus expose itself to death in the political [*la politique*], that is to say, for Schmitt, in the State, which never determines itself without an enemy, in other terms, with what could be called its being-for-death. Now Heidegger, who does not speak of this very often, also names the destiny of the State (*das Geschick des Staates*) in the *Rectorate Discourse* (*SU* 16), when he defined the three duties.

The passage in which we are interested at this moment is one of the most voluntarist of the *Rectorate Discourse*. Its essence proceeds from the will for essence:

> Elaborating the figure (*Ausgestaltung*) of the primordial essence of science, however, demands such a degree of rigor, responsibility (*Verantwortung*), and superior patience that, in comparison, matters like the conscientious pursuit or zealous reform of the traditional procedures hardly carry any weight.
>
> But if the Greeks took three centuries just to put the *question* of what knowledge can be upon the right basis and on a secure path, then *we* have no right to presume that the elucidation and unfolding of the essence of the German university could take place in the current or in the coming semester. (*SU* 17–18; *SAU* 478 [modified])

This allusion to the long time leaves open the possibility of a reevaluation beyond the rhythm of so-called political events, in the narrow sense, for example, beyond Nazism in its Hitlerian moment, beyond also a reform of academic institutions, beyond all institutional militancy. But this reevaluation of the duration is based again on a Greek model. Heidegger continues:

> *One thing* [eines, underscored], however, we do know from the indicated essence of science; we do know that the German university will take shape and come to power [*Gestalt und Macht*: this word *Macht* that *Sein und Zeit* connects with *Kampf* as the essence of the *Mitdasein*] when the three services—Labor Service, Armed Service, and Knowledge Service—primordially gather together in *one* [underscored, einer] striking force (*ursprünglich zu* einer *prägenden Kraft sich zusammenfinden*). (*SU* 18; *SAU* 478 [modified])

On two occasions, after an interval of seven lines, in the first and the last phrase of the same paragraph, Heidegger underscores the word "one": the unique thing we are sure of from now on is the unifying unity and uniqueness of the striking force that must gather, with the three duties, the German university in its unity with being-German. This gathering force that in truth gathers Heidegger's whole work and that, like *Versammeln*, is constantly associated with λέγειν, to wit, with φιλεῖν as ὁμολογεῖν (as will be said in 1955), this force is what we are going to see is maintained, in 1933, homologous to *Kampf*, just as two years later, in 1935, λόγος as *Versammlung* will be said to be homologous to πόλεμος. This gathering force, like λόγος, gathers in advance both Πόλεμος and φιλεῖν. All that is going to be specified in a moment, but I underscore in passing that *Kampf*, as the war toward which it points, is not limited to its military phenomenon. In this sense, it is not even a war, at least in the sense of an armed war. Since the struggle (*Kampf*) gathers the three services—of which military service is then only one determination—the tropical status of the word *Kampf* is difficult to assign. It is not a military or militant metaphor displaced toward the civil, that opposition no longer having any pertinence. But it is not either a simple generality of which military service (*Wehrdienst*) would be only a particular case. Such is the profound stake, the consequence or decisive premise of Heidegger's so insistent proposition on the unity, the co-originary character, and the equal rank of the three services. All hierarchization and all derivation would destroy the very logic of the *Rectorate Discourse*, that is, a logic that configures in the same pragmatico-discursive event three types of indissociable motifs: some belong to the great tradition of German philosophy of the university, others to the keenest interpretation of a certain modernity, others to the equivocal strategy of accommodation to National Socialism.

After recalling this "one striking force," Heidegger moves on: "Das will sagen . . ." 'That means, that wants to say . . . ,' an apparently neutral and innocent little phrase, like a modest expletive of discourse. But its place, the scansion one imagines in the *Rectorate Discourse*, the fact that after this little phrase there is a colon and that Heidegger begins a new paragraph—all that gives to this "Das will sagen" a strong resonance and tunes [*accorde*] it to the deliberately voluntarist accent of what is going to follow. That phrase wants to say not "in other words," "in other terms," but it wants, it must want and want to say how we must want to want, how you are called here to want to hear and understand [*entendre*], and with what ear, what this will, this want, says or what is said in the name of will as wanting to say and wanting to be, etc. For beginning a new paragraph after "Das will sagen:" and the colon, Heidegger goes on:

> *Der Wesenswille der Lehrschaft*, the teaching corps' will to essence must awaken and strengthen (*erstarken*) and thus gain the simplicity and breadth necessary to knowledge about the essence of science [*um das Wesen der Wissenschaft*: then the will for essence must mobilize itself around the essence of knowledge]. The student body's will to essence (*Der Wesenswille der Schülerschaft*) must force itself (*sich hinaufzwingen*) to rise to the highest clarity and rigor of knowing and, demanding and determining, integrate its engaged understanding (*Mitwissenschaft*) of the people and its State (*um das Volk und seinen Staat*) into the essence of science. Both wills must be reciprocally compelled to struggle (*Beide Willen müssen sich gegenseitig zum Kampf stellen*). (*SU* 18; *SAU* 478–79 [modified])

The two, the "both" of these two (*Beide*), the duo or the dual of these two wills to essence are in rapport with one another, call one another to the struggle. *Zur Kampf stellen* wants to say "to oblige to struggle," to force to struggle, to engage, as one says an enemy has been engaged, forced to begin fighting on the front. "Beide Willen müssen sich gegenseitig zum Kampf stellen": the "gegenseitig" can recall the "wechselweise" of the texts on φιλεῖν; whether a matter of struggle or lovence [*aimance*], of *Kampf* or φιλία, there must be two, and the two must be a reciprocal two. "Both wills must be reciprocally compelled to struggle. All faculties of will and thought, all the forces of the heart and all the skills of the flesh (*Leib*) must be deployed *through* struggle, heightened *in* struggle, and preserved *as* struggle (*müssen durch Kampf entfaltet,* im *Kampf gesteigert und* als *Kampf bewahrt bleiben*)" (*SU* 18; *SAU* 479 [modified]).

The underscored prepositions (*durch, im, als*) clearly mark that it is not a question of *entering* the *Kampf* or of *leaving* it. Both wills, the two of the will, are born as wills to essence and as such in the struggle, through the struggle. They do not exist before the struggle; they would cease to be what they are or have to be outside of the struggle, in peace. These are propositions at once very close to those of Carl Schmitt, but, as we shall see, withdrawn in principle from Schmitt's secularized anthropotheology. At the opening of the following paragraph is another Karl that Heidegger judges opportune to invoke even if he does not cite the proverbial phrase of a theoretician of war for whom war alone exists, peace being only war pursued by other means. That in 1933 Heidegger cites Karl von Clausewitz is what sets the tone, but it is also interesting that Heidegger does this by tying to *Kampf* not only the knowledge but also the experience of the *question*:

> We elect (*Wir wählen*) the informed struggle (*den wissenden Kampf*) of those that question (*der Fragenden*) and profess with Karl von Clausewitz: "I declare I forsake any futile hope in salvation by the hand of chance (*Ich sage mich los von der leichtsinnigen Hoffnung einer Errettung durch die Hand des Zufalls*)." (*SU* 18; *SAU* 479 [modified])

Once more, in this discourse to the university, it is certainly not a matter of just any struggle, above all not only or first of all of armed war. The struggle (*der Kampf*) is much more essential, interior, irreducible insofar as it is inherent to knowledge and even to the question. It is the struggle of those that question. And it is the struggle for education, struggle as education itself, in the same way that ten years later φιλεῖν, but furthermore φιλεῖν as Ἔρις, will appear essential to education (*Erziehung*) as well as to philosophical questioning. All that implies [*laisse entendre*] that there is not only no knowledge without questioning, but no questioning with a view to knowledge without the will to essence, that is, without this *Kampf*. One can then ask oneself once again, thinking of the schema of *Was ist das—die Philosophie?*: Does not this moment of the question as struggle essentially belong to that moment of *Eros* when philosophy becomes a question tensed or plunged into mourning, inquisitive and jealous about being? In other terms, if *Kampf* is essential to the very questioning of the question, as would be a certain πόλεμος; if πόλεμος is λόγος as gathering; if thereby πόλεμος is homologous to the homology of φιλεῖν, does the knowledge or the question that carries the struggle in itself still have an affinity with the Heraclitean φιλεῖν that Heidegger will say in 1955 is more originary than the nostalgic tension, than the philosophical *Streben* and *Suchen?* Is the *Kampf*, the πόλεμος, or, another translation, the *Auseinandersetzung*, as originary as the Heraclitean φιλεῖν, that is, more originary than the question and than knowledge as φιλοσοφία? Or else, does *Kampf* belong to that moment of discord and nostalgia that would be the very gestation of φιλοσοφία? Or else, is φιλεῖν not yet what gathers the *Auseinandersetzung*, the *Kampf*, the πόλεμος, in the memory of a lost homology?

If, as I think, there is no clear response by yes or no to such a question, that is not only because the Heraclitean φιλεῖν is also, in 1943, determined as discord ("Ερις) and because that would cause all the distinctions to oscillate; but because in all the limits, epochal or not, that Heidegger deliberately wants to determine, from 1933 to 1955, each time he says "originary" or "nonoriginary," this oscillation introduces an irreducible inconsistency and a nonformalizable equivocation. This nonformalization or perhaps the nonformalizable character of this discourse are not at all, in any case, not sufficiently, thematized. And it is partly in such an equivocation that precisely are the political strategies played out, lost, stopped or carried along.

Before leaving the *Rectorate Discourse* to move on toward the *Einführung* . . . , I would like to situate two other paragraphs. They name, *on the one hand*, the community of struggle (*die Kampfgemeinschaft*)—in a single word, for it is community *insofar as* it struggles. The community does not first exist and then come round to struggle as one enters into war. The community is struggling or it is not community, it is the struggle itself. These two paragraphs name, *on the other hand*, a logic of opposition that Heidegger shares, on another level, with Schmitt and that seems to me to be the condition-limit, the very condition and the very limit, the positive condition and the positive limit, too positive and too positional, perhaps, of the very force of this thought. The struggle is what holds and keeps the opposition (*Gegensatz*). The struggle keeps the opposition open, which can mean both open to the two of the difference and open, in and through difference, beyond the two or between the two. It is the opening of the two that maintains not only the difference, the interval between two, but the *entre-deux*, the space-between-the-two, as the face-to-face of the dual, contradiction in one another, of one against the other, of one encountering or running counter to the other. No community gathering [*Pas de rassemblement communautaire*] if there are not two, but there are not two if there is not opposition (*Gegensatz*). In the community of professors and students, the opposition is not only their common struggle against the other, but the inner struggle in each of them. Each community carries with itself, in its ear, the voice of the adversary, a sort of interior resistance. The verb *tragen*, this time *in sich tragen*, reappears in a significant way. Concerning "resistance" (*Widerstand*), it is also Heidegger's word, one could make him say much.

The community of struggle (*Die Kampfgemeinschaft*) of professors and students [Heidegger says], however, will only transform the German university into a place of spiritual legislation (*der geistigen Gesetzgebung*) and establish in it the center of the most disciplined and focused preparation for the highest service to the people in its State, when the teaching corps and the student body lead their existence (*ihr Dasein*) more simply, harder, and freer of needs than all the other members of the people [*als alle anderen Volksgenossen*: thus the academic corps must raise themselves exemplarily above the people they are part of; they are the "few" we spoke about above]. All leading (*Alle Führung*) must grant [accord to, *zugestehen*] those that follow (*der Gefolgschaft*) their own proper force (*die Eigenkraft*). But all following carries resistance within itself (*trägt in sich*). This essential opposition (*Wesensgegensatz*) in the *Führen* and the *Folgen* must not be obscured, let alone eliminated.

Struggle alone holds the opposition open (*Der Kampf allein hält den Gegensatz offen*) and alone implants in the entire body of teachers and students that basic mood (*Grundstimmung*), which lets self-limiting self-assertion empower resolute self-examination to genuine auto-nomy (*die sich begrenzende Selbstbehauptung die entschlossene Selbstbesinnung zur echten Selbstverwaltung ermächtigt*). (*SU* 19; *SAU* 479 [modified])

Let us leave for later the analysis of such words as *Verwaltung*, certainly a very ordinary word in the sense of "administration," but which, like *Walten* in general, is always very actively overdetermined by Heidegger. Everything that is said and reverberates here with such an insistence on *selbst* or αὐτό (self-affirmation, self-definition, auto-nomy, etc.) signifies indeed that the self-rapport, the self-relation, the self-appropriation, the authentic return to self, passes through the opening of this opposition of the inside that is struggle, this internal disagreement [*differend*] that carries in itself or with itself the resistance of the adversary, and hears [*écoutant*] and obeys it at once. Struggle gathers with itself, it is self-rapport as disagreement [*differend*]. And the *Selbst*, this self-rapport, is clearly determined, at least in this text, as will and oppositional logic of the will. This will not cease to be confirmed, for Heidegger immediately adds:

Do we, or do we not, will the essence of the German university? It is up to us whether, and to what extent, we concern ourselves (*uns bemühen*) with self-examination (*Selbstbesinnung*) and self-assertion (*Selbstbehauptung*) not just casually, but penetrating to their very foundations. . . . (*SU* 19; *SAU* 479)

Voluntarism signifies here that it depends on us to be us, to be thus what we are and must be. The αὐτός is we, depends on us, but on us as we carry the resistance of the adversary in us. Whence the necessity of a fundamental effort. We must be what we are in order to make the effort. But we shall be what we are, we, only if we want to make the effort. The force of the effort, the will, is at once the name of that circle in which we listen to ourselves, hear ourselves, understand ourselves, obey ourselves, our internal ear, if you wish, but also what the *Selbst* needs in order to enter into the circle in which nevertheless it is already wound and in order to set the circle moving, in its own proper movement. The will must hear itself as force, the force of resistance and of resistance to resistance, which sets and holds this circle in its essential movement. This movement is also, in its essence, a struggle, *der Kampf*. As that will be repeated a little farther on, this force is also the spiritual force of the West, what gives to the German people the exemplary unity of its historial mission in order to make the people of spiritual historiality a people "geschichtlich-geistige" (*SU* 19).

4.

That was in 1933. In 1935, in the *Einführung* . . . , the style is certainly different, the contextual aim changes a little, since this concerns a seminar and not a rectorate address. But don't we find again an analogous conceptual armature when, reading Heraclitus, Heidegger says again of *Kampf*, one of the translations for πόλεμος, that it constitutes the opposition (*Gegeneinander*), maintains in it an "opening"— that is again his word—and at the same time, by just that, gathers in a *Sammlung* that is a λόγος?

Fragment 53 is the matter at hand and was the subject of an exchange of letters with Carl Schmitt during the summer of 1933. I am going to cite this fragment and first translate it traditionally or conventionally, but Heidegger does not hear it with this ear and the retranslation he proposes and never ceases to retranslate in its turn, from 1935 to 1955, will be the place of essential decisions. Here is the text assumed to be well known and its common translation:

> Πόλεμος πάντων μὲν πατήρ ἐστι 'Πόλεμος, war, is the father of all things,' πάντων δὲ βασιλεύς 'the king of all things,' καὶ τοὺς μὲν θεοὺς ἔδειξε τοὺς δὲ ἀνθρώπους, τοὺς μὲν δούλους ἐποίησε τοὺς δὲ ἐλευθέρους 'of certain things it establishes— or proves—that they are gods, of other things that they are men; of some it makes slaves, of others free beings.'

What war is in question under the name πόλεμος? Certainly not a human war, then not a war, according to Heidegger, since πόλεμος precedes the men to which it gives birth. Immediately after translating the fragment in a certain way that we will read in a moment, Heidegger adds: "The πόλεμος named here is a conflict (*Streit*) that prevailed [the French translation says *un conflit qui perdomine* for *waltender Streit*] prior to everything divine and human, not a war in the human sense (*kein Krieg nach menschlicher Weise*)" (*EM* 47; *IM* 62).[8]

The argument is strong since πόλεμος is clearly situated by Heraclitus *at the origin*, before the gods and before men. Heidegger will always refuse the coarse hearing that would translate this fragment into an anthropology of war, a polemology as human discourse on war, a war discourse or a politics of war. Whatever the affinities, the analogies, or homologies between Schmitt and Heidegger, Heidegger would mark here an irreducible gap [*écart*] concerning the sense and the aim of what he understands [*entend*] and of what he means [*entend dire*]. Whether it is a matter of men or gods, of the anthropology or theology of war. The Heraclitean πόλεμος comes up to the origin, *before* gods and men. Now the discourse of Schmitt on politics and on the State is not only an anthropology of war, an anthropolemology. He interprets political conceptuality as the secularization of theological concepts. It is a theoanthropolemology. Exactly what Heidegger will not cease to resist in the name of this Heraclitus fragment. Heidegger cites it a great many times; and still twenty years after, in 1955, in *Zur Seinsfrage*, he protests against every appropriation of the Heraclitean πόλεμος by a discourse of war. This is in an apparently very different context, and on the topology of being that is henceforth written crossed out [*sous la rature en forme de croix*] (*kreuzweise Durchstreichung*), Heidegger writes: "This is not a war, but the πόλεμος, which alone makes appear Gods and men, the free and the slaves, in their respective essence, and which leads to an *Aus-einander-setzung* [in three words, Heidegger's most continual translation for πόλεμος] of ~~being~~ [crossed out].

Compared to which world wars remain superficial. They are always all the less capable of providing [*apporter*] a decision as they are more technically prepared" (*W* 418 [252]). Insofar as πόλεμος destabilizes the subject/object representation, against which Heidegger also proposes this crossing out of being, one can think that πόλεμος is not a stranger to this *kreuzweise Durchstreichung* and that it also participates, like the *Durchstreichung*, in the play of the fourfold, in the play of its opposable regions (*Gegenden*), or rather in the very place (*Ort*) of the crossing through (*in die vier Gegenden des Gevierts und deren Versammlung im Ort der Durchkreuzung* [*Zur Seinsfrage*, in *W* 405 (239)]) for sky and earth, gods and mortals (see, for example, "Bauen Wohnen Denken," in *VA* 145; *PLT* 150–51).

What are Heidegger's meaningful initiatives in the translation of 1935? After citing the fragment, he begins a new paragraph and proposes, without quotation marks, a paraphrastic equivalence that does not officially assume the conventional status of translation and is inscribed then already as an *Auseinandersetzung*, a πόλεμος, with the ordinary translations. Πόλεμος is already rendered, precisely, by *Auseinandersetzung*, in one single word: it is a matter of explicating oneself, of struggling, of debating with the other agonistically. For all, all things (πάντων), Heidegger says "allem," but adds actively between parentheses "(Anwesenden)": for all being present, for all that comes to present itself, πόλεμος is πατήρ and βασιλεύς. The most meaningful innovations concern precisely πατήρ and βασιλεύς, which are ordinarily heard and understood as father and king. Πατήρ, Heidegger does not hear or understand as "father," as those that think they know, familiarly, what is a father, but as "Erzeuger," the one that produces or engenders; and he adds between parentheses: "(der aufgehen läßt)": the one that makes bloom, rise, come to presence—and we have recognized above the stake of this word. In βασιλεύς, Heidegger hears and understands not "king," as those that, speaking or not of politics, believe they know what king means (to say), but "waltender Bewahrer" (*EM* 47), the guardian that governs, rules across [*perdomine*], reigns over presence. *Walten* is there again very marked.

In saying generator and guardian in place of father and king, Heidegger deanthropologizes understanding, as if these human figures of father and king were only rhetorical figures to which, if not their literal [*propre*] sense, at least their own proper enigma or difference would have to be rendered; as if in sum they were an anachronic anthropologization abusively reappropriating Heraclitus's word [*parole*] in the field of a philosophy, an anthropology, or a political science [*une politique*] that will always remain latecomers and strangers to the originarity of its λόγος. Heidegger's understanding can seem violent, his ear speaks and writes, but it claims to restore an originary sense against another violence, that of a deafness, of an *Überhören* that would have closed up the tympanum, buried the clarity of an early [*matinale*] resonance under layers of wax, archive, and reproduction.

At the beginning of this lecture, Heidegger multiplies the calls to revolution— that is his word (*Revolution*)—an actual (*wirkliche*) (*EM* 41) revolution in our hearing and our experience of the tongue. In particular, of the Greek and German tongues, the most powerful and spiritual (*die geistigsten*) (*EM* 43) of tongues. This revolution passes through teachers and must begin with revolutionizing the teaching corps itself (*Aber dazu müssen wir die Lehrer revolutionieren*) (*EM* 41) and with transforming the university. One must condemn a science of language that would only be the technical knowledge of a dead mechanics, the history of grammatical forms that have the cold rigidity of a corpse. Heidegger's accent and rhetoric recall the Nietzsche of the *Lectures on the Future of Our Educational Institutions*.[9] As soon as one refinds an "originary rapport with language," one "scents" (*spürt*) the trace of the dead (*das Tote*) (*EM* 40) in the grammatical forms, which have become pure mechanisms. Despite his well-known distrust with regard to vitalist or organicist discourse, Heidegger opposes here, in a traditional way, the originary to technical machination, as the living to the dead. His conclusion, political and pedagogical at once, carries him in 1935, as was already the case at the beginning of the 1920s, in the direction of those, above all students, that want to change the university. That doubtlessly does not reduce to an academic demagoguery. Heidegger not only searches to seduce or to involve the most impatient and most revolutionary students, whether it be a matter of the Nazi "revolution" underway or of a revolution that would wish itself more radical. He does not abstractly condemn the deadly technologization of our rapport with the tongue caught in a "steel network" (*Stahlnetz*). In place of a teaching "without spirit" (*geistlose*) (*EM* 40) of the grammatical technology, he would prefer that one initiate the students into the prehistory and the ancient history of the Germans. But one would fall back into the same ennui if one did not convert the school to the "world of the spirit," in a "spiritual and nonscientific atmosphere" (*EM* 41).

At that time Heidegger is no longer rector. Yes or no, is he already deceived by what is called the "revolution underway"? The strategy of his discourse is made to render this question too simple. Whether a matter of the nonanthropological interpretation of Heraclitus's πόλεμος or of the revolution in the experience of language, his statements are intended to respond to several expectations. They are consonant with certain expectations that are immediate or narrowly determined in a political and anthropological context, while they are dissonant with them at the same time, if one hears and understands with another ear, that is, by hearing beyond this immediate field of consonance toward the horizon of a more open future. Heidegger would claim thus that his reading of Heraclitus is already an act of spiritual revolution in the rapport with language, beyond the grids of dead knowledge, of philosophy, of history, of anthropology. Let us take an example, doubtless the privileged example in Heidegger's eyes. The meditation devoted to the grammar of the word *Sein* describes the Greeks' experience of being, and in being their experience of the language that is for them a being. This Greek experience would be a nonquestioning (*fraglos*) experience of "Dastehen, zum Stand kommen und im *Stand* bleiben," that is, of οὐσία as παρουσία, which Heidegger hears and translates here as *Anwesenheit* (*EM* 46). There again, Heidegger claims to go back short of what he calls "Greek philosophy," which would stop at the *Anwesende* without questioning it. To determine the originarily Greek apprehension of being as φύσις, before all the later concepts tied to "nature," Heidegger insists on the tension of a double movement: to stand up, to rise, to unfold itself toward the outside while remaining enveloped within itself (*das aufgehende Sichaufrichten, das in sich verweilende Sichentfalten*) (*EM* 47), the originary unity of repose and movement. Now the word that Heidegger privileges to say this originary unity of two contraries is *Walten*: to govern, to rule, *perdominer*: to rule across (a somewhat strange French translation), prevail, exercise in any case a power or a force, and not without a certain violence. Very difficult to translate, this word carries a weight all the heavier since, on the one hand, the word is inseparable from a certain πόλεμος, preparing and thus legitimating the citation of Heraclitus, and since, on the other hand, Heidegger makes of this word quite simply, at a certain point, the synonym of *An-Wesen*, in two words, of presence, indeed of ἀλήθεια. The *An-* of *An-Wesen*, what makes come to presence this unfolding of a φύσις remaining however in itself, is the force or the violence of this *Walten*.

One has trouble translating the sentences that introduce the Heraclitus fragment on πόλεμος to the very extent that the idiomaticity of *Walten* plays a decisive role in them, the role of decision, the role of the very truth enveloped in the tension of the two contraries:

In diesem Walten sind aus ursprünglicher Einheit Ruhe und Bewegung verschlossen und eröffnet. "In this *Walten* repose and movement are enclosed and open on the basis of their originary unity." Dieses Walten ist das im Denken noch unbewältigt überwältigende An-Wesen, worin das Anwesende als Seiendes west. "This *Walten* is pre-sence (*An-Wesen*) governing (*überwältigende*) yet untamed [ungoverned] by thought [in other words, *Walten* is already governing in presence without having been thought or governed by thought; *Walten* is at a given moment stronger than thought], *An-Wesen* in which *das Anwesende west*, the present presents itself, if you wish, as being." Dieses Walten aber tritt erst aus der Verborgenheit heraus, d. h. griechisch: ἀλήθεια (Unverborgenheit) geschieht, indem das Walten sich als eine Welt erkämpft. Durch Welt wird das Seiende erst seiend. "But this *Walten* does not proceed outside of the dissimulation, that is to say in Greek that ἀλήθεια (nondissimulation) comes about only as this *Walten* '*sich erkämpft*,' obtains itself as a world through struggling [*lutte*]. It is through world alone that beings become beings." (*EM* 47)

Walten thus becomes truth, the truth of the struggle for truth, the nondissimulation, insofar as, preceding or prevailing over as it were itself, it obtains itself by a struggle, it *sich erkämpft* as world. The world is the opening for beings. *Walten* first conceals itself, forgets itself. It goes out of its crypt, comes about as *truth* only insofar as it wins itself, obtains itself through struggling (*sich erkämpft*), carries the day in traversing resistances, putting itself to the test of its own proper resistance. It carries the day over itself, carries itself and carries itself along in itself beyond itself. The power, the force, or the violence of this *Walten* is the originary φύσις that can come about only in *striving, s'efforçant*. The force forces itself, strives, *s'efforce*. Here I am playing with the French idiom to try to get back to Heidegger's idiom. As in the *Rectorate Discourse*, *Walten, Kampf, sich erkämpfen*, is articulated with the lexis of force, but of spiritual force (*geistige Kraft*). In *Sein und Zeit* the word *Kampf* was associated with that of power (*Macht*) or superpower (*Übermacht*) as the proof of freedom for finitude. The self-winning and self-struggling—with self and with the other, with self as with the other—is an absolutely originary struggle, φύσις itself. Further on, Heidegger will say: "Der hier gemeinte Kampf ist ursprünglicher Kampf" (*EM* 47): "The struggle meant here is an originary struggle." The "self-winning" does not come [*arrive*] to being, being comes [*arrive*] in the "self-winning."

Let us return to the transcription of what Heidegger hears and understands in tuning into [*entend à l'écoute du*] the Heraclitean πόλεμος. The Heraclitean πόλεμος is then *Auseinandersetzung*, debate, agonistic explication with the other, struggle of all, for all (πάντων) (*allem*). Heidegger, as we have seen, adds, between parentheses, after "allem": "(Anwesenden)": for all being, for all that comes to present itself. This addition of a parenthesis is intended to confirm the interpretation according to which the predominance of the *Walten*, which merges with the *Anwesen* itself, is at the origin of presence. For all being-present, the πόλεμος is *Erzeuger*, not the father, a concept too anthropological for a πόλεμος that gives birth to gods and men, but the producer, the generator. Heidegger continues: "aber (auch) waltender Bewahrer," but (also) the prevailing guardian. Whereas the little word "auch" is added between parentheses, "waltender" is not between parentheses. Heidegger adds this "auch" as a matter of course for reasons that are now evident to us. If *Walten* also means (to say) "reign," the translation of βασιλεύς by guardian-who-reigns, by reigning guardian, reconstitutes to be sure the conventional signification, the royal signification that the simple *Bewahrer* could somewhat attentuate, depoliticize, and de-anthropologize. But at the same time, the translation renders to the German *Walten* all its force. The πόλεμος, the *Auseinandersetzung*, Heidegger then continues, makes appear (*läßt . . . erscheinen*) some as God, others as men. *Erscheinen lassen*, to make appear, to emerge, to unfold—for ἔδειξε—all that clearly means this father does not procreate. The πόλεμος, the *Kampf*, is not a creative father, it is a power that brings to light [*faire paraître*]. End of the transcription: "die einen stellt sie her(aus) als Knechte, die anderen aber als Frei": The same πόλεμος, the same *Auseinandersetzung*, this time as *waltender Bewahrer*, "produces some as slaves, but others as free." In saying *heraustellen*, with the "(aus)" between parentheses, Heidegger plays between: (1) *herausstellen*, to *produce* in the sense of placing outside, manifesting, exposing; (2) *herstellen*, to *produce* in the sense of fabricate, make; and perhaps also (3) *ausstellen*, to *produce* in the sense of expose, exhibit, issue, emit.

The Heraclitean πόλεμος then can no longer have the sense of war: neither between men, nor between men and gods, nor between gods. This dehumanization or this detheologization does not suffer from the faulty interpretative violence that some would be tempted to see in it. There is nothing more "logical." Nothing more "logical" between quotation marks, for we are here at the very place of the originary λόγος as πόλεμος, whose internal contradiction has no more to protect itself against incoherence or to search itself for the guarantee of a logic of good sense, both of which do nothing but derive from the λόγος.

Is there in effect nothing more logical? The πόλεμος, the producer or the prevailing guardian that engenders gods and men, is neither a god nor a man. It is more originary than the human or the divine, precedes the opposition that places them face to face. In the beginning, there will have been πόλεμος, a "waltender Streit," the reign of a conflict that is not a war in the human manner (*kein Krieg nach menschlicher Weise*). Πόλεμος will have made upsurge between men and gods, slaves and freemen not only opposition, faults, gaps [*écarts*], distances, but also joints and couplings. The conflict, such as it is thought by Heraclitus (*Der von Heraklit gedachte Kampf*), is that by which the being-present (*das Wesende*) is separated in opposing itself (in the *Gegeneinander*, the *Auseinandertreten*). Conflict gives to the being-present, in presence, its position (*Stellung*), its status, its stance (*Stand*), and its rank (*Rang*), the hierarchy, for example, between freemen and slaves. Dissociation, disjunction, scission, dissension, or secession: in this schiz, this split, of the *Auseinandertreten* or of the *Auseinandersetzung* are no doubt opened the faults, the intervals, the gaps, the distances, but also are formed the joints or the couplings (*Fugen*). For the schiz produced by the πόλεμος must also gather, join up, join together, ally, combine, hold together what it separates or spaces. This will permit concluding that πόλεμος and λόγος, it is the same (*dasselbe*), the λέγειν of λόγος always being heard and understood in its originary signification of gathering. If one recalls here what will be said of the Heraclitean φιλεῖν as λέγειν in 1955, one can conclude from this that πόλεμος and φιλεῖν, it's originarily the same. And what assures the homology of this τὸ αὔτον, of this reversible tautology between πόλεμος and φιλεῖν, what gathers the tautology with itself, is the λόγος, the power of concentrating of the λόγος, the lovence [*aimance*] of λόγος, I dare not say the "philology" of Heideggerian hearing; I dare even less to say, while yielding to the temptation, its "otology."

This tautology is otology, for it supposes not only a discourse on the ear, but a discourse of the ear, and of the ear that speaks, of poetizing (*dichtende*) hearing. If this otology were a monology, it would be in the sense in which Heidegger writes at the end of *Der Weg zur Sprache*, "Aber die Sprache *ist* Monolog" (*US* 265), not in the idealist sense that he attributes to Novalis's *Monolog* cited at the beginning of this meditation, but in the sense in which speech alone speaks. Or rather: speech is *alone to speak*, one cannot speak of speech without speech already speaking, there is no metalanguage, speech is alone to speak in a solitude that alone makes possible the belonging-to-one-another of a *Zueinandergehören* (*US* 265–68), the belonging-to-one-another that makes this singular monology an autoheterology. How is this monology to be distinguished from the speculative proposition of absolute idealism whose synthesis is also heterotautological? This is much too formidable a question that I prefer to leave open here.

In the sentence of the *Einführung* . . . I am going to reread, this otophilology could replace πόλεμος with φιλεῖν or φιλία without the least inconsistency: "(Die Auseinandersetzung trennt weder, noch zerstört sie gar die Einheit. Sie bildet diese, ist Sammlung (λόγος): πόλεμος und λόγος sind dasselbe)" (*EM* 47): "(The πόλεμος (*Auseinandersetzung*) does not dissociate the unity, even less does it destroy it. It forms the unity, is gathering (λόγος). Πόλεμος and λόγος are the same.)" The word λόγος, translated by *Sammlung*, is between parentheses in this sentence that is *itself* between parentheses, somewhat like a supplementary and tautological precaution, murmured for anyone who would not yet have understood. Tautology in the tautology about a tautology, this sentence between parentheses was explaining another sentence that was saying however nothing less than world and history. It was saying the world, the becoming-world in and through πόλεμος: "In der Aus-einandersetzung wird Welt" (*EM* 47): "In the conflict with the other the world comes about." And further on, this becoming world is described as history, historical events [*l'événementialité*], historiality, the being-history of history proper and authentic: "Dieses Weltwerden ist die eigentliche Geschichte" (*EM* 48).

How is this originary history of the world to be *determined*? In other words, how to determine the rapport between the originary *Kampf* and what we identify as the history of the world, for example, political history [*la politique*]? Through concern for economy, I shall follow the track [*trace*] of a response in one single paragraph of the *Einführung* . . . , the paragraph that immediately follows the parenthesis "(. . . πόλεμος und λόγος sind dasselbe)." In the labyrinth of an ear, this paragraph takes up again and re-ties most of the threads we are following from the beginning. Heidegger recalls in this paragraph that *Kampf* is originary. Why? "for," "because" (*denn*) it makes upsurge the contenders as such. Then it precedes them. The struggle that precedes all then fights nothing, that is the very logic of this tautology. This *Kampf* does not yet have any contenders facing it. It does not make war with someone or something. It is not an "assault," Heidegger says, against something that would be present in front of or before it, against a *Vorhandenes*. Before it, there is no world, there is nothing. Then, what makes the πόλεμος originary? How does it leave this tautology? How does it leave pure tautology while remaining in otology? It projects and develops (*entwirft und entwickelt*) what is not yet heard, the unheard, *das Un-erhörte*, written in two words separated by a hyphen, as if to make the heard better heard in the unheard of what is not heard, but also, as elsewhere for *Un-gedacht*, to make better heard the not simply negative character of the *Un-*. In other words, in order to hear the originary πόλεμος, the unheard must be heard. I had recalled a short while ago, concerning the reading of Hölderlin, that *Erhören* also means (to say) answer, respond to a request, to a prayer or a wish. The originary *Kampf* sketches and unfolds then what is not yet heard or answered, what then remains yet unaccomplished as the unheard (*Un-erhörte*) of a non-said (*Un-gesagte*) and of a non-thought (*Un-gedachte*) (*EM* 47).

All that is, as it were, the logical consequence of *Kampf*'s originarity. That is why Heidegger says "denn," "for," "because." But what happens *next, then, dann*? How does the *unheard* originarity of the unaccomplished make itself heard *then*, outside of itself in itself, in a sort of heterotautology, through historical works and events? In Heidegger's elliptical response, I hear above all the "dann" and, once more, the "tragen" that will not have ceased to carry us and carry us away [*déporter*] since *Sein und Zeit*: "Dieser Kampf wird dann von den

Schaffenden, den Dichtern, Denkern, Staatsmännern getragen" (*EM* 47): "The [originary] struggle is then carried on (*getragen*) by those that open (creators), poets, thinkers, statesmen." In the course of the same year, in the seminar on *Germanien*, to which I take the liberty to refer you, Heidegger is much more explicit about what he calls the three creative "Gewalten" of historial Dasein, to wit, the "powers of poetry, of thought, of the creation of the State (*Die Mächte der Dichtung, des Denkens, des Staatsschaffens*)" (*GA* 39: 144). The triad of these creators hears and makes heard finally the unheard of the originary πόλεμος. These three creators carry this unheard, they carry it first in themselves, close by themselves, will I dare to say "*bei sich*," like a mute voice and to which they respond by taking responsibility for it. They open in this responsibility. This work is theirs, since they carry the unheard in themselves and take responsibility for it. But this work is not theirs, since they only hear the unheard. Their work carries only the seal or the signature of the originary πόλεμος that has projected and developed the unheard. I speak of work for *Schaffen*, because Heidegger does not stop, in the lines that follow, determining this *Schaffen* as *Werken* and *Werk*, without distinguishing between the three *Gewalten* of the poet, thinker, and states-man. If the figure of the statesman is somewhat artificially isolated, one can wonder what Heidegger's crafty strategy signifies in 1935. After what has been said of the originary and pre-anthropological, pre-subjective, pre-personal, pre-political, pre-polemological *Kampf*, no one should have the right to write and to sign "Mein Kampf," without ridiculous presumption, in any case without confining oneself to a very degraded sense of *Kampf*. Nevertheless, wishing himself a statesman, the institutor of a new order and of a new State, was not the author of *Mein Kampf* able to appeal to the originary πόλεμος? Supposing Heidegger finds no other objection to his politics, a hypothesis I shall not examine here, Hitler would perhaps have been able to say: the "*mein*" of *Mein Kampf* does not signify an anthropologico-subjectivistic reappropriation. In respectful listening to the origi-nary πόλεμος, concerning its most unheard aspect [*en ce qu'il a de plus inouï*], *Mein Kampf* says "my" way, that is, "our" way of carrying (*tragen*) the originary *Kampf*. I speak, like you, Heidegger, of our responsibility, of the mission (*Sendung* [*GA* 39: 151]), of the "historial spiritual mission (*Auftrag*) of the German people" (*SU* 10), I *carry* the responsibility for this mission (*Auftrag*). My response is *our* response to the originary *Kampf*, I am only hearing and developing what it has inaudibly projected. In continuing the principle of such a response, Heideggerian hearing offers no guarantee, supposing such guarantees can ever exist, against the use that the regime at that time can make of this thinking hearing of Heraclitus. Not only does Heidegger then voice agreement with those that have only the *Kampf* in their mouth, but he can furnish them the most dignified and the most thoughtful justification, which can always deepen rather than dissipate the equivocation and the misunderstanding, the mishearing, the essential *sich verhören*. Earlier I sug-gested that Heidegger had not sufficiently thematized or formalized the essential equivocation of all these strategies. But I added that in any case they are never totally objectifiable, thematizable, and formalizable. This limit is even the place of decision, of decision in general, of political decision in particular, its tragic condition of possibility, there where decision cannot finally let itself be guided by a knowledge. And then to say that a *strategy* or the calculus of a *stratagem* is not formalizable, is that not still to situate the project of formalization in what I shall call a war economy?

In order to hasten the conclusion of a lecture that is too long, I would like to situate very quickly, in the history of this philopolemology, what accords in a perhaps less visible and hardly audible way, a certain negativity of hearing (nonhearing, incapacity for *Horchen*, the deafness of the *Überhören*, of the *sich Verhören*, disagreement, misunderstanding, mishearing, unwilling- or not-being-able-to-hear) with a certain *degeneration of sight* on the one hand, with *sacrifice* on the other. In both cases, this negativity responds to the sense, to the possibility and the necessity of what Heidegger calls in general, but also in this context, *Verfall*, fall or decay.

Conflict (*Kampf*) is φύσις inasmuch as it institutes but also inasmuch as it keeps what it institutes. It is institution itself, in the double sense of this word, instituting and instituted. When conflict stops, when one no longer hears what is unheard in the conflict, the being does not disappear, but is no longer kept, affirmed, maintained (*behauptet [d. h. als solches gewahrt]*), becomes an object (*Gegenstand, Vorhandene*), an object *available* there where the world has ceased to become world (*keine Welt mehr weltet*). It becomes either an object for a gaze (*Betrachten, Anblick*), or a form or image that faces us, or the object of a calculated production. In this fall of πόλεμος, in this *Verfall*, the originary φύσις falls (*fällt . . . herab*) from the rank of model (*Vorbild*) to the rank of reproduction and imitation (*Abbilden, Nachmachen*). Φύσις, the instituting institution, becomes the Nature (*Natur*) that is opposed to Art. Φύσις was the originary upsurging of force, power, or violence, of the *Gewalten des Waltenden*, the φαίνεσθαι in the major sense of the epiphany of the world. The unheard falls now to the rank of spectacle, in the quelled visibility of objects that face us. This decay does not consist in becoming visible, it is also a decay of the eye. Like hearing, seeing suffers when the originary πόλεμος is quelled. When seeing penetrated inside *Walten* at the moment of the sketch of the work, seeing becomes superficial, an eye of the outside, the simple consideration of the spectator or examination of the inspector (*Ansehen, Besehen, Begaffen*). Sight degenerates into *optics*, that is to say, also into the technology of sight—here is the symptom, that is, the fall. This new blindness then no more excludes spectacle than deafness excludes noise; deafness goes hand in hand with a cultural din louder than before (*lauter . . . als je zuvor*). Πόλεμος degenerates into polemics. The creators (poets, thinkers, statesmen) then have been removed from the people; they are regarded as eccentrics or cultural ornaments. They are hardly tolerated (*geduldet*) (*EM* 48) when the originary πόλεμος withdraws. This tolerance, this little bit of tolerance is in truth an intolerance.

The brief remark of the *Einführung* . . . on intolerance is supported by a thought of *sacrifice*, a more radical, harder and more piercing thought that had been developed in the earlier seminar of the same year on *Germanien*, the first seminar on Hölderlin, in particular in section 10 that inscribes that poem and

Hölderlin in the horizon of a thought of Heraclitus, even if Heidegger does not neglect the difference of times between the two. The fact of not hearing (*überhören* again) the poet that announces the future being of a people is defined as a *sacrifice*. *Überhören* is in truth a sacrifice. It is even the sacrifice of truth, and this sacrifice passes through the ear. In truth, this sacrifice of the truth is the very movement of truth. The initiators or the first-born *must* be sacrificed (*müssen die Erstlinge geopfert werden*) (*GA* 39: 146). And this is as valid for poets as for thinkers and statesmen when it is a matter of a fundamental mutation or of a foundation. This necessity for sacrificial exclusion can be interpreted in Heidegger's tone, precisely when he speaks of the fundamental tone (*Grundstimmung*) or, in this *Grundstimmung*, when he speaks of the conflict of joy and mourning. But the necessity of the sacrificial foreclosure can also be formalized abstractly and in another tone, like that of Rousseau, for example, when he explains that the founders or the legislators must not belong to the very thing they found or institute: they must be strangers to it or taken for strangers, a priori excluded. Ostracism and sacrifice, suppression, repression, foreclosure, the impossibility of tolerating the founding instance and authority, are structurally part of what is founded. The institution or the foundation cannot itself be founded; it inaugurates above an inaudible abyss, and this knowledge is intolerable. Which, by definition, moreover, is not knowledge. It is the experience of the foundation as the experience of the *Abgrund*. What founds or justifies cannot be founded or justified. Let us not forget that the same year, in *Der Ursprung des Kunstwerkes*, truth states itself as an originary conflict (*Urstreit*), the thetic opposition of the clearing and of the double dissimulation (*Gegeneinander von Lichtung und zwiefacher Verbergung*). And among the four essential ways for truth to institute itself in the being it opens, there is the founding act of the State and the essential sacrifice (*das wesentliche Opfer*) (*HW* 49–50). In *Germanien*, the allusion to sacrifice comes not long after another reading and another translation of aphorism 53 of Heraclitus (*GA* 39: 123ff.). We cannot analyze it here closely. Heidegger again complains about the common translation, notably about the translation of πατήρ: by father. In 1966–67, he will no longer protest, it seems, when, in the joint seminar he devotes with Fink to Heraclitus, Fink keeps the words war, father, and king. But let us leave that for the moment. Let us retain only that the seminar on *Germanien*, in a reading of Heraclitus analogous to that of the *Einführung* . . . , proposes a translation as such, between quotation marks this time, in which the words between parentheses have disappeared. Βασιλεύς is not translated by *waltender Bewahrer*, but by *Beherrscher*, master or lord. This difference perhaps becomes more significant if one recalls that ἐλεύθερους, translated by "free" (*Freie*) in the *Einführung* . . . , which is, so to speak, normal, was found to be translated at that time by *Herren* (lords or masters), in opposition to slaves (δούλους, *Knechte*). In the context I have tried, not without violence, to delimit, we would have to, with more time, pay the greatest attention to other motifs I am briefly indicating.

At the focus of this reading, there is not only aphorism 53, but also two other aphorisms of Heraclitus that name πόλεμος. One says that justice (δίκη) is conflict (ἔρις). And the commentary of Heidegger—who writes "δίκη ἔρις—Recht *ist*

Streit"—tends to underscore, against common sense, the reciprocal belonging of justice and of conflict that are in agreement [s'entendent] between themselves, so to speak, in this Zusammengehörigkeit. The other aphorism (67) says god is war and peace, just as god is day and night, winter and summer, abundance and famine—just as god is the fire that transforms itself in this way. Fire will be an important theme of the seminar with Fink. This time translating πόλεμος by war (Krieg), Heidegger does so naturally without warmongering, just as he insists without irenicism on εἰρήνη: god is also peace. One must hear the harmony between war and peace, the Einklang, the accord to which the contradictory (Widerstreit) refers, as well as the contradiction in which the Einklang oscillates or resonates. In this whole thematic configuration, what is said, in the seminar on Der Rhein, of the Feindseligkeit would naturally have had to be meditated on. This word, Feindseligkeit, currently signifies hostility, but it lets itself be translated with difficulty here, above all according to the hearing Heidegger proposes of it. He would lead one to hear and understand a kind of originary enmity (ursprüngliche Feindschaft [GA 39: 245]) that reigns (waltet again) at the crisscross of contraries (in dieser sich überkreuzenden Gegenstrebigkeit waltet die ursprüngliche Feindschaft). But once more, this originary enmity does not produce the exploding dispersion of contraries, rather it is their originary oneness (ursprüngliche Einigkeit). And that is why enmity would also have the characteristic of beatitude, bliss, Seligkeit. The bliss of this originary enmity constituting the unity of a being, this unity must also preserve "the highest purity" (GA 39: 241). Feindseligkeit would give, so to speak, the secret, idiomatic economy, in a single word, of a reconciliation. Not of a reconciliation in friendship, but of a reconciliation between friendship and enmity, a reconciliation carried in the same ordeal [épreuve], in the non-identical-sameness-of the experience.

Heidegger almost never names the enemy, it seems, nor hatred. Why doesn't he evoke the voice of the enemy if between πόλεμος and φιλία the λόγος assures such a homology? Why this dissymmetry? If I had to try to gather this thought still more by finding again the carrying-distance of Tragen and of Austrag that we have been testing ever since the voice of the friend that each Dasein bei sich trägt, I would bring this reconciliation together with what Heidegger says elsewhere of Austrag. You know that this word plays a major role not only in certain texts I cited above, notably Die Sprache, but also in Identity and Difference, at the end of the "Onto-theo-logical Constitution of Metaphysics." In its everyday sense, Austrag would be able to be translated by distribution, settlement (for example, the settlement and the solution of a conflict). We have seen how, in Die Sprache, Heidegger also heard it as carrying, indeed the gestation and the carrying-to-term of difference as well as of intimacy (Innigkeit). The French translator of Identity and Difference recalls that Austrag, which he translates by "Conciliation," is also the "somewhat approximate etymological translation" of difference (dis-fero = aus-tragen). And he cites a text of Heidegger (Der europäische Nihilismus, p. 185) specifically stating that "Difference (Unterscheidung), as Differenz, means (to say) that there is a permanent accord (Austrag) between being and beings."

And so difference becomes in some way synonymous with peace, another name for accord, harmony or conciliation, indeed reconciliation, since Heidegger also defines *Austrag* as "the reconciliation of conflict (*Der Versöhnung des Streites*)."[10] In the last pages of "The Onto-theo-logical Constitution of Metaphysics," *Austrag*, as preamble, threshold, or preliminary place (*Vorort*) of the essence of the difference between being and beings, also becomes the threshold by which God enters philosophy. But this God of philosophy or of ontotheology is a God to which man cannot address himself: neither by prayer nor by sacrifice (*Zu diesem Gott kann der Mensch weder beten, noch kann er ihm opfern*) (*ID* 64). If I understand right, the God that can be addressed *beyond* ontotheology, the God that would no longer be the God of philosophers and scholars [*savants*], the God that would no longer be the foundation of being or *causa sui*, that God that is called by prayer and can hear (*Erhören*), indeed answer the prayer, would be a God to which it is possible and no doubt necessary to offer sacrifice.

These explicit allusions to sacrifice are doubtless rather rare and discreet. I have indicated three or four of them. But you have at least seen that they already oriented a later and more patient attempt to perceive better what Heidegger will have heard, whether he understood it or not [*sous-entendu ou non*], I mean, what Heidegger will not have heard under this word sacrifice. In order to continue on this preliminary path today, I thought I had to hear Heidegger, to hear him hearing his own tongue, struggling with it or playing with it. I thought I had to do this up to a certain point, always difficult to discern, that point where, in order to hear the singularity of the idiom, is also required the plurality, indeed the *Auseinandersetzung* of idioms. More than one ear is necessary. More than an ear. When he speaks of Hölderlin, Heidegger specifically states that each verse must be heard (*hören*) not by searching for some imitative harmony, some painting of sounds (*Klangmalerei*), but starting from the "plenitude of its truth, in which the sound and the sense are not yet disjoined (*wo Klang und Sinn noch nicht zertrennt sind*)" (*GA* 39: 240). Translation always risks this separation—which is also a war and a sacrifice, the choice perhaps being left among several qualities and several events of sacrifice.

Hölderlin's sacrifice, which the Germans have not heard and understood, is in Heidegger's eyes an exemplary sacrifice. After recalling that the initiator poets are not heard and that they are dedicated to sacrifice, Heidegger adds: "Hölderlin is a poet of this kind (*Hölderlin ist ein solcher Dichter*)" (*GA* 39: 146). But who will have heard the one that announces to his people that he has not heard the sacrificed poet? What does someone do who, while speaking, says to his people: "'You do not hear the sacrificed poet,' you do not hear the one who says 'Ich aber bin allein': 'But I am alone'; hear him at last, he is exemplary. Stop sacrificing him"? The mediator or intercessor is necessarily in the same situation, quite as exemplary as the one he would like to make heard and whom for the moment he alone hears. The mediator always says in truth: "Ich aber bin allein," you do not hear me, when will you hear me hearing Heraclitus, Hölderlin, and some others? When will you stop sacrificing me? When will you hear the voice of that strange friend that your *Dasein bei sich trägt*, of that enemy-friend that speaks to you in the heart of a *Feindseligkeit*, of this originary enmity that forever gathers us for the best and the worst?

Of course, *bien entendu*, I reserve for another time the unstable and multiple title I would have liked to give this reading: "le sacrifice *de* Heidegger," not only the sacrifice in general, but *Heidegger's sacrifice, the sacrifice* of *Heidegger*, what he has thought or not of sacrifice, of his own, for example, that he may have offered himself to or that one may still offer him to [*qu'il s'y soit offert ou qu'on l'y offre encore*]. *A bon entendeur, salut*: let the hearer beware.

NOTES

Translator's note. I consulted the English translations of Heidegger where available and cited some passages with modifications as indicated herein; the exception is the translation of *Sein und Zeit* (*Being and Time*) by John Macquarrie and Edward Robinson (New York: Harper, 1962), which gives the German pagination in the margins; for that text I have only given the German reference, although I have used the translation with modifications. However, in all the "translations" of Heidegger I have attempted to follow Derrida in his "translation," which "always risks," as he says, "a war and a sacrifice" between sound and sense.

1. G. W. F. Hegel, *Wissenschaft der Logik 2*, vol. 6 of *Werke in zwanzig Bänden* (Frankfurt a.M.: Suhrkamp, 1969), 573; *Hegel's Science of Logic*, trans. A. V. Miller (Atlantic Highlands, N.J.: Humanities Press, 1989 [1969]), 843 (modified).

2. See Christopher Fynsk, *Heidegger, Thought and Historicity* (Ithaca: Cornell University Press, 1986), 42–43; Jean-François Courtine, "Voix de la conscience et vocation de l'être," *Cahiers Confrontation* 20 (Winter 1989): 82; and Jean-Luc Nancy, "La décision d'éxistence," in *"Etre et temps" de Heidegger* (Marseilles: Sud, 1989), 239.

3. Although Heidegger in outline gives the understanding that *Ereignis* is not a mode of being, he puts us on guard against this simple "inversion (*Umkehrung*)" of the logical order, which would still be a "flight," a "refuge" (*Zuflucht*). The relations of the logical order here have no pertinence since we are trying to think the very origin of logic and ontologic. See *SD* 22–23; *TB* 21–22.

4. Since this lecture was written and delivered, my friend Maurizio Ferraris has pointed out to me another occurrence of the word "friend." In a certain way, it can be judged to be without great import [*portée*], in any case, without a common measure with the occurrence occupying us here. This occurrence in effect seems lost in another demonstrative space, in a series of examples in which the friend could easily be replaced by another figure without damaging the sense. The arrival of a friend (*die Ankunft eines Freundes*) is invoked there as an example of impending events in a series concerning *Vorhandensein* (a storm), *Zuhandensein* (the renovation of a house), as well as *Mitdasein* (the arrival of a friend): "For instance, a storm, the remodeling of the house, or the arrival of a friend, may be impending; and these are entities which are respectively present -at-hand, ready-to-hand, and there-with-us (*Bevorstehen kann zum Beispiel ein Gewitter, der Umbau des Hauses, die Ankunft eines Freundes, Seiendes demnach, was vorhanden, zuhanden oder mit-da-ist*)" (*SZ*, § 50, p. 250). It is justifiable and indispensable to dissociate this allusion to the impending coming of the friend from the allusion to the voice of the friend, the latter of having a different status and seriousness as the former.

But once that was done, once the coming of the friend, one example among others, was opposed to the exemplary voice of the friend, one could nevertheless be tempted to charge this apparently contingent example with a troubling, indeed *unheimlich (uncanny)*, signification. For the imminence Heidegger analyzes here and that he justly wants to distinguish, in all rigor, from other imminences, like that of the storm, of the renovating of the house, or of the coming of the friend, is nothing other than the imminence of death. It is a matter of distinguishing the imminence, the "not yet" of death from every other imminence. This contextual proximity obliges one to ask why the example of the arrival of the friend has been imposed on Heidegger the moment he treated in sum of the always impending arrival of death. Without citing this text, without even letting it be thought that he had paid attention to it, Christopher Fynsk, in *Heidegger, Thought and Historicity*, evokes the voice of the friend in a context in which he chooses to associate it with the death of Dasein, as if, in its very silence, the voice of the friend announced to Dasein its own proper death: "In its silence, the voice of the friend," Fynsk says, "speaks to Dasein of its death" (p. 43).

And yet however tempting and perhaps justified this reading may be, it cannot act on the authority of the allusion to the impending coming of the friend—and that is why, whether he had remarked it or not, Fynsk was right not to refer to this to back up his reading. For Heidegger puts us on guard against an assimilation between the imminence of death and the imminence of such an arrival. The passage I just cited closes thus: "Ein Sein dieser Art hat der bevorstehende Tod nicht": "The death which impends does not have this kind of Being."

That said, every association, every "logic" does not reduce itself to the association and the "logic" prescribed by a rigorous reading of argumentation, of conceptual and semantic linkings in a context regulated by meaning. Heidegger clearly explains to us how and why, *if one comprehends what he means (to say)*, one must not put on the same plane the example of the impending arrival of a friend and the imminence of death. But the choice of examples can be read beyond that meaning. This supposes a completely other protocol of reading, an other logic, an other rhetoric, a hermeneutic not only broadened but restructured by taking into account what would be called, to go quickly and in a word doubtless problematic, the "unconscious." While belonging to a rigorously heterogeneous sphere and from which one comprehends that Heidegger is anxious to distinguish it, the examples chosen have a certain type of affinity, an unquestionable relation of magnetizing with the imminence, the dread, or the anticipation of death, such as an existential analytic can describe it. This magnetizing, this law of attraction whose status remains to be defined, concerns the example of the friend's coming, but also the other two, the storm (*Gewitter*) or the topsy-turvy transformation (*Umbau*) of the house. They are not just any examples. No doubt the discourse that guides the analytic of Dasein no longer depends, in its axiomatics, on a philosophy of consciousness. But does not that discourse still resist that "logic" or that "law" that we associate here with the old word "unconscious" and that is withdrawn, that in any case we withdraw, in a fashion not very Heideggerian, I believe, from the authority of intentional meaning? Without coming under a metaphysics of consciousness, is not the Heideggerian analytic of Dasein, however, regulated by the norms of an absolute intentional meaning? Such at least is the stake of this remark.

5. I choose this word [join together, *conjoindre*] a bit conjugal—one could also say "become engaged" ["*se fiance*"]—because the Latin *spondere* signifies to promise, to promise in marriage [*fiancer*]. The spouses, the fiancé, the fiancée (*sponsi*) are first the promised, those that have been promised because they promise themselves in a place that is first that of *spondere* and of *respondere*. *Spondere*, but also *sponsare*, is to promise solemnly in prescribed forms, singularly in marriage. *Sponsio, -onis*, or moreover *sponsus,-ûs*, is the solemn promise, engagement, the "yes," the pledge [*gage*] of what is engaged. If I do not imprudently go too far, the etymology of the Latin *spondere* leads back to a family of Greek words (σπονδή, σπονδεῖος, σπονδοφόρος) that all have a certain rapport with

libation, more precisely with wine and other drinks that are offered or poured out at the moment of the sacrifice. This family of words would concern the sacrificial libation or the wine poured out on the earth, the hearth, on the altar, or on the victim: libation consecrated to god. From there the word σπονδή is thought to come to designate every alliance, the peace treaty or armistice, sworn faith, convention: from there, one is thought to have passed to the written or diplomatic document sealing an engagement, symbol or σύμβολον. The σπονδοφόρος is the herald that carries the propositions of peace or alliance.

6. Jacques Derrida, *Of Spirit: Heidegger and the Question*, trans. Geoffrey Bennington and Rachel Bowlby (Chicago: University of Chicago Press, 1989).

7. *Pli selon pli* 'fold according to fold' is a citation by Derrida without quotation marks from Mallarmé's "Remémoration d'amis belges," a citation that Pierre Boulez takes up in a composition of five pieces (see the sleeve note for the recording, CBS 75.770, a note that has been reprinted in *Orientations: Collected Writings by Pierre Boulez*, ed. Jean-Jacques Nattiez, trans. Martin Cooper [Cambridge: Harvard University Press, 1986]: 174–76).—Trans. note.

8. *Introduction à la métaphysique*, trans. Gilbert Kahn (Paris: Gallimard, 1967), 72.

9. I take the liberty of referring here to my *Otobiographies: l'enseignement de Nietzsche et la politique du nom propre* (Paris: Galilée, 1984), 73ff.; *The Ear of the Other: Otobiography, Transference, Translation*, trans. Peggy Kamuf ("Otobiographies" trans. Avital Ronell) (Lincoln: University of Nebraska Press, 1988), 19ff.

10. *Questions* I, trans. Henry Corbin, et al. (Paris: Gallimard, 1968), 256, 299.

VI

HEIDEGGER AND
THE GREEKS

KENNETH MALY

12. Reading and Thinking

Heidegger and the Hinting Greeks

The scope of this presentation is a gathering of reading, thinking, and hinting in their evocative possibilities—possibilities opened up within the work of thinking that we call "Heidegger." The early Greek context for this presentation is twofold: Anaximander and Parmenides. The textual context is threefold, three texts of Heidegger's: *"Der Spruch des Anaximander"* (called "The Anaximander Fragment" in English translation) from *Holzwege* (*GA* 5), *Grundbergriffe* (*GA* 51) (whose last section is devoted to Anaximander), and the short text on Parmenides and the ensuing discussion in the "Seminar in Zähringen 1973" from *Seminare* (*GA* 15).

Specifically, the work of thinking attempted here is a weaving of reading, thinking, and hinting into and out of those three Heidegger texts, then a weaving of the texts on Anaximander with the text on Parmenides, and finally a weaving of the whole problematic of "being" as it unfolds from out of the questions of reading, thinking, and hinting—as they are probed, tested, and tried at the fire of this first beginning with the early Greeks.

Thus this presentation, in the process of its unfolding, will be of service to two issues of paramount importance to Heidegger scholarship at the present juncture in philosophy, exactly one hundred years after his birth. First, by engaging the core issues of Heidegger's thinking in terms of texts that have appeared in the *Gesamtausgabe,* it participates in that thorough and in-depth reinterpretation and reappropriation of Heidegger's works called for by the ongoing publication of the *Gesamtausgabe.* Second, by engaging texts from different years in Heidegger's life-work and by letting the one question that runs through all of these texts be seen in its several hues, it shows the unfolding in the turns and turnings in Heidegger's work *from within the texts themselves,* rather than from the perspective of textual hermeneutics, comparison of texts, or commentary *on* these texts.

This presentation is not intended as an external commentary on Heidegger's thought—first commenting *on* Heidegger and then either dividing his thought into "periods" or placing his thinking here or there within the history of metaphysics. Rather, it wants to go underneath such commentary to the subtle but very forceful evocation of the matter for thinking (*das Zudenkende*), which is always the same (even a one?) and which a proper reading of the texts opens up.

This presentation unfolds in a series of imagings that image or show or let be seen the question that is imaged in the imagings. And, finally, since *what* gets imaged in the imaging is always the one question (the question of being/disclosure/self-showing), the imagings are always imaging being as self-showing. Since being as self-showing is itself an imaging, this presentation is a series of imagings of imaging itself.

FIRST IMAGING: THE PLACE OF OPENING

That place where the question opens up for us—what is it? Where is it? How to name, provisionally, that place where the question carries with it and within itself its own energy (*energeia*) or work?

In *Grundbegriffe* (*GA* 51) Heidegger portrays an unavoidable and unresolvable tension, the tension whereby, on the one hand, being (or the "is") is, while on the other hand, every attempt to think that being results in its being transformed into a being. Although being is somehow other than beings, when we think "being as such," we end up thinking it as *a* being, turning everything upside down, perverting, inverting, turning everything topsy-turvy—putting a misleading and inappropriate shape to the question.

In paragraph 17 of *Grundbegriffe* Heidegger says this place of tension, of unresolvability, in several ways:

(1) We stand between two equally unsurpassable limits: On the one hand, insofar as we think and say "being 'is,'" we immediately make being into a being and thereby deny the proper work (energeia) of being. *Being gets disavowed by us.* But, on the other hand, as long as we experience beings, we can never deny the "being" and the "is." (*GA* 51: 80)

(2) On the one hand being cannot be gotten around; on the other hand, when entered into, being gets immediately made over into "*a* being." (*GA* 51: 81)

(3) In every attempt to think being, being always gets turned the wrong way and changed into *a* being—and is thus destroyed in what it is in its core. And yet: Being in its otherness from beings (being other than beings) cannot be denied. (*GA* 51: 82)

(4) Being shows itself to be both at the same time: It is put forward as unavoidable and indispensable, even necessary—and at the same time incomprehensible and ungraspable. (*GA* 51: 82)

(5) [I add here a quotation from *Introduction to Metaphysics*, where the same tension is expressed]: The word *being* is undefined/indefinite [unbestimmt] in its meaning, and still we definitely [bestimmt] understand it. "Being" turns out to be (shows itself as) something highly definte, but totally indefinite, undefined—even ambiguous. (*GA* 40: 83)

The place of opening, as portrayed and laid out here, is that place where being both is and is not graspable, where being cannot be denied and at the same time gets thought as itself *a* being—and thus no longer itself: being as such—where being is disavowed and at the same time undeniable.

From the point of view of logic, this place is one of contradiction—and often gets dismissed for its impossibility. In dismissing this place, logic renounces and then loses being and its domain. (The uncanny part of this is that this renouncing, which is at its root a loss, gets taken as a gain. "Reality" is simplified, manageable—and its managers are more secure—within this renouncement. No wonder that they blindly call this loss a gain! Cf. *GA* 51: 40.) The discipline of logic will never enter into this domain.

We are presented here with an aporia, a place that is difficult or even impossible to pass through. The mode of metaphysical thinking is to think *about* this aporia, only to realize that there is no way out. What Heidegger proposes and evokes is a different way of thinking: not thinking as thinking *about*, but thinking as expanding into, having a genuine root connection to this aporia, not as a "no way out," but as what is worthy of thought (*denk-würdig*): what calls for, requires, or draws forth thinking.

Gathering up: the place of the opening of the question is the aporia (no way out) of being's always getting turned into *a* being, or of being's being unavoidable and intrinsic to what is and at the same time being incomprehensible in its "is-ness." Rather than thinking *about* this aporia, we are called to expand into the domain of being in its aporetic and unresolvable character.

It might seem as if what we are describing here is a refined and more subtle shape of the ontological difference. But it is utterly different. Although the words used and the grammar may *seem* to be about the ontological difference, what is being said is in a dimension that is fundamentally *not* that. This can be seen in two ways: first, the being that is spoken of here (speaks itself) is not the being *of* beings—it is not the difference between beings and the being of those beings. (We will later see that the very word *being* is unsuited for saying this region/domain.) Second, what is opened up in this unresolvable matter/*Sache* is not a difference at all. There is no difference here, even though language and grammar differentiate. Thus I would suggest not using such words as *discord, dispersal, dichotomy*—or even *difference*—to name this place of opening. This *Sache* in its unresolvability cannot be named *difference*, however one spells or pronounces the word.

Rather it is an opening. At work is an expanding. This gets heard in the ἐνέργεια of the opening. What is called for is a language that says this domain in its folding and unfolding, in the movement that it carries *in itself*. What is called for is to see the aspects and shapes of the tension in the imaging of weaving and nuance rather than in any imaging of juxtaposition or opposition.

SECOND IMAGING: ENTERING INTO THE CLEARING OF BEING

How to enter the question of being, the domain of being? Given that the place of opening is aporetic, *how* does thinking expand into this aporia?

The tension that we have just described in the first imaging—namely, that being, in every attempt to think it, gets turned or perverted into *a* being, thus losing its root character, while at the same time being as other than beings cannot be denied—appears to logical thought as a contraction or paradox. We, on the other hand, must try to go all the way into the tension of the two "equally unsurpassable limits," into the tension of being's being unavoidable *and* incomprehensible, into the definite indefiniteness of being, into being's otherness even as it is always thought as not other than beings, into the tension of the unresolvability.

The word that Heidegger uses for this "going all the way into" is *erfahren*. We usually translate *erfahren* as "to experience." But simply to render *erfahren* as "to experience" carries two risks: (a) that we in our thinking will miss the point of this deep penetration or entering into the dynamic of this tension, and (b) that by using the English word *experience* we fall prey to a dimension of interiority or subjectivity that the word carries with it in its usual connotation as well as in its etymology from Latin.

If we take the word *erfahren* back to its roots, we find the verb *fahren*—to travel, to wander; to let go; to ride; to move, go, travel—and then the prefix *er-*. *Er-* has a root connection growing out of the prefix *ur-*, referring to origin or source. *Ur:* from the source or origin, out-and-out, thorough, through-and-through. In this connection *er-* means: all the way into, into and out of the origin. Thus *erfahren* means:

to get by going through
to go all the way into/through
to move/pass through
to be drawn through
to become versed in
to let go into.

Erfahren means "to experience," but in the deeper sense of going all the way into and being thoroughly *in* the *Sache*.

Heidegger says that we need "to go all the way into [*erfahren*] the situation that, placed between the two limits, we are delivered into a unique situation or place from which there is no way out." (*GA* 51: 81) Thus, thinking's way into the question is to get all the way into and to stay with the fact that there is no way out of the question. This "no way out" (*Auswegslosigkeit*) or impasse presses upon us in twofold manner: (1) how the question or domain of being is both unavoidable and incomprehensible, how we are called to think being in its being other than beings, even as we always think it *as a* being, and (2) how, once our thinking has entered this domain, there is no way out. (Again, logic will not help; for it gets out by jumping the fence!)

In presenting the unresolvability of this question, Heidegger opens up a pathway with several clues or steps as to how we in our thinking might enter into this space of unresolvability.

First " . . . this extreme 'no way out' might come from being itself" (*GA* 51: 81). "Being itself unfolds in such a way that *it* brings . . . thinking into this 'no way out'" (*GA* 51: 82). Our entry into the unresolvability is granted by being itself as it emerges in the dynamics of unresolvability.

Second, one possible response is to close our eyes to the aporia. Another possible response is to eliminate the aporia by disallowing the question of being. But there is a third possibility: to move into and to stay with the "no way out" situation abandoning all haste to get out of it. (Cf. *GA* 51: 82.)

Being has cast itself upon us as the "light" by virtue of which beings appear and get seen. We cannot fight against or refuse this casting of being—nor would we want to, Heidegger says. But at the same time being withdraws when we try to say it—and we are left only with beings. This continual tension is our proper dwelling place; its name is Da-sein.

Thus, by staying in and with the "no way out," we find that, as humans thinking, we are left in a region that simply has/is this utter openness, dynamically in tension. In this context Heidegger says: "In a strange sort of way being has exploded our own *human* essence" (*GA* 51: 89).

Third, staying within this domain of unresolvability, "the recollecting of being (gathering oneself unto being) is remembering or becoming wakeful to the first origin of Western thinking. This remembering or being wakeful to the first origin is a preparatory thinking (*Vordenken*) into the more originary origin" (*GA* 51: 92). This preparatory thinking needs to be *unbeeilt:* unrushed, needing its own time (not the hasty moving from one thing to another). It also needs to be *ungerahmt:* unframed, not de-fined, needing its own opening and expanding (not the limitation of the space of positions or niches, as in "this niche" and then "that niche"). This remembering is being transported into the being itself which still unfolded in that origin and which always still unfolds, even when thinking's focus is on beings alone. Thus being in its originary character is always close to us—as close as can be. Therefore, what seems like being transported *into* that domain is really only remembering and being awake to our being always already there.

Fourth, to be awake to, being within or expanding into the domain of "no way out," is to be gathered into being. This "being gathered into" is, very simply and in each case, a transformation (*Wandlung*) in our way of being. This transformation needs beforehand a preparedness, the state of being prepared (*Bereitschaft*). This preparedness needs beforehand a preparation, getting prepared (*Vorbereitung*). This preparing needs beforehand an attentiveness (*Aufmerken*). Finally, this attentiveness needs beforehand that first reminder of being (*erste Erinnerung in das Sein*). (Cf. *GA* 51: 93.) All of this remains anticipatory.

In the *Der Spiegel* interview Heidegger said that this preparing a readiness is really all that we can do. Thinking is awakening the preparedness of awaiting. Central to this awaiting is the character of the domain as showing to those who stay with it that being reveals itself as what we precisely feel the lack of. It shows that we carry a want, we miss something. (Think of *Angst* in *Being and Time*.) Heeding this want—or what we miss—brings us into the simple and straightforward way of a region that is not beings-oriented. (Cf. *GA* 51: 4f.)

The dynamics of tension is always at play. The thinking called for in this dynamic, in the claim that it makes upon us in our thinking, is not logical or rationally oriented. It is an "other thinking." This other thinking might awaken and clarify this preparedness.

But what kind of thinking is this?

THIRD IMAGING: FROM DIALECTICAL TO TAUTOLOGICAL THINKING

In a little piece called *"Zeichen"* (first published in 1969 in the *Neue Zürcher Zeitung,* now in *Aus der Erfahrung des Denkens, GA* 13) Heidegger writes:

> The method of dialectical mediation misses the phenomenon. . . . By itself keen wit cannot get to what still withdraws from our thinking. . . . Dialectic is dictatorship over the unquestioned; and in its net every question is choked off (stifled, smothered) and suffocates. (*GA* 13: 13)

Dialectical thinking is the thinking with which we in our epoch have to deal. With Fichte, Schelling, and Hegel—prepared for in Kant—Western thinking reached its pinnacle in dialectical thinking. In the historical unfolding of Western thinking, "thinking becomes knowingly dialectical."[1] But dialectical thinking misses the phenomenon, and does not keep open the question in which root thinking persists.

How can we move all the way into (*erfahren*) dialectical thinking—which *is* the thinking of our historical unfolding—such that it gets shown to be in need? How can we move all the way into dialectical thinking such that our "experience" expands into and calls for another thinking?

What *is* dialectical thinking? When thinking becomes dialectical, it enters that realm "within which it can think itself completely."[2] Thinking thinks itself, mirrors itself to itself, is reflective. This can be seen by looking at how dialectical thinking alters the traditional principles of logic. In dialectic the principle of identity, A = A, takes on a new dimension. For dialectic A = A has to be more than simply a static identity, an identity of something with itself that cannot be unfolded further. Dialectic introduces something *more* than that. Thus Hegel in the *Science of Logic* writes: "There resides in the *form of the proposition* in which identity gets expressed *more* than simple abstract identity."[3] In order for A to equal A, there has to be a setting up of an opposite. This leads to contradiction, but now not simply *formally* logical. Rather, the contradiction is itself in motion and sets in motion. This movement is essential for the unfolding of spirit. Hegel writes in the Preface to the *Phenomenology of Spirit:* "Spirit achieves its truth only in that it finds itself in the absolute split (i.e., contradiction)."[4]

This dialectical thinking is self-enclosed. By being a thinking that thinks itself and is self-reflective in an absolute sense, dialectic cannot reach the strange and estranging character of the unresolvability of the being-question. It cannot reach what is profferred in the phenomenon and what persists as questionable.

In dialectical thinking, reason defines identity, not taking into account movement or transformation that goes beyond it. In dialectical thinking, change gets explained in an infinite series of *positions*—one and then the other (as is "logical"). As self-enclosed, dialectical thinking takes on a superiority since it resides in the subject. In this superiority and priority, given to itself by itself, dialectical thinking shows itself to be in the calculative mode in its heightened form. Dialectical calculative thinking, finally, overpowers human beings, driving them back from their core-being and reducing them to orderable and disposable items in the "resource-bank" of the way of "technique"—disposables within the age of *Ge-stell.* In this domain the flight from another, noncalculating thinking has become hardened (hard and fast) and thus institutionalized.

What is called for in the unresolvability of the being question, in the thinking that is called to respond to the aporia, and in the going all the way through and into unresolvability, is another way of thinking. What is called for is a thinking that thinks the movement or ἐνέργεια in the aporia of being, but not as an oppositional movement. What is called for is a thinking that does not go back and forth between differences, but one that expands into the clearing of the onefold of being in its own unique movement. What is called for is a preparation for the preparedness for transformation—an awakening of the preparedness.

In one of the very last pieces of writing by Heidegger, the short text on Parmenides that he read during the seminar in Zähringen in 1973, Heidegger names this other kind of thinking: tautological thinking, Τὸ-αὐτὸ-λόγος.

The Greek word αὐτός means, generally, "self, the very one, the same." Within these general meanings are hidden some other meanings that open up what tautological thinking might be. Αὐτός also means "of itself, natural, not made." Αὐτος sometimes has the character of the whole, taken together, as in αὐτόρριζος, roots and all. Αὐτοῦ means "in this very place, on the spot, the core movement." Αὔτως means "even so, just as it is."

In speaking of being (ἐόν), *Parmenides,* fragment 8:, 29, says: "ταὐτόν τ'ἐν ταυτῷ τε μένον καθ' ἑαυτό τε κεῖται (The self-same, together with itself, just as it is in this very place, is situated within the core movement/tension of itself)." The thinking of τὸ αὐτό is tautological thinking, a thinking that stays with the self-same movement/ἐνέργεια, together with itself. We say that a tautology is a redundant saying, one that repeats the same. Ταυτολογέω: I repeat the said, or I say the same. Ταυτολογία is a repeating of what was already said. But what happens in the repetition? It is saying over again that which has already been said. It is a seeking again (*re-peto*) that which has already been sought. It is doing over again. Τὸ αὐτό λέγειν is to say/gather up the same as before, in common, a sharing, in the same place. Emphasis is added in the repeating saying, but the question and its place are the same. Tautological thinking is precisely a thinking that not only does not demand proof but also is outside the realm of proof. It thinks the same movement/ἐνέργεια that is, together with itself, in the very place where it is the same with itself.[5]

To move out of dialectical thinking into tautological thinking is *not* a turn or return to identity or unity. Dialectical thinking injected movement and ἐνέργεια *into* the principle of identity that it inherited from Aristotle. Still, dialectical movement duplicates identity in its very opposition to it, by being self-enclosed and by keeping and enhancing the *positions* in and from which it operates. Tautological thinking does not renounce the movement of difference but sees another, deeper movement—not merging differences, but thinking from a space where the difference-character of differences does not hold/bind/determine its own unfolding. (Thus tautological thinking *does* call into question the *irreducibility* of difference.)

In tautological thinking and saying there is a lack of positions and of certainty. The words of semantic/logical consistency yield a certain certainty, but the imaging of tautological thinking extends and expands beyond the words, always to a "more," an excess. That excess images the no-position, always ongoing and expanding, of being.

Rather than dialectical, this thinking moves in terms of the preciseness of a point within space, of the point of focus/attentiveness within the expanding opening, of the self-unfolding of the one/same within ongoing connectedness/gathering.

The question remains: Is tautological thinking legitimate? From where does it take its bearings? What is its measure? The single response is: from being, of course. But with the transformation in the shape of thinking, there is a concomitant transformation in the way that being gets said. Along with the move from dialectical subjective thinking to tautological thinking—and part and parcel of that move—is a call for *re-naming* the question of being. This re-naming stems from the ever tighter and more rigorous binding that binds a thinker to the same. In the *Der Spiegel* interview Heidegger says: "All great thinkers think the same— this same is so essential (deep) and rich that no single thinker accomplishes (exhausts) it; rather every thinker is bound even tighter and more rigorously [*strenger*] to it" (*SP 212*).

FOURTH IMAGING:
RE-NAMING THE QUESTION OF BEING

In persisting in the question of how to enter into the clearing of being, a return to the beginning or origin is called for. In the seminar in Zähringen Heidegger says: "As I see it, the entry into the root domain of Dasein . . . that entry which would enable going all the way into (*die Erfahrung*) standing within the clearing of being, can take place only with a return, in the form of a detour, to the origin" (*GA* 15: 394).

Heidegger sees this same, this deep, rich, and enriching same that all thinkers are so rigorously bound to—this place of opening, the unresolvability of the "no way out," being situated in the "no way out" regarding thinking being in its suchness (i.e., the enigma that being, when thought, gets perverted into *a* being)—as that hidden dimension that lies underneath all shapings of Western philosophy and functions as the sustaining origin of all these shapings. Thus Heidegger's thinking returns to the first beginning with the early Greeks, with the provocation that thinking carry a way of being that is *not* reduced or perverted.

Within the network of the historical transformations of being, there is indeed a kind of lineage of being; there is historical variation. However, the question, Why did being unfold in a certain way and not in another—or What "caused" this particular unfolding—is not answerable. But in *each* shaping of the unfolding, reflection can take us back to the original (*das Anfängliche*)—not to retrieve what was then, but to respond to it from here, to think it in its "futural" sense, i.e., as coming upon us (*das Zukommende*).

How is this re-turn (turning back) to the first beginning with the early Greeks possible and appropriate? This re-turn takes place within an echo. It "takes place as that hearing which opens itself to the saying[s] . . . [of this first beginning] from out of our (today's) era. . . . " (*GA* 15: 394). This turn is in echo as it turns to the echo of the first beginning with the early Greeks.

An echo is a reverberation. It is a repetition, in which the style or play of the original question resounds—without the emergence of the original question as originally asked. Within that resounding—from there to here—and within our thinking's response lies the provocation and evocative possibility. In the re-turn, in echo-thinking, to the saying/showing of the first beginning is the possibility (the only one? the most fruitful one?) of entering that place of opening described in the first imaging.

It is in this sense of the place of opening that I quote a sentence from "The End of Philosophy and the Task of Thinking":

> Accordingly, the day may come when thinking will not shun (will be able to hear) the question of whether . . . the free open [the opening as such, the place of opening as the place of being] may not be that alone within which . . . everything emerging into presence and falling away from presence in them truly occupies the place which gathers and shelters everything. (*SD* 72f.)

In *Beiträge zur Philosophie* (paragraphs 81 and 82) Heidegger addresses this return and echo in terms of a *Zuspiel*, literally "a pass to (us)." In its root sense *Spiel* is "moving freely" (as in *Spielraum*, a place/space in which to move freeely). Thus *Zuspiel*: freely moving to, from there to here. This free movement of the first beginning with the early Greeks "is not a historical contribution or the start of a 'new system', but is in itself the root preparation for the other beginning—the preparation that initiates transformation" (*GA* 65: 170).

The earliest name for being is τὸ χρεών in Anaximander, followed by ἐόν in Parmenides. In reading these texts from early Greek thinking, Heidegger's own work has been to open up the domain of being as such, to think being for what it is: not defined in terms of beings, but rather told in its own right. Thinking this domain was an ongoing work for Heidegger, enjoining many years and spanning the history of metaphysics, from its start to its extreme possibility in the root-character of technology. Underlying this whole history is the decisive move in thinking whereby beings and being were no longer distinguished, whereby *what* emerged into presence and the emergence as such were no longer thought different. What was not thought was being or the emerging as such.

In *Der Spruch des Anaximander* Heidegger writes: "The real core of emerging, and with that the difference between emerging and *what* emerges, got forgotten" (*GA* 5: 364). A marginal note here says: "The difference [*Unter-schied*] meant here is infinitely other than all being that remains being *of* beings. Thus it is no longer appropriate (no longer in accordance) to name the difference with the word *being/Sein*. . . . " (*GA* 5, 364). And in *Grundbegriffe, Unterscheidung* is read as an expanding and an opening.

If we read this passage in accordance with the unresolvability of the question as presented earlier, then (1) *Unter-schied* is always already dynamic, a being at work (ἐνέργεια), even self-oscillating—thus saying "opening" rather than "difference," and (2) once Heidegger's thinking has delved this deeply into the question that guides all his thinking—into the same to which every thinker is bound so tightly—the word *being/Sein* is no longer fitting or appropriate. This calls for a re-naming of being, a re-naming of the *Sache* at the heart of the work of thinking that we call "Heidegger."

Heidegger does this re-thinking and re-naming in the three texts that provide the context or encircling for my presentation. He does this by re-thinking τὸ χρεών in Anaximander and ἐόν in Parmenides. (Heidegger's texts in which he reads Heraclitus do the same re-thinking, each in its own way.)

The way into these early Greek sayings initially takes us aback; we are surprised, startled, and confused. Everything is strange. Rather than trying to make these sayings accessible to us in our terms, we need to go all the way into (*erfahren*) *our* being exluded—seeing ourselves as distanced from them.

This distance is not a nonrelation. On the contrary this distance, when properly entered into, brings us nearer. Today's priority given to knowledge or information reduces and contracts the questions of these sayings of the first beginning into answers of metaphysics. Dialectic diminishes (reduces) over against the hidden fruitfulness (possibility) of the shapings of this originary opening. Thus these sayings of Anaximander and Parmenides demand of us to get some distance from the usual interpretations (or "readings"). We are called to something quite different: "Simply listening to that from out of which the saying there comes" (*GA* 51: 100).

Let me here—all too briefly—let Heidegger's reading of τὸ χρεών and ἐόν emerge for the reading that it is: one that re-opens the matter/*Sache* named in the German word *Sein* and the English word *being* and, in that re-opening, re-names the *Sache*. To ask the question, What is the name of the *Sache?* is to point to something most essential in the *Sache*. For the name of anything says the deepest root character of that thing. The name is not merely an arbitrary label but is essentially an imaging of the thing itself. *Therefore, to re-name the matter/Sache or being is to s a y that deep root character in a deeper, more originary way.*

The Anaximander fragment reads:

ἐξ ὧν ἡ γένεσίς ἐστι τοῖς οὖσι, καὶ τὴν φθορὰν εἰς ταῦτα γίνεσθαι κατὰ τὸ
χρεών διδόναι γὰρ αὐτὰ δίκην καὶ τίσιν ἀλλήλοις τῆς ἀδικίας κατὰ τὴν τοῦ
χρόνου τάξιν.[6]

Heidegger's rendering into German reads:

Von woheraus aber der Hervorgang ist dem jeweilig Anwesenden auch die Entgängnis
in dieses (als in das Selbe) geht hervor entlang dem Brauch; gehören nämlich lassen
sie Fug somit auch Ruch eines dem anderen (im Verwinden) des Unfugs entsprechend
der Zuweisung des Zeitigen durch die Zeit.[7]

My rendering of the German into English reads:

The place from out of which emergence comes is, for everything that emerges, also
the place of disappearance into this (as into the same)—in accordance with exigence
(brook); for they let enjoining and thereby also reck belong to each other (in the
getting over) of disjoining, responding to the directive of time's coming into its own.

The first step into this saying is taken with the words γένεσις and φθορά:
emerging and disappearing, coming forth into presence and withdrawing. Traditionally these words were taken to be about things, beings: the coming forth of
beings and their going away. To think in a Greek way, we must think the "forth"
and the "away." When we do that, however, we see that emerging and disappearing
do not refer primarily to beings but to the movement itself, i.e., the words are
to be taken *in themselves* as describing *being* and therefore they say the emerging
as such, rather than emerging/disappearing things/beings.

This takes place κατὰ τὸ χρεών: in accordance with τὸ χρεών. The usual
translation is "necessity": what compels and what must inescapably be. But if
thinking expands into this word in its Greek-ness, the word suggests χράω,
χράομαι—and the ἡ χείρ, the hand. Χράω: I reach for, extend my hand—and
then I hand over, let something belong. "Thus τὸ χρεών is the handing over of
emergence; this handing over hands out (furnishes) emergence *to* what emerges
and thus holds (in its "hand") and preserves what emerges as precisely what it
is, holds it in its hand, i.e., in emergence itself" (*GA* 5: 366; *EGT* 52).

The German word for emergence is *das Anwesen*. The more usual English
translation of *Anwesen* is "presencing" or "presence." I deliberately use the word
emergence, to avoid the danger of implying a "presence" in "presencing"—thus
letting thinking think in terms of presence rather than "presencing." The *Sache*
in Heidegger is clearly *not* presence, but *Anwesen* in its work of emergence, i.e.,
in its work as *being*. The published English translation fell and slipped on this
very danger. It reads: "Tὸ χρεών is thus the handing over of presence [*Anwesen*],
which presencing delivers to what is present . . . " (*EGT* 52). This translation
suggests that there are two realms named here: the realm of what comes to presence
(beings) and the realm of presence, with *Anwesen* (presencing) as the movement
between these two realms. Much of Heidegger scholarship has stumbled on this
rock by not staying long enough or working closely enough with this realm of
Anwesen itself, thus getting lost by taking the *Sache* of *Anwesen* to be one of

presence. Frankly, *presence as such*—separated out from emerging ("presenc*ing*," if you will) is only an issue for metaphysics (named by Heidegger as *Anwesenheit*) and is never the *Sache* of being.

Τὸ χρεών as handing over or furnishing Heidegger ventures to call in German *der Brauch* (use/usage, making use of, service, serving oneself with something, the reach over); *brauchen* (to reach over, require); *sich gebrauchen* (lend oneself to). *Brauchen* is *bruchen*, the Latin *frui:* to enjoy by having at hand. "'Brauchen' thus says: to let something that emerges emerge as emergent . . . to hand out (furnish) something unto its own essence and to hold it as thus emerged in its preserving hand" (*GA* 5: 367; *EGT* 53).

Given that γένεσις and φθορά name the work of being as such—and not of beings—so too does τὸ χρεών, that in accordance with which γένεσις and φθορά are what they are, name the opening of being. Enjoying by having at hand, furnishing, handing over (*der Brauch*) is not said of human comportment, but rather names they way in which being itself unfolds in its connection with what emerges, a connection that has to do with and deals with what emerges as it is: τὸ χρεών. (Cf. *GA* 5: 368; *EGT* 54.)

This word, τὸ χρεών/*der Brauch* is not easy to render into English. The more obvious words *need* or *use/usage* hardly convey any of this rich nuance of furnishing, handing over, allowing to emerge. English has two, not readily accessible words: *exigence* (from *exigo, ex-ago;* I drive forth/out, carry forth/out, dispatch, turn out) and *brook* (from Middle English *broc*, breaking/bursting forth, yielding, bearing forth). I offer both of these words, each somewhat awkward, as a way to say what Heidegger says here, in the German word *der Brauch*.

In the Anaximander fragment τὰ πολλά and τὰ πάντα are the names for τὰ ὄντα (beings) in general. However, ὄν and ὄντα were originally ἐόν and ἐόντα. With that their rootedness in the world εἶναι was secured. Indeed, Parmenides and Heraclitus always use ἐόν and ἐόντα. The move from ὄν to ἐόν is the decisive move into the region of being. And this move in our thinking is a echoing re-turn to the place of opening within the first beginning in the thinking of Parmenides and Anaximander.

"But ἐόν ("being") is not simply the singular of the participle ἐόντα ("beings")" (*GA* 5: 345; *EGT* 33). Rather ἐόν names the region of being as such, the one, the same, that binds all thinking. Everything depends on a proper reading of ἐόν. "Without exaggeration . . . we could say that the [whole] unfolding of the West depends on how the word ἐόν gets translated, provided that the trans*lation* rests on the *trans*lation to the truth of what comes to language (gets said) in ἐόν" (*GA* 5: 345; *EGT* 33). Τὰ ἐόντα, the word that really names what comes to language in Anaximander, "names that which, unspoken in thinking, speaks in all thinking, even as it itself remains unspoken. The word names that which from then on lays claim to all of Western thinking, whether expressed or not" (*GA* 5: 351; *EGT* 38).

A few decades after Anaximander, in Parmenides, the word ἐόν and εἶναι is named explicitly as the fundamental root word for Western thinking.

In *Der Spruch des Anaximander* Heidegger says that Parmenides thinks ἐόν—as the emerging of what emerges—in terms of the "hidden and unresolved fullness of the disclosure of beings—unresolved as it is thought from out of ἀλήθεια, "the disclosing sheltering" (*GA* 5: 352; *EGT* 39). Here ἐόν is thought from out of the disclosure of ἐόντα (beings) and is thought in terms of *Unverborgenheit* as disclosing/revealing/concealing. Disclosure is named "the open region." The focus here is on the expanding/staying of the opening (*Unter-scheidung*) that comes to language in the word ἐόν. (Cf. *GA* 5: 363; *EGT* 48.)

Unspoken in Anaximander, spoken in Parmenides, the word ἐόν/εἶναι says: "Emergence into disclosure [*Anwesen in die Unverborgenheit*]. Hidden in that statement is [the imaging that] *Anwesen* itself brings disclosure with it. Disclosure itself is emergence. Both are the same, but not identical" (*GA* 5: 370; *EGT* 55).

Thus the first stage in Heidegger's thinking ἐόν in Parmenides is in terms of *Unverborgenheit*/disclosure: ἀλήθεια/*entbergendes Bergen* (as the fullness of *Unverborgenheit*)/emerging sheltering (as the fullness of disclosure). The second stage in Heidegger's thinking ἐόν in Parmenides is in terms of *Anwesen*/emergence. It is ἐόν as *Anwesen*/emergence to which the small piece read at the seminar in Zähringen turns. This piece of writing (*GA* 15: 401–07)—one of Heidegger's last pieces of writing—along with the transcript of the discussion that followed Heidegger's reading of the text during the seminar, opens up a new dimension or turn in the work of thinking that we call "Heidegger." There his thinking works explicitly tautologically, saying the same as indeed it itself. That same is ἐόν.

The context in which Heidegger read this brief text on Parmenides was the question of entering into being. It is the same theme as the one named with *Dasein;* for both have to do with clearing/*Lichtung*—with opening.

Parmenides names this theme or realm for thinking: τὸ ἐόν—which, Heidegger says, names neither *beings*/*das Seiende* nor *being*/*das Sein,* but rather τὸ ἐόν. *Anwesend, Anwesen selbst:* Emergent (coming forth, unfolding); emerging (coming forth, unfolding) itself.

He begins with fragment 6: 1:

ἔστι γὰρ εἶναι

Is: that is to say, being.

The saying refers to being, not to beings. Being is. Heidegger hesitates on this, because one can say "it is" only of beings. Being precisely is not. But Parmenides says here: Being/*das Sein* is. Heidegger asks: Are we capable of hearing this Greek word, that speaks of ἔστι and εἶναι, with a Greek ear (*GA* 15, 397)? Or: Do we think the Greek saying of the words ἔστι and εἶναι in a Greek way? Finally, in using the words "is" and "being," do we think precisely enough at all (*GA* 15: 405)?

Thought in its Greek way, the word εἶναι says: *anwesen*/to emerge. This verb speaks more precisely. It brings us, in a greater revealing, closer to the *Sache* to be thought. In accordance with this we must render ἔστι γὰρ εἶναι as: *anwest nämlich anwesen:* emerges, that is to say emerging. (*GA* 15: 405)

What is being thought here is not being in its difference from beings, but rather only emerging: being as emerging, or simply, emerging itself.

The word of Parmenides that names this *Sache* is τὸ ἐόν. Heidegger says τὸ ἐόν as *anwesend: anwesen selbst* or *anwest nämlich anwesen* (emerging: the emerging itself; or unfolding: the unfolding itself, emerges). That is to say emerging; unfolds, that is to say unfolding—emerges emerging.

Where and how does emerging[8] emerge?—". . . into disclosure." But then ἐόν is the "heart" of disclosure/ἀλήθεια. Τὸ ἐόν, "itself residing in itself, is decisive for and disposes disclosure through and through" (Parmenides, fragment 8:4, as Heidegger reads it in *GA* 15: 405).

What does this say with regard to ἀλήθεια? Heidegger says: we must think ἀλήθεια as τὸ ἐόν: emerging, emerging itself.

Heidegger finishes his short text on Parmenides with this remark:

> The remark in the poem of Parmenides lets us see:
> The emergent emerging itself disposes
> the revealing unfolding disclosure that encircles.

> *Das anwesend: anwesen selbst durchstimmt*
> *die schicklich entbergend es umkreisende*
> *Unverborgenheit.* (*GA* 15: 407)

This says, not so much that ἐόν/emerging lies at the core of ἀλήθεια/disclosure—it does say that—but more that to think ἀλήθεια is to think it as emergent emerging. Thus on the one hand it is helpful to think ἀ-λήθεια in its two components, λήθη and the ἀ-. Thus: hiddenness/closure and revealing/disclosure. The danger in that way of thinking is that the *Sache* remains a twofold, a dichotomy, with two positions. Heidegger explicitly tells us that he himself fell prey to this danger in "The End of Philosophy and the Task of Thinking," when he suggested that λήθη is the heart of (lies at the root of) ἀ-λήθεια. In the discussion that followed his reading of the Parmenides text (in Žahringen), Heidegger says that what he suggested in that earlier essay—that λήθη lies at the heart or root of ἀ-λήθεια—is simply not true; Parmenides did not say anything like that. (Cf. *GA* 15, 395.) Rather, to think the whole of ἀ-λήθεια is to think ἐόν: emergent emerging.

Τὸ ἐόν allows thinking to think the one, the same, in its ongoing work of emerging. Thus it never rests anywhere, neither thinking nor the *Sache;* it never allows one or the other dimension to settle out and be "at the bottom" or "at the top." Tautological thinking is needed to do this kind of thinking work. The word *emerging/Anwesen/*τὸ ἐόν names tautologically in that there is within it no dichotomy, even as it carries within it the highest tension and movement.

The way of thinking that Parmenides calls for here is πυθέσθαι: *erfahren,* going all the way into. Parmenides names this more precisely (goes further into it) in fragment 6: 1:

> χρὴ τὸ λέγειν τε νοεῖν τε . . .
> Incumbent is
> saying (letting the self-showing) and

(thereby ensuing) facing up to
and taking it in. (*GA* 15: 406)

Heidegger names this kind of thinking a *reines Erblicken:* pure beholding, simply
taking it in, being awake to.

In thinking (as pure beholding) τὸ ἐόv (as emergent emerging), the question
of being (the place of its opening) is expanded beyond being (as being, *Sein,*
ὄv, *ens*) and beyond being (as in *Sinn des Seins*) to ἐόv: emergent emerging.
In fact the word *being* no longer names the *Sache.*

With this kind of thinking there is no proving, no logical argument, no dialectical thinking, no foundational explaining. Rather what holds this thinking is what
comes over against it, what turns its gaze to it. Simply put, this kind of thinking
is phenomenological.

FIFTH IMAGING: HINTING'S MANY HUES

Being as a *question* opens up within that point where being as other than beings
is unresolvable; dialectical thinking opens out into tautological thinking; and being
is renamed as ἐόv/*Anwesen*/emerging. Saying these several imagings cannot happen within the confines of logic or calculative thinking. Rather, saying shows itself
as suggesting, intimating, surmising—in short, saying is hinting.

The most revealing word from early Greek thinking, for showing this imaging
of hinting, is in Heraclitus, fragment B93:

ὁ ἄναξ, οὗ τὸ μαντεῖόv ἐστι τὸ ἐv Δελφοῖς, οὔτε λέγει οὔτε κρύπτει ἀλλὰ
σημαίνει.

The work of thinking that we call "Heidegger" comes back to this fragment again
and again. An English rendition that pulls together several of Heidegger's German
renderings of this fragment might go something like this.

Ths sublime one whose place for intimating saying is at Delphi neither discloses (only)
nor conceals (only), but rather hints, gives signs, points to, intimates.[9]

Heidegger renders the crucial word, σημάινει, into German as *winken (bedeuten)* and as *Zeichen geben.* In *Erinnerung an Hans Jantzen* Heidegger says,
simply: "Hinting [*Der Wink*] is the revealing and simultaneously concealing showing.[10]

In *Hölderlins Hymnen "Germanien" und "Der Rhein"* Heidegger says:

Originary saying does not only immediately reveal, nor does it only simply and plainly
conceal; rather this saying is both at once. And in this way it is a hinting [*ein Winken*]
in which what is said intimates what is unsaid and what is unsaid intimates what
is said and *to be said.* It is a hinting in which what is in tension intimates the accord
[*Einklang*] that it is and the accord intimates the tension within which alone it oscillates
(flourishes). (*GA* 39: 127f.)

In *Heraklit* Heidegger says:

A marking [Zeichen] is something that is shown or revealed . . . [which] unfolds essentially in a not-showing. . . . The showing of markings is the originary way in which what later gets differentiated—disclosing for itself and concealing for itself—*still holds sway unseparated.* . . . thought in a Greek way, "markings" are the *self-showing* of *emerging itself,* to which this self-showing belongs. (*GA* 55: 179—Italics mine)

Emerging itself emerges as the ταὐτόν τ' ἐν ταὐτῷ τε μένον καθ' ἑαυτό τε κεῖται: the self-same, together with itself, just as it is in this very place, within the core movement/tension of itself. Its proper way of showing itself is as a hinting/intimating.

At the end of a series of poems entitled *"Winke"* ("Hintings," privately printed in 1944, now in *GA* 13: *Aus der Erfahrung des Denkens*) Heidegger writes: "'Hintings' are words of a thinking that (1) in part needs this expression but (2) is not fulfilled in the expression" (*GA* 13: 33). Why? Because such a thinking thinks being—now ἐόν/*Anwesen*/emerging.

It belongs essentially within the αὖτο of the free open/opening—that opening named in ἐόν/*Anwesen*/emerging—that it can only be said tautologically. Tautological thinking is a hinting thinking.

In *Grundbegriffe* Heidegger uses the word *ahnen* for this hinting: hinting as intimating or surmising. What is intimated has no position and is not conclusive. To intimate is to have a feel for what comes over or befalls one. This is only intimateable but is more essential than any certainty in calculating what is not-essential. What is called for is to surmise (let befall one) that from out of which beings emerge (emerging itself) and to say with what is so surmised/intimated: "Thinking in and for intimating/surmising is essentially stronger and lays greater claim than any formally conceptual discrimination in whatever realm of the calculable" (*GA* 51: 12).

This kind of thinking can only be practiced; it cannot be talked about or "ascertained." In the lecture course text of 1923 entitled *Ontologie* (GA 63) Heidegger says simply: "Phenomenology can be appropriated only phenomenologically" (*GA* 63:46).

SIXTH IMAGING: WHAT BELONGS TO READING AS ITS OWNMOST

The look of that which has claimed us—the look of being, now named emergent emerging, ἐόν—is the deepest possible confirmation of the thereness of being as emergent emerging. And the look of being continually proffers and confirms our relation to that thereness—manifesting and nourishing it in its disclosure, in its "truthing."

Proper reading—reading in its ownmost—has its appropriate concern in this look. As Heidegger says in *Was heißt Lesen?*, "Without proper reading we cannot see what turns its gaze to us" (*GA* 13: 111). We cannot gaze on what emerges.

Do we know at all anymore what reading is? Where do we read unto—and where from? Why do we read at all? How is proper reading? What is called forth and evoked in proper reading? These are the unspoken questions with which the work of thinking presented here began some months ago.

There are two areas of concern in opening up proper reading. First, normally and traditionally, we in our thinking are held back from proper reading by *our* own comportment. Our comportment does not heed what turns its gaze to us. Rather we assume a certain definition and normally have always already comprehended (conceptualized) the what of the words read. In this sense proper reading is a matter of a renewed attentiveness. Reading is not based on "our" ability to decipher and interpret. It goes deeper than that. It calls for a detachment from "personal" inclinations and in that detachment opens out to that which claims reading/thinking in its look/gaze. The look of things always already shows the look of ἐόv, of the emergent emerging. In reading we are called (evoked) to foster a fertilizing contact with the pregnancy of ἐόv, to be open to what we read in our reading in *its* turning its gaze to us. Reading in this way, we "fall into round"— to use a potter's expression—and thinking reading takes its shape *from* that which gazes upon it. This is the ἐόv/emergence in the first beginning with the Greeks. Indeed, the hinting character of that first beginning stems from attentiveness to precisely this domain, which calls for a thinking that reads properly, rather than a thinking that runs roughshod over the written text, always already knowing what is to be found there. Think of this mode of thinking/reading as a handicraft. It works by handling the words, the reading. This is the place of ἐόv as such—ἐόv in its suchness, the suchness of ἐόv. Ἐόv is what turns its gaze and touches us; it is the name for the opening cast to us in the unresolvability of being-beings; it is thinkable tautologically, and not dialectically; and it calls for a hinting/intimating thinking, rather than for the direct hit of a calculating, resolving thinking.

The second area of concern in opening up what proper reading is is that traditionally we are entangled within the web of ordinary grammar. We usually allow "grammar" to give us the definitive word on language and how it speaks. What we have been trying to do here has actually been held back by grammar. Sentences in their sentence-structure cannot reach far enough into which turns its gaze to us. Though having grammatical shapes, words and sentences always carry an imaging that is not bound to that grammar. Words then become guidewords for imaging beyond grammar; this imaging is evoked by what turns its gaze to reading. Thus we are called to be more attentive, more gathered, for what lies deeper in the words, though not deeper *than* the words. (Cf. *GA* 51: 68.) If we hear language within the deeper saying of the word, only then is it on the mark—and the affordance of the origin hidden in the first beginning (i.e., the neighborings of the first and the other beginnings, both as original beginnings) hints and haunts it.

Proper reading is attentive to the evocative character in what turns its gaze to us. Thus pure beholding evokes the deeper root saying. Words take on the shape of the clearing/opening. Words do not grasp (conceive) objects, but rather evoke. Words render seeable and hearable and touchable. The reader is thus led into the region or regioning of opening that imaging words image.

For this to take place, words move away from their grammatical expression into evocative saying. In evocative saying words do not show a ready-made content, but rather carry an appeal—by indirection and hinting. This appeal carries the reader over to evocation—and thus to a transformation in thinking.

In hinting saying, that which casts its gaze on the reader, there is no defined or definitive content. Rather there is the free receiving and discerning of the opening/clearing. This is the opening/clearing that lets beings be, that lets echoing words resonate with silence/stillness. This resonance of echoing words and of stillness names the one, the same, self-oscillating ἐόν: emerging.

SEVENTH IMAGING: DRAWING TO A CLOSE

This presentation has carried the intention, not to resolve the question, but to be attentive to its re-shaping, to come closer or nearer to the question in its own ἐνἐργεια.

In thinking as well as in hinting and in proper reading there is a responding, not only to the known, but also to the unknown. Thinking and the hidden are inseparable—and require the ongoing work of our response. Thus thinking always takes place in and is a response to a showing extending and expanding beyond the shown. This is the torso-dimension of all root thinking: it always points beyond. In reading, the writing that one reads always points beyond—this excess is not something beyond the text. Rather it is carried in the text as the process or ἐνἐργεια of emerging itself.

Recognizing the ambiguity in this expanding beyond the shown—and letting that ambiguity be what it appears to be—opens a deeper way of showing, of self-showing.

In a sense what we do here *is* a construction—even and ambiguity—but more fundamentally than that it heeds/respects/even honors a trace "naturally" left within.

I am reminded of a poem by Rilke, in which he sings of a torso of Apollo. The torso glows like a candelabra in which the look/gaze of the torso is held and sparkles and shines. If the torso did not so glisten, did not so carry within itself the life of the eye or the chuckle of the heart, then it "would not break out of all its borders, like a star: for there is therein no point that does not see you."[11] It is this ἐνἐργεια of expanding beyond that is carried in language that says/shows; and it is in proper reading that this expanding emerging turns its gaze upon the reader.

Within the context of such an opening, the question of being cannot at all any longer be taken or read as a metaphysical question. Given this bond to the expanding of opening, all forms of Heidegger's question open out beyond the metaphysical—be it the move from *Sinn des Seins* to *Wahrheit des Seins* to *Wahrnis des Seins* to *Unverborgenheit* to ἐόν/*Anwesen selbst*, be it the move from subject to Dasein and *Erschlossenheit* to *Geschick des Seins* to *Ereignis*.

In every case the work of thinking is held to this opening. In order to see this, we must take very seriously Heidegger's own "corrections" of his work. Examples of Heidegger's "corrections" come up in the several texts that we have worked with here:

1. As already mentioned, in the seminar in Zähringen in 1973 Heidegger says that his statement (in "The End of Philosophy and the Task of Thinking") that λήθη is the heart of ἀλήθεια simply does not work. That is not how Parmenides says/thinks/ intimates the *Sache*.

2. There is clearly a re-thinking of the Anaximander fragment from the time of the lecture-course *Grundbegriffe* (1941) to the writing of *Der Spruch des Anaximander* (1946). This is seeable (a) in that in the later text Heidegger no longer considers the whole of the Anaximander fragment as handed down to be authentically by Anaximander himself, and (b) much more importantly, in that the central word for naming the *Sache*, τὸ χρεών, is thought in its root unfolding as *Brauch* only in the later text.

3. In *Grundbegriffe* Heidegger tries to uncover a deeper sense to the words *be-greifen* and *Begriff*, whereby they might be able properly to name the *Sache*. In the seminar in Zähringen he no longer holds out this possibility for the word *Begriff*. "The Greeks do not have *Begriffe*. *Begreifen* is a way of comportment that takes possession of. The Greeks do not grasp [*be-greifen*]" (*GA* 15: 399).

4. In 1973 Heidegger explicitly states that the phrase *Sinn des Seins* from *Being and Time* does not say the *Sache* that is to be thought. (*GA* 15: 345 and 373).

How will we read these changes? The question is not Is Heidegger metaphysical here? Or just where and how is Heidegger a metaphysician? Rather, the question is: How to read underneath and deeper than the *grammar* to what is evoked in the saying? Evocative thinking is always directed toward the *Sache* and emerges from out of the *Sache*. To hone in on a word or concept—or even a phrasing—as metaphysical is to miss the point. Heidegger above all grants the indeterminate dimension, the perhaps in the look of ἐόν. Thus the way is involved in the undeterminable and nonconceptualizeable—therefore always hinting. The way is always open to revision (a re-seeing) and thus to a new opening to the same.

Again we hear the *Zuspiel* from *Beiträge zur Philosophie*: "Coming to grips with the necessity of the *other* beginning from out of the originary bearing of the first beginning" (*GA* 65: 169). This thinking is always ongoing, playing one beginning out for the other—always attentive to the *Sache* of being, now named ἐόν/*anwesen*/emerging. The issue is not how Heidegger "has changed his mind," but rather how the work of thinking that we call "Heidegger" comes to grips with the *Sache* by staying always more decisively and more rigorously with the same.

Finally, reading, thinking, and hinting call for forgetting Heidegger for Heidegger's sake and becoming involved in the onefold of the always oscillating expanding into the clearing of being, the opening that is named in ἐόν: emergent emerging. To think in the "Heideggerian mode," then, is to expand into the one question and to respond thinkingly to it.

Hinting reading thinks along with the text. Hinting thinking reads the text for what it evokes. Thinking reading hints in such a way that what turns its gaze *evokes*. Thus, in proper reading is *der Einsprung in die Wesung des Seins*—or *Einsprung in die Anwesung des Anwesens*.

NOTES

1. Martin Heidegger, "Grundsätze des Denkens," in *Jahrbuch für Psychologie und Psychoterapie*, 4 (1958), 34.

2. Ibid., 37.

3. G. W. F. Hegel, *Wissenschaft der Logik*, 2. Buch, Lass, Bd. 2, S. 31.

4. Hegel, foreword to *Phänomenologie des Geistes*, ed. Johannes Hoffmeister (Hamburg: Felix Meiner Verlag, 1952), 29/30.

5. The preceding several paragraphs appeared earlier, in a slightly different form, in my essay "Parmenides: Circle of Disclosure, Circle of Possibility," *Heidegger Studies* 1 (1985): 13.

6. In *GA* 51 Heidegger takes this whole fragment to be authentic and by Anaximander himself; in the *Holzwege* essay he says that he is inclined to consider only . . . κατὰ τὸ χρεών διδόναι γὰρ αὐτὰ δίκην καὶ τίσιν ἀλλήλοις τῆς ἀδικίας as from Anaximander himself. However, he adds that the first part of the saying, though probably not from the hand of Anaximander, should not be simply excluded, but rather kept as an indirect witness to Anaximander's thought by virtue of the strength and saying-power of his thought (*GA* 5: 341). For my purposes here the philological question—significant as it might be—has no bearing, in that the earlier part remains "Anaximandrian" if not by Anaximander himself.

7. The first and the last part of this German rendition by Heidegger comes from *GA* 51: 101; the middle part (that part *alone* that Heidegger considers to be by Anaximander himself) comes from *GA* 5: 372.

8. Heidegger's own text here—the one that he read to the group assembled for the seminar—reads: *Anwesen*/emerging (*GA* 15: 405). The *transcript* of the text reads: *Anwesenheit*/presence (*GA* 15: 398). I find this discrepancy to reveal a significant difference in meaning. The word *Anwesenheit* covers up the poignant and sharply focused dimension of Heidegger's thinking in this short text.

9. For a complete listing of Heidegger's many readings of this fragment, see Kenneth Maly and Parvis Emad, eds., *Heidegger on Heraclitus: A New Reading* (Lewiston: The Edwin Mellen Press, 1985), 54ff.

10. "Erinnerung an Hans Jantzen: Wort der Freunde zum Freund in die Abgeschiedenheit" (Freiburg i. Br.: Universitäts-buchhandlung Aberhard Albert, 1967), 20.

11. Rainer Maria Rilke, "Archaischer Torso Apollos," in *Der neuen Gedichte Anderer Teil:* quoted here from R. M. Rilke, *Gesammelte Gedichte* (Frankfurt a.M.: Insel-Verlag, 1962), 313.

JEAN-FRANÇOIS COURTINE

13. Phenomenology and/or Tautology

Translated by Jeffrey S. Librett

I.

In the last private seminar of 1976, known as the Zähringen seminar, Heidegger evokes tautological thought as the final word of phenomenology. Though I shall not do so here, one ought to follow in detail the zigzagging path of this seminar. Heidegger recalls first of all how he gained access to Being through Husserl and the doctrine of categorical intuition ("Being was given to me . . . phenomenally present in the category") and then how he returned to the fundamental utterances (*paroles*) of Greek philosophy, to Parmenides. The path of the seminar—and indeed more generally the path of Heidegger's thinking, only certain stations of which the seminar marks—is a regressive path: return to the source or the beginning (*Anfang*), in search of the chance for another, new, more originary beginning (*der andere Anfang*).

But concretely, profiting from the free retrospection of the seminar, the return to the beginning takes a detour (*Umweg*) by way of Parmenides.

In order to illustrate the question of the access to Being *by way of* Parmenides or rather turned *toward* Parmenides, Heidegger proposes to reread a text he has recently written (winter of 1972–73) thematically centered on "the heart of ἀλήθεια." This theme, one will learn, is consonant with the theme of *Dasein*, understood as *die Lichtung-sein* to the extent that here too it is a question of *Lichtung*, of *Da-sein* and *Lichtung*. Heidegger announces that in a sense it is a matter of seeing how the consonance (*Zusammenstimmung*) of Being-there and clearing will have presented itself to Parmenides.

This text read by Heidegger in 1976 contains, above all, an essential correction of what he had said, already in the mode of the *retractio*, at the end of the lecture, "The End of Philosophy and the Task of Thinking."

I shall take up briefly here the thread of this lecture from 1964: there too the debate was centered principally on the interpretation of the maxim or call: *Zur Sache Selbst*. Straight to the question! But what *about* this question, affair, or matter (*Sache*) of philosophy (or of phenomenology)? To the determination of the matter corresponds the determination of method: it is the matter that is supposed to decide the method or the path (*SD* 69–71). In a word, the lecture moves from the matter of philosophy as it was fixed from the beginning ("the Being of beings, its state of presence in the figure of substantiality and subjectivity") to *Lichtung* (as the dimension of opening and freedom from which anything whatsoever can come to show itself).

Heidegger specifies that *Lichtung*, if understood in the fullness and originality of its sense, is not simply a word or play of representations, but the *Ur-sache*, "the one-of-a-kind thing that is named appropriately by the name *Lichtung*." *Lichtung* is understood here, then, not in terms of *Licht* (light as opposed to dark), but of *leicht* (light as opposed to heavy) and of *lichten* (to liberate, to detach or set free).

"All philosophical thinking which explicitly or inexplicitly follows the call 'to the thing itself' ['*Zur Sache selbst*'] is already admitted to the free space of the clearing in its movement and with its method. But philosophy knows nothing of the clearing. Philosophy does speak about the light of reason but does not heed the clearing of Being" (*SD* 73). Ἀλήθεια has certainly been *named* since the beginning of philosophy, but in the course of time it has not been *thought* properly and as such by philosophy. It is the clarification of this point, more than a mere "nuance," that is the task of the remarkable self-criticism contained in the text of 1964: it had been misleading, Heidegger now avers, to speak of ἀλήθεια in the sense of *Lichtung*, as truth. The question of ἀλήθεια in the sense of unconcealment (*Unverborgenheit*) is not the question of truth. The "everyday" concept of truth, even among the first Greek philosophers, does not in any way allude to *Unverborgenheit*. Heidegger here gives Friedländer's objections their due:[1] "It must be acknowledged that ἀλήθεια, unconcealment in the sense of the clearing of presence [*Unverborgenheit im Sinne der Lichtung von Anwesenheit*], was originally experienced only as ὀρθότης, as the correctness of representations and statements. But then the assertion about an essential transformation of truth, that is, from unconcealment to correctness, is also untenable. Instead one must say: ἀλήθεια, as clearing of presence and presenting in thinking and saying, originally comes under the perspective of ὁμοίωσις and *adaequatio*, that is, the perspective of adequation in the sense of the correspondence of representing with what is present" (*SD* 78). But what ἀλήθεια is in itself remains withdrawn from our grasp.

Is this the effect of chance, the consequence of a particular negligence on the part of the thought of mortals? Or is it the effect of the fact that *self-withdrawal, remaining in reserve*, in a word, λήθη, belongs to ἀλήθεια, not as a simple addition (*Zugabe*), but as *the very heart* of ἀλήθεια? "And does not even a sheltering and preserving [*Bergen und Verwahren*] hold sway in this self-concealing of the clearing of presence, from which unconcealment can first be granted, so that what is present can appear in its presence?" (*SD* 78).

The clearing (*Lichtung*) is thus to be understood, not as *Lichtung von Anwesenheit*, but as *Lichtung der sich verbergenden Anwesenheit*, or better, as *Lichtung des sich verbergenden Bergens*: clearing of a sheltering that remains in reserve.

A double task for thinking is thus sketched out: to experience ἀλήθεια in the Greek mode as unconcealment (*Unverborgenheit*); and to think *Lichtung*, beyond Greek thought (*über das Griechische hinaus*), as *Lichtung des Sichverbergens*. The new title which defines this task for thinking is no longer *Sein und Zeit* but *Lichtung und Anwesenheit*: clearing and presence.

Immediately the following questions arise: "Where does the clearing come from and how is there [*gibt es*] clearing? What speaks in this 'there is' [*es gibt*]?" (*SD* 80). It is precisely to these questions that the Zähringen seminar attempts to respond by echoing Parmenides' fragment 8, 1–2: Unique, however, remains the saying of the path that leads to the "that there is" (μόνος δ' ἔστι μῦθος ὁδοῖο λείπεται ὡς ἔστιν).

That there is, or that it is. But, again, *what* exactly? τὰ ἐόντα? No. The nontrivial response is given by verse 1 of fragment 6: χρὴ τὸ λέγειν τε νοεῖν τ' ἐόν ἔμμεναι . ἔστι γὰρ εἶναι. Being, in fact, is. And, as Heidegger emphasizes, this is indeed an "unheard-of thought." The question is whether or not we are capable of hearing this Greek speech with Greek ears. Heidegger translates this speech as: "anwest nämlich Anwesen." This is certainly a tautology. It names the self-same as the same as *itself*. Hence this new translation, even more accentuated: *anwest nämlich Anwesen selbst.*

What is the name for that which is neither simply a being nor simply Being? The answer proposed here, echoing Parmenides, is this: τὸ ἐόν. And Heidegger, in turn, restores or explicitates τὸ ἐόν thus: *anwesend: anwesen selbst.* "Coming to presence : presence itself."

Heidegger renders this formula more precise by evoking Goethe's emphatic insistence on *die reine Bemerkung*: "This thought of Parmenides is neither a judgment nor a proof nor a grounded justification. It is rather a *grounding oneself on what has appeared to view*." The entire difficulty here consists in managing to get a view (but according to what phenomenological gaze?) of the fact that *anwesend : anwesen* are one word (a not-yet explicitated or redoubled tautology): τὸ ἐόν.

Heidegger renders these considerations still more precise as follows: "I call the thought that is demanded here tautological thought. It is the original sense of phenomenology." "Understood in this way, phenomenology is a path that leads to . . . and lets itself be shown that before which it is led. This phenomenology is a phenomenology of the nonapparent."

Here again a number of urgent questions arise: what appears to the gaze with or through the ἐόν or the ἐόν ἔμμεναι? What is given to see or to *remark* on the path of the goddess, in accordance with the μῦθος ὡς ἔστιν, even if it is provided with signs in great number (σήματα πολλά)? In the Poem, is it not a matter, not so much of viewing, but rather primarily of κρίναι (κρινεῖν) λόγῳ, of deciding λογικῶς, as Aristotle said, in a controversial argumentation (fragment 7: 5): ἔλεγχος πολύδηρις, to know whether or not it is possible *to be*: ἔστιν ἤ οὐκ ἔστιν?

In any case, this is how the sophists understood it, in particular Gorgias in his Περὶ τοῦ μὴ ὄντος. But even if one sets this problem aside, since one could consider it to be merely a matter of Parmenides exegesis, the question remains of what a phenomenology of the nonapparent might be, and in what sense or with what right such a phenomenology could or ought to be achieved in the form of a "tautological thinking" itself interpreted as the "original sense" of phenomenology.

Concerning the first question, that of whether or not there can be a phenomenology of the nonapparent, and in what sense phenomenology can be said to be the phenomenology of the nonapparent—and this essentially and principally, not in the way one speaks of a phenomenology of this and that, of religion, work, or carnival—concerning this first question, then, a first answer immediately imposes itself which does not offer, it seems to me, any major difficulties.

2 .

In the period of *Sein und Zeit* Heidegger's phenomenological project is as such and expressly linked to language (*Sprache, Logos*). It is first of all linked to language through the fact that it is directly a project of the deconstruction or "destruction" of logic (*GA* 26: 70). For the destruction of logic will always be accompanied by the destruction of the (Aristotelian?) determination of man as ζῷον λόγον ἔχον.

But to what exactly is the destruction in question applied? It has become easier to answer this question since the publication of the courses which led to the elaboration of *Sein und Zeit* in the Marburg period: the destruction is applied essentially to the "theory of proposition," i.e., the traditional interpretation of the apophantic utterance (*énoncé*) as "saying something about something" (λέγειν τι κατά τινος), as predication which attributes a determination, a predicate, to a subject (cf. *GA* 21, 24, 26, 29/30). For the Aristotelian tradition, the proposition or the statement (*Aussage*) is in fact considered to be "the primordial and proper place of truth" ("der primäre und eigentliche Ort der Wahrheit"). Heidegger's entire effort will consist first of all, as is well known, in disengaging—beneath this derivative sense of the statement as predication, i.e., as determination (*Bestimmung*) of a subject by a predicate—a more original sense of ἀπόφανσις as showing (*monstration*) (*Aufzeigung*).[2]

Heidegger's procedure here, on which we can touch only very briefly, consists in making evident the primary articulation of signifying or significance which is directly linked to Being-in-the-world, not "beyond language" or before language, but in and through an original type of "discursivity"—*Rede*—which does not have to be expressed in either "words" or "sentences."[3]

Language, speaking in language, is possible only on the basis of this fundamental prearticulation that Heidegger calls *Rede* (discourse, discursivity, speech?). Speaking is possible only as "redendes Sprechen."[4] *Rede* implies in turn, as a constitutive element, "listening," listening to or for . . . (*Das Hören auf . . .*) and, correlatively, silence, the possibility of remaining silent (*Das Schweigen*). Listening and silence: passing by way of the analysis of *Gewissen* and its call

(*Ruf*), these are doubtless the motifs that connect the analyses of *Sein und Zeit*—rapid, elliptical, and certainly insufficient as they are—to Heidegger's second meditation on *Sprache*, the meditation that he undertakes after the *Kehre*.[5] To the achievements of *Sein und Zeit* belongs, to be sure, the conquest of the concept of ἑρμένεια in the fullness of its sense and in all of its breadth: the manifestation of the radical hermeneutic *als* in the apophantic *als* of propositional articulation. This conquest results in the guiding thread of a phenomenological reinterpretation of ἀπόφανσις. The statement (*Aussage*) is a derivative mode of *Auslegung* (*SZ* §33), itself understood as primitive articulation of sense (*Sinn*). The *Auslegung* which is always already at work can either formally accomplish and realize itself as enunciation or not.[6]

All of these threads come together in Heidegger's determination of the concept of the *phenomenon* or of phenomenology as ἀποφαίνεσθαι τά φαινόμενα. Heidegger thus takes three steps in a continuous progression moving from *Aussage* to *Rede* and from *Rede*, in its new sense, to *Wahrheit*.[7]

In the background, to be sure, remains the reconsideration of the question of the multiple senses of Being in Aristotle and the primacy accorded to Being in the sense of the true or the manifest: τὸ ὄν ὡς ἀληθές.

One can say that from this point on, in a sense, everything turns around ἀλήθεια. The new determination of the phenomenon is here the true "phenomenological" point of departure for the meditation on the truth of Being—"That which, beginning with itself, shows itself from itself"—and on the counter-concept (*Gegenbegriff*) of the truth of Being—*Verdecktheit* in its various forms. The phenomenon, in the phenomenological sense, is precisely that which does not show itself first of all and for the most part (*zunächst und zumeist*). Indeed, as Heidegger forcefully insists (*SZ* §7), it is precisely because phenomena *are not given* that we need phenomenology, or better, that we need work and research in phenomenology.[8]

Phenomenology (as a destructively or deconstructively hermeneutic enterprise) will be understood as a work of showing, of bringing to light (*Aufweisung, Aufzeigung*), which must ever and again struggle against the tradition and its obfuscation: one must ever and again rediscover, draw forth from withdrawal, prevail over obfuscation, and fight against deterioration and degeneracy, in order to find again the "giving" originality, the living source. Repetition (*Wiederholung*) is precisely this combat—ever to be recommenced—against a mere parroting (*Weitersagen*) that covers up what it parrots. From the first, Heidegger's phenomenological project is centered on "destruction." *Abbauen der Verdeckungen*: this is not merely an excessive or "violent" formula which Heidegger will later correct in function of a more serene climate of thought.

What covers up, deforms, and dissimulates is, in a sense, simply what is said, the utterance, that which deposits itself in the words of the language, insofar as these words are regarded as things to be taken up again, passed on, repeated, and communicated as prefabricated formulae within the public sphere. Phenomenological work, then, turned toward "things themselves," consists in rediscovering the original power of saying and its function as "opening" beyond the fixed formulae of a mechanical repetition.

Heideggerian phenomenology intends thus to struggle against the entropy and the inevitable disintegration of the evocative power of words: the exhaustion of words through overuse, their progressive loss—precisely through repetition (parroting), transmission, and communication—of their original, presentifying power. The word, exactly discovered, as if newly created, opens access to the experience of giving [l'experience donatrice].

The struggle against the exhaustion of words, against their unthinking use, is in reality one with the critique of "idle talk" (Gerede) as it is thematized in Sein und Zeit (§35) on the basis of the analysis of Verfallen. (One cannot indeed sufficiently emphasize the importance of the analysis of Verfallen for Heidegger's elaboration of his problematic, an importance on a par with that of the related oppositions of authentic and inauthentic, proper and improper.) Communication (Mitteilung) is what renders possible Weitersagen, the parroting which does not directly draw what is said from the thing itself as originally apprehended.

3.

In Sein und Zeit the reflection on language remains, as is well-known, rather enigmatic, reduced in fact to certain rapid indications. Notably, Heidegger evokes, at the end of section 7, the linguistic difficulties with which phenomenological hermeneutics and the project of fundamental ontology are confronted. These difficulties are not merely terminological (the creation of new words or the establishment of links between words), but rather logical or grammatical, logicogrammatical. It is a matter of finding a new syntax, i.e., a mode of organization or articulation which escapes precisely the control of predicative or propositional analysis. It is a matter, Heidegger notes, of delivering grammar from Aristotelian— or rather, as Heidegger attempts to show, pseudo-Aristotelian—logic. He returns to this point in section 34, emphasizing there the privileged status of the statement in the tradition of Aristotelian metaphysics:

> But because the λόγος came into their philosophical ken primarily as assertion, *this* was the kind of λόγος which they took as their clue for working out the basic structures of the forms of discourse and its components. Grammar sought its foundations in the 'logic' of this λόγος. But this logic was based upon the ontology of the present-at-hand. . . . But if on the contrary we take this phenomenon [viz., *Rede*] to have in principle the primordiality and breadth of an *existentiale*, then there emerges the necessity of reestablishing the science of language on foundations which are ontologically more primordial. The task of *liberating* grammar from logic requires *beforehand* a *positive* understanding of the basic a priori structure of discourse in general as an *existentiale*. (SZ 165)

The scope and import of Heidegger's reflection on language in the period of Sein und Zeit is limited from the first, however, as many commentators have observed, by his failure to consider the "aesthetic" or "poetic" dimensions of language. *Dichtung* is almost completely absent from the "pragmatist" perspective of *Sein und Zeit* as is moreover the *Kunstwerk*. Instead, the artisan's workshop constitutes the horizon of the analyses of *Sein und Zeit*.

It is necessary, certainly, to underline inflections, to mark stages, even to indicate reversals (*Kehre*), but it is possible also to make a certain continuity appear between, on the one hand, the conception of phenomenology, the determination of the phenomenon *cum emphasi*, and the new approach to *Rede* (with the theme of the call in the background) in the period of *Sein und Zeit*, and on the other hand, Heidegger's "final word" on phenomenology as "tautology," as phenomenology of the nonapparent, at the time of the Zähringen seminar. Is it a matter of an increasingly profound or radical fidelity to the maxim of phenomenology (*Zu den Sachen selbst—Zur Sache selbst*), or on the contrary, of a fatal involution of Heidegger's thought? This is the question I shall address in what follows, without of course pretending to provide a conclusive answer. But I would like first of all to follow several of the paths that traverse this space.

One can notice, after the fact no doubt, the first tautology in Heidegger's determination of the preconcept of phenomenology as λέγειν τὰ φαινόμενα = ἀποφαίνεσθαι τὰ φαινόμενα. To show what shows itself, to show oneself what shows itself! Why this redoubling? Why is it necessary at all to *show oneself* if that which precisely of itself shows itself, appears? Is it perhaps permissible to see here a kind of anticipated return to that mirror-structure which states itself in such formulae as "to speak speech," "to say the said"?—*Die Sprache als Sprache bringen*.

To what extent is Heidegger's project in *Sein und Zeit*—the project of a new grammar liberated from the (predicative) logic of (the) metaphysics (of *Vorhandenheit*)—realized by the paratactic constructions for which the later Heidegger had such a predilection when it came to saying the profoundest or simplest things (the "wonder of wonders": that the being is: *dass es ist!*) or to commenting upon the sayings of the first thinkers (Heraclitus, Parmenides)?

What do the Heideggerian tautologies say? Nothing or the same. Tautology is always a particularly subtle strategy when it comes precisely to *not saying*.[9] The destruction of logic is accomplished here as a sigetics (cf. *GA* 65: 78–79). But tautology says also precisely the same in a possible play of substitution (against the using up of usage?): the thing, the world, space, time, language or speech, and last but not least—since it is perhaps the endpoint of the entire tautology— the gift of giving (the *Gabe* of the *es gibt*) or the *ereignen* of the *Ereignis* (*SD* 24, 46–47).

Let us recall some of the Heideggerian tautologies: the oldest perhaps: "die Welt weltet"—"die Sprache spricht"—"die Zeit zeitigt"—"der Raum räumt" (*US* 213)—"das Ding dingt" (*VA* 172)—"Das Ereignis ereignet" (*US* 258f.; ID 30). And already, in *Sein und Zeit* the "call calls." One must insist on the essential indeterminacy, the disidentification of the one who calls (or of that which calls:

Es ruft): "The author of the call escapes absolutely all possible identification." It is not I who calls me, but that itself (*Das Selbst*) calls in me from a depth beneath myself. Indeterminacy is a constitutive trait of the call. It calls: what calls is here nothing other than the call itself. Tautology hence obviously imposes itself here: the call calls. "The author of the call is one with the call addressed to . . ." But the call is in its turn a call only as *addressed* to . . . What is at stake here is always essentially the *address*, the injunction.

That is, within the horizon of the interpretation of Parmenides, who paradigmatically provides the entire tautology in one single word: τὸ ἐόν, the tautology, goes like this: ἔστι γὰρ εἶναι: τὸ γὰρ αὐτό ἐστι: νοεῖν τε καὶ εἶναι. For the tautology, here again *cum emphasi*, is precisely what says: the Same— *Das Selbe*: thinking and Being.

What is, after the *Kehre*, the new thematization of language that henceforth governs the paratactic mode of speech or, asymptotically, the tautological utterance (itself a contradictory formulation)? Tautology always responds to the possibility/ necessity of escaping from the discursive mode of propositional enunciation (*SD* 27). Language is in a sense essentially tautological: it says (itself) in its power of denomination and of showing: "In a general manner," Heidegger writes, "language is not this and that, that is, it is not something other and more than itself" (*WD* 99). Language is language, language is itself.[10] The *Letter on Humanism* has already insisted—in answer to the question: What is Being?—on the necessity of tautology whenever one would thematize "simple" things (*Einfaches*). Being?: "It is itself" (*GA* 9: 331). The Simple itself requires also, if it is to emerge as such, *reduplicatio*, redoubling. In the lecture course, *Was heisst Denken?*, Heidegger still recognizes the danger of tautology, i.e., its unlimitedness: "The peculiarity of sentences of this sort is that they say nothing and that, at the same time, they bind thinking to its matter [*Sache*] in the most decisive manner. The fact that nothing limits the possible abuse of such sentences corresponds to the unlimitedness to which they expose the mission of thinking" (*WD* 99).

Does tautology, understood in this way, constitute the primitive, original level of language to which a regressive procedure ought to lead us, this side of the Aristotelian tradition? Is it necessary to see here the final consequence of the rendering evident of ἀληθεύειν (e.g., *Nicomachean Ethics*) as it precedes all λόγος ἀποφαντικός? But what new interpretation of λέγειν is thus proposed? Can one restrict oneself, as Heidegger sometimes seems to suggest, to the Platonic δῆλουν (e.g., as in the *Sophist*), and above all—this time this side of Plato and the συμπλοκή of the *Sophist*—to the ὄνομα or to the ὀνομάζειν? To name authentically is to cause the being to appear in its Being by summoning it: "to spread out before, in the light in which a thing holds itself by the very fact that it has a name."[11] It is still the privilege granted to the denominative function of the word (*Nennen heisst hervor-rufen*) that governs the resolute interpretation of speech as φάσις—or *Sage*, as Heidegger will later say.

It is no doubt important to specify here that the accentuation of the linguistic structure of experience (*Worthaftigkeit, Sprachlichkeit*), of Being-in-the-world, and of perception—which is certainly an acquisition of *Sein und Zeit*, in the tradition of W. von Humboldt—in no way implies this quasi-exclusive privilege accorded to the word. One can emphasize the linguistic structure of perception (against Husserl), as for example, Heidegger does in *Die Grundprobleme der Phänomenologie*, and one can even radicalize this idea to the point of maintaining, as Heidegger does in *Holzwege*, that: "When we go to the fountain, when we go through the forest, we always go through the word 'fountain', through the word 'forest', even if we do not pronounce these words and do not think of anything that would be of the order of language" (*HW* 286). One nonetheless does not need to reduce language to denomination—not even to an essentially monstrative denomination.

In the lecture, "The Origin of the Work of Art," Heidegger still emphasizes, above all, that language is not a means of communication, but rather "what makes beings as beings emerge into the open." The mode of discourse in terms of which Heidegger explicitly regulates himself here is poetic discourse, or better: a certain highly determined type of poetic discourse, the hymnic speech of Hölderlin. It would be superfluous to evoke here the forms of "poetry" for which an analysis thus centered on the call, denomination, and invocation (of the gods, the sacred, the fatherland, etc.) would not be appropriate. Can one nonetheless hold to the idea of a persistence of romantic thematics: poetry defined as *Ursprache*?[12]

4.

The expression, "phenomenology of the nonapparent," can take still another sense: the task of such a phenomenology would no longer be to make appear that which does not appear initially or that which has fallen into oblivion or become eclipsed, but to leave the nonapparent to its nonappearance, or better, to its nonappearing, to shelter rather than to get a view of, to preserve the secret (*Geheimnis*) of Being, the *Bergen* or the *sichverbergen* of the λήθη at the heart of ἀλήθεια. Phenomenology would thus have to be understood no longer as ἀποφαίνεσθαι τὰ φαινόμενα, that is, τὰ ἀδηλά, or in a word, ἀληθεύειν, but—if one may be permitted to put it in Greek: μελατᾶν τὴν λήθην.

Although I shall not do so here, one would have to follow step by step the long elaboration by means of which Heidegger develops this phenomenology of the nonapparent, from the final note of the *Platonslehre*: "What is above all necessary is a positive appreciation (*Würdigung*) of the positive content of the privative essence of ἀλήθεια. This positive content ought to be apprehended above all as the fundamental trait of Being itself" (*GA* 9: 238)—to the meditation on the *Es gibt*, the *Geben* in "Zeit und Sein": the *Geben* of the *es gibt* in distinction from the *Gabe*, the gift, is what is in no way susceptible of being given or presented. Giving is never given. There is no question of following here this complicated thread, which runs through nearly all of Heidegger's corpus. I shall merely mention very briefly the principal governing terms: one passes from Earth as *Grund* (background or resource) in "The Origin of the Work of Art" to the secret (*Geheimnis*) in the Hölderlin commentaries and the enigma (*das Rätsel*) in the Nietzsche lectures (*N* 2: 372), to *Entzug* in the essay on Anaximander, to absence (lack, failure) (*Ausbleiben*) again in the course on Nietzsche, to forgetfulness (*Vergessenheit*), retention or reserve (*Vorenthalten*), refusal (*Verweigerung*), and ἐποχή (again from the Anaximander essay) (*HW* 311). To the ἐποχή of Being understood in this way there will have to correspond a new determination of the *Schrittzurück*: the αἰδώς which is the shelter of this *Ausbleiben des Seins*, of this suspension or abandonment of Being (*N* 2: 368, 481).

One can ask, furthermore, whether, in the elaboration of this phenomenology of the nonapparent, this aphano-ology, the tutelary figure will have been not so much Parmenides as Heraclitus. For Heidegger attempts to think conjointly the three fragments of Heraclitus which he takes to be determinant of the latter's thought: fr. 123 (φύσις κρύπτεσθαι φιλεῖ), fr. 16 (τό μὴ δῦνόν ποτε πῶς ἄν τις λάθοι), and fr. 54 (ἁρμονία ἀφανής φανερῆς κρείττων).

To think the coherence and interconnectedness of these three fragments is in particular to ask oneself about the identity or the sameness of, on the one hand, the φιλία and πλεῖν named in fragment 123 and, on the other hand, the ἁρμονία ἀφανής named in fragment 54. In doing so one must presuppose—as Heidegger notes in *Vorträge und Aufsätze*—that the joint (*die Fuge*) owing to which unveiling and veiling are turned toward and belong to each other must remain in nonapparent (*das Unscheinbare alles Unscheinbaren*), for it is this joint that grants appearing to all that appears.[13]

Ἁρμονια, the joint, is necessarily, essentially nonapparent; it is indeed the nonapparent κατ᾽ ἐξοχήν; it is that instance the nonappearance of which grants appearing, grants phenomenality to all phenomena; it is that instance the nonappearance of which makes a present or a gift of the present—and the task of thought is consequently to shelter in its retreat or suspension precisely this ἁρμονία, to safeguard or to preserve it, as one does a secret, since it is what can never be made to appear, uneclipsed, in the light of day.

In the same essay from *Vorträge und Aufsätze* on which I have been drawing here, entitled "ἀλήθεια," Heidegger quotes in passing another fragment of Heraclitus (fragment 11): asses prefer hay to gold. Heidegger comments on this fragment as follows: "But the golden gleam of the lighting's invisible shining [*des unscheinbaren Scheinens der Lichtung*] cannot be grasped, because it is not itself something grasping. Rather, it is the pure propriating [*Ereignen*]."

The nonapparent appearing, unseemly seeming, or rather simply the nonappearing, of *Lichtung* here receives its "proper" name, the name which emerges more and more clearly (so to speak) as the "word" of a long path of thought: *das Ereignis*.

Thanks to this latter term (and also to its essential polysemy, accentuated by a double etymology: *er-äugnen, Auge, eigen*),[14] the question of tautology can perhaps at last be clarified.

For precisely on the subject of the *Ereignis*, of the *Geben*, of the *Es* of the *Es gibt*, there can be no statement that would not be tautological: how can one in fact recognize and say the *Ereignis*, the event of the gift, if the gift as such, the giving of the gift annuls itself and withdraws into or in favor of what it gives (its *Gabe*): "A giving which gives nothing other than its gift but which, giving itself thus, retains and withdraws itself—we call such a giving: destining (*das Schicken*)."[15]

In order that there should be giving, the gift (the giving) must not appear as gift; it must be forgotten. How does one guard or safeguard giving, if precisely the gift as gift is pure nonappearing, if the gift only "gives" itself in the ἐποχή of a *Geben* which, precisely through this suspension, liberates what is given (*die Gabe*)?

"In the *Ereignen*—in the ad-propriation (the event of the gift)—the singular property of the *Ereignis* announces itself: that it withdraws what is most properly its own from limitless disclosure."[16] The gift withdraws from disclosure: this is what is proper, and even most proper to it; it disappropriates itself of itself: *Zum Ereignis als solchem gehört die Enteignis*. What remains to be said of the *Ereignis*, Heidegger proceeds to ask, if one cannot say of it either that it is (*das Ereignis ist*) or that there is *Ereignis* (*es gibt das Ereignis*)? What can one say other than this: *Das Ereignis ereignet*: the appropriating arrival, the central property of which is its dis-propriation, makes or lets arrive? That this is the only thing that remains to be said, Heidegger adds in the Protocol of the seminar on "Zeit und Sein"— does not exclude but rather, to the contrary, includes thinking a whole wealth of what is to be thought in *Ereignis* itself" (*SD* 45–46).

Perhaps. Or even: no doubt! But the question is not now: "what remains to be thought?" but rather "what remains to be said, what remains to be said for a thought which, as Heidegger demands, is engaged in *Ereignis*, in order 'to say it from itself and toward itself'"? The thought that engages with *Ereignis* ought both to say it tautologically, and principally, if it is to have above all the value of a warning, to say "how the arrival must not be thought"! It will say: ταὐτόν τ᾽ ἐν ταυτῷ τε μένον καθ᾽ ἑαυτό τε κεῖται—"The same, sojourning in the same, reposes in itself" (fragment 8).

Such thought, then, can or even ought to explore, to explicitate, the entire tautology. To say from itself and toward itself what only gives in order to withdraw, to say what, as this gift, subtracts itself in and from what it gives—this *may* be to devote oneself eminently to the task of thinking Being without beings. But what seems to me less probable is that this saying or this thought could still define itself rigorously as a phenomenology—even if specifically as a phenomenology of the nonapparent or nonappearing—and a fortiori that it could indicate the path phenomenology ought to take in order to arrive at what it properly is. One is perhaps compelled to conclude that phenomenology and aphanology, phenomenology and apophantism are two very different things.

To be sure, it would be fitting or seemly here to attempt to designate as precisely as possible the point of rupture, the decisive reversal that takes place in Heidegger's interpretation of ἀλήθεια, around which the interpretation of phenomenology in its truth must turn. One will object: but why does Heidegger so stubbornly and belatedly insist on reaffirming his limitless allegiance to the principle of phenomenology, its governing call? It would certainly not suffice to respond to this objection by merely invoking the violence of the self-interpretation that induces Heidegger to transcribe the Dasein of the existential analytic first as *Da-sein* and then as *die Lichtung-sein*, or even by demonstrating the initial presence of the motif of the "es gibt" in a text as early as *Sein und Zeit*. Just as the *Kehre*, as Heidegger underscores, does not represent a fortuitous or extrinsic episode but is at work at the heart of the *Seinsfrage* which *Sein und Zeit* attempts to "position," so phenomenology is in its Heideggerian pre-determination (*Vor-begriff*) secretly meant or destined to veer into tautological thinking. But this would not yet mean that one could legitimately speak of the latter as *die eigentliche Phänomenologie*. For would not speaking in this way amount to exposing oneself to equivocation pure and simple?

5.

Tautology gives nothing to be seen; it no longer shows a thing. Does it give to be heard and thus be understood? It is the totally purified figure through which emerges the pure "articulation" of sense, that is, accentuation. Tautology appears thus to impose itself precisely when what is to be said is the nonapparent pure and simple: *das Ereignis* as *das Unscheinbare des Unscheinbaren* (*US* 259).

Is tautology then this singular showing, which without ever forcing out of its retrenchment that which escapes its grasp, lets appear (at a distance, "shyly"— *Züruckhalten*, Scheu, αἰδώς) what does not show itself, what remains essentially in retreat? It would thus respond in an exemplary manner to the injunction that the eagle addresses to the goddess in Hölderlin's hymn *Germania*:

> And name what you see before you:
> No longer now the unspoken
> May remain a mystery
> Though long it has been veiled;
> For shame behoves us mortals
> And most of the time to speak thus
> Of gods indeed is wise.
>
> . . . .
> For once between Day and Night must
> A truth be made manifest
> Now threefold circumscribe it,
> Yet unuttered also, just as you found it
> Innocent virgin, let it remain.[17]

Speech is always the response to a call, self-effacement before what calls.[18] It is obvious what still connects this movement of thought to the phenomenological procedure: loyalty to the thing-itself which one takes as one's rule, reduction of the natural thesis, retreat, ἐποχή. But one can see here too the obvious danger entailed by conceiving the "response" to the call only in terms of *echoing* (this will be Heidegger's word with regard to Parmenides at the end of the Zähringen seminar). According to such a conception, response would be mere acquiescence to the address within an empty purity. "Yes" would thus be the first and last word of thinking.

In this intimate relation of mutual belonging to language as address, injunction, and proffered speech, one can discover the final point of Heidegger's destruction of man's essence as ζῷον λόγον ἔχον: man's essence is once again defined by language: he is reduced to his essential property, appropriated in terms of the speaking of language (*ereignet aus dem Sprechen der Sprache*) (*US* 30). Man is inducted, conducted, induced or seduced into his propriety or essential property by speech. He is thus appropriated in order that he should remain assigned to, re-placed within, the *Wesen der Sprache*.[19] "Such an appropriation takes (its own proper) place insofar as the essential unfolding of language, the *tolling of silence, needs and uses* mortal speech in order to be heard from, as the tolling of silence, for the hearing of mortals." ("Solches Ereignen ereignet sich, insofern das Wesen der Sprache, das *Geläut der Stille*, das Sprechen der Sterblichen *braucht*, um als Geläut der Stille für das Hören der Sterblichen zu verlauten") (*US* 30). The essential unfolding as tolling of silence? Is not this again what programs tautology? Tautology, founded on the word and its demonstration, thus takes over the relay from the Greek language to which a singular phenomenological privilege had initially been granted.

"The word is not one thing among others," Heidegger notes (*US* 193). The word *is* not. When one says, "Das Ding ist," the word, "is," is itself not a thing.[20] One cannot say, of the word, "es ist," but only "es gibt"; this, not certainly in the sense that there are words in language, thus not in the sense that "es Worte gibt," but in the sense that "das Wort selber gibt": speech gives, is giving.[21] Hence the nontranslatable formulation: "Das Wort be-dingt das Ding zum Ding" (*US* 232).

The word "be-dingt"—*das Ding zum Ding*.[22] It at once contributes to the "gest(icul)ation" of the world (*das Gëbarden der Welt*) and grants things the "favor" of Being: *das Gönnen von Dingen*.

Gift, giving, and donation characterize in general the word: to give—speech, to give—the word. *Es gibt—das Wort* (*US* 155). What is the story here on the "Es" of the "es gibt"? What is it that does the giving here? Or simply, what gives? Precisely, the word. There is the word that gives. The giving opening of the "there is" (*es gibt*) is always already the opening giving of speech. It is above all the "word" here that bears the burden of the primary articulation of understanding and signifying, and no longer *die Rede*, the discourse of which Heidegger spoke in the period of *Sein und Zeit*.

In *Unterwegs zur Sprache*, and in particular in the commentary on George's poem, "Das Wort," Heidegger radicalizes his conception of language: language or speech (*Das Sprechen*) is what makes things come into the world, but also what makes world: speech makes the world come to things. Speech is the interval (*das Zwischen*) or the Difference, the Di-mension (*der Unter-schied*) of the world and things. Language bears the burden of the mutual belonging of *Welt* and *Ding*,

Ding and *Welt* (*US* 25–28). *Sprache*, Heidegger will say further, is *Verhältnis*, or better: *das Verhältnis aller Verhältnisse* (the relation of all relations) (*US* 176, 188, 267). *Die Sage* (the saying or the saga) holds everything together, but as such it does not state itself, does not express itself, and does not expose itself: quite to the contrary, it retains-itself-within-itself (*Ansichhalten*): it is entirely such a reserve, retention, and silence (*Geläut der Stille*). The mortals are those who guard and preserve speech (*das Wort*). It is thus a matter (phenomeno-logy?) of giving speech to speech, of finding the word for saying the saying, *die Sage*, which is precisely silence, reticence: *Geläut der Stille*: the reception/collection in which silence and peace (re)sound. The command thus takes quite naturally the form of the following double bind: find the word for *not* saying: leave *ungesprochen* the true which one must (*braucht*) nonetheless also name! (cf. *GA* 51: 77).

One can pursue here again the displacement with respect to the thematics of *Sein und Zeit*. Although this involves a considerable simplification, one can say that Heidegger's procedure consists in deepening the strict mutually belonging of, on the one hand, the humanity of man (the insistence in the clearing of Being, if you will) and, on the other, speech as addressed to man. Man is man to the extent that he is involved in the dialogue (or better: in the monologue of language) and responds to it, in making himself, if one can put it this way, *le porte parole de la parole*, the vehicle and representative of speech.[23] It is necessary to add, however, that the "dialogue" which we are (in the sense declared by Hölderlin as read by Heidegger) only comes about as this correspondence: as an *envoi*, address, and call which arrives at its destination only in and through the response. The call truly calls only in the response to the call. The call gives and gives itself, but it gives itself silently only for the response. The response, in an essential sense, *responds from out of* the call itself.

To say that speech speaks is also and at once to dethrone man from the position of speaker, the position of the one who would master discourse as an instrument of communication, that is, of experience or knowledge. If speech speaks, it speaks to us and through us only because first of all it is addressed to us. Man speaks only in response to, in correspondence with the address.[24]

It is this address, this claim, which constitutes us in and as dialogue. Hence, Heidegger's predilection for commenting upon the beginning of the preparatory version of Hölderlin's "Friedensfeier" ("Versöhnender, der du nimmer geglaubt . . ."):

> Viel hat erfahren der Mensch.
> Der Himmlischen viele genannt,
> Sein ein Gespräch wir sind
> Und hören können voneinander.

> Man has experienced much,
> Named many of the gods,
> Since we are a dialogue
> And can hear from one another.

As Heidegger frequently underscores, the dialogue which we are consists in the denomination of the gods. We are not in dialogue with one another, but we can address ourselves to one another, because from the start we are required, claimed by the address of the language in which world and gods conjointly appear.[25]

The phenomenon of this tautological phenomenology will no longer be *das sich Zeigende*, but rather that which gives itself to be heard and understood. *Entsprechen* now takes the place of the "show oneself what shows itself" which defined the task of phenomenology in the period of *Sein und Zeit*.[26]

Just as the Heidegger of the Marburg Period attempted to surpass the Aristotelian tradition by returning to Aristotle and the hermeneutic interpretation of speech as φάσις, so the later Heidegger does not hesitate, within or beyond Greek thought, to think speech in a horizon which is no longer quite that of λόγος. Playing off Hölderlin against Homer he notes: "The Aristotelian analysis of language achieves in a certain sense the most originary comprehension of language as it already governed Homer's poetry . . . In Greek, to name always already means to state, *aussagen*; and to state is to manifest something as something. It is in this hidden comprehension that Homeric poetry moves. . . ." But Heidegger underscores that for Hölderlin, on the contrary, "to name is to call out (*bei Hölderlin ist das Nennen ein Rufen*), and one sees hereby the deeply nonpoetic nature of the Greek comprehension of language. . . ." (*GA* 15: 336).

It is time that I conclude; but at the end of this rapid trajectory, instead of proposing a conclusion, or a final word, I shall confess my difficulty and share with you my hesitation. One can see clearly along what path of deepening and radicalization Heidegger undertakes the tautological transmutation of phenomenology. Even if, from one to the other, there is not a passage properly speaking but a leap, this leap, which is also an interruption, is still governed by the project of the destruction of logic. However, can one go so far as to admit the idea that tautology is the accomplished logic of phenomenology? To have an experience of speech, to experience language in its power of denomination, in its poetic dimension (not, however, as Heidegger specifies, in its "literary" dimension), to attempt to surpass metaphysics to the point of determining a mode of saying beyond the *Satz vom Grund*—this assuredly amounts to a kind of completion of an ever more enduring meditation on the language of metaphysics. But one can still wonder whether the—admittedly indispensable—abandonment of the propositional form that we inherit from the Aristotelian tradition ("the cat is on the mat" is the formula Heidegger mocks during the Marburg period) permits one to do justice to *Dichtung* in its Hölderlinian dimension (a Hölderlinian dimension).

In a magnificent letter addressed to Heidegger in July 1942, Max Kommerell concludes an examination of the commentary on the hymn, "Wie wenn am Feiertage . . . ," by risking the notion that Heidegger's essay might well be a "disaster" (*Unglück*) for his thought as well as for Hölderlin's poetry. I am tempted to end with an analogous question by asking whether the tautological transmutation of phenomenology does not itself also have a disastrous or catastrophic character, both for the very *possibility* of phenomenology and for the immense critical potential of Heidegger's thought.

NOTES

1. S. Friedländer, *Platon*, vol. 1 (Berlin: n.p., 164).
2. "Jede Prädikation ist, was sie ist, nur als Aufseigung." Heidegger recapitulates in these terms his analysis of the statement which distinguishes three moments: "Aussage ist mitteilend bestimmende Aufseigung" (*SZ* §33).
3. "Die Hinausgesprochenheit der Rede ist die Sprache." See also *SZ* 161: "Die befindliche Verständlichkeit des In-der-Welt-seins spricht sich als Rede aus. Das Bedeutungsganze der Verständlichkeit kommt zu Wort. Die Bedeutungen wachsen Worte zu. Nicht aber werden Wörterdinge mit Bedeutungen versehen." See also *GA* 21: 151.
4. As is well known, Heidegger later investigates the "Wesen der Sprache"—an investigation which indeed leads to a complete reinterpretation of the *essence*—but in *Sein und Zeit*, on the contrary, he criticizes all attempts to apprehend the "Wesen der Sprache," except for the analytic of Dasein and of *Rede*, the originary discursive articulation which this analytic brings to light (*SZ* 162–63). Before any investigation of the essence of language, Heidegger notes, the decisive point is to "work out in advance the ontologico-existential whole of the structure of discourse on the basis of the analytic of Dasein" (*SZ* 163).
5. One can ask to what extent Heidegger has realized in *Sein und Zeit* the program thus outlined or announced of an approach to *Rede* in its total structure and on the basis of an analytic of Dasein. The question amounts here to asking oneself whether or not Heidegger has succeeded in thinking the equi-primordiality he affirms of *Verstehen*, *Befindlichkeit*, and *Rede*. In the *Beiträge zur Philosophie*, Heidegger returns again to this question: "Mensch (Da-sein)—Sprache, beide gleichursprünglich dem Sein zugehören" (*GA* 65: 497); Sprache und Mensch bestimmen sich wechselweise. Wodurch wird das möglich? Sind beide in gewisser Hinsicht dasselbe, und in welcher Hinsicht sind sie dies? Kraft ihrer Zugehörigkeit zum Seyn? Zum Seyn gehören?" (*GA* 65: 499).
6. The combat ought to center on the λόγος for it is also in following the guiding thread of λόγος that in antiquity the fundamental ontological determinations have been conquered. See *SZ* 154: "Sodann hat die Analyse der Aussage innerhalb der fundamentalontologischen Problematik eine ausgezeichnete Stelle, weil in den entscheidenden Anfängen der antiken Ontologie der logos als einziger Leitfaden für den Zugang zum eigentlich Seienden und für die Bestimmung des Seins dieses Seienden fungiert."
7. Cf. *GA* 21: 134—"Nicht von Sprache zur Rede, sondern von Rede zur Sprache."
8. The task of phenomenology defined as research is "die Arbeit des freilegenden Sehenlassens im Sinne des methodischen geleiteten Abbauens der Verdeckungen." The necessary and privileged—if not exclusive—theme of phenomenology in Heidegger's sense is the phenomenon of "Being," i.e., precisely that which does not show itself. Or rather—as is indicated by a marginal note to paragraph 7 of *SZ*, a note which is of course utterly determined by Heidegger's own retrospective, interpretive reappropriation—the phenomenon of phenomenology is "the truth of Being."
9. See J. Derrida, "Comment ne pas parler. Dénégations," in *Psyché: Inventions de l'autre* (Paris: Galilée, 1987).
10. One has here of course the fundamental principle of tautological "logic."

11. "Das vom λέγειν her gedachte Nennen (ὄνομα) ist kein Ausdrücken einer Wortbedeutung, sondern ein Vor-liegen-lassen in dem Lichte, worin etwas dadurch steht, dass es einen Namen hat" (*VA* 224). See also *EM* 11.

12. In reality, Heidegger does not invoke the romantic idea (already in Rousseau and Herder) of a primitive poetry, linked, for example, to expressivity or figurality. If *Dichtung* is the privileged figure of language, this is because it responds rigorously to the essential determination of language: "Man speaks only insofar as he responds to language by listening to what it says." But what does "speaking" mean here? Speaking is speaking in response to. . . . But the correspondence in which man listens truly to the call of language is this saying which speaks in the element of *Dichtung*" (*VA* 190).

13. ". . . dank deren sich Entbergen und Verbergen gegenwendig ineinanderfügen, das Unscheinbare alles Unscheinbaren bleiben muss, da es jedem Erscheinenden das Scheinen schenkt" (*VA* 272).

14. The ultimate metamorphosis of phenomenological seeing? The "eyes of Husserl"?

15. "Ein Geben, das nur seine Gabe gibt, sich selbst jedoch dabei zurückhält und entzieht . . ." (*SD* 8).

16. ". . . bekundet sich das Eigentümliche, dass es sein Eigenstes der schrankenlosen Entbergung entzieht" (*SD* 23).

17. Hölderlin, *Poems and Fragments*, trans. Michael Hamburger (Ann Arbor: University of Michigan Press, 1968).

18. As Heidegger already indicated in the letter to H. Buchner, published in *VA* 182–83: "'Sein' denken heisst: dem Anspruch seines Wesens entsprechen. Das Entsprechen entstammt dem Anspruch und entlässt sich zu ihm. Das Entsprechen ist ein Zurücktreten vor dem Anspruch und dergestalt ein Eintreten in seine Sprache."

19. Man = "das so Ereignete: durch die Sprache in sein Eigenes gebracht."

20. "Ist das 'ist' selber auch noch ein Ding? Wir finden das 'ist' nirgends als ein Ding an einem Ding. . . . Dem 'ist' geht es wie dem Wort. So wenig wie das Wort gehört das 'ist' unter die seienden Dinge."

21. "Das Wort: das Gebende. Das Wort = das Gebende selbst, aber nie Gegebene. Es, das Wort, gibt . . ."

22. See also "Das Wort—die Bedingnis" (*US* 232–33).

23. On the monologue of language which is concerned only with itself, cf. the quotation from Novalis in *US* 241.

24. "Denn eigentlich spricht die Sprache. Der Mensch spricht erst und nur, insofern er der Sprache entspricht, indem er auf ihren Zuspruch hört" (*VA* 190).

25. "Hölderlin sagt: 'Seit ein Gespräch wir sind' (*Friedensfeier*). Deutlicher ist zu sagen: Insofern wir Gespräch sind, gehört zum Menschensein das Mitsein" (*SZ* 123).

26. "Unser Vernehmen ist in sich ein Entsprechen" (*SG* 88).

ADRIAAN T. PEPERZAK

14. Heidegger and Plato's Idea of the Good

Although the conceptual pair of authenticity *(Eigentlichkeit)* and inauthenticy *(Uneigentlichkeit)*, which structures the composition and all the analyses of *Sein und Zeit*, reminds us of Plato's ethics-oriented metaphysics, Heidegger has repeatedly defended himself against the reader's suspicion that his existential ontology also contained the outline of an ethics.[1] He showed even slight contempt for the discipline called "ethics," classifying it with "philosophical psychology, anthropology, "politics," poetry, biography and history" *(SZ* 16),[2] with sociology *(GA* 26: 21, 241), or even with *Weltanschauung (GA* 26: 19) on one level. On the other hand, Heidegger maintained clearly that the primary task of philosophy did not lie in a theoretical philosophy that should subsequently be completed by a philosophy of the human πρᾶξις and ποίησις, but rather in an investigation of the originary dimension preceding the distinction between theory, practice and poetics.[3]

Plato's philosophy, too, was an attempt to think the unity of theory, practice and ποίησις through their unfolding from a gathering and giving origin. The philosopher is in love with the "whole of sophia," which includes the practical and poietical virtues as well as all scientific, philosophical and empirical forms of knowledge *(Rep.* 475b).[4] The good dominates all beings by shedding truth and being upon them. Every idea has something of the resplendent but secret generosity that constitutes the excellence of the good. The central thesis of the *Republic*, proclaimed in the very center of its text, states that no human society will be saved unless philosophy and politics become one *(Rep.* 473c11–e5),[5] and the portrait of the perfect philosopher is not the contemplative who stays in the margin of the troubles suffered by his polis but the well-formed intellectual who, having caught sight of the good, consents to take part in the ruling of his fellow citizens *(Rep.* 519b–c; cf. 516c).

How did Heidegger's encounter with Plato initiate and develop? The question is an important one since Heidegger saw early on the whole of western philosophy as the elaboration of its original Platonism. In his course, *Basic Problems of Phenomenology* (summer 1927), for example, he already declared "that philosophy, with regard to its cardinal question *(Kardinalfrage)* has not proceeded further than where it was with Plato" *(GA* 24: 399–400), and in *The End of Philosophy and the Task of Thinking* (1964) we read that "throughout the whole history of philosophy Plato's thought in various transformations remains the leading one," and "all metaphysics, as well as positivism, its antagonist, talks the language of Plato" (*SD* 63, 74).

Although we do not yet possess the full documentation necessary for a genetic survey of Heidegger's retrieval of Plato's dialogues and letters, the available texts permit us to have an idea of the orientation of Heidegger's reading. In this paper I will draw attention to the ways in which Plato's well-known "allegory of the cave" (*Rep.* 514a1–517a7) was interpreted by Heidegger shortly after *Sein und Zeit* and later on, in 1940–42. After a brief review of some pages of the two courses held in the summer semester of 1927 and 1928 and of the essay *On the Essence of Ground* of 1929, I will concentrate on the essay *Plato's Doctrine of Truth*, published in 1942 but written in 1940.

In his course, *Basic Problems of Phenomenology* (summer 1927), Heidegger gives an interpretation of Plato's story of the cave (*Rep.* 514a1–517c7) and of some statements about the idea of the good (*Rep.* 509b2–10) as part of his ongoing reflection on the transcendental conditions of the possibility of *Seinsverständnis* (*GA* 24: 400ff.). The understanding of Being presupposes a projection that is different from all projections toward modes and possibilities of being; it demands a "beyond being." Plato's characterization of "the good" as "beyond being" (ἐπέκεινα τῆς οὐσίας) seems to point to the similarity of his research (*GA* 24: 404; *Rep.* 509b9). Hence, Heidegger can state: "with the seemingly very abstract question of the conditions of the possibility of the understanding of Being, we, too, want nothing other than to bring ourselves out of the cave to the light." As if he is afraid that his students might expect some dim or solemn speculations, he immediately adds the warning: "but in all soberness and in a realistic questioning that avoids all magic."

Heidegger's meditation on "the good" is focused on the meaning of the "beyond" as the pre-ontic horizon of all ontic and ontological projections (*GA* 24: 402–403). This brings him to the attempt of identifying "the good" of Plato with "the world" as explained in *Sein und Zeit*. Dasein's transcendence to world, made possible by original temporality, is equated with the orientation of the ψυχή toward the good as its τέλος (*GA* 24: 425–26). "Temporality in its exstatic-horizonal unity is the fundamental condition of the possibility of the ἐπέκεινα, i.e., of the transcendence that constitutes *Dasein* itself" (*GA* 24: 436). Finite time is the beyond: the ultimate horizon of all understanding and so the origin and outset of all possibilities of projection (*GA* 24: 436–37). The retrieval of Plato's "good" in "world" and "time" has an anti-Neoplatonic ring to it. The same sound is heard in the closing pages of the course, where Heidegger quotes a long passage from Kant's essay "On a Superior Tone Recently Adopted in Philosophy," in which the "academic Plato" is honored, while the "letterwriting Plato" and his sentimental followers are condemned as "mystagogical" *Schwärmer* (*GA* 24: 468–69).[6] Heidegger must have recognized in this passage an attempt to save Plato's sober truth from the mask that covers it.

In his course of a year later on the *Metaphysical Foundations of Logic* (summer 1928) the idea of the good and its qualification as "beyond being" are again interpreted (*GA* 26: 143–44, 236–38) as pointing into the direction of the "world" in which we are, but another feature of "the good" is now seen as expressing the affinity between both.

First, a difference is stressed. Since, according to Heidegger, "the character of totality (*Ganzheit*) belongs somehow to the concept of world" (*GA* 26: 233), the good, which is beyond the totality of beings and their Being, seems to be a less well-placed candidate for being paralleled with the "world" than the ideas, which form one community (κοινωνία).[7] For several reasons, however, the "world" cannot be equated with a realm of ideas (*GA* 26: 236): first, because the world is an ontological, not an ontic structure; and second, because the idea stresses the visual and contemplative aspect of Being too much, thus limiting the perspective to a primarily theoretical one (*GA* 26: 236–37). It is noteworthy—and for the appraisal of Heidegger's further evolution, important—that Heidegger in 1928 accuses Plato of privileging the theoretical over the practical and the aesthetic. He states firmly that it is the task of philosophy to disclose the common root from which contemplation (*Anschauung*, θεωρεῖν) and action (*Handeln*, πρᾶξις) unfold. The Greeks called this root itself πρᾶξις. It is the proper, primordial and authentic acting (*das eigentliche Handeln*), which precedes the split between thought (νόησις) and striving (ὄρεξις). Although, according to Heidegger, Plato did not explicitly thematize this common root of knowledge and action, we can see a trace of it in the fact that he interprets the fundamental transcendence as orientation toward the *good*. The predominance of intuition and theory, expressed in the leading role of the ideas, is tempered by the good's leaning toward the practical side of human existence.

There is, however, another trait by which "world" and "the good," according to Heidegger, can be heard as two names for the same. It is the structural determination of the good as the "for-the-sake-of" (*das Umwillen*, οὗ ἕνεκα). Heidegger does not justify his use of this Aristotelian category as an interpretative key for Plato's texts on the good, in which it rather appears as a giving source or granting and initiating ἀρχή than as the τέλος of some desire or ἔρως; he could, however, have pointed out that Plato, in introducing the long discussion about the nature of the good, calls it "that, which every soul pursues and for its sake does all that it does (*Rep.* 505e).[8] However, although Plato apparently takes it for granted that the word "good" is used as a synonym for "loved," "desired," and "pursued," one can hardly maintain that, as far as the *Republic* is concerned, his own thematization stresses this aspect, and not at all that the οὗ ἕνεκα constitutes the primary ontological structure that is brought out in the context of the ἐπέκεινα.

Although the "for-the-sake-of" is primarily a category of action, Heidegger applies it here (*GA* 26: 237) to Plato's ontology of the good. The meaning of the *Umwillen* is determined as "that for the sake of which something is or is not or is such or otherwise." He interprets Plato's good consequently as that for the sake of which the realm of the ideas all beings are what they are. Stressing the κοινωνία of the ideas (not thematized either in the *Republic*) he declares that the good, for the sake of which all things are what they are, is the proper determination which transcends the collectivity (*Gesamtheit*) of the ideas and hence, at the same time, organizes them in their totality (*Ganzheit*). The "for-the-sake-of" surpasses ἐπέκεινα as κοινωνία, the ideas, but in surpassing it determines them and gives them the form of totality, their κοινωνία, their belonging together" (*GA* 26: 237–38).

At this point, Heidegger establishes a connection between Plato's "doctrine of ideas"—as he calls it—and his own analysis of Dasein's transcendence to the world: "The fundamental character of the world, to which the totality (*Ganzheit*) owes its specific transcendental form of organization, is the for-the-sake-of. World, as that to which Dasein transcends, is primarily determined by the for-the-sake-of" (*GA* 26: 238).

As these lines show, Heidegger wants to distinguish his concept of *Umwillen* sharply from the traditional concept of an end in the sense of a most desired being or *causa finalis*. As ontological structure of Dasein, the for-the-sake-of, which is the world, is not to be confounded with the ontic concept of an ultimate end or goal of human existence. The question of an ultimate concern of human life can only be solved through existenti*ell* decisions of human individuals who accept the responsiblity for their own possibilities. As far as human existence is concerned, the only genuinely philosophical questions are those concerning its ontological or existent*ial* structures among which "being-for-the-sake-of" is a fundamental one. Philosophy is neither a "world vision" (*Weltanschauung*) nor a faith, nor a wisdom prescribing the way to live a good life. The content of the ultimate end of human existence is a question that cannot be answered objectively (*GA* 26: 238). Heidegger even states that "the search for an objective answer . . . is the main misunderstanding of human essence as such (*des menschlichen Wesens überhaupt*) (*GA* 26: 239). Philosophy should, however, be able to explain *why* the existenti*ell* questions and answers must be left to the decisions of the single existences engaged in them.

As the recurrence of the expression ἐπέκεινα τῆς οὐσίας in the last part of the course (*GA* 26: 246, 249) and in the closing section of the course (*GA* 26: 284) shows, Heidegger remains fascinated by them, while continuing his meditations on transcendence, freedom, world and ground.[9] "The good" seems to be another name for the world as "the whole of the essential inner possibilities (*das Ganze der wesenhaften inneren Möglichkeiten*) of Dasein, a whole which—as we know from *Sein und Zeit*—surpasses all real beings (*alles wirklich Seiende*) (*GA* 26: 248–49). The οὗ ἕνεκα, with which the good was equated (*GA* 26: 237) is also defined as the originary and utlimate *ground*, which was the category from which the course had started: "The *Umwillen*, as primary character of the world, i.e., of transcendence, the archphenomenon of ground as such" (*das Urphänomen von Grund überhaupt*) (*GA* 26: 276). Therefore, it "transcends all beings in it various *modi essentiae* and *existentiae*" (*GA* 26: 276). "The archphenomenon of ground is the 'for-the-sake-of' that belongs to transcendence" (W 56–57).

Two pages of the 1929 essay *On the Essence of Ground* (W 21–71) are dedicated to Plato's concept of the good as beyond εἶναι and οὐσία. Heidegger detects a certain ambiguity in Plato's work by seeing it as a combination of two orientations. On the one hand, the transcendence of Dasein is stated in the ἐπέκεινα τῆς οὐσίας; on the other hand, Plato's philosophy carries the seeds of a tradition that distorts the proper meaning of transcendence by its conception of the ideas as most objective entities belonging to a heavenly realm or, also, as most subjective entities innate in the soul. How does Heidegger show that τὸ ἀγαθόν signifies Dasein's transcendence as a source of Dasein's being possible as such? He reminds us of the context in which the good[10] was introduced by Plato, namely, as the summit of a search that was guided by the central question of the *Republic*, the "question of the fundamental and guiding possibility of the existence of *Dasein* in the polis" (W 56). Thus rendering Plato's often repeated question about the essence of δικαιοσύνη and ἀδικία and their connections with εὐδαιμονία, Heidegger reformulates it by saying that it is—at least implicitly—the search for the originary ground by which the ontological projection (*Entwurf*) of Dasein toward its metaphysical foundation and constitution is made possible. As coinciding with this projection, the understanding of Being is "the originary act (*Urhandlung*) of human existence, in which all existing among beings must be rooted" (W 56).

We are here confronted with a new description of the common root of theory and πρᾶξις but Heidegger immediately passes to another formulation, in which the inherent connections of the "arch-action" with the virtues of the polis and the individuals do not manifest themselves. The pretheoretical and prepractical transcendence is called "the originary and unique foundation of the possibility of the truth of the understanding of Being," or shorter: "the possibility of truth, understanding and Being" (W 56).

In a renewed attempt to liberate Plato from his Neoplatonic pupils, Heidegger again identifies the world with Plato's ἀγαθόν by mediation of the "for-the-sake-of," in which he sees the "primary character of the world" (W 57). This time Heidegger tries to justify his identification by pointing to the expression ἡ τοῦ ἀγαθοῦ ἕξις in a sentence which has caused some difficulty for translators.

Heidegger declares that ἕξις means the powerfulness (*Mächtigkeit*) of the good, which as a "source of possibility as such" (W 57), has power over itself and over the possibility of truth, understanding, and Being. Because possibility is higher than effective reality, the ἕξις of the good is more honorable.

As a consequence of his former explanations about the "for-the-sake-of," good is not seen as the ἀρχή of all light behind our backs, but uniquely as the "power" that opens up a future of possibilities. Instead of an ἀρχή or beginning in the sense of a "from what" (ὅθεν)—as Aristotle would say—the good is understood as τέλος without content, i.e., as a future which grants us the possibility of existing as worldly Dasein.

Plato's pure thought of the good as equivalent to the ultimate for-the-sake-of, which is the world, has been contaminated and concealed by the doctrine of ideas that, starting from Plato, has become the core of traditional metaphysics. The world as possibility granting power has been transformed into a realm of entities whose interpretation vacillates between objective and subjective accounts on the basis of the well-known subject–object relation and the reduction of all Being to *Vorhandenheit*. The most authentic thought of Plato must be saved by a destruction of all these distortions and their root, i.e., by a rethinking of the truth of Being, ground, essence, truth, and thought.

It would be revealing to follow from year to year how Heidegger's meditations on "the good" and "the ideas" developed. The recently published winter semester course of 1931–32, *On the Essence of Truth* (*GA* 34), would then especially deserve study. Such a genetic study would, however, exceed the limitations of a lecture. Therefore, I have chosen to dedicate the rest of my paper to the text of *Plato's Doctrine of Truth*, which, in a way, is the outcome of Heidegger's struggle with Plato, although—as we shall see—later writings have made clear that this outcome, too, was only a station on the way of a never ceasing thought (*W* 109–44).

In the essay on *Plato's Doctrine of Truth*, written in 1940 and published in 1942, Heidegger gives a new interpretation of Plato's allegory of the cave, in which he tries to show that it testifies to a shift in the essence of truth. For a good understanding of Heidegger's interpretation, it is necessary to have a clear idea about the function of the selected fragment and its connection with the rest of the dialogue form which it is taken. Therefore, I would like to start by providing a scheme of those parts of the *Republic* that cannot be ignored if we want to understand the meaning of the cave story and its exegesis in Heidegger's essay.

In 473c–d Socrates has formulated the most fundamental but also most difficult condition of a perfect πολιτεία: the unity of philosophy and political government in one or a few rulers to which the polis is entrusted. This thesis dominates not only the "third wave," which overwhelms the discussion partners from 471c until the end of book 7 (541a), but in the whole of the *Republic*. The first part of the following, central, section of the dialogue, is dedicated to its defense, especially against the objection that it expresses a utopian impossibility (471c–502c). The main condition for the possibility of its realization, the philosophical character of the ruler(s), demands a complete philosophical education. Parts of this have been treated in the lengthy discussions of traditional culture and pedagogy in the earlier books 2–5 (376e–427c and 451c–457b), especially everything that has to do with gymnastics, sport, health care, literature, music, dance, theater, morality, mythology and religion, but from 502c to 545b the scientific and philosophical part receives full attention. This part can be represented schematically in the following way, which shows some inclusions that are important for an adequate interpretation.

502c (505c)–509b: the greatest μάθημα: the good.
509b–511e: the hierarchy of sciences (the "divided line")
514a–517a: the "έικων" of the cave.
517a–521b: explanation of this έικὼν.
521c–531c (532d): preparation for dialectics through the sciences (mathematics, etc.).
531c (532d)–534e: dialectics as knowledge of the good.

As we shall see, Heidegger's interpretation uses parts of 507a–509b and 517a–518c, but he does not refer to the divided line (509b–511e) and the scientific curriculum that is designed in 521c–532d, nor to the determination of dialectics as knowledge of the good (532d–534e), in which the dialogue culminates. Yet Plato himself refers the reader of the cave story in 517a and 532bc to the sections by which it is preceded and followed. The latter passage, not used by Heidegger, especially proves that Plato's reference is not limited to the still rather imaginative explanations referred to by Heidegger's interpretation, but stresses the relations between his "eikonic" discourse on the knowledge of truth and the good, and the more "technical" or "academic" exposition of the philosophical curriculum.

'Αλήθεια

Heidegger's translation of *Republic* 514b2–517a7, with which the essay begins, after a very short introduction, does not pose many problems, although several renderings can be challenged on philological grounds. The most debatable and debated translation is, of course, that of the word ἀλήθεια as *Unverborgenheit* (unhiddenness, unconcealedness, unconcealment) and of τὸ ἀληθές as *das Verborgene* (the unhidden).[11] Already in *Sein und Zeit* Heidegger defined truth (*Wahrheit*) as originary disclosedness or unhiddenness (*Entdecktheit, Unverborgenheit*). In section 44 he stresses the fact that Dasein, at the same time, is in truth and in untruth, an that the truth must be robbed, torn away and wrested form its being unhidden by which it is preceded. He refers to fragment 1 of Heraclitus, in which the λόγος that says how beings are and behave (*wie das Seiende sich verhält*) is contrasted with the hiddenness (λανθάνει) into which they fall back (ἐπιλανθάνονται) for the one who does not have understanding (*SZ* 219; cf. 222, 226). The word ἀ-λήθεια is thus understood as composed of a root also found in λανθάνομαι (being concealed) and an *alpha privans*. Heidegger has maintained this explanation and translation throughout his writings. As unconcealment truth is the coming into the open from a hiddenness that can never be completely clarified. As unconcealing (*Entbergung*), ἀλήθεια preserves and heeds the concealment (*Verbergung, Verborgenheit*) of the secret (*Geheimnis*) that belongs to it. The essence of "truth" is its governing all being and thought by its concealing and unconcealing, robbing and heeding powerfulness (*SZ* 219; cf. 222, 226). In his later writings, Heidegger will stress more and more the overriding importance of ἀλήθεια as another name for the open (*das Offene*) or clearing (*Lichtung*) that precedes all possibility of being and manifestation (see below).

Heidegger's explanation of the word ἀλήθεια has been challenged by several specialists of Greek language and philosophy.[12] Paul Friedländer has dedicated a thorough discussion to it in the first volume of his *Plato* and revised it for every new edition in German and English.[13] His discussions are disappointing insofar as their author does not quite seem to understand what Heidegger means by the originary essence of ἀλήθεια. Friedländer's concessions, too, are less important than they might appear at first sight, for they rest upon an identification of Heidegger's concept of "unconcealedness" with the "objective" truth of the thing (the being or the idea) distinct from the "subjective" truth of the human mind. Friedländer seems to equate the difference between truth as adequacy and truth as ἀλήθεια with the distinction between the νόησις as the νόημα of an act of knowing. This is also shown by the summary of his investigations,[14] in which he gives the following three meanings of ἀλήθεια:

1. the correctness of revealing speech or writing;
2. the manifested reality of things;
3. the unforgetful and nontreacherous honesty of a human subject.

The contrary features, which constitute ψεῦδος, can be summarized then as:

1. lying, cheating, or error by words or silence;
2. forms of unreality, like dreams, imitations, falsifications;
3. unreliability and dishonesty.

Frideländer replaces Heidegger's "ambiguity" (*Zweideutigheit*) by the bipolarity (*Zweiseitigkeit*) of an equilibrium.[15]

One conclusion at least seems guaranteed by the discussions occasioned by Heidegger's translation of ἀλήθεια as *Unverborgenheit*: we do not know and cannot know whether the etymology of the word leads us back to an *alpha privans* and a root that is also found in λανθάνομαι (being hidden) and λήθη (oblivion), but it is true that some Greek authors, mainly of the Hellenistic period, were aware of this possibility. In this situation the presumed etymology can of course not provide any proof for any phenomenological or conceptual explanation. Heidegger himself recognizes later on that the meaning he formerly read into the Greek use of ἀλήθεια was not there, but he continued to translate it by *Unverborgenheit*. Already in 1943, in a paper ἀλήθεια (*VA* 257–82) he decisively rejects the idea that one could justify his philosophical explanation by appealing to the mere word ἀληθεσία, as he writes constantly in this essay (*VA* 258–59, 262). He maintains, however, his etymology (*VA* 259) and the essential connection between ἀλήθεια and λήθη as concealment (*Verbergung*). According to this essay the unity of concealedness and unconcealedness, although not thought (*gedacht*) as such by "the Greeks"—not even by Parmenides—has, however, been experienced (*erfahren*) by them. Heidegger's argument here is not etymological, but rather hermeneutic: it is impossible to understand the coherence of presence and absence, manifestation, emergence, production and being-there, as the Greeks and their language understood it, unless one postulates that sort of experience. (*VA* 262)[16]

The argument that was given in the 1954 essay on 'Αλήθεια returns in a paper on *Hegel and the Greeks* (W 255–72) which dates from 1958: "The experience of 'Αλήθεια as unconcealedness and unconcealing is not founded at all on the etymology of an isolated word, but on the "thing" (*die Sache*) that ought to be thought here (W 267). "The 'Αλήθεια or Unconcealing does not play solely in the fundamental words of the Greeks; it plays in the whole of the Greek language, which speaks differently as soon as we discard in their interpretation the Roman and medieval and modern modes of representation. . . ." The global understanding of "the Greeks" to which Heidegger here appeals is then opposed to those interpreters of the Greek world who are scandalized by the enigmatic ἀλήθεια "because they stick to this single word and its etymology, instead of thinking from out of the issue [*Sache*] towards which we are sent by Unhiddenness and Unhiding and the like" (W 269–70).

Whereas Heidegger maintains in *Hegel and the Greeks* that the association of ἀλήθεια with verbs of affirmation, as stated by Friedländer, does not prevent it from meaning "Unconcealedness" since Homer (W 271), we read a further retraction in a paper on *The End of Philosophy and the Task of Thinking* (SD 61–80) of 1964:

> The natural concept of truth does not mean unconcealedness, not even in the philosophy of the Greeks. It is often and rightly pointed out that Homer already uses the word ἀληθὲς always for verba dicendi only, for assertions, and therefore, in the sense of correctness [*Richtigheit*] and reliability [*Verlässlichkeit*], not in the sense of unconcealedness. . . . Neither the poets, nor the everyday language use, and not even philosophy have seen themselves confronted with the task of asking to what extent the truth, i.e., the correctness of the assertion [*die Richtigkeit der Aussage*] is granted in the element of the clearing of presentiality [*der Lichtung von Answesenheit*] only. . . . In any case this one point has become clear: the question of the 'Αλήθεια, the unconcealedness as such, is not the question of the truth. Therefore it was not appropriate, and consequently misleading to call the 'Αλήθεια in the sense of the clearing 'truth.' "
> (SD 77–78)

Whereas, in *Sein und Zeit* and *On the Essence of Truth*, Heidegger distinguished correspondence and the originary essence as two closely related meanings of "truth," now he clearly distinguishes "truth" (*Wahrheit*), defined by the tradition as adequacy of a statement with regard to the stated, from the clearing (*Lichtung*) as the enigma of the unconcealment that precedes and preserves, as well as grants both presence and absence.

When Heidegger continued "stubbornly" to translate the name ἀλήθεια as "unconcealedness" (SD 75–76) he did this in honor of the goddess who—by that name invoked by Parmenides in fragment 1, 29—stands at the beginning of Western philosophy (SD 74; cf. W 267). But even Parmenides did not think this ἀλήθεια as clearing and unconcealing, although he named and experienced it as such (W67; SD 75).[17] Heidegger seems to suggest that the word ἀλήθεια is wiser than the philosophers who pronounced it. Its power dominates the history of philosophy without the philosophers knowing it. Ἀλήθεια holds sway over the beginning of Greek philosophy in no matter how veiled and unthought way" (*W* 267). But even if the first philosophers did not explicitly think the secret that governed their thoughts, the conclusion must be that philosophy has not been able to accomplish its task, namely, to think the clearing. "Right from its beginning and even because of its beginning" the task of philosophy has been hindered and afterwards it has progressively withdrawn itself (*SD* 66).

Since Heidegger in *The End of Philosophy and the Task of Thinking* abandons his attempt to find his concept of unconcealment expressed in Plato's use of the word ἀλήθεια, he can no longer maintain that its difference from ὀρθότης is by itself a clear indication of a turn or an ambiguity in Plato's meditations on truth. As Heidegger himself declares ". . . one must recognize that [. . .] unconcealedness in the sense of the clearing of presentiality was experienced from the outset and uniquely as ὀρθότης, i.e., as the correctness of representation and assertion. But then one cannot either maintain the affirmation of an essential change of truth, namely, from unconcealedness to correctness. Instead, we ought to as: Ἀλήθεια, as clearing of presentiality and presentation [*Gegenwärtigung*] in thinking and saying has, from the beginning, been caught in the perspective of ὁμοίωσις and *adaequatio*, i.e., the perspective of assimilation [*Angleichung*] in the sense of conformity of representation and the present" (*SD* 78).

The consequences of this development for a renewed reading of Plato's text seem to be the following:

First, the meaning intended by Plato when he used the words ἀληθής and ἀλήθεια is not "unconcealed" and "unconcealment," but "true" and "truth." In Heidegger's understanding, the words *name*, however, a forgotten and hidden unconcealment which Plato, and even Parmenides, were not able to think. However, Heidegger concedes too much when he, in the *The End of Philosophy* (*SD* 77), wrote that ἀλήθεια had always had the meaning of correct (*richtig*) or reliable (*zuverlässig*). He forgot the meaning which he himself had listed as the first meaning in his essay *On the Essence of Truth* and which—as we shall see—is the most important one in the text and in the context of the parable of the cave: the *Sachwahrheit* or truth of being itself (*W* 75). In this sense, ἀληθές and true are synonyms of genuine (*echt*) or authentic (*eigentlich*); ἀλήθεια and ἀληθές signify the "real thing," that which "truly is" (τὸ ἀληθῶς ὄν), that which "beingly is" (το ὄντως ὄν) or simply "what is" (ὁ ἔστι, το ὄν).

Second, the impossibility of attributing to Plato the thought of unconcealment does not exclude the thesis that Plato's texts on truth permit a double reading.[18] His thematization of the truth might still show a repression or oblivion of the originary or unconcealedness hidden behind the equivalence of truth with correctness, reliability, and genuine beingness. Though unrecognized and not thought as such, the "well rounded Unconcealment" of Parmenides (*SD* 74 and *Parmenides*, fr. 1:29) might still be operative in Plato's discourse. As "unthought" it would cause an equivocation or ambiguity that permeates all the texts of our history (*W* 137).[19] If Plato is one of the Greeks who "experienced" the unconcealedness in the sense of clearing *"as"* correctness of representation and assertion only (*SD* 78), it is the task of a good interpreter to show how that experience permeates its semantical and conceptual masks, its closures and distortions.

Heidegger's description of unconcealment, as contained in *Plato's Doctrine of Truth* is not exactly the same as the one brought out in the later studies. However, to save time I will not dwell on the differences but only point out one difficulty in Heidegger's use of the word "unconcealment" in *Plato's Doctrine of Truth* as related to Plato's supposed experience of the same. There are a few passages in Heidegger's essay in which he seems to use the word "unconcealed" in a relative sense: Τὸ ἀληθές is different for the unliberated prisoners, for the recently liberated ones and for the well-guided and well-educated, "truly free" people. There are, thus, three forms or sorts of "unconcealment." This word seems to express that which sets the standard (*das jeweils massgebende* ἀληθές) for a particular stage of life or history, the "truth" of a period, or even perhaps of the moment. Those who still live in the realm of shadows consider their "truth" as *more "unconcealed"* (ἀληθθστερα) than any other truth (cf. *W*126 with *Rep.* 515d 6–7), whereas as others, living on another level, deem different appearances unconcealed and have only contempt for the pseudo-truths of the former. The problem created by this use of "unconcealed" becomes clear when we ask how ἀλήθεια can be a standard for judging the "quality" or the degree of culture, education, knowledge and . . . truth (as it, without any doubt, is meant by Plato), if it is completely dependent on the opinions and customs of a *factual* state of affairs. Unconcealed-ness would be equivalent to what the public opinion or the traditional mores *see* in fact or *hold as* true. But then the expressions "to deem unconcealed" (515c2: νομίζειν τὸ ἀληθὲς), "to regard as more unconcealed" (515d6–7: ἡγεῖσθαι . . . ἀληθέστερα) and "that which is said to be true" (516a3: τα νῦν λεγομένα ἀλήθα) are redundant, because the unconcealed would already include the relativizing clause that it is *deemed* to be unconcealed (or "true") only. This "unconcealment" would coincide with an opposite of Plato's ἀλήθεια: not its contrary, ψεῦδος, but the form of opinion most often expressed through the word δοκεῖν, for instance, in phrases like: "It appears (or seems) to me that . . . ," "I am of the opinion that. . . ." It is, however, precisely to overcome the government of opinion and mere appearance—a government which Plato sees as a terrible tyranny—that he used the words ἀλήθεια and ἀλνθές: Only authentic truth, i.e., only *true* uncon-cealment, can protect us against the terror of *das Man* and its false revelations.

Heidegger, too, recognizes that—at least according to Plato—ἀλήθεια has a normative essence when he affirms that the prisoner, even after his liberation, errs (*sich verschätzt*) in his determination of the "true," and that this failure is due to the fact that his first liberation "is not yet the real freedom."[20] Plato's use of ἀληθές is much closer to Heidegger's "wirklich" in the quoted phrase than to the "unconcealed." Indeed, the last word does not express by itself any normative or evaluative connotation, which is essential to Plato's use of ἀλήθεια as a standard by which someone—for instance, a philosopher or a god—can judge the authenticity of all sorts of revelations and concealments, truths, opinions and pseudotruths about everything, and especially about the good. Since the word "unconcealedness" seems to imply that there is something seen or known, without giving an answer to the question whether the seen or the known is authentically or "truly true," or maybe only a dream, an illusion, a claimed but not authentic truth, the word seems unfit for rendering the full meaning of ἀληθές as it is understood by Plato, and not by Plato alone. It needs a further qualification in order to know whether the unhidden is solid, safe, transparent, superficial, frivolous, misleading, solemn, only shining, pure glitter, kitsch, fake, or (truly) true.

The question just asked is intimately connected with the question of the origin as preceding all duality of the theoretical and the practical. If Heidegger's interpretation neglects the "normative" moment, which is so essentail to Plato's concept of truth, must we understand that interpretation as a purposely one-sided approach to the more originary question? In the course of his essay (*W* 132–33), Heidegger has some polemical, antimoralistic words about a conception of the good which, according to him, is radically different from its Greek understanding, and in the closing pages (*W* 143–44) he suggests that it would be possible to sketch a genealogy of "values" parallel to the genealogy of "truth" outlined in the essay. There are, however, also a few passages where he insists on the transformations which the "whole ψυχή," according to Plato's text, must undergo in order to learn not only new insights, but a general mode of comportment. Must we understand Heidegger's plea for unconcealment as an attempt to name and think the granting source to which πρᾶξις and production no less than knowledge owe their emergence from the silence of Hades without any light? Or is Heidegger himself "Platonic"?

Παιδεία

A hint in the direction of an answer to that question can be found in Heidegger's ignoring all Plato's indications of ethical and political importance in his "'εἰκών" of the cave. What does this "likeness" represent? According to the first sentence of the story, Socrates invites the reader to see "our ψύσις" in relation to παιδεία and its opposite, ἀπαιδευσία, as similar to and pictured by the experience undergone by those who, in the cave, . . . , etc. From this sentence one could gather that the story tells a parable about human nature in need of education and culture, but we should not forget that the story and the explanations which surround it are presented as the explantion and justification of a παιδεία by which a well-bred elite of boys and girls should be transformed into the best human beings who excel in philosophy *as well as in political wisdom and practice*, or who are—in one word—accomplished in δικαιοσύνη. The last word is awkwardly translated as "justice," but it is the main purpose of the *Republic* to show that it encompasses all the practical, emotional, and theoretical elements that compose human excellence or perfection in individuals and in the collectivity of the polis. That the intellectual and contemplative element of this formation is stressed in the central books of the *Republic* is typical for Plato and most of Western philosophy, but it should neither be forgotten that σοφία and φιλοσοφία do not have the unilateral theoretical meaning we moderns hear in it, nor that they are inseparably tied to the "gymnastic" and "musical" παιδεία treated in books 2–4. The context as well as Plato's own explanation of the cave image do not agree with Heidegger's taking the cave as an allegory of the cosmos between the vault of heaven and the earth (cf. *Rep.* 517a, 9ff, 521 cff., 532 a–c, 540 a–b, with *W* 119–20). According to Plato, the cave is the political situation wherein "we"—and here he thinks primarily of the Greeks—find ourselves. It is not a very good situation, and we cannot escape from it, but the desire for a better one can be met: genuine philosophy—not the fake revelations of the sophists, and even less the ethos and the moral lessons of common sense—can transform us into reformers of the society provided we are of a healthy, well-disciplined, harmonious and well-educated character. It is noteworthy that Plato's own explanation of the parable in 519bff. insists rather heavily on the necessity that the accomplished philosopher is not allowed to stay out and above the political πρᾶξις and the society of unconverted people. Participation in the common life is an essential part of δικαιοσύνη; those who dedicate themselves only to the joys of pure contemplation are no more able to rule the city than the uneducated cave dweller, because they are attached too much to the fake πρᾶξις of souls that imitate a bodiless existence.

When Heidegger stresses the unbreakable unity of παιδεία and ἀπαιδευσία (*W* 123, 128), his argument for it is different from Plato's. Since he eliminates all references to those persons without whom no prisoner can be freed or turned around, he cannot explain them otherwise than as events that might happen. Once turned toward the light, he says, one might fall back into the realm of shadows (*W* 122). The *Republic* states clearly that all formation demands a certain violence done to the amorphic and chaotic striving of human spontaneity, a violence which comes—at least in part—from other humans who have already been formed and enlightened sufficiently to awaken and guide their fellow people.[21] The way up and the way down form, indeed, one essentially connected whole—not, however, because of the inevitable mixture of truth and untruth alone. There are in fact three motivations for the participation of a truth-lover in the everyday life of the existing society, (1) because of our "somatic" existence; (2) because it is an integral moment of δικαιοσύνη (519b–c); and (3) because of ἔλεος (516c), "compassion," i.e., care (or nonindifference) for others' δικαιοσύνη and εὐδαιμονία.

Heidegger quotes the expression ἐμφρόνως πράξειν (to act wisely, or—as Heidegger translates—"to act with insight and circumspection"), in which Plato summarizes the results of a successful παιδεία, but he neglects the opposition "in private or public" (ἢ ἰδίᾳ ἢ δημοσίᾳ) (*W* 135, with *Rep.* 443a, 517c5, 540b, etc.) which, as a sort of refrain, runs through the *Republic* and all the references to public life contained in Plato's explanation of the cave story (518e–521b). Without its imaginative presentation of an overall formation of human behavior the εἰκὼν of the cover is truncated and the temptation becomes strong to read a certain intellectualism into it. To a certain degree, this could be prevented by Plato's clear distinction between an insufficient form of φρόνησις and a sufficient one (518e ff.). Although the former, too, is a virtue, it is useless, because it is not oriented by the good. This orientation is the true end of all παιδεία, the excellence of all excellences, a metavirtue that consumes and founds a whole composed of an excellent πρᾶξις including the virtue of σοφία and all excellences of theory. The dimension of the good—unique and ultimate issue of formation—is presented by Plato as the transcendence sought by the earlier Heidegger, but overwhelmed by his later concern for the orginal struggle between hiding and unhiding.

And yet, Heidegger, too, insists on the conversion and transformation of the *whole* soul (*W* 123) and their effect on our most fundamental attitude and behavior (*W* 122–23).

THE IDEA

As a picture of the average polis the cave symbolizes the inauthentic praxis in everyman's society. Just as with most of Plato's work it can be read as an expression of his central experience: that of the contrast between the inauthenticity of the existing individual and social life on the one side and the idea of that same life in a purified form on the other. Although this idea is neither realized nor realizable among us, it commands and translates in an imaginative form our most authentic desire. Plato's search for a force that could "liberate" and "heal" us (515c)—at least to a certain extent—was a search for authenticity and truth. The "idea" is first of all a name for the genuine or the true (τὸ ἀληθὲς).

In his interpretation of the things that can be seen outside the cave, Heidegger states that they are the image of "the proper and authentic being of beings" (*das eigentlich Seiende des Seienden*) (*W* 120). This expression reminds us of Plato's expression το ὄντως ὄν (that which "beingly" is). Immediately afterwards Heidegger says that this proper being of a being is that thanks to which a being shows itself in its "look" ("*Aussehen*"). This "look" is not a mere appeal; it still has something of the self-presentation by which all beings "present" themselves. Heidegger's statement is not accompanied by an argumentation. It is obvious that ἰδέα and εἶδος are etymologically related to ἰδεῖν (to see). It is also clear that Plato calls our perceiving (νοεῖν) of the being of beings very often a vision or contemplation of their truth or being, but these indications insufficiently define the idea as a "look." When Plato uses the words "ἰδέα" or "εἶδος," he mostly stresses the fact that they can neither be heard, nor seen nor touched, etc. The ἰδέα is not "given" in the sense of an aesthetic form or sound or smell. It must be discovered by a capacity that passes through the senses without being essentially dependent on them because it transcends their possibilities of perception.

In order to see to what extent Heidegger's understanding of Plato's ἰδέα coincides with Plato's analyses, a long discussion of the huge literature on the subject would be necessary. Due to the limitations of this paper, only a few insufficient remarks are possible.

To stay within the *Republic*, it is a striking fact that the words ἰδέα and εἶδος occur very rarely in more than a vague sense, in which they are also used by contemporaries such as Thucydides and Isocrates. If Heidegger had restricted himself to the text of the cave story, he could not even have mentioned Plato's "doctrine of ideas," for neither ἰδέα nor εἶδος appear one more time in the text of 514a1–517a7. If we take Plato's own commentaries on this text into account and consider the whole of 502c–541b, the word ἰδέα appears there five times together with the ἀγαθόν as ἡ τοῦ ἀγαθοῦ ἰδέα (*Rep.* 505a, 508e, 517b, 526e, 534b–c) and in other combinations in only 507b, 507c and 507e. "The idea of the good" is equivalent to the expression το ἀγαθὸν or τἀγαθὸν, which is found in many more places.[22] The places where εἶδος occurs in these same texts are probably not many more.

To briefly sum up the most striking features by which Plato in the *Republic* characterizes the ἰδέα, we may start by saying that it is a sort of "secret" by which a φαινόμενον fascinates someone who has been surprised or amazed. "Ἰδέα" is the name for that in being which, though not invisible, audible or touchable, is more genuine than that which appears to those immediate acquaintances, insofar as they are not purified by "thinking" (νοεῖν). The ἰδέα is "the truth" of such a being. In discussing questions such as "What is justice?" or "What is ἐπιστήμη (or σῶμα or αἴσθησις or ἀρετή)?" Plato uses very often a series of synonyms instead of appealing all the time to εἶδος or ἰδέα. Instead of the "idea of the καλόν" he also writes "the καλόν itself" (αὐτὸ το καλόν or αυτὸ καλόν), "the καλόν according to itself" (τὸ καλόν καθ᾽ αὐτό), "what καλόν is" (ὁ καλόν ἐστι) or "the καλόν as it is" (ὡς ἐστι). By generalizing these expressions, they become "that which each thing is" (ὁ ἐστι ἕκαστον) or simply "that which truly is" (τὸ ἀληθῶς ὄν) or "that which 'beingly' is" (τὸ ὀντῶς ὄν) or, still simpler, "the true" (τὸ ἀληθές) and "the being" (τὸ ὄν). By taking these equivalences seriously, we will avoid the silly interpretation of Plato's thought as a "doctrine" about two realms or as the defense of an invisible cosmos of ideal entities distinct from the unique corporeal and aisthetic world in which we live. The idea is neither a thing above the phenomena nor simply given to our spontaneity. It is not a look, but rather an astonishing secret, which urges us to discover and admire its genuine but hidden presence. No aisthetic phenomenon is ever separated from the ideality of its idea; if it were, it would not even be perceptible at all, since it would have been swallowed by a black and soundless night without touch or taste or smell. On the other hand, no idea is separated from its audible, smellable, touchable, visible, or edible appearances since it would—just as pure light—not be perceptible, lacking things to be reflected upon. The truth of the shadows cannot be known unless they are illuminated by the shining of their own true secret, whose dim and approximate unhiding they are. The shining of their truth is, however, not possessed in property; it is granted as a splendor which generates θαυμασία.

The synonymy of the quoted expressions with "εἶδος" and "ἰδέα" shows that the etymological reference to seeing is not essential to their understanding. On the contrary, Plato's opposition of the thinkable (τὸ νοητόν) to ther sensible (τὸ ἀισθητόν) is reinforced.

Concerning the optical character of the metaphysical system in which the thinking of true Being is caught, it must be stressed that Plato in 507c very explicitly states that vision and visibility are used as *pars pro toto* for the whole range of senses. Vision represents all the "aisthetic" or sensible possibilities of immediate contact, including even all imaginative, "eikonic" or "phantasmic" representations, insofar as they are not yet thought and understood *as* phenomenal presence of their unseen, unheard, and unfelt truth.

Plato's privileging of vision and visibility over the other senses is defended in 507c–508a on the basis of their qualitative superiority. This is concluded from the intermediary reality needed for any act of seeing: the light (τὸ φῶς), which is called "not a small idea." The bond (ζύγον) that joins the sense of seeing and the capacity of being seen is more honorable (τιμιωτερόν) than the other junctions (*Rep.* 507e–508a). It is not clear from this text whether all sense and sensibilia are dependent on specific junctions. Glaucon denies that any other sense has something comparable to the light which illuminates vision and the visible (*Rep.* 507d), but Socrates is more prudent when he leaves the question open (*Rep.* 507d, 508a: τῶν ἀλλῶν). It is obvious that sound and hearing cannot be united without an intermediary, as Plato himself in the *Timaeus* (*Tim.* 67b) seems to presuppose, but it is not as easy to find an equivalent of light for touch and the touched. Anyway, the force of the argument for the superiorty of vision lies not in its being the only one of the senses needing a third element as bond but in the quality of this bond: it is on the basis of a very Greek—but not exclusively Greek—experience that the light is perceived and thought of as the most precious of all elements.

All other characteristics of "the idea" ought to be understood from the perspective of this first one, i.e., from the truth or the (authentic) Being of things: its being free from corruption and its transcending the endless play of birth, growth, decay and death; its "being always"; and its gathering unity, which certainly does not coincide with the generality induced or guessed by the most attentive cave dwellers (516c–d) or with the abstract universality of a Wolffian logic, etc.

One feature—which is not a feature but the very essence of the idea—must be stressed, especially because it is very often forgotten and neglected in the explanation of Plato's ontology. The idea, or οὐσία is not merely a descriptive category. As the hidden genuineness of courage, a polis, an animal, music. or a god, their idea is the perfection and purity of that which this courageous behavior, that roaring lion, those melodies, etc., realize within the limitations of a mixture with impure, obscure, defective, and corrupting elements. Every being is and is not quite (and sometimes hardly is) what it—in truth and according to its authentic essence—is. Everything is and is not what it is. The idea is the ideal in the light of which every being appears as being more or less its οὐσία. This means that the idea simultaneously and originally is that which something *is* and what it *ought to* be; it is the union of being (*Sein*) and ought (*Sollen*) before their difference—and, thus their proper meaning—arises. The ἰδέα or οὐσία, the essence of all phenomena is the primordial ἀρχή in which the existing and the ethical are still one; the transcendental origin of the unity holding theory and practice together—an original unity without which no ethics would be as primordial as ontology. Plato's concept of the idea as an ideal of authenticity is a necessary presupposition of any philosophy that tries to establish tasks, norms or duties on an analysis of the οὐσία or the φύσις of a being. If original being or truth *includes* its own perfection, the first command for every being is: "Be what you are!" The whole cosmos is then permeated by Eros: the passion of being as good (i.e., as "true" or as "beingly being") as one can be.

Which elements of the idea are stressed in Heidegger's reading? In the first place, it simultaneously (re)presents and represses ἀλήθεια. The idea provides beings with the possibility of appearing in the brightness of a given light. This grants them the showing of a face or a look. The idea is neither something behind the aisthetic appearance (in that case, it would be aisthetic itself), nor a facade behind which something else would be going on; it is the brightness within which a being manifests itself, thanks to which it can be perceived and understood as that which it is (*W* 131). Knowing a house as a house, a god as a god, the tree as a tree, is made possible by the idea (*W* 120). In the light of the idea beings can show *what* they ("really," in truth) *are*. They present their being-what, their *essentia* (οὐσία) in the sense of *quidditas* (*W* 131). Thus, the idea restricts ἀλήθεια to the presence of a "look" caught in the network of being looked at, to perception and determination (*W* 143).

Heidegger's interpretation tends to blur the Platonic distinction between the idea as such and the ("idea" of the) good. Plato attributes the gift of light and brightness in the first place to their ultimate source, the good but the idea also is shining. So, for instance, in *Rep.* 508d, where the same word καταλάμπει (to spread light) is used of ἀλήθεια, τὸ ὄν, and the sun (ἥλιο). If we accept the equivalence of ἀλήθεια and τὸ ὄν with the ἰδέα, we may identify the latter, too, as a source of light. It is however, obvious that Plato's telling about the cave and explaining his story is entirely dominated by the thought that "the ideas" (i.e., the beings as they are) constantly receive all the light and shining from the good that possesses it because of its essence.

A second moment of the idea that is lost in Heidegger's interpretation is its paradigmatic and commanding, appealing, or (pro)vocative character, which they also owe to the good. By their purity and perfection the ideas (i.e., the essences of beings) are not only structures or models of empirical things, but also tasks that ought to be realized. By their very essence, they bring the impurities, lies, and distortions of the existing world to the fore. The truth of an idea is, thus, in its accusation of the inauthenticity that belongs to a "somatic," i.e., an idolatrous existence.

THE GOOD

The idea of the good is interpreted by Heidegger on *W* 132–35 and 141. Instead of stressing the "beyond" (ἐπέκεινα), by which the good is distinct from Being (εἶναι, οὐσία) truth and ideas—as he did in the texts of 1927–29, he now stresses the proximity between the good and the idea. In fact, the whole idea of the "beyond Being" (i.e., of the "determination" by which all "ὁ ἔστι," i.e., all possible determinations, are removed from the "the good") has disappeared and the phrase "ἐπέκεινα τῆς οὐσίας" is not even quoted. Before analyzing his interpretation, let us briefly summarize what Plato himself says about the idea of the good.

Since the entire text of the *Republic* is dominated by the question of the essence of δικαιοσύνη, i.e., of that which makes the polis and the psyche well-balanced, harmonious, strong, wise, beautiful and "good," the word ἀγαθός ("excellent" or "good") has in this context primarily an *ethical* meaning, in the Greek, or at lease in the Socratic, Platonic and Aristotelian sense of the word ἠθικός. It is, therefore, surprising—to put it euphemistically—to read Heidegger's peremptory declaration that the interpretation of "the good" as the "ethical good" (*das "sittlich Gute"*) "falls short of Greek thought" (*W* 132–33). Now, it is true that ἀγαθός (excellent) initially, for instance, in Homer, did not have the moral connotation of καγός, but Plato's dialogues provide abundant evidence for its having taken on that meaning also and having become a synonym of καγός (beautiful, fair, nice, good, etc.). This is, for example, clearly shown in Plato's criticism of the traditional mythology. It is impious and immoral, he says, to represent the gods as causing damages to human beings or other gods; for the good is never cause (αἴτιον) of bad things (κακά); good is the contrary of harmful (βλαβερόν); it is a cause of doing good (εὐπραξία) (*Rep.* 379a–c). It is, therefore, not suprising that ἀγαθος and καλός are very closely associated[23] and even can join into one word καλοκάγαθός, καλοκἀθία.

"Good" can also be synonymous with "useful" or "favorable." Then it refers to another thing or state ot event that is—good. In *Rep.* 357b, Plato distinguishes carefully between three sorts of good (αγαθά): (1) "goods" we desire because of themselves only (αὑτοῦ ἑνεκά); (2) goods that are desired because of their consequence; and (3) goods desired for both reasons. The second and third sort of goods are useful. As such, the good appears, for example, when Socrates that all useful and favorable things, even δικαιοσύνη itself, are what they are thanks to the good only (*Rep.* 505a). As desired and sought for itself, however, the good appears in the description of it as "that which the whole pysche hunts for and for the sake of which (τουτοῦ ἑνεκά) she does all she does" (*Rep.* 505e),—a description which I have already quoted in the margin of Heidegger's earlier interpretation of the good as "for-the-sake-of" (τὸ οὗ ἑνεκά). In the same sense, the good is also said to be the one thing that in any case must be considered to be the most εὐδαιμόν in all that is (*Rep.* 526d), the τέλος of the whole search (*Rep.* 532e) and the τέλος of all that can be known (*Rep.* 532b).

Being the excellent and the ultimate, the ἀγαθόν is also "the most shining" (*Rep.* 518c). In comparison with this qualification the epithet "goldy" or "divine" (θεῖον, not as Heidegger says in *W* 141, "τὸ θεῖον, *the* divine"), is much less impressive and important, since many outstanding beings, like men, forces, pleasures, mores, laws, etc., are called "divine."[24]

As "greatest μάθημα" the (idea of the) good is the summit of what has to be discovered along the pedagogy of truth, which therein possesses its ultimate (τελευταῖα) perfection and its most fundamental orientation. Although the good itself can hardly (μόγις) be seen (*Rep.* 517c1) we bathe in the "light," which is its gift; if we love this "light," we will be in the truth, not because the good *is* the truth, but because the truth and our knowledge of it testify—through the light in which they appear—to their common source that is beyond the dimension

of knowing and being known, neither an αἰσθητόν, nor a νοητόν, but . . .
"the good."

In contrast to Plato's emphasis on the difference between the good and the
truth of τα ὄντα, Heidegger now stresses the idea that the good is called an
ιδέα. By calling it "the highest idea" and "the idea of the ideas" he tends to
restrict its function to the supreme form of a shining that is proper to all the
ideas. The word τελευταῖα, used in a sentence that resumes the cave story by
saying that "the idea of the good in the [dimension of the] knowable is the ultimate"
(Rep. 517b8), is translated as "that which consummates all shining" (die alles
Scheinen vollendende) (W 132). Accordingly, the consummate perfection is interpreted as belonging to the good "because in it the essence of the idea is perfectly
accomplished, i.e., [in the good the essence of the idea] begins to be and rule
(wesen), such that only from it [namely, the good] emerges the possibility of all
other ideas" (W 134). According to this reading the ἀγαθόν has, in a perfect
and total way, the same function as all other ideas, but the degree or extent to
which they practice it is differrent. Every idea grants a look on beings as beings.
Therefore, the idea of the good is nothing other than the ultimate condition of
possibility of all shining and manifestation. In this sense, it is the source of all
ideas or also "the idea of all ideas" (W 133).

Although Plato has made it very clear that the good is not just an idea, but
the origin of οὐσία, truth, and idea, on the one hand, and knowledge, discovery,
and science, on the other, Heidegger tries to justify his interpretation by another
peremptory remark on the meaning of "good." "Thought in the Greek way, τὸ
ἀγαθόν means that which is good (or of use) for something and makes good
(or of use) for something"²⁵ (W 133). Plato, thus, seems not to be Greek, if Heidegger's translation of ἀγαθόν is the only permissible one. Does the latter want
to get rid of the thought that the ultimate and the consummation of all things
and events has essential connotations of an ethical character and that it can be
loved for itself, without any thought of its possible use? On the basis of his restrictive definition, Heidegger defends that the good is "that which makes useful (or
good for) in general" (das Tauglichmachende schlechthin),²⁶ and because he restricts its function to the condition of the possibility of ideas (or "looks") alone,
he concludes that the use granted by the idea of the good is uniquely the shining
of the ideas. However, when Plato considers the good to be that which grants
εἶναι, νοῦς, and ἀλήθεια, but also δικαιοσύνη, καλλός, and εὐδαιμονία of
the whole ψυχή and the πόλις, and even of all shadows, mirrorings and εἴδωλα,
does he only think of their splendor, or is he also astonished by the contrast between
an unshining good and bad behavior? An indication of there being some hidden
and unshining dimension of genuine quality may be found in a clause that more
than once accompanies his statements about the goodness of δικαιοσύνη. In
Rep. 367e we read that the issue at stake is not whether the δικαῖος is or must
be praised by gods and people, but whether δικαιοσύνη indeed is stronger and
better for ψυχή and πόλις than its contrary, ἀδικία (ἐάν τε λάνθανῃ ἐάν τε
μὴ θεούς τε καὶ ανθρώπους). Whether the δικαῖος is hidden or not for gods

and men." The same clause is found in another important passage (*Rep.* 427d), in which the discussion partners, having accomplished the building of a good polis, ask again where δικαιοσύνη and ἀδικία should be found. The only difference is that Plato adds now "all" to "gods and men." In both places the word λανθάνειν (to be concealed)—so important for Heidegger's interpretation of ἀλήθεια—is used to bring out the authenticity, i.e., the truth of "justice," its οὐσία or ιδέα, the ἀλήθεια of what (truly, beingly, or essentially) is. The real question is "what justice *does* to the one that has it" (*Rep.* 367e), not whether it shines forth in a human world protected by the gods. It is, however, true that the second passage appeals to our visual abilities for determining the essence of "justice" and its being "good," Socrates "looks" for "light" in order to "see" what it and its contrary are. The hiding of the essence and its *hidden truth* must be brought to the light of a *true, i.e., adequate, discourse*. The essential truth distinguishes itself form all unconcealment by its hiddenness. The unconcealed is put at a distance, because it could be a false shinining forth, a fake shining lacking truth.

Based on his understanding of the good as origin of all shining, Heidegger draws a conclusion that makes the resemblance between the good and the idea almost perfect. Since the good provides all shining, Heidegger suggests, it itself must be visible. Since its essence consists in granting shining, it must be that whose essence it is to shine most of all (*das Scheinsamste*): "This grants shining to everything that is essentially shining *and is therefore* itself the very appearing, that which in its shining is the most shining."[27] That the good is not only the source but also is itself the most shining of all beings would be the reason why Plato calls it τοῦ ὄντος τὸ φανότατον, which expression—instead of translating it as the "brightest of beings"—Heidegger renders by the words "the most appearing of beings (whose essence it is to shine)."[28] In the same vein, he translates *Rep.* 517b8 thus: "In the dimension of the knowable the idea of the good is that which consummates all shining *and therefore also the essentially visible which only at the end can be truly seen*, in such a way, however, that it hardly (only with great effort) can be seen in itself" (*W* 132). The italicized phrase is an interpreting clause added to the text in which the visibility of the good is stressed. Now, it is true that Plato himself—in flagrant contradiction to his own characterizations of the good—states the "visibility" of the good and the possibility of knowing it,[29] but, from a thematic point of view, the *therefore* in Heidegger's explanatory clause is certainly wrong. It is not true that the condition of the possibility of something (for example, of language, time, or utility) itself possesses the functions or features or modes of being of that something made possible by it. If we take Plato's analogies concerning the good seriously, it *cannot* be *known* as a νοητόν, an ουσία, a truth or an ἰδέα, for if it were, it would presuppose *another* "light" and *another* source of "light" to make it knowable. The good cannot be an idea in the normal "Platonic" sense of the word. Is this the reason why Plato prefers to speak of "the good" instead of "the idea of the good"? Or does the word "idea" still have that early, very vague meaning which permits analogy, homonymy, or ambiguity? The answer to this question is less important than the solution of the riddle with which Plato confronts us by treating the good as something knowable or "visible" in an analogic sense, as something that we at any rate must know ("see") if we want to be perfect philosophers.

In his study of *Plato's Doctrine of Truth,* John Sallis has pointed out that the expression μόγις ὁρᾶσθαι in *Rep.* 517b8 (it—the good—can "hardly be seen") is a hint that should be followed up by saying that the good is not an idea, but an ἀρχή.[30] It is indeed Plato's own ambiguity that expresses itself in his naming the ἀγαθόν an idea and treating it as such. Both his *eikonic* story and his more conceptual commentaries present the good as the presence of a beyond of light and essence, that, notwithstanding its beyondness, can and must be "seen" and "known" as if it were a being, a truth, an essence, or a virture. Plato's clear consciousness of the radical difference between the good and all that can be known has not prevented him from looking at the good as if it were to be known. Is this an instance of Plato's irony? A paradox, the highest or the original paradox by which he wants to test the best of those whom he has "compelled" and "forcefully dragged"[31] out of a cave? In any case we will miss the whole secret of "the good" if we betray all of Plato's efforts by leveling "the good" to the dimension of essences and their manifestation.

TRUTH

Since we have already dealt extensively with Heidegger's translation and interpretation of the *word* "ἀλήθεια," I can restrict myself here to a short summary of the main meanings of ἀλήθεια in the *Republic.*

Besides the meaning of "true," as a qualification of assertions that state how things really are, and the meaning by which we characterize persons as truthful, ἀληθής is used—and this might be the most-used meaning—to indicate the genuine reality of things, events, situations, virtues, or persons, that which they "really" or "truly" are. In this sense (of *Sachwahrheit*), the ἀληθές is synonymous with οὐσία and ἰδέα.[32] Often ἀλήθεια indicates the side of a being over against the γνῶσις or ἐπιστήμη had by the person who admires or contemplates that being.[33] It is an authentic being itself which manifests itself to the researcher who looks for it. A philosopher is hunting for ἀλήθεια (*Rep.* 490c), as if it were something out there (or also here, very close to me, but very hidden) that must be discovered or "found" (*Rep.* 538e–539a). The "objective" or "essential" character of "the true" is connected with its hiding from bad or mediocre presons (such as the cave dwellers). A long and strenuous discipline is demanded for its becoming unconcealed. 'Αλήθεια is primarily the hidden secret of authentic being that remains always concealed to a certain extent because it manifests itself only to its pure and authentic lovers (*Rep.* 501d).

If "the true" and the idea are essentially shining, their splendor must be thought as for the most part hidden. The authenticity of a well-balanced philosopher—not the pseudo-science of a philodoxos (*Rep.* 480)—is called forth by the good, as τέλος of all knowledge, to discover and receive the self-revelation of the true.

Immediate appearances generate fascination because their truth is not immediately apparent; they have a depth because of their truth withholding itself in its shining forth.

To what extent and on the basis of which motivations does Heidegger find traces of unconcealment, as *he* understands it, in Plato's staging of the cave?

According to Heidegger, the whole scene of the story is by itself an imaginative evocation of unconcealment (*W* 128, 130–31). For what else could this underearthly cave symbolize than a space which at the same time is enclosed and opened up towards its entrance? Its hiding in half-darkness is essentially related to an outerworld of brightness. Heidegger assures us that "the Greeks"—on the basis of their "fundamental and undebatable experience of ἀλήθεια" necessarily understood this εἰκὼν as the visualizing (*Veranschaulichung*) of the unconcealment of Being. In cultures "where truth is of a different essence and not unconcealment or at least not co-determined by unconcealment, a 'cave allegory' does not have a support for [its] visualizing" (*W* 130). The argument relies, thus, on Heidegger's claimed acquaintance with what he calls "the fundamental experience that was self-evident for the Greeks."[34] Although Plato himself still shared that experience, he did not give it an adequate expression; for him the meaning of his image did not lie in the twofold unity of concealment and unconcelament, but rather in the things and events, the sun and the light, the idea and the possibility of determining what there is to see and to think about (*W* 130–31).

A second motivation is given by insisting on the unbreakable unity of παιδεία and ἀπαιδευσία analyzed above.

The third motivation lies in Heidegger's interpretation of a particular sentence from Plato's own commentary on his story (*Rep.* 517b7–c5). According to Heidegger "the ambiguity (*Zweideutigkeit*) in the determination of the essence of the truth can be read off from this single sentence" (*W* 137).

THE YOKE OF THE IDEA

If, from Plato to Nietzsche, the unconcealment as "fundamental trait of Being" has been neglected, while the role of the subject's disposition and adjustment was overempahsized, this is due to the domination of the idea as "look" which demands for its being "seen" a "correct" (ὀρθός *richtig*) regard (*W* 136–37). Since Plato's text is still inhabited by the unrecognized but named and experienced Ἀλήθεια, it is equivocal (*zweideutig*). "This equivocation reveals itself in all its intensity by the fact that the text treats and speaks about ἀλήθεια but intends the ὀρθότης which is promoted to be the standard" (*W* 137).

For the domination of the idea over unconcealment Heidegger uses the word "yoke," for which he refers to a sentence in which Plato uses the word ζυγόν and two verbs with the same root[35] to characterize the *light*—*not* the idea or the good—as the bonding element of vision and the visible. In Plato's context the word "yoke" fits only insofar as it indicates a (favorable) junction. There is no hint of any oppression or mastery; on the contrary, the light is the most generous, gentle, and friendly condition for the possibility of perception and admiration. By a similar sort of reading Heidegger takes the word κυρία, by which Plato in *Rep.* 517c4 characterizes the primacy of the good (and *not* the idea), to indicate a mastery of the idea, (*W* 136; cf. 137), but his real argument is the exegesis of a sentence that in my translation reads thus:

> In the [dimension of the] knowable, the idea of the good is the ultimate (τελευταια), something that can hardly be seen; once it has been seen, however, one must conclude that it is indeed the origin of all that is right and fair (ὀρθῶν τε καλῶν αἴτια) in all things; in the visible it generates light and the source thereof (the sun), while, in the thinkable, it is the source that grants truth and thought; that (scil., the idea of the good) one must see, if one wants to act wisely in private or in public. (*Rep.* 517b7–c5)

Heidegger sees in this sentence an expression of Plato's equivocation with regard to truth. The two word pairs τὰ ὀρθά τε καὶ τὰ καλά and ἀλήθεια καὶ νοῦς, translated by him as *das Richtige und Schöne* and *die Unverborgenheit aber auch das Vernehmen* form in his reading a chiasmus: νοῦς (thought) corresponds to ὀρθά (correct) and ἀλήθεια (the unconcealed) to καλά (*W* 137). The identification of τὸ καλόν with ἀλήθεια-as-unconcealment is based on a sentence of the *Phaedrus* (*Phaedr.* 750b) in which beauty (τὸ καλλός) is said to be ἐκθανέστατον (the most resplendent). This is for Heidegger a name for "that which most of all shows the purest shine from out of itself, and thus, showing its look, is unconcealed" (*W* 137). The affinity of the "correct" (ὀρθός) and νοῦς would, on the contrary, express the essence of truth-as-correctness or adequacy of statements. The sentence would be marked by the trace of 'Αλήοεια, which is already losing the battle to the forces of the presencing and representing subject and to the correctness of its discourse.

The philological basis of Heidegger's motivation is weak. In the first place, it is not correct that both pairs are about knowledge, as Heidegger presupposes when he writes: "Both sentences speak of the precedence of the idea of the good as the condition of the possibility of the correctness of knowing (*Erkennens*) and of the unhiddenness of the known" (*W* 137–38). Second, they form neither a parallel nor chiasmus. And third, the conclusion is incorrect, insofar as it identifies the good with "the idea" and characterizes it as a yoke in the sense of an oppressing and repressing force: "Truth is here still simultaneously unconcealedness and correctness, although the unconcealedness already stands under the yoke of the ἰδέα" (*W* 138). I have already given my argument for the last objection. The second one is the denial of a gratuitous affirmation that will appear false if the following defense of my first objection is true.

The affirmation that the idea of the good grants "ἀλήθεια and νοῦς" repeats a "doctrine," affirmed in numerous places and in almost identical wordings,[36] according to which true beings (the truth of the idea) and the thinking ψυχή are powerless (hidden and blind) if the "light," which comes from the good, does not enable them to become actual knowledge and unhidden οὐσία (i.e., ἀλήθεια). The phrase "τὰ ὀρθά τε καὶ τα καλά", however, is not immediately related to questions of perceiving or knowledge, but rather to the ethicopolitical questions that dominate the whole of the *Republic* and to which Plato's exegesis of the cave story (*Rep.* 517a8ff.) from which the quoted sentence is taken, draws the reader's attention. The end of the sentence, quoted earlier by Heidegger in another context (*W* 135), warns the reader against a one-sided epistemological interpretation: ἐμφρόνως πρᾶξειν ἢ ἰδίᾳ ἢ δημοσίᾳ (*Rep.* 517c4–5). Heidegger translates this as "to act with insight and circumspection" (which diminishes perhaps the practical meaning of εμφρόνως) and his explanation concentrates on the regard for ideas (*die Ideenblick*) instead of Plato's "seeing" the good; the most surprising feature of his exegesis is that on one page he takes the pair ὀρθά τε καὶ καλά to mean the "right and beautiful" with regard to comportment (*Verhalten, W* 135), whereas a few pages further (*W* 137–39) he understands it as related to knowledge theoretical discourse.

The "right (or correct) and beautiful" as a summary of the good praxis analyzed in the ten books of the *Republic*, are one side of the "wise doing" (ἔμφρων πρᾶξις) in which Plato summarizes the lesson of his cave image. The necessity of truth and thought is its other side, but both sides need each other, for neither knowledge is possible without authenticity in virtue, nor virtue without genuine contemplation of the truth.

AMBIGUITY AND STRATEGIES

From the preceding analysis several hints may be elaborated into a revision of our interpretation of the *corpus Platonicum* and of our own history—if our history, be it only in part, is a history of Platonism. This revision might then also include a reappraisal of the *corpus Heideggerianum,* insofar as it has marked the Platonic, anti-Platonic, Neoplatonic or Platonistic reflexes of our thinking.

Since the limits of this paper do not permit a full account of the questions that spring from the three preceding considerations, I will concentrate on two topics: *the idea* and *the good.*

THE IDEA

In defending the fact that the idea is the hidden secret of the genuine and not less the "beauty" of a task or call than the core of Being or *Sein,* I wanted to stress the fact that the idea brings a movement into the phenomena by which they reveal and hide, offer and protect, promise and hold back the truth of their being—a movement that seems more akin to the unconcealment than Heidegger seems to concede and manifests more clearly the binding or even vocative character of a certain καλοκαγαθία encompassing the entire cosmos of beings.

THE GOOD

As we have seen, Heidegger's reflections about "the good" show a difference between his understanding of it in the courses he taught in the late twenties and in his essay of 1970. Where he first took "the good" to be a name for the world as a transcendental condition of Dasein's *Seinverständnis,* he later did not reinterpret it as a name for unconcealment but tended instead to reduce it to the perfect idea. Why did he reject or repress his early retrieval?

The answer seems to be: because the good is presented as something that can be "seen," thematized as an object, thought as the presence for the mind's eye of a νοητόν. An idea is a being, be it the highest of all beings. This, however, can never be understood as the originary, which is neither a highest being, nor the beingness of beings. The reason why Heidegger no longer sees τό ἀγαθόν as a trace of that which precedes all beingness and being seems, thus, to lie in the rejection of what he later calls onto-theo-logy.[37]

Now if there is any ambiguity in Plato's search for the true, it is certainly in his discourses on the good. For, on the one hand, τό ἀγαθόν is, just as τό καλόν and το δικαῖον, one of the ideas whose features and connections can be studied as pertaining to one common dimension (cf., e.g., Rep. 484d); on the other hand, τὸ ἀγαθόν stands above and outside the dimension of τὸ καλόν and τό δικαῖον and all other ideas (e.g., Rep. 505a, 506a). If we maintain the designation of the latter "good" by the word "idea," then this word must be understood in an equivocal way, or even as a homonym applicable to radically different "things." In the expression "the idea of the good" the word "idea", then, has a completely different meaning from "the idea" in "the ideas of horse, god, virtue, etc." But then the whole constellation of expressions with which Plato explains the "place," "the function," and "the essence" of the good must be understood as an equivocal language, whose meanings cannot be clarified easily, and perhaps not at all. The good, as outlined by Plato, is neither an idea nor a being, a truth, an invisible "light," or a spiritual source. It is not a virtue, a god, or cosmos either, for all these and other beings presuppose a "light" that should come from "something" that cannot be thought as a—be it "metaphorical"—"sun," a highest being, an open space, a Lichtung, or a blinding "light."

The most fundamental difficulty with which Plato and all of philosophy is confronted may be seen more clearly if we ask whether it is an essential necessity of thought or solely the contingent peculiarity of a particular tradition, often called "philosophy" or "Western philosophy," that urges us to gather all things, events, societies, conversations, and persons in the name of a substantive or hypostatic One that cannot be a being nor the essence, and yet inevitably is treated— "seen," "perceived," "thought," and said—as such. One of the questions that arises in the course of such an investigation asks why Heidegger, much more than Plato, collects and recollects his and others' thoughts in the name of impersonal yet fascinating substantives such as 'Αλήθεια, Λόγος, Μοῖρα, Geheimnis, Seyn, Ereignis, Austrag, Sage, or Sprache.

Was it Plato's "failure," was it the fate of metaphysics that, at the very moment of a great disclosure, it hid the nonessential and nonideal good which it began to perceive, behind the traits of an idea, a being, a truth, a telos, a "source" of "light"? We cannot answer this question if we do not first take into account the whole arsenal of strategies by which Plato tried to prevent himself and his readers from thinking that the good (and—since the good grants and determines the entirety of Being—also Being and all beings) could be treated as a theme or topic of a thetic and a systematic theory. Since even a complete list of these strategies would exceed the limits of this paper, I restrict myself to a few remarks.

As Plato states in the Seventh Letter (341c–e), he never wrote a doctrine, neither a doctrine of the good nor a "doctrine of the truth." What he wrote was never said in his name but in different names. Of course, Socrates is a teacher and his interlocutors rarely show any independent thought, but still we are invited either to participate in the ongoing disucssions or to stay outside and treat them as the dead corpus of a dead philosopher.

With regard to the good, the exemplary teacher, whose self-confessed ignorance is well known, states very explicitly: that he does not sufficiently know what the good is, although it is quite necessary to know it (*Rep* 505a–c, 506a; cf. 517b); that he will not speak about the good, but about its offspring (*Rep*. 506e) and simile only; and that his discourse on the good lacks the necessary rigor and expresses only an opinion instead of a well-thought-out doctrine.[38]

I bypass the eikonic and mimetic character of Plato's discourse, not only in his parable of the cave but also throughout the whole of the *Republic*, because they have not been thematized by Heidegger's interpretation or in my comments. It would, however, be very revealing to apply the analysis of the μιμητικός, as given in book 10, to the maker (ποιητής) of constitutions and texts himself and to ask what he wants to show by multiplying *eikons* and *eikons* of *eikons*, similarities, shadows, statues, pictures, imitations, φάντασματα, εἴδωλα and so on.

In order to save the ἀγαθόν from falling back into the dimension of ideas, beings, essences, and beingness, Plato resorts to superlatives and exaggerations: the good is "the brightest" (φανοτατόν), "the ultimate," (τέλος), "the summit," "the perfect" (τελευταῖα), etc. Although this hyperbolic language in fact encloses the good within the dimension of ideas and οὐσία, it is meant to be a way of separating its excellence from them. In order to express this, such superlatives should be accompanied by negations and denials of its belonging to that dimension. This has been understood by such Neoplatonists as Plotinus and Pseudo-Dionysius, who systematically combined the strategy of negation, denying that "the good" is Being, a being, light, spirit, essence or . . . good, with the strategies of hyperbolic and of eikonic language. Since "the good" is neither a highest being or light nor Being or Space or Clearing, it is neither "high" nor "low," neither *Sache* nor *Ur-sache*, neither last nor present nor first. But now, then, is it possible to refer to it at all?

A clear consciousness about the impossibility of considering that which Plato, for lack of a better word, called "the good," as a sort of light or being has prevented the greatest philosophers of our history from falling under the all too encompassing verdict that they moved within the framework of onto-theo-logy in the Heideggerian sense of this word. Although most of them were rooted in another tradition than the Athenian and pre-Hellenistic one, they welcomed Plato's name for the ultimate and did in their way what Plato did when he conceived τὸ αγαθόν as being neither an idea or Being itself nor subject to the generation and corruption of fascinating phenomena.

It may be time to revise again the schemes that rule our remembrance of the past. By giving up a perspective which tends to become dogmatic, we liberate a wealth of Greek and un-Greek thoughts willing to welcome us into a dialogue.

NOTES

1. Cf., for example, *SZ* 175ff., 28off., 289–301.
2. Cf. *GA* 26: 22, 171, 241, 245; *EM* 108.
3. *SZ* 300; *GA* 26: 172, 230–31, 235–37, 285; cf. *SZ* 320; *W* 187–89, 191–93.
4. Cf. *Rep*. 521d ff. All quotations from Plato in this paper are taken from the *Republic* (hereafter *Rep*.), unless another dialogue explicitly is indicated.
5. A count of the lines of which the dialogue is composed shows that *Rep*. 471c where this thesis (as the third condition for the realization of the ideal state) is introduced is (almost exactly?) its material center. Cf. A. Diès in his introduction to Platon, *Oeuvres completes* 7, 5th ed. Trans A. Chambry. (Paris: Les Belles Lettres, 1965), 10 and 147–51.
6. Heidegger's quotations can be found on pages 387–89 and 396 of Weischedel's edition of Kant's work in *Studienausgabe*, vol. 3 (Wiesbaden: Insel, 1958).
7. The κοινωνία of ideas does not receive any special attention in the *Republic*, but certain interconnections are implied by *Rep*. 476a and 511c.
8. Cf. also *Rep*. 357b: "Some good, which we choose to have . . . loving it for its own sake [αὐτὸ αὐτοῦ ἕνεκα]."
9. In order not to complicate this summary of Heidegger's investigation, I have left out his transition from "transcendence" to "freedom" (Freiheit), which is a synonym of the former. The exact relationship between both concepts is clarified in: W. Richardson, "Heidegger and the Quest of Freedom," in *A Companion to Martin Heidegger's "Being and Time,"* ed. J. J. Kockelmans (Washington, D.C.: Center for Advanced Research in Phenomenology and University Press of America, 1986), 161–82.
10. In these pages Heidegger does not call to τὸ ἀγαθόν an idea.
11. In the story of the cave, the word ἀληθής occurs only in *Rep*. 515c2, 515d6–7, and 516a3. In *GA* 34: 41, δοξαζεῖν (Rep. 516d7) is translated by the phrase "für das Wahre halten."
12. See R. Bernasconi, *The Question of Language in Heidegger's History of Being* (Atlantic Highlands N.J.: Humanities Press, 1985), 26 n. 7.
13. Cf. the account Friedländer's discussion given by Bernasconi, op. cit., 19 and 27 n. 8, and by J. Sallis in *Delimitations* (Bloomington: Indiana University Press, 1986), 176–80.
14. Cf. P. Friedländer, *Plato* I, 3rd German ed. (Berlin: De Gruyter, 1964), 236.
15. See also Bernasconi, 21.
16. In *Sein und Zeit* (*SZ* 219), the presumable etymology of ἀγήθεια was not the basis, but a confirmation of phenomenological analysis that stood firm by itself. The course of the winter semester 1942–43 attaches more importance to the etymological explanation, but suggests that *Entbergung* might be a better expression for the process of disclosure and unconcealing; cf. *GA* 54: 17ff.
17. *W* 67 and *SD* 75. For this reading Heidegger bases himself on a general understanding of Parmenides and on the word πυθὲοθαι in fragment I, line 28, which he translates in *SD* 74 as *erfahren* (experience).
18. Cf. also Bernasconi, 22–26, and Sallis, op. cit., 180–85.
19. Cf. Sallis, 18off. on this *Zweideutigkeit*.
20. *Die wirkliche Freiheit* (*W* 126); cf. also *die echte Bindung* (*W* 125).
21. Against the violence of the "bonds" (*Rep*. 515c5) of the "prison" in which the "heads"

of the prisoners are "compelled" (*Rep.* 515a9–b1), another "violence" (*Rep.* 515e6) is needed to "compel" (*Rep.* 515c6, d5, e1, 516a1) them to freedom. Who are the "forces" that bring slavery or "redemption" and "healing" (*Rep.* 515c4)?

22. *Rep.* 357b, 462a, 490a, 505b (three times), 508b&e, 509a&b, 517b, 526d–e, 531c, 532b, 534b&c, 540a.

23. *Rep.* 425d, 484d, 489e–490a, 497a–c, 505b, 531c, 569a.

24. For example, *Rep.* 492e–493a (ἦθος), *Rep.* 500d (philosopher), *Rep.* 433e (πόλις).

25. For this meaning Heidegger could appeal to *Rep.* 505a.

26. Most elements of Heidegger's interpretation of the good are already present in the course of 1931–32, to which he refers in W 397. Cf. *GA* 34: 95–116. esp. 100 and 106: "the good" is not a moral or ethical concept; *GA* 34: 106–107: it is *was tauglich macht.*" The interpretation of the "ἕξις τοῦ ἀγαθοῦ" as *Macht, ermächtigend*, and *Ermächtigung* is, however, closer to the texts of 1928–29 than to the later essay.

27. W 134: *Dieses bringt jedes Scheinsame zum Scheinen und ist daher selbst das eigentlich Erscheinende, das in seinem Scheinen Scheinsamste.* (Emphasis in the translation is mine.)

28. W 134: *das Erscheinendste (Scheinsamte) des Seienden.*"

29. For example, in *Rep.* 517b, 517c4–5 (cf. W 135), 517c1, 518c, 526d, and 532c. In the story of the cave alone there are more than twenty occurrences of "seeing" or "eyes."

30. J. Sallis, 181.

31. See note 21 and *Rep.* 515c6, 515e1&6–8, and 516a1.

32. Cf., for example, *Rep.* 495c, 508d, 520c, 525c, and 579d.

33. For example, *Rep.* 475e, 508b&e, 509a, 517a–b, 517c, 527e, and 539c.

34. The appeal to "Greek thought" as such (*griechisch gedacht*) occurs also in W 134 and twice in W 133.

35. W 132 refers explicitly to *Rep.* 508a1; cf. W 135–36. In *GA* 34: 102 the yoke is correctly understood as image of the light, not of the idea.

36. For example, in *Rep.* 501e, 508b&e, 509a, 517a8–b1.

37. Cf. W 141 on "the divine" and theology.

38. Rep. 504a–b, 506c–e, 509c, 532d–533a, 534a, 536b–c; cf. 376d, 435d, 443b–c, 444a, 450a–451b, 472b–473a, 484a, 501e.

KLAUS HELD

15. Fundamental Moods and Heidegger's Critique of Contemporary Culture

Translated by Anthony J. Steinbock

Thanks to the speedy and steady appearance of the *Gesamtausgabe*, Heidegger's "Collected Works," we can form a concrete picture of Heidegger's creative development in the decade which followed *Being and Time* and which culminated in the *Contributions to Philosophy* (*Beiträge zur Philosophie*) written in 1936–38. In this period, Heidegger made his way to his definitive, i.e., ontohistorical, understanding of the present age. It is his fundamental thesis that we live in an epoch of transition: behind us we have the age of metaphysics which emerged from the "first beginning" of the philosophically shaped culture of the Greeks. Before us lies the "other beginning" (*anderer Anfang*) of an entirely new thinking and culture in a future which can only be intimated.

The thinking basic to our present culture of the first beginning was made possible by Being keeping-to-itself, the "withdrawal" (*Entzug*). It belongs to the essence of the withdrawal that it withdraw itself in an abysmal concealedness for metaphysical thought. Today the forgetfulness of the withdrawal, which is conditioned by this abysmal concealedness, reaches its extreme, its ἔσχατον. On this occasion a transformation could take place through which the human being becomes an other, namely, able and ready to experience the self-withdrawing withdrawal *as* withdrawal, i.e., as "mystery" (*Geheimnis*). If human beings enter into the mystery of the withdrawal, it is possible for them to acquire the force to fashion a new beginning historically through the three areas in which the work of creating a new awakening can take place: poetry and art, thinking, and politics.[1] This new awakening could form the origin of a new culture (though Heidegger himself avoids the concept "culture").

Presented in broad strokes, this is Heidegger's vision which he has nowhere in earlier published work expressed so candidly as in the *Contribultions to Philosophy*. This vision is founded on the supposition that the historical "moment" (*Augenblick*), the καιρός, draws nigh for a thought gifted with the experience of the withdrawal as withdrawal. Heidegger's entire ontohistorical thinking is guided by this supposition. What can guard such as supposition from the suspicion that it is an arbitrary notion? What supplies it with a bindingness for thinking? Heidegger occasionally warded off the importunity of this question, but it must be entertained if ontohistorical philosophizing is not to give way to pseudopoetic promulgations.

Heidegger's confidence that the human being today could embark on a new culture is an extraordinarily high aspiration. The courage, drive, and readiness to make the sacrifices required for such a new departure presupposes a real and not merely imagined experience that makes working to bring about the new culture via the works of the type just mentioned a binding task. Thus, Heidegger cannot evade the question concerning bindingness. In order to respond to it, he must advance an experience that accounts for the bindingness of the hypothesis concerning the withdrawal and, at the same time, for the effort involved in embarking upon the historical new beginning. Heidegger specified this experience and expounded upon it in the decade following *Being and Time*; it is the experience of a certain "fundamental mood" (*Grundstimmung*). Until recently, Heidegger's phenomenological analysis of this experience could not have been sufficently well known. Now it is to be found in the *Contributions to Philosophy* and in the texts of the lectures which either preceded this work or were held at the same time. This finally puts us in a position to evaluate concretely the actual phenomenological foundation of bindingness in Heidegger's late philosophy.[2]

For the first time such an evaluation also presents us with the possibility of exposing the deepest philosophical roots of his position on National Socialism, and thereby presenting the possibility of getting beyond the superficial and philosophizing chatter triggered by the publication of Farias's unsound work. Unquestionably, Heidegger believed for a time that National Socialism would establish the novel work in the sphere of politics, the field through which the desired new age of the other beginning could dawn. This belief was accompanied by a profound distrust of democracy, from which Heidegger—until the end of his life—expected nothing. At the conclusion of my reflections I would like to suggest a new explanation for Heidegger's basic political position. In my view, this position is based upon a one-sidedness in his phenomenology of fundamental mood, a one-sidedness that can nonetheless be exposed and amended by means provided in Heidegger's own analyses.

Bindingess means that which binds our thinking. In binding lies a compulsion, a necessity (*Notwendigkeit*). The ontohistorical forethinking with respect to the καιρός of the other beginning possesses a necessity because it obeys the compulsion of a need or distress (*Not*). The experience of the withdrawal as withdrawal puts in question a human being's wonted power of disposal. In this way, the withdrawal leads human beings into a abysmal need or distress which is reflected only superficially in the varied and diverse needs of our time. Every deep need leaves us dumbfounded at first. And this is also what happens to a philosophizing that keeps its distance from the loquaciousness of learned chatter. The abysmal need makes it speechless but thereby leaves it free precisely to hear the voice of need.[3] Every need "speaks" to us because it overcomes us in corresponding moods (*Stimmungen*). Their taciturn voice tells how our situation is fundamentally faring. "Fundamental moods" (*Grundstimmungen*), according to Heidegger, are characterized by the fact that they even inform us about our general historical situaton by making the abysmal need of the forgetfulness of the withdrawal audible (i.e., experienceable).[4] Thus, it is because the "hearkening" to fundamental moods understood is in this way that, in the decade following *Being and Time*, Heidegger's ontohistorical reflection and "readiness to embark" receive their bindingness.

Now moods have been regarded, in the light of truth-claims in the philosophical tradition, precisely as that which is nonbinding par excellence; consequently, they remain largely neglected phenomena. They could rise to the status of being guide-posts for ontohistorical thinking in Heidegger because of the unbiased seeing of the phenomenological method. In *Being and Time* Heidegger took over Husserl's pioneering insight that any being whatsoever is encounterable only in the universal indicating referential context of the "world." Heidegger radicalized this discovery[5] with the insight that the world horizon stands open in moods to the human being prior to every object-consciousness.[6] In this way Heidegger can define human beings as Dasein, i.e., as the place of openness—as "Da" or "there"—for the world.[7] Dasein exists as being-in-the-world by the world as horizon offering to Dasein possibilities of existence. Dasein has the elementary experience in moods that, as existing world-openness, is nothing other than a being-in-possibilities: its mode of being is able-to-be (*Seinkonnen*), self-projection. Moods reveal to Dasein that it cannot exempt itself from the weight of always being itself given up as able-to-be. This thrownness in the "having-to-project-itself" manifests itself in the moods which tell Dasein how it fares with respect to its factical situatedness in the open range of possibilities, or "world."

What is revealed to Dasein in this way is the prepredicative truth which founds all predicative truth. The bindingness of philosophical propositions is thereby placed on an entirely new foundation that runs counter to the tradition. When truth basically takes place prepredicatively as world-openness in moods, every predicative truth—including the truth of philosophical propositions—is ultimately dependent upon how the mood primarily opens the world to us. Traditionally, truth has its place in judgment, i.e., originally in a speaking. This already points to the fact that moods can also be true precisely because they speak to us in some way. Certainly, this speaking cannot be a discoursing. It is a saying and as such a taciturn showing[8] of the particular temperment[9] of being-in-the-world.

To be sure, Dasein normally flees in the face of the weight of the thrownness into everdayness whose noisy bustle drowns out that taciturn voice. But Dasein can also, in its being-possible, bring itself before its thrownness and summon up the readiness to appropiate being-possible expressly as being-possible. The ability-to-be comes into relief *as* being-possible only in explicit contrast with the possibility of its own impossibility. Dasein must directly face the closing of the dimension of openness, "world," which threatens in death. This happens in the resoluteness of the "moment" in which Dasein comes to itself, and in this becoming-its-*PROPER*-self (Sich-zu-*EIGEN*-werden) becomes "authentic" (*eigentlich*).[10]

Husserl's analysis of the horizon character of appearing objects remained essentially trained on the paradigm of perceptual and theoretical seeing. Through Heidegger's analysis of mood, hearing or "hearkening" received, for phenomenology, a significance essentially on a par with seeing. This extension of the paradigm signals the methodical title "hermeneutical phenomenology." In fact, Heidegger was only able to discover the systematic import of the phenomenon of mood because he appropriated, from the hermeneutical tradition, the notion that thinking as interpretation is dependent upon a hearing. Historical existence demands an openness to the historical "moment,"[11] the καιρός, i.e., the readiness to experience a readied situation as a summons to essential action.

This thought from Heidegger's earlier "Hermeneutik der Faktizität" makes easy passage into the phenomenology of being-in-the-world via the analysis of mood, and comes to fruition beginning with *Being and Time*, in the development of the following decade. Moods overcome us; how they disclose our temperment to us in this process does not come under our power, and is not at our disposal. They compel us to hearken to its taciturn voice. Through the recognition of this compulsion to hearken, the hermeneutical phenomenology of mood from *Being and Time* prepares the *Kehre*, that is, the interpretation of Dasein as a response to be historical exhortation that withdraws itself from Dasein's power of disposal.[12] Thus, the analysis of mood becomes the foundation for bindingness and the guidepost for the inculcation of ontohistorical thinking in the decade following *Being and Time*.

In *Being and Time* itself, the historical referentiality of moods does not yet emerge, but it is, to be sure, unmistakably articulated in terms of the systematic structure of the work. The latter culminates in resoluteness for authenticity which constitutes the "moment." It can only come to the explicit confrontation with the possible impossibility of being-possible, that is, to "advancing toward death" (*Vorlaufen zum Tode*) because from the beginning, the ability-to-be is constantly tempered by the possibility of its impossibility. This fundamental temperment, anxiety (*Angst*), reveals to Dasein that, as being-in-the-world, it hovers over the abyss of the nothing. In the resoluteness of advancing toward death, Dasein musters up the courage to let the voice of anxiety (which latently tempers Dasein) be determinative for existence.

No one can take over my death. Resoluteness therefore brings Dasein into a radical individualization in which it discovers itself as self. Yet this does not imply solipsism, for anxiety is not a subjective state of mind; it is, rather, like an atmosphere in which the whole of being-in-the-world is immersed. This whole would not be the whole were it simply to concern my world. In fact, human beings remain alone with themselves in fleeting moods, in superficial "humors" that overcome them in the process of everyday life. But a fundamental temperment such as anxiety, to which Dasein hearkens in the resoluteness of the moment, opens Dasein for the whole of the world, for being-in-the-world as being-with-one-another.[13]

The world is historical as a communal horizon, as a world of *Volk*—as Heidegger intimates in *Being and Time*. This historical dimension discloses itself in the "moment." This concept is introduced in *Being and Time* as an expression for the transhistorical possibility of humanity, that is, as the situation of resoluteness.

By virtue of the ecstatic structure of its temporality in view of its death the whole of its world relations is revealed to Dasein, as it were, in one stroke. But the concept of "moment" in *Being and Time* also implies the meaning of historical "moment," the καιρός. It is characterized by the ability, mentioned at the outset, to institute historical beginnings in works of thinking, art, and political communal formations.

This capability develops out of resoluteness. As the openness for what the taciturn voice of fundamental temperment has to say to Dasein, it consists in an openness as ready for action in the historical world; and it forms the foundation of experience through which the creation of works that have the power of initiating historical change becomes the binding task for Dasein. This is to say that mood of the "moment" in which the fundamental temperment manifests itself must itself be historically related. The Da of Dasein, the place of the dawn of the general world horizon, transforms itself historically and is disclosed in the authenticity of the mood of the "moment."

Thus the way is paved for the analysis of fundamental mood in the decade following *Being and Time*. We must now inquire into the fundamental mood of the present in which the fundamental temperment of our communal being-in-the-world comes bindingly to light. In responding to this question, we should surely take into account the fact that as long as Dasein does not attain resoluteness it misses (*überhört*) what the fundamental temperment of anxiety can say to it about its historical situation. Dasein represses its fundamental temperment in inauthentic everydayness and, therefore, in the historical reference of the "moment."

Neither in the relevant sections in *Being and Time* nor in the exposition of anxiety in Heidegger's Freiburg inaugural lecture of 1929 did he make explicit the systematic connection between the fundamental temperment of anxiety of the historical referentiality of the "moment" just sketched. The connection is, nevertheless, there; for this reason, when Heidegger expresses this connection for the first time in the afterword to the inaugural lecture in 1943, it does not concern a subsequent reinterpretation: fright (*Schrecken*) manifests itself in anxiety in the face of the abyss of the historical withdrawal of Being.[14] According to the *Contributions to Philosophy* and to the lecture course in the winter semester of 1937–38 concurrent with it, fright is the mood into which our age is tuned by the abysmal need of that withdrawl.[15] Thus this historical need calls for readiness for authentic anxiety.

The exposition of deep boredom in the lecture course in the winter semester of 1929–30, which takes up the Inaugural Lecture, shows that Heidegger already had this connection in mind at the time of the latter. Deep boredom is a fundamental temperment like anxiety; the difference is that, from now on, the expression "fundamental mood" replaces the concept of fundamental temperment. Deep boredom initially appears in the inaugural lecture, as does essential anxiety, as a, so to speak, transhistorical possibility of being-tuned. But then it turns out that by entering into this possibility, we become ready for an experience of the fundamental condition of our age.[16]

Things no longer appeal to us in the fundamental mood of deep boredom;[17]

all beings, as a whole, including ourselves, sink into an abysmal indifference.[18] The real reason for this stems from the fact that there is no longer anything to occasion essential questions. In the enterprise of all-encompassing, organized scientificotechnical management of Dasein—what Heidegger characterized in the period of the *Contributions* as "machination"[19] and later as the "framework" or "setting up" (Gestell)—all questions are viewed as tasks that are, in principle, solvable. The sense of the dimension of the mysterious disappears. We rarely experience anything as a need, or the distress of an unsolvable enigma. In this way, the distressful situation of lack of distress, the need of need-lessness (*Notlosigkeit*),[20] i.e., ultimately the abyss of the withdrawal, is that which manifests itself in the fundamental mood of boredom. In the *Contributions to Philosophy* Heidegger returns explicity to this historical referentiality developed in the lecture course of 1929–30 (*GA* 65: 157).

Decisive here with respect to the systematic consistency of the matter is that fundamental moods are not historically referential as long as they are simply latent in Dasein as mere possibilities for an authentic being-tuned and, moreover, as long as they are superimposed on everydayness with inauthentic derivatives of themsleves. In *Being and Time* this was authentic anxiety as covered up by fear. In the lecture course of 1929–30 this is illustrated in the repression of deepboredom by the superficial familiar forms of boredom: being-bored-with-something, for example, when waiting for a train in the train station or being-bored-by-something, e.g., when at a party. In this connection, despair is mentioned (*GA* 29/30: 211)—as well as an evasion of the onset of deep boredom.

The same construction is behind the systematic presentation of "leading mood" (*Leitstimmung*) and "fundamental mood" which emerges later in the *Contributions to Philosophy*. Leading moods are temperments that "put thinking in the mood" or tune thinking epochally into its respective basic position.[21] The history of metaphysics arose from a series of such leading moods surpassing one another, the latest of these leading moods is fright, just mentioned, to which Nietzsche's nihilism responds.[22] But fright as such in no way places Dasein in the resoluteness of the "moment." As we all know, fright normally petrifies and occludes all creative action: This petrifaction is overcome for the first time in the resoluteness of the "moment" that makes us hearken to that which leaves us speechless from fright. Only when this occurs does this leading mood become authentic; only then is it able to call forth historically powerful action.

Our age bears the signatures of the moods of boredom, anxiety and fright. But these only characterize it incompletely and onesidedly, for in them merely the departure from the age of the first beginning manifests itself. We can also detect a mood in our age that prepares the other beginning. The mystery of withdrawal experienced as withdrawal is already discernible in fright.[23] The mood that opens itself to the mystery fully and gratefully is awe (*Scheu*).[24] This timidbeing-in-awe is Dasein which keeps to itself, and this keeping to itself is the response to the essence of Being itself experienced as keeping-to-itself, i.e., as withdrawal. In the present historical "moment" of the possible transition to the other beginning, thinking is set the task of preserving what was experienced as heard

in authentic fright in the new leading mood of awe.[25] This task manifests itself
in the authentic mood of our transitional epoch: holding-back (*Verhaltenheit*).[26] But
here holding-back takes over the same systematic function as resoluteness. For
resoluteness is understood both as the readiness for essential anxiety[27] and as
that readiness (which remains nameless in the lecture course of 1929–30) by virtue
of which we let the latent boredom of our age become effective in its authenticity
as deep boredom.[28]

Just as petrifying fright in its inauthenticity—fright not experienced as holding-
back—remains ineffective for historical action, and indeed is even destructive,
anxiety in its modification as the inauthentic mood of fear loses the force for
creative action in the historical "moment." And the same holds for boredom in
its superficial forms.[29] Every fundamental mood can only then become the experience of an historical need and thereby make an historical act necessary and binding
when it meets Dasein's readiness for authenticity in the "moment"—characterized
in *Being and Time* as resoluteness.[30] But here we are faced with the unavoidable
question as to how this readiness can be specified more precisely.

Readiness is a comportment of the will. However, already in *Being and Time*
this will is not to be understood as a spontaneous, active power of disposal, but
as the ability to hearken to and thus experience what is said to Dasein in a fundamental mood. In order to keep itself open to this experience that occurs in hearkening, the will that presses toward the power of disposal must keep to itself. Thus,
we are concerned with a readiness to be receptive to being overcome by a fundamental mood. To be sure, this readiness demands us to surmount inauthenticity.
But the effort required for surmounting inauthenticity consists precisely in letting
loose of oneself and giving in unreservedly to the fundamental mood. In other
words, it consists of abandoning the strenuous efforts of inauthentic everyday affairs, not wanting to pursue them in a new striving—in striving to reach authenticity. Although the diction of *Being and Time* seems to imply a heroic "existential"
straining of the will, it is clear from the internal sense of the work that resoluteness
entails a peculiar relaxed willfulness, the placid self-abandonment to a fundamental mood that allows it to pendulum out, as it were, thus granting to Dasein historically formative vigor for the "moment."[31]

Yet we must still address a decisive question: how does this letting loose of
oneself and this self-abandonment get its start? We pose the question in the first
place because there appear to be many fundamental moods which lie ready in
Dasein as concealed possibilities and, so to speak, waiting to be awakened. It
could seem as if resoluteness hit upon these possibilities through a sort of selection
process. In an age of transition such as ours, and indeed in accordance with the
nature of transition—especially of transiton that is only possible in such an age—
the fundamental mood cannot be univocal. Therefore, many possible moods offer
themselves as the signature of our age. Heidegger especially draws our attention
to this fact in the *Contributions to Philosophy*.[32] And he confirms it again later
in the lecture "Was ist das—die Philosophie?" that he delivered in 1955 in Nor-
mandy.[33] In the *Contributions to Philosophy* Heidegger remarks that in the analysis
of fundamental mood we cannot pre-judge or even deduce which of the possible

forms of the contemporary fundamental mood will become the actual experience for Dasein. It would contradict the essence of moods, upon whose inaccessible attendance we depend, if we believed we could philosophically explain away their contingency.[34]

Nevertheless, even if we accept this insuperable contingency, the question still remains: What brings Dasein to the readiness to break through the superficial, fleeting moodedness of the everyday, which for the most part takes the shape of a "waning nonmoodedness," as it is called in *Being and Time* (*SZ* 134)? What brings Dasein to abandon itself to a fully necessary experience of a fundamental mood? One could maintain that this just goes to show that, contrary to Heidegger's contention, the mood cannot have the last word in human Dasein: here the reason-driven will of the tradition would have to be restored to its time-honored position of privilege, for only it could be considered to be the motivating factor for the transition from inauthenticity to authenticity.

Against this hypothesis it would do well to consider that Dasein is fundamentally open to the world through its moodedness. Moods are not occasional attendants of human existence but constitute it as being-in-the-world. Dasein is "tuned" through and through, and that means, as it is called in *Being and Time*, Dasein can only become master of a pregiven mood "by a counter-mood."[35] There is no appeal beyond authentic moods. If the reason-directed will leads Dasein out of everyday moodedness, it can only do so because it can, for its part, be determined by a mood which tunes Dasein into the readiness for authenticity.

This brings the question just posed to a head: What kind of mood is this? Only the following alternatives come into consideration as an answer: either it is the authentic fundamental mood itself, for which readiness is being awakened and which motivates the readiness (as yet concealed) from the very start to its explicit efficacy, or it is another mood.

Let us consider the first assumption. As latent possibility, every fundamental mood is ambivalent. Dasein can evade it in inauthenticity by covering it up and replacing it by its deficient form, and this is what ordinarily occurs. But Dasein can also be attentive to it in the authenticity of the "moment" by moving counter to this prevalent tendency of covering-over and thereby creating the strength for historical powerful action. This strength and the readiness for authenticity are not two different things. Dasein receives both together from the same mood. It provides the impetus for the transition to authenticity and for engaging in historically formative action. That transition and this engagement possess the same character: the character of beginning. This is what is essential in the historical "moment": Dasein makes a beginning. The sought-after mood enables Dasein to be able-to-begin in the authenticity of the "moment."

The ability-to-begin is the condition of reality for a fundamental mood emerges out of its deficient mode, out of its inauthenticity, and obtains historical force. Fundamental moods wait in deficiency, as it were, for their awakening to authenticity. That means, however, that it cannot be these fundamental moods themselves, latent, lying in wait, that tune Dasein to the ability-to-begin. It must be a proper fundamental mood, a fundamental mood of the ability-to-begin from which Dasein receives the readiness and the strength for latent fundamental moods to become authentic.

Do we find this fundamental mood in Heidegger? I think we do; Heidegger has also named it θαυμάζειν, that state of wonder or being astounded from which, according to Plato and Aristotle, philosophy began.[36] According to Heidegger, this wonder was the fundamental mood of the first beginning from which metaphysics and our philosophically formed culture arose.[37] One can surmise what Heidegger means from a few clues in the *Contributions to Philosophy*. If the strength for the other beginning were to be granted to us at all, it would only accrue to us insofar as the fundamental mood of the first beginning is not past but, to speak in the language of *Being and Time*, is something having-been (*Gewesenes*) that is still historically efficacious.[38] However, there is another systematic consideration that does not seem to accord with this assumption. Even the wonder which called forth the first beginning was, like every fundamental mood, ambivalent before it was brought forth out of its latency as a mere possibility for Dasein. By what means, then, was Dasein tuned to the readiness and ability to let wonder come into relief in its authenticity? The question seems to lead us to an infinite regress, an unending questioning back to the most incipient mood. But phenomenologically this is a mere appearance. Wonder in the sense of θαυμάζειν, which institutes the beginning is a unique mood: it is in itself in the position to attune Dasein to authenticity. It distinguishes itself from all other moods by the fact that it harbors within itself the force to institute the beginning. It thereby dispels any fear of an infinite regress. Certainly, one can still ask why the immanent strength of wonder to begin became factically effective precisely at the time of the Greeks. But here we must once again recall that it would be an improper and therefore futile effort for philosophical thinking to want to dissipate the contingency of the historical efficacy of a fundamental mood with an answer to this question.[39]

The unique character of wonder, namely, that it carries in itself the force to institute the beginning authentically, can be gleaned from the phenomenal content of this mood. Heidegger described the fundamental trait of wonder in the lecture course of the winter semester of 1937–38 in the following manner: wonder lets the familiar appear as unfamiliar (cf. GA 45: 167) and therefore plunges the human being into the aporia[40] of which Aristotle speaks in the *Metaphysics*.[41]

Although Heidegger's account was correct, he overlooked something decisive. When the familiar becomes unfamiliar, the world in its entirety comes forth to the person struck with wonder as though it were appearing to him for the first time, as though it were something entirely new and surprising. As mentioned, according to *Being and Time*, fundamental moods have a reflexive trait, so to speak, insofar as they bring Dasein face-to-face with its self. Because it is the unexpected new emergence of the world that throws the person struck with wonder back on himself, he experiences his self as a newborn child for whom the light of the world has just dawned. At the same time, there is a movement of awakening; the day of the world breaks forth and invites the person struck with wonder to fashion a new beginning by entering into the possibilities which the world holds ready in its morning freshness. Heidegger, in his lecture course of 1937–38, did indeed perceive the unexpectedness and the freshness which characterize the world, but he did not see that they attune the self in a movement of awakening.[42]

To be sure, this awakening has two faces. On the one hand, the world entices the person struck with wonder by the freshness of its novelty. On the other hand, the unexpectedness of this novelty captivates him and instills in him a reservedness with respect to the world, a reverence in the face of the wonder "that there is something at all rather than nothing," an awe[43] in the face of the mystery that the dimension of openness, "world," has been freed from the reticence of the nothing.[44] In this way, a countermovement manifests itself in awe. The person struck with wonder is carried along in the movement of the wonderful new emergence of the world and becomes attuned to the awakening to the world. In this connection, it lets him hold on to himself in the face of the abyss exposed by the new emergence.[45]

The countermovement between being carried away and being in awe in relation to the world founds the ambivalence between inauthenticity and authenticity; as a latent possibility for Dasein, it is an ambivalence that belongs to wonder as to every fundamental mood. The deficient, inauthentic form of wonder is an enchantedness with the world devoid of awe or timidity. That is, uninhibited, driving curiosity chases down everything that appears in some way as surprising or "wonderful" in this superficial sense (cf. *GA* 45: 180).

Heidegger took note of the aspect of awakening peculiar to wonder only in its deficient mode. And this is probably the reason why he hardly glimpsed the fundamental trait of authentic wonder, the being attuned to the ability-to-begin. He tacitly equated this fundamental trait with that of just any driven curiosity devoid of awe. Thus he did not notice that there is also an ability-to-begin, which is tuned and tempered by an awe-inspired wonder. I shall address this phenomenon of authentic wonder at the end of my reflection. But first I should like to pursue with Heidegger wonder in its inauthenticity.

Being and Time makes this inauthenticity thematic as that curiosity which Augustine had already described as the vice of *curiositas*, that flies in the face of itself in its avarice for ever new things (cf. *SZ* 170ff.). In the ontohistorical turn after *Being and Time*, we encounter this curiosity as ἱστορίη, that worldwide circumspective knowledge-gathering already criticized by Heraclitus as the "learning of many things" and said by him to be characteristic of the "polymath" and peculiar to the earliest science.[46] This self-criticism is the historical example for the fact that wonder, which institutes the beginning, was indeed from the very start accompanied by a deficient mode of itself. Knowledge gathering can be carried away without awe in the movement of the dawning of the world. Wonder abandons itself onesidedly and focuses exclusively on the emergence of beings out of concealedness into presence.[47]

Heidegger occasionally characterizes this emergence as presencing (*Anwesung*).[48] Taken by presencing, the Greeks elevated φύσις, ἀλήθεια, and ἰδέα to the key terms of beginning philosophy. Because they were thoroughly enchanted with and carried away by presencing, the Greeks were thwarted, in preserving their wondering awe, in considering expressly the concealedness of the withdrawal out of which beings are delivered over into presence.[49] Thus, Being came to be understood primarily as presence, thereby leading metaphysics down the path of the forgetfulness of the withdrawal.

Heidegger therefore directed his full attention to the ambivalence of incipient wonder and especially toward inauthenticity interpreted ontohistorically, in order to make the anticipation of another beginning phenomenologically binding. The hope of such another beginning could not be sustained were an ambivalence not able to be shown in the phenomenon of origins on which the philosophy of the tradition depended. A possibility for thought was in play in the origin which went unnoticed; but from the very beginning it could have been seized.[50] This ambivalence can be seen concretely in the phenomenon of incipient wonder. It adumbrates the horizon of expectation for the thinking peculiar to the other beginning. Against this background, the other beginning stands out as that historical situation in which awe could for the first time come to the fore in its authenticity, whereas in the wonder of the first beginning, awe remained devoid of historical efficacy.

One can follow Heidegger's characterization of the present situation of philosophy from this phenomenological foundation. But then one must revise his thesis that the fundamental mood of wonder has definitively vanished from the present scene (cf. GA 45: 184). Only in the readiness and strength needed for the historical ability-to-begin is it possible for contemporary fundamental moods, e.g., anxiety, boredom, fright, not to lead to petrifaction or doubt, as one normally expects when such moods dominate. Heidegger maintains that this normal expectation arises from the perspective of inauthenticity, and that those fundamental moods, which are viewed inauthentically as destructive, grant to Dasein the strength for historically formative works. But then this contention can only be seriously maintained when one presupposes the persistence of the fundamental mood of the ability-to-begin, through which the destructive inauthenticity of those fundamental moods can be mastered.

From this it inevitably follows that Heidegger's assessment of the present situation cannot be our own. Though our age may be regarded as an *epoch* of transition, it is not a transition to a wholly other beginning; rather—to employ the language of *Being and Time*—it is a transition to the reenactment (*Wieder-holung*, "repetition") of the first beginning which has-been. A restoration of Greek beginnings is in no way implied here. The clarity of the θαυμάζειν in the first beginning of the Greeks was from the outset clouded by a falling into the inauthenticity of that curiosity peculiar to ἱστορίη. Nothing would be gained, therefore, by merely entering into this type of wonder for a second time.

History viewed in terms of being-attuned in moods demands today a thoughtful reflection on the awe which resonates in authentic wonder, an awe, that is, which tunes Dasein into the readiness and the ability to accord with withdrawal as withdrawal. In this sense, it is proper to re-enact (re-peat) the wonder of the first beginning in a thoughtfully reflective wonder. But thinking can be thoughfully reflective only by virtue of historical experience since the time of the Greeks. This experience speaks as a need and a necessity out of the fundamental moods of the modern world: anxiety, fright, boredom. Thus we cannot refrain from going through such fundamental moods. It seems to me that we cannot contest the correctness of Heidegger's phenomenological analysis of fundamental mood insofar as he insisted upon the unavoidability of modern fundamental moods; we can only question the fact that—with some intimations aside—he did not recognize the persistence of the authentic historical force of beginning, unique to wonder, in the overall project of his thought.

Perhaps from the very beginning Heidegger had the tendency to underplay the continuity between the task of beginning incumbent upon us today with the first beginning of the Greeks. He therefore already admits in *Being and Time* to *a* fundamental temperment wherein the ontological modality of being-possible *as* being-possible is opened up to Dasein, namely, as anxiety. In anxiety, being-possible as such, the Da or *there* of world-openness, is confronted with the possibility of its impossibility, with the reticence of the nothing. Certainly, the conflict between these poles is constitutive of Dasein. But it can be regarded systematically as it were from two directions: toward the way in which the nothing holds its own against the Da, and vice versa.

The first instance concerns the way in which the impossibility, the nothing, which withdraws every type of support from us, tempers the ability-to-be in the fundamental temperment of anxiety. In the resoluteness of the moment, anxiety makes possible advancing toward death, that is, authentic futurity. This is the direction of Heidegger's thought. But it is also possible to cast a glance in the opposite direction by considering how Dasein as able-to-be is released from the reticence of the nothing, of the world. This releasing likewise tempers Dasein in a fundamental temperment with respect to wonder as the triumph of being-possible over impossibility, i.e., wonder as being in "high spirits" for the ability-to-begin. This fundamental temperment makes possible in the "moment" the authentic having-been, the ecstatic coming back to the emergence of the ability-to-be and of the world-openness out of beginning reticence.[51] But this, corresponding to the advancing toward death, is the reenactment (re-petition) of birth; for birth is the emergence of being-possible from the reticence, the withholding of the womb.

Dasein exists as being-possible, as project (*Entwurf*), in the confrontation with the withdrawal of being-possible. Dasein is attuned through this process by birth and death. The thrownness (*Geworfenheit*) of the project is primarily the thrownness of birth, that is, release out of the dark protective enclosure of withdrawal into the ability-to-be as ability-to-begin. Thrownness understood in this way attunes Dasein to wonder in the fundamental temperment of the ability-to-begin. Only through the fundamental temperment of anxiety can conscience call Dasein into authenticity. But this does not yet explain the readiness and capability to act historically in the resoluteness of the moment. Dasein can do this because, from the fundamental temperment of wonder, it can re-peat birth in the inauguration of beginnings.[52]

In *Being and Time* Heidegger only intimated that birth is the authentic having-been of Dasein, but later he clearly expressed it.[53] In his first Hölderlin lecture course of 1934–35, he commented on the fourth stanza of the "Rhein-Hymne" which reads: "Das Meiste nämlich vermag die Geburt und der Lichtstrahl, der dem Neugebornen begegnet." Heidegger reads the *und* (and) between *Geburt* (birth) and *Lichtstrahl* (ray of light) as the expression of a correlation between two powers which are at the same time interdependent and conflictual (cf. *GA* 39: 244, 248, 428). Opposing birth as the power of origin out of the reticence of the womb (cf. *GA* 39: 247) is the ray of light as "essential in-sighting" "in which the profusion of a great willing thrusts toward becoming-form."[54] The creative power of the "moment" appears in this way to be opposed to the power of birth-related origin. It seems to me, however, to be more appropriate to the sense of the matter and more consistent with the text to understand "birth and ray of light" as the double name for one and the same thing: the historically founding power of the "moment" that flashes forth as a ray of light is nothing other than birth, namely, the emergence from the reticence of the womb into the openness of the ability-to-be. This is expressed in its authenticity as the ability-to-begin.

Just as no one can take over my death for me, a death which I look in the face in "advancing", I also experience my birth authentically as something inexchangeably my own. In the ability-to-begin I am also put in relation purely to myself. But the "moment" precisely opens the communal world to me in this radical individualization. The resoluteness of the ability-to-begin founds the authenticity of being-with-one-another. Wonder in the mode of authenticity, that is, awe as retained, tunes Dasein to being in awe of the birth-related mystery of others' ability-to-begin. In being-with, this awe is the refusal to want to take control over the radical individualization of the other in the authenticity of his ability-to-begin.

An intimate form of this awe, when it takes place among a small number of people, is love. The Greeks discovered another form in the πόλις that was suited for human beings in their plurality; and in this decisive respect they had the good fortune to retain the authenticity of this wonder. Heidegger could not do justice to the preservation of authentic wonder with his interpretation of the fundamental mood of the Greek beginning because his phenomenology of Dasein did not receive its due with respect to being-born.

The strength to create works which lies in the "moment" shapes a historical world. Authentic wonder enabled the Greeks to inaugurate and institute a new type of common world which was determined exclusively by the ability-to-begin. The open dimension of being-in-the-world is disclosed in this type of world precisely through the mutual recognition, in reciprocal awe, of a plurality of human beings who are able-to-begin. Although Heidegger often spoke about the Greek πόλις,[55] that which actually pertained to the πόλις—namely, the "political,"[56] the world of the πόλις that reveals itself as the public space of those who are-able-to begin—this world phenomenon remained closed owing to his one-sided view of wonder.

Thus, he employed the concept "public" exclusively in a pejorative sense and misunderstood the world character of the πόλις-publicness which his student Hanna Arendt discovered.[57] Through the mutual recognition of those who are able-to-begin, on account of their birth-relatedness, their natality, as Hannah Arendt formulates, the πόλις becomes a public community. It has the unique instituting sense of making possible and preserving the integration of being-possible as being-possible, that is, as being able-to-begin in being-with. Democracy was the name the Greeks gave to the novel and unique world-historical form of community which does justice to this authentic phenomenon of the political.

The mutual recognition of those who are able-to-begin is reflected in democracy by a peculiar countermovement. In order to maintain the world character in its public community, individuals must be ready to step out into the public qua political world. As able to begin, they can only do this by publicly expounding, in their respective views, the grounds for which communal action should begin. The Greeks called this oral public exposition of the grounds for beginning λόγον διδόναι, rendering account. But in this public exposition of the reasons for beginning, the birth-related mystery of individuals' ability-to-begin, the abyss of withdrawal out of which the ability-to-begin authentically takes place, remains withdrawn from publicness. The abyss (*Abgrund*) tempers and determinately tunes the public account given in terms of reasons (*Gründe*). But the abyss is publicly in play only as that nameless inaccessibility by virtue of which those rendering account never ultimately coincide in their reasons; there is always a surplus. Thus, they are never fully successful in reaching unity about communal action. Democracy recognizes precisely this point. It is always ready to let the conflict of accounts begin again. As long as this readiness is kept alive, democracy is tempered by the fundamental mood of awe. Through this awe, the "many" are all recognized at the same time as the individuals who are able-to-begin. The plurality of the "many" creates the public sphere in democracy—the form of the state of the many. Here, the alternative between the individualized authentically existing few and the inauthentically existing many is overcome. Heidegger offered two possible interpretations of λόγος, account, in λόγον διδόναι. Behind these two interpretations lie the alternatives of authenticity and inauthenticity. Λόγος appears in Heidegger, on the one hand, as the gathering unity that releases beings out of the concealedness of the withdrawal in the openness of presencing.[58] Λόγος thus understood is already in Heraclitus a matter for the few in the individualization of their resoluteness for the first beginning, just as in Heidegger's *Contributions* it is once again the solitary few who go toward the other beginning (cf. *GA 65*: 28, 96f., 319, 343, 414). On the other hand, λόγος appears in the mode of inauthenticity; whether with the Greeks or with us today, it appears as the computing, calculating account of the many related to curiosity—which, likewise, Heraclitus already criticized (cf. *GA 39*: 165).

In both interpretations, Heidegger misses the λόγος harbored in the Greek conception of the πόλις.[59] Λόγος is that type of speaking with one another through which awe enters into the public community of the many, making possible the authenticity of the few. The modern declaration of "the rights of man" and specifically of the freedom of the individual, has its original philosophical justification in awe; it tempers the mutual recognition of those who, since the time of ancient Greece, are able *to* begin on account of their natality.[60]

Contrary to Heidegger's predominant assumption, the birth-related fundamental mood of awe in the scope of Western history is not extinct but shows itself above all in this context. Heidegger could not see the uniqueness still distinguishing the liberal democracy of "the rights of man" rooted in the Greek beginning.[61] Thus, it could appear to him as just another "machination," another manifestation of the forgetfulness of Being.[62] He saw no reason in the decade following *Being and Time* to make it the criterion for a critique of National Socialism nor, in his late period, the occasion to expect from democracy anything more advantageous for the future than could ensue from any type of totalitarian system. Here we must go beyond Heidegger. But we can only do so precisely because he took the philosophy of our century a decisive step further through the phenomenology of being-in-the-world with respect to fundamental mood.

NOTES

1. In the thirties Heidegger continually resorted to these three types of work; cf., for example, *GA* 39: 144.

2. Without knowledge of the texts from the 1930s which were not yet published, I attempted initially and provisionally in 1980 to find Heidegger's answer to the question concerning bindingness. See my article "Heideggers These vom Ende der Philosophie," in *Zeitschrift für philosophische Forschung* 33 (1980). With this work I hope to have offered a critique which is more just in regard to Heidegger's intentions.

3. Regarding this point see Michel Haar, "Stimmung et pensée," in *Heidegger et l'idée de la phénoménologie* (Dordrecht: Kluwer, 1988); *Phaenomenologica* 108: 267; hereafter cited as "Stimmung." The following expostion is indebted to the significant clarification of the concept of mood presented in Haar's article.

4. Cf., for example, *GA* 65: 21, 45f., 96ff., 123, and *GA* 45: 129, 155.

5. I have attempted to explain in what sense the development of Heidegger's thought from *Sein und Zeit* can be interpreted as a consistent radicalization of the "world-problematic" inaugurated by Husserl in the work, "Heidegger und das Prinzip der Phäno-menologie," in *Heidegger und die praktische Philosophie*, eds. A. Gethmann-Siefert and Otto Pöggeler (Frankfurt: Suhrkamp, 1988).

6. See *SZ* 138: "Wir müssen in der Tat *ontologisch* grundsätzlich die primäre Entdeckung der Welt er 'blossen Stimmung"uberlassen," and *GA* 39: 82: "Die Stimmung als Stimmung lasst die Offenbarkeit des Seienden geschehen"; *GA* 39: 141: Die Welteröffnung geschieht in der Grundstimmung."

7. With a view to this elementary context, Heidegger can write in *GA* 45: 154: ". . . die recht verstandene Stimmung führt zu einer Überwindung der bisherigen Auffassung des Menschen."

8. See *US* 252.

9. Translator's note: Heidegger's expression *"Befindlichkeit"* is rendered here as "temperment." The standard rendition "state-of-mind" suggests a static, subjective, internalized "condition." And although the term "situatedness" would be much less misleading in this regard, I believe the term "temperment" is more adequate, first, because it resonates well with the German *Stimmung* and the English translation "mood"; and second, because temperment also plays on the active sense of the verb, "to temper" as with glass or metal, which is again similar to the sense of "to tune" (*stimmen*). Thus, as tuned or mooded (*gestimmt*) being-in-the-world, Dasein is "tempered." Accordingly, temper-ment is the way in which the world is opened or disclosed to Dasein.

10. In the authenticity I am inescapably myself, and that attains prominence that is unmistakeably my own. "My own" is expressed in Greek by αμτός, from which the English word "authentic" is derived. By not evading what is my own, my self-being as it were, or in Greek my "αμτός-being," my own existence becomes authentic.

11. Cf., for example, *GA* 4: 173: ". . . die rechte Zeit, wann es die Zeit ist: der geschichtliche Augenblick."

12. Cf. *WP* 36: ". . . erst auf dem Grunde der Gestimmtheit . . . empfängt das Sagen des Entsprechens . . . seine Be-stimmtheit."

13. Cf. *GA* 39: 143: "In der Stimmung geschieht die eröffnende Ausgesetztheit in das Seinde. Darin liegt zugleich, dass das Dasein des Menschen in sich schon versetzt ist in das Dasein Anderer, d.h. nur *ist*, wie es ist, im Mitsein mit den Anderen. Das Dasein ist wesenhaft Miteinandersein, Für-und Gegeneinandersein." Similarly, Heidegger had already explained in *SZ* that resoluteness ". . . gleichursprünglich die in ihr fundierte Entdeckheit der 'Welt' und die Erschlossenheit des Mitdaseins der Anderen (modifiziert). Die zuhandene 'Welt' wird nicht 'inhaltlich' eine andere, der Kreis der Anderen wird nicht ausgewechselt, und doch ist das verstehende besorgende Sein zum Zuhandenen und das fürsorgende Mitsein mit den Anderen jetzt aus deren eigenstem Selbsteinkönnen heraus bestimmt." In this connection also see clarification in F.-W. von Herrmann, *Heideggers Philosophie der Kunst* (Frankfurt a.M.: Klostermann, 1980), 342f.

14. See the afterword to "Was ist Metaphysik?" in *GA* 9: 307: ". . . nahe bei der wesenhaften Angst *als* dem Schrecken des Abgrunds wohnt die Scheu" (my emphasis). See also the introduction to "Was ist Metaphysik?" of 1949 in *GA* 9: 371, where he writes that anxiety is 'sent' by fright.

15. In *GA* 65: 204 Heidegger speaks of the thrownness of human Dasein, which manifests itself, according to *SZ*, in an authentic manner through the fundamental temperament of anxiety: "Die Geworfenheit geschieht und bezeugt sich zumal in der Not der Seinsverlassenheit und in der Notwendigkeit der Entscheidung." Cf. *GA* 45: 197f.

16. See *GA* 29/30: 242: "Wir fragen nach einer tiefen Langeweile, nach *einer*—d.h. einer *bestimmten,* d.h. einer solchen *unseres* Daseins, nicht nach der tiefen Langeweile so überhaupt und im allgemeinen." The relationship between fundamental moods as, so to speak, transhistorical possibilities of Dasein and their historical referentiality is the main topic of the investigation of Michel Haar in his "Stimmung."

17. See Heidegger's marginal note form 1949 to "Was ist Metaphysik?" in *GA* 9: 111.

18. See *GA* 29/30: 244f.: Deep boredom and authentic anxiety have indifference in common. Cf. "Was ist Metaphysik?" in *GA* 9: 111.

19. See, for instance, *GA* 65: 126.

Translator's note: Unfortunately, the English term "machination" does not convey the sense of the German *Machenschaft* which has as its root, *machen,* which means "to do" or "to make."

20. See, for example, *GA* 65: 11, 24, 125.

21. In this sense every leading mood arises from the "Lust der fragenden wechselweisen Übersteigerung der Anfänge" (*GA* 65: 169).

22. See, for example, *GA* 65: 396.

23. Thus, this fundamental mood is awe in the face of reminiscent sounding (*Aklang*) of the *Ereignis* (*GA* 65: 396).

24. Concerning awe, see *GA* 4: 131f. in addition to *GA* 65.

25. See, for example, *GA* 65: 8, 14ff., *GA* 107: 395f., and *GA* 45: 2: "Die Verhaltenheit ist jene Stimmung, in der jenes Erschrecken nicht überwunden und beseitigt, sondern durch die Scheu gerade bewahrt und verwahrt ist."

26. See, for example, *GA* 65: 31: "Die Verhaltenheit ist der ausgezeichnete augenblickliche Bezug zum Ereignis im Angerufensein durch dessen Zuruf," *GA* 65: 34: "Verhaltenheit stimmt den jeweiligen gründenden Augenblick . . ."

27. M. Haar already suspects the same connection in his investigation, "Stimmung."

Because holding-back (to speak the language of *SZ*) is the mood of authenticity, Heidegger can say in *GA* 65 that it would let the leading moods of fright and awe arise.

28. See *GA* 29/30: 245ff.

29. See *GA* 39: 142: ". . . ich bin zu nichts aufgelegt—die Urform der Langeweile, die ihrerseits bis zu einer Grundstimmung sich entfalten kann."

30. In the sense in which Heidegger speaks of the diverse ambiguity of the contemporary fundamental mood in *WP* 42f.

31. According to *GA* 65: 304, as projecting itself and opening to the world and as being thrown, what Dasein accomplishes is "nothing . . . other than the beginning of the counter-swing in Being (Seyn)."

32. See *GA* 65: 14ff., 21ff.

33. See *WP*, 42f.

34. See *GA* 65: 22: The "tuning idea *as to the onset*" [*Stimmende Einfall*] of the fundamental mood must "fundamentally remain a coincidence [*Zu-fall*]."

35. Cf. *SZ* 136: ". . . Herr werden wir der Stimmung nie stimmungsfrei sondern je aus einer Gegenstimmung," and *GA* 39: 142: "Weil das Dasein—sofern es ist—gestimmt ist, deshalb kann die Stimmung je nur durch eine Gegenstimmung umgestimmt werden, und eine Umstimmung von Grund aus vermag nur eine Grundstimmung zu erwirken. . . ."

36. See *Theaetetus* 155d and *Metaphysik* A 2, 982b12ff.

37. See above all, *WP* 38f., as well as *GA* 45: 155ff. and 170: "Das Erstaunen versetzt erst in und vor das Seiende als ein solches. Solche Versetzung selbst ist das eigentliche Stimmen der Grundstimmung. Grundstimmung heisst sie, weil sie stimmend den Menschen in Solches versetzt, worauf und worin Wort, Werk, Tat als geschehende gegründet werden und Geschichte anfangen kann."

38. Cf. *GA* 65: 186: "Hätte diese Not (scil.: der Seinsvergessenheit) nicht die Grösse der Herkunft aus dem ersten Anfang, woher nähme sie dann die Kraft der Nötigung in die Bereitschaft für den anderen (scil.: Anfang)?" See also *GA* 65: 434f. and *GA* 45: 197: Fright as fundamental mood of the other beginning ". . . harbors in itself its way . . . of the new wonder."

39. According to Heidegger, the Aristotelian determination of wonder as πάθος also essentially tends toward this contingency of being overcome by the need of the fundamental mood. See *GA* 45: 175.

40. This helplessness is a holding-fast of the inexplicable in the face of which Dasein finds itself in wonder: cf. *GA* 175 and 168.

41. See *Metaphysics* A 2, 982d17–18.

42. In *GA* 65: 434, Heidegger does characterize that which is new in the other beginning, but nevertheless as the "freshness of the originariness of beginning again."

43. M. Haar also emphasizes the connection between wonder and awe in his "Stimmung," 274 n. 3.

44. See "Was ist Metaphysik?" in *W* 121.

45. See *WP* 40: θαυμάζειν "ist, als dieses Zurücktreten und dieses Ansichhalten, zugleich hingerissen zu dem und gleichsam gefesselt durch das, wovor es zurücktritt."

46. For Heidegger's later critique of curiosity and ἱστορία see, for instance, *GA* 45: 134 and 156, and *GA* 4: 76. Concerning the critique of the "learning of many things" in Heraclitus (fragment Diels B 40), see my *Heraklit, Parmenides und der Anfang von Philosophie und Wissenschaft. Eine phänomenologische Besinnung* (Berlin: De Gruyter, 1980), 75 and 188ff.

47. Even in his latest period, Heidegger interprets it in the same sense; cf. *GA* 15: 331f.

48. In addition to *GA* 65, see, for example, *GA* 45: 19.

49. According to the *GA* 65: 189, self-withdrawing, which is to say, the fact that the primacy of presence remained unquestioned in the Greeks, "verbirgt sich selbst als solches und lässt für das anfängliche Denken einzig das Un-geheure des Aufgehens—der ständigen

Anwesung in der Offenheit (ἀλήθεια) des Seienden selbst—die Wesung ausmachen. Wesung, ohne als solche begriffen zu werden, ist Anwesung."

50. See, for example, *GA* 65: 169, 179, 187. According to *GA* 65: 434f., the inauguration of beginning in the "other beginning" is something that "in die verborgene Zukunft des ersten Anfangs sich hinauswagt."

51. Concerning the authentic having-been as coming-back-to-birth, see F.-W. von Herrmann, *Heideggers Philosophie der Kunst* (Frankfurt a.M.: 1980), 77.

52. In this sense one could say with Arendt—contrary to Heidegger's one-sided determination of authentic Dasein regarding the "advancing towards death"—that "men, though they must die, are not born in order to die but in order to begin," *The Human Condition* (New York: Doubleday, 1959), 222.

53. See *SZ* 391 in connection with *SZ* 373f., and *GA* 39: 242ff.; see also *GA* 4: 148f. n.

54. See *GA* 39: 243.
Translator's note: ". . . steht der Lichtstrahl als der 'Wesensblick' gegenüber, 'in dem die Überfülle eines grossen Wollens der Gestaltwerdung entgegendrängt.'"

55. Above all, on the occasion of his repeated interpretation of the first chorus from Sophocles' *Antigone:* see *EM* 161f. and *GA* 53: 97.

56. Heidegger also employs this concept, for example, in *GA* 4: 88: "Die polis bestimmt 'das Politische.'"

57. That Heidegger could have developed an authentic, i.e., political concept of publicness on the basis of his expansive knowledge of the history of ideas seen, for example, in his definition of the Latin "res publica" in *VA* 173: ". . . das, was jeden im Volke offenkundig angeht, ihn 'hat' und darum öffentlich verhandelt wird."

58. See, for instance, the article "Logos" in *VA*, esp. 211 and 228f.

59. Concerning the historical-systematic clarification of the early concept of λόγος, see my book on the Pre-Socratics (cited above in n. 46), 174ff. I have attempted to clarify the sense of the political λόγον διδόναι in the Greeks from the beginning of philosophy in the following articles: "Die Zweideutigkeit der *Doxa* und die Verwirklichung des modernen Rechsstaats," in *Meinungsfreiheit—Grundgedanken und Geschichte in Europa und USA,* eds. J. Schwardtländer and D. Willoweit (Kehl a. Rh. and Strassburg: 1986); and "Husserl und die Griechen," in *Phänomenologische Forschungen* 22 (1989). I have already presented my critique of Heidegger's interpretation of λόγος διδόναι in another form in the article "Heidegger und das Prinzip der Phänomenologie" (see n. 5 above).

60. The dignity of individuals declared in the declaration of the Rights of Man is, according to Arendt, based on "being born" (*Human Condition,* 158).

61. The typical Western tradition of freedom is renewed again and again from the birth-related ability-to-begin; it is therefore a result of "Renaissances"; see Hannah Arendt, *The Life of the Mind* (New York: Harcourt, Brace, Jovanovich, 1978), 2: 212, 217. For the significance of being-born for the European tradition of thought, see my "Husserls These von der Europäisierung der Menschheit," in *Phänomenologie im Widerstreit,* eds. C. Jamme and O. Pöggeler (Frankfurt a.M. Suhrkamp, 1989).

62. Nevertheless, in *GA* 65: 38, Heidegger does admit once that in the self-opinionatedness of the democratic conflict of opinion, which "requires leaving everyone to their own opinion," a remnant of genuine philosophy makes itself felt. Concerning the philosophical interpretation of the modern declaration of the Rights of Man from the Greek beginning, see my article mentioned above in n. 59.

VII

HEIDEGGER IN
CHINA

S H I - Y I N G Z H A N G

16. Heidegger and Taoism

TAOIST INVOLVEMENT WITH OUTSIDE THINGS AND HEIDEGGER'S *VERFALLEN*

As a being in the world, it is necessary for each man to have dealings with outside things and with other men. The modern German philosopher Martin Heidegger called such a situation "Verfallen." Since human being, or using Heidegger's term, "Dasein," is not an isolated being but a "Being-in-the-world," so *Verfallen* is unavoidable, belonging necessarily to care (*Sorge*), the most fundamental state of man's "Being-in-the-world." The ancient Chinese philosophical school of Taoism and its forerunner Yang Zhu called such a state "involvement with outside things," and Zi Hua Zi—as quoted by Lu Shi Chun Qiu—called it "suffering tortures from life."

Facing such a situation, according to Heidegger, Dasein cannot but make one choice: "to win itself"—which means that Dasein is unwilling to fall, or "to lose itself" (BT 68). In Chinese philosophy this choice is called "for oneself"; its opposite is called "for others." But "for oneself" is by no means selfishness, and "for others" is by no means simple sacrifice.

In *Lun Yu Ji Zhu*, Zhu Xi, the Chinese philosopher of the Sung Dynasty, commented that "'for oneself' means that one seeks for self-satisfaction, while 'for others' means that one seeks for fame." If one searches for fame, he will "finally lose himself"; while if one searches for self-satisfaction, he will "finally become a person-able man." "For others"—which means "to lose oneself"—corresponds in Heidegger's language to Dasein's losing itself, while "for oneself"—which means "to become a person-able man"—corresponds to Dasein's winning itself.

Also, "for others" and "for oneself" are two different attitudes toward life. Liu Zong Yuan (773–819), the Chinese writer and thinker of the Tang Dynasty, once said, "When I was young, I was full of dashing spirit and could not detect the danger of the mind of man and the subtlety of the mind of Tao, did not mind what others had said, but stated my views frankly." Such behavior results from the attitude "for oneself." On the contrary, if one follows the will of others and is simply a yes-man without an independent personality who lives for others, such behavior results from the attitude "for others." A man who behaves in this way will "lose himself." This is deplored in China because it means losing one's personality. Heidegger also held that ordinary men were all inclined to fall—namely, "to lose oneself" in Chinese terms, but he advocated that man, Dasein, should choose the way by which to win itself, which is similar to being "for oneself" or to "valuing oneself" and "valuing life" in Chinese Taoism. Both Heidegger and Taoism held that the real value of man's life lies in being "for oneself" instead of "losing oneself." These concepts resulted from dissatisfaction with reality and hatred of the world and its ways, and all had positive significances in their own times and for their own people. It is well known that Heidegger was not satisfied with the situation of losing oneself in modern industrial societies, and I need not dwell on this. What I want to stress here—in relation to Heidegger—is the background and influences of Taoism and its forerunner Yang Zhu's thought in the history of Chinese philosophy.

Yang Zhu advocated "each for himself," which does not mean simply selfishness, but "completeness of living and preservation of what is genuine," and not becoming involved with outside things. Mencius, a representative of the Confucian school, once condemned Yang's thought for being "without a sovereign," which indicated that Yang opposed sovereignty, opposed following the will of others, and that he intended to be a man "for himself" and not to "lose himself." As a successor of Yang Zhu, Lao Tse also said much about "valuing one's person" and "valuing life and despising wealth." What he taught was that man should choose the way of being "for oneself" (which is similar in Heidegger to Dasein's winning itself) and not that of losing oneself (which is quite analogous to Dasein's losing itself). Lao Tse's philosophy was the antithesis of the Confucian doctrine that declared "subdue one's self and return to propriety" and that means that everyone should conform to the propriety of the rulers, even at the price of "losing oneself." We can say that valuing self, valuing one's life, and each being for himself are a counterattack on the Confucian doctrine "subdue one's self."

Chi Kang (223–262) and Yuan Ji (210–263) of the Wei-Jin period, who interpreted Taoist philosophy, advocated that "one should conform to nature in disregard of the classical Confucian tradition." Yuan Ji said, "If the sage has no house, Heaven and Earth will contain him; if the sage has no master, Heaven and Earth will own him; if the sage has nothing to do, he is free to walk under Heaven and on the Earth." "The sage will not get involved with fame and wealth." Both Chi Kang and Yuan Ji were noble and refined scholars who were not resigned to the loss of self or *Verfallen*. Tao Yuan Ming (365–427), the writer and thinker of the Eastern-Jin period, also despised fame and wealth and refused to lower himself to make a living, and many of his poems expressed the Taoist appreciation of quiet and freedom, valuing living and despising wealth. So, although belonging to different times and different countries, the Taoist philosophy of "valuing one's life," "valuing oneself," and Heidegger's philosophy of not being resigned to *Verfallen* and loss of self can reflect and inspire each other and have a similar spirit and historical influence. Heidegger's philosophy does not accord with the traditional German thought represented by Hegel, just as Taoist philosophy flies its own colors in the history of Chinese philosophy. Both Heidegger and the Taoists were against tradition.

Unfortunately, at all times and in all countries, those who are not resigned to *Verfallen*, to loss of self, are often blamed or even killed. Why? At the early stage of the history of human thought, Taoism, being naive and simple, could give no detailed theoretical analysis and answer to this phenomenon, while Heidegger as a modern Western philosopher offered a profound explanation. In Heidegger's view, since Dasein is "Being-in-the-world," it is necessarily thrown into the state of "entering the world," in which it is inclined to act according to external criteria and the will of others that correspond to such Chinese declarations as "it has been so since ancient times," "everyone thinks and does so," "this is the custom," and "the final conclusion has been reached." If we call the above-mentioned criteria "others" (*der Andere*), we can describe this situation in another way: in everyday life, the words, deeds, and even moods of ordinary people are inclined to depend on others, or in other words, on *das Man* ("they"), (*BT* 163), not on themselves. That is to say, ordinary people always give up and lose themselves and live for others. Heidegger regarded the state of *Verfallen* as inauthenticity, which is similar to the Chinese term "losing oneself"; and the state of throwing off *Verfallen* and refusing to bend to others he regarded as authenticity, which is similar to what Taoism called "preservation of what is genuine." Heidegger argued that since all ordinary people acted according to others, everything conspicuous or outstanding was noiselessly suppressed and everyone lived by approximating to the average, or in Chinese terms, went "the middle way," which killed man's personality and independent action. In China we have a proverb: "The highest tree in a forest is bound to be blown down by the wind." Here the "wind" is similar to Heidegger's "others" or "they." Among the world's teeming millions, those who can fly their own colors are few and far between, and only a few of the "highest trees" dare to defy public opinion, preferring to be killed rather than to lose themselves. On the other hand, ordinary people are always inclined to live for others at the price of losing themselves and thus fall into inauthenticity for fear of authenticity. In the history of Chinese philosophy, Confucianism, being the orthodox school of thought, advocated "the middle way," which is similar to Heidegger's "average," and warned those "higher trees" of the danger of being blown down by the wind, while Taoism valued the nobility of refusing to cater to current fashion and becoming enfettered by the Confucian ethical code. I wholeheartedly hope that we in China will succeed in sweeping aside the Confucian tradition and will develop Taoism, at the same time absorb Heidegger's thought of not being resigned to *Verfallen*, absorb it in such a way as to enrich Taoist thought.

TAOIST RETURN TO INFANCY AND HEIDEGGER'S RETURN TO AUTHENTICITY

How can we avoid getting involved with outside things, or in Heidegger's words, succumbing to *Verfallen*? Taoism and Heidegger had different views and answers.

Heidegger advocated the primacy of praxis and opposed the subject-object separation. In his view, Dasein as Being-in-the-world is not, first of all, defined by the subject-object relation nor by cognition; it is rather essentially care or concern: "Ontically as well as ontologically, the priority belongs to Being-in-the-world as concern" (*BT* 85). "Knowing is a kind of Being which belongs to Being-in-the-world" (*BT* 90). "The kind of dealing which is closest to us is, as we have shown, not a bare perceptual cognition, but rather that kind of concern which manipulates things and puts them to use; and this has its own kind of 'knowledge'. The phenomenological question applies in the first instance to the Being of those entities which we encounter in such concern" (*BT* 95). "The ready-to-hand is not grasped theoretically at all" (*BT* 99). Heidegger held that the mathematicalization and calculation of science would make Being as φύσις forgotten, so he attached importance to the incalculable. But this does not mean that his thought is antiscientific; what he stressed is only that we first grasp things through being alongside them rather than by thinking about them. According to Heidegger, the subject-object dichotomy tends to take the self out of the world, placing it before the world as a spectator stands before a picture. But to be a self is, according to Heidegger, to experience the things from within the world. What Heidegger said here is quite similar to what the Taoist Chuang Tse once said: "The universe and I came into being together; and I, and everything therein, are One." The subject-object dichotomy is the antithesis between everything and I. In Heidegger's view the difference between the being of Dasein as Being-in-the-world and the being of other things lies in the fact that Dasein is the being to whom the world, including all things, can reveal itself. Man, or Dasein, is not a substance, but a nothingness, a gap, an in-between, a place of revelation of all things or of Being. Man is not merely one being among many. Rather he is, as a Chinese proverb says, "the soul of all beings." Of the same proverb "man is the soul of all beings," there are two different interpretations: one is that man is a being among many, with the sole difference that he has a soul while other beings have not (an interpretation that does not correspond to Heidegger's thought); the other interpretation is that man is the soul of all beings, neither apart from nor among all beings, but immersed in the beings of the world; this interpretation is similar to Heidegger's thought. If the relation between man and other beings is that of subject and object, then man will be determined by other beings and other men, and will not reach authenticity and freedom, and thus will "fall." Only when one has realized the union of subject and object, transcended scientific knowledge, and made himself the place where beings disclose themselves, can he return to authenticity and "become One with all things." Scientific knowledge cannot grasp "Nothingness," which is not the object of knowing. But this does not mean that we should deny Nothingness, to which we gain access through anxiety, not through scientific knowledge. Anxiety reveals Nothingness. Nothingness is superior to science, intelligence, and knowledge. "Intelligence depends on Nothingness."

Nothingness is authenticity, which is not separated from things, which does not escape from things, but which is an attitude toward things and life. Being in authenticity is called *Angst* (anxiety), which is not thinking, but a kind of mood. Dasein in the mood of anxiety is "so far from the displacement of putting an isolated subject-thing into the innocuous emptiness of a worldless occurring that in an extreme sense what it does is precisely to bring Dasein face to face with its world as world, and thus bring it face to face with itself as Being-in-the-world" (*BT* 233).

Such a realm of life is, according to Heidegger, that of holding oneself aloof from the world, and such an attitude toward things is that of indifference. But authentic existence is not something that floats above falling everydayness; existentially, it is only a modified way in which such everydayness is seized upon. Authenticity does not demand that the self withdraw from the world. Such dissociation from the social environment may be called "transcendence." The transcendence here—which is an immanent transcendence[1]—and "dissociation from the social environment" can be understood as holding oneself aloof from the world. In short, this attitude towards things rids one of entanglement in things and with other men, but does not abolish or cancel things and other men. So to return to autheticity is to get rid of the situation of *Verfallen* such as "desire, alienation, and self-yoke" and to reach the realm of maintaining independence and keeping the initiative in one's own hands, not depending on others, not getting involved with outside things, and not fearing any concrete things. "The world as such is that in the face of which one has anxiety. The utter insignificance which makes itself known in the 'nothing and nowhere', does not signify that the world is absent, but tells us that entities within-the-world are of so little importance in themselves that on the basis of this *insignificance* of what is within-the-world, the world in its worldhood is all that still obtrudes itself" (*BT* 231). "In anxiety what is environmentally ready-to-hand sinks away, and so, in general, do entities within-the-world. . . . Anxiety throws Dasein back upon that which it is anxious about—its authentic potentiality-for-Being-in-the-world" (*BT* 232). This is to say that authenticity, which cannot be grasped by theoretical thinking, can only be attained in the mood of anxiety.

In what circumstances can man reach authenticity? Heidegger held that only in the face of, and through the understanding of, death can man grasp authenticity and undo relations to others. "Its death is the possibility of no-longer-being-able-to-be-there. If Dasein stands before itself as this possibility, it has been *fully* assigned to its ownmost potentiality-for-Being. When it stands before itself in this way, all its relations to any other Dasein have been undone. This ownmost nonrelational possibility is at the same time the uttermost one. . . . Death is the possibility of the absolute impossibility of Dasein. Thus death reveals itself as that *possibility which is one's ownmost, which is nonrelational, and which is not to be outstripped*" (*BT* 294). Anxiety in the face of death must not be confused with fear in the face of one's demise. Fear is "an accidental or random mood of 'weakness' in some individuals," while anxiety is "a basic state of mind of Dasein; it amounts to the disclosedness of the fact that Dasein exists as thrown Being towards its end" (*BT* 295). Man is inclined to fall, to flee from and fear death. But "factically one's own Dasein is always dying already; that is to say, it is in a Being-towards-its-end" (*BT* 298). In other words, the authentic human being deeply understands that "Death is a way to be, which Dasein takes over soon as it is," that "as soon as man comes to life, he is at once old enough to die" (*BT* 289), and "factically,

Dasein is dying as long as it exists, but proximally and for the most part, it does so by way of *falling*" (*BT* 295). What Heidegger said here is quite similar to a succinct saying of the Taoist Chuang Tse, "When one is born, he is dying." So man has to die bravely in order to get rid of *Verfallen* and reach authenticity. By facing death, man can get rid of the trammels of other men and the yoke of everydayness which is inauthenticity and thus show his authentic existence, independence, and individuality. "Death is Dasein's *ownmost* possibility. Being towards his possibility discloses to Dasein its *ownmost* potentiality-for-Being, in which its very Being is the issue. Here it can become manifest to Dasein that in this distinctive possibility of its own self, it has been wrenched away from the 'they'. This means that in anticipation any Dasein can have wrenched itself away from the 'they' already" (*BT* 307). Our everydayness, according to Heidegger, always "makes no choices, gets carried along by the nobody, and thus ensnares itself in inauthenticity." Only in the face of death, in Heidegger's view, can Dasein return to "authenticity," namely, to bring "itself back to itself from its lostness in the 'they'" (*BT* 312). Death means that *Verfallen* is no longer possible and the situation of being entangled with other men and other things including fame, status, and wealth is no longer possible. So man, at this time, necessarily returns to authenticity, maintains independence, and keeps the initiative in his own hands.

In a lecture entitled *Gelassenheit*, Heidegger once talked of the threat of science and technology toward man. He held that we should keep science and technology from destroying our authenticity and disturbing the heart of our hearts. In his annotation to the lecture, Heidegger put forward the saying "Will das Nicht-Wollen," which was a concrete description of the mood of the authentic man. If we comprehend man's life in such a mood, then we can call it a kind of game. We all like games but not necessarily those having a definite purpose. We may get nothing from games, yet we like games and play them seriously. Coming to this point, we can say that man has reached the profound depth of life and complete realization of his self.

The later Heidegger emphasized the analysis of thinking and poetry and talked little about death, but his basic philosophical thought remained unchanged. As Heidegger himself once said, every great thinker has just one thought.

Since Plato, thinking seemed to refer only to knowledge, the result of which, according to Heidegger, is the lostness of the real meaning of thinking. Thus, Heidegger raised the issue of rescuing thinking. To rescue thinking, we should realize that it is the tyranny of everyday language that strangles thinking. Everyday language has to abide by the logic of the public and use the words of the public and thus conceal Being. So Heidegger advocated the rescue of thinking with poetry, since only poetry can express the essence of thinking. Thinking and poetry are not opposed to each other, as thinking originally should be poetry and revelation of Being. Thinking is not knowledge. Heidegger once said through the mouth of Hölderlin: "Poetry is the purest among man's activities." Poetry makes it possible for human beings to go beyond gains and losses, to hold themselves aloof from the crowd, to be immersed in imagination and not to be constrained by reality. In poetry, man can throw off the trammels of outside things and other men and return to authenticity and freedom. The poetic language makes solid things vigorous and grasps Being through the meaning of words. Poet and thinker are selfsame. Heidegger, in effect, asked us to be poetic philosophers and philosophical poets.

There exist many similarities between Lao Tse's philosophy of "return to infancy" and Heidegger's thought of return to authenticity; and Lao Tse's declaration, "extinguish sacredness and give up intelligence" should not be treated onesidedly nor simply. It is true that Lao Tse did not touch the topic of modern science and technology, that he could not analyze the limitations of knowledge in terms of the subject-object relation, and that he had existed in his philosophy the idea of "keeping the people simple-minded." In these respects his thought cannot be compared with Heidegger's. But Lao Tse, after all, noticed the characteristics and weaknesses of knowledge, namely, that knowledge prevents man from knowing how to stop—that "the pursuit of knowledge increases daily." Neither Heidegger nor Lao Tse attached importance to knowledge, since both of them held that there is something higher than knowledge. In Heidegger's view, learning how to investigate Nothingness and Authenticity is philosophy, which is superior to science. Knowledge cannot lead man to authenticity, which can only be gained in the face of death or by poetic thinking, both of which are superior to knowledge. What is superior to knowledge, according to Lao Tse, is the understanding of Tao (also translated as the Way), which cannot be grasped by knowledge, no matter how hard one seeks for knowledge. With a certain similarity to Lao Tse's philosophy, Chuang Tse once put forward the theory: "My life has a limit, but my knowledge is without limit. To drive the limited in search of the limitless, is fatal."[2] Lao Tse said, "do not escape from the steady virtue but return to infancy."[3] Lao Tse was, in effect, asking us to go beyond the infinite knowledge and to return to the ignorant state of infancy through self-training. "Return to infancy" certainly does not mean that one should remain in the state of infancy from the beginning, but that, in Lao Tse's words, one should "learn to be unlearned." One who is "unlearned" is ignorant, while "to learn to be unlearned" requires self-improvement and self-training. This is similar to the thought of Heidegger; he did not oppose science but held that science could not lead man to authenticity, that it could not bring man before the "Nothing," which can only be attained through anxiety, the understanding of death, and poetry that goes beyond the everyday language. Lao Tse once made a vivid contrast between the "ordinary man" who specially sought for knowledge and the "foolish man" who went beyond knowledge and thus reached a higher realm. "I am foolish. Sincere and seeming confused. When ordinary men are bright, I alone am dull. When ordinary men are inquisitive, I alone am confused."[4] Knowledge makes man "bright" and "inquisitive" but cannot make him a sage of a "foolish man," that is, one who, though "dull" and "confused," would have gone beyond knowledge and reached the higher state of having grasped the "Tao." Lao Tse also said, "when there is wisdom, there is hypocrisy."[5] "Hypocrisy" here is analogous to Heidegger's inauthenticity. The sage, who does not get entangled with fame, wealth, knowledge, and desire, and thus is a higher "foolish man," is similar to Heidegger's authentic man.

As to the ways leading to the highest realm, Lao Tse and Heidegger have different views, although both of them agree that such a realm cannot be reached through knowledge. Heidegger advocated the understanding of death, while Lao Tse stressed "mystical seeing." As to the meaning of "mystical seeing," He Shang Gong, a famous commentator in the Western Han-Dynasty, observed that "mystical seeing means that the mind dwells in the mystical and obscure state and sees and knows all things." "Mystical seeing" is the practice of "staying in no-reality and maintaining quiescence."[6] Chuang Tse called the way of receiving Tao "the fasting of the heart" or "forgetfulness" ("to get rid of everything"). He said, "I have freed myself from the body, I have discarded my reasoning powers. And by thus getting rid of body and mind, I have become One with the Infinite. This is what I mean by getting rid of everything."[7] The aim of "forgetfulness" is emptiness of mind and "to become One with the Infinite," namely, to receive the Tao. On the contrary, if one is vulgar, only out for power, fame, and wealth and, as Heidegger says, falls into the world, then, according to Lao and Chuang, one is far from using "mystical seeing" and "forgetfulness," and thus cannot reach the highest realm of life.

Lao Tse and Chuang Tse's way of reaching the highest realm of life is, in my opinion, superior to that of Heidegger's: Heidegger held that only in the face of death can man understand the true meaning of life, which, I think, is impractical. Along this line, one can hardly avoid *Verfallen*; Lao Tse and Chuang's "mystical seeing" and "forgetfulness" are, on the contrary, possible anywhere and at any time. "Mystical seeing," to use a common expression, is "foresight-seeing" which can be achieved through self-training, not necessarily in the face of death. Tao Yuan Ming, who admired Lao Tse and Chuang Tse and mastered the essence of their thoughts, once wrote a poem, now well-known, in order to expound their lofty ideal of life: "To live in this world, but not be disturbed by noises of horse and cart; Why can I do so? The world will be remote as long as you keep aloof." "To live in this world" is being in the state of *Verfallen*. In such a situation, according to Tao Yuan Ming, man can rid himself of the entanglement of everydayness and the noises of horse and cart and thus attain the state of freedom, that is, a state in which "the world is remote," a state of "holding aloof from the world," without the understanding of death. Of course, Heidegger did not mean that it is only in fact on the eve of death that man can understand it, and his real meaning is that everyone can understand death in everyday life. However, one seldom thinks of death in everyday life. Lao Tse and Chuang Tse's "mystical seeing" and "forget-fulness," however, can be achieved through self-training, and once man has prac-ticed self-training he can adopt the attitude of holding aloof from the world, just like Tao Yuan Ming who "lived in this world" but still enjoyed the pleasure of "not being disturbed by the noises of horse and cart." Having, perhaps, realized that the understanding of death was not the best way of rescuing man, the later Heidegger laid emphasis, not on understanding death, but on poetic thinking which, according to him, was the feasible way of rescuing man and avoiding *Verfallen*.

The philosophy of the later Heidegger was quite similar to the theory of "the unspoken single meaning" of the metaphysician Wang Bi of the Wei-Jin period, who was greatly influenced by Lao Tse and Chuang Tse. Wang Bi advocated "having got the meaning, forget the words" and "having got the fish, forget the fishing net"—which means that true meaning is always beyond words, so once man had grasped the true essence of things, he should forget the words, just as a fisherman, once he has caught the fish, may forget the fishing net. The essence of Heidegger's "poetic thinking" is, so to speak, "having got the meaning, forget the words." According to Heidegger, the single poetic statement "always remains in the realm of the unspoken" (*US* 38). Tao Yuan Ming once wrote a poem entitled "Drinking," in which there is a famous thought-provoking sentence: "Here is the real meaning, which is however unspoken." The "real meaning" here is similar to Heidegger's authenticity—namely, a realm of holding aloof from the world. Chuang Tse once said, "Our original purity is given to us from Heaven. It is as it is, and cannot be changed." This authentic realm of having thrown off all the hypocrisies of the world can be sensed but not explained in words. Tao Yuan Ming himself had the makings of Lao Tse and Chuang Tse, and was free from passions and desires and kept his mind quiet. The reason why his poems move people lies in "the real," which is Lao Tse's "return to infancy" and Heidegger's return to authenticity. Tao Yuan Ming was both a thinker and a poet, and his poetry and thinking are in perfect harmony. So in Tao Yuan Ming we can see a splendid model of the poetic philosopher or the philosophical poet commended by Heidegger.

There are two major similarities between Heidegger's understanding of death and "poetic thinking," Lao Tse's "mystical seeing," Chuang Tse's "forgetfulness," and Tao Yuan Ming's "keeping one's mind aloof": the first is that all of them advocated reaching the highest realm of life by intuition, instead of by knowledge; the second is that none of their methods is isolated from man's everyday life. Heidegger advocated "Mitsein"—declaring that men could not be isolated from other men. So we can see that Heidegger is different, in this respect, from the Chinese recluses who tried to escape reality, and from Yang Zhu who asked man to withdraw from society and live in solitude in order to "complete living and preserve what is genuine." As Heidegger said of Dasein, "'as long as it is', right to its end, it comports itself towards its potentiality-for-Being" (*BT* 279). The process of man's living is also the process of going toward death, but it is a process in which Dasein can comport itself. "In Being-towards-death, Dasein comports itself *towards itself* as a distinctive potentiality-for-Being" (*BT* 296). Lao Tse's and Chuang Tse's "Wu-Wei"—which means "letting things take their own course"—does not mean doing nothing, nonaction or nonexertion, but submitting to nature. Lao Tse's "return to infancy" does not ask man to be separated from everyday life, but describes a higher foolish man's attitude toward everyday life; and Heidegger's authenticity is also not separated from inauthenticity: Heidegger takes care to guard against an interpretation of authenticity that would demand that the self withdraw from the world. The dominant traditional Chinese schools of thought regarded "entering the world" positively as the highest standard of politics and life. The Confucian school held that "we cannot understand death unless we have understood life," and "one cannot serve ghosts if he cannot serve man." Taoism differed from this tradition. Lao Tse advocated holding aloof from the world and Chuang Tse advocated "to even life and death" and "to regard all things as One," but both of them differed from Yang Zhu who asked man to escape the world. The Neo-Taoism of the Wei-Jin and the Northern and Southern Dynasties, which originated from the thought of Lao Tse and Chuang Tse, favored holding aloof from the world but did not ask men to "become monks" or "to die to the world." On the contrary, it criticized the Buddhist doctrine of "dying to the world" or "forsaking the world" and advocated the theory of "holding oneself aloof from the crowd without forsaking the world." This is similar to what the metaphysician Guo Xiang once said in his annotations to Chuang Tse: "Although the sage stays in the temple, he keeps his mind on the mountains and forests." This is to say that the ideal personality should possess the breadth of mind for transcending everyday life, even though holding a high office in the government, just as if living in the mountains and forests, and not getting involved in worldly affairs. There is a proverb in China that means exactly the same: "The body is in the palace of Wei while the mind rests on rivers and lakes," and that is similar to Heidegger's return to authenticity. Heidegger's understanding of death and the Confucian theory—"we cannot understand death unless we have understood life"— are opposed to each other. What Heidegger advocated is, in Confucian terms, "we cannot understand life unless we have understood death." Of course Heidegger by no means asks man to commit suicide, and the essence of his thought is the concept that man should have a quiet and far-reaching mind in everyday life and worldly entanglements. We can see that Heidegger is different from Confucius who, being a representative of the old tradition, advocated "we cannot understand death unless we have understood life," and knew only "entering the world," but not "holding oneself aloof from the crowd without forsaking the world." Although there are shortcomings in Heidegger's understanding of death, we can, I think, regard it as the closest ally of Taoism and use it to attack the traditional Confucian theory that "we cannot understand death unless we have understood life." Incidentally, I do not believe that we should contrast Confucian thought with the Buddhist concept of "becoming monks" and "dying to the world."

HEIDEGGER'S ANTI-METAPHYSICS AND LAO AND CHUANG'S METAPHYSICAL TAO

Since the Renaissance, man's emancipation in the history of modern Western philosophy has gone through the following stages: man was discovered during the Renaissance, human rights were emancipated from the yoke of theocracy; another achievement of the Renaissance was the discovery of nature, which people were encouraged to study. During the seventeenth and eighteenth centuries, modern science was in its infancy and so was metaphysical. Therefore, the philosophers of the seventeenth and eighteenth centuries regarded man as completely in the power of causality. Descartes, for example, regarded animals as machines. La Mettrie regarded even man as a machine. Thus the free nature of man was first stifled by theocracy and then by the inevitability of the causality of nature. Great achievements were made in all fields of historical dialectics during the late eighteenth century (the time of the French Revolution) and in natural science, especially in the theory of evolution, during the period from the late eighteenth to the early nineteenth centuries. These achievements caused modern Western philosophy to reach its highest stage; the theory of development and evolution now replaced the mathematical method of Galileo and the metaphysical method of Newton that had prevailed until then. The German Idealist philosophers, to different extents and in different ways, summed up the ideas of their predecessors with dialectics and established classical German Idealist philosophy as represented by Kant, Fichte, Schelling, and Hegel. They were not satisfied with the way in which the mechanical causality of the seventeenth and eighteenth centuries decisively trammeled the subjectivity and free will of man. They stood on the side of idealism and struggled once more to protect the free nature of man in the field of abstract philosophy. The former struggle was aimed at theocracy, but this time the struggle was mainly aimed at mechanical causality, while at the same time struggling against theocracy in different ways. The classical German Idealist philosophers agreed that the nature of the world was spiritual, and the spirit, the self, self-awareness, and the subject constituted the central focus of their philosophy. But they inherited and developed the tradition of metaphysical ontology stemming from Plato, and they dealt only with abstract, metaphysical man, placed man's free nature in the transcendent, eternal world, and thus denied the concrete existence of real, lifelike man. The most evident essentialism was displayed in the philosophy of Hegel. Essentialism holds that the abstract idea and essence are superior to beings, and the ideal, unreal possibilities are superior to reality. Although Hegel talked much about concreteness and opposed abstractness, his supreme "absolute spirit" was not the real existence of concrete man; and since he overemphasized the whole, he finally denied individuality. We can see that the classical German Idealists trammeled man's further emancipation with the eternal spirit and abstract man, and so the development of the history of Western philosophy demanded a third struggle aiming at man's further emancipation. Nietzsche opposed transcendent free will and claimed that his philosophy was antimetaphysical. But he did not fully get rid of metaphysics, although his philosophy, especially in the later period, was, in effect, opposed to metaphysics to some extent. Heidegger regarded Nietzsche as the last great metaphysician in the history of Western philosophy since Plato— a thesis which once gave rise to objections but which is, nevertheless, to some extent accurate. In fact, Heidegger was the first philosopher in the history of modern Western philosophy who systematically opposed metaphysics. His theory of "individuation" and "Dasein" further emancipated man's free nature, marked the real beginning of the third struggle for man's emancipation in the history of modern Western philosophy, and demonstrated an important characteristic of modern Western philosophy.

Heidegger held that the development of metaphysics from Plato to Hegel involved a forgetting of the concrete existence of Dasein, that the concrete and the real were higher than the abstract and the possible and, further, that man could only be understood in the development of time, namely, in history. His Dasein was concrete and individual, and thus plural. He refused to speak about man's eternal and abstract general essence. His return to authenticity through the understanding of death means that man can realize his independent self in the face of death.

> Death *lays claim* to it as an *individual* Dasein. The non-relational character of death, as understood in anticipation, individualizes Dasein down to itself. This individualizing is a way in which the 'there' is disclosed for existence. It makes manifest that all Being-alongside the things with which we concern ourselves, and all Being-with-Others, will fail us when our ownmost potentiality-for-Being is the issue. Dasein can be *authentically itself* only if it makes this possible itself of its own accord. (*BT* 308)

In short, in the face of death man must not get involved with outside things and other men; only then can he exist as authentic and thus fully demonstrate his personality, independence, and initiative. We can see that Heidegger's theory of individuation and Hegel's metaphysical theory of attaching importance of man's abstract general essence are diametrically opposed to each other.

There exist significant distinctions between Lao and Chuang's[8] Tao and Heidegger's authenticity. Tao, in Lao and Chuang's views, was the cardinal principle by which all things on Earth and under Heaven existed. Lao Tse said, "There was a completed indefinable thing whose birth was before Heaven and Earth. Silent and empty, it exists alone and is unchanging, it moves along in a circular way without stop. It may be called the mother of the universe. I don't know its name. Forcing a name upon it, I call it the Tao and the omnipotent."[9] Chuang Tse also said, "Before Heaven and Earth were, Tao was. It has existed without change from all time. . . . no point in time is long ago, nor by lapse of ages has it grown old."[10] Tao, according to Lao and Chuang, was the "constant Tao" and the universal essence that were eternal and transcendent, and the abovementioned "before" must be understood as logical priority and not as temporal priority. That is to say, Tao is logically prior to heaven and earth. So it is clear that Lao and Chuang's Tao is exactly the metaphysical category of substance which prevailed from Plato to Hegel, to which Heidegger, as a modern Western philosopher, was opposed.

In Lao Tse and Chuang Tse, the intuitional methods such as "mystical seeing" and "forgetfulness" were means to reaching Tao—namely, to grasp the transcendent and eternal general essence—while through the understanding of death and "poetic thinking," what Heidegger intended was to reach a state of mind, and not an abstract substance or essence. Of course, Lao Tse and Chuang Tse also wanted to reach a state of mind in the end, but such a state of mind could be reached, in their views, only by reaching Tao, while Heidegger held that it could be reached directly by intuition, and not through an eternal essence—Tao. Both Lao Tse and Chuang Tse held that all things in the world changed forever and that "the life of man passes by like a galloping horse, changing at every turn, at every hour."[11] But man could overcome impermanence and reach the state of "though the body decays, the spirit is ever-lasting"[12] by reaching Tao. Lao Tse said, "when I am not conscious of my body, I shall not be troubled."[13] This was, in effect, asking man to look at things from the point of view of Tao so as to realize "valuing self." Chuang Tse's "to even life and death" and "to even others and I" was, in fact, also asking man to look at things from the point of view of Tao in order to realize that all things are the same, and to reach the state of not being troubled by impermanence. It is thus clear that Lao and Chuang's Tao is eternal and universal reason and, if one knows such reason, one can transcend impermanence and not be disturbed by grief and happiness, which can be called "controlling feelings with reason." On the contrary, in Heidegger's philosophy there is no place for universal and eternal reason, and he asks man to return to individualized authenticity through the understanding of death and poetic thinking and not to be troubled by things or other men. Also, Heidegger sees the dynamism of human beings in the temporal-ecstatic character of Dasein. This may be called "to devaluate reason with feeling," namely, to overcome the abstract and universal reason with poetry or the understanding of death. Many Chinese scholars who compare Heidegger with Lao Tse and Chuang Tse see only the similarities between them— namely, they see only that both Heidegger's authenticity and Lao and Chuang's Tao are the realms of the unspoken prior to science and knowledge and aloof from the world, and overlook the differences between them due to different times and peoples: Lao and Chuang's philosophy attached importance to transcendent essence, which is similar to the metaphysical ontology stressed by the philosophical tradition from Plato to Hegel and thus belongs to the ideology of old times; Heidegger, however, marked the beginning of contemporary philosophy which lays special emphasis on the concrete being and individual in the development of time and history. In the West, metaphysical ontology dominated the history of philosophy until Heidegger who, along with Nietzsche, began to make a break with this old tradition and expressed the living fervor of individuals; Lao and Chuang's Tao was exactly the antithesis of Heidegger's opposition to metaphysics. Although Lao Tse and Chuang Tse also attached importance to man's individuality to a certain extent—which was different from Confucian thought—they did not explicitly raise the principle of individualization. On the contrary, they held that man should act according to the metaphysical Tao, while Heidegger explicitly advanced and laid emphasis on individualization, and his Dasein necessarily implies a "will" in the sense of freedom. It has the meaning of free choice. Lao and Chuang belong to the tradition of Eastern philosophy, while Heidegger belongs to that of the West. The principle of individuality, rooted in ancient Greece, was revived during the Renaissance and has begun to shine since Heidegger. Although Heidegger stressed *Mitsein*, namely, man's sociality, the plurality of Dasein showed the individualistic character of his philosophy. In contrast, Lao and Chuang, opposed man's sociality and thus indicated their individualistic tendency, on the one hand, but attached importance to the "constant Tao," on the other hand, thus demonstrating their nonindividualism.

As regards the status quo and the future of Chinese thought and culture, I think that we in China should both carry on and develop the Taoist philosophy while also taking Heidegger's philosophy into account, considering the similarities between them, namely, that both of them, representing the antithesis of orthodox thought, stress "valuing oneself," "returning to authenticity," and not getting involved with outside things, and emphasizing the close kinship between poetry and thinking. I also think that we should absorb Heidegger's philosophy, in particular, considering the differences between it and Lao and Chuang's philosophy—namely, that Heidegger attacks metaphysical ontology and attaches importance to the principle of individuality, while Lao and Chuang advocate the abstract metaphysical Tao. Such is my conclusion from having compared Heidegger with Taoism.

NOTES

1. See Stanley Rosen, "Thinking about Nothing," in *Heidegger and Modern Philosophy, Critical Essays*, ed. Michael Murray (New Haven: Yale University Press, 1978), 182.
2. Chuang Tse, "Nourishment of the Soul," in *Taoist Philosopher and Chinese Mystic*, trans. Herbert A. Giles (London: Mandala Books, 1926), 48.
3. Lao Tse, *Tao Teh Ching* (Szechwan: Canadian Mission Press, 1936), 46.
4. Lao Tse, 33.
5. Lao Tse, 29.
6. Lao Tse, 26.
7. Chuang Tse, "The Great Supreme," in *Taoist Philosopher and Chinese Mystic*, 85.
8. Taoism, as a philosophical movement, appeared twice in the history of Chinese philosophy. Lao Tse and Chuang Tse were the major representatives of the Pre-Chin period. The second time was in the Wei-Jin period. Taoism of this time is also called Neo-Taoism. The achievement of Neo-Taoist philosophers lies in protecting Taoist thinking from employing metaphysical language as well as from absolutizing Nothingness. Most of the Neo-Taoist way of thinking is nonmetaphysical.
9. Lao Tse, 40.
10. Chuang Tse, "The Great Supreme," 76.
11. Chuang Tse, "Autumn Floods," in *Taoist Philosopher and Chinese Mystic*, 165.
12. Lao Tse, 26.
13. Lao Tse, 21.

VIII

HEIDEGGER AND
TRANSLATION

PARVIS EMAD

17. Thinking More Deeply into the Question of Translation

Essential Translation and the Unfolding of Language

To Friedrich-Wilhelm von Herrmann
on his 55th Birthday

. . . the difficulty of a translation is never
merely a technical one, but pertains to the
relation of man to the root unfolding of the
word and to the dignity of language.
Heidegger, *Hölderlins Hymne "Der Ister"*

Heidegger's thinking comes into contact with the question of translation in at least five significant ways: First, as a thinker Heidegger is involved in the activity of actual translation of texts in many places in his work. Not counting translations that appear in the lecture courses prior to *Being and Time*, we can say that Heidegger is engaged in actual translation of texts at least as early as the Foreword to *Being and Time*. Second, Heidegger's translations differ significantly from existing versions of those texts—an obvious and often misconstrued fact. For example, his rendition of part of the *Antigone* differs significantly from any existing translation; and his translation of certain portions of Plato's work differs from that of Schleiermacher. Third, unlike many philosophers who translate without stating their own viewpoints on translation, Heidegger does not take the process of translation for granted. In Heidegger's works there are sporadic and brief inquiries into the process itself. As he comes to grips with the essential character of language, he also comes to grips with the question of translation. Translation itself becomes philosophically significant. Fourth, for Heidegger translation is a form of interpretation. Very early in his work he abandons the naive assumption that translation is a detached and objective reproduction of immutable "facts" that appear in interlingual space. Finally, there is Heidegger's well-known practice of hyphenating the German word *übersetzen* and emphasizing either the prefix *über* or the suffix *setzen*, thus indicating that translation implies a process of crossing over and transposition. Adopted in the 1940s, this practice allows Heidegger to point out a process which the English word *translation* cannot easily say.

Reflecting on these five dimensions of the issue, we come to realize that Heidegger carefully, concisely, and specifically thinks through the question of translation at various junctures in his work. These various turns towards the question of translation have one important thing in common: They all explicate translation in terms of the root unfolding of language (*das Wesen der Sprache*).[1] Heidegger is fully aware that translation is a commerce and an exchange between different languages. But it is not in this exchange per se that he finds the essential character of translation. Translation shows its essential character when it becomes an occasion for language to unfold in its core. (It goes without saying that translation of a business letter or legal document does not deal with essential translation.) Heidegger is not concerned with problems that dominate the discussion of translation in the "sciences" of language. Rather, he takes translation as a unique opportunity for the root unfolding of language. And this opportunity presents itself in the way in which translation responds to the very foreignness or strangeness which calls for a deeper translation in the root unfolding of language.

In Heidegger the question of translation has two poles. At one pole there are translation's undeniable attachments to the foreignness which rules between languages. At the other pole is the root unfolding of language as a response to that foreignness. Our co-enactment with Heidegger's thinking on translation requires that we consider what gathers at each of these poles.

Thus we lay out the course of the following reflections in terms of these two poles. First, we must grasp Heidegger's appraisal of the foreignness which rules between languages in translation. We grasp this best by looking at how Heidegger views the problem of semantic equivalency of translated terms. Heidegger's opening up of this problem (which plays an important role in the conventional approach to translation) helps us to understand his thinking on translation as such. Second, we must consider how this foreignness can elicit a response from language by holding it (the foreignness) to its (language's) root unfolding in and through translation. Here we must consider Heidegger's characterization of translation as "essential or originary translation" (*wesentliche oder ursprüngliche Übersetzung*) and examine some instances of his work as a translator.

THE PROBLEM OF VALIDITY IN TRANSLATION

The problem that occupies a central place in the long and interesting history of reflection on translation is the problem of validity—the problem of semantic equivalency of translated terms. The conventional approach to translation takes this problem so seriously that it is preoccupied solely with the equivalency of translated terms. Are the chosen terms fully representative of the original, or do they cover the original terms only partially? Is the translation an accurate and reliable version of the original? Does the translation replace the original relatively or absolutely?

From Cicero and Goethe to Walter Benjamin and beyond, conventional "wisdom" about translation is plagued with the desire to have the words of one language cover fully those of the other language. This desire has given rise to at least three distinct positions: (1) that translations are nothing but distorted versions of the original and that all translations are to be rejected; (2) that it is possible to produce a translation that is absolutely identical with the original, i.e., that absolute identity with the original is a goal worth striving for; and (3) that translations are to be neither rejected out of hand nor accepted absolutely, for they take their place next to the original and do not replace it.[2]

Heidegger neither rejects translation as a distorted version of the original, nor does he take the translation to be absolutely identical with the original. He prefers to preserve to the fullest degree the difference between languages as this difference erupts within the problem of semantic equivalency in translation. When taken as they are, the differences between languages and the problem of semantic equivalency must be retained as a difference and must be seen for the problem that it is. The recourse to the dictionary, by which we try to alleviate or resolve the problem of semantic equivalency, is a recourse made in the hope that at some point we may do away with this problem and with the difference between languages. But a dictionary is not the ultimate authority, and it cannot resolve the problem of semantic equivalency and thus eliminate the differences between languages.

To consider a dictionary as an undisputed arbiter is to overburden the dictionary with expectations that it cannot fulfill: "A dictionary can provide an indication for understanding a word . . . [but] it is never a simple [*schlechthin*] authority that would be binding a priori" (*GA* 53: 75). A dictionary cannot be the ultimate authority because it is the product of a particular way of looking at language and of interpreting it. No dictionary has descended from heaven; rather it results from a certain style of reflecting and interpreting language: "The appeal to a dictionary is always an appeal to an interpretation of language which is often not grasped at all in its style [*Art*] and limits" (*GA* 53: 75). Certainly dictionaries have an important function to fulfill. But this function takes place only when there is traffic (*Verkehr*) between languages and when they are turned into means of transportation (*Verkehrsmittel*) (cf. *GA* 53: 75). But before languages enter this traffic, they have a historical spirit that dictionaries cannot grasp: "Considered in view of the historical spirit of language as a whole, no dictionary provides an immediate standard; and none is binding" (*GA* 53: 75). To expect dictionaries to resolve the problem of semantic equivalency ignores the historical spirit of a language. Rather than attempting to "resolve" this problem, we must see the semantic non-equivalency of translated terms for what it is, namely a confirmation of the ineradicable difference between languages. Translation is precisely the place where this difference shows itself to be ineradicable. For no translation can be perfect enough to minimize this difference: "There is no translation at all in which the words of one language could or should fully cover the words of another language" (*GA* 53: 75). The difficulty of attaining a total identity between translated terms, along with the existing differences between languages, provides translation with a unique revealing power. The difficulty of attaining total identity between languages and the irresolvable difference between them are not entirely negative: they bring to the fore "interrelations/interconnections [*Zusammenhänge*] which lie in the translated language but are not brought out" (*GA* 53: 75). These difficulties and differences reveal translation as a way of dealing with language in which we not only see interrelations in the translated language but also come to terms with our own language. As Heidegger puts it, "Translation is an awakening, clarifying, and unfolding of one's own language by coming to grips [*Auseinandersetzung*] with the foreign language" (*GA* 53: 80). This means that there is more to translation than just a transfer of words from one language to another. To initiate the move in such a transfer is to face the difference between languages as the foreignness that rules between them. By forcing us to see the foreignness and unfamiliarity of the languages under translation, the activity of translation clarifies our relationship to our own language. Thus, rather than serving as a means for transporting "meanings" across the so-called language barrier, translation invites us to return to our own language. When we, in translation, turn back from the foreignness of another language, we discover another *translation*, one that occurs *within our own language*.

TRANSLATION AT THE CORE OF LANGUAGE

In the general context of translation between languages and *in the very process* of translation between languages, this "other" translation shows that language unfolds in an even deeper way than translation between languages. The fact that translation between languages is at all possible—regardless of its validity—points to a translation which occurs at the core of language itself. To see this "other" translation properly, we must stop thinking of *inter*lingual translation as the only form of translation. For, before translation takes the direction between two languages, it already occurs within our own language.

> Initially we grasp the process [of translation] from the outside as a technical-philological procedure. We believe that translation is the transfer of a foreign language into another tongue or, conversely, transfer of a mother tongue into another language. However, we fail to see that we constantly translate our own language, the mother tongue, into its own words. (*GA* 54: 17)

Thus, in contrast to the conventional approach to translation, which considers it solely as interlingual, Heidegger sees translation as occurring *first* within our own language. As interlingual, translation does not manifest itself in its deepest sense, even though the occasion for such a manifestation is made possible when thinking confronts the problem of the validity of interlingual translation.

Having observed what is gathered around that pole which is marked by the foreignness of languages and by translation's validity, we are then led to see what transpires in or around the other pole, which shows that language unfolds in its core in the process of translation. When we speak with ourselves or with others, we are always involved in translation:

Speaking and saying are in themselves a translation whose essential unfolding is by no means exhausted by the fact that translated words and the words to be translated belong to different languages. An originary translation prevails [*waltet*] in every dialogue and monologue. (*GA* 54: 17)

It goes without saying that, in order to gain access to this "other"—which we call "innerlingual"—translation, we cannot be guided by the questions that are concerned with validity of interlingual translation and semantic equivalency of translated terms. Rather, we are guided by what Heidegger calls *'reformulation'*. Originary or "innerlingual" translation includes the process of "replacing one expression with another one of the same language and so using a 'reformulation' [*Umschreibung*]" (*GA* 54: 17–18). Originary translation which occurs within language and is innerlingual occurs in the closest proximity to reformulation. This involves changing the chosen words, sometimes even choosing a more appropriate word-context. This change indicates that thinking is already moved, crossed over (is "translated") into "another truth, another clarity, or even another matter calling for questioning" (*GA* 54: 18). How else could reformulation be possible? In and of itself reformulation shows a proximity to and a connection with the "words" that make up the reformulation. Thinking must *be* with those words if reformulation is to occur. To *be* with those words means that thinking crosses over to those words, translates itself into them. Thus reformulation indicates an originary or innerlingual translation.

In addition to reformulation, poetizing and thinking offer other possibilities for grasping the process of crossing over which is essential to *inner*lingual translation. To take thinking and poetizing as they occur in our own language in a manner that is appropriate to them, we must cross over and get translated into the word which originally harbors a work of poetizing or thinking. Understanding poetry or following along in thinking requires innerlingual translation: "The poetry of a poet and the treatise of a thinker reside in their own unique and singular [*einzig*] word. They force us to hear this word again and again, as if we hear it for the first time" (*GA* 54: 17). In order to read a poem or a work of thinking, we must be "translated" innerlingually into their essential word.

What distinguishes the word in a work of poetizing is that it requires our being "translated" into this word. What is called reformulation is also marked by a crossing/translating. Both movements occur when we cross over to the essential word of poetizing and to the word which is essential to reformulation; and both of these movements are movements of innerlingual translation which occur *prior to* interlingual translation. Long before language enters the arena of interlingual translation, it must be heard in innerlingual translation. This is a translation which occurs independently of interlingual translation, whose validity is questioned by the problem of semantic equivalency. Occurring within language itself, this translation directs us to the root unfolding of language.

What is this root unfolding of language all about? Before we respond to this question, we must take another look at reformulation and what it reveals—for two reasons: (1) Reformulation could be taken as a "doubling" of language which shows that language is not co-extensive with itself;[3] (2) Reformulation could also be taken as an essential indicator of what happens in the experience of being *and* language. Reflecting on this second point helps to put the first point into proper focus.

If reformulation indicates the occurrence of an originary translation within language, then it is incumbent upon us to take the phrase "truth of being, *die Wahrheit des Seins*" as a reformulation of the phrase "meaning of being, *der Sinn von Sein.*" The change that occurs in the movement in language from "meaning of being" to "truth of being" indicates an originary translation within the language of thinking. (It goes without saying that this occurrence of originary translation is appropriately thought only when reformulation is placed in the context of the experience of being and language, i.e., as an indicator of originary translation within language. If we take reformulation as a mere "rewording," then of course thinking ceases to address this significant aspect of Heidegger's thinking.) If we consider the proximity of Heidegger's thinking to the "truth of being" as he is coming to grips with the question of the "meaning of being," then we have to say that the first phrase is a reformulation of the second. This presupposes that Heidegger considers the question concerning the "truth of being" as already within the perimeter of the work which deals with the "meaning of being." As we gather from *Beiträge zur Philosophie (Vom Ereignis)*, this is indeed and precisely the case: truth of being already falls within the perimeter of *Being and Time* (cf. *GA* 65: 182).[4] If the intention of this work is "the concrete elaboration of the question of the meaning of being" (*GA* 2: 1) and if "truth of being" already falls within the perimeter of this work, then "truth of being" presents a reformulation of the "meaning of being." Originary translation as a translation that occurs within language already translates thinking of the question of the "meaning of being" *into* a thinking of the "truth of being" and thus reformulates it.

Seen in this light, reformulation does not present a "doubling" of language; rather, it testifies to its showing power. To take reformulation as a "doubling" amounts to blocking access to the originary translation that makes reformulation possible. If one insists on seeing reformulation as a "doubling"—as an indication that language is not co-extensive with itself—then one runs the risk of missing entirely what Heidegger says about translation, what he means by originary translation, and what his thinking shows us about translation and the root unfolding of language, *das Wesen der Sprache*[5] in its relation to *ursprüngliche Übersetzung*, originary translation. Occuring within language itself, this translation directs us to the root unfolding of language.

ROOT UNFOLDING OF LANGUAGE AND ORIGINARY TRANSLATION

In order fully to understand originary or innerlingual translation as one which occurs in response to the foreignness of another language, takes place in every dialogue and monologue, sustains reformulation, and upholds an appropriate entry into works of poetizing and thinking, we must determine the way in which this translation reflects the root unfolding of language. This determination is necessary because it prevents misconstruing originary translation as a "linguistic" episode isolated from the root unfolding of language. This determination allows originary translation to be seen as an innerlingual event that is sustained by the root unfolding of language and is one of its most accessible indicators. Considering Heidegger's work on language as a whole, we can say that what distinguishes originary translation and reveals it to be an intricate and relatively accessible indicator of the root unfolding of language is the occurrence of "way-making" that initiates and guides this translation. Thus to grasp originary translation broadly and essentially, we must focus on this occurrence of "way-making." This requires nothing less than outlining the fundamental way of Heidegger's thinking about language.

First, we must note that for Heidegger language is not adequately and appropriately grasped when it is construed merely in anthropological and instrumental terms. For Heidegger language has a unique showing power that goes deeper than that. When language unfolds essentially, it allows things to show themselves and be manifest. Second, the root unfolding of language occurs as a "way-making" (*be-wëgen*) so that things may appear and show themselves. What Heidegger means by the word *way/Weg* is captured by the word *way-making*. When the word *way/Weg* appears at various junctures in Heidegger's work (for example, in the last lines of *Being and Time*) or when it appears as an adjunct to thinking (such as in *Denkweg*, pathway of thinking) or when it, finally, is used in designating the *Gesamtausgabe* as *Wege, nicht Werke* (pathways, not works)—these various uses of the word *way/Weg* receive their ultimate justification and meaning from "way-making" as an occurrence which is central to the root unfolding of language. In its simple construction the word *way-making* refers to the word *way*. For Heidegger this is not a metaphor that alludes to the task of thinking and to the incomplete and provisional character of its "results"—thus implying relativism and perspectivism. Third, and in view of what we have just said about this word—*way/Weg* perhaps as no other word in Heidegger's language directs us to what transpires in the thinking of the question of being as a thinking of *both* being *and* language. This thinking is a thinking of being and language insofar as being is thought in stretches of the way that is laid out in language's way-making movement. The word *way* and what it indicates requires that we think of being and language not as two separate and independent entities but as always connected and in accord. They are distinct from each other but are not separate and independent of each other. It is language's way-making movement that takes us underneath language as an ontologically neutral and independent tool of communication. It is also the manifesting/showing/appearing of the being of things that keeps us from thinking that being occurs in a language-free zone. To think of language as an ontologically neutral tool and to think of being as appearing in a language-free zone is to overlook the fact that, as von Herrmann puts it: ". . . Heidegger thinks being as being in the horizon of the root unfolding of language; and, conversely, he thinks the root unfolding of language in the horizon of being as being."[6] This means that to think of language, we must think of its words' showing power, which is always a showing power that shows things in their being. When we state something in words, we always show something in its being. In short, every statement in language is stated in the horizon of the root unfolding of being; and being appears within the horizon of the root unfolding of language. Language's stating/showing/manifesting of things is a way-making. Heidegger captures way-making showing/stating in one word: *Sage/saying*.

We must recall—and this is our fourth point—that the word *saying/Sage* is appropriate for showing what transpires when language unfolds in its core because *Sage* in its original form, *sagan*, maintains close ties with the word *zeigen/showing*. As it unfolds in its core, language shows things and makes them manifest. Unfolding in its core, language is a saying/*Sage* which lets things be manifest for what they are. When it unfolds as saying/showing, language makes way for things to be manifest. Thus, ". . . language . . . receives its determination from saying as from that which makes way for everything [*Sprache . . . empfängt seine Bestimmung aus der Sage als dem alles Be-wëgenden*]" (*GA* 12: 191). This suggests that way-making occurs as saying in the realm of showing/manifesting, which is always the realm of being.

Having outlined—albeit briefly as is required here—the essential issues that are involved in the root unfolding of language, we can now turn to the question which prompted the outline in the first place: to what extent and in what manner is the way-making/saying/showing of language involved in originary translation? And to what extent is originary translation involved in the way-making/saying/showing of language? Our response is simply: originary translation occurs *as* way-making/saying/showing. Further, since this translation precedes interlingual translation, translating for Heidegger *in its core* implies, manifests, and is sustained by way-making/saying/showing. We can see the fittingness of this response in two ways: (1) by returning once again to what reformulation reveals; and (2) by considering translation of a work of thinking into its own language.

What Reformulation Reveals

Reformulation occurs when the matter that appears in the initial formulation (say as the "meaning of being") reappears differently (say as the "truth of being"). The mutual unfolding of being and language in their respective horizons "makes a way" which requires a different saying. Heidegger's choice of word and its special spelling corroborates this essential occurrence of way-making. He chooses the word *bewegen*, which he hyphenates and to which he adds an umlaut, showing that he is concerned with a movement in language that is more than ordinary movement. This spelling is intended to stress the movement as a way-making movement. Hyphenated and with an umlaut, *be-wëgen* indicates *Wege allererst ergeben und stiften*: yielding and bringing about ways in an originary way (*GA* 12: 186). Reformulation depends on and represents one such yielding and bringing about of ways. In reformulation saying is not something that is added to the matter that reappears differently and needs reformulation. Rather, saying is just this appearing/showing itself. Thus reformulating or re-saying the question of being in terms of the "truth of being" indicates that thinking moves along a path in language which opens unto the "truth of being." The path that thinking takes in reformulation points out an altered appearing and a translating into this appearing. Reformulation is called for, becomes necessary, and can be accomplished only because language "makes ways" in this deep sense.

TRANSLATING A WORK OF THINKING

Besides reformulation, the special circumstance of translating a work of thinking into its native language involves originary translation (language's "way-making"/showing/saying). We can see this involvement by considering what transpires in such a translation. Translation of a work of thinking into its native language involves originary translation because it requires translating the language of this work into words that belong to its own language. And this is a task that is quite different from translating this work into another language. This task is different because

> to translate one's own language into its ownmost [*eigenstes*] words is always more difficult. For instance, translation of the words of a German thinker into the German language is particularly difficult because here the obstinate prejudice holds sway that we are supposed to understand the German word automatically [*von selbst*], since it belongs to "our" own language . . . (*GA* 54: 18)

This difficulty is directly proportional to the "way" that the thinker's language of thinking "makes" in the thinker's own native language, i.e., is proportional to the extent that language is unfolded essentially and in its core. Insofar as his work shows/manifests things in a special manner, his language of thinking "makes" special "ways" in his own native language. The difficulty of translating/interpreting the work of a thinker into his own native language consists in the fact that the translator/interpreter must translate himself (here the German *über*-setzen, with emphasis on the prefix *über*, works much better than the English word *translate*) into the saying, i.e., into the "ways made" by the work of thinking in his native language.

Here the success of the translator/interpreter depends largely on his grasping that a work of thinking presupposes the mutual and horizonal root unfolding of being and language. A work of thinking represents such an unfolding, and its language is a measure of that. A translation of a work of thinking into its own native tongue requires as its first step that the translator/interpreter gain access to the "ways made" by that work in its own native tongue. Once these "ways" are ascertained, then the language of the interpreter unfolds essentially and in its core. In this root unfolding, the originary translation of a work of thinking takes place as a translation into the "ways made" by a work of thinking in its native tongue. Thus the difficulty of translating a work of thinking into its own language consists in gaining access to the "ways made" in that language and in unfolding the interpreter's language in accordance with those "ways."

Here is the place to offer a brief criticism—proceeding from this understanding of originary translation—of the contemporary hermeneutic and structuralist theories of interpretation. Contemporary hermeneutic and structuralist theories of interpretation struggle with that distance that separates the interpreter from the work to be interpreted.[7] But they do not seem to succeed in overcoming that distance. On one level, the interpreter is certainly separated and thus distanced from the work that he wishes to interpret. However, if we understand the interpreter's response to the "ways made" in the language of the work to be interpreted as a response within the root unfolding of language, then we find that the distance which separates the work from its interpreter is already overcome in and through originary translation. Originary translation overcomes this distance in its character as a translation into way-making/showing/saying that occurs when the "foreign sounding" character of the language of the work of thinking elicits a response from its own native language. The distance between translator/interpreter and the work to be interpreted is already bridged by the originary translation as a response to the language of the work of thinking—a response that lets language unfold in its core.

This means that it is language—and *not* the interpreter—that initiates, carries through, and completes originary translation. Thus originary translation confirms Heidegger's basic position: "It is not man who speaks, but language. Man speaks only by resonating with language within the root unfolding of being [*geschicklich*]" (*SG* 161).[8] This way of saying originary translation confirms Heidegger's stance on the priority of language in that this translation reveals a level of "linguistic activity" that lies deeper than what usually happens in speaking and writing within a multiplicity of meanings. We tend to think of this multiplicity as something that is at our disposal as we speak. But considering the deeper "linguistic activity" (as revealed in originary translation), we realize that the opposite is actually the case:

> Multiplicity of meanings of a term does not originate in the fact that, in speaking and writing, we humans occasionally mean different things with the same word. The multiplicity of meanings is in each case an historical [*geschichtlich*] multiplicity. It emerges from the fact that, when we speak the language, we are addressed and claimed by the being of beings in different ways, depending upon the root unfolding of being. (*SG* 161)

Thus originary translation of a work of thinking into the words of its own language reveals the language of this work as one which "makes ways" in its native tongue in accord with the root unfolding (*Geschick*) of being. Accordingly, this originary translation reveals being's most intimate involvement with language. This way of saying originary translation reveals that the language of a work of thinking is molded in closest proximity to how language essentially unfolds in a work of thinking.

Let us show how this happens with an example from Kant. We can say that this unfolding takes place when Kant interprets *ratio* as both *Vernunft* and *Grund* and translates *principium reddendae rationis sufficientis* as *der Satz vom Grund*. But stepping over to the "way made" by the Latin *ratio*—first in Latin and then in German, with *Vernunft* and *Grund*—is moving into a "way" wherein interlingual translation (i.e., the translation of the Latin *ratio* into German) and innerlingual translation (i.e., the translation within Latin and within German) intersect. This means that translation of a work of thinking into its native tongue sometimes requires stepping over to the "way made" by a word which is *not* a native word in a thinker's native tongue, but is nonetheless an essential word and gets translated into a thinker's native tongue. (In Kant's case this occurs when the word *ratio* is translated into German both as *Vernunft* and as *Grund*.) Heidegger regards this latter kind of translation—the one in which a foreign and essential word gets translated into another language, the one in which interlingual and innerlingual translations meet—as an instance of essential translation (*wesentliche Übersetzung*). In order to understand more fully what translation is all about, we must take a quick look at essential translation.

TRANSLATION AS ESSENTIAL TRANSLATION

The linguistic event which we pursued up to this point and which Heidegger calls "originary translation"—which we call "innerlingual translation"—takes place in reading a work of thinking or a work of poetizing, in essential reformulation, and particularly in that translation that occurs when a work of thinking is translated into the words of its own native language. However, sometimes translation of a work of thinking into the words of its own language unexpectedly brings us face to face with interlingual translation, insofar as the originary translation of that work comes upon a translation which takes place within the language of that work but involves another language—as is the case in Kant's rendition of the Latin *ratio* into German. What happens *in* and *as* translation, when translation is interlingual and hands over to an historical epoch a "way" of showing/manifesting that is "made" by essential words of another language? In short, what sort of interlingual translation is essential translation? In order to respond to these questions, we must draw attention to a naive assumption that often plays a quiet yet persistent role in the debate on interlingual translation. (When this assumption is rightly understood, then we can see interlingual translation as a particular occasion for language to unfold essentially and in its core.) Debate on the interlingual translation of a work of thinking sometimes naively assumes that essential words and concepts of a work of thinking are clearly circumscribed and reside without ambiguity on the other side of the so-called "language barrier," simply waiting to be transmitted to this side of the "language barrier" clearly and unambiguously. But this assumption overlooks the fact that essential words of a work of thinking are not instances of clear and unambiguous circumscription: they are cases of way-making/saying/ showing power. These cases of way-making/showing/saying power emerge from "being's root unfolding within the horizon of language and from language's root unfolding within the horizon of being."

Seen within the context of this mutual and horizonal root unfolding, interlingual translation of basic words of thinking is not primarily a matter of transmission of "well-defined meanings" from one language into another. Interlingual translation as essential translation involves primarily being's root unfolding along with language's root unfolding. In view of this involvement, we can say that, strictly speaking, no wholesale transmission takes place in essential translations of *works* of thinking because way-making/saying/showing power of elemental *words* of thinking cannot be transmitted intact. The most that essential translation can achieve is to convey a sense of what the way-making/saying/showing is—that way-making that occurs in strict correspondence with the unfolding of the language which is to be translated. Essential or interlingual translation deals with being's unfolding within a given language as this unfolding shines through its words. Essential translation indicates that being's unfolding (*das Geschick des Seins*) corresponds to a certain way of speaking and that a certain way of speaking corresponds to being's manner of involvement in language. In Heidegger's words: "An essential translation corresponds [*entspricht*] in each case to the manner in which language speaks within an epoch of unfolding of being and, in so doing, corresponds to the root unfolding of being" (*SG* 164). The word *entsprechen* (correspondence) that appears in this characterization of essential translation marks the unfolding of language within the horizon of being. As a language, German corresponds to being's unfolding when this language puts forth *Vernunft* and *Grund* as translation/reception of the Latin *ratio*. If this unfolding/corresponding would not take place, then the "way" of showing/manifesting things that is peculiar to *ratio*— i.e., the "calculative way"—would not be conveyed into modern German thought. Deliberately exaggerating, Heidegger says that there would then be no critique of pure reason. "If in modern [German] thought *ratio* would not speak in translation equivocally as *Vernunft* and as *Grund*, then there would be no critique of pure reason as delimitation of the possibility of the object of experience" (*SG* 164). In order that the way-making/saying/showing peculiar to *ratio* be received by German thought, two words are utilized, a utilization whose philosophical justification may be found in Kant's work. By undertaking the project of a critique of pure reason, Kant lays out the principles and rules that heighten and intensify the "calculative way" that was originally displayed in the word *ratio*. Critique of pure reason (the process, not the book) heightens the calculative way and thus sets the stage for the maximization of calculation as it occurs in modern technology.

As a language Latin unfolds within the horizon of being; thus it is in correspondence with the unfolding of being when this language puts forth *actualitas* as a translation of ἐνέργεια. But the Latin word is not and cannot be the exact replica of the Greek term because the mutual and horizonal root unfolding of being and language is not a selfsame and repetitive process. Being's unfolding as it gives rise to ἐνέργεια occurs in Greek as a language which unfolds within the horizon of being. Being's unfolding as it gives rise to *actualitas* occurs in Latin as a language which unfolds within the horizon of being. Being's unfolding within the horizon of Latin as a language is the unfolding of a withdrawal that marks the end of the First Beginning, the Beginning which initiates philosophy. This means that translation of the Greek ἐνέργεια into *actualitas* mirrors the unfolding of being which is distinguished by this withdrawal. We can see this by contrasting the "way" made in Greek by ἐνέργεια—for showing/manifesting things—with the "way" made in Latin by *actualitas*. The Greek ἐνέργεια makes a "way" of showing/manifesting of "the this" and "the that" "as unfolding in work as work [*das im Werk als Werk-Wesen*]" (*N* 2: 404). The Latin *actualitas* also makes a "way" of showing/manifesting things as work, but *actualitas* accentuates the work aspect only in terms of "what is effected in effecting, what is accomplished in accomplishing." (*N* 2: 412). Thus *actualitas* covers over the work aspect as unfolding by stressing the "*opus* of *operari*" and the "*actus* of *agere*" (*N* 2: 412).

Although *actualitas* covers over the showing/manifesting of ἐνέργεια (unfolding in work as work), the Latin word is not entirely devoid of the original root unfolding of being: "Beyond the indefinite relation to work, *actualitas* no longer preserves anything of the root unfolding of ἐνέργεια. And yet in *actualitas*, too, the initiatory root unfolding of being holds sway. . . ." (*N* 2: 413). The initiatory root unfolding of being holds sway in *actualitas* because, originating in a language which unfolds within the horizon of being, this word too "makes a way" and has showing power.

When Heidegger focuses on the translation of these two words, he demonstrates that the root unfolding of language extends into actual cases of interlingual translation. This extension is not an artificial imposition of a "new" meaning into an already existing word. Rather, it involves forming a word which conveys (does not duplicate) the "way-making"/showing/saying power of the original word. This extension tells us that, when a word of thinking is a foreign word, language of thinking unfolds in its core by corresponding to being's unfolding and by putting forth a word that evokes the original word's way-making/saying/showing power. Since this unfolding occurs as language's way-making/saying/showing, the very notion of an interlingual translation of the words of thinking no longer implies transportation of a word from one language into another. Rather, interlingual translation of words of thinking is a response which, for example, Latin provides in accordance with being's unfolding to the way-making/saying/showing that is Greek. Thus we can now respond to our earlier question, namely, "What happens *in* and *as* translation when translation of the words of thinking is interlingual?" The response is: When it is essential, interlingual translation of the words of thinking is a translation into way-making/saying/showing. We come upon a specific case of this translation when we consider Heidegger's rendition into German of a segment of the *Theaetetus* which differs sharply from Schleiermacher's rendition.

We begin by putting together a chart which enables us to survey at a glance a number of central Platonic concepts and their renditions into German by Schleiermacher and then by Heidegger. (For details see *GA* 34: 149–240.)

Plato	*Schleiermacher*	*Heidegger*
δίανοειν	Denken	Vernehmen
επισχέψασθαι	Erforschen	Im Hinsehen etwas einer Sache ansehen
λέγειν	Reden, Sprechen	Sammeln, gesammelt etwas darstellen und offenbar machen
ἀγάθος	gut	tauglich
ἐπολέγεσθαι	aufsuchen[9]	auf etwas zustreben

ἔρως	Liebe	Erstrebnis
ἀναλογίζεσθαι	zu Schlüssen gelangen	hin und her überrechnen
ἀλήθεια	Wahrheit	Unverborgenheit
οὐσία	Dasein	Seiendes

Just as the translation of the Greek ἐνέργεια into *actualitas* mirrors the unfolding of being which marks the end of the First Beginning, so also translation of Platonic concepts into German must occur in such a way as to mirror the unfolding of being *as* (not *at*) the end of the First Beginning and the beginning of philosophy proper in Plato. Just as in "*actualitas* the initiatory root unfolding of being holds sway," so also these central Platonic concepts must be translated by an unfolding of language which mirrors the initiatory root unfolding of being in the First Beginning, since this unfolding still holds sway in Plato. What is striking about Schleiermacher's translation of Plato's words of thinking (gathered in the above chart) is that his renditions of these words fail to mirror the initiatory root unfolding of being which still holds sway and is sheltered in Platonic words. True to the language that dominates the tradition that he inherits, Schleiermacher translates (to consider just a few) διανοεῖν with *Denken* (intellection), λέγειν with *Reden* (speaking), and ἀλήθεια with *Wahrheit* (truth). Despite the unmistakeable "accuracy" of his renditions, Schleiermacher's language is essentially repetitive and traditional. He does not seem to be shaken by the "foreignness" of Plato's Greek to the extent that is needed in order to come to terms with the root unfolding of his own language. His renditions are "good and accurate" interlingual translations, but they are not essential ones. Perhaps we can shed some light on this difficult and intricate issue by briefly examining Schleiermacher's and Heidegger's choice of terms for διανοεῖν.

Schleiermacher follows the prevalent practice of translating διανοεῖν with *Denken* (intellection). In Heidegger's words this is ". . . not only ungreek, but also fails to see all the issues that we face here . . . . such a harmless rendition, though correct according to the dictionary, undermines the poignancy and ground of the whole question" (*GA* 34: 181). For Schleiermacher the word διανοεῖν is not primarily a "way-made" for saying/showing/manifesting things, but denotes an "activity" by which things are intellectually grasped. For Heidegger διανοεῖν is primarily a "way-made" for showing/saying/manifesting things. He translates διανοεῖν as *Vernehmen*, i.e., taking in, interrogating, and hearing. Heidegger keenly attends to the ambivalence (*Zweideutigkeit*) of the word διανοεῖν, which on the one hand indicates "receiving" as "taking in" (*Hinnehmen*) and on the other hand stresses interrogating (as in "*Vernehmung von Zeugen im Gericht*, interrogating witnesses in court"):

In διανοεῖν we come upon [the occurrence of] "receiving/taking in" of what *shows itself* as a receiving that interrogates. This interrogating takes something in and receives it in that this interrogating takes up something in view of something [else]. [*Im* διανοειν *liegt dieses vor-nehmende, eine Sache auf etwas hin durchnehmende Hinneh-men dessen, was sich dabei zeigt.*] (GA 34: 181)

There is a world of difference between translating διανοειν with *Denken* and with *Vernehmen*. If we translate διανοειν with *Denken*, then we lose sight of the initiatory character of this word which places it at the end of the First Beginning. That this word shelters such an initiatory character is born out by the fact that, when *Beiträge zur Philosophie (Vom Ereignis)* offers a series of hints and indications for understanding how the First Beginning "plays forth" (*zuspielen*) into the "Other Beginning," this work mentions *Vernehmen* and *Vernehmung* as *words* that still reverberate with the initiatory root unfolding of being (as *Ereignis*). (Cf. *GA* 65: 198 and *passim*.)

Thus the question that emerges from the above chart is not whether Schleiermacher's renditions are accurate—they obviously are—but rather this: Are Schleiermacher's renditions into German "an essential translation which hands over to an historical epoch a 'way' of saying/showing/manifesting, or are his renditions repetitive and traditional?" Schleiermacher's translation does not unfold the German language in accordance with the root unfolding of being which occurs *as* the Other Beginning. His translation is accurate and takes over the existing and circulating reserve of words of the German language, and by that very token his translation is not an essential translation.

By contrast Heidegger's renditions of Platonic terms is the unfolding of the German language in such a way as to correspond to the root unfolding of being which marks the Other Beginning. Because the First Beginning "plays forth" into the Other Beginning—and this means that the end of this Beginning which occurs in Plato also "plays forth" into the Other Beginning—Heidegger's renditions of Platonic terms unfold the German language in such a way as to allow the initiatory character of these terms to emerge and reverberate. That is, the very words *Vernehmen, Sammeln, Erstrebnis, Unverborgenheit*, etc., are in each instance essential translation, i.e., move within the root unfolding of language within the horizon of the root unfolding of being (*das Wesen der Sprache im Geschick des Seins*).

If essential translation is a translation into way-making/saying/showing within an historical epoch, then language's unfolding as saying could be viewed as a formative power in that epoch. But how formative is saying that occurs in essential translation? We see the formative character of saying appropriately when we recall that saying occurs as soundless showing and as stillness (*GA* 12: 243ff.) Thinking more deeply into the question of translation, we realize that innerlingual translation turns us away from the differences between languages and leads us to a saying which is soundless showing and occurs right at the core of language. Thinking more deeply into the question of translation, we get a glimpse of this soundless and still showing. Gathering all of this, we can say: the unresolveable foreignness that always remains in interlingual translation is the occasion for experiencing the root unfolding of language as a soundless saying/showing within the horizon of being.

NOTES

1. Obviously the word *Wesen* presents great difficulties for translation. Rendition of this term with "essence" does not reflect the movement of emerging in its ongoing character which is crucial for this word. In *Beiträge zur Philosophie (Vom Ereignis)* Heidegger points out that *essentia* (hence also the English word *essence*) is a word that belongs to metaphysical thinking as a thinking that is concerned with "beingness of beings" (*GA* 65: 270). Speaking of τί ἐστιν and ὅτι ἐστιν, he says that the distinction between *essentia* and *existentia* "springs from the beingness of beings and thus pertains to the *Wesung* of being." Then he adds: "*Essentia* and *existentia* are not richer and do not originate from something simple. On the contrary [this distinction] is a definite impoverishment of the richer *Wesen* of being and its truth . . ." These remarks of Heidegger make it quite clear that, although the word *essence* pertains to the *Wesung* of being, there is a vast difference between *Wesen* and "essence," which difference translation must not overlook.

Several approaches to the translation of *Wesen* point out the difficulty that this word presents for translation: (1) Gail Stenstad proposes that this word be left untranslated (see her unpublished dissertation "*Heidegger's Question of Language: From Being to Dwelling*"). The disadvantage of retaining the German word is that, by keeping it intact, no translation actually takes place. (2) Wilson Brown translates the word *Wesen* with "issuance and abidance." This comes somewhat close to the movement of emerging and unfolding that the word displays. But by using two nouns instead of a verb, this translation stifles the movement character of *Wesen*. (See Wilson Brown, "The Selfsame and the Differing of the Difference," *Research in Phenomenology*, 14 [1984], 225). (3) Kenneth Maly suggests the use of the expression "root unfolding," which preserves the movement of emerging in its ongoing character. (See his "Imaging Hinting Showing: Placing the Work of Art," *Kunst und Technik: Gedächtnisschrift zum 100. Geburtstag von Martin Heidegger*, ed. F.-W. von Herrmann and W. Biemel [Frankfurt am Main: Klostermann Verlag, 1989], 195.) In this essay we shall follow Maly's practice and refer to *Wesen* throughout as "root unfolding." Although the word *root* runs the risk of indicating some lower/deeper place/thing "from out of which" the *Wesen* takes place—thus intimating a stability that runs counter to *Wesen*—nevertheless the expression "root unfolding," when heard in the resonance of the phrase taken as a whole, comes closest to indicating the significant movement which occurs in *Wesen*.

2. Miguel de Cervantes, among others, articulates the first position; Jorge Luis Borges, the second; and Goethe, the third. Cervantes advocates the first view when he suggests that reading a work in translation is like "viewing a piece of Flemish tapestry on the wrong side" (*The Ingenious Gentleman Don Quixote de la Mancha*. Trans. Peter Motteux. New York: Random House, 1950, 869). For Cervantes reading translation is equal to reading a distorted view of the original.

On the other hand, Borges suggests that translation is possible without distortion. His fictional Pier Menard envisions such a perfect translation in terms of actual writing, *not* rewriting the original. Three hundred years after Cervantes, Pier Menard plans to write *Don Quixote* in French. He knows "Spanish well, 'recovers' the Catholic faith, 'fights' against the Moors and the Turks, and 'forgets' the history of Europe between the years 1602 and 1918"; in short, he plans to be Miguel de Cervantes. This is a project which he "should only have to be immortal" in order "to carry out." (*Ficciones* (New York: Grove Press, 1962) 49f.)

Johann Wolfgang Goethe's position is somewhere between the two extremes just mentioned. He assesses the status of translation and equivalency in different terms, in that he sets a different goal for translation. In *Westöstlicher Diwan* (München: Deutscher Taschenbuch Verlag, 1961, 244) he designates as the last and third period in the history of translation one in which "we would want to make translation identical with the original in such a way that the new text does not exist instead of the original [*anstatt*], but in its place [*an der Stelle*]." (DTV Edition, p. 244) Goethe's view on translation touches the crucial points in Cervantes as well as in Borges. Unlike Cervantes, Goethe considers translation to be reliable and strong enough to be identical with the original. Unlike Borges, Goethe sees this identity, not as an absolute, but only a partial and functional identity. Insofar as Goethe does not envision the possibility of an absolute identity of translation with the original—as Borges seems to do—(translation, he says, does not exist instead of the original, but in its place) Goethe's identity of translation and original is partial and functional. He leaves open the access to and the need for a return to the original.

3. Cf. Eliane Escoubas, "Ontology of Language, Ontology of Translation in Heidegger," in the present volume.

4. To say that the "truth of being" is a "reformulation" of the "meaning of being" is to heed the occurrence of originary translation (which indicates language's "way-making") and to heed what Heidegger says about *Being and Time* in sections 42 and 91 of *Beiträge zur Philosophie (Vom Ereignis)*. In section 42 we are told that in the field of the question of being there "are no straightforward 'developments'. There is much less *that* relationship between what comes later [*das Spätere*] to what comes earlier [*das Frühere*], according to which relationship the former is contained in the latter" (*GA* 65: 85). In the light of this statement we can say that the "truth of being" is not contained in the "meaning of being" in *Being and Time*. However, this does not exclude taking "truth of being" as a reformulation of the "meaning of being." That *Being and Time* falls within the perimeter of the "truth of being" emerges clearly from section 91 of *Beiträge zur Philosophie (Vom Ereignis)*, where Heidegger characterizes *Being and Time* as "the first step toward creatively overcoming metaphysics" and adds that this step "had to be undertaken by holding firm, in one respect, to the posture of thinking (*Denkhaltung*) while at the same time, in another respect, basically overcoming this posture." Both happen in *Being and Time* insofar as this work "holds to the posture of thinking by inquiring into the *being of a being* and overcomes metaphysics insofar as [this work] inquires in advance into the truth of being . . ." (*GA* 65: 182). Inquiring in advance into the "truth of being" manifests a proximity to this truth in language which allows an originary translation into it, in the reformulation of the "meaning of being."

5. See note 1 above.

6. F.-W. von Herrmann, *Subjekt und Dasein*, 2d. ed. (Frankfurt a.M.: Vittorio Klostermann Verlag, 1985), 169.

7. Only when thinking fails to experience originary translation—whose very occurrence denies the distance between interpreter and work—as translation into "ways made" by the work, only then can thinking propose a "fusion of horizons" (*Verschmelzung der Horizonte*), as Gadamer does, or utilize a "deconstructive strategy," as Derrida is doing. (See H.-G. Gadamer, *Wahrheit und Methode*, 2d. ed. Tübingen: J. C. B. Mohr, 1965 289ff.; *ET* 269ff.; and J. Derrida, "Plato's Pharmacy," *Dissemination*, trans. B. Johnson (Chicago: University of Chicago Press, 1981). We can go one step further and suggest that, when originary translation does *not* take place, the distance which operates prior to this translation manifests itself by the demand for a "fusion of horizons" or for Derrida's concern for detecting "binary oppositions"—manifesting a certain insecurity of thinking that grows out of the very distance from the matter to be thought. For, in order for the interpreter's "horizon" to be "fused" with the "horizon" of the work, the two must be separated from each other by this distance. Likewise, identification and detection of "binary oppositions" in the text— as well as other elements of the "deconstructive strategy"—presuppose a distance and an *assessive* posture, which weigh and value one thing against another. (Is not this assessive posture what enables Derrida to detect "binary oppositions" in every work that he reads?) However, originary translation is not assessive because it is simply this: moving/stepping into "ways made" by a work of thinking.

8. The German word *das Geschick* and *geschicklich*, as used by Heidegger, presents significant trouble for translation. The usual way of translating the word into English, i.e.,

as "destiny," is inadequate—for it covers over the *movement* character of the word. Moreover, the dimension of the *unfolding* in any given epoch gets hidden and covered over. In this essay I have opted for the translation of *Wesen* as "root unfolding." In view of the immense light that *Beiträge zur Philosophie (Vom Ereignis)* sheds on Heidegger's work, I find it necessary to use the word "unfolding" also for translating the word *Geschick*. For, throughout *Beiträge zur Philosophie (Vom Ereignis)* Heidegger's use of the terms *Wesen* and *Wesung* suggests that *Geschick* too is a way of *Wesen* and *Wesung*, i.e., is a way of unfolding. This means that the movement named in *Geschick* emerges in the same place as the movement named *Wesung*, as this word is used in *Beiträge zur Philosophie (Vom Ereignis)*. The possibility of originary translation requires that interlingual translation focus precisely *not* on terms that are semantically equivalent, but rather simply heed that way of originary translation that takes place innerlingually, as the root unfolding of language. On this point, see my discussion and translation of the term *Betroffenheit* (a term that appears in Heidegger's *Nietzsche*, volume 2) as presented in my paper "The Question of Technology and Will to Power," in *Kunst und Technik: Gedächtnisschrift zum 100. Geburtstag von Martin Heidegger*, ed. F.-W. von Herrmann and W. Biemel, (Frankfurt a.M.: Klostermann Verlag, 1989), 137ff. See also by contrast translation of this term by David F. Krell in M. Heidegger, *Nietzsche*, vol. 3 (New York: Harper and Row, 1987), 189ff.

9. In this text Heidegger uses the word *erfassen*, using an earlier edition of Schleiermacher's translation. The Rowohlt edition of the Schleiermacher translation replaces *erfassen* with *aufsuchen*. See *GA* 34: 30, 203, 337.

ELIANE ESCOUBAS

18. Ontology of Language and Ontology of Translation in Heidegger

The topic of "translation" appears in the Heideggerian texts around 1935 and receives explicit development in the course on Parmenides (1942–43). At the same time appear the themes of *Dichtung* and of "the history of being," the epochality of being. The theme of *Dichtung* appears in the reading of the poets (the course on Hölderlin), and also in the lecture on "The Origin of the Work of Art," in which *Dichtung* ranks as the essence of all art. The theme of the history of being, of the "epochs" of being, appears throughout the courses on Neitzsche. So the thinking of language and the thinking of the history of being appear together in Heidegger's texts between 1935 and 1940. Where are the thinking of language and the thinking of the history of being tied to each other in the Heideggerian "text"? Where is the knot that joins the forms of language and the historic modes of the λόγος? Our hypothesis is that this knot is a thinking of "translation." "Translation" refers at one and the same time to the question of language and *Dichtung* and to the question of the history of being. "Translation" becomes the *name* of the history of philosophy. In fact, from 1935 onward the topic of the "epochs" of being—a reintroduction under a different guise of that of the "destruction of ontology" announced in *Sein und Zeit*—becomes the main focus of Heidegger's attention. It may seem odd that this "history" and this "destruction" should be carried out by the work of "repetition" (*Wiederholung*) and that this latter should be called "translation" (*Übersetzung*). So odd indeed that "translation," through this coincidence with the "repetition" of the history of being, is stretched well beyond its acceptation as a secondary and subsequent activity of thought. Thanks to this excess, "translation" names at once the *unthought* of the history of ontology and the very mode of this history. Hence "translation" and "thinking" coincide. To "translate" the early Greeks: such is the Heideggerian requirement of the "repetition" and/or "destruction" of the history of being. So it is essential that the topic of "translation" be addressed explicitly in a course on Parmenides—that is to say in a course on ἀλήθεια truth. It is essential that "translation" receives its second treatment in the "question" posed at the beginning of the 50s: *Was heisst denken?*" (which, moreover, brings Parmenides together with Nietzsche)—and that it receive perhaps its final development in *Der Satz vom Grund* (1956) through the articulation "translation-tradition" (*Übersetzung-Überlieferung*). We submit, then, that the topic of translation constitutes the reopening of the topic of hermeneutics—the topic of hermeneutics whose disappearance, or transformation after *Sein und Zeit* is emphasized by Heidegger himself (cf. "Conversation with a Japanese," in *Unterwegs zur Sprache*).

I propose therefore to analyze the course on Parmenides of 1942–43 (*GA* 54). Two themes are here interlaced: the theme of truth—ἀλήθεια—as a Permenidean "basic word" (*Grundwort*) and the theme of *translation* (*Übersetzung*) as a mode according to which *truth* is thought and unfolded in the course of the history of being. "Translation" and "history of truth": these are the two themes that we shall pursue and try to tie together.

TRANSLATION

The theme is explicit in the introduction to the course, *Parmenides* (*GA* 54: 17–18). What do we call translating? Two issues are conjugated in the text with a view to illuminating this question: the "doubling" of "to translate" (the double sense of *übersetzen*) on the one hand and, on the other, the rendering explicit of three "forms" of translation.

The First Issue: The "Doubling" of "To Translate"

The German language has in fact a double *Übersetzen*: über*setzen* with the stress on *setzen* and with *über* as an inseparable prefix, and *über*setzen with the stress on *über* which is then a separable prefix. The first *übersetzen* designates "translation" in the usual meaning of the term: the transition (*Übergang*) from one language to another—the "between-two-languages," or the advent of the "foreign." The second *übersetzen* affirms a crossing, a carrying over to "another shore." This is what Heidegger calls "originary translation" (*ursprüngliches übersetzen*). What does this consist of? It consists of the inner *movement* of a language—the incessant metamorphosis of a language into itself, the reshaping of an entire language always prior to each statement made in it. No doubt the expression "originary translation" can be understood in terms of the Humboldtian theory of language: language is a "force" (*Kraft*), language is ἐνέργεια. This *übersetzen*, this "originary translation," is not the advent of the "foreign," the translation between-two-languages, but rather the *autoproduction* of the language: the spacing constitutive of language, its noncoincidence with itself—hence its temporality or its "historiality." Let us say, therefore, that "originary translation" is a translation *prior* to all translation; it is related to something *untranslatable*, to what has no equivalent in another language. I shall call it "intraidiomatic translation" (I must emphasize that the term *idiom* is not Heidegger's). For example, the question of etymology, so important for Heidegger, would doubtless go back to this "intraidiomatic translation"; the ἔτυμον would be a function of the idiom, a spacing of the word with itself which opens up the *Spielraum* of a language.

This unfolding of the schema of a double *übersetzen* yields both a linguistic (or interlinguistic) difference (between-two-languages); and an idiomatic (or intraidiomatic) difference (in one and the *same* language), which according to Heidegger is the only "founded" difference. If we analyze this double difference as a play of the translatable and the untranslatable, we find that: (1) a language comprises something translatable; it cannot be altogether idiomatic (untranslatable). A language is not a language unless it is *exposed* to another language (exposed to translation); and (2) a language comprises something untranslatable, some idiom, for a language that is entirely translatable would not be a language but a code of behavior. I shall call these two features ekstaticness and idiomaticness, which are inseparable constituents of the essence of language. From this we infer that a language is not coextensive with an idiom, and an idiom is not coextensive with a language; this "space" between language and idiom is the basis of the essence of language in every language.

THE SECOND ISSUE: THE THREE FORMS OF TRANSLATION

I continue to follow the introduction to the course on Parmenides. We must now explain the processes contained in nonoriginary translation, translation in the usual sense. They can be expressed by three terms: *Übertragung* (transfer); *Umschreibung* (rewording); and *Umdeutung* (reinterpretation).

Übertragung (Transfer). *Übertragung* is the transition from one language to another. Two principles, the principle of equivalence and the principle of substitution, govern this transition and allow the advent of foreignness to be "overcome" (*aufgehoben*, "sublated"). *Übertragung* expresses the possibility of the indefinite reduplication of meaning, ideally without any loss, the possibility of replacing one language by another, which therefore implies that language is a support separable from its meaning.

Umschreibung (Rewording). *Umschreibung* is refiguration in the same language, the passage from the literal to the figurative, and is the general mode of allegory—paraphrase, commentary, metaphor—in other words, *rhetorical* difference. Here once more language is a separable support.

Umdeutung (Reinterpretation). As Heidegger observed, "It is through the Roman reinterpretation [*Umdeutung*] of the essence of man such as it appears in Greek experience that, from the λόγος, that is to say from the word, *ratio* has come" (*GA* 54: 101). The transition from Greek λόγος to Roman *ratio* is not just an example of *Umdeutung*; it is the very essence of all *Umdeutung*. *Umdeutung* is the "change of the domain of experience", so between the Greek ἀλήθεια and the Latin *veritas*, the "expressions" ("words") are substitutable whereas the "domain of experience" is totally different. I propose to call this difference a hermeneutic difference, the inverse of rhetorical difference. (In fact with *Umschreibung* the meaning remains the same with different "expressions"; with *Umdeutung* the "expressions" are substitutable but the domains of experience (hence the meaning) are incomparable. With *Umdeutung* (which Heidegger describes as "the event strictly so called" "*das eigentliche Ereignis*,") we enter upon history: it founds a successive temporality which is also a catastropic history, a history of "misunderstanding" and "failure to understand." What do these three forms of "translation"—*Übertragung, Umschreibung, Umdeutung*—jointly imply if they imply that language is in each of them a separable support? They imply a theory of the *sign* (*Zeichen*): a theory of language as an ensemble of signs endowed with signification, that is, the separation of the sign from the sense. In a word, they imply Platonic χωρισμός—this is why later, in *Der Satz vom Grund*, Heidegger makes the following well known statement: "the metaphorical exists only within the limits of metaphysics"—which means "the separation of the sensible and nonsensible as two domains each subsisting for itself" (*SG* 88–89). On the other hand, "originary translation"—the other translation, translation *prior* to all "effective" translation—is based on a theory of language as *undivided* language. The undividedness of language is the definitive critique of Platonic χωρισμός. Yet, as we have seen, there is *plurality* in every language, but a language is not divided on the basis of the separation of the sensible and the nonsensible, sign and sense; the plurality resides in the play of "forces," the divisions of ἐνέργεια (to employ the Humboldtian terms). Thus the notion of "originary translation" eliminates a theory of the sign: against this it initiates a theory of the *name*—so perhaps Humboldt and Cratylus agree with each other in the Heideggerian text: the Cratylic theory is perhaps nothing other than a theory of "translation" and would be another astonishing moment of the "Greek beginning."

Another stage in the critique of χωρισμός is discussed in *Der Satz vom Grund* in which we are told that "translation is not just an interpretation [*Auslegung*] but a tradition [*Überlieferung*]" . . . "which means that an essential translation [*wesentliche Übersetzung*] always corresponds, at an epoch of the destiny of being, to the way in which a language speaks of the destiny of being"; and also: "when one translates, it is a matter of knowing not only what one is translating but also from which language and into which language one is translating it."

Let us bring together the features of "originary translation": (1) A language is always in the course of translation; it is itself and in itself a process of translation. "To translate" is not in the first place to express or produce *meaning*, but in the first place *to produce a language*. In other words, at the origin of language is language—a language is always *exposed* to its origin, *exposed* to the *other* which is in it or outside it: a language is always *ekstatic*. This exposition is history; (2) A language is a monologue with itself (cf. the Novalis fragment, "Monologue"). *Poetry* is that which sets going this "monologue" or this intraidiomatic difference. When Heidegger affirms in *Parmenides*, "the poet himself is only the hermeneut, the interpreter of the word" (*GA* 54: 188), he calls the poet a "translator" and not a "user" of language. So "originary translation" entails this opposition: the poet is a translator, and the translator (in the conventional sense of the term) is a user of language. Note that an example of "monologue" or intraidiomatic translation is given to us by Heidegger himself in the process of the "doubling" of "to translate": the word *übersetzen* is "translated" in the same language—in which the difference is governed by homology, which is neither the principle of equivalence nor the principle of substitution; and (3) An *idiom* is not a language. An idiom exceeds language; not confined within a language, an idiom can pervade and run through several languages. This feature is explained in the Heideggerian analysis of truth and of the mutation of truth: Heidegger passes from Greek to German as though there were no linguistic difference between these two languages, no interlinguistic difference: he brings out a *common idiom* which is however *exposed* only in the between-two-languages.

THE MUTATION OF THE ESSENCE OF TRUTH

Let us now pursue schematically the second theme of the *Parmenides*. The mutation of the essence of truth is not a simple example in which the forms of translation as established in "the introduction" would receive confirmation; on the contrary, it is the very foundation of the elaboration of these forms. The Heideggerian text is here itself a tissue of "translations." Let us summarize the text by distinguishing three stages.

THE FIRST STAGE

The point of departure is the "fragment" of Parmenides on ἀλήθεια. Heidegger "translates" ἀλήθεια directly by the German word *Unverborgenheit* (*unconcealedness*). What takes place in this translation? To all appearances we remain in the same language: it is as if *Unverborgenheit* were a citation of the Greek in German. Ἀλήθεια/*Unverborgenheit* constitutes, then, an idiom common to Greek and German: the passage from the one to the other is an "originary translation"—an intraidiomatic translation. This is not all. *Unverborgenheit* permits the deployment of the essence of ἀλήθεια: as "combative essence"—as "combat against concealedness" (*GA* 54: 27). What has happened? We have passed from Greek *to* Greek *through* German; German plays the role of *relay language* permitting the repetition of the Greek into Greek.

The Second Stage

So we come back to the Greek language. The Greek language offers two "contraries" (*Gegenwesen*) of ἀληθές: ληθής (λᾶθον) and ψευδής. There is, then, an operation of displacement which is an *Umschreibung* (rewording) in the Greek language; ψευδής replaces ληθής (λᾶθον) as the "contrary" of ἀληθές. Let us, like Heidegger, analyze the term ψευδής. (1) ψευδής loses a dimension contained in ληθες (λᾶθον): the dimension of forgetting, but retains the dimension of the hiding-dissimulating; and (2) ψευδής includes another dimension: that of showing, "bringing-to-appearance" (*scheinen*). (Heidegger says, for example, that a *sign* is a ψεῦδος; so it is a question of a "showing" that dissimulates or a "dissimulating" that shows: it is a question of showing something in dissimulating something else.) Thus, although ψευδής and ἀληθές are "contraries" they have "showing" in common. As a result of this displacement of the "contrary" of ἀληθές—from ληθής (λᾶθον) to ψευδής—the *a* of ἀληθές loses its negative-privative connotation. The German translation of ἀληθές is not simply *unverborgene* but *entborgene* (where the prefix *ent-* marks not privation but *spacing*). Hence a displacement that is *readable* in the German language permits the redeployment of the essence of the *a* of ἀλήθεια—and so we read in the *Parmenides*:

> GA 54: 20: *Un-*is expressed in Greek by *a-*
> GA 54: 56: *Ent-*is expressed in Greek by *a-*

So only German, the relay language, has allowed the "doubling" of the Greek. Not only does one and the same idiom occur in Greek and German but German also allows the reading of *Greek into Greek*.

THE THIRD STAGE

The German translation of ψεῦδος is *das Falsche*—the false. Heidegger appeals to the authority of Grimm's dictionary for saying *das Falsche* is an un-German word (*undeutsches Wort*), because *das Falsche* comes from the Latin *falsum*. Now the Latin falsum occupies a domain of experience quite different from that of ἀλήθεια. While the domain of experience of ἀλήθεια is "bringing-to-appearance," the domain of experience of *falsum* is *failure. Fallere* means to fall, to bring down, to cause to fail. This is the domain of experience of the *Imperium Romanum.*

This is why with *falsum/das Falsche* it is a matter of reinterpretation (*Umdeutung*): "the Roman *falsum* is something foreign (*etwas Fremdes*) to the Greek ψεῦδος." *Etwas Fremdes*: with the Latin one leaves the intraidiomatic difference in order to embark upon the advent of the "foreign," and that is "the event properly so called" (*das eigentliche Ereignis*) in the history of being. The advent of the "foreign," of reinterpretation or mutation (*Wandlung*) of the essence of truth: this event becomes "reversal" (*Umschlag*), for the Latin *verum* means the "closed," the "covered"—hence precisely the opposite of the Greek ἀληθές which means the "open," the "noncovered," the "discovered." With the Latin we have therefore passed from intraidiomatic translation to interlinguistic translation. But the Latin *veritas*, by which in interlinguistic translation the Greek ἀλήθεια is translated, says precisely the opposite of ἀλήθεια. The term-for-term correspondence between ἀλήθεια and *veritas* amounts, then, to a "bad translation." So interlinguistic translation, cut off from "originary translation," inaugurates a "history": it opens a successive temporality, a temporality of "failure of understanding" and "misunderstanding."

But what is a "foreign language"? And what is one's "own language"? And how are we to understand this astonishing passage from *Was ist das—die Philosophie?* (1955): "The Greek language, and it alone, is λόγος . . . what is said in it is at the same time in a privileged way what is said names (*nennt*) . . . Through the word heard with a Greek ear we are directly in the presence of the thing itself there before us, and not first in the presence of a mere verbal meaning." Why is this at first appearance, exorbitant privilege accorded to the Greek language? Is it only a question of a privilege accorded to *one* language among *others*?

And how could a language, if it is a *language*, put us in the presence of "the things themselves"? The Heideggerian text must be heard differently: the Greek language is "language" on account of what is *untranslatable*—idiomatic—in it: the *names*. The opposition on which the Heideggerian text is based is the opposition of *naming* and *signifying* (*nennen/bedeuten*). Now there is no interlinguistic translation of the name; the name depends on a *translation-citation*: it is cited in several languages. A name, as idiom, can pervade and pass through several languages. Thus, what we must read in the privilege accorded to the Greek language is a determination of language in general: the essence of language consists in *nomination* prior to *signification*. What else does this determination imply if not the rejection of a theory of the sign (Zeichen), that is, a rejection of χωρισμός? It is therefore necessary to rework the Heideggerian notion of "foreign language": there is "foreignness" in every language, the foreign is the realm of χωρισμός. What is foreign in language is the ψεῦδος (the sign), the withdrawal of ἀλήθεια. So a translation always has to do with *truth*.

Therefore the history of the mutation of truth and the duplicity of "to translate" (as paradox of the translatable and the untranslatable, or paradox of the ekstatic and the idiomatic) are related to each other. Translation is not *the betrayal* (*treason*) that certain languages assert: in Italian *traddutore-traditore*. Translation, in all its Heideggerian forms, goes back to another τόπος: the τόπος of the unthought (*Ungedachte*). The *unthought* is not what would be purely and simply to be thought, but it is what calls for and forth thought: as what opens the *Spielraum* for "repetition" throughout the history of being. The unthought is the mode proper to tradition (Überlieferung). Does not translation therefore constitute the "hermeneutic circle" of the texts of the second Heidegger?

Let us conclude by bringing a few threads together.

(1) To Platonic χωρισμός—which is *Spaltung*—Heidegger opposes the *Zwiefalt*: the fold, the "doubling"-"redoubling" of "to translate."

(2) "Plurality" is inscribed in every language; a language is always plural, always "several"—the "foreign," as the ekstatic, inhabits every language.

(3) *Inversely*, there is a relation of *kinship* among languages: *idiom* can circulate from one to the other; it can be common to several languages.

(4) The "task" of the translator lies in bringing into play the paradox of the simultaneous *foreignness* and *kinship* of languages. This paradox is that in which the *unthought* is inscribed. Hence the task of the *translator* is doubtless no different from the task of the *historian*.

NOTE

I am very grateful to John Llewelyn for his help in translating this very work.

19. Mimesis and Translation

It is rather astonishing that Heidegger—who subjected almost all fundamental words of Greek thinking either to a critical analysis or to a retrieval that lets them say what they might have originally said—never mentions *mimesis*, which without doubt is one of the most important words in the philosophical and rhetorical tradition of antiquity. There are only twenty pages, found in the Nietzsche lectures, in which the subject of *mimesis* is explicitly thematized (*N* I 198–17). In those pages he gives a lucid but very limited and rather traditional exposition of one aspect of Plato's ideas on *mimesis*. Heidegger finds Plato's understanding of *mimesis* to be a reflection of Plato's doctrine of truth as adequation, or ὁμοίωσις. In his *Introduction to Metaphysics* Heidegger writes: "The basic concepts ἰδέα, παράδειγμα, ὁμοίωσις, and μίμησις foreshadow the metaphysics of classicism" (*GA* 40:194; *IM* 185).

Phillipe Lacoue-Labarthe speaks about a "persistent refusal by Heidegger to take the concept of *mimesis* seriously."[1] This refusal of Heidegger's parallels his refusal to take seriously the Sophists, who were masters in *mimetic* art and the rhetorical tradition in which *mimesis* plays a central role. On the other hand, Lacoue-Labarthe remarks, and in my view correctly, that it is difficult not to see that there is a fundamental *mimetology* at work in Heidegger's thinking. A *mimetology* that in fact betrays many Platonic traits, which means that the *mimetic* is seen as the inauthentic, the nonoriginal,—or, better, as that which has removed itself from the original given origin. Therefore, it is no accident that Heidegger only speaks of *mimesis* in relation to Plato and neglects Aristotle and the entire rhetorical and literary tradition.

Heidegger's reservation about speaking of *mimesis* goes so far that in his essay "On the Essence and Concept of φύσις" he quotes and comments on a long passage from Aristotle's *Physics* and breaks off the quotation precisely where Aristotle begins to speak about *mimesis* (*GA* 9: 239–40). Even more remarkably, in "The End of Philosophy and the Task of Thinking," Heidegger refers to ἐνάργεια to clarify the *Lichtung des Seins* (*SD* 73). This ἐνάργεια not to be confused with ἐνέργεια, means something like the sparkling, glimmering, shimmering, and is one of the basic notions of the rhetorical tradition. According to this tradition, ἐνάργεια is an affect of *mimesis*. This is how it happens: a good speaker— a storyteller or writer—knows how to render events, situations, persons, and deeds in such a way that the listener (reader) has the impression of being present as an eyewitness to the event, situation, etc. In and through the rendering (*narratio*, which is a form of *mimesis*), events, situations, persons, and deeds appear in a lucid, sparkling, glimmering, shimmering way. But where they appear, namely in the rendering, is not, of course, where they are in fact. Cicero and Quintillian speak here about *evidentia in narratione* (narrative evidence). In the narrative (rendering, exposition, discourse), which means, in *mimesis*, that there is a certain displacement of so-called reality that takes place so that reality can appear, and it can appear precisely because it appears at another place, namely, in the rendering. The capacity to speak and write in such a way that this takes place is, for obvious reasons, held in the highest regard in the rhetorical and literary tradition. It is a high point in *mimetic* art.

Heidegger remains silent as always about this rhetorical and mimetic aspect of ἐνάργεια. He speaks only about the *Lichtung des Seins* and about the translation of the Greek word ἐνάργεια by Cicero with *evidentia*, two things which are related in Heidegger.

About *Lichtung des Seins*: according to Heidegger, the Greek word ἐνάργεια means that something sparkles in itself and on its own (*leuchtet und scheint*). Heidegger adds that in order for something to be able to sparkle and shine, a more original openness is necessary, an openness in which something can sparkle and shine. An openness in which a giving and a yielding is granted. This openness is called the *Lichtung des Seins*. With all the caution and prudence that is here necessary, one could perhaps say that *Lichtung*—as well as "ἀλήθεια," which is concealment and disclosure, as well as *Ereignis* which is also always *Enteignis*— are names for what occurs in the various forms of *mimesis*. Without doubt Heidegger would protest against this kind of interpretation due to his Platonic interpretation of *mimesis*. But another interpretation than the Platonic one is possible. John Sallis writes in a recent article on *mimesis* in Heidegger that "*mimesis* can be rethought and reinscribed within Heidegger's poetics."[2] Indeed *mimesis* must be rethought, but not in terms of a more or less perfect adequation as Plato does; rather, it must be rethought in terms of what we mentioned above, namely, a displacement, the appearing of beings at a place where they are not in fact. That means, in terms of ἀλήθεια as concealment and disclosure or *Ereignis*, which is equally *Enteignis*. I would like to add that a radical reflection on *mimesis* within Aristotle and the rhetorical tradition could perhaps shed a new light on what Heidegger calls ἀλήθεια. Perhaps one should be more prudent when speaking of an original presence, an authentic proximity, a true word that names being, than Heidegger seems to be when he persists in speaking of these things.

Translation: in the quoted passage on ἐνάργεια, Heidegger remarks that Cicero translated this word with *evidentia*, thereby giving it another meaning, which is Roman (*übersetzt, d.h. ins Römische umdeutet*). This is one of the many remarks that Heidegger makes regarding the translation into Latin of Greek words such as ἀλήθεια, λήθη, λόγος, δίκη, φύσις, οὐσία, ὑποκείμενον, ψεῦδος, etc., which in each case is, according to him, a perversion of meaning (*Umdeutung*), a displacement (*Verstallung*), a covering over (*Verdeckung*). Heidegger develops this in his lecture on Parmenides in 1942–43.

To introduce a more fundamental problem, some prefatory remarks are in order. (1) Translation in Heidegger is never only a question of language. Words are not only translated but relocated (*übersetzt-übergesetzt*) to another context, another world. So the Greek words were relocated in a Roman world, and that means in an imperial, curial, and ultimately Roman Catholic world; (2) Heidegger makes a decisive but not very clear distinction between the translation of Greek words into a Roman world and into a Germanic world; (3) The translation of Greek into Roman (*die Römanisierung des Griechentums*) goes together with a transformation of the essence of truth and being (*ein Wandel des Wesens der Wahrheit und Seins*), and this transformation is, according to Heidegger, the "genuine event in history (*das eigentliche Ereignis in der Geschichte*) (*GA* 59: 66). In this context Heidegger says "being originally gives itself word" (*das Sein gibt sich anfänglich ins Wort*), (*GA* 59: 113), and this event takes place in and through a translation. This event is the event of disclosure and concealment, and disclosure and concealment are fundamental traits of being (*Entbergung und Verbergung sind ein Grundzug des Seins*) (*GA* 59: 105). Those are my prefatory remarks.

To translate is an hermeneutic and mimetic activity. It is hermeneutic in the two senses of the Greek word ἑρμηνεία: first, to render in words, and this is the topic of Aristotle's Περὶ Ἑρμηνείας; second, to interpret what is already rendered in words, which means, to say it in other words, eventually in another language. To translate is also *mimetic* in the two senses of that word: first, among other things, *mimesis* is the rendering of events and deeds in words—this is the topic of Aristotle's *Poetica*. This last work speaks about ἔπος and tragedy which consists of rendering possible and probable events into words. These events are brought to another level in and through *mimesis*. This other level is not necessarily a lower level, as Plato says, nor a higher level, as Hegel and perhaps Aristotle think. Second, "mimesis" also means to repeat what is already rendered into words, for instance, on the stage, in a quotation, or in a repetition of something using different words or in a different manner. *Variatio*, which means to say it in a different way, and *aemulatio*, which means to surpass the example in excellence, play an important role in this last form of *mimesis*. Translation is always a kind of *variatio* and *aemulatio*.

Heidegger takes up the hermeneutical aspect of translation but remains silent, as always, about its mimetic and rhetorical aspect. It is true that he frequently speaks about repetition, both in the sense of retrieval and mere repetition. The possibility of repeating words that at one time were original pertains, according to Heidegger, to the nonessence of language (*Unwesen der Sprache*), as he says in his *Germania und Der Rhien* (*GA* 39: 63). To speak about the nonessence of language is Platonic in a certain sense. If to translate is to reiterate something on another level, and if translation is a mimetic act, it seems then that Heidegger views translation—at least when it pertains to the translation of Greek into Latin—as a reiteration on a lower level. Perhaps the Platonic interpretation of *mimesis* also plays a role here.

To conclude, Heidegger has without doubt made extremely important remarks concerning translation, and every remark calls for a very careful analysis. But

I think that a radical reflection on what the Greeks—and not only Plato—understood by "mimesis" would shed a different light on the problem of translation and, at the same time, on the transformation of the essence of truth and being (*das Wandel des Wesens der Wahrheit und des Seins*) that takes place in translation.

NOTES

1. Philippe Lacoue-Labarthe, *l'Imitation des modernes* (Paris: Galilée, 1986) 170.
2. J. Sallis, "Heidegger's Poetics: The Question of Mimesis," in *Kunst und Technik. Gedächnisschrift zum 100. Geburtstag von Martin Heidegger*, eds. W. Biemel and F.-W. von Herrmann (Frankfurt a.M.: Vittorio Klostermann, 1989), 188.

IX

LANGUAGE AND
ART

FRANÇOISE DASTUR

20. Language and *Ereignis*

Sprache und Ereignis. Aufklang der Erde,
Widerklang der Welt. Streit, die
ursprüngliche Bergung der Zerklüftung,
weil der innigste Riss. Die offene Stelle.
Sprache, ob gesprochen oder geschwiegen,
die erste und weiteste Vermenschung des
Seienden. So scheint es. Aber *sie* gerade
die ursprünglichste Entmenschung des
Menschen als vorhandenes Lebewesen und
"Subjekt" und alles Bisherigen. Und damit
Gründung des Da-seins und der
Möglichkeit der Entmenschung des
Seienden.

Heidegger, *Beiträge zur Philosophie*

In "A Dialogue on Language" dating from 1954, Heidegger acknowledges to his
Japanese interlocutor that "[his] questions circled around the problem of language
and of Being" and that "reflection on language and Being has determined [his]
path of thinking from early on" (*US* 91, 93). He goes back as early as 1915 to
his dissertation, *Duns Scotus's Doctrine of Categories and Theory of Meaning*
to show that his primary interest already focused on the discussion of the Being
of beings under the traditional name of "doctrine of categories" and on the reflection on language in its relation to Being under the heading of "theory of meaning"
whose metaphysical name is *grammatica speculativa*. He admits, however, that
"all these relationships were at that time still unclear to [him]" (*US* 92). In fact,
the relationship between language and Being was still not quite clear after a twelve-
years' silence because even though *Being and Time* developed at length the question
of Being, that is not the case with the theme "Language and Being" that stayed
in the background in 1927: as the Japanese inquirer points out further on in the
dialogue, "in *Being and Time*, [Heidegger's] discussion of language remains quite
sparse" (*US* 7) because section 34 about discourse and language (*Rede und
Sprache*) is regrettably short.

Heidegger, however, finds retrospectively in this section "an indication about
the essential dimension of language" as he already said in 1946 in the *Letter on
Humanism*[1] so that he does not seem to see any contradiction between the existential conception of language in *Being and Time* and his later determination of the

essence of language as Being itself. He even explains that, because reflection on language and Being has determined the path of his thinking from early on, the discussion of their relationship has stayed as far as possible in the background (*US* 93) as if he had been waiting for the time when he would be able to see and to say clearly what the real theme of his thinking was. We know that this kind of retrospective reading belongs to Heidegger's self-interpretation and to his understanding of his own thinking as one way[2] that can and must "turn" and change (*wenden*) but not break off suddenly to begin again from another starting point. But for us the question remains: is the fundamental theme of Heideggerian thinking "language and Being" rather than "Being and time," and is there a way that leads from the first theme to the second one, from the "timebook" of 1927 to the "languagebook" published in 1959 under the title *Unterwegs zur Sprache* (*On the Way to Language*)?

In 1927 Heidegger's purpose was to show that time is the transcendental horizon of Being—in other terms, that Being is intrinsically "temporal." This goal was not reached, as we know, in the published part of *Being and Time*, which remained an incomplete book[3], but later, in the following period, from 1927 to 1929, when Heidegger developed his project of an ontology as a transcendental and temporal science in his lectures.[4] Heidegger, however, was not satisfied with his answer to the "fundamental question" (*Grundfrage*) of the "and" of Being and time which understands Being as the horizontal or rather horizonal scheme projected by the transcendence of the *Dasein*. He therefore renounced the publication of the famous third section in which, as its title "Time and Being" suggests, "the whole [that is to say the relation between Being and time] is reversed" because, he says in the *Letter on Humanism*, "the thinking failed to express this reversal in an adequate manner and did not succeed in saying it with the help of the language of metaphysics."[5] This means, in particular, that the old words of "transcendence," "horizon," and "scheme" were not appropriate to name the relationship between Being and time.

Consequently, it is clear that in order to think the "temporality" of Being, another language beside the language of tradition is needed. But, as Heidegger points out in *On the Way to Language*, the needed transformation of language "does not result from the procurement of newly formed words and phrases" (*US* 267)—as if we should try to give better names to things and to change the structure of our statements in order to express the phenomena more accurately. If that were the case, it would mean that Heidegger remained caught in the logical and grammatical conception of language, in what commentators on Wittgenstein's *Philosophical Investigations* called "the Augustinian image of language," i.e., a nominalistic conception of language that sees in words only names and referential lexemes or even morphemes.[6] The required transformation of language is the transformation of our relation to language: we need to undergo an experience with language in which we learn to renounce our usual understanding of the relation of word to thing as a connection between two beings or two objects (*US* 170). Because words (*Worte*) are not similar to things, they only seem to consist essentially in sounds or letters (in phonemes or graphemes) when we identify them with terms (*Wörter*) instead of paying attention to the soundless voice of that which is said in that which is spoken (see *US* 192: *WD* 88–89).[7] The word, the saying, has no being, is nothing that is because it not only stands in a relation to the thing but also is the relation itself that makes it possible for a thing to be (*US* 170, 188).[8] The word does not stand for the thing, it is not a way of grasping what is present by giving it a name or a means of portraying what lies before us; it is, rather, that which first bestows presence and Being on things (*US* 227): it is the source, the fount of Being (*US* 169).

By breaking with the pictorial conception of language, we no longer tend to oppose in the metaphysical way "being" and "becoming" and to understand Being as something already present (*vorhanden*) that we should subsequently try to express. Insofar as we learn to inhabit the language, instead of using it as a mere means of designation and communication, we withdraw from the metaphysics of pre-sence, i.e., from ontotheology, that conceives Being as the already present ground of beings instead of seeing in it the happening of lighting on the basis of an abysmal occultation. We open ourselves to another conception of Being, to Being as *Ereignis*, as far as this word—which I will leave untranslated—names that which determines the belonging together of Being and time.[9]

Language and *Ereignis*: This is therefore the name of the proper theme of Heidegger's thinking, which does not replace the former theme "Being and time" but confers on it a more initial form, in the sense that it makes more explicit its central problem: that of the relationship—of the *Verhältnis*—between man and Being. This is at least the leading hypothesis of my attempt to read Heidegger. But in order to try to verify this hypothesis, I must now retrace Heidegger's path of thinking and start again from *Being and Time*.

DISCOURSE AND LANGUAGE (*REDE UND SPRACHE*)

In section 34 of *Being and Time*, language is understood as a constitutive element of Dasein as Being-in-the-world, i.e., as a specifically human mode of Being, and in this respect Heidegger does not hesitate to rely upon the Greek determination of the human being as ζῷον λόγον ἔχον. However, this definition does not mean for him that the human being has the capacity to speak, i.e., to utter vocal sounds, but rather that the disclosing of world and of Dasein constitutes its mode of being. Λόγος does not mean in fact "language" but "discourse," and has the sense of manifestation (*offenbar machen*) (*SZ* 32): Heidegger stresses that "the Greeks have no word for language (*Sprache*), they 'first of all' understood this phenomenon as discourse (*Rede*)" (*SZ* 165), which means that for them the φωνή—even the φωνή σημαντική which is, according to Aristotle, the element of discourse[10]—does not constitute the essence of λόγος. We should not therefore translate the word *Rede* as *speech*, in spite of the fact that it is the usual meaning of the word in German. Heidegger understands this word in light of its etymology[11] as "articulation" in the sense of fitting together and structuring (*gliedern*), which is better expressed—better but not really well expressed—by the word *discourse*, which means an ordained succession of propositions.

Heidegger defines discourse as "the articulation of what is comprehensible,"[12] but this does not mean that it comes after comprehension as a kind of post-structuration of what has been already understood. We should become aware of the fact that comprehension is always already articulated exactly in the same sense that disposition always involves a certain comprehension: the three existential elements of the disclosedness of Dasein—comprehension, disposition and discourse—are co-original (gleichursprünglich)[13] and not founded on one another. On the contrary, language in Being and Time is not an original but a "founded phenomenon,"[14] whose existential-ontological foundation is to be found in discourse.[15] We can consequently understand why the phenomenon of language has already been analyzed under the form of the statement (Aussage) in section 33, i.e., before discourse becomes a theme: statement can be an extreme derivative of explicitation (Auslegung)[16] only because explicitation, which is nothing else than the development of comprehension,[17] and the appropriation of what has been comprehended,[18] is possible only on the ground of discourse.[19]

Discourse is the condition of possibility of language and, conversely, language is the "wordly" being of discourse, its oral exteriorization (die Hinaus-gesprochenheit der Rede), so that meanings become words instead of being attributed to words considered as things.[20] Language is therefore to be found within the world as if it were a being ready-at-hand (ein Zuhandenes), i.e., a mere instrument, whereas discourse, which can remain unspoken, possesses the existential possibilities of keeping silence and hearing. Hearing can neither be identified with acoustic perception, nor can keeping silence be identified with dumbness. The perception of "pure sounds" is only possible on the basis of hearing, exactly as speaking is only possible on the basis of discourse because hearing always means comprehension of a being-ready-at-hand inside the world and not the interpretation of the internal sensations of a subject who has only a mediate relation to the world. Keeping silence does not mean lack of the ability to speak, but presupposes, on the contrary, the possibility of saying, i.e., of disclosing, so that silence is the original mode of discourse that can convey comprehension even better than speech itself (SZ 164). Therefore, the constitutive elements of discourse should not be identified with the constitutive elements of speech: the former are existential characters, and the latter ontic ones.[21]

After this very brief recapitulation of the analysis of discourse in section 34, the question remains: How could Heidegger retrospectively find in this section, in which language has only a subordinate position, "an indication of the essential dimension of language"? It is, in fact, only at the end of section 34 that Heidegger asks the question concerning the mode of Being of language. Because spoken or written words are found within the world, they can be seen as present-at-hand things, and language can be taken as the ready-at-hand instrument of communication. But are presence-at-hand and instrumentality the proper mode of Being of language, and is not language a mode of Being of Dasein, an existential element like discourse and not only an existentiel phenomenon? Or has language neither the mode of Being of an instrument nor the mode of Being of Dasein? In that case, language should not be included among the different modes of Being but should be referred directly to Being itself in its unity. Heidegger does not develop this question as explicitly as I have tried to do but finally declares that, because the object of the science of language remains so obscure and ontologically undecided, the time has come for philosophy to stop considering language as the special domain of the "philosophy of language," and to question the "things themselves," i.e., to submit language to the ontological problematic (*SZ* 166).

The only purpose of section 34 is to show that the ontological "locus" (*Ort*) of the phenomenon of language has to be looked for within Dasein's ontological constitution. But in Chapter 4 of the second division, in which the existential analysis is repeated in terms of temporality, we see that the ontological locus of what constitutes the condition of possibility of language, i.e., discourse, remains undecided within the fundamental structure of Dasein. The principal difficulty comes from the fact that discourse is the third moment of Being-in-the-world, but it is not the third moment of the Being of Dasein, i.e., care. Care, along with existentiality (i.e., comprehension as project) and facticity (i.e., disposition as thrownness), includes as a third moment, fallenness (*SZ* 191). This cannot mean that discourse is excluded from the fundamental structure of care which should constitute the unity of all structural elements already analyzed, but it indicates that discourse cannot form a separate element of the total structure of Dasein. But if discourse is always already "contained" in project and thrownness,[22] it is not possible to assign to it a definite primary mode of temporalization,[23] as is the case for comprehension, which is primarily adventive (*zukünftig*), for disposition which is primarily grounded in having-been-ness (*Gewesenheit*) and for fallenness, which finds its existential sense in the present (*Gegenwart*).[24]

It is possible, however, to assign a privileged constitutive function to the present in regard to the facticity of discourse, i.e., language of everydayness (*SZ* 349). Everyday language is linked to the positive phenomenon of loquacity (*Gerede*) which is the fallen mode of discourse (see *SZ* § 35). As such, it gives a one-sided privilege to an existential character of discourse, which is the tenor of discourse (*das Geredete*) and address (*Anreden*), and it remains satisfied with a superficial comprehension of the "object" of discourse (*Das Worüber, Das Beredete*). This does not mean that communication (*Mitteilung*), which is another existential character of discourse and not only an existentiel dimension of speech, has been privileged; on the contrary, in loquacity there is no communication because nothing is really communicated: dictum (*Das Gesagtsein*) becomes the only instance of discourse without any original appropriation of its "object." When the relation to the "thing itself" has been lost, dictum (the having-been-said) takes on an authoritative character so that there is an inversion of what should constitute the finality of discourse: instead of disclosing, it closes up access to the being that matters and covers it up. In spite of all these negative aspects of loquacity, we should not underestimate its "positivity": we can by no means completely avoid loquacity—not even here, not even now—and always withstand the seduction of the state of interpretation prevailing in everydayness because discourse has always already factually become language: factual discourse is language[25] and we always already find ourselves under the domination of ordinary language. But the facticity of discourse as language does not mean that language is merely present-at-hand in the world but that it is, on the contrary, founded on the ontological structures of Dasein: discourse includes in itself—as a fourth structural element besides object of discourse (*Beredetes*), tenor of discourse (*Geredetes*), and communication (*Mitteilung*)—the existential possibility of enunciation and manifestation (*Bekundung*), i.e., of speaking. We cannot therefore escape ordinary language or fallenness in general. The best we can do is to become aware of our constant "uprootedness" (*Entwurzelung*), i.e., of the cutting off of our primary relation to Being and of the strangeness of the state of suspendedness (*Unheimlichkeit der Schwebe*) involved in the everydayness of Being-in-the-world (*SZ* 170).

Sections 34, 35 and 68d, however, are not the only ones in *Being and Time* in which discourse is analyzed. Discourse is once more mentioned, under the form of the call of conscience (*Ruf des Gewissens*), in the second division, when the question is to find in Dasein itself the testimony of the possibility for it of an "authentic" existence (*SZ* § 54). Conscience is the phenomenon by which disclosedness (*Erschlossenheit*) can become resoluteness (*Entschlossenheit*) in the sense that Dasein takes upon itself its own being and brings it to comprehension. And this relation with itself can only take the form of the voice of conscience. Heidegger stresses that this way of speaking of the call or voice of conscience is not at all metaphorical, precisely because it is not essential to discourse to be phonetically enunciated: the German *Stimme* has not primarily the vocal sense of the Greek φωνή,[26] but means merely to disclose, to "give-to-comprehend."[27] That is why voice and call can be modes of discourse and not only of language, exactly in the same sense as hearing, that does not mean primarily acoustic perception. But the soundless voice of conscience, because it has the character of a call, cannot be simply and solely understood as the mode of an immediate self-presence: a call is always a shock and a shake, because it calls from a distance and in the distance (*aus der Ferne und in die Ferne*) (*SZ* 271).[28] Self-presence of Dasein—and not of subject—can only mean proximity in distance and not, as seems to be the case in Husserlian soliloquy, absolute proximity of the subject to itself: because Dasein is temporality and transcendence, self-affection through the call of conscience does not happen in the intimacy of solitary life but in everydayness, i.e., in a being preoccupied with the "world," whose self is not pure interiority but temporalization, i.e., self-differance and self-differing.[29]

The call of conscience, which calls up (*aufruft*) Dasein to become what it is, does not say anything, does not communicate anything to the self, but only calls Dasein back out of its dispersion in "inauthenticity," which does not mean cutting off its relationship with others but access to a more original Being-with-others. Because the phenomenon of conscience is not similar to a dialogue with oneself, the call of conscience discourses in the strange mode of keeping silence.[30] The strangeness here—*die Unheimlichkeit*—comes from the foreign character of the voice which is calling. It is true that in the call of conscience Dasein—and not a transcendent being—calls itself, and that the being who is called is at the same time the being who calls. But the calling happens abruptly and unwillingly: "there is" a calling (*"Es" ruft*) (*SZ* 275) and it is not the call of the other. Who then is calling finally? Not a present-at-hand being, that does not mean no being at all, because Being is not to be identified with presence-at-hand which is only one mode of Being. It means, therefore, that the voice calling cannot come from within the world, from Dasein in everydayness who is immersed in a world familiar to it. Nevertheless, it does not come from somewhere out of the world, it comes from Dasein as being thrown into the world and whose original relation to world is not familiarity, but the "feeling"—i.e., *Angst*—of not being at home.[31] The voice calling, although foreign to everydayness, is friendly in the sense that it calls up Dasein to its most proper power-to-be.[32]

The "identity" between what calls and what is called, between the voice of the foreigner and the voice of the friend,[33] is the expression, in the structure of discourse, of the duality of Dasein in its temporalizing self-differance: Dasein is at the same time project and thrownness, comprehension and disposition, disclosing and factually disclosed, adventive and having been. This duality has to be thought of as the co-originality of the ek-stases of temporality,[34] which means that self-temporalization can never be understood as a separate process emanating from a being closed in itself and present-at-hand: Heidegger's solipsism is existential (see *SZ* 188) and the solitude of "authenticity" does not exclude but includes the essential dimension of world and of the Other in a more original manner than dispersedness of inauthenticity does. Even more profoundly, this duality is the expression of the radical finitude of temporality that defines the human being in its difference from the animal. Human finitude is not only the fact of not being the origin of Being, because being dependent on the pre-donation of the beings constitutes also animal condition: human finitude is the need[35] of comprehending Being which becomes manifest as Dasein. Finitude is therefore not a characteristic of human reason, but the fact that human being is summoned to comprehend Being. Radical finitude alone explains why there is ontological "creativity" in the human being who, like the animal, is ontically noncreative. The conjunction of powerless dependence upon predonated beings and of overpowerful summoning to the comprehension of Being is what constitutes properly the historicality of Dasein, i.e., fate (*Schicksal*) (*SZ* 384–85). Only a being who has a fate can hear the soundless voice of conscience and therefore keep silence. The animal, that cannot speak because it cannot discourse, cannot hear anything else than vocal sounds: it is not open to the silent call of conscience because its powerlessness is not creative—because it does not need to create the ontological horizon in which beings can appear. The human being has to anticipate, i.e., to schematize, in order to be receptive. He sees and hears only what he has already understood, i.e., articulated in a discourse. Man shapes the world—*Der Mensch ist weltbildend* (*GA* 29/30: § 42)—means that he needs to give himself a scheme, i.e., a special kind of image (*Bild*), to give a direction to his intentionality so that it can encounter beings. The animal, on the contrary, is directly open to the realm of the sensible but not to beings as beings: its specific way of being open is quite different from human openness to Being, which does not mean that it is inferior.[36]

Whereas the ekstase of "inauthentic" present can be assigned to language as a primary mode of temporalization—which means that silence only seems to constitute the "authentic" or proper mode of discourse—we have seen that discourse as such does not find its temporalization in one particular ekstase. Discourse is the origin of the expliciting articulation which makes beings manifest as beings.[37] It does not, consequently, reveal a specific character of Being—as is the case for comprehension, which reveals possible Being, and disposition, which reveals factual Being—but only what Heidegger later calls the ontological difference.[38] Discourse can therefore find its primary temporalization either in the future in "authentic" existence or in the present in "inauthentic" existence, because in both cases the ontological difference is fully accomplished as it is nothing else than existence itself.[39] Therefore, it is only after *Being and Time*, when Heidegger begins to develop the problematic of the ontological difference, that the relation of language to Being can come to the fore. And this leads Heidegger to a complete transformation of his concept of language.

LANGUAGE AS *EREIGNIS*

I would like to try now, after such a long journey through *Being and Time*, to approach the theme of this lecture, i.e., the explanation of the relation between language and *Ereignis* in Heidegger's late thinking. By carefully reading the 1927 work, we have been able to measure the importance of discourse—which is not only a specific existential element but one that is related to Dasein as a whole—in spite of the "sparseness" of its indications concerning discourse and language. Language itself and not only discourse can become an essential theme only if it is no longer understood as the phonetic enunciation of words, but, like discourse, as a showing, i.e., a saying. In section 7 of *Being and Time* Heidegger, following Aristotle, understands the Greek λόγος as discourse in the sense of the manifestation (*offenbar machen*) of what is in question in discourse.[40] After *Being and Time* Heidegger will deepen his analysis of λόγος in order to carry out the phenomenological "destruction" of traditional logic in reconducting logic to its fundament which is λόγος in its initial, i.e., Greek sense.[41] In this way,[42] he will come to think language itself no longer as a phonetic process of expression and communication—which is in fact the metaphysical conception of language that in a way still prevails in *Being and Time*—but as showing in itself, that is to say, as the happening of lighting.

Indeed, the Greek word λόγος has something overpowering (*bestürzend*) in itself: "It speaks simultaneously as the name for Being and for Saying" (*US* 185). What happened at the beginning of Western thinking with Heraclitus was a naming of the relation of Being and a saying in the single word of λόγος (*VA* 228). The Greek dwelt in this being of language but did not have a thinking experience of it. That is why when they began thinking the essence of language they understood it as an expression based on its phonetic character. Language was therefore defined by Aristotle as φωνή σημαντική—as a sound that signifies something, and since then language has been understood in this way as the title of the Husserlian first Logical Investigation "Expression and Signification" shows. The "superiority" of the Greek language that Heidegger emphasized in his Cerisy lecture of 1955[43] has nothing to do with a special quality of the Greek language in itself, as if it were more appropriate to the saying of Being than other languages. We should remember in this respect Heidegger's statement in *Der Spruch des Anaximander*: "Being speaks everywhere and always and through all languages. The difficulty is not so much to find in thinking the word for Being but rather to retain purely the found word in the proper thinking" (*H* 388). The "superiority" of the Greek language comes merely from the fact that the Greeks (in fact, some Greeks) were dwelling in their language, which means that through Greek words they were immediately near the thing itself and not caught in a realm of arbitrary signs—in short, that they did not have a superior language but a different relation to their language, a relation of dwelling and not an instrumental relation. That is the reason why they invented philosophy—because for them dwelling in language did not mean being familiar with their own language and mastering it but being open to its strangeness and being forced to appropriate it, i.e., to translate Greek into Greek as is the case for all thinkers in relation to their native tongue.[44] For proper dwelling—in Greek ἦθος—does not mean only familiarity. It requires the ability to see the unfamiliar (*das Ungeheure*) in the familiar (*in dem Geheuere*), δαίμων in ἀνθρώπῳ—God in man—and the foreigner in the friend.[45] Dwelling means to maintain distance in proximity and strangeness (*die Unheimlichkeit*) at home (*in der Heimat*).

But in following the Greeks who said it without thinking it that language is a dimension of Being, Heidegger is led completely to reverse his former determination of language: from a phenomenon belonging to the human being, it apparently becomes an independent power dominating man.[46] The instrumental relation that metaphysical man has with language seems to be diametrically inverted insofar as, now, it is language which "needs" and "uses"—in German *braucht*—man to his service (*US* 260). Such a reversal of the metaphysical viewpoint could only lead—as Heidegger himself points out in the *Letter on Humanism* with the example of Sartrean existentialism[47]—to a new form of metaphysics and not at all to its destitution. It would therefore mean the return of the phantoms of metaphysics under the form of a language separated from human speaking and represented as "a fantastic, self-sustained being which cannot be encountered anywhere as long as our reflection on language remains sober" (*US* 255–56). The risk of the return of metaphysics is clearly involved in the tautological statements by which Heidegger enunciates the new essence of language: "language speaks" (*US* 12, 20, 254) and "language is language" (*US* 12–13) as well as in the goal he gives to himself in *Unterwegs zur Sprache*: to "reflect on language itself, and on language only" because "language itself is: language and nothing else besides" (*US* 12–13). The attempt to make it clear that language has no other ground than itself could lead to an idealization of language, to a Platonism of a new kind. This is in fact the risk involved in the phenomenological way of thinking—i.e., the Greek way of thinking—and the reproach of "Platonic realism" addressed to Husserl after the publication of his *Logical Investigations* showed it clearly.[48] But if the Husserlian essence is not a Platonic "hypostasis" because it does not "exist" in the same way as things do—as Plato himself already declared—it does not mean that Husserl does not remain "authentically" Platonic in a more profound sense in his eidetic and to some extent ahistoric way of thinking. Heidegger breaks more decisively with Platonism (and goes in this way "beyond the Greeks"[49] in thinking the "essence"—in German *Wesen*—no longer as *quidditas*, as genus, but as the unfolding of the being of something, in the sense of the old German word *wesan*. *Wesen*, understood no longer in its nominal, but in its verbal sense, cannot refer to the permanence or invariability of the εἶδος but only to the duration of the unfolding of the being of something.[50] Consequently what Heidegger calls *"das Wesen der Sprache"* is no longer the essence of language, understood as a nonhistorical entity from which the human being could be separated, but the happening of language—the unfolding of its being that requires human speaking. This change in the understanding of what *Wesen* is is already in itself the thought of *Ereignis*.

We now know for sure, after the publication this year of the *Beiträge zur Philosophie*, that Heidegger, under the name of *Ereignis*, developed as early as 1936 (see *US* 260) a new conception of Being, no longer considered the ground of beings but the happening of lighting on the basis of an abysmal occultation. Man is no longer the thrown ground of the lighting but remains exposed to it and owes his own being to it. Being as such and the being of man no longer coincide: the There of Being can no longer be understood as the result of man's self-projection and transcendence but as the address (*Anspruch*) of Being to man, to which man has to respond (*ent-sprechen*). The *Verhältnis* of Being to man should not be understood as a mere relation between two separate entities but as the way in which Being reserves itself in letting Da-sein be: to the withdrawal of Being, the nonmetaphysical man responds by his reserve (*Verhaltenheit*) that becomes his fundamental tonality (*Grundstimmung*). Heidegger gives the name *Ereignis* to this belonging together, which is neither coincidence nor dialectical intertwining but being-for-one-another and con-stellation of man and Being (*ID* 25f.). *Ereignis* is not one event among others, as the ordinary meaning of the word suggests, but is used by Heidegger as *singulare tantum* (*ID* 29) to name the happening of lighting. It is the happening of the disclosing of beings, i.e., the coming of beings to their own (*Eigen*), or proper manifestation. But this *Er-eigen*, this propriation, is not a process that takes place by itself but requires man's participation. Propriation is therefore to be understood, according to the true etymology of the word *Ereignis* that does not refer to *eigen* (own) but to *Auge* (eye), as the calling look of Being toward man: *Ereignis er-aügt den Menschen*—*Ereignis* calls man by looking at him. This being-called-and-looked-at constitutes the true specificity of humanity in relation to animality: man no longer needs to comprehend Being in a transcendental way; he is now needed by *Ereignis* for the propriation of beings. As such, man is led to vocal speech, which is no longer a secondary phenomenon but the proper response of man to the saying of Being which happens only as the sounding of the word through the mouths of mortals (*US* 260).

Thus there are not two different languages: the language of Being, on the one hand, and the language of mortals on the other hand. There is not the silent voice of Being on one hand and the sounding of human word on the other hand. There is neither first listening and then saying in response. The listening happens in saying and responding, and silence happens in speaking. There is only one language, neither human, nor nonhuman, which is the τόπος of the differance— of the intimate self-differing of responding.

With the thought of *Ereignis* as language, i.e., of a durable unfolding of Being as language which, because it is lasting (*während*) without being permanent (*fortwährend*), can only be a donation—in German, *Nur das Gewährte währt*—[51] all the phantoms of metaphysics should disappear. Such a donation without a "subject" of donation in which the donating instance can never itself be given is also what Heidegger calls *Geschick*, destination. Because destiny is a donation which gives only its donation and in giving holds itself back and withdraws,[52] it can only be expressed by the idiomatic impersonal form *es gibt*—"there is"— but understood in the sense of "is granted." And what is granted to the human being is above all the word. But such an expression could lead again to a Platonic hypostasis if we stay at the level of the mere statement, i.e., if we remain unable to inhabit language.

To conclude, I would like to quote a passage from *On the Way to Language*:

> We are familiar with the expression "there is, there are" in many usages, such as "There are strawberries on the sunny slope" *il y a, es gibt*, there are strawberries; we can find them as something that is there on the slope. In our present reflection, the expression is used differently. We do not mean "There is the word"—we mean "by virtue of the gift of the word, there is, the word gives . . . The whole spook about the "*Es*" [the giving instance], which many people justly fear, is blown away. But what is memorable remains, indeed only now does it come to radiant light. (So verfliegt der ganze Spuk mit dem "Es," vor dem sich viele mit Recht ängstigen; aber das Denkwürdige bleibt, kommt erst zum Scheinen) (*US* 194).

What is properly memorable—*Das eigentlich Denkwürdige*—is the *Ereignis* of language. It shows itself only after the last phantom of the metaphysics of pre-sence has vanished—for all phantoms are the offspring of the spirit of re-venge[53]—revenge against time and becoming.

NOTES

1. "Nur darum enthält *Sein und Zeit* (§34) einen Hinweis auf die Wesensdimension der Sprache und rührt an die einfache Frage, in welcher Weise des Seins denn die Sprache als Sprache jeweils ist" (*W* 149–50).

2. "The lasting element in thinking is the way [*Das Bleibende im Denken ist der Weg*]" (*US* 99).

3. The last sentence of *Being and Time* is still a question: "Führt ein Weg von der ursprünglichen *Zeit* zum Sinn des *Seins?* Offenbart sich die *Zeit* selbst als Horizont des *Seins?*"

4. See above all *Die Grundprobleme der Phänomenologie, GA* 24, a lecture course from the summer semester 1927, which is presented as "a new elaboration of the third section of the first part of *Being and Time*" (note p. 1), but also *Metaphysische Anfangsgründe de Logik, GA* 26, a lecture course from the summer semester 1928, as well as *Kant und das Problem der Metaphysik*, published in 1929, and *Vom Wesen des Grundes*, published in the same year.

5. "Hier kehrt sich das Ganze um. Der fragliche Abschnitt wurde zurückgehalten, weil das Denken im zureichenden Sagen dieser Kehre versagte und mit Hilfe der Sprache der Metaphysik nicht durchkam" (*W* 159).

6. See Ludwig Wittgenstein, *Philosophische Untersuchungen* (Frankfurt a.M.: Suhrkamp, 1967), 13. The very beginning of the *Investigations* is a quotation from Augustine, *Confessions*, I, 8, commented upon by Wittgenstein as follows: "In diesen Worten erhalten wir, so scheint es mir, ein bestimmtes Bild von dem Wesen der menschlichen Sprache. Nämlich dieses: Die Wörter der Sprache benennen Gegenstände—Sätze sind Verbindungen von solchen Benennungen.—In diesem Bild von der Sprache finden wir die Wurzel der Idee: Jedes Wort hat seine Bedeutung. Diese Bedeutung ist dem Wort zugeordenet. Sie ist der Gegenstand, für welchen das Wort steht."

7. This opposition between words and terms (*Worte und Wörter*) may remind us of the Saussurian distinction between a linguistics of language and a linguistics of speech (see F. de Saussure, *Cours de linguistique générale* [Paris: Payot, 1969], introduction, chap. 4: "Linguistique de la langue et linguistique de la parole," where Saussure points out that historically, speaking always precedes language and constitutes the element of creativity in language but considers that only language can be the object of linguistics in the proper sense of the word). The opposition between soundless saying and speaking can be linked to the Husserlian difference between expression (*Ausdruck*) and indication (*Anzeige*). In the first Logical Investigation, Husserl refers the indicative sign (*Anzeichen*) to the communicative speech where the phonetic instance is necessary to reciprocal understanding, but shows that in soliloquy we do not really *speak* to ourselves as if we were somebody else, but make use of irreal words immediately connected with ideal significations. See the analysis of this first Investigation in J. Derrida, *La voix et le phénomène* (Paris: Presses universitaires de France, 1967).

8. In the *Letter on Humanism* Heidegger says in the same manner that Being is not only related to eksistence but is itself the relation in which Being destines itself to itself ("Das Sein selber ist das Verhältnis. . . , als welches das Sein sich selbst schickt") (*W* 163).

9. See *SD* 20: "Was beide, Zeit und Sein, in ihr Eigenes, d.h. in ihr Zusammengehören, bestimmt, nennen wir: *das Ereignis.*"

10. Περὶ Ἑρμηνείας, 16b27

11. The German *Rede*, as well as the Latin *armus* and *ars*, the Greek ἀρθμός, ἀρθρον, ἁρμονία, and the Vedic *rta* (order) all derive from the Indo-European root *ar- which means fitting together.

12. "Rede ist die Artikulation der Verständlichkeit" (*SZ* 161).

13. "*Die Rede ist mit Befindlichkeit und Verstehen existential gleichursprünglich*" (*SZ* 161).

14. This determination of language as a non-original phenomenon will be later rejected by Heidegger. See the relevant marginalia in the 1977 edition of *Sein und Zeit* (*GA* 2: 87) where Heidegger declares "untrue" his previous statement concerning the foundation of words on "significations" and declares that "language is not an added storey but *is* the

original coming-to-being of truth as There [Sprache ist nicht aufgestockt, sondern *ist* das ursprüngliche Wesen der Wahrheit als Da]."

15. *"Das existenzial-ontologische Fundament der Sprache ist die Rede"* (*SZ* 160).

16. "Mit der Aussage wurde ein extremes Derivat der Auslegung sichtbar gemacht" (*SZ* 160).

17. "Die Ausbildung des Verstehens nennen wir Auslegung" (*SZ* 148).

18. "Verstehen birgt in sich die Möglichkeit der Auslegung, das ist der Zueignung des Verstandenen" (*SZ* 160).

19. "Sie [Die Rede] liegt daher der Auslegung und Aussage schon zugrunde" (*SZ* 161).

20. "Den Bedeutungen wachsen Worte zu. Nicht aber werden Wörterdinge mit Bedeutungen versehen" (*SZ* 161).

21. See on this point the analysis of discourse in F.-W. von Herrmann, *Die Selbstinterpretation Martin Heideggers* (Meisenheim am Glan: Anton Hain, 1964), 183–85.

22. I am following here F.-W. von Herrmann's interpretation (*Die Selbstinterpretation Martin Heidegger*, op. cit., 187) with which I am fully in agreement.

23. "Die volle, durch Verstehen, Befindlichkeit und Verfallen konstituierte Erschlossenheit des Da erhält durch die Rede die Artikulation. Daher zeitigt sich die Rede nicht primär in einer bestimmten Ekstase" (*SZ* 349).

24. See *SZ* §68 a, b, and c. The determination of the third moment of the care-structure as fallen-ness constitutes another difficulty. Fallen-ness is in fact not a separate moment of this structure but the "inauthentic" or non-proper (*uneigentlich*) modality of the *whole* structure as such, so that we should strictly distinguish between a fallen Being-near the beings that are encountered within the world (*Sein-bei innerweltich begegnendem Seienden*) and an "authentic" one. If this distinction is not clearly established (Heidegger does not mention it in *Being and Time*, but only later, in *Vom Wesen des Grundes*), then it becomes difficult not to understand "authentic" care as a mere self-care which has no relation with the world. Heidegger stresses, on the contrary, that care always includes Being-near (*SZ* 193) so that it becomes necessary to admit that there is an "authentic" Being-near beings, an "authentic" way of being preoccupied with the world.

25. As Heidegger points out in the margin of his own copy of *Sein und Zeit* (*GA* 2: 161), "Throwness is essential for language [*Für Sprache ist Geworfenheit wesentlich*]"

26. The Greek φωνή comes, like φημί, from the Indo-European root **bha* which means to speak (for example in Sanskrit *bhan* = to speak). The German *Stimme*, whose etymology is unknown, was first used (fifteenth century) in the sense of vote, of given opinion.

27. "Wenn die alltägliche Auslegung eine 'Stimme' des Gewissens kennt, dann ist dabei nicht so sehr an eine Verlautbarung gedacht, die faktisch nie vorfindlich wird, sondern 'Stimme' ist aufgefasst als das Zu-verstehen-geben" (*SZ* 271).

28. See the end of *Vom Wesen des Grundes*, where the human being is called *Wesen der Ferne*.

29. See Husserl, first *Logical Investigation*, §8, and Derrida's commentary in *La voix et le phénomène*, op. cit., chap. 6.

30. "Der Ruf redet im unheimlichen Modus des Schweigens" (*SZ* 277).

31. See also p. 189: "Das beruhigt-vertraute In-der-Welt-sein ist ein Modus der Unheimlichkeit des Daseins, nicht umgekehrt. Das Un-zuhause muss existential-ontologisch als das ursprünglichere Phänomen begriffen werden" (*SZ* 276).

32. "Das Hören konstituiert sogar die primäre und eigentliche Offenheit des Daseins für sein eigenstes Seinkönnen, als Hören der Stimme des Freundes, den jedes Dasein bei sich trägt" (*SZ* 163).

33. We can find in *Being and Time* another occurrence of this "identity": there is also an identity of the "agent" and "patient" in anxiety (see *SZ* 188).

34. At least on the level of "authentic" temporality, it is possible to speak of the *duality* of the ekstase of "future" and of the ekstase of the "past," because the third *ekstase*, the ekstase of present remains included in the two others as the authentic present of the

Augenblick (see *SZ* 328). Inauthenticity, on the other hand, tends to elude the duality in finding shelter in a unidimensional present.

35. See *Kant und das Problem der Metaphysik* (Frankfurt a.M.: Vittorio Klostermann, 1973), 229: "In der Transzendenz bekundet sich das Dasein sich selbst als des Seinsverständnisses bedürftig. Durch diese transzendentale Bedürftigkeit ist im Grunde dafür "gesorgt", dass überhaupt so etwas wie Da-sein sein kann. Sie ist die innerste, das Dasein tragende Endlichkeit." This need is also what German idealism has understood as "need of philosophy" (*Bedürfnis der Philosophie*). See Hegel, *Differenz des Fichteschen und Schellingschen Systems der Philosophie*.

36. See *GA* 29/30: 371–72, where Heidegger emphasizes that there is no hierarchical meaning in his analysis of animal life: "Vielmehr ist das Leben ein Bereich, der einen Reichtum des Offenseins hat, wie ihn vielleicht die menschliche Welt gar nicht kennt." There is also no hierarchy within the animal world. See *GA* 29/30: 287: "Jedes Tier und jede Tierart ist als solche gleich vollkommen wie die andere."

37. Heidegger considers the as-structure as a schema (*SZ* 360). Schematization and articulation should therefore be identified.

38. First during the summer semester 1927 in *Die Grundprobleme der Phänomenologie*, *GA* 24, second section.

39. "Der Unterschied von Sein und Seiendem *ist*, wenngleich nicht ausdrücklich bewusst, latent im Dasein und seiner Existenz *da*. Der Unterschied *ist da*, d.h. er hat die Seinsart des Daseins, es gehört zur Existenz. Existenz heisst gleichsam 'im Vollzug dieses Unterschied sein'" (*GA* 24: 454).

40. *SZ* 32: "Λόγος als Rede besagt vielmehr soviel wie δηλοῦν, offenbar machen das, wovon in der Rede 'die Rede' ist" (*SZ* 32).

41. See my article, "Logic and Ontology: Heidegger's 'Destruction' of Logic," in *Research in Phenomenology* 17 (1987): 55–74.

42. In "A Dialogue on Language" (*US* 91–93 & 128f.), some indications concerning this way are given. His Japanese interlocutor reminds him of a lecture held in 1921 under the title "Expression and Appearance" or "Expression and Signification" in which Heidegger already suggested his turning away from the metaphysical conception of language as "expression." But it is only in the lecture course from the summer semester of 1934 that Heidegger dared discuss the question of language under the form of a reflection on the λόγος. See also, concerning the same lecture course, *WD* 99–100.

43. "Langsam dämmert nämlich für unsere Besinnung, dass die griechische Sprache keine blosse Sprache ist wie die uns bekannten europäischen Sprachen. Die griechische Sprache, und sie allein, ist λόγος . . . Wenn wir ein griechisches Wort griechisch hören, dann folgen wir seinem λέγειν, seinem unmittelbaren Darlegen. Was es darlegt ist das Vorliegende. Wir sind durch das griechische gehörte Wort unmittelbar bei der vorliegenden Sache selbst, nicht zunächst bei einer blossen Wortbedeutung" (*WP* 20).

44. See *Parmenides*, *GA* 54: 17: "Man meint, das Übersetzen sei die Übertragung einer Sprache in eine andere, der Fremdsprache in die Muttersprache oder auch umgekehrt. Wir verkennen jedoch, dass wir ständig auch schon unsere eigene Sprache, die Muttersprache, in ihr eigenes Wort übersetzen . . . In jedem Gespräch und Selbstgespräch waltet ein ürsprüngliches Übersetzen." When in the *Spiegel* interview from 1966, Heidegger mentions "the special internal affinity of German language with the language of the Greeks and *their thinking*" (emphasis mine), and adds in all seriousness that the French can think only in German, it could be something else than "insolence" as J. Derrida interprets it in *De l'esprit* (Paris: Galilée, 1987, 111f.). The privilege of German and Greek languages can be understood in a more "matter of fact" fashion, as resulting from the capacity of the two peoples (in fact of some Greeks and some Germans) to inhabit their own language in a more original fashion than other people's. And the proof of it is *the fact* that they were able to have great philosophers. The privilege of Greek and German languages is neither absolute nor inborn: it results merely from history.

45. See *Brief über den "Humanismus,"* (*W* 187): "ἦθος ἀνθρώπῳ δαίμων, sagt Heraklit selbst: 'Der (geheure) Aufenthalt ist dem Menschen das Offene für die Anwesung des Gottes (des Un-geheuren).'"

46. See, for example, *VA* 146: "Der Mensch gebärdet sich, als sei *er* Bildner und Meister der Sprache, während *sie* doch die Herrin des Menschen bleibt. Vielleicht ist es vor allem anderen die vom Menschen betriebene Verkehrung *dieses* Herrschaftsverhältnisses, was sein Wesen in das Unheimische treibt."

47. "Aber die Umkehrung eines metaphysischen Satzes bleibt ein metaphysischer Satz" (*W* 159).

48. See Husserl, *Ideen 1*, §22, Der Vorwurf des platonischen Realismus.

49. "Was heisst Grund und Prinzip und gar Prinzip aller Prinzipien? Lässt sich dies jemals zureichend bestimmen, ohne dass wir die ἀλήθεια griechisch als Unverborgenheit erfahren und sie dann, über das Griechische hinaus, als Lichtung des Sich-verbergens denken?" (*SD* 79). See also *US* 134–35: "[the] clearing itself, as occurrence, remains unthought in every respect [in Greek thinking]. To enter into thinking this unthought occurrence means: to pursue more originally what the Greeks have thought, to see it in the source of its reality. To see it so is in its own way Greek, and yet in respect of what it sees is no longer, is never again, Greek." To think "beyond the Greeks" does not mean in fact only breaking with Platonic idealism, but thinking the unthought of Heraclitus himself, i.e., the *happening* of φύσις (Being) on the basis of a *lasting* κρύπτειν (see *Heraclitus*, fragment 123).

50. See *VA* 38: "Vom Zeitwort 'wesen' stammt erst das Hauptwort ab. 'Wesen', verbal verstanden, ist das Selbe wie 'währen'; nicht nur bedeutungsmässig, sondern auch in der lautlichen Wortbildung. Schon Sokrates und Platon denken das Wesen von etwas als das Wesende im Sinne des Währenden. Doch sie denken das Währende als das Fortwährende (ἀεὶ ὄν). Das Fortwährende finden sie aber in dem, was sich als das Bleibende durchhält bei jeglichem, was vorkommt. Dieses Bleibende wiederum entdecken sie im Aussehen (εἶδος, ἰδέα), z.B. in der Idee 'Haus.'"

51. *"Nur das Gewährte währt. Das anfänglich aus der Frühe Währende ist das Gewährende"* (*VA* 39).

52. "Ein Geben, das nur seine Gabe gibt, sich selbst jedoch dabei zurückhalt und entzieht, ein solches Geben nennen wir das Schicken" (*SD* 8).

53. And, who knows, perhaps there is no other spirit than the spirit of revenge.

WALTER BIEMEL

21. Elucidations of Heidegger's Lecture *The Origin of Art and the Destination of Thinking*

Translated by Joan Stambaugh

The text of Heidegger's lecture, *The Origin of Art and the Destination of Thinking*, consists of an introduction and three sections. In the introduction Heidegger asks the question: How can thanks be expressed to the Greek academy of sciences for their invitation to Athens? That seems to be a matter of courtesy. The person invited gives thanks for the invitation. Not so for Heidegger. He takes the question of thanks seriously. Thinking and thanking belong together: "We thank by attempting to think with you."

What is to be thought in common by the members of the Berlin academy of arts and the members of the Athenian academy of sciences? At this particular place—Athens, at this time, in this age, namely, the age of "scientific technology"? It is important to remember this. It is not just a matter of some presentation; it is a matter of thinking the present age as the age of technology. Here in Athens, the Greek world is to be thought about, not because we happen to be in Greece but because the world originated in Greece, "which once established the beginning for the Western-European arts."

In the manuscript that Heidegger gave me as a present, which, as in all of his manuscripts given as lectures contains exact underlining for emphasis (like a musical composition with its accents and directions for performance), the word *beginning* is doubly underlined. The emphasis is on it. That is not a matter of chance but is key to Heidegger's thinking and questioning. We can say that Heidegger's whole way of thinking consists of a questioning of the beginning. This beginning should not simply be understood as what precedes in time. Many things can precede the present without being able to claim to be a beginning. For Heidegger a beginning means an origin.[1]

Heidegger's demand for searching after the origin generates a polemic that asserts the impossibility of finding the origin. Heidegger's thinking about Greece constantly searches for the origin: thus his return to Parmenides, Heraclitus, and

Anaximander whom he does not call Pre-Socratic philosophers but rather incipient thinkers (*anfängliche Denker*). He expresses this in the next sentence: "Reckoned historiographically, this world is indeed past. But historically experienced as our destiny, it still remains and becomes ever a new presence: what waits for us to think toward it and measure our own thinking and forming" (*HK* 135f.). And this thought reaches a crescendo when Heidegger continues: "For the beginning of a destiny is the greatest. It holds sway before everything that follows" (*HK* 136). What ignites Heidegger's thinking is succinctly expressed here: asking and searching for the true beginning. At the same time it becomes clear why the Greeks have such a significance for Heidegger. It is not a matter of romantic enthusiasm for the Greeks, or for the time of Greece as the golden age. The Greek world is significant for the whole of German Idealism.[2] But the Greek world has a distinctive position because it is the beginning of European history, of European philosophy, which then became metaphysics with Plato and Aristotle. Heidegger in no way doubts that there is a Chinese world, but he does doubt that Chinese thought is philosophy in the sense that Greek thought was for Europe. (It is misunderstanding him to accuse him of Eurocentrism. There are undoubtedly echoes of East-Asian thought in his own thought. But what is incontestable is the domination of world civilization, its domination today, on the basis of modern European science and technology.) The possibility of falling away from the beginning also belongs to Heidegger's thinking of history. Forgetting and denying the origin— that is a constant danger in which a historical humanity stands. To this danger Heidegger opposes the necessity of returning to the source in order to make a new origin possible. For the first origin cannot simply be repeated.

The lecture invites us to reflect upon the origin of art in Greece. Right at the beginning we are given a reference to the dimension which, according to Heidegger, precedes art "and grants art its own" (*HK* 136). Heidegger wants to point to the occurrence of ἀλήθεια—to the fundamental occurrence of history as such. We are trying to indicate this cautiously and of necessity insufficiently when we remember how for Heidegger the relation to λήθη as original concealment is also thought in Ἀ-λήθεια and how clearing occurs in the happening of unconcealment, a clearing that first makes appearing possible for each being, and how the essence of man is thus determined as Da-sein.[3]

At the end of his short introduction Heidegger sketches out the plan of the lecture. To begin with, the question of the origin of art is to be discussed, starting with the pointers that we can experience from Athena, the goddess of Athens and the Attic country.

The second question, "How is art related today to its former origin?" leads into the third question, "From where is the thinking determined that is now reflecting on the origin of art?"

What is Athena's relation to the arts? She is the goddess who gives advice. When something is realized as a work, set into the light, in action and deed, she is the adviser, the helper. She especially helps those "who produce implements, vessels and jewelry" (*HK* 136). They are the τεχνίτης. We should not define them as handworkers. A τεχνίτης is he whose "decisive deed is guided by an understanding" (HK 137). The Greeks call this understanding τέχνη. Heidegger emphasizes the fact that what is decisive here is the knowledge guiding the production, and has the following to say about knowledge: "To have that in view which is important for the production of a structure and a work" (HK 137). This knowledge also concerns the production of works of science and philosophy, poetry, and public speech: "Art is τέχνη, but not technology. The artist is τεχνίτης, but neither a technician nor a handworker" (HK 137). What is distinctive about τέχνη is the fact that it is a kind of knowledge. This knowledge looks toward something not yet present in such a way that it makes it possible to give form to the work. Heidegger says that this knowledge looks ahead to "what is still invisible, what is first to be brought into the visibility and perceptibility of the work" (HK 137). Such looking ahead needs "sight and brightness in a distinctive way" (HK 137).

Here Heidegger connects the Aristotelian knowledge about τέχνη with the presentation of Athena—Athena the γλαυκῶπις, where γλαυκός expresses both the shining of the sea, the stars, the moon, and the gleaming of the eye. The owl is Athena's animal—its eyes are fiery and glowing. The owl can see even at night, a fact that Heidegger characterizes as making the invisible visible. His reference to Pindar's seventh Olympic ode names the art of the island-dwellers of Rhodes: "But the bright-eyed one helped them to outdo the earth's dwellers with the best handwork in every art" (V, 50). A further characterization of Athena is as σκεπτομένη, the musing one. This musing seeks to find the limit: "However, the limit is not only an outline and a framework, not only where something stops. A limit is that by which something is gathered into its Own in order to appear in its fullness, to merge into presence" (HK 138). This definition of the limit— which by no means was thought up by Heidegger and attributed to Athena— is a decisive concept in Greek thought.[4] It is the limit that makes it possible for beings to appear and become present. What is without limit is without essence. The creator can only work by looking ahead to the limits of what is to be created. When we speak of giving form, we mean giving limits. Here limit is not related to the edge, to the end, but is the best way of holding together. This is especially clear in the work of a sculptor. But Heidegger does not stop with this realm. Not only does he say that Athena has the limit realized by man in view, the form which at the beginning of the work process is precisely not there but also he goes a step further and thinks of beings that are not produced by man but already lie present—φύσις—we can say what lies present of itself, the natural. He does not want us right away to adduce the Roman meaning of natura in order to understand the essence of φύσις.[5] A being belonging to φύσις is for the Greeks "what emerges of itself in its actual limit and lingers therein" (HK 138).

In his elucidation of φύσις Heidegger cites the experience of the traveler in Greece: how an island suddenly appears, then a mountain, an olive tree. The reference to the special light is only in the foreground, although it undoubtedly belongs to Greece:

Only here in Greece where the whole of the work has addressed man as φύσις and claimed him could human perception and deed co-respond to this claim. This had to be when it was pressured, of its own capability, to bring that to presence which as a work should let a world appear that had never yet appeared. (*HK* 138f.)

What does this mean? A special experience of being occurs in φύσις. It is not the case that things simply lie present and then the totality of things is given the name φύσις, as is later the case when world is characterized as the totality of beings; rather, in φύσις beings open themselves to Greek man in a unique way. In his elucidation of Hölderlin's poem "As on a Holiday" Heidegger says about φύσις:

> Φύσις, φύειν signifies growth. But how do the Greeks understand growth? Not as quantitative increase, nor as "development," nor as the succession of a "becoming." Φύσις is emerging and rising, the self-opening that, rising, at the same time returns to the emergence and thus closes itself in that which gives presence to a present being . . . Φύσις is the rising return to itself, and names the presence of what lingers in the emergence as the open. (*GA* 4: 56).

Heidegger wants to remind us of the fundamental Greek experience of being as φύσις. He himself reflected upon this experience in his attempt to comprehend the Greek world in a Greek way, not to interpret it in a modern way as, for example, Hegel did in spite of his love for Greece. It is by no means just the Mediterranean light that made beings as φύσις accessible to the Greeks but also a mysterious experience of beings in which rising and coming to appearance is decisive. It is an event in which being reveals itself, thus determining the Greek world. For this reason, Heidegger uses the formulation that "the whole of the world addressed itself to man as φύσις" (*HK* 138). It is a matter of a moment in the history of being which cannot be made by man but merely experienced when it opens itself to him. We shall not discuss this further here. We must not overlook the fact that human life (*das menschliche Verhalten*) was shaped by the Greek's experience of φύσις and that the Greeks thus understood their actions and production as co-responding to this experience—namely, as "bringing to presence" (*HK* 139). What is to be brought to presence? This new experience of world that we should attempt to distinguish from other contemporary experiences—the Egyptian and the Semitic. That is not possible here but should at least be mentioned.

These points are decisive. What is at stake here? The Greek artist does more than create "beautiful objects" that are then paradigmatic and thus effective for the future, for a co-responding to the fundamental experience of φύσις takes place in their production. Thus Heidegger can say: "Art co-responds to φύσις and is yet not an imitation or copy of what is already present" (*HK* 139).

The belonging together of art and φύσις determines the Greek world, "but the element in which φύσις and τέχνη belong together and the realm, with which art must be engaged in order to become what it is as art, remains concealed" (*HK* 139). That is a thought that shaped the reflection of the late Heidegger and that he expresses in "The End of Philosophy and the Task of Thinking": that ἀλήθεια was the fundamental word of Greek thought but at the same time was not thought expressly by the Greeks: "What else does this mean but that presence as such and all the more the clearing granting it remain unnoticed? Only what ἀλήθεια as clearing grants is experienced and thought, not what it is as such" (SD 78). Heidegger strives to bring what has not been thought face to face with thinking. He refers to the significance of the lightning flash in Heraclitus's thought: "The brightness which grants to all that is present its presence shows its gathered ruling suddenly appearing in the lightning flash" (HK 139). Zeus hurls the lightning flash; Athena is his daughter. She "knows the key to the house where the lightning flash is enclosed and sealed."[6] The relation to Zeus, the knowledge about the house of the lightning flash distinguishes Athena—giver of manifold advice, πολύμητις, the goddess who sees clearly, the γλαυκῶπις, the σκεπτομένη, who reflects upon the limit (HK 139).

The remarks about Athena are supposed to bring us to the realm that is decisive for the origin of art in Greece. Here the interpretation of φύσις as the fundamental character of the Greek world has emphasized the dimension in which φύσις and τέχνη are at play together.

The second part of Heidegger's lecture brings us to the present: "What is the situation of art today with respect to its former origin?" Heidegger asks the question: "After two-and-a-half-thousand years is art still claimed in the same way that it was in Greece?" (HK 140). He continues: "If not, from what realm does the claim come to which modern art in all its areas co-responds?" (HK 140). From this we can see that art is no arbitrary production and creation. It cannot be understood simply as the utterance of a subject that needs to express itself, as is usually the case. Heidegger does not refer now to the connection of art with the realm of the godlike as in his beginning remarks on Athena. Rather, he speaks of world civilization and contrasts it with the national and folk world: "Its world no longer originates from the decisive limits of the folk and national world" (HK 140). The concept of the limit is retained but does not refer to the limit of what was created—it refers, rather, to the limit of the people, here the Greek people in whom Greek art and philosophy originated.

We must understand our present situation. Our stay in the world is determined by scientific technology. Heidegger's work on technology in the sixties newly defined technology in connection with modern metaphysics.[7] Heidegger cannot expand on the whole topic here, so he goes back to interpreting a passage from Nietzsche: "What distinguishes our nineteenth century is not the triumph of science, but the triumph of the scientific method over science" (Will to Power, no. 466). Method must not be understood as an instrument of research. Method is "rather the way the actual area of the objects to be investigated are delimited in advance in their objectivity. Method is the anticipatory project of the world that determines the only way the world can be investigated" (HK 141). We are reminded of the introduction to Kant's Critique of Pure Reason in which Kant investigates the scientists' procedure, the factor of the project.[8] The relationship of science with nature is not that of a teacher and student but that of a judge ordering nature to answer his questions. Kant contrasts with this project the experiment that is supposed to confirm the project. Heidegger also speaks of project and experiment in his interpretations of Nietzsche. The work-project is determined by the "thoroughgoing calculability of everything that is accessible and can be checked in the experiment" (*HK* 141). The sciences are subordinate to it. Heidegger now shows succinctly how the essence of the real is determined by its calculability. The consequence is this: the world is available and can be dominated by man. This development began with Galileo and Newton in Europe in the seventeenth century. Heidegger does not stop with this discussion of knowledge, which he presents elsewhere in more detail, but asks: Where has this development led us? How do we experience it today? This leads to his characterization of cybernetics.

In the text, "The End of Philosophy and the Task of Thinking," the sciences are characterized as taking over the task of philosophy in the sense of regional ontologies (nature, history, art):

> The interest of the sciences is directed toward the theory of necessary structural concepts of the coordinated areas of investigation. 'Theory' means now: supposition of the categories which are allowed only a cybernetical function, but denied any ontological meaning. The operational and model character of representational-calculative thinking becomes dominant. . . .
>
> The end of philosophy proves to be the triumph of the manipulable arrangement of a scientific-technological world and of the social order proper to this world. The end of philosophy means: the beginning of the world-civilization based upon Western European thinking. (*SD* 65).

The scientific world is determined in the Athens lecture as the cybernetic world: "The cybernetic work-project has in advance the supposition that the fundamental trait of all calculable world processes is steering" (*HK* 141). The representation of the mediation of information belongs to steering: "Since the steered process for its part reports back to what steers it, thus informing it, steering has the character of feedback information" (*HK* 141). The fundamental trait of the cybernetically understood world is the feedback control system. Because of the circuit of feedback control and the possibility of the self-controlled system of movement, automatically working machines can be designed: more precisely, machines with the signification of automata that control their courses themselves. Automation increasingly determines the modern places of production from which man as worker disappears and in which he is needed only as the supervisor of functions. Today, when people speak of "streamlining" in industry, they mean this relinquishing of man as worker. (What this leads to, what consequences it ultimately has, cannot be discussed here, but they are noticeable all over the world as unemployment.)

With the cybernetic stance (this world-project), "the distinction disappears between automatic machines and living beings" (*HK* 142). (See also the work on artificial intelligence.) The relation of man to the world is understood according to the model of the feedback control system (Regelkreis). The complete calculability of "the inorganic and organic world" (*HK* 142) belongs to it. In this scientific stance it is important to gain control not only of the world but, above all, of man as well. Contemporary anthropology has its foundations in biochemistry and biophysics, in the sciences in which the demand for calculability can best be realized. One asks about the cell, the structure of the genes in which man's plan of life is contained, not just to gain knowledge but to influence this life plan, to change breeding. "Biochemistry's entry into the structure of the genes of human cells and nuclear physics' splitting of the atom are on the same course of the triumph of methods over science"' (*HK* 143). Nietzsche's statement about man, that "Man is the still undetermined animal," is reinterpreted by Heidegger to mean that he is the animal who can steer his evolutionary course. Since that is not yet possible today, man is a "disturbing factor." And man's possible actions must also be considered, starting with information thus gained—that happens in futurology.

Heidegger asks about the presupposition of the cybernetic-futurological science of man. His answer is: man is a social being. By society he means industrial society. The illusion that man's subjectivity is relinquished is, with this first point, immediately refuted: "Rather, industrial society is the most extreme form of egoity, i.e., subjectivity. Man stands exclusively on his own and on the institutionalized areas of his world" (*HK* 144). Industrial society is subordinate to "science dominated by cybernetics and to scientific technology" (*HK* 144). Heidegger asks what all of this has to do with the topic and answers: "The references to the existence of contemporary man have prepared us for asking more reflectively about the origin of art and about the destination of thinking" (*HK* 144). This is one of the few places where Heidegger makes a statement about our form of society. We have not been accustomed to this from him; this seemed to be the privilege of philosophers who base themselves on Marx's interpretation of history. But he is not speaking about the alienation of man in society in the Marxist sense; rather, this form of society is related to modern metaphysics and its interpretation of subjectivity, and more precisely, to the dominance of subjectivity, which is something else. When Heidegger says "man stands exclusively on his own," he implies that the relation to Being does not hold sway. The question is bracketed of how the association with beings always already stands in a certain clearing, of what kind of clearing this is, and whether it is an essential concealment, an essential withdrawal.

In the first section of his lecture, Heidegger had explicated the connection of art with the experience of beings as φύσις. The remarks about Athena, the goddess who guides man's production, the mistress of the action that the knowledge of τέχνη underlies, were presented in this context. Art does not copy and imitate φύσις, but co-responds to it. Freely formulated: the Greek experience was outlined from which the Greek world originated and to which art belongs decisively. Indeed, the Greek world is the origin of European history, but this history has since essentially distanced itself from the Greek world if it has not fallen away from it altogether. The question now is: From what realm does a claim for art come today to which it is to co-respond? This introduces the third section.

In the second section of his lecture Heidegger characterized the contemporary world as determined by the cybernetic project. Now, resuming this thought, he tries again to consider the modern world, what determines it, what happens in it with regard to its relation to art. To put it another way, if art is to co-respond to the modern world, if this world is, so to speak, the source for modern art, we have to think about this relation: "The world relations of man and with them the whole social existence of man are locked in in the area of domination of cybernetic science" (*HK* 145). This factor of being locked in is central. The world project that determines our time is ordinarily measured only by the successful accomplishments attained by the technological mastery of nature. These accomplishments are admired and celebrated as constant progress. For Heidegger matters are different. It is not that he does not acknowledge the accomplishments of technology; but at bottom they remain on the surface, quite apart from the fact that the questionability of a consistently exploitative mentality is coming to attention in our time to large circles of people. Man's being locked in as prisoner is elucidated with the example of futurology, the science that attempts to predict and anticipate the future. The future is by no means understood as the horizon of a possible transformation; it "necessarily exhausts itself in what is calculated by and for the present" (*HK* 145). It is a "prolonged present," and "Man is locked in in the scope of possibilities calculated by and for him" (*HK* 145). Formulated differently, the realm of what is coming can be nothing other than what becomes accessible in the calculating, dominating association with beings. One does not take into account how a demarcation in the sense of a restriction, if not a limitation, results from this behavior. It would not be difficult to show how this limitation and limitedness burdens our world as a whole today without our thinking of the consequences, since we are accustomed to them.

In the second section of his lecture Heidegger referred to the fact that the modern (contemporary) world has become an industrial society. The real power lies not with the politicians, who are often just puppets of society, but with the representatives of this new power. Heidegger now resumes the thought that industrial society must be understood in terms of the development of modern subjectivity as the dominant form of this subjectivity: "Industrial society has inflated itself to the unconditional criterion of all objectivity" (*HK* 145). This means that industrial society forces its way of seeing upon people; it determines how beings are to be understood, and what the criterion is for an appropriate association.

That criterion is success in the sense of economic efficiency without regard to what is happening to nature and man. Heidegger does not develop this idea in detail; he just points out that "Industrial society exists on the basis of being locked in in its own manipulations" (*HK* 145). Thus we cannot expect it to bring about a transformation in the relation of man to beings or in the relation of men to one another.

What is the situation of art? Is it nothing but a wheel in the cybernetic world determined by the feedback control system (*Regelkreis*)? To quote just one of Heidegger's numerous questions, "Are the productions determined by having to suffice for the process character of the industrial feedback control system and its constant applicability?" (*HK* 145). Is the significance of work then preserved? There is a backward reference here to the origin of the artwork and its character as work, as truth's setting itself into the work.[9]

The art business is denounced as the consistent ordering of art into this world and is viewed, according to the paradigm of the feedback control system "as a feedback of information in the feedback control system of industrial society and the scientifico-technological world" (*HK* 146). Although Heidegger formulates this as a question—it is not as a rhetorical question but as a danger.

Heidegger asks the decisive question about the connection between art and thinking:

> What about man's being locked in in his scientifico-technological world? Does not perhaps this being locked in close men off from that which first sends man to the destination peculiar to him so that he may unite with his destiny instead of calculatively taking control scientifically and technologically over himself and his world, over himself and his technological self-production? (*HK* 146)

Here, Heidegger clearly expresses a criticism of the technological and scientific world. It is not an external, superficial criticism since Heidegger has said elsewhere that technology is the completion of metaphysics.[10] It is rather a matter of first thinking about our being locked in in the contemporary world in its form of world civilization, of not allowing ourselves to be numbed by technological feats and acting as if all questions could be solved by technological means. The technological-scientific world does not question its own limitation; it cannot. When Heidegger speaks of "man's being closed off from that which sends man to the attunement peculiar to him," he is thinking of man's fundamental relation to Being. A relation in which man always already stands without seeing or contemplating it. That is the foundational criticism of metaphysics expressed again and again in "The Overcoming of Metaphysics" (and other places).

Heidegger once coined the phrase "forgottenness of being" which he later gave up because it could easily be misunderstood merely as a question omitted, as a mistake easily corrected, whereas according to Heidegger something like a withdrawal of being holds sway in this forgottenness over which man by no means has arbitrary control. For Heidegger it is important for man to think about being locked in in the technological-scientific world project and not to view this world project as the only possible one.

In this connection we must recall Heidegger's interpretation of history. For him, history is not the history of power and politics but the history of the transformation of the relation of man to beings. For the Greeks this relation is decisive as perceiving (*Vernehmen*); in the medieval period, beings are conceived as being created by God; in the modern age, as something represented. Beings become ob-jects and are ultimately conceived as the standing reserve that can be ordered. For this notion, Heidegger coined the term *Framing* (*Ge-stell*). We find the following passage about destiny in the lecture on technology:

The essence of modern technology sets man on the path of that revealing through which the real everywhere becomes, more or less perceptibly, standing reserve. To set on a path is calling sending. We call that gathering sending which first sets man on a path of revealing *destiny* (*VA* 32).

Heidegger also refers to his lecture "On the Essence of Truth":

"Only where beings are raised and preserved expressly in their unconcealment, only where this preserving is understood in terms of the questioning of beings as such does history begin. The incipient revealing of beings as a whole, the question of beings as such and the beginning of Western history are the same . . ." (*GA* 9: 190).

The connection between history, truth, and freedom, first stated in "On the Essence of Truth," is taken up in the technology lecture in reference to the connection between the occurrence of revealing (or truth) and Freedom: "Freedom is the realm of the destiny that brings a revealing on its way" (*VA* 25). The difficult problem that Heidegger faces on the one hand, is that man is not able to change his stance toward beings arbitrarily, thus to control his destiny, so to speak; on the other hand, this destiny is not to be accepted as fatality.[11]

We now come to the passage in the lecture in which Heidegger discusses the second half of the title of his lecture: "the destination of thinking." What kind of thinking is this that Heidegger clearly differentiates from philosophy? In the text, "The End of Philosophy and the Task of Thinking," Heidegger asks, when characterizing "world civilization" and the development of philosophy into the sciences:

is there a *first* possibility for thinking apart from the *last* possibility we characterized (the dissolution of philosophy in the technological sciences), a possibility from which the thinking of philosophy would have to start out, but which as philosophy it could nevertheless not experience and adopt? (*SD* 65)

Heidegger discusses this in the second part of this text, in which he asks, "What task is reserved for thinking at the end of philosophy?" He reminds us of a characteristic of thinking—that it is less than philosophy. Its task is "only of a preparatory, not of a founding character. It is content with awakening a readiness in man for a possibility whose contour remains obscure, whose coming remains uncertain" (*SD* 66). That sounds vague and mysterious at first. Heidegger's aim is as follows: "We are thinking of the possibility that the world civilization which is just beginning might one day overcome the technological-scientific-industrial character as the sole criterion of man's world sojourn" (*SD* 67). To repeat, this overcoming cannot be brought about by man. But by understanding what is occuring in the present (in technological world civilization), what its limits are, what fatal destruction is at work in it, man can prepare himself for a possible transformation, can keep himself ready for a transformation of destiny. When Heidegger then goes back to the beginning of philosophy with the Greeks, he does so because ἀλήθεια, the clearing that first grants the possibility of truth, was experienced in this beginning: "We must think ἀλήθεια, unconcealment, as the clearing which first grants being and thinking and their presencing to and for each other" (*SD* 68). According to Heidegger, this clearing has remained unthought in philosophy.

We have digressed from the Athens lecture in order to make accessible what Heidegger expresses there suggestively and concentratedly. In the lecture Heidegger continues with the demand that the locked-in-ness ruling world civilization be thought. He does not say that this step is difficult and requires great exertion because we are so engrossed and trapped in this civilization that we no longer surmise any other possibility of the relation to beings. But he does say that such thinking cannot be dismissed to the theoretical realm that is powerless as opposed to action. Expressly formulated, he states: "Such thinking is not a mere prelude to action, but is the decisive action itself through which man's world relation can first begin to be transformed" (*HK* 146f.). This sounds presumptous. But only as long as we take technological efficiency as our criterion and are blinded and dazzled by technological success. What Heidegger demands is that thinking "concern itself with the realm with which today's planetary world civilization began" (*HK* 147). That is the historical moment of the thinking of ἀλήθεια with the Greeks. He calls it the "step back" as it became visible with the elucidation of Athena. We need to gain distance from world civilization but not by denying it. If we did that, we would not be able to see what it is all about, what is happening in it. At the same time, however, we must go back to the beginning of thinking in order to think—and that is Heidegger's claim—"that which had to remain unthought in the beginning of Western thought, yet was already named there and pronounced for our thinking" (*HK* 147). It is a matter of the experience of ἀλήθεια. It was already present in the discussion of the character of Athena—the factor of limitation, the belonging together of φύσις and τέχνη, the meaning of light in the experience of things. But we must not stop with the meaning of light, for "Light can illuminate what is present only when what is present has already arisen in what is open and free and can expand there" (*HK* 147). This openness that makes both light and darkness accessible, "the Freeing of the free that first grants everything open" was thought by the Greeks as Ἀ-λήθεια. Heidegger translates it as un-concealment: "It does not remove concealment. On the contrary, revealing needs concealment" (*HK* 148). Heidegger then refers to Heraclitus's saying, "φύσις κρύπτεσθαι φιλεῖ" (*B* 123), which he interprets quite differently from the dominant translations in terms of his understanding of the Greek beginning, as "What arises of itself has the peculiar property of concealing itself" (*HK* 148). The lecture finally climaxes with a series of questions about the essence of unconcealment and the concealment belonging to it, and the historical fact that because unconcealment still remains unthought we do not know our destiny of remaining shut out of it. I shall choose a few of them:

"Is being locked out of destiny the withholding of unconcealment that has lasted a long time? Does the beckoning (*Wink*) into the mystery of the still unthought Ἀ-λήθεια point at the same time into the realm of the origin of art? Does the claim to produce works come from this realm?" (*HK* 148)

That is the goal of this lecture: to see the thinking of Ἀλήθεια in its connection with the origin of art with the Greeks, to think and interpret art in terms of the occurrence of Ἀλήθεια in order, then, to make visible the need of our time, in which art is confined in cybernetic world civilization: "Will it be granted to man on this earth to find a world sojourn remaining on it, i.e., a dwelling that is attuned by the voice of unconcealment concealing itself?" (*HK* 148f.). That is the questioning look ahead into the future after the return to the origin.[12]

A second reading of the text must follow the first elucidating one—starting with Heidegger's questions at the end. Its central focus must be on whether a transformation of dwelling in the world is possible originating with art—for example, whether Beethoven's last string quartets do not transpose us into a world, or open up a world for us, that is no longer determined by the absolute dominance and exploitation of the world, by this form of cybernetic subjectivity that determines our social life. But who has an ear for this art, beyond all planning and all efficiency, and who allows himself to be addressed and transformed by it? Perhaps it is as far away from us as the primordial art of the Greeks whose significance we can scarcely grasp.

NOTES

1. See the Hölderlin interpretations (*GA* 4, 39, 52, 53) on the meaning of the origin, the source, especially for becoming at home.

2. See Jacques Taminiaux, *La nostalgie de la grèce à l'aube de l'idéalisme allemand* (The Hague: Martinus Nijhoff, 1967).

3. Cf. "On the Essence of Truth" (*GA* 9: 177–202) and the Parmenides and Heraclitus lecture courses of 1942–43 (*GA* 54 and *GA* 55). These are only examples since the question of ἀλήθεια is a fundamental question for Heidegger. See also my monograph, *Martin Heidegger in Selbstzeugnissen und Bilddokumenten* (Reinbeck bei Hamburg: Rowohlt, 1973), 142ff.

4. Cf. the meaning of πέρας and ἄπειρον in Aristotle.

5. See "On the Essence and Concept of φύσις, Aristotle, *Physics* B, 1" (*GA* 9: 239–301).

6. Aeschylus, *The Eumenides*.

7. See "The Question concerning Technology" (*VA* 13–44). References to technology are also found in the essays "What are Poets For?" and "The Time of the World Picture" (*HW* 248–95, 69–104).

8. See *Die Frage nach dem Ding: Zu Kants Lehre von den transzendentalen Grundsätzen* (Tübingen: Max Niemeyer, 1962).

9. "In the work the happening of truth is at work in the manner of a work" (*H* 59).

10. See my Leiden lecture, "Heidegger's Interpretation of Technology," Bonn, 1988.

11. Cf. Heidegger's interpretation of Descartes, the way in which the development that followed was shaped by Descartes and what the consequences of it were.

12. The concept "destination of thinking" ["*Bestimmung des Denkens*"] has a double meaning. If Heidegger's third question reads "From whence is destined the thinking that now reflects on [*nachdenkt*] the origin of art?" then this proves that this thinking is sustained by the relation to ἀλήθεια. The second meaning is that this thinking has a special destination; here destination has the sense of task. This is clearly expressed in the question: "What

task is reserved for thinking at the end of philosophy?" This task is to comprehend the age of world-civilization and thus to prepare for a possible transformation by way of insight into the danger in which we stand unawares: a transformation that man certainly cannot force, for it presupposes a transformation of Being itself.

DOMINIQUE JANICAUD

22. The "Overcoming" of Metaphysics in the Hölderlin Lectures

Concluding his preliminary remarks to his first course on Hölderlin (*Germanien*), Heidegger writes:

> One considers Hölderlin historiographically and one fails to recognize the only essential point: his work—which has not yet found its space and time—has already overcome our historiographical embarrassment and has founded the beginning of another history, that history which starts with the contest concerning the advent or the vanishing of God.

> Man nimmt Hölderlin "historisch" und verkennt jenes einzig Wesentliche, dass sein noch Zeit-raum-loses Werk unser historisches Getue schon unberwunden und den Anfang einer anderen Geschichte gegründet hat, jener Geschichte, die anhebt mit dem Kampf um die Entscheidung über Ankunft oder Flucht des Gottes. (*GA* 39: 1)

In this sentence, Heidegger provides a clue to understanding his work on Hölderlin: the well-known distinction between *historisch* and *geschichtlich*. For him, it is not a mere formal distinction: he claims that Hölderlin's poetry has *already grounded* another history (in the sense of *Geschichte*). This is a daring claim which we have to consider and make clearer.

As for "metaphysics," the word does not appear in this quotation and it is not so frequent in the Hölderlin lectures. I nevertheless venture the hypothesis that Heidegger's relationship to metaphysics must be scrutinized to understand fully the Hölderlin lectures and, more radically, to throw a light on Heidegger's most originary presuppositions.

The title of this paper seems to imply that an "overcoming" of metaphysics takes place in the Hölderlin lectures. Is this obvious? The text I just quoted only allows us to answer that Hölderlin's poetry has fulfilled a certain kind of "overcoming," but it does not say that it is the overcoming of metaphysics as such. What is overcome by closely listening to Hölderlin's poems? What is the radical change that is performed through Heidegger's attempts? This is the first question I shall try to answer, by taking into account what is not modified in Heidegger's projects between 1934–35 and 1941–42. One remembers that chronologically the texts we are studying may be divided into two parts: the courses upon *Germanien, Der Rhein* were taught in 1934–35 and are published in *GA* 39; the lectures concerning *Andenken* and *Der Ister* were delivered in 1941–42: we find them in *GA* 52 and 53.

My first approach to these four courses as a whole will then lead to a consideration of remarkable differences between the two sets of lectures and eventually to a questioning of Heidegger's most radical presupposition.

Allow me to formulate the title of the following first part in a paradoxical way.

THE CHANGE WHICH DOES NOT CHANGE

I mean by this that what does not change through all the Hölderlin lectures (and this could also be said of the *Erlauterungen* and of "Hölderlins Erde und Himmel") is the project of a poetic dwelling or, better said, the assumption that Hölderlin's poetry, provided we listen to its most intimate message, offers a radically new experience, i.e., a new world and, first, a new space-time relationship (a new Zeit-Raum). To experience it, we have to perform a massive methodological change in our approach to space and time: we have to pass from combining geography and historiography to coupling topology and historicity.

What is at stake is a dwelling, a poetic dwelling. Is a dwelling just an arrangement within a space? *Germanien* is a hymn to the fatherland and not to a mere territory:

> Denn voll Erwartung liegt
> Das Land
> (*Germanien*, 6–7)[1]

The criticisms over against the usual abstract representations of space, of the landscape and, above all, of the flow of the rivers are various in the Hölderlin lectures. In the Rhine lecture, Heidegger writes:

> The river is not a watercourse which passes along the place where people live, but its stream, in so far as it gives its shape to the country, provides the possibility of the foundation of the human settlements.

> Der Strom ist nicht ein Gewässer, das an dem Ort der Menschen nur vorbeifliesst, sondern sein Strömen, als landbildendes, schafft erst die Möglichkeit der Gründung der Wohnungen der Menschen). (*GA* 39: 264)

The geographical descriptions presuppose representations of dimensions and inscribe in them the drawing of surfaces, of the relief, of the curves, etc. Heidegger says that these representations are, in fact, "obscure and questionable" (see *GA* 53: 65). People think they know what the river does because they are able to describe it; but Hölderlin writes in the *Ister* hymn:

Was aber jener thuet der Strom
Weis niemand.[2]

Heidegger quotes these last verses of the poem to invert the usual "geographical" representations of the river: the poem reveals something which is far deeper than a description: "The stream *is* the situation . . ." (*Der Strom "ist" die Ortschaft* . . .) (*GA* 53: 22–23). The stream is not part of the landscape; the stream is the poem as grounding dwelling and wandering (see *Der Ister*, section 7: "Der Strom als Ortschaft und Wanderschaft der Ortschaft"). The stream is not a metaphor of poetic dwelling on this earth: it *is* this dwelling and, as such, it reveals and offers what is near and far (see *GA* 53: 204–205). For instance, the modification of the watercourse of the Rhine (which first goes east and then suddenly turns west) is interpreted by Heidegger as a poetic appropriation of the essential German dwelling according to the hints suggested by Hölderlin in his letter to Böhlendorff (December 4, 1801): the Rhine is a destiny as the sign of a calling and of a poetic task (see *Der Rhein*, p. 205ff. and p. 291ff.). Heidegger insists even more strongly on the change concerning time. In section 6 of the commentary concerning *Germanien*, he makes a radical distinction between the measurable time of the individual and the originary time of peoples: the historical time of peoples is thought of as the time of the creators (founders of the State, poets, thinkers): the essential time will be a "long time" (Die wesenhaft lange Zeit: *GA* 39: 55). At the end of the same course on *Germanien*, he explicitly refers to his own conception of the originary time as *das EK-statikon* (he quotes *Sein und Zeit*, §§ 65ff.) as opposed to the measurement of a flux or, more precisely, "our squatting on every changing day" (ein in sich Zusammenhocken auf einem je wechselnden Heute) (*GA* 39: 109). In the same passage, he assumes the closeness of this approach of time with the Hölderlinian qualification of time as *die "reissende"*, that rapture which violently tears us along into the future. But this essential time is not only the repetition of a rapture; it is a maturing, the maturing of the "long time," which also may correspond to the convenient time of the Feast, such as is the case in the *Andenken* lecture. In the second part of this lecture, Heidegger deals with the "feast-day and the feast in Hölderlin's poetry"; section 4 is devoted to the temporality of the *Weile* in contrast with the usual duration which Heidegger characterizes as divided into the opposite sides of constancy or evanescence. "Die Weile" is usually considered as transient. Calculative thought is thus not able to understand the true and secret duration of the "Weile." Heidegger writes that in this true duration (as opposed to *Rechnung*, computation) "what is unique finds the fitting way of lasting in the uniqueness of its originary essence" (In der Weile hat das Einzige aus der Einzigkeit seines anfänglichen Wesens die gemässe Art des Bleibens) (*GA* 52: 104).

We are thus led to a sharp dichotomy between the space-time of the ordinary representative logics (that produce both geography and historiography) and the originary space-time that brings out both *Ortschaft* and *Weile* (the sense of "situation" and of duration or *Zeitigung*). The search for "universality and legality" may reduce space to a mere ordering of disposable space (*Abstellraum*: see *GA* 39: 108, 227). On the contrary, the great methodological change that Heidegger both performs and requires from his listeners leads to the topology of the originary "middle." In the Rhine lecture, this topology is worked out through the theme of the demigod: the stream of the Rhine itself is poetically raised to the status of *ein Halbgott*. The demigod is the mediator between gods and mortals, but not in the Hegelian sense of a dialectics: he opens up the new space-time of the originary "middle": "To think the demigods means: from the originary middle to guide our thought down to the earth and up to the gods" (Halbgötter denken heisst: aus der ursprünglichen Mitte auf die Erde zu und auf die Götter hin denken) (*GA* 39: 226).

There would be much more to say concerning the demigod, the ambiguity of his "function" and of his embodiments, and also concerning the other aspects of the methodological change performed in the Hölderlin lectures (especially, the status of language and the overcoming of the classical rhetorical distinctions between form and content, metaphor and direct expression, etc.). I choose to follow the leading thread which Heidegger himself proposed at the outset of his lecture on *Germanien*: Hölderlin has founded a new experience and first of all new space-time relationships. Let me stress that this entire set of assumptions and the very project of a "conversion" to poetic dwelling remain unchanged in all the Hölderlin lectures and essays.

In so doing, I have intentionally been silent about the differences between the two sets of courses on Hölderlin. We should not underrate them, and all the less as the focus of these differences turns out to be the relationship toward metaphysics.

THE GREAT CHANGE:
THE RELATIONSHIP TO METAPHYSICS

As we now have to question whether Hölderlin's poetry is metaphysical or not, we should already acknowledge that Heidegger's position on this point changed between 1934–35 and 1941–42.

First, it cannot be denied that Heidegger was conscious that a philosophical teaching on a poet and his poetry was not only an academic revolution but involved the danger of cutting Hölderlin's poems into conceptual pieces (see *GA* 39: 5). He justified his daring attempt by claiming that his aim was not philosophical in the traditional sense and that the meditation on Hölderlin's message implied a kind of conversion and a complete submission to the poet's *thought*:

Hölderlin is one of our greatest, that is: one of our most promising thinkers, because he is our greatest poet. The poetical turning toward his poetry is only possible as *meditative* debate with the *revelation of Being* which has been achieved in this poetry

Hölderlin ist einer unserer grösster, d.h. unser zukünftigster Denker, weil er unser grösster Dichter ist. Die dichterische Zuwendung zu seiner Dichtung ist nur möglich als denkerische Auseinandersetzung mit der in dieser Dichtung errungenen Offenbarung des Seyns. (*GA* 39: 6; see also 39: 4)

Although Heidegger already makes the distinction between this meditative confrontation and a mere philosophical debate, he assumes that the fundamental determination of the poem *Germanien* (its *Grundbestimmung*) is metaphysical. Or in more proper terms: "The fundamental determination comes from the specific metaphysical situation of any given poetry" (Die Grundbestimmung aber erwächst aus der jeweiliger metaphysischen Ort der jeweiligen Dichtung) (*GA* 39: 15). This hidden metaphysical ground of Hölderlin's poetry is thus set up as the aim of Heidegger's research.

This hermeneutical project is quite paradoxical: the philosopher acknowledges he is tied up in a kind of double bind; his attempt is open to the risk of reducing the poem to concepts of traditional or even just daily representations (including *Erlebnisse* or biologism: see *GA* 39: 27), but it is also supposed to lead to a *metaphysical* ground. The word *überwinden* is not yet applied to metaphysics: we have to overcome the reading of the poem as a "mere present piece of work" (nur vorhandenes Lesestück): see *GA* 39: 19.

As we unfortunately cannot reread the whole *Germanien* lecture, I would like to recall that Heidegger's reading of Hölderlin's *Germanien* leads to the *Grundbestimmung* of the poem: the "sacred sorrow" which brings out the openness to the "historical" distress (*Not*) of the German people. Concerning metaphysics, many passages of the *Germanien* lecture show that Heidegger is still looking for "another metaphysics," according to his own words (see *GA* 39: 196 and *GA* 39: 85, 121, 288).

This is in sharp contrast with the negative, if not pejorative, connotation which will characterize metaphysics in the *Ister* lecture (1942): the representative mode of thinking is not only attributed to metaphysics (and even to a blocking within the metaphysics of subjectivity) (see *GA* 53: 19, 203), but Hölderlin's poetry is said to be, in its very core, "outside metaphysics" or "no longer metaphysical" (see *GA* 53: 21, 99). Similarly, Heidegger writes in the *Andenken* lecture that in the poetry of Hölderlin "the domain of art and beauty and every metaphysics— where they are both exclusively grounded—is exceeded" (überschritten wird) (see *GA* 52: 63).

What is the meaning of this great change? It is neither a superficial modification of the terminology nor a giving up of Heidegger's fundamental project. We have seen that he has constantly been looking for a poetical dwelling and has been aware of the gap between that experience and our everyday world.

In 1942, Heidegger no longer believes that the original site of Hölderlin's poetry has anything to do with an originary metaphysics that would imply references to both Heraclitus and Hegel, as he did less than ten years before. As Jacques Taminiaux has pointed out, the field of thought as well as the vocabulary of 1934–35 still remain those of fundamental ontology and are very close to the well-known themes of *Being and Time*: the criticism of *das Man*, of everyday life attitudes and of *Vorhanden-sein*, as opposed to the authenticity of *Entscheidung* and of ex-static temporality. As Taminiaux puts it, the first reading of Hölderlin still falls under the division between *das Verfallen* and resolute authenticity (see Jacques Taminiaux, "La première lecture de Hölderlin," *Lectures de l'ontologie fondamentale*, Grenoble: Millon, 1989, p. 258ff; and in Heidegger's *GA* 39: 15, 23, 33, etc.)

The first result of our inquiry is not so surprising: it shows that the turn toward metaphysics as such has not taken place in the Hölderlin lectures but in between the two sets of lectures concerning the poet. However, this is not enough. We have not yet really answered the ultimate question about the meaning of this great change. Should it be thought as part of Heidegger's "turn" (Kehre)? But more, should it not help to think this turn the radicalization of a hidden presupposition?

THE PRESUPPOSITION

Be it called *Umwandlung, Überwindung,* or *Überschreiten*, the transformation which the reading of Hölderlin requires is thought by Heidegger (in 1941–42) as exceeding metaphysics and even as being *outside* the whole metaphysical domain (including art and beauty). If the way *we* might take to join this move is not yet designated or thought of as *Verwindung*, something is now more explicit than ever: Hölderlin's poetry has *already grounded* another possibility. To try a comparison, this overcoming does not resemble a construction game in which we fit together the different parts; we already have gotten the aim and the frame; we know that Hölderlin's poems are the shrine of our future possible poetic dwelling on this earth.

But, in so doing, we have not yet isolated the presupposition that makes Heidegger's attempt so original and that makes it so different from the "poetical inspirations" of philosophers. For instance, Marx and Freud were inspired by Shakespeare; Alain was inspired by Valéry; Bachelard was inspired by Hugo, Keats, Shelley, and others. Heidegger is not only inspired by Hölderlin. The privilege he gives him is not only and not properly aesthetic. To capture it in a word: this privilege is *geschichtlich*.

What does this mean? It would not make sense to translate it by saying that Heidegger endows Hölderlin with an historical privilege. According to Heidegger, the uniqueness of Hölderlin's poetry comes from its relationship to history and destiny. But not to history and destiny *in general!* In the foreword to the *Erläuterungen zu Hölderlins Dichtung* (Frankfurt: Klostermann, 1951, 7), Heidegger writes that the specific quality of Hölderlin's poetry is its *geschichtliche Einzigkeit*, the uniqueness of its relationship to German history and to Western destiny. He has not said anything less in the four Hölderlin lectures.

In the *Ister* lecture, after having assumed that the poetic stream determines the coming back home of Western man, Heidegger explains this point:

> When here and everywhere we speak about "man," we always mean the essence of the historical man of the history to which we belong: the essence of Western humanity.

"Man" does not mean "man in general" or "universal humanity," neither a form of unification reserved for an elite, nor any form of mass unification. But in the concept of the essence of Western man are necessary and constantly implied the essential relationships in which this humanity is involved: the relationship to the world, to the earth, to gods, "antigods," and false gods. Yet these relationships are not added to man from the outside in order to make him man, but "being a man" is being the unity of this articulation. The "becoming at home" (*Heimischwerden*) of man includes at once the full essence of the human being

Wenn hier und überall in den Anmerkungen von "dem Menschen" die Rede ist, dann meinen wir stets das Wesen des geschichtlichen Menschen der Geschichte, in die wir selbst gehören: das Wesen des abendländischen Menschentums. "Der Mensch" bedeutet weder "der Mensch überhapt" und die "allgemeine Menschheit," noch auch nur den "einzelnen" Menschen, noch auch nur irgendeine Form der Einigung mehrerer und vieler. Aber im Begriff des Wesens des abendländischen Menschentums sind auch notwendig und daher stets die wesentliche Bezüge mitgedacht, in denen dieses Menschentum steht der Bezug zur Welt, der Bezug zur Erde, der Bezug zu den Göttern und zu den Gegengöttern und Abgöttern. Diese Bezüge sind jedoch "dem Menschen" nicht ausserdem, dass "er" der Mensch ist, noch angefügt, sondern die Einheit dieses Gefüges zu sein, ist das Menschsein selbst. Das Heimischwerden des Menschen begreift somit die volle Wesen des Menschenseins in sich (*GA* 53: 52).

Forgive this long quotation which is intended to stress how historicity, thought as a unique becoming and "sending," now grounds the essence of man. Although the word "essence" is still metaphysical, as is the act of grounding, Heidegger assumes the uniqueness of a move which is a destiny we are supposed to share with Hölderlin, or rather: with Hölderlin's poetry.

The grounding of poetic dwelling on *Geschichtlichkeit* presupposes the fastening of an extremely tight link between three terms: Hölderlin's poetry, the act of founding, and historicity. This link may be found in the last verse of *Andenken*, a verse which is the motto of the *Andenken* lectures as well as the focus of Heidegger's meditations:

Was bleibet aber, stiften die Dichter.[3]

How to understand this "stiften"? It would not be enough to define it as a grounding, although Heidegger writes that it is "die Gründung im Heimischen" (*GA* 52: 196). It is not a grounding on principles, not even on language in general, but on the word, the poetic sign: what is sacred is *ins Wort gegründet* (*GA* 52: 193); and consequently its grounding is said to be the "sending of the originary" (Die gründende Schenkung des Anfänglichen ist Stiftung) (*GA* 52: 193). This indicates that the axis or the center-line of this grounding is historical, in that it is bound up with a hidden law of essential history. The expression *Gesetz der Geschichte* is not mine: one can find it on page 155 of the *Ister* lecture where Heidegger writes that to experience the true law of history means to be touched by the necessity and distress of historicity (von der Not der Geschichtlichkeit getroffen werden).

On the one hand, the scheme of a direct foundation of all reality by the three creators (the political, the poetic, the philosophical) has been dropped in 1942; on the other hand, the necessity of a new historical foundation has been radicalized and the priority of *Geschichtlichkeit* is still deeper, if such is possible. But the privilege of the poet seems now unchallenged, insofar as this poet obeys the hidden law of history and is secretly looking for a radical *Ereignis* (the expression *lichtend-Ereignende* appears at the end of the *Ister* to characterize the openness of a new space-time) (see *GA* 53: 204).

"What remains," *was bleibet*, will be this new space-time experience, the poetic dwelling.

There is, thus, between 1934 and 1942, a double move: a step backward from fundamental ontology, from metaphysics and from its involvements with the will to power (see *GA* 52: 180); and a radicalization of the presupposition or rather the chain of presuppositions which binds Hölderlin's poetry, the act of founding and historicity. It seems that the latter gives a support to the former, that the radicalization of Heidegger's own attempt has helped him greatly to get some distance on the metaphysical presuppositions he still conceded in the *Introduction to Metaphysics*; however, it does not imply his surrender of every kind of presupposition and, to be sure, it does not imply that we should declare the most intricate set of presuppositions obvious. In other words, we may find Heidegger's search for a new space-time extremely suggestive, without being as sure as he was that Hölderlin has already founded a new historicity or even announced a new epoch.

A reference to Max Kommerell might help to question this chain of presuppositions Heidegger forged in his Hölderlin lectures. Kommerell's letter of July 29, 1942, to Heidegger is very dense and remarkable. I will just quote the sentences which are most significant for us. Kommerell writes: "What we have to learn from you is that Hölderlin is a destiny . . . Like Empedocles, he does not leave anything unchanged . . ." This is the positive side. But Kommerell also raises sharp criticisms, reproaching Heidegger for having created a new esoteric language, for having committed a kind of philosophical suicide by suggesting that even Heidegger's own philosophy becomes empty in the face of the Hölderlinian grounding. Kommerell also charges that Heidegger monstrously insists on "literality." He dares to conclude that Heidegger's attempt could be an *Unglück* (I quote Kommerell's letter according to the French translation given by Marc Crépon in *Philosophie*, no. 16: 10ff.).

Kommerell's questions deserve close examination, but my present task is not the same as his, for I am not concerned with all the questions raised by a literary critic.

I prefer merely to suggest three questions which focus on the difficulties we have faced in this paper:

(1)   Should Hölderlin's poetry as such be *unified* in a new eschatology of Western destiny?

(2)   Should Hölderlin's poetry be considered as grounding the totality of a world and, more generally, can a poetical creation *ground* a world?

(3)   How are we to think not only the differences but also the link between our present metaphysical world and the reserved dimensions of language?

I will not conclude by hastily answering these questions that require care and time. A division between what we have to keep and what we should drop from the legacy of a great thinker cannot be decided at once.

> Lang ist
> Die Zeit, es ereignet sich aber
> Das Wahre.[4]

Commenting on this famous quotation from Hölderlin's *Mnemosyne*, Heidegger insists on the "long time" which the meditation on Hölderlin requires. And thinking of the sailors in the poem *Andenken*, he strikingly differentiates them from mere adventurers: the figure of the adventurer is modern and metaphysical; Ulysses was not yet an adventurer; Hölderlin's companion travellers are no longer adventurers, they have dropped all will to power. *Ihr Herz trägt Scheue* (see *GA* 52: 180).[5]

As Hölderlin's and Heidegger's companion travellers, we should not forget this teaching concerning the patience, care, and even awe of the search for truth. *Scheue*: this word is hard to translate, but its meaning is not so difficult to catch, once we have started to listen to Hölderlin. If Heidegger is right to assume that the Hölderlinian sense of historicity is full of *Scheue*, it has nothing to do with the brutal and cynical history of the "adventurers." It echoes the *Scheue* of Being itself in its truth. This remark encourages us to think that there is not *one* law of history, but rather that our history is still open, still full of undecidable voyages downstream, upstream.

NOTES

I would like to thank David Krell for his kind assistance with my text.

1. "For, full of expectations, lies the land."
2. "Yet what it is that the stream does/No one knows."
3. "Yet what endures/The poets institute."
4. "Long is the time, but Truth/will reveal itself/come to pass."
5. "Their heart bears awe."

JACQUES TAMINIAUX

23. The Origin of "The Origin of the Work of Art"

I remember Heidegger saying in passing during the Zähringen seminar held in September 1973 that the meditation on the origin of the work of art had played a decisive role in the *Kehre*, the turn that occurred in his thought in the thirties. In this paper I would like in a provisional way to elucidate in what sense and to what extent the texts dealing with the question of the origin of the work of art bear evidence of a turn, or at least of a shift in Heidegger's thought.

To what texts are we to look for such evidence? As a matter of fact, we now have three texts about the origin of the work of art, which are, taken in chronological order:

1. The first elaboration of the lecture given by Heidegger on November 13, 1935, at the *Society for the Sciences of Art* in Freiburg im Breisgau. This text is now available since it was published in the last issue of *Heidegger Studies*.
2. The second elaboration of the same lecture. This version came out in France in 1987, together with a translation into French by Emmanuel Martineau, based upon a photocopy of the typewritten transcript of Heidegger's own manuscript. It comprises the text of the lecture as it was actually pronounced by Heidegger in November 1935, and repeated without change in January 1936 at the University of Zürich in Switzerland, under the title *Vom Ursprung des Kunstwerkes*.
3. Finally, we have a third elaboration of the topic, namely the text of the three lectures offered in November and December of 1936 at the *Freie Deutsche Hochstift* in Frankfurt am Main. This version was published in the Fall of 1945 in the *Holzwege* under the title *Der Ursprung des Kunstwerkes*.

My purpose in this paper is to take literally what Heidegger suggested in passing in 1973: to look for the evidence of a shift in the texts dealing with the origin of the work of art. In other words, and more precisely, I propose to look for such evidence by comparing the two 1935 versions to the 1936 version. But before proceeding, tentatively of course, to the outline of a comparison, a short investigation about the place of art in Heidegger's writings before the fall of 1935 would be helpful.

FUNDAMENTAL ONTOLOGY

If we consider the writings and the now published lecture courses of the period of Fundamental Ontology, we might say that art taken in the sense of the Greek word τέχνη is everywhere present as a topic but that it is in no way originary, *ursprünglich*. Let me try to clarify this point.

The project of Fundamental Ontology intended to prove that there is only one focus for understanding the various meanings of Being, namely, the finite time of the being that we ourselves are, the Dasein. To prove that the question of the meaning of Being reaches an answer in the finite and mortal time, which at bottom is the Dasein, amounts to considering the very Being of Dasein as the ground of ontology. It amounts to making the ontology of Dasein into the basis of Fundamental Ontology. Thanks to the publication and/or widespread diffusion of the lecture courses offered by Heidegger in Marburg before the publication of *Being and Time*, particularly the lecture course on Plato's *Sophist* and the lecture course on the *Basic Concepts of Greek Philosophy*, it is possible today to realize that Heidegger discovered the articulation of his Fundamental Ontology above all thanks to a decade-long meditation on Aristotle, and more specifically thanks to a peculiar reappropriation of the *Nicomachean Ethics*, a work indeed which, for Heidegger at that time, was the first ontology of Dasein.

Now art, the Greek word for which is τέχνη, is among the topics of the *Nicomachean Ethics*. How does this work deal with art? Aristotle's treatise scrutinizes the dianoetic excellences, or intellectual virtues, in order to determine their rank. The intellectual virtues have two levels: at the lower level are the deliberative virtues, at the higher one are the epistemic virtues. Τέχνη, art, is an intellectual virtue, but it is located on the lowest level, at the lower level of the deliberative virtues. It is an intellectual virtue in the sense that it is a way of disclosing, of discovering, of ἀληθεύειν, of revealing. It is thus a way of knowing truth. As a way of knowing truth, and even of being-in-truth; however, τέχνη is strictly linked with a specific activity, the activity of producing, ποίησις, which consists in setting into a work (ἐνέργειν) what τέχνη reveals. In the Aristotelian framework, the origin of the work of art, of the ἔργον of the τεχνίτης, is ποίησις, the productive activity, but the productive activity itself has its origin in art, in τέχνη as a way of unconcealing, of ἀληθεύειν. "The origin of the work of art is art" is a strictly Aristotelian statement. Likewise, it is strictly Aristotelian to state that the essence of art lies in a happening of truth. However, in Aristotle's *Ethics* both art and the activity ruled and permeated by it, i.e., ποίησις, suffer from an intrinsic deficiency. They are deficient because the end, the τέλος of the productive activity ruled by τέχνη is not in the agent but outside it. It is the ἔργον. To be sure, the principle for the productive process is within the agent (it is the model the agent has in view) and to that extent it is an excellence. But it is a deficient excellence since its end is a product, the ἔργον, outside of the agent.

Such deficiency does not characterize the highest deliberative excellence, namely, φρόνησις, a way of ἀληθεύειν, of unconcealing, that is adjusted to an activity which is no longer ποίησις but πρᾶξις, action in the sense of the conduct by an individual of his life among other individuals and in their presence. Φρόνησις, practical judgment, is the highest deliberative virtue insofar as neither its principle, its ἀρχή, nor its end, its τέλος, fall outside the agent himself. Indeed, the principle of φρόνησις is a prior option of the agent for well-doing, its end is the well-doing of the agent. Φρόνησις is nothing other than resoluteness in well-doing.

For Aristotle, however, φρόνησις is not at all the highest excellence. Both art and φρόνησις are linked to the realm of the perishable in general. And φρόνησις is strictly confined within the realm of human affairs, which cannot be the highest realm since human beings, because they are mortal, are not what is highest in the world. Higher than the αἰών, the finite time of the mortals is the ἀεί, the imperishable which is forever what and how it is.

Two dianoetic excellences or virtues are concerned with the ἀεί. They are the epistemic virtues: ἐπιστήμη and σοφία. Both of these virtues are adjusted to a way of behaving which is higher than both ποίησις and πρᾶξις. That way of behaving is θεωρία. The two disclosing or unconcealing virtues of θεωρία have nothing to do with the perishable. Indeed ἐπιστήμη is concerned with unchangeable entities, like the mathematical figures. And σοφία, the highest intellectual excellence, is concerned with the ontological structure of the totality of beings and with the highest being, the prime mover, which is the principle of all the movements among the beings of φύσις. According to Aristotle, the contemplation of that immutable realm is, for a mortal being, the most authentic way of being. As long as such contemplation lasts, the mortal spectator comes close to the divine. He reaches εὐδαιμονία or authenticity, in the sense of being himself with excellence.

Heidegger's Fundamental Ontology is both a reappropriation and a critique of Aristotle's views. He thoroughly agrees with Aristotle's distinction between τέχνη as a mode of disclosing adjusted to the production of artifacts or of effects, and φρόνησις as a mode of disclosing adjusted to the conduct of human life. In other words, he agrees with Aristotle's distinction between art as adjusted to production and φρόνησις as adjusted to πρᾶξις. But he reappropriates the distinction in ontological terms, which means that it is metamorphosed into the distinction between, on the one hand, an everyday way of being that is concerned and preoccupied by ends to be attained by utensils and their readiness-to-hand and that is revealed by a specific circumspection and, on the other hand, an authentic way of being that cares for the very Being of Dasein, existence, and is illuminated by resoluteness.

Heidegger's reappropriation also includes an agreement with Aristotle about the privilege of θεωρία. But this reappropriation again implies an ontological metamorphosis.

What is at stake in Aristotle's concept of the highest form of θεωρία is the knowledge of the Being of beings; such knowledge in Aristotle is conflated with the science of the highest being, theology. This view, Heidegger claims, involves both an equivocation and an indeterminacy. An equivocation, since the science of Being (ontology) gets confused with the science of the divine (theology). An indeterminacy, since for Aristotle as for all of the Greeks, the meaning of Being is limited to οὐσία, presence, in the sense of *Vorhandenheit*, presence-at-hand, a presence whose privilege presupposes, moreover, that only one mode of time is taken into account. The aim of Fundamental Ontology is to overcome both the equivocation and the indeterminacy. It overcomes equivocation by showing that the eternity of the prime mover is but a concept derived from everydayness, in which indeed our art, our know-how, our circumspective and projective disclosure of our environment, again and again requires a permanence, i.e., the stable persistence of Nature. But such interest and fascination for permanence, Heidegger claims, is nothing else than a way of escaping our own Being, of falling away from our own existence and its finite time. Now it is by taking into account our own finite time as originary, a time in which prevail the projection upon a future and the retrieval of a past, that Fundamental Ontology also overcomes what remains indeterminate in the meaning of Being when the latter is limited to sheer presence.

This schematic recall is sufficient, I trust, to show that, in the framework of Fundamental Ontology, art is in no way originary, even though it is understood as a mode of unconcealment. Quite the contrary, art, as τέχνη, and the activity of setting into work ruled by it, are secondary; they are derived, they are in a position of fallenness with respect to what is our own, our existence and its finite time.

We find confirmation of this, as far as the fine arts are concerned, in the way Heidegger deals with *The Notebooks of Malte Laurids Brigge* in the lecture course of 1927, *The Basic Problems of Phenomenology*. Heidegger's comments prove that for him, at that time, the poet cannot be on an equal footing with the thinker. The poet cannot go beyond an improper or inauthentic understanding of existence, because, while he has the presentiment of what existence is, he either projects existence upon things or projects upon existence the mode of being of things (*BP* 171–73, 289).

THE RECTORAL ADDRESS

Hence in Fundamental Ontology τέχνη as a whole is minimized and downgraded. There is no significant change for that matter before the *Rectoral Address* of 1933. But here things change dramatically. We indeed find in the Address a major correction to the hierarchy of the ranks of active life as articulated in *Being and Time*, a major correction as far as τέχνη is concerned. Τέχνη, which formerly was narrowly confined within the inauthentic and fallen realm of everydayness, now suddenly climbs to the top on the ladder of authenticity. Let us consider this transformation more closely.

At the beginning of the Address, Heidegger recalls the following in strict agreement with Aristotle, and in continuity with what he already developed in the Marburg period about philosophy as the highest way of existing, and the authentic principle of individuation. The Greeks, he says, conceived of θεωρία as "the highest implementation of genuine πρᾶξις" (*SU* 12). Indeed, Aristotle and Plato before him conceived of θεωρία as a βίος, a way of existing or behaving, i.e., a πρᾶξις. There is nothing new in Heidegger's statement for that matter. But earlier in the same Address, Heidegger claims that there was an old Greek legend according to which Prometheus would have been the first philosopher, and he recalls in this context the works of Prometheus in Aeschylus's tragedy. "τέχνη δ'ἀνάγκης ἀσθενεστέρα μακρῷ." Heidegger translates: "Knowing (*Wissen*) however is much weaker than necessity." This means, he says, that all knowledge concerning things is first of all delivered to the over-power (*Übermacht*) of destiny and falters in the face of such supreme over-power. That is precisely why, if it is to genuinely falter, knowledge must display its highest challenge, in front of which only the power of concealment of beings stands up (*SU* 11). Hence philosophy, the highest knowledge, the knowledge of the Being of beings, is both θεωρία, and as such the highest form of βίος or of πρᾶξις, and τέχνη, which obviously means a mode of disclosing adjusted to a peculiar ποίησις, that is to some setting-into-work over that which it rules. This is quite a correction of the previous hierarchy.

Does it mean that the link formerly established between τέχνη and fallen everydayness disappears? Not at all. Indeed, a distinction has to be made between a lower form of τέχνη which is unable, ontologically speaking, to overcome *Vorhandenheit* (or presence-at-hand), and a higher form of τέχνη adjusted to the unconcealment of the Being of beings. Concerning the higher form of τέχνη, we find developments and precisions in the two lecture courses offered by Heidegger right after the Rectorate period, namely, the first lecture course on Hölderlin (winter semester 1934–35), and the lecture course, *Introduction to Metaphysics* offered during the summer semester of 1935, i.e., just before the elaboration of the first lecture, *The Origin of the Work of Art* (*Vom Ursprung des Kunstwerkes*). Let me summarize those developments.

FIRST LECTURE COURSE ON HÖLDERLIN AND THE INTRODUCTION TO METAPHYSICS

As far as the first lecture course on *Hölderlin* is concerned, it is obvious to me that its articulation stems directly from Fundamental Ontology, in the sense that it is entirely dominated by the contrast between fallen everydayness and resolute authenticity. This reading of Hölderlin proposes to discard right away the various figures of fallen everydayness which were described by *Being and Time* as building a dam against the question: *Who is Dasein?* The difference with *Being and Time* is that the Dasein at stake is no longer the individual, but "the authentic gathering of individuals in a community" (*GA* 39: 8) Hölderlin's poetry raises the question "Who are we?"—(*GA* 39: 48) not as individual beings, but as this singular German people to whom the poet addresses himself. In order to appropriate the question, "What about the Being of this very people?" (*GA* 39: 22), one should, Heidegger insists, be capable of "withdrawing from everydayness" (*GA* 39: 22) and of maintaining what the *Rectoral Address* called an attitude of radical questioning over against the "they" who immediately object: No, "The answer is what is decisive" (*GA* 39: 41).

Now how does Heidegger characterize everydayness here? The answer is: by τέχνη. In the sense, of course, of a circumspection dedicated to the management of an environment. A rigorous opposition, he says, should be preserved between, on the one hand, "the authentic Dasein" as "exposed to Being" and, on the other hand, "the everyday operations of the producing man, who then uses his products and contributes to the progress of culture" (*GA* 39: 38). This lower level of τέχνη includes, in the context of the Hölderlin course, the everyday life of the Nazi regime: cultural activism, subordination of thought and poetry to specific political needs, the rulings of the ministries. But on the level of authentic Dasein, there is place for a quite different τέχνη. Once again what is at stake in this reading of Hölderlin is no longer the finite time of individuals but "the historical Dasein of a people, experienced as the authentic and unique being, from which the fundamental position towards beings in their totality grows and owns its articulation" (*GA* 39: 121–22). Now there is a difference between the finite time of individuals and the ownmost time or historicality of a people: each individual can temporalize the former; only a few individuals can temporalize the latter. Those few are the *creators*.

In his interpretation of Hölderlin's sacred mourning—i.e., the awareness that the gods have vanished—Heidegger tries to show that such a basic mood, *Grundstimmung*, reveals the truth of the German people "and opens it to the decision of standing ready in the acceptance of a return of the divine" (*GA* 39: 102). In this context he writes the following:

> The *Grundstimmung*, and this means the truth of the Dasein of a people, is originally instituted by the poet [*gestiftet*]. But the Being thus disclosed of beings is understood and articulated, and thus opened for the first time by the thinker, and Being thus understood is laid to rest in the last and original seriousness, which means a determined [*bestimmt*] historical truth, by this only that the people is led to itself as people. This occurs only thanks to the creation by the State-creator of a specific State adjusted to the essence of that people. . . . Those three creative powers of the historial Dasein are the ones realizing that which solely deserves to be acclaimed as great. (*GA* 39: 144)

This triad, the poet, the thinker, and the State-founder, embodies the Promethean τέχνη that the *Rectoral Address* was talking about. Insofar as they are aware of the over-power of destiny, they are aware of finiteness. Insofar as such awareness incites them to the highest challenge, they rise to the level of the demigods. The Promethean τέχνη, the great τέχνη of poet, thinker and State-founder is thus separated by an abyss from the low and petty τέχνη of everydayness.

The lecture course, *Introduction to Metaphysics*, focuses upon the same topic in the light of the Pre-Socratics. We already know that there is no τέχνη without ποίησις, without a production of a work, without a setting into work (ἐνέργεια) of what τέχνη discloses. As a result of the elevation of a peculiar τέχνη to the highest ontological level, the convergences that Heidegger now detects between Parmenides, Heraclitus, and Sophocles can be summarized in the following way:

> Being human determines itself from out of a relation to beings as a whole. The human essence shows itself here to be the relation which first opens up Being to man. Being-human, as the need for apprehending and gathering, is a being-driven into the freedom of undertaking τέχνη, of the setting-into-work of Being, a setting-into-work which is itself knowing. Thus is History (*Geschichte*) (*EM* 130)

In other words, there is now an ontological compulsion or assignment to τέχνη and to setting-into-work what τέχνη knows. Why such a necessary assignment to τέχνη? Because Being itself (φύσις) is essentially *polemical*. It is an unconcealment which, on the one hand, retains itself in itself and which, on the other hand, in its very appearing is again and again threatened by sheer appearances, deception, illusion. Being itself is an "intricate struggle" (*EM* 81) between powers: concealment and unconcealment, unconcealment and sheer appearance, Being and Non-Being. Because of this intricate struggle between powers, Being is an over-power requiring a "creative self-assertion" (*EM* 81), *Selbstbehauptung*, an over-power which places man before a "constant decision" (*Entscheidung*) by which is meant a "separation in the togetherness of Being, between unconcealment and appearance, non-Being" (*EM* 84). Such a decision is the way man is called to be responsive to the over-power of Being. And since that over-power is a violence, he can be responsive by being himself *the* disrupting and *the* violent one. The issue for him is to operate "a taming and ordering of powers by virtue of which beings open up as such when man moves into them. This disclosure (*Erschlossen-heit*) of beings is the power that man must master in order to become himself amid beings, i.e., in order to be historical" (*EM* 120). In the context, "himself" means "the wielder of power," the one "who breaks out and breaks up, he who captures and subjugates" (*EM* 120).

This violent activity is that of τέχνη in the high and essential sense. Heidegger writes: "It is τέχνη which provides the basic trait of δεινόν, the violent: for violence is the use of power against the overpowering: through knowledge it wrests Being from prior concealment into the manifest as Being" (*EM* 122).

Thus understood, τέχνη is again, as it was during the Marburg period, a knowledge and a power. But the difference is that τέχνη in Marburg was reduced to everydayness and therefore fascinated by presence-at-hand and in a position of fallenness with regard to authentic Dasein. By contrast the celebrated τέχνη, which is now reinterpreted with the help of the Pre-Socratics, turns out to be the countermovement against the falling tendency of everyday and petty τέχνη. The τέχνη that is now acclaimed is great τέχνη as opposed to petty τέχνη. As a knowledge, instead of being limited by the present-at-hand, it is "the initial and persistent sight looking beyond what is directly given before the hand (*Vorhan-dene*)" (*EM* 122). And as a power, it is the "capacity to set-into-work Being as a being which each time is so and so" (*EM* 122), and consequently the work stemming from τέχνη is "a manifesting implementation [*Er-wirken*] of Being in beings" (*EM* 122).

This great τέχνη, as opposed to the petty business of the many or the They, has only three fundamental modalities: artistic, philosophical, and political. Heidegger writes: "Unconcealment occurs only when it is achieved by work: the work of the word in poetry, the work of stone in temple and statue, the work of the word in thought, the work of the πόλις as the historical place in which all this is grounded and preserved" (*EM* 146). These works are those of the creators who were celebrated in the first course on Hölderlin: the poet, the thinker and the State-creator. In addition, there is now the architect of the temple and the sculptor of the gods of a people. Only the works of these creators deserve the qualification of greatness insofar as they are foundational.

The State-creator grounds the πόλις, i.e., "the place, the there, wherein and as which historical Dasein is." He is the one who first creates "institutions, frontiers, structures and order" (*EM* 117). The great poet is the one who is dedicated to the "original institution [*Stiftung*] of the historical Dasein of a people" (*EM* 126), and "the great poetry by which a people enters into history" (*EM* 131). The great thinker is the one who takes upon himself the very essence of philosophy, namely, "a thinking that breaks the paths and opens the perspectives of the knowledge that sets the norms and hierarchies, of the knowledge in which and by which a people fulfills itself historically and spiritually . . . " (*EM* 8). Or:

It is the genuine function of philosophy to challenge the historical Dasein and hence, in the last analysis, Being pure and simple. Challenge [*Erschwerung*] restores to things, to beings, their weight (Being). How so? Because challenge is one of the essential prerequisites for the birth of all greatness, and in speaking of greatness we are referring primarily to the destiny of a historical people and to its works. There is destiny, however, only where a truthful knowledge about things dominates Dasein. And it is philosophy that opens up the path and perspectives of such knowledge. (*EM* 8)

Heidegger even suggests that it is because of that foundational role with regard to his people, that his own work up to that moment deserved the heading of Fundamental Ontology (*EM* 133). In this context, at that time Heidegger liked to quote, with full agreement, Hegel's words in the *Logic* of 1812: "A people without a metaphysics is like a temple without a Holy of Holies."

As to the artistic setting-into-work of ἀλήθεια, we find the following:

The Greeks called with special emphasis τέχνη art in the proper sense and the work of art because art is what most immediately brings Being (i.e., the appearing that stands in itself) to stand in something present, in the work . . . It is through the work of art as essent being that everything else that appears and is to be found is *first* confirmed and made accessible, explicable, and understandable as being or not being. Because art in a pre-eminent sense stabilizes and manifests Being in the work as a being, it may be regarded as the ability, pure and simple, to put-into-work, as τέχνη. (*EM* 122)

Such is the background of the lecture of November 1935 about the origin of the work of art.

All the key words and topics of the actual lecture, as well as of its first undelivered draft, are already uttered in the first lecture course on Hölderlin and/or in the *Introduction to Metaphysics*. Those topics are the historical Dasein of a people, the struggle at the heart of Being and at the heart of the work, the setting-into-work of unconcealment, the institution (*Stiftung*) of history by the work, the greatness of such institution in its three basic modalities, the necessity of a decision (*Entscheidung*) "for Being against Not-being, and thus of a struggle with appearance" and "against the continuous pressure of involvement in the everyday and common place" (*EM* 128), the necessity of preserving the unconcealment "against cloaking and concealment" (*EM* 133), the obligation, since art is disclosure of the Being of beings and not the representation of the beautiful in the sense of the pleasing, to fight aesthetics and to "provide the word 'art' with a new content" on the basis of a *"recaptured originary relation* to Being" (*EM* 101. Emphasis mine). Even the topic of the origin is a decisive one in the *Introduction to Metaphysics*. Indeed, in the preliminary consideration on the basic questions of metaphysics, we read that the question "Why are there beings rather than nothing?" recoils upon itself, and "has its ground in a leap through which man thrusts away all the previous security of his life." And Heidegger adds the following: "The leap [*Sprung*] in this questioning opens up its own source . . . We call such a leap, which opens up its own source or origin [*Ursprung*], the finding of one's own ground" (*EM* 5).

On the basis of what I have recalled so far, the preliminary discussion about the origin of the work of art that took place before the Fall of 1935 and which started with the *Rectoral Address* does not yet indicate any turn in Heidegger's thought. On the contrary, the introduction of a distinction between a petty τέχνη, which is blind toward Being and trapped within everydayness, and a great τέχνη that sets-in-work Being itself as unconcealment, not only leaves untouched but even reinforces the articulation of Fundamental Ontology, i.e., the contrast between the inauthentic and the authentic, and more deeply between vulgar time and originary time. For that matter, the fact that the Dasein at stake is now the Dasein of a people does not introduce any significant discontinuity with respect to the early problematic of Fundamental Ontology. The Dasein of the people, either Greek or German, is still understood in the light of the key sentence of Fundamental Ontology: "Das Dasein existiert umwillen seiner." Instead of introducing a discontinuity, the abovementioned modification even brings Fundamental Ontology to a sort of metaphysical climax. To be sure, Heidegger introduces in his approach to the Greek world several discrepancies between the Pre-Socratics on the one hand and Plato on the other hand. He thus seems to take sides with them against Plato. But this, in a sense, is perhaps still a semblance insofar as obviously it is from Plato that he derives the assertion that philosophy is not only the true principle of individuation but also the foundational work by which the thinker conceptually discloses the totality of beings taken in its ground and claims to be able to be a ruler for a people. In other words, Plato's *Republic* is still, in spite of several corrections, one of the most influential texts at the core of Heidegger's thought.

LECTURE OF NOVEMBER 1935

What about the lecture of November 1935: *Vom Ursprung des Kunstwerkes, On the Origin of the Artwork?* As I have said, there are two versions of it. Since they follow one another within a limited period of time, one can suppose that the first is the draft of the second. And since they are separated from the lecture course, *Introduction to Metaphysics* by a short lapse of time, one may suppose that they both pursue the train of thought developed in that lecture course. However, the weight of the legacy of Fundamental Ontology, including the modifications I have mentioned, is more obvious in the draft than in the manuscript of the actual paper.

The point here is not, as it will be the case later on, to "see the enigma of art" but, as Heidegger insists at the beginning of the draft, "only to prepare an alteration of the basic stand [*Grundstellung*] of our Dasein towards art" (This same sentence is already present in the *Introduction to Metaphysics*) (*UKa* 2). The preparation of such an alteration implies an overcoming of the approach to works of art in terms of *Vorhandenheit*, presence-at-hand. Such an approach is blind toward the very meaning of the word 'origin', *Ursprung*, primal leap. For if 'origin' simply means the cause of the art-product in the psychological processes of the artist, it therefore does not let the work be itself. And when the usual approach seems to do so, it treats the work as an object for an artistic business in which the work is explained, maintained, restored, criticized, and enjoyed. The work, however, is neither an object nor a product. By seeing it in that way, we miss its origin. We approach the origin only by a leap away from the public agitation of the *Kunstbetrieb*. Clearly the leap here is understood as a move away from the publicity of the They (*das Man*) in everydayness. This shows the continuity between this lecture and Fundamental Ontology. And indeed, as soon as Heidegger, in the first part of the first draft, approaches the artwork as work, he stresses that the being-manifest of the work has nothing to do with the availability to a public. He writes: "The only relation of the work towards a public, where there is one, is that the former destroys the latter. The greatness of a work is measured by this destructive power" (*UKa* 3). In other words, what is at issue here as in Fundamental Ontology is the distinction between everydayness and authenticity, between presence-at-hand and existence. This is confirmed by the way Heidegger describes the two basic features of the work-being of the work, namely, world and earth.

The world that is set up by the work is neither the sum of the present-at-hand, nor the frame of it, nor an object in front of us. It is like an escort (*Geleit*) which is "more being than all the things present-at-hand and graspable amid which in everydayness we believe to be at home. World is the ever unfamiliar [*Unheimische*]." What is at work in the work, as it sets up a world, is the "rejection [*Abweisung*] of the usual present-at-hand" (*UKa* 4).

The other feature is the pro-duction (*Herstellung*) of the earth. The earth here is described as "the unison of an unsurpassable fulness" which is "both a Ground and an Abyss which essentially closes itself" (*UKa* 5–6). But it is also a hardness (*Härte*) which, because it is in a trial or conflict (*Streit*) with the world, requires in order to come to the fore, the counterhardness of what is usually called a Form, a sketch (*Riß*). Such dispute opens a play-space, a There (*Da*) in which a people comes to itself. "The works thanks to which such a There is opened are the *temple* around the *statue* of the God, and the *poems*" in which "are pre-coined [*vorgeprägt*] for a people its great concepts of the totality of beings." Poetry is thus the anticipation of philosophy, as it was in Hölderlin's *Hyperion* or in Hegel's chapter on the Religion of Art in the *Phenomenology of Spirit*.

This description of the work of art gives Heidegger the opportunity to criticize the classical approaches of the work in terms of matter and form—concepts that are adjusted to utensils, not to artworks. Likewise, the approach of the work in terms of representation (*Darstellung*) is rejected. This is a notion in which, however elaborate it might be, "the presence-at-hand of everyday things operates as a standard" (*UKa* 9). And at the end of this description, in continuity with a basic scheme of Fundamental Ontology, Heidegger insists on the "solitude" (*Einsamkeit*) of the work of art, over against "the common reality" (*UKa* 9) that is shaken and frightened by it.

The second part of the first draft deals with the origin. The origin is art taken in its essence. Taken in its essence, art as the origin is the very historicality of truth, its *Geschehen*. Here again the continuity with both the early Fundamental Ontology and its recent broadening and transposition to the Dasein of a people is obvious. Heidegger insists that the setting-into-work is a necessity because truth only occurs with and thanks to the work. And it only occurs with the work because Truth has to be projected. In other words the aletheic and historical traits which in *Being and Time* were the properties of authentic πρᾶξις or fully temporal existence turn out now also to be the properties of the recently discovered high form of ποίησις and τέχνη.

But that poietic project—*Dichtung* in Heidegger's German—requires a locus which itself is what it is depending on the impact of the work of the poietic project. That locus is the *Dasein of a people*, which means that the *There* as the very open-ness of truth, or as truth itself in its historization, has no other locus than the people. So that ultimately there is a knowledge of the essence of art insofar as the people is willing to win "clarity as to who we are and who we are not." This clear knowledge taken as a will is also a decision as to "what is great and what is petty, what is brave and what is cowardly, what is durable and what is transitory, what is Lord and what is Slave." It is this clear *knowledge* taken to be the decision by which a people wills itself, that is the decisive leap into the proximity of the origin" (*UKa* 13).

Up to this point, I cannot see any significant adumbration of a turn. To be sure the opening of the There, its grounding character, is rooted in a "dark abyss," in the earth itself which is for a people "its earth" closing itself and resisting open-ness? To be sure "the leap of the origin essentially remains a secret." But in spite of several new words, all of this is already present in *Vom Wesen der Wahrheit* and *Vom Wesen des Grundes*. And it seems to me highly significant to find at the end of the first draft the following sentence which sounds as an echo of the essay of 1929 on Truth: "The origin is a mode of that ground whose necessity we have to call *Freedom*" (*UKa* 14).

There is no adumbration of a turn, either, in the actual lecture of 1935. A few sentences suffice to show this. "The world is that in which a people comes to itself" (*OA* 26). "The world is never the everybody's world of a universal humanity; it is for a people its world, the task which is assigned to it" (*OA* 36). "The open-ness of the There, Truth is only as History. And only a people can be historial, as projected upon its future by retrieving what it is. The people takes over the task to be the There" (*OA* 36). "Truth occurs only in so far as it is so and so decided, thereby grounding new domains of decision" (*OA* 44). "The work is a leap ahead [*Vor-sprung*] pointing toward what a people decides to be" (*OA* 48).

LECTURES OF 1936

Hence, instead of being attentive to the *enigma* of Art, these two versions of the 1935 lecture turn out to be voluntarist proclamations to the German Dasein. However, those who only know or knew *The Origin of the Work of Art* on the basis of the third version will no doubt object that the tone of a voluntarist proclamation to a people is not obvious in the third version. They are right. Though interrogation is claimed to be a central issue in all the texts I have mentioned beginning with the *Self-Assertion of the German University*, it is obvious from the tone of these texts that Self-Assertion prevails upon questioning. Not so in 1936. This change of tone, occurring in the final version, deserves consideration.

To be sure, the "people" is still an issue as well as its gods, and "greatness" is still mentioned as well as the founder of the State. Likewise, decision is still an issue. But all of these topics seem to lose the harshness they had in the previous versions. Or at least their harshness seems to be diluted by a tone which is more meditative than assertive or proclamatory, and certainly not Promethean. Moreover, the *circle* emphasized by the early versions was in the last analysis a device for showing the circular character of Dasein, as a being existing for its own sake, and becoming what it already was. By contrast, the circle in 1936 loses this voluntarist connotation and now seems to mean that Being is neither beings, nor outside them, and that human beings are concerned by the difference of both. In addition, the previous contempt for everydayness and its pettiness has almost vanished. It is highly significant that the first third of the final version is devoted to the question: What is a thing in its thingly character? In the frame of Fundamental Ontology, paying attention to the Being of things was clearly not a central issue for the task of thinking. Things did not deserve interrogation since their Being had nothing enigmatic. It was defined either by presence-at-hand or by readiness-to-hand. These easy answers are no longer mentioned. Instead it is now stated: "The unpretentious thing evades thought most stubbornly. Can it be that this self-refusal of the mere thing, this self-contained independence, belongs precisely to the nature of the thing? Must not this strange feature of the nature of the thing become what a thought that has to think the thing confides in? If so, then we should not force our way to its thingly character" (*GA* 5: 17). In other words, everydayness is no longer the "familiar, all too familiar" that resoluteness has to avoid and overcome. It is now strange despite being familiar. Likewise, the tool previously defined once and for all by its readiness-to-hand now turns out to be a witness, in its very reliability, of the deepest truth, the interplay of unconcealment and concealment. Obviously, if the unpretentious character of things and tools now deserves meditation, it no longer makes much sense to despise everydayness and its petty τέχνη.

We can also observe a remarkable shift in the second third of the final version. Formerly, ἀλήθεια was connected with the There that a people is entrusted to take upon itself, so that the Dasein of a people was the locus of truth. This is what now disappears. Dasein is no longer the locus of truth. Unconcealment is now taken to be a *clearing* in the midst of beings, a clearing to which humans belong and are exposed, instead of instituting it. Consequently, resoluteness also undergoes a deep change of meaning: it forsakes its initial call to the will, to its decisions, its project to be a Self. It now becomes dis-closure or exposure to the reserve which is at the core of the clearing. By the same token, truth itself is no longer a matter of human decision between Being and not-Being, or between unconcealment and mere appearance. And if it is no longer a matter of human decision, it is because the very distinction between concealment and deception or mere appearance has now become undecidable. "Concealment can be a refusal or merely a dissembling. We are never directly certain whether it is the one or the other. Concealment conceals and dissembles itself" (*GA* 5: 41). To be sure, the word *decision* remains in use. But the decision now belongs to Being, no longer to Dasein.

Finally, the last section of the final version deals with creation but in a tone from which the Promethean inspiration has disappeared. What is seen as most essential in the work inasmuch as it is created, what is valued as most extraordinary in it, is no longer its capacity for anticipating in a leap what a people wills to be and for affixing in the register of greatness what its rank and standards should be. Much more modestly, what is most essential in it, as created, is this: "that such work *is* at all rather than is not" (*GA* 5: 53). The most essential, now is "this '*that* it is' of createdness" (*GA* 5: 53). In other words, the coming to presence now seems almost to erase the previous privilege of the futural projection.

As for the creator, it is still a striving that he sets into work, the struggle of world and earth, but he himself is no longer a struggler. Creating, Heidegger says, is "receiving and borrowing within the relation to Unconcealment." These verbs are in no way Promethean.

Notes on Contributors

ROBERT BERNASCONI is Moss Professor of Philosophy at Memphis State University, He has edited a collection of Gadamer's essays titled *The Relevance of the Beautiful and Other Essays*. With David Wood he has edited *Derrida and Difference*, and with Simon Critchley he has edited *Re-Reading Levinas*. He is the author of *The Question of Language in Heidegger's History of Being*, as well as a number of essays on various aspects of continental philosophy and the history of social thought. He is currently completing a book called *Between Levinas and Derrida*. Before coming to Memphis, Robert Bernasconi taught at the University of Essex for thirteen years. He has also held visiting positions at Loyola University of Chicago, Vanderbilt University, and Braunschweig University in Germany.

WALTER BIEMEL, now Emeritus at the Staatliche Kunstakademie Düsseldorf, served for many years as an editor at the Husserl Archives in Louvain and in Köln. In addition to editing several volumes in the *Husserliana* and the *Phaenomenologica* series, he is editor of two volumes of Heidegger's *Gesamtausgabe: Logik: Die Frage nach der Wahrheit* (GA 21) and *Hölderlins Hymne "Der Ister"* (GA 53). His own writings include *Le concept du monde chez Heidegger, Kants Begründung der Asthetik und ihre Bedeutung für die Philosophie der Kunst, Philosophische Analysen zur Kunst der Gegenwart*, as well as monographs on Sartre and on Heidegger.

JEAN-FRANÇOIS COURTINE is Professor at the Université de Paris-X (Nanterre) and Director of the Husserl Archives in Paris. He is the author of *Suarez et le système de la métaphysique, Heidegger et la phénoménologie*, and *Extase de la raison: Essais sur Schelling*. He has also published several French translations of works by Heidegger and by Schelling.

FRANÇOISE DASTUR is Maître de conférences at the Université de Paris-I (Sorbonne). She is the author of *Heidegger et la question du temps* and of numerous articles on Heidegger, Husserl, and Merleau-Ponty. She is currently finishing a French translation of Heidegger's *Logik: Die Frage nach der Wahrheit* (GA 21).

JACQUES DERRIDA currently teaches at the École des Hautes Études en Sciences Sociales in Paris. He is also a regular Visiting Professor at the University of California at Irvine. Among his many books are *La voix et le phénomène, L'écriture et la différence, De la grammatologie, La dissémination, Marges de la philosophie, Glas, La vérité en peinture, La carte postale*, and, most recently, *De l'esprit, Psyché*, and *Du droit à la philosophie*.

PARVIS EMAD, Professor of Philosophy at DePaul University, is founding co-editor of *Heidegger Studies*. He is author of *Heidegger and the Phenomenology of Values* and co-editor of *Heidegger on Heraclitus*. He has translated into English Heidegger's lectures on Hegel (GA 32) and (with Kenneth Maly) is currently translating Heidegger's lectures on Kant (GA 25) as well as *Beiträge zur Philosophie* (GA 65).

ELIANE ESCOUBAS is Maître de conférences at the Université de Toulouse. She is the author of *Imago Mundi: Topologie de l'art* and the editor of several collections on Heidegger, Husserl, and the phenomenology of art. She has translated Husserl's *Ideen 2* into French.

R O D O L P H E   G A S C H É is Professor of Comparative Literature at the State University of New York at Buffalo. His publications include *Die hybride Wissenschaft, System und Metaphorik in der Philosophie von Georges Bataille*, and *The Tain of the Mirror: Derrida and the Philosophy of Reflection*. He is currently completing a book entitled *Rethinking Relation: On Heidegger, Derrida and De Man*.

M I C H E L   H A A R is Professor of Philosophy at the Université de Paris-XII. He has published two major books: *Le chant de la terre. Heidegger et les assises de l'Histoire de l'Être* (to be published in English translation by Indiana University Press), and *Heidegger et l'essence de l'homme*. He is also the author of numerous articles on Heidegger, Nietzsche, Hölderlin, Derrida, and Levinas. He is editor of the Cahiers de l'Herne volume on Heidegger.

K L A U S   H E L D is Professor of Philosophy at the Bergische Universität Wuppertal. Since 1987 he has been President of the Deutsche Gesellschaft für Phänomenologische Forschung. His major publications include *Lebendige Gegenwart* and *Heraklit, Parmenides und der Anfang von Philosophie und Wissenschaft*. He is the editor of Heidegger's *Metaphysische Anfangsgründe der Logik im Ausgang von Leibniz* (*GA* 26).

S A M U E L   I J S S E L I N G is Professor at the Katholieke Universiteit Leuven and Director of the Husserl Archives at Leuven. He is the author of *Heidegger, denken en danken, geven en zijn*, of *Retoriek en filosofie* (translated into English as *Rhetoric and Philosophy in Conflict*), and of *Mimesis. Over schijn en zijn*. He has also published numerous papers on Heidegger, Husserl, Schelling, Novalis, Freud, and Derrida.

D O M I N I Q U E   J A N I C A U D is Professor of Philosophy and Director of the Research Center on the History of Ideas at the Université de Nice. His major publications include *La métaphysique à la limite: Cinq études sur Heidegger* (in collaboration with J.-F. Mattéi), *La puissance du rationnel* (to be published in English translation by Indiana University Press), and *L'ombre de cette pensée: Heidegger et la question politique*.

D A V I D   F A R R E L L   K R E L L is Professor and Chair of Philosophy at DePaul University in Chicago. Former Chair of Philosophy at the University of Essex, England, he also taught literature and philosophy at the Universities of Freiburg-im-Breisgau and Mannheim, Germany. He is the author of *Of Memory, Reminiscence, and Writing: On the Verge, Intimations of Mortality: Time, Truth, and Finitude in Heidegger's Thinking of Being*, and *Postponements: Woman, Sensuality, and Death in Nietzsche*. He has published numerous articles on subjects ranging from the Presocratics and Plato to Nietzsche, Heidegger, and Derrida, and on themes such as metaphysics, human embodiment, and the literary text. He is editor and translator of several books and articles by Martin Heidegger, including *Basic Writings, Nietzsche*, and *Early Greek Thinking*, and co-editor (with David Wood) of *Exceedingly Nietzsche*. His latest book is entitled *Daimon Life: Heidegger and Life-Philosophy*.

K E N N E T H   M A L Y is Professor of Philosophy at the University of Wisconsin—La Crosse. He is founding co-editor of *Heidegger Studies* and co-editor of *Heraclitean Fragments* (with John Sallis) and of *Heidegger on Heraclitus* (with Parvis Emad). He is co-translator of several volumes of Heidegger's *Gesamtausgabe*, including the lectures on Kant (*GA* 25) and on Hegel (*GA* 32), and, currently in preparation, *Beiträge zur Philosophie* (*GA* 65).

A D R I A A N   T.   P E P E R Z A K is Arthur J. Schmitt Professor of Philosophy at Loyola University of Chicago. Previously he was Professor of Philosophy at the Universities of Nijmegen and Amsterdam and has taught at several other universities in the United Sates. Among his publications are *System and History in Philosophy,* three books on Hegel (*Le jeune Hegel et la vision morale du monde, Philosophy and Politics,* and *Hegels praktische Philosophie*), as well as numerous articles on Levinas and on the relations between metaphysics, epistemology and ethics.

W I L L I A M J. R I C H A R D S O N is Professor of Philosophy at Boston College and a practising psychoanalyst. He is the author of *Heidegger: Through Phenomenology to Thought* (1974) and several articles on Heidegger. He is also co-author (with John P. Muller) of *Lacan and Language. A Reader's Guide to the Écrits* (1982) and *The Purloined Poe: Poe, Lacan, Derrida, and Psychoanalytic Reading* (1988).

J O H N S A L L I S is currently W. Alton Jones Professor of Philosophy at Vanderbilt University. He formerly held the Arthur J. Schmitt Chair at Loyola University of Chicago. His books include *Phenomenology and the Return to Beginnings, Being and Logos: The Way of Platonic Dialogue, The Gathering of Reason, Delimitations, Spacings—of Reason and Imagination, Echoes: After Heidegger,* and *Crossings: Nietzsche and the Space of Tragedy.*

C H A R L E S E. S C O T T is Professor of Philosophy at Vanderbilt University. His books include *Boundaries in Mind, The Language of Difference,* and *The Question of Ethics: Nietzsche, Foucault, Heidegger.* He has also edited several collections including (with Edward Ballard) *Heidegger in Europe and America.*

J A C Q U E S T A M I N I A U X is Professor of Philosophy at the Université de Louvain-la-neuve and a regular Visiting Professor at Boston College. His books include *La nostalgie de la grèce à l'aube de l'idéalisme allemand, Le regard et l'excédent, Recoupements,* and *Dialectic and Difference.* He translated into French Heidegger's *Die Frage nach dem Ding* and was one of the participants in Heidegger's last private seminar, the Zähringen seminar.

F R I E D R I C H - W I L H E L M V O N H E R R M A N N is Professor of Philosophy at the Universität Freiburg. He worked very closely with Heidegger during the preparation of the *Gesamtausgabe* during the last years of Heidegger's life. He has played a major role in the publication of the *Gesamtausgabe* and has edited ten of the thirty-five volumes published so far. His own writings focus on the philosophical works of both Heidegger and Husserl, as well as on texts from the tradition. His works include: *Bewusstsein, Welt und Zeitverstandnis, Husserl und die Meditationen des Descartes, Subjekt und Dasein, Heideggers Philosophie der Kunst, Der Begriff der Phänomenologie bei Heidegger und Husserl, Hermeneutische Phänomenologie des Daseins: Eine Erläuterung von "Sein und Zeit"* (the first of a series of volumes that will eventually provide detailed commentary on the entirety of *Being and Time*).

J I R O W A T A N A B E is Professor and Chairman of the Philosophy Department at the University of Tokyo in Hongo. He is the author of numerous books in Japanese dealing with German philosophy, including *Existential Analysis in the Early Heidegger, The Thought of Being in the Later Heidegger, Nihilism,* and *Phenomenology of the Inner Life.* He has also translated several major texts of German philosophy into Japanese, including Nietzsche's *Philosophenbuch,* Heidegger's *Sein und Zeit,* Husserl's *Ideen 1,* and Schelling's *Philosophische Untersuchungen über das Wesen der Menschlichen Freiheit.*

D A V I D W O O D is Senior Lecturer in Philosophy at the University of Warwick. He is the author of *The Deconstruction of Time* and *Philosophy at the Limit.* He is co-editor of *Heidegger and Language, Time and Metaphysics, Derrida and Difference, Exceedingly Nietzsche,* and *The Provocation of Nietzsche.*

S H I - Y I N G Z H A N G is Professor of Philosophy in the Institute of Foreign Philosophy at Beijing University. He is also Director of the Institute of Philosophy at Hubei University in Wuhan and is President of the Association for the Study of Chinese and Western Philosophy and Culture. He is the author of seven books dealing with Kant, Hegel, and other Western philosophers.

General Index

Index of Greek Words